FORTRAN 77

WITH NUMERICAL METHODS
FOR ENGINEERS AND SCIENTISTS

FORTRAN 77

WITH NUMERICAL METHODS FOR ENGINEERS AND SCIENTISTS

D. M. ETTER

Dept. of Electrical & Computer Engineering
University of Colorado, Boulder

The Benjamin/Cummings Publishing Company, Inc.
Redwood City, California • Menlo Park, California • Reading, Massachusetts
New York • Don Mills, Ontario • Wokingham, U.K. • Amsterdam
Bonn • Sydney • Singapore • Tokyo • Madrid • San Juan

Dedicated with love to Virginia and Herbert Etter.

Sponsoring editor: Lisa Moller
Production editors: Eleanor Renner Brown and Laura Kenney
Text designers: Linda Robertson and Victoria Ann Philp
Cover designer: Mark Ong
Cover image: The Magellan satellite at Venus, courtesy of NASA
Compositor: Graphic Typesetting Service, Inc.
Cover and insert printer: New England Book Components
Text printer and binder: R. R. Donnelley and Sons

Library of Congress Cataloging-in-Publication Data

Etter, D. M.
    Fortran 77 with numerical methods for engineers and scientists /
D.M. Etter.
        p.   cm.
    Includes index.
    ISBN 0–8053–1770–8
    1. FORTRAN 77 (Computer program language)   I. Title.
QA76.73.F25E847   1992
005.13′3—dc20   91-44065
                                                                         CIP

1 2 3 4 5 6 7 8 9 10—DO—95 94 93 92

The Benjamin/Cummings Publishing Company, Inc.
390 Bridge Parkway
Redwood City, California 94065

PREFACE

This introductory text has been written to show you how to solve engineering and science problems using FORTRAN 77 and numerical methods. The material has been divided into two parts. Part I contains nine chapters that cover the complete FORTRAN 77 language; Part II contains six chapters that cover a variety of numerical methods commonly used in solving engineering and science problems. The material in all 15 chapters is framed in real-world applications so that you can immediately begin to see the usefulness of the computer in solving problems. However, knowing a computer language is to no avail if you cannot break a problem solution into the properly ordered steps that a computer can perform; therefore, we present a top-down design approach to problem solving that is used throughout the text. Our specific objectives are the following.

1. To acquaint you with the capabilities of computers and the types of problems that computers can solve.
2. To teach standard FORTRAN 77 so that you can use it to solve problems on essentially any computer system, in both academic and nonacademic environments.
3. To develop the numerical methods necessary to solve many engineering and scientific problems and to understand the applications and limitations of the numerical methods.
4. To establish good problem-solving techniques applicable to any problem, whether computer related or not.
5. To use practical, real-world engineering and science problems while accomplishing the first four objectives.

DISTINGUISHING FEATURES

Engineering and Science Applications The examples and problems have been selected to introduce you to a wide range of engineering and science applications from disciplines including electrical engineering, mechanical engineering, aerospace engineering, environmental engineering, optical engineering, robotic engineering, and acoustical engineering. The specific applications include topics such as equipment reliability, quality control analysis, cryptography, terrain navigation, water treatment, spacecraft data analysis, robot arm control, adaptive optics for telescopes, wind tunnel data analysis, sounding rocket trajectories, and sonar signals. Many of the examples and problems also contain sample data files.

Problem-Solving Design Process A five-step process for solving problems is introduced in Chapter 1 and then used throughout the text. The five steps are:

1. State the problem clearly.
2. Describe the input and the output.
3. Work the problem by hand for a specific set of data.
4. Develop an algorithm using top-down techniques.
5. Test the algorithm with a variety of data sets.

This design process is used consistently in the development of all complete programs.

Complete FORTRAN 77 Coverage Complete coverage of FORTRAN 77 makes this book suitable not only as a learning tool for the first-time computer user but also as a comprehensive reference for the experienced user. In addition, only standard FORTRAN 77 statements and structures are used, so all programs and statements are compatible with any FORTRAN 77 compiler. Another advantage of using only standard FORTRAN 77 is that all programs will work properly on the new Fortran 90 standard because the new version is upward-compatible. Appendix D discusses the new features in Fortran 90.

Graphical Description of the Numerical Methods A wide range of numerical methods are presented, including the Newton-Raphson method, Gauss elimination, cubic spline interpolation, least-squares modeling, Euler's method, and the Runge-Kutta method. Each method is illustrated with diagrams and drawings to help you visualize the concepts and thus more easily understand the techniques.

Digital Signal Processing A unique chapter is included that introduces the area of digital signal processing (DSP). The chapter discusses how to generate digital signals, including signals with noise, and how to reduce the noise in a signal using a digital filter.

Appendix on Plotting   Since graphs are so useful in interpreting engineering data and computational results, an appendix is included that illustrates the steps in plotting information from data files using both MATLAB and Lotus 1-2-3.

Program Diskette   A diskette that accompanies the text contains all the programs and engineering data sets from the application sections in the text. Thus, you have immediate access to the programs so you can both experiment with them to be sure you understand the key concepts and easily modify them to add new capabilities or solve other problems. These files are ASCII files and can therefore be uploaded to any computer system.

Motivational Problems as Chapter Openers   Each chapter begins with a specific problem that cannot reasonably be solved with the FORTRAN statements presented up to that point; hence, we establish motivation to develop new elements of the language in order to solve the described problem. The introductory problem is solved after the new topics are covered.

Engineering Case Studies   The application sections represent 41 engineering case studies. Each case study includes a detailed development of the problem solution along with sample data to illustrate testing the algorithm developed in the section.

Top-Down Design Techniques   The five-step design process that appears throughout the text stresses top-down design techniques. A problem is first decomposed into general steps shown in a block diagram. Then, using stepwise refinement, the steps are translated into computer language. Both pseudocode and flowcharts contribute to the development of the stepwise refinements so that students become acquainted with both techniques. Structure charts illustrate the modular structure of programs containing functions and subroutines.

Structured Programming Approach   To promote simplicity in solutions and reduce the time spent in testing and debugging programs, all problem solutions use structures with one way into the structure and one way out of the structure. All programs are implemented as either WHILE loops or iterative loops (DO loops). Thus, GO TO statements are used only to implement WHILE loops.

Software Tools   Algorithms for common techniques are presented and used in numerous applications. Several forms of algorithms for averaging data and for determining the maximum and minimum are developed. Sort algorithms are presented for selection sorts, insertion sorts, and bubble sorts. Search algorithms for searching both ordered and unordered lists are presented with sequential and binary searches. Algorithms for inserting and deleting from ordered lists are also included. After subroutines and functions are covered, these algorithms are all developed into modules so that you can utilize these software tools in other programs. Many of the numerical techniques in Part II are also developed as modules. The reuse of existing software tools is stressed throughout the text.

FORTRAN Statement Summaries   Each chapter in Part I contains a summary of the FORTAN statements presented in that chapter. The summary contains the general form of the statement, specific examples of the statement, and a brief discussion of the rules for using the statement.

Self-Tests and Solutions   Chapters 2–15 contain a number of short self-tests that allow you to check your understanding of the new material. You can immediately determine whether you are ready to proceed to the next section by comparing your answers to the solutions at the end of the text.

Style/Technique Guides   Each chapter in Part I (except for Chapter 1) contains a style/technique guide to promote good programming habits that stress readability and simplicity. This short discussion is included in each chapter on the premise that developing good style and technique is an integral part of learning the language. In addition to this special section at the end of each chapter, a number of examples in the text have multiple solutions, thereby exposing you to different approaches to solving the same problems. If one of these solutions has better style or technique than the others, it is pointed out in the accompanying discussion.

Debugging Aids   Debugging aids are included in every chapter after Chapter 1. This section outlines efficient methods for locating and correcting program errors relevant to the programming techniques described in the chapter. With guidance from this section, you learn consistent methods for spotting and avoiding the common errors associated with each new FORTRAN statement or numerical method. In addition to debugging aids, a number of examples in the text include an incorrect solution to a problem along with the correct solution. The incorrect solution is used to highlight common errors, thus helping you avoid the same mistakes.

Error Analysis   Each chapter in Part II contains a section on error analysis. These sections discuss the types of errors that can be introduced by the complicated techniques and present methods for minimizing the errors.

Key Words and Glossary   A list of key words appears at the end of each chapter. For easy reference, the definition of each of the 240 key words is in the glossary at the end of the text.

Large Number of Problems   Over 600 problems are included in the self-tests and end-of-chapter problems. These problems vary in degree of difficulty, from simple to more challenging problems. Solutions to all the self-tests and to many of the end-of-chapter problems are included at the end of the text.

I/O Flexibility   List-directed input statements and simple formatted output statements are used throughout the text. This choice provides maximum flexibility in the form in which data is entered and maximum control over the form of the output data. We encourage the use of list-directed output for the testing and debugging phases, but we always use formatted output for printing final results.

Use of Color   Color is used throughout the text to emphasize important material. Pedagogically, the use of color in emphasizing certain statements within a computer program is especially significant. Without using arrows or lines or distracting symbols, we can clearly stress the use of a new statement or point out the differences in two similar program segments. All pseudocode and flowcharts are highlighted in color for easy reference. End-of-chapter problem numbers appear in color to indicate that the solution is included at the end of the text.

ORGANIZATION

The first seven chapters contain the material necessary to build a solid foundation in FORTRAN 77. Chapters 8 and 9 contain additional material on data types and advanced file handling, but some topics may be omitted if desired. The numerical methods chapters in Part II can be covered sequentially, or the material may be introduced as the necessary FORTRAN topics are presented. The following chart lists the FORTRAN chapters along with the various numerical methods that could be presented at the end of the indicated FORTRAN chapter.

FORTRAN CHAPTER	NUMERICAL METHODS
Chapter 4 (Data Files)	Sinusoid Generation—Sonar Signals (Chapter 15, Sections 1–3)
Chapter 5 (Arrays)	Linear Interpolation—Wind Tunnel Data (Chapter 12, Sections 1–2)
	Least-Squares Methods—Accelerometers (Chapter 12, Sections 6–7)
	Numerical Differentiation—Sounding Rocket (Chapter 13, Sections 4–5)
	Euler's Method—Radioactive Decay (Chapter 14, Sections 1–2)
	Digital Signal Processing—Filtering (Chapter 15, Section 6)
Chapter 6 (Functions)	Numerical Integration—Frequency Bands (Chapter 13, Sections 1–3)
Chapter 7 (Subroutines)	Roots of Equations—Digital Filter Design (Chapter 10, Sections 1–4)
	Gauss Elimination—Deformable Mirrors (Chapter 11, Sections 1–4)
	Gauss-Seidel Method—Electrical Circuits (Chapter 11, Sections 5–6)
	Cubic Splines—Robot Path Generation (Chapter 12, Sections 1–4)

	Runge-Kutta—Air Pollution
	(Chapter 14, Sections 3–5)
	Random Signals—Communications
	(Chapter 15, Sections 4–5)
Chapter 8	Newton-Raphson Method—Robot Arm Control
(Data Types)	(Chapter 10, Sections 5–7)

PREREQUISITES

The text is intended for engineering and science students who have no prior computer background. In general, only college algebra and trigonometry are assumed; however, a few sections in Part II assume a calculus background.

SUPPLEMENTS

Instructor's Guide An instructor's guide is available to instructors on request to the publisher. This supplement contains viewgraphs, new computer projects, and complete solutions to the end-of-chapter problems.

Test Bank A test bank is also available to instructors on request to the publisher. This supplement contains over 200 quizzes that are printed one per page to allow photocopying of the pages for use in the classroom. Midterm and final exams are also included for class distribution as actual exams or practice exams. Complete solutions to the quizzes and exams are included.

ACKNOWLEDGMENTS

After writing several textbooks, I appreciate more than ever the suggestions, guidance, and constructive criticism provided by reviewers. The group of especially helpful reviewers for this text were Professors Betty J. Barr, Nels Madsen, William J. Kubitz, Levon Minnetyen, Jeanine Ingber, Thomas Kisko, and Skip Fletcher. Previous reviewers of the FORTRAN 77 material were Professors W. F. Beckwith, Lawrence J. Genalo, John Cowles, Mike Manry, Josann Duane, Ronald Danielson, William Holley, John Goda, Lee Maxwell, John R. Zimmerman, Susanne M. Shelley, Ted Wahstaff, Glen Williams, Edward T. Ordman, Elizabeth Unger, Joe Jefferis, Robert Aiken, Enrique A. Gonzales, and William Harlow. I want to thank Alan Apt (former editor) for getting me off to a good start with this book. I also want to thank the following people at Benjamin/Cummings Publishing Company: Lisa Moller, Jake Warde, and Dan Joraanstad (Editorial); Eleanor Brown, Laura Kenney, and Erika Nelson (Production); and Mary Tudor and Liane Shayer (Marketing). Special thanks also go to my husband Jerry (a mechanical/aerospace engineer) who gave a great deal of assistance in the development of the numerical methods chapters and who developed many of the engineering applications. Finally, I would like to thank Sheralyn Esparza and Amy Etter for their assistance in word processing and proofreading.

D. M. Etter

BRIEF CONTENTS

1 An Introduction to FORTRAN 77 and Problem Solving   1
2 Arithmetic Computations   13
3 Control Structures   71
4 Data Files and More I/O   143
5 Array Processing   191
6 Implementing Top-Down Design with Functions   243
7 Implementing Top-Down Design with Subroutines   299
8 Additional Data Types   347
9 Additional File Handling   401
10 Roots of Equations   441
11 Matrices and Systems of Simultaneous Equations   477
12 Curve Fitting and Interpolation   525
13 Numerical Integration and Differentiation   571
14 Integration of Ordinary Differential Equations   601
15 Introduction to Digital Signal Processing   631
Appendix A   FORTRAN 77 Intrinsic Functions   667
Appendix B   Additional FORTRAN 77 Topics   671
Appendix C   Printing Data Files with MATLAB and Lotus 1-2-3   685
Appendix D   An Introduction to Fortran 90   691
Glossary of Key Words   695
Answers to Self-Tests   707
Answers to Selected Problems   725
Index   769

DETAILED CONTENTS

Each chapter begins with an opening problem and an introduction and ends with a summary and key words. Chapters 2–15 also contain:
- *debugging aids*
- *style/technique guides*
- *problems*

A FORTRAN statement summary is included in chapters 2–9, and an error analysis section is included in chapters 10–15.

1 AN INTRODUCTION TO FORTRAN 77 AND PROBLEM SOLVING   1

1 – 1   Computer Organization   2
1 – 2   Computer Languages   4
1 – 3   Running a Computer Program   6
1 – 4   Top-Down Design Techniques   8

2 ARITHMETIC COMPUTATIONS   13

2 – 1   Constants and Variables   15
          Scientific Notation   16
          Magnitude Limitations   17

2–2 Arithmetic Operations   18
   Evaluating an Arithmetic Expression   19
   Truncation and Mixed-Mode Operations   22
   Underflow and Overflow   25
2–3 Intrinsic Functions   26
2–4 Simple Input and Output   29
   List-Directed Output   30
   List-Directed Input   32
   Formatted Output   33
2–5 Complete Programs   45
2–6 Application—Bacteria Growth (Biology)   47
2–7 Application—Carbon Dating (Archeology)   50
2–8 Application—Railroad Track Design
   (Transportation Engineering)   52
2–9 Application—Equipment Reliability (Electrical
   Engineering)   54

3 CONTROL STRUCTURES   71
3–1 Algorithm Structure   72
   Sequence   73
   Selection   74
   Repetition   76
3–2 IF Structures   83
   Logical Expressions   83
   IF Statement   84
   IF-ELSE Statement   87
   IF-ELSEIF Statement   88
3–3 WHILE Loop Structure   91
3–4 Application—Rocket Trajectory (Aeronautical
   Engineering)   95
3–5 Application—Suture Packaging (Biomedical
   Engineering)   100
3–6 DO Loop   104
   Structure of a DO Loop   106
   Execution of a DO Loop   107
3–7 Application—Timber Regrowth (Environmental
   Engineering)   115
3–8 Application—Cable Car Velocity (Mechanical
   Engineering)   119
3–9 Nested DO Loops   124

4 DATA FILES AND MORE I/O   143
4–1 Data Files   144
   Trailer and Sentinel Signals   148
   End Option   151

4 – 2   Application—Critical Path Analysis (Manufacturing Engineering)   153
4 – 3   Application—Population Study (Sociology)   158
4 – 4   Formatted Input   162
    X Specification   162
    I Specification   162
    F Specification   164
    E Specification   165
4 – 5   Additional FORMAT Features   168
    Repetition   168
    Slash   168
    Tab Specification   171
    Number of Specifications   171
4 – 6   Application—Quality Control (Manufacturing Engineering)   173

5 ARRAY PROCESSING   **191**
5 – 1   One-Dimensional Arrays   192
    Storage and Initialization   192
    Input and Output   194
5 – 2   Data Statement   199
5 – 3   Application—National Park Snowfall (Meteorology)   201
5 – 4   Sorting Algorithms   205
    Selection Sort   205
    Bubble Sort   205
    Insertion Sort   205
5 – 5   Application—Earthquake Measurements (Civil Engineering)   213
5 – 6   Two-Dimensional Arrays   218
    Storage and Initialization   218
    Input and Output   221
5 – 7   Application—Power Plant Data Analysis (Power Engineering)   223
5 – 8   Application—Terrain Navigation (Aeronautical Engineering)   227
5 – 9   Multidimensional Arrays   231

6 IMPLEMENTING TOP-DOWN DESIGN WITH FUNCTIONS   **243**
6 – 1   Intrinsic Functions   244
6 – 2   Statement Functions   245
6 – 3   Application—Temperature Conversions (Chemistry)   249
6 – 4   Top-Down Design and Structure Charts   254
6 – 5   Function Subprograms   256

6 – 6   Application—Oil Well Production (Petroleum Engineering)   270

6 – 7   Application—Traffic Flow (Transportation Engineering)   277

6 – 8   Functions for Search Algorithms   281
        Unordered List   282
        Ordered List   285

7 IMPLEMENTING TOP-DOWN DESIGN WITH SUBROUTINES   299

7 – 1   Subroutine Subprograms   300

7 – 2   Application—Simulation Data (Computer Science/ Engineering)   306

7 – 3   Application—Waste Water Treatment (Chemical Engineering)   312

7 – 4   Subroutines for Inserting and Deleting   319
        Inserting in an Ordered List   319
        Deleting from an Ordered List   323

7 – 5   Application—Computer Security (Computer Science/Engineering)   330

7 – 6   Common Blocks   337

8 ADDITIONAL DATA TYPES   347

8 – 1   Character Data   348
        Character I/O   350
        Character Operations   352
        Character Intrinsic Functions   357

8 – 2   Application—Cryptography (Computer Science/ Engineering)   362

8 – 3   Double-Precision Data   370
        Double-Precision I/O   371
        Double-Precision Operations   372
        Double-Precision Intrinsic Functions   373

8 – 4   Application—Temperature Distribution (Mechanical Engineering)   375

8 – 5   Complex Data   383
        Complex I/O   383
        Complex Operations   384
        Complex Intrinsic Functions   384

8 – 6   Application—Electric Circuit Model (Electrical Engineering)   386

9 ADDITIONAL FILE HANDLING   401

9 – 1   Internal Files   402
9 – 2   Sequential Files   403
     OPEN Statement   404
     CLOSE Statement   405
     REWIND Statement   406
     BACKSPACE Statement   406
     ENDFILE Statement   406
9 – 3   Application—Voyager Spacecraft Data Analysis (Electrical Engineering)   407
9 – 4   Application—Whooping Crane Migration (Biology)   414
9 – 5   Direct-Access Files   423
9 – 6   Application—Computer Parts Inventory (Computer Science/Engineering)   424
9 – 7   Inquire Statement   429

10 ROOTS OF EQUATIONS   441

10 – 1   Incremental-Search Method   447
10 – 2   Bisection Method   449
10 – 3   False-Position Method   451
10 – 4   Application—Digital Filter Design (Electrical Engineering)   453
10 – 5   Newton-Raphson Method   461
10 – 6   Secant Method   464
10 – 7   Application—Robot Arm Control (Mechanical Engineering)   465

11 MATRICES AND SYSTEMS OF SIMULTANEOUS EQUATIONS   477

11 – 1   Matrix Operations   479
11 – 2   Cramer's Rule   486
11 – 3   Gauss Elimination   492
11 – 4   Application—Deformable Mirrors (Optical Engineering)   501
11 – 5   Gauss-Seidel Method   508
11 – 6   Application—Electrical Circuits (Electrical Engineering)   512

12 CURVE FITTING AND INTERPOLATION   525

12 – 1   Linear Interpolation   527
12 – 2   Application—Wind Tunnel Data (Aerospace Engineering)   529
12 – 3   Cubic Spline Interpolation   534

12 – 4   Application—Robot Path Generation (Robotic Engineering)   541

12 – 5   Discussion of Single Polynomial Interpolation   549

12 – 6   Least-Squares Methods   551

       Linear Models   552

       Polynomial Models   555

       Nonlinear Models   556

12 – 7   Application—Accelerometer Model (Mechanical Engineering)   558

13   NUMERICAL INTEGRATION AND DIFFERENTIATION   571

13 – 1   Integration Using the Trapezoidal Rule   572

13 – 2   Application—Frequency Bands   575

13 – 3   Integration Using Simpson's Rule   580

13 – 4   Numerical Differentiation   583

13 – 5   Application—Sounding Rocket Trajectory (Aerospace Engineering)   587

14   INTEGRATION OF ORDINARY DIFFERENTIAL EQUATIONS 601

14 – 1   Euler's Method   602

14 – 2   Application—Radioactive Decay and Carbon Dating (Archeology)   605

14 – 3   Runge-Kutta Method   611

14 – 4   Application—Air Pollution Control (Environmental Engineering)   616

14 – 5   Discussion of Advanced Techniques   623

       Higher-Order Ordinary Differential Equations   623

       Partial Differential Equations   625

15   INTRODUCTION TO DIGITAL SIGNAL PROCESSING   631

15 – 1   Sampling a Continuous Signal   632

15 – 2   Sinusoid Generation   634

15 – 3   Application—Sonar Signals (Acoustical Engineering)   639

15 – 4   Random Signal Generation   643

       Uniform Random Numbers   643

       Signal-to-Noise Ratios   649

15 – 5   Application—Communications Channels (Electrical Engineering)   650

15 – 6   Application—Digital Filtering (Electrical Engineering)   654

Appendix A FORTRAN 77 Intrinsic Functions   667
Appendix B Additional FORTRAN 77 Topics   671
Appendix C Printing Data Files with MATLAB and Lotus 1-2-3   685
Appendix D An Introduction to Fortran 90   691
Glossary of Key Words   695
Answers to Self-Tests   707
Answers to Selected Problems   725
Index   769

ENGINEERING AND SCIENCE APPLICATIONS

ACOUSTICAL ENGINEERING

Sonar Signals (Sec. 15-3, p.639; Probs. 15.1–15.4, p.662).

AERONAUTICAL AND AEROSPACE ENGINEERING

Rocket Trajectory (Sec. 3-4, p.95; Probs. 3.1–3.5, p.132).
Retrorocket Performance (Prob. 3.29, p.135).
Wind Tunnel Data (Prob. 6.31, p.295).
Terrain Navigation (Sec. 5-8, p.277; Probs. 5.16–5.20, p.236).
Hot-Air Balloons (Ex. 8-2, p.355).
Wind Tunnel Data (Sec. 12-2, p.530; Probs. 12.1–12.5, p.567).
Sounding Rocket Trajectory (Sec. 13-5, p.587; Probs. 13.6–13.10, pp.597–598).

BIOMEDICAL ENGINEERING

Suture Packaging (Sec. 3-5, p.100; Probs. 3.6–3.10, p.133).

CHEMICAL ENGINEERING

Radioactive Decay (Prob. 2.39, p.66).
Pressure Chambers (Probs. 4.18–4.19, p.183).
Waste Water Treatment (Sec. 7-3, p.312; Probs. 7.6–7.10, p.341).
Sensor Data (Probs. 9.16–9.22, p.433).

CIVIL ENGINEERING

Beam Analysis (Probs. 4.26–4.27, p.185).
Earthquake Measurements (Sec. 5-5, p.213; Probs. 5.6–5.10, p.235).
Tremor Averages (Prob. 5.29, p.237).
Ground Motion Detection (Probs. 15.14–15.17, p.664).

ELECTRICAL ENGINEERING

Energy Conversion (Ex. 2-14, p.46; Probs. 2.1–2.5, p.60).
Equipment Reliability (Sec. 2-9, p.54; Probs. 2.21–2.25, pp. 62-63).
Parallel Resistance (Prob. 2.31, p.64; Ex. 4-1, p.146; Ex. 4-2, p.147).
Circuit Inspection (Probs. 3.27–3.28, p.135).
Diodes (Prob. 3.33, p.138).
Communication Channels (Prob. 5.38, p.240)
Electric Circuit Model (Sec. 8-6, p.386; Probs. 8.11–8.15, p.393).
Transfer Functions (Probs. 8.20–8.22, p.394).
Digital Filtering (Sec. 10-14, p.453; Sec. 15-6, p.654; Probs. 10.1–10.5, p.474; Probs. 15.9–15.13, p.663, Sec. 15.21–15.24, pp.665–666).
Electrical Circuits (Sec. 11-6, p.512; Probs. 11.11–11.15, p.522; Probs. 14.11–14.16, p.629).
Frequency Bands (Sec. 13-2, p.575; Probs. 13.1–13.5, p.597).
Sinusoid Generation (Sec. 15-2, p.634).
Communication Channels (Sec. 15-5, p.650; Probs. 15.5–15.8, pp.662–663).
Telephone Communications (Probs. 15.18–15.20, pp.664–665).
Voyager Spacecraft Data Analysis (Sec. 9-3, p. 407; Probs. 9.1–9.5, p.432).

ENVIRONMENTAL ENGINEERING

Timber Regrowth (Sec. 3.7, p.115; Probs. 3.11–3.15, p. 133).
Air Pollution Control (Sec. 14-4, p.616; Probs. 14.6–14.10, p.628).

MANUFACTURING ENGINEERING

Critical Path Analysis (Sec. 4-2, p.153; Probs. 4.1–4.5, p.181).
Quality Control (Sec. 4-6, p.173; Probs. 4.11–4.15, p.182).
Equipment Maintenance (Prob. 5.32, p.238).

MECHANICAL ENGINEERING

Cable Car Velocity (Ex. 3-4, p.87; Sec. 3-8, p.119; Probs. 3.16–3.20, p. 133).
Solar Device (Prob. 4.16, p.182).
Fuel Analysis (Probs. 4.21–4.22, p.183; Prob. 8.26, p.395).
Temperature Distribution (Sec. 8-4, p.375; Probs. 8.6–8.10, p.393).
Materials Testing (Probs. 9.23–9.27, p.434).
Robot Arm Control (Sec. 10-7, p.465; Probs. 10.6–10.10, pp. 474–475).
Robot Path Generation (Sec. 12-4, p. 541; Probs. 12.6–12.10, pp. 567–568).
Accelerometer Model (Sec. 12-7, p.558; Probs. 12.11–12.15, p.568).

OPTICAL ENGINEERING

Deformable Mirrors (Sec. 11-4, p.501; Probs. 11.6–11.10, pp.521–522).

PETROLEUM ENGINEERING

Seismic Drilling (Probs. 4.23–4.25, p. 184).
Oil Well Production (Sec. 6-6, p.270; Probs. 6.6–6.10, p.293).

POWER ENGINEERING

Power Plant Data Analysis (Sec. 5-7, p.223; Probs. 5.11–5.15, p.235).
Nuclear Plant Cooling System (Prob. 5.35, p.239).

TRANSPORTATION ENGINEERING

Railroad Track Design (Sec. 2-8, p.52; Probs. 2.16–2.20, pp.61–62).
Traffic Flow (Sec. 6-7, p.227; Probs. 6.11–6.15, p.293).

COMPUTER ENGINEERING/ COMPUTER SCIENCE

Sorting (Sec. 5-4, p.205; Ex. 7-2, p.303; Ex. 8-7, p.360; Probs. 8.28–8.29, p.395; Prob. 8.40, p.398).
Computer Security (Sec. 7-5, p.330; Probs. 7.11–7.15, p.341).
Character Editing (Ex. 8-3, p.335; Ex. 8-4, p.357; Ex. 8-5, p.358; Probs. 8.16–8.17, p.394; Probs. 8.24–8.25, p. 395; Probs. 8.27, p.395; Probs. 8.30–8.32, p.396; Probs. 8.34–8.36, p.397).
Collating Sequences (Ex. 8-6, p.359).
Cryptography (Sec. 8-2, p.362; Probs. 8.1–8.5, p. 392; Probs. 8.38–8.39, p.397).
Printer Plotting (Prob. 8.33, p.396).
Computer Inventory (Sec. 9-6, p.424; Probs. 9.11–9.15, p.433)
Searching (Sec. 6-8, p.281; Ex. 6-7, p.282; Ex. 6-8, p.283; Ex. 6-9, p.287)
Inserting and Deleting (Sec. 7-4, p.319; Ex. 7-3, p.320; Ex. 7-4, p.324).

ANTHROPOLOGY AND ARCHEOLOGY

Carbon Dating (Sec. 2-7, p.50; Probs. 2.11–2.15, p.61).
Radioactive Decay and Carbon Dating (Sec. 14-2, p.605; Probs. 14.1–14.5, p.628).

ASTRONOMY

Solar Distances (Ex. 8-8, p.371).

BIOLOGY

Bacteria Growth (Sec. 2-6, p.47; Probs. 2.6–2.10, p.61).
Nutrition Study (Prob. 2.30, p.64; Ex. 4-8, p.166; Prob. 4.17, p.182).
Germ Growth (Prob. 3.30, p.136).
Whooping Crane Migration (Sec. 9-4, p.414; Probs. 9.6–9.10, p.432).

CHEMISTRY

Temperature Conversions (Sec. 6-3, p.249; Probs. 6.1–6.5, p.292).

MATHEMATICS

Rectangle Properties (Prob. 2.26, p.63).
Slope of a Line (Prob. 2.27, p.63).
Circle Properties (Prob. 2.28, p.63).
Metric Conversions (Prob. 2.29, p.63).
Coordinate Distances (Prob. 2.32, p.64).
Volume of a Sphere (Prob. 2.35, p.65).
Triangle Area (Prob. 2.38, p.66; Ex. 6-2, p.246).
Polynomials (Ex. 3-9, p.108; Ex. 3-10, p.109; Ex. 3-11, p.112; Probs. 10.11–10.16, p.475).
Factorials (Ex. 3-13, p.127; Prob. 3.32, p.137; Prob. 6.26, p.294).
Infinite Series (Prob. 3.31, p.137; Probs. 6.28–6.30, p.294; Prob. 8.18, p.394).
Polar Coordinates (Probs. 4.28–4.30, p.186).
Matrix Operations (Ex. 5-7, p.220; Ex. 11-1, p.480; Ex. 11-2, p.480; Ex. 11-3, p.482; Ex. 11-4, p.483; Ex. 11-5, p.485; Probs. 11.16–11.18, p.522).
Airline Reservations (Prob. 5.34, p.239).
Gregorian–Julian Dates (Probs. 5.36–5.37, p.240).
Data Analysis (Prob. 7.27, p.342).
Quadratic Formula (Ex. 8-10, p.384; Prob. 8.19, p.394).
Equation Roots (Probs. 10.17–10.19, p.475).
Simultaneous Equations (Probs. 11.1–11.5, p.521).
Interpolation (Probs. 12.16–12.18, p.568).
Data Modeling (Probs. 12.19–12.23, pp.568–569).
Numerical Integration (Probs. 13.11–13.12, p.598).
Numerical Differentiation (Probs. 13.13–13.15, p.598).
Computation of Pi (Probs. 13.16–13.18, pp.598–599).

METEOROLOGY

National Park Snowfall (Sec. 5-3, p.201; Probs. 5.1–5.5, p.235).
Yearly Rainfall Analysis (Prob. 5.33, p.239).

PHYSICS

Rectifier Tube (Prob. 2.34, p.65).
Spherical Mirror (Ex. 8-9, p.373).

SOCIOLOGY

Weight Category (Ex. 3-5, p.89).
Population Study (Sec. 4-3, p.158; Probs. 4.6–4.10, p.181).

STATISTICS

Averages (Sec. 1-4, p.8; Ex. 3-1, p.79; Ex. 3-6, p.92; Ex. 4-3, p.149; Ex. 4-4, p.152; Ex. 6-4, p.263).

Labor Force Percentages (Prob. 2.33, p.64).

Gaussian Density (Prob. 2.36, p.65; Prob. 2.37, p.66).

Maximum, Minimum (Ex. 3-2, p.81; Ex. 3-7, p.94; Ex. 6-6, p.266; Prob. 7.26, p.342).

Random Number Generation (Sec. 15-4, p.643).

Experimental Sums (Ex. 3-12, p.125).

Scatter Reduction (Prob. 5.31, p.237).

Median Value (Ex. 6-5, p.264).

Array Statistics (Ex. 7-1, p.301).

Random Number Generation (Sec. 7-2, p.306; Probs. 7.1–7.5, p.340).

Variance, Standard Deviation (Probs. 7.28–7.29, p.343).

Bias Adjustment (Prob. 7.30, p.343).

PART I

FORTRAN 77

Part I of this text is designed to begin your computer education by introducing you to the process of problem solving with the computer. The first nine chapters contain a comprehensive coverage of the FORTRAN 77 language and its capabilities.

Chapter 1 is an introduction to computers and the types of problems they can solve. It also presents a five-step problem-solving approach that we will use throughout the text. If you have some prior computer experience, you will find that you can cover this chapter quickly. Beginning with Chapter 2, we present the features of FORTRAN that make it such a versatile and powerful language. Our presentation includes many examples, with an emphasis on the problem-solving technique presented in Chapter 1. Chapters 2–7 should be covered sequentially because they present the fundamental components of FORTRAN that are commonly needed to solve problems. Chapter 8 contains discussions of three additional data types: character data, double-precision data, and complex data. Chapter 9 is a detailed discussion of advanced file-handling statements and techniques.

A number of special features have been added to the text to help you focus on the important concepts. *Color* is used to identify pseudocode solutions throughout the text. Key statements in FORTRAN programs are also highlighted in color. Solutions to some end-of-chapter problems are included at the end of the text, and those problems are identified with colored problem numbers. We have also printed all FORTRAN statements, output from programs, and data file contents in a special *font* (or typeface) to distinguish them clearly from other material.

Most sections are followed by short *self-tests*. You should complete each self-test after reading the corresponding section and then check your answers with those in the back of the text. If you have trouble completing a self-test, reread the section before continuing to the next section.

Each chapter contains a *debugging section* and a *style/technique section*. The debugging section points out errors commonly made with the FORTRAN statements presented in the chapter and makes suggestions for avoiding them. The style/technique section includes guidelines for developing a programming style that stresses readability and simplicity. A list of *key words* also appears at the end of each chapter, with the definitions included in the *glossary* at the end of the text for easy reference.

At the end of each chapter that presents new FORTRAN statements we have included a *statement summary* that gives the general form of each new statement, examples of the statement, and a discussion of the rules associated with the statement. These statement summaries appear at the very end of the chapter.

The *diskette* that accompanies the text contains all the programs and data files from the application sections. These files are ASCII files and thus can be used on any computer system. With these files, you can run the programs to be sure that you understand how they work; you can also easily make modifications and test them.

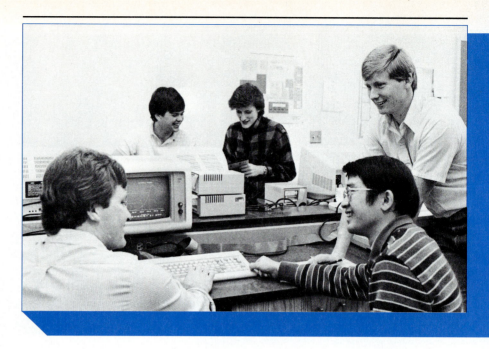

APPLICATION — Experimental Data Analysis

The analysis of laboratory data often involves time-consuming
computations that must be performed before the final results of an
experiment can be determined. Many of these computations can be
performed quickly and easily with a computer. Therefore, one of
the benefits of learning to use the computer is that you can then
use this tool to help you with other tasks and in other coursework.
In this chapter, we use the familiar problem of computing an
average from a set of measurements to illustrate the steps in the
development of a FORTRAN solution to a given problem. (See
Section 1–4 for the solution.)

Photo courtesy of D. M. Etter.

1

AN INTRODUCTION TO FORTRAN 77 AND PROBLEM SOLVING

Introduction
1–1 Computer Organization
1–2 Computer Languages
1–3 Running a Computer Program
1–4 Top-Down Design Techniques
Summary

INTRODUCTION

Problem solving is an activity in which we participate every day. Problems range from analyzing our chemistry lab data to finding the quickest route to work. Computers can solve many of our problems if we learn how to communicate with them in computer languages such as FORTRAN 77. Some people believe that if we describe a problem to a computer, it will solve it for us. Programming would be simpler if this were the case; unfortunately, it is not. Computers only perform the steps that we describe. You may wonder, then, why we go to the effort of writing computer programs to solve problems if we have to describe every step. The answer is that although computers can perform only simple tasks, they perform them extremely accurately and at fantastic rates of speed. In addition, computers never get bored. Imagine sitting at a desk analyzing laboratory data for eight hours a day, five days a week, year after year. This is a pretty dismal thought, and yet thousands of laboratory results must be analyzed every year. Once the steps involved in performing a particular analysis (such as computing an average) have been carefully described to a computer, however, it can analyze data 24 hours a day, with more speed and accuracy than a group of technicians.

We must not forget that someone must first describe the steps to the computer using proper computer language statements before the computer can be used to solve the problem. We will spend much of Part I of this text teaching you the FORTRAN 77 language, but any computer language is useless unless you can break a problem into steps that a computer can perform. Therefore, techniques for problem solving will also be presented and illustrated in each chapter.

In this first chapter we discuss the different types of computers, from the supercomputer to the personal computer. We compare different computer languages and discuss some of the reasons why there are so many languages. We then present a design process for problem solving that we will use throughout the text. This design process will be illustrated by the problem of computing the average of a set of data values mentioned in the introductory chapter application.

1-1 COMPUTER ORGANIZATION

Computers come in all sizes, shapes, and forms, as illustrated in the color section in this chapter. All these computers have a common internal organization, shown in the block diagram in Figure 1-1. Each part is likely to be physically distinguishable from the others in large computer systems. In a microcomputer or minicomputer, all the parts within the dotted line may be combined in a single, integrated circuit chip.

The processing unit or *processor* is the part of the computer that controls all the other parts. The processor accepts input values and stores them in the memory. It also interprets the instructions in a computer program. If we want to add two values, the processor will retrieve them from the memory and send them to the *arithmetic logic unit* or *ALU*. The ALU performs the desired addition, and the processor then stores the result in the memory. If we desire, we may also direct

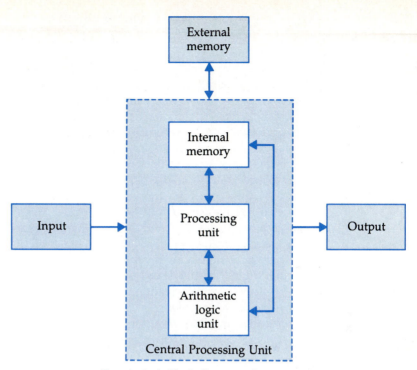

FIGURE 1-1 Block diagram of a computer.

the processor to print the result on paper. The processing unit and the ALU use a small amount of memory, the *internal memory*, in their processing; most data is stored in *external memory*. The processor, internal memory, and ALU are collectively called the *central processing unit* or *CPU*. Thus, a microprocessor is a CPU, but a microcomputer is a CPU with input and output capabilities.

The size of a computer system needed to solve a particular problem depends on the type and number of steps required to solve a problem. If the computer is to be part of a home security system, a microcomputer is sufficient; if the computer is to handle airline reservations for a major airline, then a large computer system may be required. Because FORTRAN 77 is available on most computers, we will be able to use a variety of computers for our programs.

When working with computers, you will often hear the terms *software* and *hardware*. Software refers to the programs that direct computers to perform operations, compute new values, and manipulate data. Hardware refers to the physical components of the computer, such as the memory unit, the processor, and the ALU. A person who works with software might write computer programs, and a person who works with hardware might design new components or connect devices. For example, a hardware engineer might design the interface equipment necessary to connect a microprocessor to an input terminal.

1-2 COMPUTER LANGUAGES

Computer hardware is based on two-state *(binary)* technology; that is, computers are built from components that have two values (such as open or closed, on or off, plus or minus, or high or low). These two values can be represented by the numbers 0 and 1. Thus, computers are often defined as machines capable of interpreting and understanding sequences of 0's and 1's, called binary strings.

Because we have been trained to think in terms of English-like phrases and formulas, we use English-like languages such as FORTRAN 77 to tell the computer the steps we want it to perform. A special program called a *compiler* then translates the FORTRAN 77 program into binary strings that the computer can understand. This compilation procedure is discussed in Section 1-3.

FORTRAN (FORmula TRANslation) was one of the first computer languages. Originally developed in the 1950s for technical applications, FORTRAN 77 is a specific version of FORTRAN based on a set of standards established in 1977. These new standards greatly improved the language by adding new features and structures that allow us to write powerful yet readable programs. (See Appendix D for information on Fortran 90.) COBOL was designed to handle business-related problems and file manipulations. BASIC is commonly used with personal computers. Pascal and C are more recent languages that are *structured languages* because of special structures included in the language. (FORTRAN 77 is also a structured language, but the original FORTRAN was not.) Ada is a language designed for the U.S. Department of Defense for use in technical applications. All these languages are considered high-level languages because their instructions are in English words as opposed to binary strings.

Learning a computer language is similar to learning a foreign language. Each step that you want the computer to perform must be translated into "computer language." Fortunately, computer languages have small vocabularies and no verb conjugations; however, computers are unforgiving in punctuation and spelling. A comma or letter incorrectly placed will cause errors that keep your program from working properly. You will discover that you must pay close attention to many such details.

We have discussed *high-level languages* (such as FORTRAN 77) and *low-level languages* (binary or machine language). At another level are *assembly languages*. Assembly languages are between high-level and low-level languages and do not require a compiler to translate them into binary code. A smaller program, the *assembler*, translates the assembly language into machine language.

Most assembly languages do not have many statements, which make them inconvenient to use. For example, you might have to add a series of numbers to perform a single multiplication. You would also have to understand certain elements of your computer's design to use an assembly language. For these reasons, when given a choice, most people prefer to write programs in a high-level language. Assembly language is used primarily when it is necessary to minimize a program's memory requirements and its execution time.

Some of the statements in various high-level languages are illustrated in Table 1-1. Each section of code represents the calculation of a water bill based on

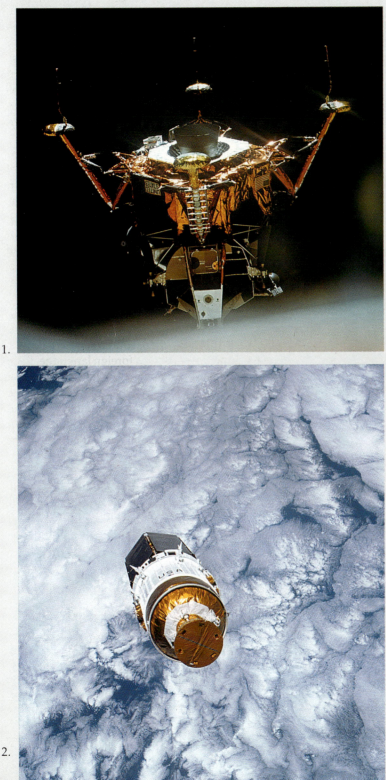

1.

2.

The moon landing was probably the most complex and ambitious engineering project ever attempted. Several major technological advances occurred in a number of areas that made the Saturn/Apollo system possible. For example, the Apollo spacecraft required a new inertial navigation system; the lunar lander ascent engine had to work perfectly because there was no backup; the space suits had to be designed to protect the astronauts in a hostile environment and still allow flexibility for movement; and the Saturn V rocket had to be 15 times more powerful than the biggest rockets available in the early 1960s. Given all these major technical problems to solve, the program was clearly successful. A total of 9 spacecraft and 12 astronauts landed on the moon between 1968 and 1972.

The National Academy of Engineering recently selected what it considers to be the 10 most important engineering achievements during the past 25 years. This photograph gallery recognizes each of these 10 achievements, beginning with the moon landing and covering a wide range of advances and breakthroughs.

1. **Moon Landing** The lunar lander, photographed from the Apollo 11 Lunar Module as it prepares to descend to the lunar surface, was the first manned vehicle designed to fly solely in space. One of its most critical parts (which had no backup) was the small ascent engine that was used to return the astronauts to the Command Module. (Photo courtesy of NASA.)

2. **Application Satellites** Satellite systems ring the earth today giving weather information, relaying communication signals, mapping uncharted terrain, and providing navigational information. This Tracking and Data Relay satellite was used to communicate with spacecraft in low-earth orbit. (Photo courtesy of NASA.)

3. **Microprocessors** A microprocessor is a tiny computer smaller than your fingernail. With its size and capabilities, the applications range from operating remote television controllers or VCR recorders to providing the computational power in hand-held calculators or personal computers. This microprocessor is used for document image compression. (Photo © Melgar Photography, Inc.)

4. **Jumbo Jet** Much of the success of the jumbo jet (747, DC-10, L-1011) can be attributed to the high-bypass fanjet engine that allowed the planes to fly farther using less fuel and with less noise than previous jet engines. The jumbo jets also have an increased emphasis on safety, with four main landing-gear legs on a 747 instead of two. A middle spar was added to the wings in the event one is damaged, and redundant hydraulic systems operate the critical system of elevators, stabilizers, and flaps that control the motion of the plane. (Photo courtesy of Boeing.)

3.

4.

5. **CAT Scan**   A CAT scan (computerized axial tomography scanner) is a machine that generates three-dimensional images or slices of an object using x-rays. A series of x-rays is generated from many angles, encircling the object or patient. Each x-ray measures a density at its angle, and by combining these density measurements with sophisticated computer algorithms, an image can be reconstructed that gives clear detailed pictures of the inside of the object. (Photo © Matthew Borkoski.)

6. **Advanced Composite Materials** Composites consist of a matrix of one material that has been reinforced by the fibers or particles of another material. Examples include using straw in mud bricks to make the bricks stronger and using steel rods in concrete to reinforce bridges and buildings. This composite bicycle wheel is made of epoxy resin reinforced with carbon fiber, Kevlar® aramid fiber, and glass fiber. (Photo courtesy of DuPont.)

7. **CAD/CAM**   CAD (computer-aided design) typically refers to the use of the computer to generate designs, particularly using computer graphics. CAM (computer-aided manufacturing) uses design parameters (sometimes produced by CAD systems) to automatically control the machinery or industrial robots in manufacturing the parts assembling components and moving them to the desired locations. These three CAD views show a solid model of a crane lifting mechanism. (Photo courtesy of Aries Technology.)

5.

6.

7.

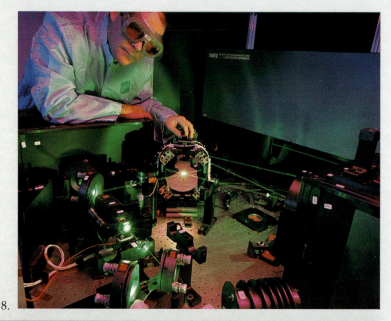

8.

8. **Lasers** Light waves from a laser have the same frequency and thus create a beam with one characteristic color. More importantly, the light waves travel in phase, forming a narrow beam that can easily be directed and focused. CO_2 lasers can be used to drill holes in materials such as ceramics, composite materials, and rubber. Medical uses of lasers include repairing detached retinas, sealing leaky blood vessels, vaporizing brain tumors, removing warts and cysts, and performing delicate inner-ear surgery. This laser beam is being aligned by an optical system. (Photo courtesy of Ball Aerospace Systems Group.)

9.

9. **Fiber-Optic Communications** An optical fiber (a transparent glass thread) is thinner than a human hair but can carry more information than either radio waves or electrical waves in copper telephone wires. In addition, fiber-optic communication signals do not produce electromagnetic waves that cause "cross-talk" noise on communication lines. The first transoceanic fiber-optic cable was laid in 1988 across the Atlantic. It contains four fibers that can handle up to 40,000 calls at one time. This undersea cable contains six optical fibers. (Photo courtesy of AT&T.)

10. **Genetically Engineered Products** Genetically engineered products are created by splicing a gene that produces a valuable substance from one organism into another organism that will multiply itself and the foreign gene along with it. Once the new organism has been created, a system has to be designed to produce and process the product in large quantities at a reasonable cost. The first commercial product of genetic engineering was the production of human insulin, which appeared commercially under the trade name Humulin. The molecules are produced by the genetically engineered bacteria and are then crystallized into human insulin. (Photo courtesy of Eli Lilly & Co.)

10.

the number of gallons of water used. In order to encourage conservation of water, many communities charge a higher rate per gallon if the usage is over a specified amount. In this example, we assume that one rate is used if the number of gallons is less than or equal to 5000; another rate is used for each gallon over 5000. The different names used to represent gallons used, water rates, and total water bill reflect the various rules within the individual languages. Also note the differences in punctuation among the various languages.

TABLE 1-1   Examples of High-Level Languages

LANGUAGE	EXAMPLE STATEMENTS
| FORTRAN 77 | ```
IF (GALLNS.LE.5000.0) THEN
    BILL = GALLNS*RATE1
ELSE
    BILL = 5000.0*RATE1 +
        (GALLNS - 5000.0)*RATE2
ENDIF
``` |
| Pascal | ```
IF GALLONS <= 5000.0 THEN
    BILL := GALLONS*RATE1
ELSE
    BILL := 5000.0*RATE1 +
        (GALLONS - 5000.0)*RATE2;
``` |
| C | ```
IF (GALLONS <= 5000.0)
    BILL = GALLONS*RATE1;
ELSE
    BILL = 5000.0*RATE1 +
        (GALLONS - 5000.0)*RATE2;
``` |
| Ada | ```
IF GALLONS <= 5000.0 THEN
    BILL := GALLONS*RATE1;
ELSE
    BILL := 5000.0*RATE1 +
        (GALLONS - 5000.0)*RATE2;
``` |
| BASIC | ```
    IF G > 5000.0 THEN 200
    LET B = G*R1
    GO TO 250
200 LET B = 5000.0*R1 + (G - 5000.0)*R2
250
``` |
| COBOL | ```
IF GALLONS IS LESS THAN 5000.0 OR
    GALLONS IS EQUAL TO 5000.0,
        COMPUTE BILL = GALLONS*RATE1
ELSE
        COMPUTE BILL = 5000.0*RATE1 +
            (GALLONS - 5000.0)*RATE2.
``` |

1-3 RUNNING A COMPUTER PROGRAM

In the previous section, we defined a compiler as a program that translates a high-level language to machine language. This compilation step is the first step in running a computer program. As the compiler translates statements, it also checks for *syntax errors*. Syntax errors, also called compiler errors, are errors in the statements themselves, such as misspellings and punctuation errors. If syntax errors (often referred to as "bugs") are found, the compiler will print error messages or diagnostics for you. After correcting the errors ("debugging"), you must rerun your program, again starting with the compilation step. Once you have compiled your program without errors, a *linkage editor* program performs the final preparations so that it can be submitted to the execution step. It is in the execution step that the statements are actually performed. Errors can also arise in the execution step; these are called *logic errors*, run-time errors, or execution errors. These errors (also called "bugs") are not in the statement syntax but are errors in the logic of the statements, which are detected only when the computer attempts to execute the statement. For example, the statement

$$X = A/B$$

is a valid FORTRAN 77 statement that directs the computer to divide A by B and call the result X. The statement contains no syntax errors. Suppose, though, that the value of B is zero. Then, as we try to divide A by B, we are attempting to divide by zero, which is an invalid operation; we will get an execution error message. Logic errors do not always generate an error message. For instance, if we were supposed to divide by 0.10 and instead we multiplied by 0.10, no error would be detected by the computer although our answers would be wrong.

A computer program is often called the *source program*. After it is converted into machine language by the compiler and prepared for execution by the linkage editor, it is in machine language and is now called the *object program*. A diagram of this *compilation-linkage-execution process* is shown in Figure 1-2.

It is uncommon for a program to compile, link, and execute correctly on the first run. Do not become discouraged if it takes several runs to get your answers. When you do get answers from your program, do not assume they are correct. If possible, check your answers with a calculator, and always check to see if the answers make sense. For example, if the answer represents the weight of a

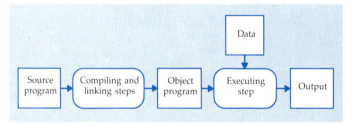

FIGURE 1-2 Compilation-linkage-execution process for running a computer program.

boxcar, then 5 pounds is not reasonable and suggests that you have given the computer incorrect information or an incorrect program to execute.

Two methods are used for running computer programs: *batch processing* and *time sharing*. In batch-processing systems, the computer stores the program in its memory and compiles and executes it completely before executing another program. In time-sharing systems, the program is typed into the terminal, followed by a command such as RUN, which immediately begins the processing. This technique is called time sharing because the computer does a few steps of a program from one terminal, then a few steps of a program from another terminal, and so on until it is back to the first terminal. The computer then performs another cycle of steps in each program. We usually do not notice the time between cycles because the computer executes statements so quickly. We seem to have the undivided attention of the computer, although we are actually sharing it with many other terminal users. Interaction with either type of system is generally by means of a terminal. Hard-copy terminals use paper to record the input and output from the computer, and CRT (cathode ray tube) terminals use a video screen to display the input and output.

Most time-sharing systems allot each user a specified amount of memory to be used as a workspace in the computer. This workspace is usually divided into a temporary workspace and a permanent workspace. As you enter programs or data into the temporary workspace you can edit the information, which means you can add to it, delete portions of it, or modify it with the use of an editing program (called an editor). When you have the program or data in the form that you want, you can save it in the permanent workspace. You can then clear the temporary workspace and begin entering new information or you can ''log off'' the terminal. The next time you ''log on,'' you can load any information that was previously saved in your permanent workspace into your temporary workspace.

Time sharing or using a personal computer is called *interactive computing* because we are interacting with the computer more than in a batch-processing system. This increased interaction results in more efficient use of your time— you have fewer delays.

We can also interact with computers using workstations. A *workstation* is a computer that can do many types of processing by itself, and thus can function as a standalone computer. However, a workstation is also connected to other computers via a *computer network* that allows the computers to communicate with each other. The access to the network can be used to increase the resources available to the workstation. For example, a workstation may have a dot-matrix printer attached to it for general printing. If the user wishes to print an important report on a laser printer attached to the network, the workstation can request that the information be transmitted across the network and printed on the laser printer. Workstations can also share programs or data files with other computers on the network. For example, instead of every computer on a network maintaining its own FORTRAN 77 compiler, the compiler could be stored on one computer and then copied to other workstations that wanted to use it. After each user finished using the compiler, it would then be deleted from all the individual workstations, but it would still be retained on the original computer system.

1-4 TOP-DOWN DESIGN TECHNIQUES

Having discussed computer hardware and software, we now turn to developing a procedure for solving problems using the computer. Our procedure has five phases; we will use it each time we present a complete problem solution. Understanding the phases will be easier if we go through them using a familiar problem, such as computing an average. This problem arises when we are computing our homework average in one of our courses or when we are summarizing experimental data from a lab experiment.

The first phase of our design process is to state the problem clearly. It is important to give a clear, concise statement of the problem to avoid any misunderstandings. For our example, the problem statement is

Compute the average of a set of experimental data values.

The second phase is to describe carefully any information or data needed to solve the problem and then describe how the final answer is to be presented. These items represent the input and the output for the problem. Collectively, they are called *input/output*, or *I/O*. In our example, the input information is the list of experimental data values. The output is the average of these data values.

The third phase is to work the problem by hand or with a calculator, using a simple set of data. An example of a set of data values and the computed average is

LAB MEASUREMENTS	4/23/89
NUMBER	VALUE
1	23.43
2	37.43
3	34.91
4	28.37
5	30.62
Sum	154.76

Average = Sum/5 = 30.95

The fourth phase is to describe, in general terms, the steps that you performed by hand. The sequence of steps that solves the problem is called an *algorithm*. The procedure that we use in our algorithm development is called *top-down design*. Top-down design is composed of two techniques: *decomposition* and *stepwise refinement*. We break the problem into a series of smaller problems (decomposition), and address each smaller problem separately (stepwise refinement). Decomposition is a form of "divide and conquer" in which each part of the overall problem is described in general terms. Stepwise refinement begins with this general description and successively refines and describes each step in greater detail. The refining continues until the solution is specific enough to convert into computer instructions.

The advantage of decomposition is that we can initially think of the overall steps required without getting lost in the details. Details are introduced only as we begin the refinement of our algorithm. We will show the decomposition in block diagrams to emphasize that we are breaking the solution into a series of sequentially executed steps. Two tools assist us in refining the general steps of the decomposition: *flowcharts* and *pseudocode*. A flowchart shows the steps in an algorithm in graphic form, and pseudocode presents algorithm steps in a series of English-like statements. For the development of our example solution, we will describe the steps in a longhand form similar to pseudocode. The details of flowcharts and pseudocode are presented in Chapter 3.

Applying the concept of "divide and conquer," or decomposition, to our problem of computing an average, we first break the problem into a series of smaller problems.

DECOMPOSITION

Read data values and sum them.
Divide sum by the number of data values.
Print the average.

The second part of top-down design is to refine each step in the decomposition into more detailed steps. As you read the following algorithm, remember the steps you just performed in the longhand example; they should be similar to these steps:

ALGORITHM FOR COMPUTING AN AVERAGE

Step 1. Set the sum of the values to zero.
           Set a count of the values to zero.
Step 2. As long as there are more data values, do the following:
               Add the next data value to the sum.
               Add 1 to the count.
           When there are no more values, go to the next step.
Step 3. Divide the sum by the count to get the average.
Step 4. Print the average.
Step 5. Stop.

Once the solution steps, or algorithm, are detailed, they are ready to be converted into FORTRAN 77. The statements for solving this problem will not all be presented until Chapter 3, so there are items in the solution that you probably won't understand at this time. We present the solution here so that you can see how similar it is to the refined steps previously described. We assume that a data value of zero is used to indicate that we have reached the end of the data values.

```
*---------------------------------------------------------------*
        PROGRAM   COMPUT
*
*   This program computes the average of
*   a set of experimental data values.
*
        INTEGER   COUNT
        REAL   X, SUM, AVERG
*
        SUM = 0.0
        COUNT = 0
        READ*, X
      1 IF (X.NE.0.0) THEN
            SUM = SUM + X
            COUNT = COUNT + 1
            READ*, X
            GO TO 1
        ENDIF
        AVERG = SUM/REAL(COUNT)
        PRINT 5, AVERG
      5 FORMAT (1X,'THE AVERAGE IS ',F6.2)
        END
*---------------------------------------------------------------*
```

The fifth phase of problem solving is to test the solution steps (or algorithm) that you have just described. Testing an algorithm is not easy. We can usually find data for which our algorithm works correctly, but it is just as important to determine if there are sequences of data that cause our algorithm to fail — so that we can correct the steps in the program. A correct algorithm to average data should work properly for any set of data. If the data from our longhand example were used in the FORTRAN program presented here, the output on our terminal screen would be

THE AVERAGE IS   30.95

Algorithm testing is discussed further in later chapters.

These five phases for algorithm development are used in the special application sections throughout the rest of the text.

SUMMARY

In this chapter we discussed the fundamental concepts of computers. The process of converting a computer program into a form the computer can understand and execute was described, and the five-phase procedure for developing problem solutions (algorithms) was presented. The five phases are

1. State the problem clearly.
2. Describe the input and output information.
3. Work the problem by hand (or with a calculator) for a specific set of data.
4. Develop a solution that is general in nature.
5. Test the solution with a variety of data sets.

The solution is developed using top-down design. Decomposition assists in describing the general steps that have to be performed to solve the problem. Stepwise refinement guides us in refining the steps and adding necessary details.

KEY WORDS

algorithm	FORTRAN 77
arithmetic logic unit (ALU)	hardware
assembler	high-level language
assembly language	input/output (I/O)
batch processing	interactive computing
binary	logic error
bug	machine language
cathode ray tube terminal (CRT)	memory
central processing unit (CPU)	object program
compilation	problem solving
compiler	processor
computer network	program
data	software
debug	source program
decomposition	stepwise refinement
design phases	syntax error
diagnostic	time sharing
editor	top-down design
execution	workstation

APPLICATION — Equipment Reliability (Electrical Engineering)

If you have a personal computer, or if you have a friend who has one, open the back of the computer system and look at the computer board(s) that contain its circuitry. Each board contains a large number of components. You might wonder how computers can be so reliable when so many different components could malfunction. Much of their reliability is due to the quality control maintained during their manufacture. Also, during the design of the computer, or any other complicated piece of instrumentation, the reliability is analyzed. This analysis depends both on the reliability of the individual components and on the manner in which the components are connected. Write a FORTRAN program to compute the reliability of a design with many components connected serially. (See Section 2–9 for the solution.)

Photo © Mark Antman, The Image Works.

2

ARITHMETIC COMPUTATIONS

Introduction

2–1 Constants and Variables

2–2 Arithmetic Operations

2–3 Intrinsic Functions

2–4 Simple Input and Output

2–5 Complete Programs

2–6 Application — Bacteria Growth (Biology)

2–7 Application — Carbon Dating (Archeology)

2–8 Application — Railroad Track Design (Transportation Engineering)

2–9 Application — Equipment Reliability (Electrical Engineering)

Summary

INTRODUCTION

Arithmetic operations (adding, subtracting, multiplying, and dividing) are the most fundamental operations performed by computers. Engineers and scientists also need other routine operations, such as raising a number to a power, taking the logarithm of a number, or computing the sine of an angle. This chapter discusses methods of storing data with FORTRAN 77 and develops the statements for performing arithmetic calculations with that data. We also introduce statements for simple data input and output. With this group of statements, we can write complete FORTRAN 77 programs.

Before we discuss which types of numbers can be stored in computers and some specific statements, we need to outline the proper form for entering FORTRAN statements. These rules generally apply to FORTRAN statements entered on both time-sharing systems and batch systems. Each statement is entered on a new line. We refer to specific positions within the line by column number: The first position in a line is column 1, the second position in a line is column 2, and so on.

1. Columns 1 through 5 are reserved for statement numbers (also called labels), which must be nonzero positive integers. Not every statement requires a number, but as you will see in later chapters, some statements need numbers so they can be referenced. If column 1 contains an asterisk or the letter C, the line is a comment line. Comment lines are used for entering general comments and are printed in a listing of the program; comment lines are not converted into machine language or used during execution of the program.

2. Column 6 is used to indicate that a statement has been continued from the previous line. Any nonblank character except a zero can be used in the second line in column 6 to indicate continuation. A FORTRAN statement may have several continuation lines if it is too long to fit on one line.

3. FORTRAN statements start in column 7 and can extend to column 72. In general, blanks can be inserted anywhere in the statement for readability. All information beyond column 72 is ignored.

These rules are summarized in Figure 2–1.

Some terminal editors require you to number each line. These line numbers are used in editing but cannot be referenced by a FORTRAN statement. If you are using one of these editors, all statements will have a line number, and statements referenced in your program will also have a FORTRAN label.

FIGURE 2–1 General form of a FORTRAN statement.

2-1 CONSTANTS AND VARIABLES

Numbers are introduced into a computer program either directly with the use of *constants* or indirectly with the use of *variables*. Constants are numbers used directly in FORTRAN 77 statements, such as -7, 3.141593, and 32.0. Constants may contain plus or minus signs and decimal points, but they may not contain commas. Thus 3147.6 is a valid FORTRAN constant, but 3,147.6 is not. Constants are stored in memory locations but can be accessed only by using the constant value itself.

A variable represents a memory location that is assigned a name. The memory location contains a value; we reference that value with the name assigned to that memory location. We can visualize variables, their names, and their values as shown:

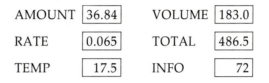

Each memory location to be used in a program is given a name and may be assigned a value using a FORTRAN statement. In the preceding example, the memory location named RATE has been assigned the value 0.065.

Each variable must have a different name, which you provide in your program. The names may contain one to six characters consisting of both alphabetic characters and digits; however, the first character of a name must be alphabetic. The following are examples of both valid and invalid variable names:

DISTANCE	Invalid name — too long
TIME	Valid name
PI	Valid name
$	Invalid name — illegal character ($)
TAX−RT	Invalid name — illegal character (−)
B1	Valid name
2X	Invalid name — first character must be alphabetic

Numerical values in FORTRAN can be one of four types: integer, real, double precision, or complex. Integer-type values are those with no fractional portion and no decimal point, such as 16, -7, 186, and 0; they are also called fixed-point values. On the other hand, real-type values contain a decimal point and may or may not have digits past the decimal point, such as 13.86, 13., 0.0076, -14.1, 36.0, and -3.1; these real values are also called floating-point values. Double-precision values and complex values are discussed in Chapter 8.

A memory location can contain only one type of value. The type of value stored in a variable is specified by two methods: *implicit typing* or *explicit typing*. With implicit typing, the first letter of a variable name determines the value type that can be stored in it. Variable names beginning with the letters I, J, K, L, M, or N are used to store integers. Variable names beginning with one of the other letters, A–H and O–Z, are used to store real values. Thus, with implicit typing, AMOUNT represents a real value and MONEY represents an integer value. An easy way to remember which letters are used for integers is to observe that the range of letters is I–N, the first two letters of the word integer.

With explicit typing, a special FORTRAN statement is used to specify the variable type. For example, the statements

```
INTEGER  WIDTH
REAL  ITEM, LENGTH
```

specify that WIDTH is a variable containing an integer value and that ITEM and LENGTH are variables containing real values. These *specification statements* have the following general forms:

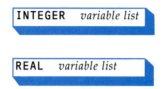

INTEGER *variable list*

REAL *variable list*

The variable lists in the previous statements contain variable names separated by commas. These statements are *nonexecutable* because they are used by the compiler to specify the type of value to be stored in a variable and are not translated into machine language. Specification statements are placed at the beginning of the program—before any executable statement.

It is helpful to select a variable name that is descriptive of the value being stored. For example, if a value represents a tax rate, name it RATE or TAX. If the implicit typing of the variable name does not match the type of value to be stored in it, then use a REAL or INTEGER statement at the beginning of your program to specify the desired type of value. Some programmers prefer to list all variables in specification statements, including those correctly typed by the implicit rules. In the example programs used in this book, all variables are included in specification statements. When individual statements are used as examples, you can assume that the variables are typed according to their names unless otherwise indicated.

SCIENTIFIC NOTATION

When a real number is very large or very small, decimal notation does not work satisfactorily. For example, a value that is used frequently in chemistry is Avogadro's constant, whose value to four significant places is 602,300,000,000,000,000,000,000. Obviously, we need a more manageable notation for very large values like Avogadro's constant or for very small values like 0.000000000042. *Scientific notation*, commonly used in science, expresses a value as a number between 1 and 10 multiplied by a power of 10. In scientific notation, Avogadro's constant becomes 6.023×10^{23}. Elements of this form are commonly referred to as the mantissa (6.023) and the exponent (23). The FORTRAN form of scientific notation, called *exponential notation,* expresses a value as a number between 0.1 and 1 multiplied by an appropriate power of 10. Exponential notation uses the letter E to separate the mantissa and the exponent. In exponential form, Avogadro's constant becomes 0.6023E24. Other examples of decimal values in scientific and exponential notation are

DECIMAL VALUE	SCIENTIFIC NOTATION	EXPONENTIAL NOTATION
3,876,000,000	3.876×10^9	0.3876E10
0.0000010053	1.0053×10^{-6}	0.10053E−05
−8,030,000	-8.03×10^6	−0.803E07
−0.000157	-1.57×10^{-4}	−0.157E−03

Although FORTRAN uses an exponential form with a mantissa between 0.1 and 1.0, it will accept mantissas beyond that range; for instance, the constant 0.16E03 would also be valid in the forms 1.6E02 or 0.016E04.

MAGNITUDE LIMITATIONS

There are limitations on the magnitude and precision of values that can be stored in a computer. All limitations on values depend on the specific computer. For instance, pi is an irrational number and cannot be written with a finite number of decimal positions; in a computer with seven digits of accuracy, pi could be stored as 3.141593. In addition to limits on the number of significant positions in the mantissa, there are also limits on the size of the exponent.

Table 2−1 compares the approximate range of values that can be stored in several large computers. Check a reference manual to find the ranges of real and integer values for the computer you will be using.

TABLE 2-1 Typical Ranges for FORTRAN Data Values

COMPUTER	REAL VALUE RANGES	MAXIMUM INTEGER
IBM 360/370	Mantissa: 6 significant digits Exponent: −77 to 75	2,147,483,647
VAX	Mantissa: 7 significant digits Exponent: −38 to 38	2,147,483,647
CRAY-1	Mantissa: 13 significant digits Exponent: −2465 to 2465	2.8×10^{14}
CDC 6000/7000	Mantissa: 14 significant digits Exponent: −293 to 322	9.2×10^{18}

2-2 ARITHMETIC OPERATIONS

Computations in FORTRAN may be specified with the assignment statement whose general form is

$$\textit{variable name} = \textit{expression}$$

The simplest form of an expression is a constant. Hence, if the value of pi is needed frequently in a program, we might choose to define a variable PI with the value 3.141593. We could then refer to the variable PI each time we needed the constant. An assignment statement that assigns a value to PI is

$$PI = 3.141593$$

The name of the variable receiving a new value must always be on the left-hand side of the equal sign. In FORTRAN, the equal sign can be read as "is assigned the value of." Thus, this statement could be read "PI is assigned the value 3.141593." The term "initialized" is often used to refer to the first value assigned to a variable in a program; this statement could also be read "PI is initialized to the value 3.141593."

TABLE 2-2 Arithmetic Operations in Algebraic Form and in FORTRAN

OPERATION	ALGEBRAIC FORM	FORTRAN
Addition	$A + B$	A + B
Subtraction	$A - B$	A − B
Multiplication	$A \times B$	A*B
Division	$\dfrac{A}{B}$	A/B
Exponentiation	A^3	A**3

It is important to recognize that a variable can store only one value at a time. For example, suppose the following statements were executed one after another:

```
WIDTH = 36.7
WIDTH = 105.2
```

The value 36.7 is stored in the variable WIDTH after the first statement is executed. The second statement replaces that value with the new value 105.2, and the first value is lost.

Consider these statements:

```
TEMP1 = -52.6
TEMP2 = TEMP1
```

The first statement stores the value −52.6 in TEMP1. The second statement stores the same value in TEMP2 that is stored in TEMP1. Note that the value in TEMP1 is not lost; both TEMP1 and TEMP2 now contain the value −52.6.

Often we want to calculate a new value using arithmetic operations with other variables and constants. For instance, assume that the variable RADIUS has been assigned a value and we want to calculate the area of a circle having that radius. To do so, we must square the radius and then multiply by the value of pi. Table 2−2 shows the FORTRAN expressions for the basic arithmetic operations. Note that an asterisk (instead of a ✕) represents multiplication; this avoids confusion because AXB (commonly used in algebra to indicate the product of A and B) represents a variable name in FORTRAN. Division and exponentiation also have different symbols that allow us to write these arithmetic operations on a single line.

EVALUATING AN ARITHMETIC EXPRESSION

Because several operations can be combined in one arithmetic expression, it is important to determine the priorities of the operations (the order in which the operations are performed). For instance, consider the following assignment statement that calculates the area of a circle:

```
AREA = PI*RADIUS**2
```

TABLE 2–3 Priorities of Arithmetic Operations

Priority	Operation
First	Parentheses
Second	Exponentiation
Third	Multiplication and division
Fourth	Addition and subtraction

If the exponentiation is performed first, we compute $PI \times (RADIUS)^2$; if multiplication is performed first, we compute $(PI \times RADIUS)^2$. Note that the two computations yield different results. The order of priorities for computations in FORTRAN is given in Table 2–3 and follows the standard algebraic priorities.

Operations in parentheses are performed first. When executing the previous FORTRAN statement, the RADIUS is first squared, then the result is multiplied by PI — correctly determining the area of the circle. Remember that we assume that both PI and RADIUS have been initialized. The following statements also correctly compute the area of the circle:

```
AREA = PI*RADIUS*RADIUS
```

or

```
AREA = 3.141593*RADIUS*RADIUS
```

If a minus sign precedes the first variable name in an expression, it is computed on the same priority level as subtraction. For example, $-A**2$ is computed as if it were $-(A**2)$; $-A*B$ is computed as if it were $-(A*B)$; and $-A+B$ is computed as if it were $(-A)+B$.

When two operations are on the same priority level, as in addition and subtraction, all operations except exponentiation are performed from left to right. Thus, $B - C + D$ is evaluated as $(B - C) + D$. If two exponentiations occur sequentially in FORTRAN, as in $A**B**C$, they are evaluated right to left, as in $A**(B**C)$. Thus, $2**3**2$ is 2^9, or 512, as opposed to $(2**3)**2$, which is 8^2, or 64.

A more complex arrangement is represented by the following expression for one of the real roots of a quadratic equation:

$$X1 = \frac{-B + \sqrt{B^2 - 4AC}}{2A}$$

Recall that A, B, and C are coefficients of the quadratic equation ($AX^2 + BX + C = 0$). Because computers cannot divide by zero, we assume A is not equal to zero. The value of X1 can be computed in FORTRAN with the following statement, assuming that the variables A, B, and C have been initialized:

```
X1 = (-B + (B**2 - 4.0*A*C)**0.5)/(2.0*A)
```

To check the order of operations in a long expression, you should start with the operations inside parentheses; that is, find the operation done first, then second, and so on. The following diagram outlines this procedure, using braces to show the steps of operations. Beneath each brace is the value calculated in that step:

$$\text{X1 = } \underbrace{(\underbrace{-B}_{-B} + \underbrace{(B**2 - 4.0*A*C)**0.5}_{B^2 - 4AC})}_{\substack{-B + \sqrt{B^2 - 4AC} \\ \\ \dfrac{-B + \sqrt{B^2 - 4AC}}{2A}}} / \underbrace{(2.0*A)}_{2A}$$

As shown in the final brace, the desired value is computed by this expression.

Parentheses placement is important. If the outside set of parentheses in the numerator in the previous FORTRAN statement were omitted, our assignment statement would become

$$\text{X1 = } \underbrace{-B}_{-B} + \underbrace{(B**2 - 4.0*A*C)**0.5}_{\substack{B^2 - 4AC \\ \sqrt{B^2 - 4AC}}} / \underbrace{(2.0*A)}_{\substack{2A \\ \\ \dfrac{\sqrt{B^2 - 4AC}}{2A} \\ \\ -B + \dfrac{\sqrt{B^2 - 4AC}}{2A}}}$$

As you can see, omission of the outside set of parentheses causes the wrong value to be calculated as a root of the original quadratic equation. Omission of a different set of parentheses would result in the following expression:

$$\text{X1 = } \underbrace{(-B + B**2 - 4.0*A*C**0.5)}_{\substack{-B + B^2 - 4A\sqrt{C} \\ \\ \dfrac{-B + B^2 - 4A\sqrt{C}}{2A}}} / \underbrace{(2.0*A)}_{2A}$$

Again, the wrong value would be calculated. If all parentheses were omitted, the expression would become

$$\text{X1 = } \underbrace{-B}_{-B} + \underbrace{B**2}_{B^2} - \underbrace{4.0*A*C**0.5}_{\substack{\sqrt{C} \\ \dfrac{4A\sqrt{CA}}{2}}} / \underbrace{2.0*A}_{\substack{\\ \\ -B + B^2 - \dfrac{4A^2\sqrt{C}}{2}}}$$

Still another incorrect value would be computed.

Omitting necessary parentheses results in incorrect calculations. Using extra parentheses to emphasize the order of calculations is permissible even though they may not be needed. It is advisable to insert extra parentheses in a statement if it makes the statement more readable.

You also may want to break a long statement into several smaller statements. Recall that the expression $B^2 - 4AC$ in the quadratic equation is called the discriminant. Both roots of the solution could be calculated with the following statements after initialization of A, B, and C:

```
DISCR = B**2 - 4.0*A*C
X1 = (-B + DISCR**0.5)/(2.0*A)
X2 = (-B - DISCR**0.5)/(2.0*A)
```

In the preceding statements we assume that the discriminant, DISCR, is positive, enabling us to obtain X1 and X2, the two real roots to the equation. If the discriminant were negative, an execution error would occur when we attempted to take the square root of the negative value. If the value of A were zero, we would get an execution error for attempting to divide by zero. In later chapters we learn techniques for handling these situations.

We often use variables as counters in our FORTRAN programs. We first initialize the counter to a certain value and later, under certain conditions, change it to another value. For example, a counter named COUNTR, which we assume was listed in an INTEGER statement, is incremented by 1:

```
COUNTR = COUNTR + 1
```

This statement may look invalid because, algebraically, COUNTR cannot be equal to COUNTR + 1. But remember, in FORTRAN, this statement means "COUNTR is assigned the value of COUNTR plus 1." Hence, if the old value of COUNTR is 0, the new value of COUNTR after executing this statement is 1.

TRUNCATION AND MIXED-MODE OPERATIONS

When an arithmetic operation is performed using two real numbers its intermediate result is a real value. For example, the circumference of a circle can be calculated as

```
CIRCUM = PI*DIAMTR
```

or

```
CIRCUM = 3.141593*DIAMTR
```

In both statements, we have multiplied two real values, giving a real result, which is then stored in the real variable CIRCUM.

Similarly, arithmetic operations between two integers yield an integer. For instance, if I and J represent two integers, and if I is less than or equal to J, then the number of integers in the interval I–J can be calculated with the following statement:

```
INTERV = J - I + 1
```

Thus, if I = 6 and J = 11, then INTERV will contain 6, the number of integers in the set {6, 7, 8, 9, 10, 11}.

Now consider the statement:

$$\text{LENGTH = SIDE*3.5}$$

Assume that SIDE represents a real value and that LENGTH represents an integer value. We know that the multiplication between the real value SIDE and the real constant 3.5 yields a real result. In this case, however, the real result is stored in an integer variable. When the computer stores a real number in an integer variable, it ignores the fractional portion and stores only the whole number portion of the real number; this loss is called *truncation*.

Other computations with integers also give unexpected results. Consider the following statement that computes the average, or mean, of two integers, N1 and N2:

$$\text{MEAN = (N1 + N2)/2}$$

If we assume that all the variables in the statement are integers, the result of the expression will be an integer. Thus, if N1 = 2 and N2 = 4, the mean value is the expected value, 3. But if N1 = 2 and N2 = 3, the result of the division of 5 by 2 will be 2 instead of 2.5 because the division involved two integers; hence, the intermediate result must be an integer. At first glance it might seem that we could solve this problem if we called the average by a real variable named AVE (instead of MEAN) and used this statement:

$$\text{AVE = (N1 + N2)/2}$$

Unfortunately, this cannot correct our answer. The result of integer arithmetic is still an integer; all we have done is move the integer result into a real variable. Thus, if N1 = 2 and N2 = 3, then (N1 + N2)/2 = 2 and AVE = 2.0, not 2.5. One way to correct this problem is to declare N1 and N2 to be real values and use the following statement to calculate the average:

$$\text{AVE = (N1 + N2)/2.0}$$

Note the difference between rounding and truncation. With rounding, the result is the integer closest in value to the real number. Truncation, however, causes any decimal portion to be dropped. If we divide the integer 15 by the integer 8, the truncated result is 1, the integer portion of 1.875.

The effects of truncation can also be seen in the following statement, which appears to calculate the square root of NUM:

$$\text{ROOT = NUM**(1/2)}$$

However, since $\frac{1}{2}$ is truncated to 0, we are really raising NUM to the zero power; ROOT will always contain the value 1.0, no matter what value is in NUM.

We have seen that an operation involving only real values yields a real result and an operation involving only integer values yields an integer result. FORTRAN also accepts a *mixed-mode* operation, which is an operation involving an integer value and a real value. The intermediate result is a real value. The final result depends on the type of variable used to store the result of the mixed-mode operation. Consider the following arithmetic statement for computing the perimeter of a square whose sides are real values:

```
PERIM = 4*SIDE
```

The preceding multiplication is a mixed-mode operation between the integer constant 4 and the real variable SIDE. The intermediate result is real and is correctly stored in the real result PERIM.

Using mixed mode, we can now correctly calculate the square root of the integer NUM, using this statement:

```
ROOT = NUM**0.5
```

The mixed-mode exponentiation yields a real result, which is stored in ROOT.

To compute the area of a square with real sides, we could use the mixed-mode expression

```
AREA = SIDE**2
```

or the real-mode expression

```
AREA = SIDE**2.0
```

The result in both cases is real; but in this case, the mixed-mode form is preferable. Exponentiation to an integer power is generally performed internally in the computer with a series of multiplications such as SIDE times SIDE. If an exponent is real, however, the operation is performed by the arithmetic logic unit using logarithms; SIDE**2.0 is actually computed as antilog(2.0 × log(SIDE)). Logarithms can introduce small errors into the calculations; although 5.0**2 is always 25.0, 5.0**2.0 is often computed as 24.99999. Also, note that (−2.0)**2 is a valid operation, but (−2.0)**2.0 is an invalid operation—the logarithm of a negative value does not exist, and an execution error occurs. As a general guide when raising numbers to an integer power, use an integer exponent, even though the base number is real.

Mixed-mode expressions may still lose accuracy through truncation if operations between integers are embedded in the expression. For instance, assume that we want to calculate the volume of a sphere with radius R, where R represents a real value. The volume is computed by multiplying 4/3 times pi, times the radius cubed. The following mixed-mode statement at first appears correct:

```
VOLUM = (4/3)*3.141593*R**3
```

The expression contains integer and real values, so the result will be a real value. However, the division of 4 by 3 yields the intermediate value of 1, not 1.333333; therefore, the final answer will be incorrect.

Because mixed-mode operations can sometimes give unexpected results, you should try to avoid writing arithmetic expressions that include them. The only time that a mixed-mode expression is desirable is in an exponentiation operation in which an integer is raised to a non-integer power or when a real value is raised to an integer power.

UNDERFLOW AND OVERFLOW

In a previous section we discussed magnitude limitations for the values stored in variables. Because the maximum and minimum values that can be stored in a variable depend on the computer system itself, a computation may yield a result that can be stored in one computer system but is too large to be stored in another. For example, suppose we execute the following assignment statements:

```
X = 0.25E20
Y = 0.10E30
```

If we assume that we are using a VAX computer (see Table 2–1), both of these variables are within the range of real values that we can store (the exponent range is -38 through 38). Suppose we now execute the following statement:

```
Z = X*Y
```

The numerical result of this multiplication is .025E50. Clearly this result is too large to store in a VAX computer. The error is not a syntax error; the statements themselves were valid FORTRAN 77 statements. The error is an execution error because it occurred during execution of the program. This error is called an exponent *overflow* error because the exponent of the result of an arithmetic operation was too large to store in the computer's memory.

Exponent *underflow* is a similar error caused by the exponent of the result of an arithmetic operation being too small to store in the computer's memory. If we were using a VAX computer, the following statements would generate an exponent underflow error because the value that is computed for C has an exponent smaller than -38:

```
A = 0.25E-20
B = 0.10E+20
C = A/B
```

If you get exponent underflow or overflow errors when you run your programs, you need to examine the magnitude of the values you are using. If you really need values whose exponents exceed the limits of your computer, the only solution is to switch to a computer that can handle a wider range of exponents. Most of the time, exponent underflow and overflow errors are caused by other errors in a program. For example, if variables are initialized to an incorrect value or the wrong arithmetic operation is specified, exponent underflow or overflow can occur—but the source of the problem is elsewhere. If you consider the limits on values that can be stored in a VAX, for example, you will see that it is an unusual problem whose answer is greater than 10 raised to the thirty-eighth power or is smaller than 10 raised to the negative thirty-eighth power.

SELF-TEST 2–2

This self-test allows you to check quickly to see if you have remembered some of the key points from Section 2–2. If you have any problems with the exercises, you should reread this section. The solutions are included at the end of the text.

1. What value is stored in Y after the following statements are executed?

```
REAL   X1, X2, X3, Y
X1 = 5.0
X2 = 5.0
X3 = 0.5
Y = X1+X2/X1-X2/X3
```

2. What values are stored in the variables A and K after the following statements are executed?

```
REAL   A
INTEGER   I, J, K
I = 8
J = 3
A = I/J
K = I/J
```

3. What value is stored in T after the following statements are executed?

```
REAL   R, S, T
R = 4.0
S = 10.0
T = 1.0/(1.0/S)+(1.0/R)
```

2-3   INTRINSIC FUNCTIONS

Algorithms commonly require many simple operations such as computing the square root of a value, computing the absolute value of a number, or computing the sine of an angle. Because these operations occur so frequently, built-in computer functions called *intrinsic functions* are available to handle these routine computations. Instead of using the arithmetic expression X**0.5 to compute a square root, we can use the intrinsic function SQRT(X). Similarly, we can refer to the absolute value of B by ABS(B). A list of some commonly used intrinsic functions appears in Table 2-4, and a complete list of FORTRAN 77 intrinsic functions is contained in Appendix A, along with a brief description of each function.

The name of the function is followed by the input to the function, also called the *argument* of the function, which is enclosed in parentheses. This argument can be a constant, variable, or expression. For example, suppose that we want to compute the cosine of the variable ANGLE and store the result in another variable COSINE. From Table 2-4, we see that the cosine function COS assumes that its argument is in radians. If the value in ANGLE is in degrees, we must change the degrees to radians (1 degree = pi/180 radians) and then compute the cosine. The following statement performs the degree-to-radian conversion within the function argument:

```
COSINE = COS(ANGLE*(3.141593/180.0))
```

TABLE 2-4 Common Intrinsic Functions

FUNCTION NAME AND ARGUMENT	FUNCTION VALUE	COMMENT
SQRT(X)	$\sqrt{X}$	Square root of X
ABS(X)	$|X|$	Absolute value of X
SIN(X)	Sine of angle X	X must be in radians
COS(X)	Cosine of angle X	X must be in radians
TAN(X)	Tangent of angle X	X must be in radians
EXP(X)	e^x	e raised to the X power
LOG(X)	$\log_e X$	Natural log of X
LOG10(X)	$\log_{10} X$	Common log of X
INT(X)	Integer part of X	Converts a real value to an integer value
REAL(I)	Real value of I	Converts an integer value to a real value
MOD(I,J)	Integer remainder of I/J	Remainder or modulo function

The inside set of parentheses is not required but serves to emphasize the conversion factor.

The REAL and INT functions may be used to avoid undesirable mixed-mode arithmetic expressions by explicitly converting variable types. For example, if we are computing the average of a group of real values, we need to divide the real sum of the values by the number of values. We can convert the integer number of values into a real value for the division using the REAL function, as shown in the following statement:

```
AVERG = SUM/REAL(N)
```

If the values were integers, then the sum would also be an integer. We would still probably want the average to be represented by a real value, which could be specified by

```
AVERG = REAL(SUM)/REAL(N)
```

It is also acceptable to use one intrinsic function as the argument of another. For example, we can compute the natural logarithm of the absolute value of X with the following statement:

```
XLOG = LOG(ABS(X))
```

When using one function as an argument for another, be sure to enclose the argument of each function in its own set of parentheses. This *nesting* of functions is also called *composition* of functions.

It is important to observe that an intrinsic function and its argument represent a value. This value can be used in other computations or stored in other memory locations. It does not of itself, however, represent a memory location. A function can never appear on the left-hand side of an equal sign; it must always be on the right-hand side. For example, to compute the square root of X, we can use the statement

$$ROOT = SQRT(X)$$

but we cannot reverse the order and begin the statement with SQRT(X) because SQRT(X) is not a variable name. The intrinsic square root function could be used in the computation of a root of the quadratic equation used in a previous example, as shown:

$$X1 = (-B + SQRT(B**2 - 4.0*A*C))/(2.0*A)$$

The type of value returned by a function is specified in Appendix A. Many of these intrinsic functions are *generic functions*, which means that the value returned is the same type as the input argument. The absolute value function ABS is a generic function. If X is an integer, then ABS(X) is also an integer; if X is a real value, then ABS(X) is also a real value. Some functions specify the type of input and output required. IABS is a function that requires an integer input and returns an integer absolute value from the function. If K is an integer, then ABS(K) and IABS(K) return the same value. Appendix A contains all forms of the intrinsic functions and identifies all generic functions.

SELF-TEST 2–3

This self-test allows you to check quickly to see if you have remembered some of the key points from Section 2–2 and Section 2–3. If you have any problems with the exercises, you should reread these sections. The solutions are included at the end of the text.

In problems 1–6, convert the equations into FORTRAN assignment statements. Assume all variables represent real values.

1. Slope of a straight line between two points:

$$SLOPE = \frac{Y2 - Y1}{X2 - X1}$$

2. Correction factor in pressure calculation:

$$FACTOR = 1 + \frac{B}{V} + \frac{C}{V^2}$$

3. Coefficient of friction between tires and pavement:

$$FRICTION = \frac{V^2}{30 \cdot S}$$

4. Distance of the center of gravity from a reference plane in a hollow cylinder sector:

$$\text{CENTER} = \frac{38.1972(R^3 - S^3)\sin A}{(R^2 - S^2)A} \qquad \text{where } A \text{ is in radians}$$

5. Pressure loss from pipe friction:

$$\text{LOSS} = F \cdot P \cdot \frac{L}{D} \cdot \frac{V^2}{2}$$

6. Equivalent resistance of a parallel circuit:

$$\text{REQ} = \frac{1}{\dfrac{1}{X1} + \dfrac{1}{X2} + \dfrac{1}{X3} + \dfrac{1}{X4}}$$

In problems 7–12, convert the FORTRAN statements into algebraic form.

7. Uniformly accelerated motion:

```
MOTION = SQRT(VI*VI + 2.0*A*X)
```

8. Electrical oscillation frequency:

```
FREQ = 1.0/SQRT((2.0*3.14159)*(1.0/XL*C))
```

9. Range for a projectile:

```
RANGE = 2.0*VI*VI*SIN(B)*COS(B)/G
```

10. Length contraction:

```
LENGTH = LI*SQRT(1.0 - (V/C)*(V/C))
```

11. Mass energy:

```
C = 2.99E10
ENERGY = 1.6747E-24*C*C
```

12. Volume of a fillet ring:

```
PI = 3.14159
VOLUME = 2.0*PI*X*X*((1.0-PI/4.0)*Y-(0.8333-PI/4.0)*X)
```

2-4   SIMPLE INPUT AND OUTPUT

The input and output of information are fundamental parts of a computer program. FORTRAN has two types of statements that allow us to perform these operations. *List-directed* input/output statements are easy to use but give us little control over the exact spacing used in the input and output lines. *Formatted* input/output, although more involved, allows us to control the input and output forms with greater detail. In this section, we present list-directed input/output and simple formatted output. For our example programs, we use list-directed input statements and formatted output statements — this allows us to be flexible about the form we use for information that we enter, and at the same time allows us to be specific about the form used to print the output from our program. Refer to Chapter 4 for more information on input and output statements.

LIST-DIRECTED OUTPUT

If we wish to print the value stored in a variable, it is necessary to tell the computer the variable's name. The computer can then access the memory location and print its contents. Generally, time-sharing output is displayed on the terminal screen and batch output is either displayed on the terminal screen or printed on computer paper. The general form of the list-directed PRINT statement is

PRINT*, *expression list*

The expressions in the list must be separated by commas. The corresponding values are printed in the order in which they are listed in the PRINT statement. The output from each PRINT statement begins on a new line.

In our examples, computer output is shown inside a terminal screen, as illustrated in Example 2–1.

EXAMPLE 2-1   **WEIGHT and VOL**

Print the stored values of the variables WEIGHT and VOL.

Solution

COMPUTER MEMORY

WEIGHT 35000

VOL   3.15

FORTRAN STATEMENT

```
PRINT*, WEIGHT, VOL
```

COMPUTER OUTPUT

```
35000   3.15000
```

The number of decimal positions printed for real values and the spacing between items varies depending on the compiler used. If a value to be printed is very large or very small, many compilers automatically print the value in exponential notation instead of in decimal form, as shown in Example 2–2.

EXAMPLE 2-2   **Density Value**

Print the value stored in the variable DENSTY.

Solution

Computer Memory

DENSTY $\boxed{0.0000156}$

FORTRAN Statement

```
PRINT*, DENSTY
```

Computer Output

```
0.156000E-04
```

Descriptive information (sometimes called literal information or *literals*) may also be included in the expression list by enclosing the information in single quotation marks or apostrophes. This descriptive information is then printed on the output line along with the values of any variables also in the PRINT statement.

EXAMPLE 2-3   **Literal and Variable Information**

Print the variable RATE with a literal that identifies the value as representing a flow rate in gallons per second.

Solution

Computer Memory

RATE $\boxed{0.065}$

FORTRAN Statement

```
PRINT*, 'FLOW RATE IS', RATE, 'GALLONS PER SECOND'
```

Computer Output

```
FLOW RATE IS 0.0650000 GALLONS PER SECOND
```

EXAMPLE 2-4   **Centrifuge Information**

Print the values stored in the variables RPM and FORCE using descriptive headings.

Solution

COMPUTER MEMORY

$$\text{RPM} \quad \boxed{37.5}$$

$$\text{FORCE} \quad \boxed{6.75}$$

FORTRAN STATEMENTS

```
PRINT*, 'CENTRIFUGE RPM AND FORCE'
PRINT*, RPM, FORCE
```

COMPUTER OUTPUT

```
CENTRIFUGE RPM AND FORCE
37.5000  6.75000
```

LIST-DIRECTED INPUT

We frequently want to read information with our programs. The general form of a list-directed READ statement is

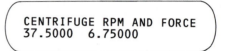

The variable names in the list must be separated by commas. The variables receive new values in the order in which they are listed in the READ statement. These values must agree in type (integer or real) with the variables in the list. If the program is run in a time-sharing mode, the system will wait for you to enter the appropriate data values when the READ statement is executed. If more than one value is being read by the statement, the data values can be separated by commas or blanks. For batch systems, the data lines follow the complete program. Batch processing usually requires extra information, called *job control information*, with your program. Typically, this extra information requires additional information lines before your program, between your program and its data, and after your program. A READ statement will read as many lines as needed to find new values for the variables in its list. Also, each READ statement begins reading from a new line.

EXAMPLE 2-5   **Capacitor Charge**

Read the beginning and ending charges for a capacitor.

Solution 1

This solution uses one READ statement; thus both values can be entered on the same line.

FORTRAN STATEMENT

```
READ*, BEGIN, ENDING
```

DATA LINE

```
186.93, 386.21
```

COMPUTER MEMORY

BEGIN   186.93

ENDING   386.21

The data values in this example could also have been entered on separate lines since the READ statement will read as many lines as needed to find values for the variables in its list.

Solution 2

This solution uses two READ statements; thus the values must be entered on different lines.

FORTRAN STATEMENTS

```
READ*, BEGIN
READ*, ENDING
```

DATA LINES

```
186.93
386.21
```

COMPUTER MEMORY

BEGIN   186.93

ENDING   386.21

FORMATTED OUTPUT

To specify the form in which data values are printed and where on the output line they are printed requires formatted statements. The general form of a formatted PRINT statement is

PRINT *k, expression list*

The expression list designates the memory locations whose contents will be printed or arithmetic expressions whose values will be printed. The list of expressions also determines the order in which the values will be printed. The reference k refers to a FORMAT statement, which will specify the spacing to be used in printing the information. The FORMAT statement has a statement label k. A sample PRINT and FORMAT combination is

```
PRINT 5, TIME, DISTNC
5 FORMAT (1X,F5.1,2X,F7.2)
```

Recall that statement labels are entered in columns 1 through 5.

The general form of the FORMAT statement is

> k **FORMAT** *(specification list)*

The specification list tells the computer both the vertical and horizontal spacing to be used when printing the output information. The vertical spacing options include printing on the top of a new page (if the output is being printed on paper), the next line (single spacing), double spacing, and no spacing. Horizontal spacing includes indicating how many digits will be used for each value, how many blanks will be between numbers, and how many values are to be printed per line.

To understand the specifications used to describe the vertical and horizontal spacing, we must first examine the output from a line printer or terminal, the most common output devices. Other forms of output have similar characteristics.

The line printer prints on computer paper that is on a perforated, continuous roll so it is easy to separate the pages. A common size computer paper page is 11 inches by 14 7/8 inches. Typically, 55 to 75 lines of information can be printed per page, and each line can contain up to 132 characters. In our discussion of printed output, we assume that an output line contains 132 characters. Most line printers print either 6 lines per inch or 8 lines per inch. The PRINT/FORMAT combination specifically describes where each line is to be printed on the page (vertical spacing) and which of the 132 possible positions will contain data (horizontal spacing).

The computer uses the specification list to construct each output line internally in memory before actually printing the line. This internal memory region, which contains 133 characters, is called a *buffer*. The buffer is automatically filled with blanks before it is used to construct a line of output. The first character of the buffer is called the *carriage control character*; it determines the vertical spacing for the line. The remaining 132 characters represent the line to be printed.

Output buffer

Carriage control character

132 characters to be printed

The following list shows some of the valid carriage control characters and the vertical spacing they generate. When needed for clarity in either FORMAT statements or buffer contents, a blank is indicated by the character b placed one-half space below the regular line.

Carriage Control Character	Vertical Spacing
1	New page
blank	Single spacing
0	Double spacing
+	No vertical spacing

Double spacing causes one line to be skipped before the current line of output is printed. When a plus sign is in the carriage control, no spacing occurs and the next line of information will print over the last line printed. On most computers, an invalid carriage control character causes single spacing.

When a terminal is used as the output device, the width of the line may be less than 132 positions. Although terminal systems do not always use carriage control, the internal buffer will contain one character more than the line width if carriage control applies. Because a terminal does not have the same capabilities as a line printer for spacing a new page, a 1 in the carriage control usually becomes an invalid control character and causes single spacing. If the terminal system does not use carriage control, then the entire contents of the buffer, including the carriage control character, will appear on the terminal screen.

We will now examine four FORMAT specifications that describe how to fill the output buffer. Commas are used to separate specifications in the FORMAT statement. Additional FORMAT specifications are included in Chapter 4.

Literal Specification The literal specification allows us to put characters directly into the buffer. The characters must be enclosed in single quotation marks or apostrophes. These characters can represent the carriage control character or the characters in a literal. The following examples illustrate use of the literal specification in FORMAT statements.

EXAMPLE 2-6 **Title Heading**

Print the title heading TEST RESULTS on the top of a new page, *left-justified* (that is, no blanks to the left of the heading).

Solution

FORTRAN Statements

```
      PRINT 4
    4 FORMAT ('1','TEST RESULTS')
```

Buffer Contents

```
1TEST RESULTS
```

COMPUTER OUTPUT

```
              111
     123456789012
```

```
  ╭─────────────────╮
  │   TEST RESULTS   │
  ╰─────────────────╯
```

The buffer is filled according to the FORMAT. No variable names were
listed on the PRINT statement; hence, no values were printed. The literal
specifications cause the characters 1TEST RESULTS to be put in the
buffer, beginning with the first position in the buffer. After filling the
buffer, as instructed by the FORMAT, the carriage control is examined to
determine vertical spacing. The character 1 in the carriage control position tells the computer to begin a new page. The rest of the buffer, 132
positions, is then printed. Notice that the carriage control character is not
printed. The row of small numbers above the computer output shows
the specific column of the output line: The first T is in column 1, the
second T is in column 4, and the third T is in column 11.

EXAMPLE 2-7

Column Headings

Double space from the last line printed and print column headings 1988
kWh and 1989 kWh, with no blanks on the left-hand side of the line and
seven blanks between the two column headings.

Correct Solution

FORTRAN STATEMENTS

```
        PRINT 3
      3 FORMAT ('0','1988 kWh        1989 kWh')
```

BUFFER CONTENTS

```
┌──────────────────────────────────┐
│01988 kWh        1989 kWh          │
└──────────────────────────────────┘
```

COMPUTER OUTPUT

```
                11111111112222
      12345678901234567890123
```

```
  ╭──────────────────────────────╮
  │  1988 kWh        1989 kWh      │
  ╰──────────────────────────────╯
```

The line shown is printed after double spacing from the previous line of
output.

Incorrect Solution

FORTRAN STATEMENTS

```
      PRINT 3
    3 FORMAT ('1988 kWh          1989 kWh')
```

BUFFER CONTENTS

1988 kWh   1989 kWh

COMPUTER OUTPUT

```
              1111111111222
    12345678901234567890 12
```

```
 ( 988 kWh          1989 kWh )
```

In this example we forgot to specify the carriage control. However, the computer does not forget: The first position of the buffer contains a 1, which indicates spacing to a new page. The rest of the buffer is then printed.

X Specification The X specification will insert blanks into the buffer. Its general form is nX, where n represents the number of blanks to be inserted in the buffer. An example using both the X specification and the literal specification follows.

EXAMPLE 2-8

Centered Heading

Print the heading EXPERIMENT NO. 1 centered at the top of a new page.

Solution

Because an output line contains 132 characters, to center the heading we determine the number of characters in the heading (16), subtract that from 132 (132 − 16 = 116), and divide that by 2 to put one-half the blanks in front of the heading (116/2 = 58).

FORTRAN STATEMENTS

```
      PRINT 35
   35 FORMAT ('1',58X,'EXPERIMENT NO. 1')
```

BUFFER CONTENTS

58 blanks

```
5666666666677777
9012345678901234
```

EXPERIMENT NO. 1

This heading could have been printed without the 58X specification by using a literal specification of 1 followed by a literal of 58 blanks and EXPERIMENT NO. 1.

I Specification The literal specification and the X specification allow us to specify carriage control and to print headings — they cannot, however, be used to print variable values. We will now examine a specification that prints the contents of integer variables: The specification form is Iw, where w represents the number of positions (width) to be assigned in the buffer for printing the value of an integer variable. The value is always *right-justified* (no blanks to the right of the value) in those positions in the buffer. Extra positions on the left are filled with blanks. Thus, if the value 16 is printed with an I4 specification, the four positions contain two blanks followed by 16. If there are not enough positions to print the value, including a minus sign if the value is negative, the positions are filled with asterisks. Hence, if we print the value 132 or − 14 with an I2 specification, the two positions are filled with asterisks. It is important to recognize that the asterisks do not necessarily indicate that there is an error in the value; instead, the asterisks may indicate that you need to assign a larger width in the corresponding I specification.

More than one variable name is often listed in the PRINT statement. When interpreting a PRINT/FORMAT combination, the compiler will match the first variable name to the first specification for printing values, and so on. Therefore, there should be the same number of specifications for printing values as there are variables on the PRINT statement list. (In Chapter 4 we will explain what happens if the number of specifications does not match the number of variables.)

EXAMPLE 2-9

Integer Values

Print the values of the integer variables SUM, MEAN, and N on the same line, single spaced from the previous line.

Solution

COMPUTER MEMORY

SUM	12
MEAN	− 14
N	− 146

```
              PRINT 30, SUM, MEAN, N
           30 FORMAT (1X,I3,2X,I2,2X,I4)
```

Buffer Contents

$$bb\,^{12}bb^{**}bb^{-146}$$

Computer Output

```
                      11111
           1234567890123
```

$$12\quad **\quad -146$$

The computer will print SUM with an I3 specification, MEAN with an I2 specification, and N with an I4 specification. The value of SUM is 12, so the three corresponding positions contain a blank followed by the number 12. The value of MEAN, -14, requires at least three positions, so the two specified positions are filled with asterisks. The value of N fills all four allotted positions. The carriage control character is a blank; thus the line of output is single spaced from the previous line.

EXAMPLE 2-10 **Literal and Variable Information**

On separate lines, print the values of MEAN and SUM, along with an indication of the name of each of the integer variables.

Solution

Computer Memory

SUM | 12 |

MEAN | -14 |

FORTRAN Statements

```
           PRINT 2, MEAN
         2 FORMAT (1X,'MEAN = ',I4)
           PRINT 3, SUM
         3 FORMAT (1X,'SUM = ',I4)
```

Buffer Contents

$$b\,^{MEAN}b^=b\,bb^{-14}$$
$$b\,^{SUM}b^=b\,bbb\,^{12}$$

```
                          11
          12345678901
```

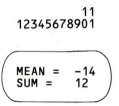

```
          MEAN =    -14
          SUM =      12
```

F Specification The F specification is used to print real numbers in a decimal form (for example, 36.21) as opposed to an exponential form (for example, 0.3621E+02). The general form for an F specification is Fw.d, where w represents the total width (number of positions) to be used in printing the real value and d represents the number of those positions that will represent decimal positions to the right of the decimal point. For example, the minimum size F specification that can be used to print 34.186 is F6.3, a total of six positions counting the decimal point with three positions to the right of the decimal point. Before the value is inserted in the buffer, the decimal point is located in the specified position; the form for F6.3 is thus

$$\underbrace{XX.\overbrace{XXX}^{\text{decimal portion} = d}}_{\text{total width} = w}$$

If the value to be printed has fewer than d decimal positions, zeros are inserted on the right-hand side of the decimal point. Thus, if the value 21.6 is printed with an F6.3 specification, the output is 21.600. If the value to be printed has more than d decimal positions, only d decimal positions are printed, dropping the rest. Thus, if the value 21.86342 is printed with an F6.3 specification, the output is 21.863. Many compilers will round to the last decimal position printed; in these cases, the value 18.98662 is printed with an F6.3 specification and the output would be 18.987.

If the integer portion of a real value requires fewer positions than allotted in the F specification, the extra positions on the left-hand side of the decimal point are filled with blanks. Thus, if the value 3.123 is printed with an F6.3 specification, the output is a blank followed by 3.123. If the integer portion of a real value, including the minus sign if the value is negative, requires more positions than allotted in the F specification, the entire field is filled with asterisks. Thus, if the value 312.6 is printed with an F6.3 specification, the output is ******.

If a value is between −1 and +1, positions must usually be allowed for both a leading zero to the left of the decimal point and a minus sign if the value is negative. Thus, the smallest F specification that could be used to print −.127 is F6.3, which would be printed as −0.127. If a smaller specification width were used, all the positions would be filled with asterisks.

EXAMPLE 2-11   **Angle THETA**

Print the value of an angle called THETA. Construct the Greek symbol for theta using a zero with a dash printed over it. The output should be in this form:

$$\theta = XX.XX$$

Solution

Computer Memory

THETA | 3.184 |

Fortran Statements

```
      PRINT 1
1 FORMAT (1X,'0')
      PRINT 2, THETA
2 FORMAT ('+','- = ',F5.2)
```

Buffer Contents

```
 0
b

+- = bb3.18
  b bb
```

Computer Output

```
123456789
```

```
θ =   3.18
```

The first PRINT statement printed a zero in the first position of the output line after single spacing from the previous line. The second PRINT statement had a plus sign in the carriage control, which caused no vertical spacing. The dash character is therefore printed on top of the character zero, giving the Greek symbol theta. The value of the variable THETA is printed on the same line.

EXAMPLE 2-12   **Sine and Cosine Computation**

Print the values of the sine and cosine of the angle THETA. Assume that THETA is in radians. Use descriptive literals.

Solution

<small>COMPUTER MEMORY</small>

THETA $\boxed{1.26}$

<small>FORTRAN STATEMENTS</small>

```
   PRINT 1, THETA, SIN(THETA)
 1 FORMAT (1X,'THE SINE OF ',F5.2,' RADIANS = ',F4.2)
   PRINT 2, THETA, COS(THETA)
 2 FORMAT (1X,'THE COSINE OF ',F5.2,' RADIANS = ',F4.2)
```

<small>BUFFER CONTENTS</small>

$_b$THE$_b$SINE$_b$OF$_{bb}$1.26$_b$RADIANS$_b$=$_b$0.95
$_b$THE$_b$COSINE$_b$OF$_{bb}$1.26$_b$RADIANS$_b$=$_b$0.31

<small>COMPUTER OUTPUT</small>

```
                1111111111222222222233333
       1234567890123456789012345678901234

     THE SINE OF   1.26 RADIANS = 0.95
     THE COSINE OF   1.26 RADIANS = 0.31
```

Suppose that the value of THETA was 1.78 radians. Then the computer output for this set of FORTRAN statements would be:

<small>COMPUTER OUTPUT</small>

```
                1111111111222222222233333
       1234567890123456789012345678901234

     THE SINE OF   1.78 RADIANS = 0.98
     THE COSINE OF   1.78 RADIANS = ****
```

The asterisks were printed instead of the correct value of -0.21 because the correct value requires a total of five positions instead of the four allotted with the specification F4.2. In order to have a solution that will work for all possible values of the sine and cosine functions, we should use an F5.2 format specification in both formats, as shown below:

```
   PRINT 1, THETA, SIN(THETA)
 1 FORMAT (1X,'THE SINE OF ',F5.2,' RADIANS = ',F5.2)
   PRINT 2, THETA, COS(THETA)
 2 FORMAT (1X,'THE COSINE OF ',F5.2,' RADIANS = ',F5.2)
```

E Specification Real numbers may be printed in an exponential form with the E specification. This specification is primarily used for very small values, or very large values, or when you are uncertain of the magnitude of a number. If you use an F format that is too small for a value, the output field will be filled with asterisks. In contrast, a real number will always fit in an E specification field.

The general format for an E specification is Ew.d. The w again represents the total width or number of positions to be used in printing the value. The d represents the number of positions to the right of the decimal point, assuming that the value is in exponential form, with the decimal point to the left of the first non-zero digit. The framework for printing a real value in an exponential specification with three decimal places is:

$$\text{decimal portion} = d$$
$$\underbrace{\text{SO.}\overbrace{\text{XXX}}\text{ESXX}}_{\text{total width} = w}$$

The symbol S indicates that positions must be reserved for both the sign of the value and the sign of the exponent in case they are negative. Note that with all the extra positions, the total width becomes ten positions. Three of the ten positions are the decimal positions and the other seven are positions that are always needed for an E format. Thus, the total width of an E specification must be at least d + 7; otherwise asterisks will be printed. The above specification is then E10.3.

If there are more decimal positions in the specification than are in the exponential form of the value, the extra decimal positions are filled on the right with zeros.

If the total width of the E specification is more than 7 plus the decimal positions, the extra positions appear as blanks on the left side of the value.

EXAMPLE 2-13

TIME in an Exponential Form

Print the value of TIME in an exponential form with four decimal positions.

Solution 1

COMPUTER MEMORY

TIME $\boxed{-0.00125}$

FORTRAN STATEMENTS

```
        PRINT 10, TIME
     10 FORMAT (1X,'TIME = ',E11.4)
```

BUFFER CONTENTS

$\boxed{\text{b}^{\text{TIME}}\text{b}^{=}\text{b}\text{ b}-0.1250\text{E}-02}$

```
          111111111
1234567890 12345678
```

```
TIME = -0.1250E-02
```

Solution 2

COMPUTER MEMORY

TIME $\boxed{-0.00125}$

FORTRAN STATEMENTS

```
        PRINT 15, TIME
     15 FORMAT (1X,'TIME = ',E13.4)
```

BUFFER CONTENTS

```
b TIME b = b bbb -0.1250E-02
```

COMPUTER OUTPUT

```
           11111111112
1234567890 1234567890
```

```
TIME =    -0.1250E-02
```

Both of these solutions use an exponential format, but the second solution will place two additional blanks after the equal sign.

SELF-TEST 2–4

This self-test allows you to check quickly to see if you have remembered some of the key points from Section 2–4. If you have any problems with the exercises, you should reread this section. The solutions are included at the end of the text.

1. What is printed by the following statements? Show the exact location of any blanks.

```
     INTEGER  SECNDS
     REAL  DIST
     SECNDS = 23
     DIST = 57.829
     PRINT 5, DIST, SECNDS
   5 FORMAT (1X,F7.4,2X,I3)
```

2. What is printed by the following statements? Show the exact location of any blanks.

```
      REAL  DIST, VEL
      DIST = 15.68323
      VEL = 0.0270043
      PRINT 5, DIST
    5 FORMAT (1X,'DISTANCE = ',F7.4)
      PRINT 6, VEL
    6 FORMAT (1X,'VELOCITY = ',E10.2)
```

2-5 COMPLETE PROGRAMS

Only one additional statement is required to write complete FORTRAN programs. This statement, the END statement, identifies the physical end of our FORTRAN program for the compiler. The compiler stops translating statements when it reaches the END statement. Every FORTRAN program must end with the END statement, whose general form is

Two other simple statements often appear in FORTRAN programs; they are optional, but are useful in documenting a program. The PROGRAM statement clearly identifies the beginning of a program and assigns the program name. The general form of this statement is

Like a variable name, the program name can be one to six characters, begins with a letter, and contains only letters and digits. Some example PROGRAM statements are

```
PROGRAM  TEST

PROGRAM  COMPUT

PROGRAM  SORT2
```

You may not use a variable in your program that has the same name as the program name.

The other optional, though useful, statement is the STOP statement, which signals the computer to terminate execution of the program. The END statement also serves this purpose but can only appear once, at the physical end of the program. The STOP statement can appear anywhere in the program that makes sense, and it can appear as often as necessary. For example, certain data values may not be valid, and we may want to stop executing the program if they occur. The general form of the STOP statement is

A program may use both a STOP and an END at the end of the program, although the STOP is not necessary if it is followed immediately by the END.

EXAMPLE 2-14   **Complete Program to Convert Kilowatt-Hours to Joules**

Write a program to convert an amount in kWh (kilowatt-hours) to joules. The amount in kWh is to be entered from the terminal. The output should be the number read in kWh and the converted value in joules. (Use the following conversion factor: joules = 3.6E+06 × kWh)

Solution

The steps in solving this problem are straightforward, but we still follow the algorithm development phases given in Chapter 1. We first decompose the problem solution into a series of steps, yielding the following:

DECOMPOSITION

Read amount in kilowatt-hours.
Convert amount to joules.
Print both amounts.

These steps are now written in more English-like phrases and some detail of the computation is included. We discuss the decomposition and pseudocode steps in detail in Chapter 3.

REFINEMENT IN PSEUDOCODE

CONVRT: Read kilowatt-hours.
        joules ← 3.6E+06 × kilowatt-hours.
        Print kilowatt-hours, joules.

FORTRAN PROGRAM

```
*--------------------------------------------------------*
      PROGRAM CONVRT
*
*   This program converts kilowatt-hours to joules.
*
      REAL   KWH, JOULES
*
      PRINT*, 'ENTER ENERGY IN KILOWATT-HOURS'
      READ*, KWH
      JOULES = 3.6E+06*KWH
      PRINT 5, KWH, JOULES
    5 FORMAT (1X,F6.2,' KILOWATT-HOURS = ',E9.2,' JOULES')
      END
*--------------------------------------------------------*
```

The following computer output illustrates a sample run of the program:

```
ENTER ENERGY IN KILOWATT-HOURS
5.5
   5.50 KILOWATT-HOURS = 0.20E+08 JOULES
```

Even though this program is simple, it illustrates some of the structure and style we will use in our programs throughout the text.

1. We will mark the beginning and end of each program with a comment line containing a series of dashes.
2. A brief discussion of the purpose of the program will follow the PROGRAM statement.
3. This discussion will be followed by specification statements to define the type of all variables used in the program. Even variables whose type matches the implicit type of their names will be included for documentation.
4. Any statement number will be right-justified within the group of columns 1 through 5.

In the program in Example 2–14, we printed a message to the user that specified the input that the program was expecting. After converting the value in kilowatt-hours to joules, we printed the value of kilowatt-hours along with the converted value in joules. This interaction between the program and the user resembles a conversation and is called *conversational computing*. Conversational computing is an effective technique and will be used in many of our example programs. Note that conversational computing is useful in time-sharing systems because both the input and the output information are displayed on the same screen. Conversational computing is not applicable to a batch system because the input information must be included along with the program.

2–6 APPLICATION—BACTERIA GROWTH (Biology)

A biology laboratory experiment involves the analysis of a strain of bacteria. Because the growth of bacteria in the colony can be modeled with an exponential equation, you are going to write a computer program to predict how many bacteria will be in the colony after a specified amount of time. Suppose that, for this type of bacteria, the equation to predict growth is

$$y_{new} = y_{old}e^{1.386t}$$

where y_{new} is the new number of bacteria in the colony, y_{old} is the initial number of bacteria in the colony, and t is the elapsed time in hours. Thus, when $t = 0$, we have

$$y_{new} = y_{old}e^{1.386 \cdot 0} = y_{old}$$

PROBLEM STATEMENT

Using the equation

$$y_{new} = y_{old}e^{1.386t}$$

predict the number of bacteria (y_{new}) in a bacteria colony given the initial number in the colony (y_{old}) and the time elapsed (t) in hours.

INPUT/OUTPUT DESCRIPTION

The input will be two values: the initial number of bacteria and the time elapsed. The output will be the number of bacteria in the colony after the elapsed time.

HAND EXAMPLE

You will need your calculator for these calculations. For $t = 1$ hour and $y_{old} = 1$ bacterium, the new colony contains

$$y_{new} = 1 * e^{1.386 \cdot 1} = 4.00$$

After 6 hours, the size of the colony is

$$y_{new} = 1 * e^{1.386 \cdot 6} = 4088.77$$

If we start with 2 bacteria, after 6 hours the size of the colony is

$$y_{new} = 2 * e^{1.386 \cdot 6} = 8177.54$$

ALGORITHM DEVELOPMENT

DECOMPOSITION

Read y_{old}, t.
Compute y_{new}.
Print y_{old}, t, y_{new}.

REFINEMENT IN PSEUDOCODE

GROWTH: Read y_{old}, t
$\quad y_{new} \leftarrow y_{old}e^{1.386t}$
$\quad$ Print y_{old}, t, y_{new}

FORTRAN Program

```
*------------------------------------------------------------*
      PROGRAM   GROWTH
*
*  This program predicts bacteria growth.
*
      REAL  YOLD, YNEW, TIME
*
      PRINT*, 'ENTER INITIAL POPULATION'
      READ*, YOLD
      PRINT*, 'ENTER TIME ELAPSED IN HOURS'
      READ*, TIME
      YNEW = YOLD*EXP(1.386*TIME)
      PRINT 10, YOLD
   10 FORMAT (1X,'INITIAL POPULATION = ',F9.4)
      PRINT 20, TIME
   20 FORMAT (1X,'TIME ELAPSED (HOURS) = ',F9.4)
      PRINT 30, YNEW
   30 FORMAT (1X,'PREDICTED POPULATION = ',F9.4)
      END
*------------------------------------------------------------*
```

TESTING

The program output using data from one of our longhand examples is

```
ENTER INITIAL POPULATION
1.0
ENTER TIME ELAPSED IN HOURS
6.0
INITIAL POPULATION =    1.0000
TIME ELAPSED (HOURS) =    6.0000
PREDICTED POPULATION = 4088.7722
```

You should try using other values in the program to see if the results appear reasonable. Very large values of TIME will result in an overflow error. Negative values of TIME represent population decreases; but if the population falls below 1, the model is no longer applicable.

2-7 APPLICATION—CARBON DATING
(Archeology)

Carbon dating is a method for estimating the age of organic substances such as shells, seeds, and wooden artifacts. The technique compares the amount of carbon 14, a radioactive carbon, contained in the remains of the substance with the amount of carbon 14 that would have been in the object's environment at the time it was alive. The age of the cave paintings in Lascaux, France, has been estimated at 15,500 years using this technique.

Assume that you are working as an assistant to an archeologist on Saturdays. Artifacts from a recent excavation have been sent to a laboratory for carbon analysis. The lab will determine the proportion of carbon that remains in the artifact. The archeologist has shown you the following equation that gives the estimated age of the artifact in years:

$$\text{age} = \frac{-\log_e \text{ (carbon 14 proportion remaining)}}{0.0001216}$$

Recall that $\log_e X$ is the natural logarithm of the value X.

The archeologist would like you to write a FORTRAN program that will read the proportion of carbon 14 remaining in an artifact and then compute and print its estimated age.

PROBLEM STATEMENT

Write a program to read the proportion of carbon 14 remaining in an artifact, then compute and print its estimated age.

INPUT/OUTPUT DESCRIPTION

The input will be a real number that represents the proportion of carbon left in the artifact. The output will be a number that estimates in years the age of the artifact.

HAND EXAMPLE

Suppose that no carbon 14 has decayed; then the carbon proportion is 1.0, and the estimated age is

$$\text{age} = \frac{-\log_e(1.0)}{0.0001216} = \frac{0}{0.0001216} = 0$$

This age makes sense because the artifact must be relatively young if no carbon 14 decay has occurred.

Let's assume now that one-half of the carbon has decayed. Thus, we will use 0.5 as the proportion of carbon left and see how this affects the formula:

$$\text{age} = \frac{-\log_e(0.5)}{0.0001216} = 5700.2 \text{ years}$$

From a reference book we learn that the half-life of carbon 14 is 5700 years, so our equation works pretty well!

ALGORITHM DEVELOPMENT

DECOMPOSITION

Read proportion of carbon remaining.
Compute estimated age.
Print estimated age.

REFINEMENT IN PSEUDOCODE

AGE: Read proportion of carbon remaining

$$\text{age} \leftarrow \frac{-\log_e(\text{proportion of carbon remaining})}{0.0001216}$$

Print estimated age

To compute the estimated age, we need to compute a natural logarithm. Using Table 2–4, we find that the intrinsic function LOG performs this operation. LOG is a generic function; thus it will return a real value if its argument is real.

FORTRAN PROGRAM

```
*------------------------------------------------------------*
      PROGRAM  DATE
*
*  This program estimates the age of an artifact from
*  the proportion of carbon remaining in the artifact.
*
      REAL  CARBON, AGE
*
      PRINT*, 'ENTER PROPORTION REMAINING FOR CARBON DATING'
      READ*, CARBON
      AGE = (-LOG(CARBON))/0.0001216
      PRINT 5, AGE
    5 FORMAT (1X,'ESTIMATED AGE OF ARTIFACT IS ',F6.1, ' YEARS')
      END
*------------------------------------------------------------*
```

TESTING

Test your program with the examples we used in the longhand examples. A typical screen display should be

```
ENTER PROPORTION REMAINING FOR CARBON DATING
0.5
ESTIMATED AGE OF ARTIFACT IS 5700.2 YEARS
```

2-8 APPLICATION—RAILROAD TRACK DESIGN (Transportation Engineering)

When a train travels over a straight section of track, it exerts a downward force on the rails; but when it rounds a level curve, it also exerts a horizontal force outward on the rails. Both of these forces must be considered when designing the track. The downward force is equivalent to the weight of the train. The horizontal force, called centrifugal force, is a function of the weight of the train, the speed of the train as it rounds the curve, and the radius of the curve. The equation to compute the horizontal force, in pounds, is

$$\text{FORCE} = \frac{\text{WEIGHT} \times 2000}{32} \times \frac{(\text{MPH} \times 1.4667)^2}{\text{RADIUS}}$$

where WEIGHT is the weight of the train in tons, MPH is the speed of the train in miles per hour, and RADIUS is the radius of the curve in feet.

Write a FORTRAN program to read values for WEIGHT, MPH, and RADIUS. Compute and print the corresponding horizontal force generated.

PROBLEM STATEMENT

Using the equation

$$\text{FORCE} = \frac{\text{WEIGHT} \times 2000}{32} \times \frac{(\text{MPH} \times 1.4667)^2}{\text{RADIUS}}$$

determine the force generated for specific values of WEIGHT, MPH, and RADIUS.

INPUT/OUTPUT DESCRIPTION

The input will be three real numbers that represent the weight of the train in tons, the speed of the train in miles per hour, and the radius of the curve in feet. The output will be the horizontal force generated.

HAND EXAMPLE

Assume that the weight of the train is 405.7 tons, its speed is 30.5 miles per hour, and the radius of the curve is 2005.33 feet. Substituting these values into the equation gives

$$\text{FORCE} = \frac{405.7 \times 2000}{32} \times \frac{(30.5 \times 1.4667)^2}{2005.33}$$

This computation yields a horizontal force of 25,303.55 pounds.

We begin the algorithm development by listing the steps necessary to reach the solution. Again, our problem solution is straightforward and the decomposition is the following:

DECOMPOSITION

Read train weight, train speed, and curve radius.
Compute horizontal force.
Print horizontal force.

We add detail in the decomposition step.

REFINEMENT IN PSEUDOCODE

TRAIN: Read train weight, train speed, and radius of curve

$$\text{FORCE} \leftarrow \frac{\text{WEIGHT} \times 2000}{32} \times \frac{(\text{MPH} \times 1.4667)^2}{\text{RADIUS}}$$

Print the horizontal force

In the FORTRAN program that follows, note the use of parentheses in the computation statement.

FORTRAN PROGRAM

```
*-------------------------------------------------------------*
      PROGRAM  TRAIN
*
*  This program computes the horizontal force
*  generated by a train on a level curve.
*
      REAL  WEIGHT, MPH, RADIUS, FORCE
*
      PRINT*, 'ENTER WEIGHT OF TRAIN IN TONS'
      READ*, WEIGHT
      PRINT*, 'ENTER SPEED OF TRAIN IN MILES PER HOUR'
      READ*, MPH
      PRINT*, 'ENTER RADIUS OF CURVE IN FEET'
      READ*, RADIUS
*
      FORCE = (WEIGHT*2000.0/32.0)*((MPH*1.4667)**2/RADIUS)
*
      PRINT 10, WEIGHT
   10 FORMAT (1X,'TRAIN WEIGHT - ',F7.2,' TONS')
      PRINT 20, MPH
   20 FORMAT (1X,'TRAIN SPEED - ',F7.2,' MPH')
      PRINT 30, RADIUS
   30 FORMAT (1X,'CURVE RADIUS - ',F7.2,' FEET')
      PRINT*
      PRINT 40, FORCE
   40 FORMAT (1X,'RESULTING HORIZONTAL FORCE - ',
     +          F8.2,' POUNDS')
      END
*-------------------------------------------------------------*
```

Also note that the FORMAT statement with reference number 40 was continued on a second line. The plus sign in column 6 specifies to the compiler that this is a continuation line.

TESTING

If the program is tested with the data that we used in the longhand example, the output is

```
ENTER WEIGHT OF TRAIN IN TONS
405.7
ENTER SPEED OF TRAIN IN MILES PER HOUR
30.5
ENTER RADIUS OF CURVE IN FEET
2005.33
TRAIN WEIGHT -  405.70 TONS
TRAIN SPEED -   30.50 MPH
CURVE RADIUS - 2005.33 FEET

RESULTING HORIZONTAL FORCE - 25303.55 POUNDS
```

2-9 APPLICATION—EQUIPMENT RELIABILITY (Electrical Engineering)

If you have a personal computer, or if you have a friend who has one, open the back of the computer system and look at the computer board(s) that contain its circuitry. Each board contains a large number of components. You might wonder how computers can be so reliable when so many different pieces could malfunction. Much of their reliability is due to the quality control maintained during their manufacture. However, before the design of a computer or any complicated piece of instrumentation is actually implemented, the reliability of the device is analyzed. In this section we will look at one way of estimating the reliability of a piece of instrumentation that may have large numbers of the same component in it. In order to perform the computations, we must know the reliability of a single component. This number is generally available from the manufacturer. For example, a company may sell transistors that are guaranteed to be reliable 98 percent of the time. This information tells us how reliable one transistor is, but it does not tell us how reliable a piece of instrumentation may be if it contains 5000 of these transistors.

Equations for analyzing reliability come from the area of mathematics called statistics and probability. However, in order to select the correct equation, we must know something about the design. For example, consider the following diagrams:

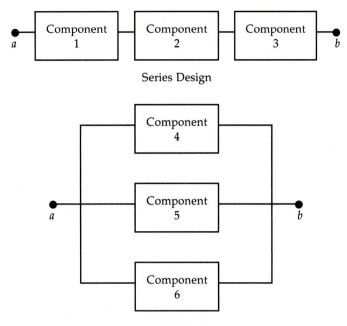

Series Design

Parallel Design

The design on the top contains three components connected serially, or in series. In order for information to flow from point *a* to point *b*, all three components must work properly. The design on the bottom contains three components connected in parallel. In order for information to flow from point *a* to point *b*, only one of the three components must work properly. If all the individual components have the same reliability, we would expect that the parallel configuration would have better overall performance. This can also be verified with mathematical equations.

In this section we are going to estimate the reliability of a piece of equipment relative to a specific component that is used in many places in the design. We are going to compute the percentage of the time that all the components will be working properly, so we are looking at a series-type design. This situation can be described using a Bernoulli equation. With the equation we can compute the probability that all the components will work properly. This probability can be expressed as the percentage of time that there will be no component failures. If this percentage is not high, we may not want to perform critical operations with the instrumentation or we may want to request that the instrumentation be redesigned.

Assume that p is the percentage of time that a single component will be good and n is the total number of components in the piece of equipment.

Then the reliability, or percentage of the time that no component will fail, is given by the Bernoulli equation below:

$$\text{percentage} = (p/100.0)^n \cdot 100.0$$

Using the Bernoulli equation, write a program that will read the reliability of a single component and the number of components in a design. Compute the percentage of time that all the components will work properly using the Bernoulli equation.

PROBLEM STATEMENT

Write a program that will compute the reliability of a piece of instrumentation relative to a specific component, using the approximation given by the Bernoulli equation.

INPUT/OUTPUT DESCRIPTION

The input will be two values; the reliability of a single component and the number of components in the instrumentation. The output will be the overall reliability of the instrumentation relative to the specific component.

HAND EXAMPLE

Suppose we are evaluating a piece of instrumentation that contains 20 transistors. Each transistor has a reliability of 96 percent. We are interested in the reliability of the instrument with no transistor failures. The calculation is performed as shown below:

$$n = 20$$
$$p = 96.0$$
$$\text{percentage} = (96.0/100.0)^{20} \cdot 100.0$$
$$= 44.2$$

where percentage is the percentage of the time that there will be no transistor failures. This number is probably lower than you expected. Even with 99 percent reliability of an individual component, the reliability of 20 of them at one time is 81.8 percent. Clearly, most instrumentation must have ways of improving reliability over that given by Bernoulli trials. Designs that use parallel features have greatly increased reliability, and different equations are used for the reliability computations.

ALGORITHM DEVELOPMENT

The algorithm for this problem is straightforward. After reading values for p and n, we are ready to compute the reliability.

Decomposition

Read reliability of component and number of components.
Compute reliability of group of components.
Print reliability.

We now refine the steps in the decomposition into pseudocode.

Refinement in Pseudocode

RELY: Read P, N
$$PERC \leftarrow (P/100.0)^n \cdot 100.0$$
Print PERC

In the FORTRAN program that follows, note the use of parentheses in the computation statement to make it easier to read.

FORTRAN Program

```
*- - - - - - - - - - - - - - - - - - - - - - - - - - - - - - - - - - - - - - - - - - - -*
      PROGRAM  RELY
*
*  This program computes the reliability of
*  instrumentation using a Bernoulli equation.
*
      INTEGER N
      REAL P, PERC
*
      PRINT*, 'ENTER RELIABILITY OF SINGLE COMPONENT'
      PRINT*, '(USE PERCENTAGE BETWEEN 0.0 AND 100.0)'
      READ*, P
      PRINT*, 'ENTER NUMBER OF COMPONENTS IN EQUIPMENT'
      READ*, N
*
      PERC = (P/100.0)**N*100.0
*
      PRINT*, 'PERCENT OF THE TIME THAT THE EQUIPMENT'
      PRINT 5, PERC
    5 FORMAT (1X,'SHOULD WORK WITHOUT FAILURE IS ',
     +          F6.2,' %')
      END
*- - - - - - - - - - - - - - - - - - - - - - - - - - - - - - - - - - - - - - - - - - - -*
```

TESTING

If we test this program with 20 components, each of which has a reliability of 96 percent, the output is:

```
ENTER RELIABILITY OF SINGLE COMPONENT
(USE PERCENTAGE BETWEEN 0.0 AND 100.0)
96.0
ENTER NUMBER OF COMPONENTS IN EQUIPMENT
20
PERCENT OF THE TIME THAT THE EQUIPMENT
SHOULD WORK WITHOUT FAILURE IS   44.20 %
```

If we test this program with 20 components, each of which has a reliability of 99 percent, the output is:

```
ENTER RELIABILITY OF SINGLE COMPONENT
(USE PERCENTAGE BETWEEN 0.0 AND 100.0)
99.0
ENTER NUMBER OF COMPONENTS IN EQUIPMENT
20
PERCENT OF THE TIME THAT THE EQUIPMENT
SHOULD WORK WITHOUT FAILURE IS   81.79 %
```

SUMMARY

In this chapter we learned how to define variables and constants in FORTRAN. We discussed the arithmetic operations and intrinsic functions that allow us to compute new values using these variables and constants. Some of the considerations that are unique to computer computations were discussed with specific examples: magnitude limitations, truncation, mixed-mode operations, underflow, and overflow. Statements for reading information from the terminal and for printing answers were covered. Several complete example programs were developed.

DEBUGGING AIDS

If a program is not working correctly, you should *echo* the values that you read in the program — that is, immediately after reading them, print them out to be sure that the values you want to give the variables are being used. A common mistake is to enter the data values in the wrong order. For example, instead of entering the initial number of bacteria followed by the elapsed time, you enter the elapsed time followed by the initial number of bacteria.

If the input portion of your program is working correctly, check your assignment statements.

1. If the assignment statement is long, break it into several smaller statements.
2. Double check the placement of parentheses. Add parentheses if you are not sure what order the computer will use to compute the operations involved.

Be sure that you always have the same number of left parentheses as right parentheses.

3. Review each variable name on the right-hand side of the assignment statement to be sure you have spelled it exactly as previously used. (Did you use VEL when you should have used VELCTY?)

4. Make sure all variables on the right-hand side of the assignment statement have been previously initialized.

5. Be sure that arguments of functions are in the correct units (for example, trigonometric functions use angles in radians, not in degrees).

If you still are not getting correct answers, check the variable names in your output statements. Do you have the correct names listed?

If these steps do not help you isolate your error, ask your instructor or a classsmate to check the program. If no one is available to check your program and you cannot find the error, start over on a clean sheet of paper. Sometimes it is hard to spot your own errors because you know what you want the statements to do and you read that into the statements when searching for errors.

STYLE/TECHNIQUE GUIDES

A program should be written so that another person who knows FORTRAN can readily understand the statements and interpret the procedures — This is especially important because the person updating the program may not always be the same person who originally wrote it. To write a clearly understood program is challenging and necessitates building good habits while you are learning a language. The following guides will help you develop a style and technique that will enable you to meet these requirements.

1. Use variable names that indicate something about the values being stored in the variable. For instance, represent velocity by VELCTY instead of V, or X, or something obscure.

2. Use a consistent number of significant digits in constants. Do not use 3.14 as a value for pi in the beginning of your program and later use 3.141593. Assure this consistency by defining a variable to store the value of these constants. Use the variable instead of the constant value in subsequent statements.

3. Break long expressions into smaller expressions and recombine them in another statement. A complicated fraction can be computed by first calculating a numerator, then calculating a denominator, then dividing in a separate statement.

4. Insert extra parentheses for readability. Inserting extra pairs of parentheses is never wrong as long as they are properly located. Extra parentheses often make arithmetic expressions much more readable.

5. Use the intrinsic functions where possible.

6. Develop the habit of echo-printing values that you have read.
7. Print the physical units that correspond to the numerical values being printed; this information is vital for proper interpretation of results.
8. Do not mix modes except for exponents. Use the intrinsic functions REAL and INT to avoid mixing types by explicit conversion.

KEY WORDS

argument	intrinsic function
arithmetic expression	left-justified
assignment statement	list-directed I/O
buffer	literal
carriage control	magnitude limitation
comment line	mixed-mode operation
constant	nested function
continuation line	nonexecutable statement
conversational computing	overflow
echo	real value
executable statement	right-justified
explicit typing	rounding
exponential notation	scientific notation
formatted I/O	specification statement
generic function	statement label
implicit typing	truncation
initialize	underflow
integer value	variable
intermediate result	

PROBLEMS

We begin our problem set with modifications to programs given earlier in this chapter. Give the decomposition, refined pseudocode, and FORTRAN program for each problem.

Problems 1–5 modify the energy conversion program CONVRT, given on page 46.

1. Modify the energy conversion program so that it converts joules to kilowatt-hours.
2. Modify the energy conversion program so that it converts British thermal units to joules. (1 Btu = 1056 joules)

3. Modify the energy conversion program so that it converts calories to joules. (1 calorie = 4.19 joules)

4. Modify the energy conversion program so that it converts joules to British thermal units and to calories.

5. Modify the energy conversion program so that it converts kilowatt-hours to calories.

Problems 6–10 modify the bacteria growth program, GROWTH, given on page 49.

6. Modify the bacteria growth program so that the time elapsed is entered in minutes even though the equation still requires a time in hours.

7. Modify the bacteria growth program so that the time elapsed is entered in days even though the equation still requires a time in hours.

8. Modify the bacteria growth program so that an initial population is read from the terminal. The program should compute and print the percent increase in population as time increases from 2 hours to 3 hours.

9. Modify the bacteria growth program so that the program reads two time values from the terminal, where the first time is less than the second time. Compute and print the amount of growth between the two times, assuming an initial population value of 1.

10. Modify the bacteria growth program so that the program reads two time values from the terminal, with no restrictions on which time is larger. Compute and print the amount of growth between the two times, assuming an initial population value of 1. (*Hint:* Review the absolute value function.)

Problems 11–15 modify the carbon-dating program DATE, given on page 51.

11. Modify the carbon-dating program so that it truncates the age to the nearest year.

12. Modify the carbon-dating program so that it rounds the age to the nearest year. (*Hint:* Review the NINT function.)

13. Modify the carbon-dating program so that it gives the age in centuries instead of in years. Use two decimal places in the output age.

14. Modify the carbon-dating program so that it gives the age in centuries instead of in years. Truncate the resulting age to the nearest century.

15. Modify the carbon-dating program so that it gives the age in centuries instead of in years. Round the resulting age to the nearest century.

Problems 16–20 modify the railroad track analysis program TRAIN, given on page 53.

16. Modify the railroad track analysis program so that the weight of the train is entered in pounds instead of in tons.

17. Modify the railroad track analysis program so that the radius of the curve is entered in yards instead of in feet.

18. Modify the railroad track analysis program so that the horizontal force printed is truncated to the nearest pound.

19. Modify the railroad track analysis program so that the horizontal force printed is rounded to the nearest pound.

20. Modify the railroad track analysis program so that the speed is entered in kilometers per hour instead of in miles per hour. (Recall that 1 mile is equal to 1.609 kilometers.)

Problems 21–25 modify the equipment reliability program RELY, given on page 57. In the modifications, if P1 is the reliability of component 1, and P2 is the reliability of component 2, then the reliability of the components connected in series is:

$$\text{percentage} = (P1/100.0) \cdot (P2/100.0) \cdot 100.0$$

The reliability of two components connected in parallel is:

$$\text{percentage} = (P1/100.0 + P2/100.0 - (P1/100.0) \cdot (P2/100.0)) \cdot 100.0$$

21. Modify the reliability program so that it reads the reliabilities of two components and then computes the reliability of the two components connected in series, as shown in the following diagram:

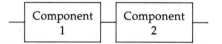

22. Modify the reliability program so that it reads the reliabilities of two components and then computes the reliability of the two components connected in parallel, as shown in the following diagram:

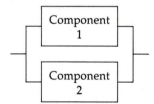

23. Modify the reliability program so that it reads the reliabilities of three components and then computes the reliability of the components connected as shown in the following diagram:

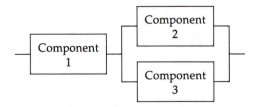

24. Modify the reliability program so that it reads the reliabilities of four compo-

nents and then computes the reliability of the components connected as
shown in the following diagram:

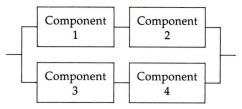

25. Modify the reliability program so that it reads the reliabilities of four components and then computes the reliability of the components connected as
shown in the following diagram:

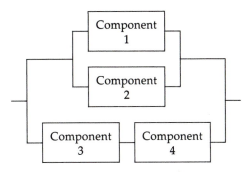

Develop programs for problems 26–39. Use the five-phase design process.

26. Write a program to read the length and width of a rectangle and compute
and print its perimeter and area.

27. Write a program to read the coordinates of two points (X1,Y1), (X2,Y2).
Compute the slope of the straight line between these two points where

$$\text{SLOPE} = \frac{Y2 - Y1}{X2 - X1}$$

Print the points and the slope of the line between the points.

28. Write a program to read the diameter of a circle. Compute the radius, circumference, and area of the circle. Print these new values in the following form:

```
PROPERTIES OF A CIRCLE WITH DIAMETER XXXX.XXX
(1)   RADIUS = XXXX.XXX
(2)   CIRCUMFERENCE = XXXX.XXX
(3)   AREA = XXXX.XXX
```

29. Write a program to read a measurement in meters. Print the value followed
by the units, METERS. Convert the measurement to kilometers and print the
value on the next line, again with the correct units. Convert the measurement to miles and print the value on the third line, with correct units. (Use 1
mile = 1.609 kilometers.)

30. A research scientist performed nutrition tests using three animals. Data on each animal includes an identification number, the weight of the animal at the beginning of the experiment, and the weight of the animal at the end of the experiment. Write a program to read this data and print a report. The report is to include the original information plus the percentage increase in weight for each animal.

31. Write a program to read three resistance values (R1, R2, R3) and compute their combined resistance (RC) for the parallel arrangement shown. Print the values of R1, R2, R3, and RC.

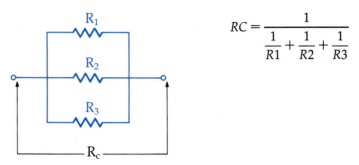

$$RC = \cfrac{1}{\cfrac{1}{R1} + \cfrac{1}{R2} + \cfrac{1}{R3}}$$

32. The distance between points with coordinates (XA,YA) and (XB,YB) is given by

$$DISTANCE = \sqrt{(XA - XB)^2 + (YA - YB)^2}$$

You are given the coordinates of three points:

$$point\ 1:\ (X1,Y1)$$
$$point\ 2:\ (X2,Y2)$$
$$point\ 3:\ (X3,Y3)$$

Write a program to read the coordinates. Next calculate and print the distance DIST12 between points 1 and 2, the distance DIST13 between points 1 and 3, and the distance DIST23 between points 2 and 3.

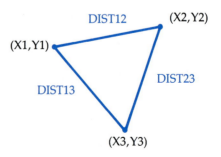

33. Write a program to read the following information from the terminal:

Year
Number of people in the civilian labor force
Number of people in the military labor force

Compute the percentage of the labor force that is civilian and the percentage that is military. Print the following information:

```
LABOR FORCE   - YEAR XXXX
NUMBER OF WORKERS (THOUSANDS) AND PERCENTAGE OF WORKERS
CIVILIAN          XXX.XXX                  XXX.XXX
MILITARY          XXX.XXX                  XXX.XXX
TOTAL             XXX.XXX                  XXX.XXX
```

34. The approximate time for electrons to travel from the cathode to the anode of a rectifier tube is given by

$$\text{TIME} = \sqrt{\frac{2 \cdot M}{Q \cdot V}} \cdot R1 \cdot Z \cdot \left(1 + \frac{Z}{3} + \frac{Z^2}{10} + \frac{Z^3}{42} + \frac{Z^4}{216} \right)$$

where Q = charge of the electron (1.60206E−19 coulombs)
M = mass of the electron (9.1083E−31 kilograms)
V = accelerating voltage in volts
$R1$ = radius of the inner tube (cathode)
$R2$ = radius of the outer tube (anode)
Z = natural logarithm of $R2/R1$

Define the values of Q and M in the constant section of your program. Read values for $V, R1$, and $R2$, then calculate Z and TIME. Print the values of $V, R1, R2$, and TIME.

Cathode ⟶   Anode
R1
R2

Rectifier Tube

35. Write a program to compute the volume of the shell of a hollow ball. Assume that the values for the radius and for the thickness of the ball are to be read. The volume of a sphere is related to the radius r by

$$\text{VOLUME} = \frac{4}{3} \cdot \text{pi} \cdot r^3$$

36. The Gaussian density function is commonly used in engineering statistics. This function is defined in the equation that follows:

$$Y = \frac{1}{\sqrt{2 \cdot \text{pi}}} \cdot e^{-0.5 \cdot X^2}$$

Write a program to read a value of X and compute the corresponding value of Y. Print the values in the following form:

```
THE STANDARD NORMAL DENSITY FUNCTION EVALUATED
AT XXX.XX GIVES A VALUE OF XX.XXXXX
```

37. A Gaussian density function is defined in problem 36. Write a program to compute and print the change in y between $x = 0.0$ and $x = 1.0$. Also compute and print the change in y between $x = 1.0$ and 2.0 and between $x = 2.0$ and 3.0. Use the following output form:

```
       STANDARD GAUSSIAN DENSITY FUNCTION

   X: 0.0 TO 1.0        CHANGE IN Y:   XXX.XX
   X: 1.0 TO 2.0        CHANGE IN Y:   XXX.XX
   X: 2.0 TO 3.0        CHANGE IN Y:   XXX.XX
```

38. Write a program to read the x and y coordinates of three points from the terminal. Then compute the area of the triangle formed from these points using the following equation:

$$AREA = 0.5|X_1Y_2 - X_2Y_1 + X_2Y_3 - X_3Y_2 + X_3Y_1 - X_1Y_3|$$

Print the coordinates and the area in the following form:

```
       TRIANGLE VERTICES:
       (1)   XXX.X,  XXX.X
       (2)   XXX.X,  XXX.X
       (3)   XXX.X,  XXX.X

       TRIANGE AREA:
            XXX.XX
```

(Be sure to give a descriptive message to the user to describe the form and order for the input values.)

39. The radioactive decay of thorium is given by the equation

$$N = N_0 \cdot e^{\left[-0.693 \frac{t}{1.65 \times 10^{16}}\right]}$$

where N_0 represents the initial amount of thorium and t represents the time elapsed. When $t = 0$, N is equal to N_0, and no decay has occurred. As t increases, the amount of thorium is decreased. Read values for N_0 and t from the terminal, and then compute and print the amount of thorium left after the specified time has elapsed. Use the following output form:

```
   INITIAL VALUE OF THORIUM:   XXX.XXX
   TIME ELAPSED:               XXX.XXX
   REMAINING THORIUM:          XXX.XXX
```

FORTRAN STATEMENT SUMMARY

Assignment Statement:

$$variable = expression$$

Examples:

```
PI = 3.141593
AREA = SIDE*SIDE
ROOT = SQRT(X)
```

Discussion:

The left-hand side of the assignment statement must be a variable name. The right-hand side can be any form of an expression, from a simple constant to a complex arithmetic expression involving other variables and intrinsic functions.

END Statement:

```
END
```

Discussion:

This statement must be the last statement in a FORTRAN program. It is a signal to the compiler that there are no further statements to translate. Program execution stops when it reaches the END statement.

FORMAT Statement:

k **FORMAT** *(format specifications)*

Examples:

```
 5 FORMAT (1X,'TEMPERATURE DATA FROM EXPERIMENT 1')
10 FORMAT (1X,'THE VALUE OF X IS ',F7.3)
15 FORMAT (1X,I3,2X,F7.1)
```

Discussion:

The FORMAT statement must always have a statement label, which is referenced in a formatted I/O statement, such as a PRINT statement. The FORMAT statement specifies the exact form of the input or output that is being requested. For output, the specifications include the vertical spacing (how many lines to skip) and the horizontal spacing (how many spaces to skip between values).

INTEGER Statement:

INTEGER *variable list*

Examples:

```
INTEGER  SUM

INTEGER  ID, TOTAL, X
```

Discussion:
The INTEGER statement explicitly lists all variables that will store integer values. Listing a variable name in an INTEGER statement overrides its implicit typing.

PRINT* Statement:

PRINT*, *expression list*

Examples:

```
PRINT*, 'DISTANCE VERSUS VELOCITY MEASUREMENTS'

PRINT*, 'SLOPE = ', SLOPE

PRINT*, X, Y, X + Y
```

Discussion:
The PRINT* statement is a list-directed output statement. The value of any literals, variables, constants, or expressions in its expression list will be printed in the order in which they are listed. The form of numeric output is pre-determined by the compiler.

PRINT k Statement:

PRINT *k, expression list*

Examples:

```
PRINT 5, ALPHA, BETA

PRINT 50, SLOPE

PRINT 25
```

Discussion:
The PRINT *k* statement is a formatted output statement. The value of any variables or expressions in its expression list will be printed in the order in which they are listed according to the specifications in the FORMAT statement with label *k*.

PROGRAM Statement:

PROGRAM *program name*

Examples:

PROGRAM   CALC

PROGRAM   REPORT

Discussion:

The PROGRAM statement is optional, but it must be the first statement in a program if it is used. It assigns a name to the program. This name must be unique and cannot be used for a variable in the program.

READ* Statement:

READ*, *variable list*

Examples:

READ*, TIME

READ*, DIST, VELCTY

Discussion:

The READ* statement is a list-directed input statement that reads values for the variables in its list. The values are stored in the order in which the variables are listed. Data values must be separated by blanks or commas, and as many lines as are needed will be read. Each READ* statement will begin searching for values with a new line.

REAL Statement:

REAL *variable list*

Examples:

REAL   FORCE

REAL   TEMP, PRESS, VOL

Discussion:

The REAL statement explicitly lists all variables that are to store real values. Listing a variable name in a REAL statement overrides its implicit typing.

STOP Statement:

STOP

Discussion:

The STOP statement is an optional statement that stops the execution of a program. Programs may have more than one STOP statement. The END statement also serves to stop program execution if it is executed.

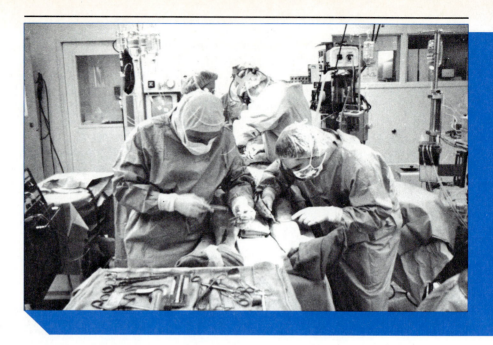

APPLICATION — Suture Packaging (Biomedical Engineering)

Sutures are strands or fibers used to sew living tissue together after an injury or an operation. Packages of sutures must be sealed carefully before they are shipped to hospitals so that contaminants cannot enter the packages. The object that seals the package is referred to as a sealing die. Generally, sealing dies are heated with an electric heater. For the sealing process to be a success, the sealing die is maintained at an established temperature and must contact the package with a predetermined pressure for an established time period. The time period in which the sealing die contacts the package is called dwell. An engineering assistant in a packaging company might be asked to write a program to analyze the data collected during the sealing of several batches of sutures. The information available would be the temperature, pressure, and dwell time for each batch, along with the acceptable range of these parameters. Write a program to generate a report analyzing the data for batches that were rejected because the packages were not sealed properly. (See Section 3–5 for the solution.)

Photo courtesy of Northridge Hospital Medical Center.

3

CONTROL STRUCTURES

Introduction

3–1 Algorithm Structure

3–2 IF Structures

3–3 WHILE Loop Structure

3–4 Application — Rocket Trajectory (Aeronautical Engineering)

3–5 Application — Suture Packaging (Biomedical Engineering)

3–6 DO Loop

3–7 Application — Timber Regrowth (Environmental Engineering)

3–8 Application — Cable Car Velocity (Mechanical Engineering)

3–9 Nested DO Loops

Summary

INTRODUCTION

In Chapter 2 we wrote complete FORTRAN programs, but the steps were all executed sequentially. The programs were composed of reading data, computing new data, and printing the new data. We now introduce FORTRAN statements that allow us to control the sequence of the steps being executed. This control is achieved through statements that allow us to select different paths through our programs and statements that allow us to repeat certain parts of our programs.

3–1 ALGORITHM STRUCTURE

In Chapter 1 we presented a five-step design process for problem solving:

1. State the problem clearly.
2. Describe the input and the output.
3. Work a sample problem by hand.
4. Develop an algorithm to solve the problem.
5. Test the algorithm carefully.

To describe algorithms consistently, we use a set of standard forms, or structures. When an algorithm is described in these standard structures, it is a *structured algorithm*. When the algorithm is converted into computer instructions, the corresponding program is a *structured program*.

Each structure for building algorithms can be described in an English-like notation called *pseudocode*, which we will soon discuss in detail. Because pseudocode is not really computer code, it is language independent — pseudocode only depends on the steps needed to solve a problem, not on the computer language being used. *Flowcharts* also describe the steps in algorithms. We use both techniques in this text so that you can choose the form that is most convenient for you. Neither pseudocode nor flowcharts are intended to be a formal way of describing the algorithm; they are informal ways of easily describing the steps in the algorithm without worrying about the syntax of a specific computer language. After we present the structures that we will be using and some examples of their corresponding pseudocode and flowcharts, we will develop problem solutions using both techniques so that you can compare them side-by-side.

The steps included in algorithms can be divided into three general structures:

1. Sequence: Contains steps that are performed sequentially. All of the programs in Chapter 2 were sequential.
2. Selection: Asks a question or tests a condition to determine which steps are to be performed next. For example, a step of this structure might be "if the data value is positive, add it to the sum; otherwise, print an error message."

3. Repetition: Allows us to use loops, which are sets of steps in an algorithm that are repeated. One type of loop, the *WHILE loop*, repeats the steps as long as a certain condition is true. Another type of loop, the *counting loop*, repeats the steps a specified number of times.

Other special structures are sometimes included in a list of algorithm structures. Generally, these other structures are special forms of the three structures already presented.

SEQUENCE

The sequence structure is a series of steps in an algorithm listed one after another. These steps are primarily computations, input, and output. We now compare pseudocode and flowcharts for these three operations.

Computations In pseudocode, computations are indicated by arrows, as in

$$\text{average} \leftarrow \text{total/count}$$

We read this pseudocode statement as "average is replaced by total divided by count" or "total is divided by count, giving average." In a flowchart, the computation is enclosed in a rectangle. The flowchart statement for the preceding computation is

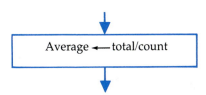

Input Input statements in pseudocode are specified by the word "Read" followed by the variables that are to be read. For example, to read a temperature value and a humidity value, we could use the following pseudocode:

$$\text{Read temperature, humidity}$$

(At this point do not worry about whether or not the names you have chosen are valid FORTRAN names).

The flowchart symbol for input is a parallelogram. The preceding pseudocode can be specified by the following flowchart statement:

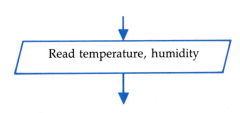

Output Output statements are specified in pseudocode by the word "Print" followed by a list of variable names and constants. The following pseudocode statement prints a literal and the value of an average:

Print 'THE AVERAGE IS', average

The flowchart symbol for output is the same as for input. Thus, the preceding statement in flowchart form would be

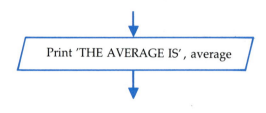

SELECTION

The selection structure is used to choose between sets of steps. It is most commonly described in terms of an IF structure that may itself have several forms. We will use three forms of the IF structure for selection. The simple IF form tests a *condition;* if the condition is true then a certain step or series of steps is performed. For example, suppose the algorithm that we are developing must count the number of students who are on the honor roll and print their student ID numbers. One step in our algorithm might be "if the grade point average (GPA) is greater than 3.0, then print the ID and add 1 to the number of students on the honor roll." This step is shown in both pseudocode and flowchart forms. Note the use of indenting in the pseudocode.

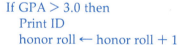

If GPA > 3.0 then
    Print ID
    honor roll ← honor roll + 1

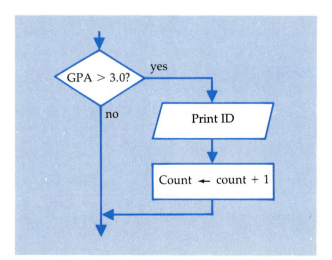

Another form of the IF structure is the IF-ELSE form. This form specifies one series of steps to be executed if a condition is true and an alternate series if the condition is false. For example, suppose that we want to modify the honor roll example to print the ID of each student; however, if the student is on the honor roll, we want to increment our honor roll count and also print the GPA beside the student's ID. We could describe this step with the following pseudocode and flowchart:

If GPA > 3.0 then
   Print ID, GPA
   honor roll ← honor roll + 1
Else
   Print ID

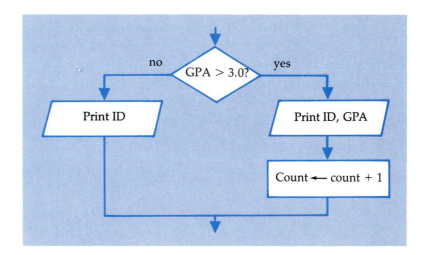

The last form of the IF structure allows us to test for multiple conditions. This IF-ELSEIF form can be illustrated by extending the honor roll example. Assume that the president's honor roll requires a GPA of greater than 3.5 and that the dean's honor roll requires a GPA of greater than 3.0. We want to count the number of students on each honor roll. Students on the president's honor roll are not to be included on the dean's honor roll. Print each student's ID and GPA if above 3.0; also include an asterisk beside the GPA if it is above 3.5. The following pseudocode and flowchart describe this set of steps:

If GPA > 3.5 then
    Print ID, GPA, '*'
    president's count ← president's count + 1
Else If GPA > 3.0 then
    Print ID, GPA
    dean's count ← dean's count + 1
Else
    Print ID

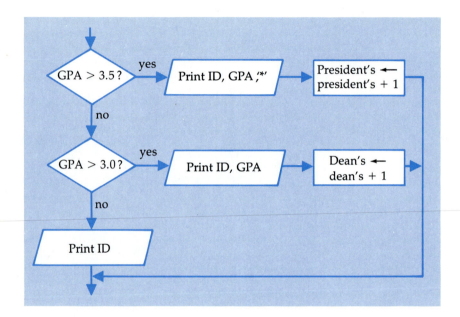

REPETITION

A WHILE loop identifies a series of steps that are to be repeated if a certain condition is true. This series is composed of sequential, selection, or other repetition steps. Suppose that we wish to continue reading data values and adding them to a sum as long as that sum is less than 1000. These steps are described in the following pseudocode and flowchart:

While sum < 1000 do
    Read data value
    sum ← sum + data value

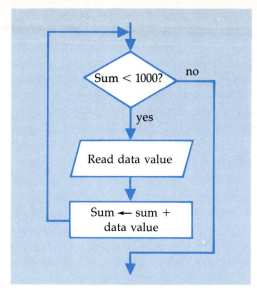

Again, note that the indenting in the pseudocode specifies the steps that are included in the WHILE loop. If we wish to print the value of the sum after exiting the WHILE loop, we can use the following pseudocode and flowchart:

While sum < 1000 do
    Read data value
    sum ← sum + data value
Print sum

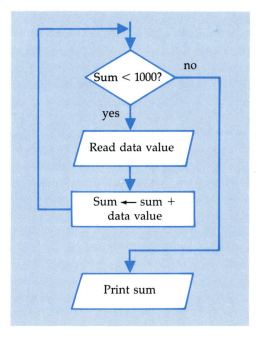

Counting loops, or *iterative loops*, repeat steps a specific number of times. For example, suppose we are going to read ten values from the terminal and perform some calculations with each value. We can describe the steps in a counting loop that is repeated ten times. However, a counting loop can be considered a special form of a WHILE loop in which a counter has been introduced. The counter represents the number of times that the loop has been executed. The counter is usually initialized to zero before the loop is executed. Inside the loop, the counter is incremented by one. The loop is then executed "while the value of the counter is less than ten." The pseudocode and flowchart for this counting loop example are

count ← 0
While count < 10 do
    (processing of data)
    count ← count + 1

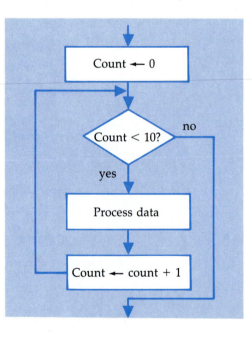

By developing pseudocode and flowcharts for the three main structures discussed, we can describe algorithms for any problem.

EXAMPLE 3-1   **Average of a Set of Data Values**

In Chapter 1 we illustrated top-down design in algorithm development with a program to compute the average of a set of data values. Let's look at that problem again and develop a flowchart for the solution. Assume that we are reading data values from the terminal. A value of zero indicates that we have reached the end of the data values.

Solution

The first step in algorithm development is to decompose the problem into a series of sequential steps. To compute an average, we need to sum and count the values. Thus, our decomposition is

DECOMPOSITION

Read data values and keep a sum and count.
Divide the sum by the number of data values to get the average.
Print the average.

The decomposition provides a top-level picture of the solution in general terms.

We now take each of the sequential steps in the decomposition and refine it using the structures that we have just discussed: sequential steps, selection steps, and repetition steps. The first step in the decomposition is "read data values and keep a sum and count." This step can be refined by recognizing that it is composed of setting a count and a sum to zero (sequential steps) followed by a loop to read the values and update the count and sum (repetition step). The loop should be structured into a WHILE loop, so we must determine the condition necessary to keep us in the loop. The problem statement tells us to assume that the data values have all been read when a zero is entered; thus, we want to stay in the loop "while the data value is not a zero." We need to read a data value before entering the WHILE loop. We then continue to read values inside the loop. After completing the WHILE loop, we need the sequential steps to compute the average and print it. We can now put this refinement into a flowchart. Note that we use an oval symbol to indicate the start and end of the flowchart for a complete problem.

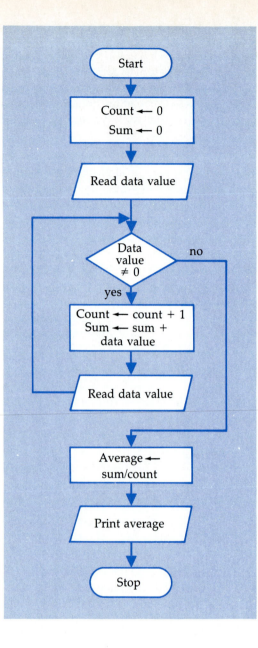

EXAMPLE 3-2   **Experimental Data Analysis**

Develop an algorithm to analyze a set of experimental data values, determine the minimum and the maximum values, and compute the range of the data values. Assume that a zero data value indicates that all the data values have been read.

Solution

Because this is a new algorithm, we start with a simple set of data in a hand-worked example. Assume that the following lab worksheet contains data from a recent chemistry experiment:

LAB MEASUREMENTS   9/30/89

40.56

55.92

66.31

58.35

62.88

41.99

49.70

53.21

Let's begin with the steps to find the maximum value. We look at the first value, compare it to the second value, and denote the larger of the two as the "maximum so far." Now we look at the third value and compare it to our "maximum so far." If the "maximum so far" is larger, we go to the fourth value; but if the third value is larger than our "maximum so far," we update the value in our "maximum so far." Continuing this process with the entire list of data results in labeling the maximum value as the "maximum so far." A similar process finds the minimum value. For the preceding data, our results are

maximum value $= 66.31$

minimum value $= 40.56$

Now we can compute the range of values by subtracting the minimum value from the maximum value:

range of values $= 66.31 - 40.56 = 25.75$

Having worked out a simple problem by hand, we are ready to begin our algorithm development. We start with decomposition of the problem; this is a good example of the "divide and conquer" concept discussed in Chapter 1.

| Read data values and determine maximum and minimum values. |
| Subtract minimum value from maximum value to get range. |
| Print maximum, minimum, range. |

For this example, we refine the solution with pseudocode. We take each step of the decomposition and decide which structures (sequential, selection, and repetition) define the step in greater detail. Clearly, our first decomposition step requires the greatest refinement because it includes sequential steps (initializing our maximum and minimum values) plus the repetition step (the loop to read values and update our maximum and minimum values if necessary). The maximum and minimum values are commonly initialized to the first data value so we only need to read one data value outside the loop to initialize them. We then read the second data value and enter the WHILE loop. "While the data value is not zero," we update the maximum and minimum values if necessary. Note that we do not need a count of the data values or a sum for this problem. Let's write these refined steps in pseudocode.

REFINEMENT IN PSEUDOCODE

```
ANALYSIS: Read data value
          maximum ← data value
          minimum ← data value
          Read data value
          While data value is not zero do
             If data value > maximum then
                maximum ← data value
             If data value < minimum then
                minimum ← data value
             Read data value
          range ← maximum − minimum
          Print 'MAXIMUM DATA VALUE = ', maximum
          Print 'MINIMUM DATA VALUE = ', minimum
          Print 'RANGE OF VALUES = ', range
```

This was a simple algorithm; only one refinement was needed. Additional refinements are often necessary for more complex problems.

In the next two sections, we present the FORTRAN statements for the IF structures and the WHILE loop. We then return to the two algorithms we have just developed and translate them into complete FORTRAN 77 programs.

3-2 IF STRUCTURES

In Section 3-1 we presented the pseudocode and flowcharts for three IF structures. In this section we present the corresponding FORTRAN statements. All forms of the IF structure use a condition to determine which path to take in the structure. Therefore, before we discuss the forms of these statements, we want to discuss logical expressions that are used as the conditions to be tested.

LOGICAL EXPRESSIONS

A *logical expression* is analogous to an arithmetic expression but is always evaluated to either true or false, instead of a number. Logical expressions can be formed using *relational operators*, which are listed:

RELATIONAL OPERATOR	INTERPRETATION
.EQ.	Is equal to
.NE.	Is not equal to
.LT.	Is less than
.LE.	Is less than or equal to
.GT.	Is greater than
.GE.	Is greater than or equal to

Numeric variables can be used on both sides of the relation operators to yield a logical expression whose value is either true or false. For example, consider the logical expression A.EQ.B where A and B are real values. If the value of A is equal to the value of B, then the logical expression A.EQ.B is true. Otherwise, the expression is false. Similarly, if the value of X is 4.5, then the expression X.GT.3.0 is true.

We can also combine two logical expressions into a *compound logical expression* with the *logical operators* .OR. and .AND.. When two logical expressions are joined by .OR., the entire expression is true if either or both expressions are true; it is false only when both expressions are false. When two logical expressions are joined by .AND., the entire expression is true only if both expressions are true. These logical operators are used only between complete logical expressions. For example, A.LT.B.OR.A.LT.C is a valid compound logical expression because .OR. joins A.LT.B and A.LT.C. However, A.LT.B.OR.C is an invalid compound expression because C is a numeric variable, not a complete logical expression.

Logical expressions can also be preceded by the logical operator NOT. This operator changes the value of the expression to the opposite value; hence, if A.GT.B is true, then .NOT.A.GT.B is false.

A logical expression may contain several logical operators, as in

```
.NOT.(A.LT.15.4).OR.KT.EQ.ISUM
```

The *hierarchy*, from highest to lowest, is .NOT., .AND., and .OR.. In the preceding statement, the logical expression A.LT.15.4 would be evaluated, and its value, true or false, would then be reversed. This resultant value would be used, along with the value of KT.EQ.ISUM, with the logical operator .OR.. For example, if A is 5.0, KT is 5, and ISUM is 5, then the left-hand expression is false and the right-hand expression is true; but these expressions are connected by .OR., thus the entire expression is true.

Another type of variable, a *logical variable,* is also useful in writing the conditions that allow us to choose different paths and to repeat parts of our programs. A logical variable can have one of two values: true or false. A logical variable must be defined with a specification statement whose form is

```
LOGICAL    variable list
```

Logical constants are .TRUE. and .FALSE.. Therefore, the statements necessary to define a logical variable and give it a value of false are

```
LOGICAL  DONE
DONE = .FALSE.
```

Logical variables are generally used to make our programs more readable; thus, they are not usually part of the input or output. In several examples in this chapter, we will compare solutions using logical variables to ones without logical variables.

IF STATEMENT

The IF form of the IF structure can be implemented in two ways: One statement handles the situation where only one step is performed when a condition is true; the other statement handles the situation where several steps must be performed when the condition is true. The general form of the IF statement with one step to perform is

```
IF  (condition) executable statement
```

Execution consists of the following steps:

1. If the condition is true, we execute the statement that is on the same line as the condition and then go to the next statement in the program.
2. If the condition is false, we jump immediately to the next statement in the program.

A typical IF statement is

```
IF (A.LT.B) SUM = SUM + A
```

If the value of A is less than the value of B, then the value of A is added to SUM. If the value of A is greater than or equal to B, then control passes to whatever statement follows the IF statement in the program. Other examples of IF statements are

```
IF (TIME.GT.1.5) READ*, DISTNC

IF (DEN.LE.0.0) PRINT*, DEN

IF (-4.NE.NUM) NUM = NUM + 1
```

The executable statement that follows the condition is typically a computation or an input/output statement—it cannot be another IF statement.

In many instances we would like to perform more than one statement if a condition is true. The form of the IF statement that allows us to perform any number of statements if a condition is true uses the words THEN and ENDIF to identify these steps. The general form is

```
IF (condition)   THEN
     statement 1
        .
        .
        .
     statement n
ENDIF
```

Execution consists of the following steps:

1. If the condition is true, we execute statements 1 through *n* and then go to the statement following ENDIF.
2. If the condition is false, we jump immediately to the statement following ENDIF.

Although not required, the statements to be performed when the condition is true should be indented to indicate that they are a group of statements within the IF statement.

EXAMPLE 3-3   **Zero Divide**

Assume that you have calculated the numerator NUM (explicitly typed REAL) and the denominator DEN of a fraction. Before dividing the two values, you want to see if DEN is zero. If DEN is zero, you want to print an error message and stop the program; if DEN is not zero, you want to compute the result and print it. Write the statements to perform these steps.

Solution

```
IF (DEN.EQ.0.0) THEN
    PRINT*, 'DENOMINATOR IS ZERO'
    STOP
ENDIF
FRACTN = NUM/DEN
PRINT*, 'FRACTION = ', FRACTN
```

IF statements can also be nested; the following construction includes an IF statement within an IF statement:

```
IF (condition 1) THEN
    statement 1
        .
        .
        .
    statement n
    IF (condition 2) THEN
        statement n + 1
            .
            .
            .
        statement m
    ENDIF
    statement m + 1
        .
        .
        .
    statement p
ENDIF
statement q
```

Again, the indenting of statements within the construction is not required but makes the logic easier to follow. If condition 1 is true, we then always execute statements 1 through n and statements $m + 1$ through p. If condition 2 is also true, we then also execute statements $n + 1$ through m. If condition 1 is false, we immediately go to statement q.

Consider these statements:

```
IF (GPA.GE.3.0) THEN
    PRINT*, 'HONOR ROLL'
    IF (GPA.GT.3.5) THEN
        PRINT*, 'PRESIDENT''S LIST'
    ENDIF
ENDIF
```

If the GPA is less than 3.0, the entire construction is skipped. If the GPA is between 3.0 and 3.5, only HONOR ROLL is printed. If the GPA is greater than 3.5, then HONOR ROLL is printed, followed on the next line by PRESIDENT'S LIST.

IF-ELSE STATEMENT

The IF-ELSE statement implements another form of the IF structure and allows us to execute one set of statements if the condition is true and a different set if the condition is false. The general form of the IF-ELSE statement is on the next page. If the condition is true, then statements 1 through n are executed. If the condition is false, then statements $n + 1$ through m are executed. Any statement can also be another IF or IF-ELSE statement to provide a nested structure.

```
IF (condition) THEN
    statement 1
       .
       .
       .
    statement n
ELSE
    statement n + 1
       .
       .
       .
    statement m
ENDIF
```

Now consider this set of statements which uses a logical variable VALID with the IF structure:

```
READ*, VOLTS
IF (VOLTS.GE.-5.0.AND.VOLTS.LE.5.0) THEN
    VALID = .TRUE.
ELSE
    VALID = .FALSE.
ENDIF
IF (.NOT.VALID) PRINT*, 'ERROR IN DATA'
```

In these statements, the variable VALID is true if the value in VOLTS is between −5.0 and 5.0; otherwise VALID is false. After determining the value of VALID, it can be used in other places in the program, such as in an IF statement to print an error message if the value is not valid. The advantage of using the logical variable is that we can reference it each time that we need to know if the value is valid, instead of repeating the test to see if value in VOLTS is between −5.0 and 5.0.

EXAMPLE 3-4   **Velocity Computation**

Give the statements for calculating the velocity VEL of a cable car. The variable DIST contains the distance of the cable car from the nearest tower. Use this equation if the cable car is within 30 feet of the tower:

$$\text{velocity} = 2.425 + 0.00175 \text{ distance}^2 \text{ ft/sec}$$

Use this equation if the cable car is further than 30 feet from the tower:

$$\text{velocity} = 0.625 + 0.12 \text{ distance} - 0.00025 \text{ distance}^2 \text{ ft/sec}$$

Correct Solution

```
IF (DIST.LE.30.0) THEN
    VEL = 2.425 + 0.00175*DIST*DIST
ELSE
    VEL = 0.625 + 0.12*DIST - 0.00025*DIST*DIST
ENDIF
```

Incorrect Solution

```
IF (DIST.LE.30.0) VEL = 2.425 + 0.00175*DIST*DIST
VEL = 0.625 + 0.12*DIST - 0.00025*DIST*DIST
```

This incorrect solution points out a common error. Suppose DIST is greater than 30, then the first logical expression is false and we proceed to the next statement to calculate VEL — this part works fine.

Now suppose the logical expression is true — that is, DIST is less than or equal to 30. We execute the assignment statement in the IF statement, correctly calculating VEL when DIST is less than or equal to 30; but the next statement that is executed is the other assignment statement, which replaces the correct value in VEL with an incorrect value.

IF-ELSEIF STATEMENT

When we nest several levels of IF-ELSE statements, it may be difficult to determine which conditions must be true (or false) to execute a set of statements. In these cases, the IF-ELSEIF statement is often used to clarify the program logic; the general form of this statement is

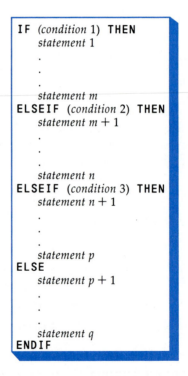

```
IF (condition 1) THEN
    statement 1
    .
    .
    .
    statement m
ELSEIF (condition 2) THEN
    statement m + 1
    .
    .
    .
    statement n
ELSEIF (condition 3) THEN
    statement n + 1
    .
    .
    .
    statement p
ELSE
    statement p + 1
    .
    .
    .
    statement q
ENDIF
```

We have shown two ELSEIF clauses; there may be more or less in an actual construction. If condition 1 is true, then only statements 1 through m are executed. If condition 1 is false and condition 2 is true, then only statements $m + 1$ through n are executed. If conditions 1 and 2 are false and condition 3 is true, then only statements $n + 1$ through p are executed. If more than one condition is true, the first condition encountered is the only one executed.

If none of the conditions are true, then statements $p + 1$ through q are executed. If there is not a final ELSE clause and none of the conditions are true, then the entire construction is skipped. The IF-ELSEIF form is also called a CASE structure because a number of cases are tested. Each case is defined by its corresponding condition.

EXAMPLE 3-5   **Weight Category**

An analysis of a group of weight measurements involves converting a weight value into an integer category number that is determined as follows:

Category	Weight (pounds)
1	weight ≤ 50.0
2	$50.0 <$ weight ≤ 125.0
3	$125.0 <$ weight ≤ 200.0
4	$200.0 <$ weight

Write FORTRAN statements that put the correct value (1, 2, 3, or 4) into CATEGR based on the value of WEIGHT. Assume that CATEGR has been explicitly typed as an integer variable.

Solution 1

This solution uses nested IF-ELSE statements:

```
IF (WEIGHT.LE.50.0) THEN
   CATEGR = 1
ELSE
   IF (WEIGHT.LE.125.0) THEN
      CATEGR = 2
   ELSE
      IF (WEIGHT.LE.200.0) THEN
         CATEGR = 3
      ELSE
         CATEGR = 4
      ENDIF
   ENDIF
ENDIF
```

Solution 2

This solution uses the IF-ELSEIF statement:

```
IF (WEIGHT.LE.50.0) THEN
   CATEGR = 1
ELSEIF (WEIGHT.LE.125.0) THEN
   CATEGR = 2
ELSEIF (WEIGHT.LE.200.0) THEN
   CATEGR = 3
ELSE
   CATEGR = 4
ENDIF
```

As you can see, Solution 2 is more compact than Solution 1: It combines the ELSE and IF statements into the single statement ELSEIF and eliminates two of the ENDIF statements.

The order of the conditions is important in Solution 2 because the evaluation will stop as soon as a true condition has been encountered. Changing the order of the conditions and the category assignments can cause the CATEGR value to be set incorrectly.

3-3 WHILE LOOP STRUCTURE

The WHILE loop is an important structure for repeating a set of statements as long as a certain condition is true. In pseudocode, the WHILE loop structure is

> While condition do
>   statement 1
>   .
>   .
>   .
>   statement m
> statement p

While the condition is true, statements 1 through m are executed. After the group of statements is executed, the condition is retested. If the condition is still true, the group of statements is reexecuted. When the condition is false, execution continues with the statement following the WHILE loop (statement p in our example). The variables modified in the group of statements in the WHILE loop must involve the variables tested in the WHILE loop's condition, or the value of the condition will never change.

Standard FORTRAN 77 does not include a WHILE statement, although many compilers have implemented their own WHILE statement. We will implement the WHILE loop with the IF statement as shown below, so that our programs will be standard FORTRAN 77 and will execute on other FORTRAN 77 compilers without any conversion.

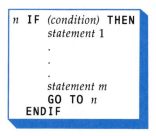

```
n IF (condition) THEN
     statement 1
        .
        .
        .
     statement m
     GO TO n
  ENDIF
```

In this implementation we used an unconditional transfer statement whose general form is

```
GO TO n
```

where n is the statement number or label of an executable statement in the program. The execution of the GO TO statement causes the flow of program control to transfer, or *branch*, to statement n.

We are now ready to write programs for the algorithms we developed in Section 3-1.

EXAMPLE 3-6 **Average of a Set of Data Values**

In Example 3–1 we developed a flowchart for the algorithm to find the average of a set of data values. This flowchart is repeated here:

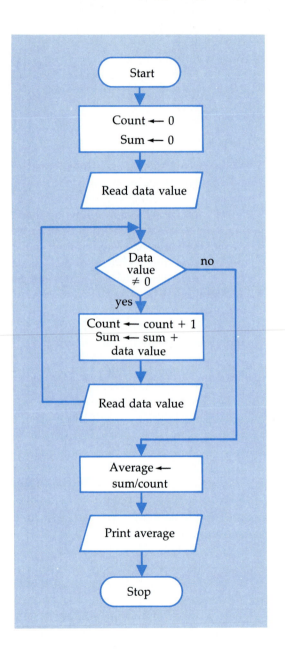

Convert this flowchart into a FORTRAN program.

Solution 1

We have covered the FORTRAN statements for the IF structures and for the WHILE loop. Using these statements, we can translate each step in the flowchart into FORTRAN.

```
*-------------------------------------------------------*
      PROGRAM  COMPUT
*
*  This program computes the average of
*  a set of experimental data values.
*
      INTEGER  COUNT
      REAL  X, SUM, AVERG
*
      SUM = 0.0
      COUNT = 0
      READ*, X
   1 IF (X.NE.0.0) THEN
         SUM = SUM + X
         COUNT = COUNT + 1
         READ*, X
         GO TO 1
      ENDIF
      AVERG = SUM/REAL(COUNT)
      PRINT 5, AVERG
   5 FORMAT (1X,'THE AVERAGE IS ',F6.2)
      END
*-------------------------------------------------------*
```

This is the program we used in Chapter 1 to illustrate the form and readability of a FORTRAN program.

Solution 2

We now present a second solution that uses a logical variable DONE to specify when we have reached the end of the data. In this solution, we initialize the logical variable to the value .FALSE.; when we find the value that indicates the end of the data, we change the value of the logical variable to .TRUE..

```
*-------------------------------------------------------*
      PROGRAM COMPUT
*
*  This program computes the average of
*  a set of experimental data values.
*
      INTEGER  COUNT
      REAL  X, SUM, AVERG
      LOGICAL  DONE
*
      DONE = .FALSE.
      SUM = 0.0
      COUNT = 0
      READ*, X
      IF (X.EQ.0.0)  DONE = .TRUE.
*
```

```
1 IF (.NOT.DONE) THEN
      SUM = SUM + X
      COUNT = COUNT + 1
      READ*, X
      IF (X.EQ.0.0) DONE = .TRUE.
      GO TO 1
  ENDIF
*
  AVERG = SUM/REAL(COUNT)
  PRINT 5, AVERG
5 FORMAT (1X,'THE AVERAGE IS ',F6.2)
  END
*-------------------------------------------------------*
```

EXAMPLE 3-7

Experimental Data Analysis

In Example 3–2 we developed pseudocode for the algorithm to analyze a set of experimental data values and determine the minimum and maximum values and compute the range of data values. This pseudocode is repeated again:

REFINEMENT IN PSEUDOCODE

ANALYSIS: Read data value
maximum ← data value
minimum ← data value
Read data value
While data value is not zero do
   If data value > maximum then
     maximum ← data value
   If data value < minimum then
     minimum ← data value
   Read data value
range ← maximum − minimum
Print 'MAXIMUM DATA VALUE = ', maximum
Print 'MINIMUM DATA VALUE = ', minimum
Print 'RANGE OF VALUES = ', range

Convert this pseudocode into a FORTRAN program.

Solution

Again, using the statements presented in this chapter for the IF structure and the WHILE loop, we can convert each step of the pseudocode into FORTRAN.

```
*-------------------------------------------------------*
      PROGRAM  ANALYZ
*
*  This program determines maximum and minimum values
*  and the range of values for a set of data values.
*
      REAL  X, MAX, MIN, RANGE
*
```

```
      READ*, X
      MAX = X
      MIN = X
      READ*, X
    1 IF (X.NE.0.0) THEN
         IF (X.GT.MAX) MAX = X
         IF (X.LT.MIN) MIN = X
         READ*, X
         GO TO 1
      ENDIF
      RANGE = MAX - MIN
      PRINT 5, MAX
    5 FORMAT (1X,'MAXIMUM DATA VALUE = ',F8.2)
      PRINT 6, MIN
    6 FORMAT (1X,'MINIMUM DATA VALUE = ',F8.2)
      PRINT 7, RANGE
    7 FORMAT (1X,'RANGE OF VALUES = ',F8.2)
      END
*-------------------------------------------------------*
```

If we use the sample data from Example 3–2, the output is

```
MAXIMUM DATA VALUE =    66.31
MINIMUM DATA VALUE =    40.56
RANGE OF VALUES =    25.75
```

3–4 APPLICATION—ROCKET TRAJECTORY (Aeronautical Engineering)

A small rocket is being designed to make wind shear measurements in the vicinity of thunderstorms. Before testing begins, the designers are developing a simulation of the rocket's trajectory. They have derived the following equation that they believe will predict the performance of their test rocket, where t is the elapsed time in seconds:

$$\text{height} = 60 + 2.13t^2 - 0.0013t^4 + 0.000034t^{4.751}$$

The equation gives the height above ground level at time t. The first term (60) is the height in feet above ground level of the nose of the rocket. To check the predicted performance, the rocket is "flown" on a computer, using the preceding equation.

Develop an algorithm and use it to write a complete program to cover a maximum flight of 100 seconds. Increments in time are to be 2.0 seconds from launch through the ascending and descending portions of the trajectory until the rocket descends to within 50 feet of ground level. Below 50 feet the time increments are to be 0.05 seconds. If the rocket impacts prior to 100 seconds, the program is to stop immediately after impact. The output is to be in the following form:

```
TIME (SEC.)      HEIGHT (FT.)

0.0000           XXXX.XXXX
2.0000           XXXX.XXXX
  .
  .
  .
```

As shown in the following diagram, several possible events could occur as we simulate the flight. The height above the ground should increase for a period and then decrease until the rocket impacts. We can test for impact by testing the height for a value equal to or less than zero. It is also possible that the rocket will still be airborne after 100 seconds of flight time. Therefore, we must also test for this condition and stop the program if the value of time becomes greater than 100. In addition, we need to observe the height above ground. As the rocket approaches the ground, we want to monitor its progress more frequently; we will need to reduce our time increment from 2.0 seconds to 0.05 seconds.

PROBLEM STATEMENT

Using the equation, compute height values and print them along with their corresponding time values. Start time at zero and increment it by 2.0 seconds until the height is less than 50 feet, then increment time by 0.05 seconds. Stop the program if the rocket impacts or if the total time exceeds 100 seconds.

$$height = 60 + 2.13t^2 - 0.0013t^4 + 0.000034t^{4.751}$$

INPUT/OUTPUT DESCRIPTION

There is no input to the program. The output is a table of time and height values in the following form:

```
TIME (SEC.)     HEIGHT (FT.)

0.0000          XXXX.XXXX
2.0000          XXXX.XXXX
.
.
.
```

HAND EXAMPLE

Using a calculator, compute the first three entries in our table as shown:

```
TIME (SEC.)     HEIGHT (FT.)

0.0000          60.0000
2.0000          68.5001
4.0000          93.7719
```

We are now ready to develop the algorithm so that the computer can compute the rest of the table for us.

ALGORITHM DEVELOPMENT

The initial decomposition comprises two sequential steps, as shown:

DECOMPOSITION

Set time to zero.
Compute heights and print report.

As we begin the refinement, we find that it is easiest to do the refinement in two steps. Our initial refinement yields:

INITIAL REFINEMENT IN PSEUDOCODE

ROCKET: time ← 0
      While above ground and time ≤ 100 do
          Compute height using equation
          Print time, height
          Increment time

In our final refinement, we replace "Increment time" with the steps that take into account our height above ground. We also replace the condition "above ground" with a specific condition based on our height above ground.

ROCKET: time ← 0
        height ← 60
        While height > 0 and time ≤ 100 do
          Compute height using equation
          Print time, height
          If height < 50 then
            time ← time + 0.05
          Else
            time ← time + 2.0

Notice that the height variable was initialized to 60.0 before entering the WHILE loop. Why? Could it have been initialized to any value? Because the condition in the WHILE loop used the height variable, it had to be initialized before the condition was tested. The height must also be set to a value greater than zero or the WHILE loop would never be executed.

We can now translate our pseudocode statements into FORTRAN.

FORTRAN Program 1

```
*-------------------------------------------------------------*
      PROGRAM  ROCKET
*
*  This program simulates a rocket flight.
*
      REAL  TIME, HEIGHT
*
      TIME = 0.0
      HEIGHT = 60.0
      PRINT 5
    5 FORMAT (1X,'TIME (SEC.)       HEIGHT (FT.)')
      PRINT*
*
   10 IF (HEIGHT.GT.0.0.AND.TIME.LE.100.0) THEN
         HEIGHT = 60.0 + 2.13*TIME**2 - 0.0013*TIME**4
     +               + 0.000034*TIME**4.751
         PRINT 15, TIME, HEIGHT
   15    FORMAT (1X,F7.4,8X,F9.4)
         IF (HEIGHT.LT.50.0) THEN
            TIME = TIME + 0.05
         ELSE
            TIME = TIME + 2.0
         ENDIF
         GO TO 10
      ENDIF
      END
*-------------------------------------------------------------*
```

As our programs become longer, we will use comment lines with only an asterisk in column 1 to separate groups of statements that have a common function. In the preceding program, the blank comment line separated the steps that initialized variables and printed the heading from the WHILE loop.

Another solution to this problem uses the logical variables introduced in Section 3–2. In this solution, we use a logical variable called DONE. As long as neither of the conditions that indicate that we want to stop the program occurs, the value of this variable remains false. Thus, as long as .NOT.DONE is true, we want to stay in the WHILE loop.

FORTRAN PROGRAM 2

```
*------------------------------------------------------------*
      PROGRAM  FLIGHT
*
*  This program simulates a rocket flight.
*
      REAL  TIME, HEIGHT
      LOGICAL  DONE
*
      TIME = 0.0
      HEIGHT = 60.0
      DONE = .FALSE.
      PRINT 5
   5  FORMAT (1X,'TIME (SEC.)     HEIGHT (FT.)')
      PRINT*
*
  10  IF (.NOT.DONE) THEN
          HEIGHT = 60.0 + 2.13*TIME**2 - 0.0013*TIME**4
     +              + 0.000034*TIME**4.751
          PRINT 15, TIME, HEIGHT
  15      FORMAT (1X,F7.4,8X,F9.4)
          IF (HEIGHT.LT.50.0) THEN
              TIME = TIME + 0.05
          ELSE
              TIME = TIME + 2.0
          ENDIF
          DONE = HEIGHT.LE.0.0.OR.TIME.GT.100.0
          GO TO 10
      ENDIF
      END
*------------------------------------------------------------*
```

It is invalid to compare two logical variables with the relation .EQ. or .NE.. Instead, two new relations, .EQV. and .NEQV., are used to represent equivalent and not equivalent. If we wanted to compare .NOT.DONE to the value .TRUE., we could use this statement:

```
IF (.NOT.DONE.EQV..TRUE.) THEN
```

Whenever arithmetic, relational, and logical operators are in the same expression, the arithmetic operations are performed first; the relational operators are then applied to yield true or false values; and these values are evaluated with the logical operators whose precedence is .NOT., .AND., and .OR.. The relations .EQV. and .NEQV. are evaluated last.

TESTING

The first few lines and the last few lines of output are shown. The values are in agreement with the hand-worked example.

```
 TIME (SEC.)        HEIGHT (FT.)

   0.0000            60.0000
   2.0000            68.5001
   4.0000            93.7719
   6.0000           135.1644
   8.0000           191.6590
     .
     .
     .
  54.0000           999.1558
  56.0000           827.4219
  58.0000           633.3003
  60.0000           418.3994
  62.0000           184.8125
  64.0000           -64.8574
```

Can you think of ways to test different parts of the algorithm? We now know that the rocket impacts before 100 seconds of flight time; we could change the cutoff time to 50 seconds to see if this exit from the WHILE loop were working correctly. How could you modify the program to check the change in the increment of the time variable from 2.0 seconds to 0.05 seconds?

3-5 APPLICATION—SUTURE PACKAGING (Biomedical Engineering)

As we mentioned in the introductory problem for this chapter, sutures are strands or fibers used to sew living tissue together after an injury or an operation. Packages of sutures must be sealed carefully before they are shipped to hospitals so that contaminants cannot enter the packages. The object that seals the package is referred to as a sealing die. Generally, sealing dies are heated with an electric heater. For the sealing process to be a success, the sealing die is maintained at an established temperature and must contact the package with a predetermined pressure for an established time period. The time period in which the sealing die contacts the package is called dwell. We want to develop an algorithm and a FORTRAN program to analyze the data collected on batches of sutures that have been rejected. We assume that we will be given the temperature, pressure, and dwell time for each batch. For the sutures that have been sealed, the following acceptable range of parameters has been established:

Temperature: 150.0–170.0 degrees centigrade
Pressure: 60–70 psi (lb/sq in)
Dwell: 2.0–2.5 seconds

All sutures in a batch will be rejected if any of these conditions is not met.

Our program will ask the user to enter the batch code, temperature, pressure, and dwell time for each batch that has been rejected during some time period. We want to collect data on the reasons why the batches were rejected to attempt to find the underlying problem. For example, if most of the rejections were due to temperature problems, then we need to check the electric heater in the sealing die. If most of the rejections were due to pressure problems, then we need to check the pressure in the air cylinder that lowers the die to the package. Or, if most of the rejections were due to dwell time, then the control information in the sealing die may be in error. Clearly, the first step in locating the source of the problem must be to get a good analysis of the data from rejected batches of sutures. The data we will compute in this program will be the percentage of rejections due to temperature, the percentage of rejections due to pressure, and the percentage of rejections due to dwell time. If a batch was rejected for more than one reason, it should be counted in the total for each rejection category.

We now use our five-phase design process to develop an algorithm and a FORTRAN solution to this problem.

PROBLEM STATEMENT

Write a program to print a report analyzing the information for all batches of sutures that were not properly sealed, where a proper seal requires the following range of parameters in the sealing process:

Temperature: 150.0 – 170.0 degrees centigrade
Pressure: 60 – 70 psi (lb/sq in)
Dwell: 2.0 – 2.5 seconds

INPUT/OUTPUT DESCRIPTION

The input to the program will be four values for each batch that was rejected: the batch number, the temperature, the pressure, and the dwell time. A negative batch number indicates the end of the data. The output from the program will be a report giving the percentages of the batches rejected because of temperature problems, pressure problems, and dwell time problems.

HAND EXAMPLE

Assume the following data represents the information on the batches rejected during one day:

BATCH NUMBER	TEMPERATURE	PRESSURE	DWELL TIME
24551	145.5	62.3	2.13
24582	153.7	63.0	2.52
26553	160.3	58.9	2.51
26623	159.5	58.9	2.01
26624	160.5	61.3	1.98

In this data, batch 24551 was rejected because of temperature, batch 24582 was rejected because of dwell time, batch 26553 was rejected because of pressure and dwell time, batch 26623 was rejected due to pressure, and batch 26624 was rejected due to dwell time. The report summarizing this information is the following:

```
SUMMARY OF BATCH REJECT INFORMATION

20.0 % REJECTED DUE TO TEMPERATURE
40.0 % REJECTED DUE TO PRESSURE
60.0 % REJECTED DUE TO DWELL TIME
```

ALGORITHM DEVELOPMENT

The decomposition contains the following sequential steps:

DECOMPOSITION

Read data and collect information.
Print report.

Using the hand-worked example solution as a guide, we can develop the initial pseudocode for this problem.

INITIAL REFINEMENT IN PSEUDOCODE

SEALS: count ← 0
      Read batch, temperature, pressure, dwell
      While batch ≥ 0 do
          Determine reject reason and add to totals
          count ← count + 1
          Read batch, temperature, pressure, dwell
      Convert totals to percentages
      Print report

We still need to refine the step further to determine which parameters were not within the specified values, and then add to the corresponding totals. This involves three different tests: one for the temperature, one for the pressure, and one for the dwell time. We will call the rejection totals rejctt (for rejections due to temperature), rejctp (for rejections due to pressure), and rejctd (for rejections due to dwell time). The final refinement in pseudocode follows.

```
SEALS: count ← 0
         rejctt ← 0
         rejctp ← 0
         rejctd ← 0
         Read batch, temperature, pressure, dwell
         While batch ≥ 0 do
             If temperature out of bounds then
                 rejctt ← rejctt + 1
             If pressure out of bounds then
                 rejctp ← rejctp + 1
             If dwell out of bounds then
                 rejctd ← rejctd + 1
             count ← count + 1
             Read batch, temperature, pressure, dwell
         Convert reject totals to percentages
         Print report
```

We now convert the pseudocode steps to FORTRAN.

FORTRAN Program

```
*----------------------------------------------------------------*
*      PROGRAM  SEALS
*
*  This program analyzes data on batches of sutures that have
*  not been properly sealed, and then prints a report.
*
       INTEGER  BATCH, COUNT, REJCTT, REJCTP, REJCTD
       REAL   TEMP, PRESSR, DWELL, PERCT, PERCP, PERCD
*
       COUNT = 0
       REJCTT = 0
       REJCTP = 0
       REJCTD = 0
*
       PRINT*, 'ENTER BATCH NUMBER, TEMPERATURE, PRESSURE, DWELL'
       PRINT*, 'FOR BATCHES THAT HAVE BEEN REJECTED'
       PRINT*, '(NEGATIVE BATCH NUMBER TO STOP)'
       READ*, BATCH, TEMP, PRESSR, DWELL
*
     5 IF (BATCH.GE.0) THEN
           IF (TEMP.LT.150.0.OR.TEMP.GT.170.0) REJCTT = REJCTT + 1
           IF (PRESSR.LT.60.0.OR.PRESSR.GT.70.0) REJCTP = REJCTP + 1
           IF (DWELL.LT.2.0.OR.DWELL.GT.2.5) REJCTD = REJCTD + 1
           COUNT = COUNT + 1
           PRINT*, 'ENTER NEXT SET OF DATA'
           READ*, BATCH, TEMP, PRESSR, DWELL
           GO TO 5
       ENDIF
       PERCT = REAL(REJCTT)/REAL(COUNT)*100.0
       PERCP = REAL(REJCTP)/REAL(COUNT)*100.0
       PERCD = REAL(REJCTD)/REAL(COUNT)*100.0
*
```

```
      PRINT*
      PRINT*, 'SUMMARY OF BATCH REJECT INFORMATION'
      PRINT*
      PRINT 10, PERCT
   10 FORMAT (1X,F6.2,' % REJECTED DUE TO TEMPERATURE')
      PRINT 15, PERCP
   15 FORMAT (1X,F6.2,' % REJECTED DUE TO PRESSURE')
      PRINT 20, PERCD
   20 FORMAT (1X,F6.2,' % REJECTED DUE TO DWELL')
      END
```
--

TESTING

The output of this program from the data used in the hand example is:

```
ENTER BATCH NUMBER, TEMPERATURE, PRESSURE, DWELL
FOR BATCHES THAT HAVE BEEN REJECTED
(NEGATIVE BATCH NUMBER TO STOP)
24551        145.5        62.3        2.13
ENTER NEXT SET OF DATA
24582        153.7        63.0        2.52
ENTER NEXT SET OF DATA
26553        160.3        58.9        2.51
ENTER NEXT SET OF DATA
26623        159.5        58.9        2.01
ENTER NEXT SET OF DATA
26624        160.5        61.3        1.98
ENTER NEXT SET OF DATA
-1             0.0         0.0        0.0

SUMMARY OF BATCH REJECT INFORMATION

20.0 % REJECTED DUE TO TEMPERATURE
40.0 % REJECTED DUE TO PRESSURE
60.0 % REJECTED DUE TO DWELL TIME
```

3-6   DO LOOP

In Section 3–3 we used the IF statement to build WHILE loops. A special form of the WHILE loop is the counting loop, or iterative loop. Implementing a counting loop generally involves initializing a counter before entering the loop, modifying the counter within the loop, and exiting the loop when the counter reaches a specified value. Counting loops are executed a specified number of times. The three steps (initialize, modify, and test) can be incorporated in a WHILE loop as we have already seen; but, they still require three different statements. A special statement, the DO statement, combines all three steps into one. Using the DO statement to construct a loop results in a construction called a DO loop.

The general form of the DO statement is

> **DO** *k index = initial, limit, increment*

The constant k is the number of the statement that represents the end of the loop; index is a variable used as the loop counter; initial represents the initial value given to the loop counter; limit represents the value used to determine when the DO loop has been completed; and increment represents the value to be added to the loop counter each time the loop is executed.

The values of initial, limit, and increment are the *parameters* of the DO loop. If the increment is omitted, an increment of 1 is assumed. When the value of the index is greater than the limit, control is passed to the statement following the end of the loop. The end of the loop is usually indicated by the CONTINUE statement, whose general form is

k CONTINUE

where k is the statement number referenced by the corresponding DO statement. Before we list the rules for using a DO loop, let's look at a simple example.

EXAMPLE 3-8　**Integer Sum**

The sum of the integers 1 through 50 is represented mathematically as

$$\sum_{i=1}^{50} i = 1 + 2 + \cdots + 49 + 50$$

Obviously, we do not want to write one long assignment statement of the form

$$SUM = 1 + 2 + 3 + \cdots + 50$$

A better solution is to build a loop that executes 50 times and adds a number to the sum each time, as shown in the following solutions.

WHILE Loop Solution

```
      INTEGER  SUM, NUMBER
      .
      .
      .
      SUM = 0
      NUMBER = 1
   10 IF (NUMBER.LE.50) THEN
         SUM = SUM + NUMBER
         NUMBER = NUMBER + 1
         GO TO 10
      ENDIF
```

DO Loop Solution

```
      INTEGER  SUM, NUMBER
      .
      .
      .
      SUM = 0
      DO 10 NUMBER=1,50
         SUM = SUM + NUMBER
   10 CONTINUE
```

The DO statement identifies statement 10 as the end of the loop. The index NUMBER is initialized to 1. The loop is repeated until the value of NUMBER is greater than 50. Because the third parameter is omitted, the index NUMBER is incremented automatically by 1 at the end of each loop. Comparing the DO loop solution with the WHILE loop solution, we see that the DO loop solution is shorter but that both compute the same value for SUM.

STRUCTURE OF A DO LOOP

We have seen a DO loop in a simple example. We now need to summarize the rules that relate to its structure.

1. The index of the DO loop must be a variable, but it may be either real or integer.
2. The parameters of the DO loop may be constants, variables, or expressions and can also be real or integer types.
3. The increment can be either positive or negative, but it cannot be zero.
4. A DO loop may end on any executable statement that is not a transfer, an IF statement, or another DO statement. The CONTINUE statement is an executable statement that was designed expressly for closing a DO loop; although other statements may be used, we strongly encourage the consistent use of CONTINUE to indicate the end of the loop.
5. We will use the following pseudocode for an iterative loop:

For index = initial to limit by step do
set of statements

The "by step" clause is omitted if the increment is 1. The pseudocode for the iterative loop we used in Example 3–8 is

For number = 1 to 50 do
sum ← sum + number

6. The flowchart symbol for an iterative loop is

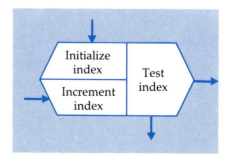

Note that the symbol is divided into three parts, each corresponding to the three steps in building an iterative loop. The flowchart for the iterative loop in Example 3–8 is

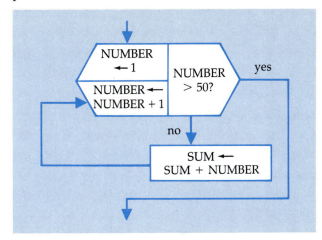

These rules define the structure of the DO loop but do not define the steps in its execution. The following discussion describes these rules.

EXECUTION OF A DO LOOP

In the following list we present a complete set of rules that relate to DO loop execution. We suggest that you read through them once and then go through the set of examples that follow the rules. Later, reread these rules. Do not worry about memorizing them; after you have gone through the set of examples, most of the rules will seem logical.

1. The test for completion is done at the beginning of the loop, as in a WHILE loop. If the initial value of the index is greater than the limit and the increment is positive, the loop will not be executed. For instance, the statement

$$\text{DO 10 I=5,2}$$

sets up a loop that ends at statement 10. The initial value of the index I is 5, which is greater than the limit 2; therefore, the statements within the loop will be skipped and control passes to the statement following statement 10.

2. The value of the index should not be modified by other statements during the execution of the loop.

3. After the loop begins execution, changing the values of the parameters will have no effect on the loop.

4. If the increment is negative, the exit from the loop will occur when the value of the index is less than the limit.

5. Although it is not recommended, you may branch out of a DO loop before it is completed. The value of the index will be the value just before the branch. (If you need to exit the DO loop before it is completed, you should restructure the loop as a WHILE loop to maintain a structured program.)

6. Upon completion of the DO loop, the index contains the last value that exceeded the limit.

7. Always enter a DO loop through the DO statement so that it will be initiated properly.

8. The number of times that a DO loop will be executed can be computed as

$$\left[\frac{\text{limit} - \text{initial}}{\text{increment}} \right] + 1$$

The brackets around the fraction represent the greatest integer value; that is, we drop any fractional portion (truncate) of the quotient. If this value is negative, the loop is not executed. If we had the following DO statement

$$DO\ 35\ K=5,83,4$$

the corresponding DO loop would be executed the following number of times:

$$\left[\frac{83 - 5}{4} \right] + 1 = \left[\frac{78}{4} \right] + 1 = 20$$

The value of the index K would be 5, then 9, then 13, and so on until the final value of 81. The loop would not be executed with the value 85 because that value is greater than the limit, 83.

The next set of examples illustrates both the structure and the execution of the DO loop.

EXAMPLE 3-9 **Polynomial Model with Integer Time**

Polynomials are often used to model data and experimental results. Assume that the polynomial

$$3t^2 + 4.5$$

models the results of an experiment where t represents time in seconds. Write a complete program to evaluate this polynomial for the period of time from 1 second to 10 seconds in increments of 1 second (that is, let $t = 1, 2, 3, 4, 5, 6, 7, 8, 9,$ and 10). For each value of time, print the time and the polynomial value.

Solution

The solution to this problem requires printing the headings of the report and an iterative loop to evaluate the polynomial.

DECOMPOSITION

Print headings.
Print report.

Refining the "Print report" step into an iterative loop yields the following pseudocode.

REFINEMENT IN PSEUDOCODE

POLY1: Print headings
    For time = 1 to 10 do
      poly ← 3 · time² + 4.5
      Print time, poly

We now convert the pseudocode into a FORTRAN program.

FORTRAN PROGRAM

```
*------------------------------------------------------------*
      PROGRAM  POLY1
*
*  This program prints a table of
*  values for a polynomial.
*
      INTEGER  TIME
      REAL  POLY
*
      PRINT*, 'POLYNOMIAL MODEL'
      PRINT*, 'TIME   POLYNOMIAL'
      PRINT*, '(SEC)'
      PRINT*
*
      DO 15 TIME=1,10
         POLY = 3.0*REAL(TIME)**2 + 4.5
         PRINT 10, TIME, POLY
   10    FORMAT (1X,I2,5X,F6.2)
   15 CONTINUE
      END
*------------------------------------------------------------*
```

The output from this program is

```
POLYNOMIAL MODEL
TIME    POLYNOMIAL
(SEC)

 1        7.50
 2       16.50
 3       31.50
 4       52.50
 5       79.50
 6      112.50
 7      151.50
 8      196.50
 9      247.50
10      304.50
```

EXAMPLE 3-10   **Polynomial Model with Real Time**

We again assume that the polynomial

$$3t^2 + 4.5$$

models an experiment where *t* represents time in seconds. Write a program to evaluate this polynomial for time beginning at zero seconds and ending at 5 seconds in increments of 0.5 seconds.

Solution

The solution to this problem requires printing the headings of the report and an iterative loop to evaluate the polynomial.

DECOMPOSITION

Print headings.
Print report.

Refining the "Print report" step into an iterative loop yields the following flowchart:

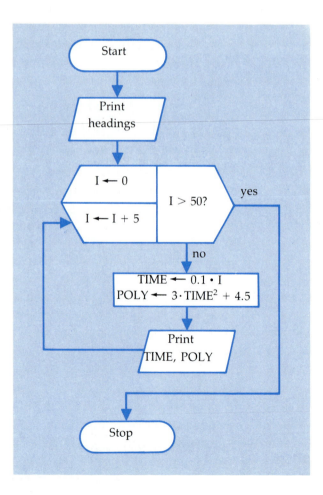

Converting the flowchart to FORTRAN gives the following program:

FORTRAN Program

```
*-----------------------------------------------------------*
      PROGRAM  POLY2
*
*  This program prints a table of
*  values for a polynomial.
*
      INTEGER  I
      REAL  TIME, POLY
*
      PRINT*, 'POLYNOMIAL MODEL'
      PRINT*, 'TIME   POLYNOMIAL'
      PRINT*, '(SEC)'
      PRINT*
*
      DO 15 I=0,50,5
         TIME = 0.1*REAL(I)
         POLY = 3.0*TIME*TIME + 4.5
         PRINT 10, TIME, POLY
   10    FORMAT (1X,F4.1,5X,F5.2)
   15 CONTINUE
      END
*-----------------------------------------------------------*
```

Note that the value of TIME is computed from an integer that varies from 0 to 50 in steps of 5. Another possibility would have been to use the following DO statement:

```
DO 15 TIME=0.0,5.0,0.5
```

However, it is wise to avoid DO statements such as this one with real parameters because these statements do not always execute exactly the way we expect because of truncation within the computer. For example, suppose that the value for 0.5 is stored as a value slightly less than 0.5 in our computer system. Each time we add 0.5 to the index, we are adding less than we intend, and the values are not those we intend; in this case, the value of TIME for the last time that we want to execute the loop would be less than 5.0 instead of exactly 5.0.

The output from this program is

```
POLYNOMIAL MODEL
TIME   POLYNOMIAL
(SEC)

0.0        4.50
0.5        5.25
1.0        7.50
1.5       11.25
2.0       16.50
2.5       23.25
3.0       31.50
3.5       41.25
4.0       52.50
4.5       65.25
5.0       79.50
```

EXAMPLE 3-11   **Polynomial Model with Variable Time**

Assume that we want to evaluate the same polynomial

$$3t^2 + 4.5$$

beginning at t equal to zero, in increments of 0.25, for a variable number of seconds. Write a program to read an integer NSEC that represents the number of seconds to be used for evaluating the polynomial. Print the corresponding table.

Solution

The solution to this problem requires reading the number of seconds that the report is supposed to cover, printing the headings of the report, and an iterative loop to evaluate the polynomial.

DECOMPOSITION

| Read number of seconds. |
| Print headings. |
| Print report. |

Refining the "Print report" step into an iterative loop yields the following pseudocode:

REFINEMENT IN PSEUDOCODE

POLY1: Read nsec
       Print headings
       For $i = 0$ to $100 \cdot$ nsec by 25 do
          time $\leftarrow 0.01 \cdot i$
          poly $\leftarrow 3 \cdot$ time $\cdot$ time $+ 4.5$
          Print time, poly

We now convert the pseudocode into a FORTRAN program.

```
*----------------------------------------------------------*
      PROGRAM  POLY3
*
*  This program prints a table of
*  values for a polynomial.
*
      INTEGER  I, NSEC
      REAL   TIME, POLY
*
      PRINT*, 'ENTER NUMBER OF SECONDS FOR TABLE'
      READ*, NSEC
      PRINT*
      PRINT*, 'POLYNOMIAL MODEL'
      PRINT*, 'TIME   POLYNOMIAL'
      PRINT*, '(SEC)'
      PRINT*
*
      DO 15 I=0,100*NSEC,25
         TIME = 0.01*REAL(I)
         POLY = 3.0*TIME*TIME + 4.5
         PRINT 10, TIME, POLY
  10     FORMAT (1X,F4.2,5X,F7.4)
  15 CONTINUE
      END
*----------------------------------------------------------*
```

If we enter the value 4 for the number of seconds, the output from this program is

```
ENTER NUMBER OF SECONDS FOR TABLE
4

POLYNOMIAL MODEL
TIME   POLYNOMIAL
(SEC)

0.00    4.5000
0.25    4.6875
0.50    5.2500
0.75    6.1875
1.00    7.5000
1.25    9.1875
1.50   11.2500
1.75   13.6875
2.00   16.5000
2.25   19.6875
2.50   23.2500
2.75   27.1875
3.00   31.5000
3.25   36.1875
3.50   41.2500
3.75   46.6875
4.00   52.5000
```

We are now ready to develop problem solutions that use the DO statement to implement iterative loops.

This self-test allows you to check quickly to see if you have remembered some of the key points from Section 3–5. If you have any problems with the exercises, you should reread this section. The solutions are included at the end of the text.

In problems 1–6, determine the number of times that the statements in the DO loop will be executed.

1. `DO 10 NUM=3,20`
2. `DO 10 COUNT=-2,14`
3. `DO 10 K=-2,-10,-1`
4. `DO 10 TIME=10,0,-1`
5. `DO 10 TIME=10,5`
6. `DO 10 INDEX=314,-52`

For problems 7–11, give the value in COUNT after each of the following loops is executed. Assume that COUNT is initialized to zero before starting each problem.

```
  7.    DO 5 I=1,10
            COUNT = COUNT + 1
        5 CONTINUE

  8.    DO 5 K=1,10
            COUNT = COUNT + K
        5 CONTINUE

  9.    DO 5 INDEX=-2,2
            COUNT = COUNT + INDEX
        5 CONTINUE

 10.    DO 5 NUM=5,0,-1
            COUNT = COUNT - NUM
        5 CONTINUE

 11.    DO 5 M=5,5
            COUNT = COUNT*M
        5 CONTINUE
```

3-7 APPLICATION—TIMBER REGROWTH
(Environmental Engineering)

A problem in timber management is to determine how much of an area to leave uncut so that the harvested area is reforested in a certain period of time. It is assumed that reforestation takes place at a known rate per year, depending on climate and soil conditions. A reforestation equation expresses this growth as a function of the amount of timber standing and the reforestation rate. For example, if 100 acres are left standing after harvesting and the reforestation rate is 0.05, then $100 + 0.05*100$, or 105 acres, are forested at the end of the first year. At the end of the second year, the number of acres forested is $105 + 0.05*105$, or 110.25 acres.

Write a program to read the identification number of an area, the total number of acres in the area, the number of acres that are uncut, and the reforestation rate. Print a report that tabulates for 20 years the number of acres reforested and the total number of acres forested at the end of each year.

PROBLEM STATEMENT

Compute the number of acres forested at the end of each year for 20 years for a given area.

INPUT/OUTPUT DESCRIPTION

The input information consists of the identification number for the area of land, the total acres, the number of acres with trees, and the reforestation rate. The output is a table with a row of data for each of 20 years. Each row of information contains the number of acres reforested during that year and the total number of acres forested at the end of the year.

HAND EXAMPLE

Assume that there are 14,000 acres total with 2500 acres uncut. If the reforestation rate is 0.02, we can compute a few entries as shown:

Year 1 $2500*0.02 = 50$ acres of new growth
original 2500 acres + 50 new acres = *2550 acres forested*

Year 2 $2550*0.02 = 51$ acres of new growth
original 2550 acres + 51 new acres = *2601 acres forested*

Year 3 $2601*0.02 = 52.02$ acres of new growth
original 2601 acres + 52.02 new acres = *2653.02 acres forested*

The overall structure is an iterative loop that is executed 20 times, once for each year. Inside the loop we need to compute the number of acres reforested during that year and add that number to the acres forested at the beginning of the year; this will compute the total number of acres forested at the end of the year. The output statement should be inside the loop because we want to print the number of acres forested at the end of each year.

DECOMPOSITION

Read initial information.
Print headings.
Print report.

INITIAL REFINEMENT IN PSEUDOCODE

TIMBER: Read initial information
       Print headings
       For year = 1 to 20 do
           Compute reforested amount
           Add reforested amount to uncut amount
           Print reforested amount, uncut amount

Clearly an error condition exists if the uncut area exceeds the total area. We will test for this condition and exit after printing an error message if it occurs. It is possible to imagine soil conditions that would have a zero or negative reforestation rate so we will not perform any error checking on the rate. However, all the values read will be printed, or echoed, so that the user can recognize an error in an input value. We now add these refinements to our initial pseudocode.

FINAL REFINEMENT IN PSEUDOCODE

TIMBER: Read identification, total, uncut, rate
       Print identification, total, uncut, rate
       If uncut > total then
         Print error message
       Else
         Print headings
         For year = 1 to 20 do
           refor ← uncut*rate
           uncut ← uncut + refor
           Print year, refor, uncut

From the pseudocode, the overall structure of the program is evident. The outer structure is an IF-ELSE structure, with a DO loop in the ELSE portion. We can now convert the pseudocode into FORTRAN.

```
*------------------------------------------------------------*
      PROGRAM  TIMBER
*
*  This program computes a reforestation summary
*  for an area that has not been completely harvested.
*
      INTEGER  ID, YEAR
      REAL  TOTAL, UNCUT, RATE, REFOR
*
      PRINT*, 'ENTER LAND IDENTIFICATION (INTEGER)'
      READ*, ID
      PRINT*, 'ENTER TOTAL NUMBER OF ACRES'
      READ*, TOTAL
      PRINT*, 'ENTER NUMBER OF ACRES UNCUT'
      READ*, UNCUT
      PRINT*, 'ENTER REFORESTATION RATE'
      READ*, RATE
*
      IF (UNCUT.GT.TOTAL) THEN
          PRINT*, 'UNCUT AREA LARGER THAN ENTIRE AREA'
      ELSE
          PRINT*
          PRINT*, 'REFORESTATION SUMMARY'
          PRINT*
          PRINT 5, ID
   5      FORMAT (1X,'IDENTIFICATION NUMBER ',I5)
          PRINT 10, TOTAL
  10      FORMAT (1X,'TOTAL ACRES = ',F10.2)
          PRINT 20, UNCUT
  20      FORMAT (1X,'UNCUT ACRES = ',F10.2)
          PRINT 30, RATE
  30      FORMAT (1X,'REFORESTATION RATE = ',F5.3)
          PRINT*
          PRINT*, 'YEAR  REFORESTED   TOTAL REFORESTED'
          DO 50 YEAR=1,20
              REFOR = UNCUT*RATE
              UNCUT = UNCUT + REFOR
              PRINT 40, YEAR, REFOR, UNCUT
  40          FORMAT (1X,I3,F11.3,F17.3)
  50      CONTINUE
      ENDIF
      END
*------------------------------------------------------------*
```

Using the test data from the hand-worked example, a typical interaction is

```
ENTER LAND IDENTIFICATION (INTEGER)
25563
ENTER TOTAL NUMBER OF ACRES
14000.0
ENTER NUMBER OF ACRES UNCUT
2500.0
ENTER REFORESTATION RATE
0.02


REFORESTATION SUMMARY

IDENTIFICATION NUMBER 25563
TOTAL ACRES =    14000.00
UNCUT ACRES =     2500.00
REFORESTATION RATE = 0.020


YEAR   REFORESTED    TOTAL REFORESTED
 1       50.000          2550.000
 2       51.000          2601.000
 3       52.020          2653.020
 4       53.060          2706.080
 5       54.122          2760.202
 6       55.204          2815.406
 7       56.308          2871.714
 8       57.434          2929.148
 9       58.583          2987.732
10       59.755          3047.486
11       60.950          3108.436
12       62.169          3170.605
13       63.412          3234.017
14       64.680          3298.697
15       65.974          3364.671
16       67.293          3431.964
17       68.639          3500.604
18       70.012          3570.616
19       71.412          3642.028
20       72.841          3714.869
```

The numbers match the ones we computed by hand. Try an example to test the error condition by using an uncut area larger than the total area. What happens if the reforestation rate is 0.00, or −0.02? Should there be an upper limit on the reforestation rate? This information is not given in the original problem so we probably should not set one arbitrarily. What happens if you enter 14,000.0 instead of 14000.0? It might be a good idea to remind the program user not to use commas in numbers. How would you do this?

3–8 APPLICATION—CABLE CAR VELOCITY
(Mechanical Engineering)

This problem involves a 1000-foot cable that is stretched between two towers, with a supporting tower midway between the two end towers. The velocity of the cable car depends on its position on the cable. When the cable car is within 30 feet of a tower, its velocity is

$$velocity = 2.425 + 0.00175d^2 \text{ ft/sec}$$

where d is the distance in feet from the cable car to the nearest tower. If the cable car is not within 30 feet of a tower, its velocity is

$$velocity = 0.625 + 0.12d - 0.00025d^2 \text{ ft/sec}$$

Print a table starting with the cable car at the first tower and moving to the last tower in increments of 10 feet. At each increment of 10 feet, print the number of the nearest tower (1 = first, 2 = middle, 3 = end), the distance from the first tower, and the velocity of the cable car.

PROBLEM STATEMENT

Write a program to print a table containing distances and velocities of a cable car as it moves from the first tower to the last tower in increments of 10 feet.

INPUT/OUTPUT DESCRIPTION

There is no input to the program. The output is a table containing distances and velocities.

HAND EXAMPLE

As we begin thinking about this problem, it is helpful to draw a rough diagram of the tower configuration:

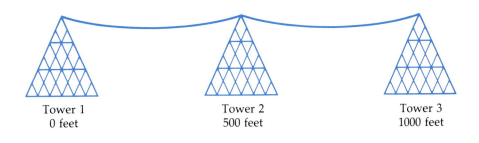

Tower 1   Tower 2   Tower 3
0 feet   500 feet   1000 feet

The cable car will be closest to Tower 1 if the total distance of the cable car from Tower 1 is 0 to 250 feet. When the total distance is greater than 250 feet but less than 750 feet, the cable car is closest to Tower 2. When the total distance is greater than or equal to 750 feet, the cable car is closest to Tower 3. (Note that when the total distance is 250 feet, we could choose Tower 1 or 2. A similar situation occurs when the total distance is 750 feet.)

Furthermore, the distance to the nearest tower is the total distance if the total distance is less than or equal to 250 feet. When the total distance is between 250 feet and 750 feet, the distance to the nearest tower is the absolute value of the total distance minus 500 feet. We use the absolute value here so that the distance is always positive. Finally, the distance to the nearest tower is 1000 feet minus the total distance when the total distance is greater than 750 feet. Pick a few values of the total distance and use these formulas to convince yourself that they are correct.

Total Distance	Distance to Nearest Tower
200	200
300	$|300 - 500| = 200$
650	$|650 - 500| = 150$
850	$1000 - 850 = 150$

ALGORITHM DEVELOPMENT

Because there is no program input, the decomposition is

Decomposition

Print headings.
Compute velocities and print report.

Using the hand-worked example solution as a guide, we can flowchart the steps needed to determine each set of entries in the table.

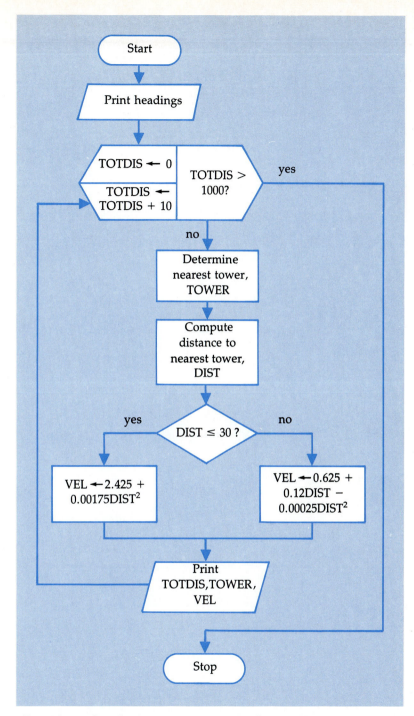

We still need to refine further two steps in the flowchart: "Determine nearest tower" and "Compute distance to nearest tower." Relying on the steps developed in our hand-worked example, we develop this refined flowchart:

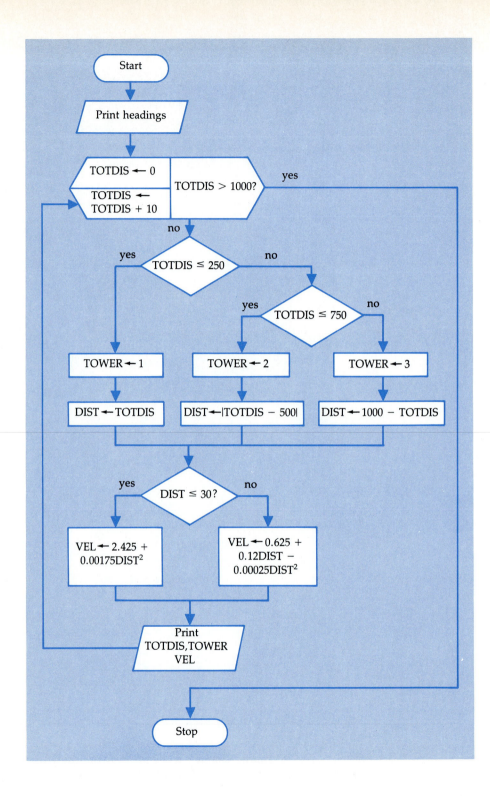

Note the use of blank comment lines to separate sets of steps in the FORTRAN solution.

FORTRAN Program

```
*---------------------------------------------------------------*
      PROGRAM  CABLE
*
*  This program computes the velocity of a cable car
*  on a thousand-foot cable with three towers.
*
      INTEGER  TOTDIS, DIST, TOWER
      REAL  VEL
*
      PRINT 1
    1 FORMAT (1X,9X,'CABLE CAR REPORT')
      PRINT*
      PRINT 2
    2 FORMAT (1X,'DISTANCE  NEAREST TOWER  VELOCITY')
      PRINT 3
    3 FORMAT (1X,'  (FT)',19X,'(FT/SEC)')
      PRINT*
*
      DO 50 TOTDIS=0,1000,10
         IF (TOTDIS.LE.250) THEN
            TOWER = 1
            DIST = TOTDIS
         ELSEIF (TOTDIS.LE.750) THEN
            TOWER = 2
            DIST = ABS(TOTDIS - 500)
         ELSE
            TOWER = 3
            DIST = 1000 - TOTDIS
         ENDIF
         IF (DIST.LE.30) THEN
            VEL = 2.425 + 0.00175*DIST*DIST
         ELSE
            VEL = 0.625 + 0.12*DIST - 0.00025*DIST*DIST

         PRINT 30, TOTDIS, TOWER, VEL
   30    FORMAT (1X,I4,11X,I1,9X,F7.2)
   50 CONTINUE
      END
*---------------------------------------------------------------*
```

A portion of the output from this program is

```
                    CABLE CAR REPORT

        DISTANCE   NEAREST TOWER   VELOCITY
          (FT)                     (FT/SEC)

            0            1           2.42
           10            1           2.60
           20            1           3.13
            .            .             .
            .            .             .
            .            .             .
          980            3           3.13
          990            3           2.60
         1000            3           2.42
```

3-9 NESTED DO LOOPS

DO loops may be independent of each other, or they may be nested within other DO loops. If loops are nested, they must use different indexes or loop counters. When one loop is nested within another, the inside loop is completely executed each pass through the outer loop. To illustrate, consider the following program:

```
*--------------------------------------------------------------------*
      PROGRAM  NEST
*
*  This program prints the indexes in nested DO loops.
*
      INTEGER  I, J
*
      PRINT*, ' I    J'
      PRINT*
      DO 20 I=1,5
         DO 10 J=3,1,-1
            PRINT 5, I, J
    5       FORMAT (1X,I3,1X,I3)
   10    CONTINUE
         PRINT*, 'END OF PASS'
   20 CONTINUE
      END
*--------------------------------------------------------------------*
```

The output from this program is

```
I    J
1    3
1    2
1    1
END OF PASS
2    3
2    2
2    1
END OF PASS
3    3
3    2
3    1
END OF PASS
4    3
4    2
4    1
END OF PASS
5    3
5    2
5    1
END OF PASS
```

The first time through the outer loop, I is initialized to the value 1. We thus begin executing the inner loop: The variable J is initialized to the value 3. After executing the PRINT 5 statement, we reach the end of the inner loop and J is decremented by 1 to the value 2. Because 2 is still larger than the final value of 1, we repeat the loop. J is redecremented by 1 to the value 1, and the loop is repeated again. When J is decremented again, it is less than the final value of 1, so we have completed the inner loop and the message 'END OF PASS' is printed. I is incremented to 2, and we rebegin the inner loop. This process is repeated until I is greater than 5.

EXAMPLE 3-12   **Experimental Sums**

Write a complete program to read 20 data values. Compute the sum of the first 5 values, the next 5 values, and so on. Print the four sums. Assume that the values are real.

Solution

Although we will read a total of 20 data values, we need only 5 values at a time; thus, an outer loop is needed to read 4 sets of data. Each set of data is 5 values; thus, the inner loop reads the 5 values. It is important to initialize to zero the variable being used to store the sum before the inner loop is begun. We then add 5 values, print the sum, and set the sum back to zero before we read the next 5 values.

The decomposition is a single step in this problem; all the other steps are performed inside the overall loop.

Print report.

The refinement in pseudocode illustrates the structure of this algorithm, which is a loop within a loop.

REFINEMENT IN PSEUDOCODE

SUMS: For i = 1 to 4 do
    sum ← 0
      For j = 1 to 5 do
        Read value
          sum ← sum + value
      Print sum

We can now translate the pseudocode into FORTRAN.

FORTRAN PROGRAM

```
*- - - - - - - - - - - - - - - - - - - - - - - - - - - - - - - - - - - - - - -*
      PROGRAM   SUMS
*
*   This program reads 20 values and prints
*   the sum of each group of 5 values.
*
      INTEGER  I, J
      REAL   VALUE, SUM
*
      DO 5 I=1,4
          SUM = 0.0
          DO 1 J=1,5
              READ*, VALUE
              SUM = SUM + VALUE
    1     CONTINUE
          PRINT 3, I, SUM
    3     FORMAT (1X,'SUM ',I1,' = ',F6.2)
    5 CONTINUE
      END
*- - - - - - - - - - - - - - - - - - - - - - - - - - - - - - - - - - - - - - -*
```

Here is a sample of the type of output that would be printed from this program:

```
SUM 1 =   23.44
SUM 2 =   10.23
SUM 3 =   -5.69
SUM 4 =    1.01
```

EXAMPLE 3-13   **Factorial Computation**

Write a complete program to compute the factorial of an integer. A few factorials and their corresponding values are shown (an exclamation point following a number symbolizes a factorial):

$0! = 1$
$1! = 1$
$2! = 2*1$
$3! = 3*2*1$
$4! = 4*3*2*1$
$5! = 5*4*3*2*1$

Compute and print the factorial for four different values that are read from the terminal.

Solution

Because the factorial of a negative number is not defined, we should include an error check in our algorithm for this condition. In computing a factorial, we use a DO loop to perform the successive multiplications. Because the overall structure of this problem solution is a loop, the decomposition is again a single step.

DECOMPOSITION

> Print report.

As you read the following pseudocode refinement, notice that the overall structure of the algorithm is a counting loop. Within the counting loop is an input statement and an IF-ELSE structure. Within the ELSE portion is another counting loop.

REFINEMENT IN PSEUDOCODE

```
FACT: For i = 1 to 4 do
         Read n
         If n < 0 then
             Print error message
         Else
             nfact ← 1
             If n > 1 then
                 For k = 1 to n do
                     nfact ← nfact*k
             Print n, nfact
```

Converting the refined pseudocode into FORTRAN gives the following program:

FORTRAN Program

```
*- - - - - - - - - - - - - - - - - - - - - - - - - - - - - - - - - - - - - - - - - - -*
      PROGRAM   FACT
*
*  This program computes the factorial
*  of four values read from the terminal.
*
      INTEGER  N, NFACT, I, K
*
      DO 10 I=1,4
          PRINT*, 'ENTER N'
          READ*, N
          IF (N.LT.0) THEN
              PRINT 2, N
    2         FORMAT (1X,'INVALID N = ',I8)
          ELSE
              NFACT = 1
              IF (N.GT.1) THEN
                  DO 4 K=1,N
                  NFACT = NFACT*K
    4             CONTINUE
              ENDIF
              PRINT 6, N, NFACT
    6         FORMAT (1X,I4,'! = ',I8)
          ENDIF
   10 CONTINUE
      END
*- - - - - - - - - - - - - - - - - - - - - - - - - - - - - - - - - - - - - - - - - - -*
```

The output from a sample run of this program is

```
ENTER N
3
    3! =        6
ENTER N
-2
INVALID N =    -2
ENTER N
11
   11! = 39916800
ENTER N
0
    0! =        1
```

This self-test allows you to check quickly to see if you have remembered some of the key points from Section 3–8. If you have any problems with the exercises, you should reread this section. The solutions are included at the end of the text.

For problems 1–3, give the value in COUNT after each of the following loops is executed. Assume that COUNT is initialized to zero before starting each problem.

1.
```
      DO 10 I=1,5
         DO 5 K=2,0,-1
            COUNT = 100
   5     CONTINUE
  10 CONTINUE
```

2.
```
      DO 10 I=5,8
         DO 5 K=-2,1
            COUNT = COUNT + 1
   5     CONTINUE
  10 CONTINUE
```

3.
```
      DO 10 I=2,0,-1
         DO 5 K=2,0,-1
            COUNT = COUNT + 1
   5     CONTINUE
         COUNT = COUNT + 1
  10 CONTINUE
```

SUMMARY

This chapter greatly expanded the types of problems we can solve in FORTRAN with use of IF statements: We can now control the order in which statements are executed. An important property of these statements is that they are entered only at the top of the structure and that they have only one exit; with only one entrance and one exit, this type of flow promotes the writing of simpler programs. We also learned to use both WHILE loops and DO loops to implement repetition steps — most of the programs in the rest of the text will use either one or the other of these loop structures.

DEBUGGING AIDS

The most helpful debugging tool is the PRINT* statement. Just knowing that your program is working incorrectly does not tell you where to begin looking for errors. If you have the computer print the values of key variables at different points in your program, however, it becomes easier to isolate the parts of the program that are not working correctly. The location of these *checkpoints*, or places to write the values of key variables, depends on the program; some of the obvious places are after reading new values for variables and after completing loops and computations.

It is also a good idea to number the checkpoints and then print the check-point number along with the other values. For instance, if you print the values of X and Y at several checkpoints, it may not be obvious which set of X and Y values have been printed. However, the following output is clear:

```
CHECKPOINT 3: X = 14.76    Y = -3.82
```

If you have narrowed the problem to an IF statement, then first check the condition. Did you use .LT. when you needed .LE.? Be careful when using NOT in an expression because the relationships can get complex. For example, .NOT.((A.EQ.1.0).OR.(B.EQ.2.0)) is also equal to (A.NE.1.0).AND.(B.NE.2.0).

Another possible error with IF statements can be traced to values being close to, but not exactly equal to, the desired value. For instance, suppose that the result of a mathematical computation should have a real value of 5.0. Because computers have limitations on the number of digits of accuracy, the result might be 4.999 or 5.001; if you check only for 5.0, you may not realize that you really have the correct value. One way to address this problem is to use the IF statement to look for values close to 5.0. For instance, if

$$|X - 5.0| < .001$$

then X is between 4.999 and 5.001. If this is close enough for the problem being solved, then replace the statement

```
IF (X.EQ.5.0) SUM = SUM + 1
```

with this statement

```
IF (ABS(X-5.0).LE.0.001) SUM = SUM + 1
```

If you believe that a programming error is within a WHILE loop, print the values of key variables at the beginning of the loop; this information will be printed each time the loop is executed, so you should be able to locate the trouble spot.

Most errors in a DO loop involve the loop parameters. When a program error seems to involve a DO loop, print the value of the index or count variable immediately within the loop. After executing the loop with this output statement, you can answer the following questions:

1. Did the index start with the correct value?
2. Did the index increment by the proper amount?
3. Did the index have the correct value during the last execution of the loop?

If the answer to any of these questions is no, check the DO statement itself; you probably have an error in the variables or expressions that you specified.

If the error is not in your original specification of the DO statement, print the values of the index at both the beginning and the end of the loop statements. After executing the loop with these two output statements, you will be able to determine if the value of the index is changed by the statements inside the loop. If the index is modified, you have either used the index inadvertently, which can be corrected, or you should replace the DO loop with a WHILE loop.

Another common error associated with DO loops occurs when a similar variable name is used instead of the index. For instance, if the index of the DO loop is INDEX, use INDEX and not I inside the loop when you intend to use the index value.

STYLE/TECHNIQUE GUIDES

The larger a program grows in size, the more apparent becomes the programmer's style—not only does bad style/technique become more obvious, it also becomes harder to correct. Practicing good style/technique in your small programs builds habits that will carry over into all your programming.

One of the best guides to good style is to use the WHILE loop and the DO loop consistently. With a little practice, you will find that all loops fit easily into one of these two forms. As we pointed out in the summary, these types of loops have only one entrance and one exit—enhancing readability and adding simplicity to your program.

Another characteristic of good style is the use of indenting to emphasize the statements in IF structures and loops. You can convince yourself of the importance of indenting if you try to follow a program written by someone else who has not indented statements within control structures. If loops are nested, indent each nested loop from the previous one.

Use the CONTINUE statement consistently to define the end of each DO loop. Although other statements are valid, the CONTINUE statement becomes an important part of the structure definition. Do not close more than one loop with the same CONTINUE statement.

Comment lines are yet another sign of good style; however, the use of comment lines can become excessive. Use only as many lines as are needed to show the program's organization and enhance its readability. Comment lines should be easy to distinguish from FORTRAN statements. We use blank lines before and after our comments and also use lowercase letters within the comment itself. You should always use initial comments to describe the purpose of the program. If needed, comments may be used throughout the program to identify processes, values, variables, and so on. You will also find that blank comment lines can be effective in separating different steps within a program— this technique is often used in our example programs.

A program that exhibits good style will save time in the long run because it is easier to debug. Programmers who may need to modify your programs in future projects will also appreciate your good style. Changing a few lines of FORTRAN code to achieve this will be time well spent.

KEY WORDS

branch	limit value
compound logical expression	logical expression
condition	logical operator
control structure	logical value
counting loop	loop
DO loop	nested loop
flowchart	parameter
IF-ELSEIF structure	pseudocode
IF-ELSE structure	relational operator
IF structure	repetition
increment value	selection
index	sequence
initial value	structured programming
iterative loop	WHILE loop

PROBLEMS

We begin our problem set with modifications to programs given earlier in this chapter. Give the decomposition, refined pseudocode or flowchart, and FORTRAN program for each problem.

Problems 1–5 modify the rocket trajectory program ROCKET, given on page 98.

1. Modify the rocket trajectory program so that it stops if the rocket impacts or if the total time exceeds 50 seconds.

2. Modify the rocket trajectory program so that it starts time at zero seconds and increments it by 1 second until the height is less than 50 feet; then increment time by 0.25 seconds.

3. Modify the rocket trajectory program so that it starts time at zero seconds and increments it by 0.5 seconds until the height is less than 80 feet; then increment time by 0.25 seconds.

4. Modify the rocket trajectory program so that it reads two values, INCR1 and INCR2. Start time at zero seconds and increment it by INCR1 seconds until the distance is less than 50 feet; then increment time by INCR2 seconds.

5. Modify the rocket trajectory program so that it does not print a table but instead prints two values. The first value is the time at which the rocket begins falling back to the ground and the second value is the time at which the rocket impacts. Start time at zero and increment it by 0.01 seconds.

Problems 6–10 modify the suture packaging program SEALS, given on page 103.

6. Modify the suture packaging program so that it also writes the total number of batches rejected.

7. Modify the suture packaging program so that it also writes the number of batches in each rejection category.

8. Modify the suture packaging program so that it prints an error message if the information is entered for a batch that should not have been rejected. Do not count this batch in the overall count of rejected batches.

9. Modify the suture packaging program so that it also counts and writes the total number of batches with ranges out of bounds on more than one of the parameters.

10. Modify the suture packaging program so that it counts and prints the total number of batches with ranges out of bounds on all three parameters.

Problems 11–15 modify the timber management program TIMBER, given on page 117.

11. Modify the timber management program so that a value N is read from the terminal, where N represents the number of years that are to be used in printing the table.

12. Modify the timber management program so that it computes information for 20 years but only prints information for every other year (second year, fourth year, and so on).

13. Modify the timber management program so that a value M is read from the terminal, where M represents the number of years that should be between lines in the output table. (Problem 12 is a special case where $M = 2$.)

14. Modify the timber management program so that instead of printing data for 20 years, it prints yearly information until at least 10 percent of the cut area has been reforested.

15. Modify the timber management program so that it prints only the final line of data after 20 years and then allows the user to input a different reforestation rate. The program should then print the final line of data after 20 years with this new reforestation rate and again allow the user to input a different reforestation rate. The program should end when a reforestation rate of 0.00 is entered. Thus, the user can compare results of several reforestation rates over the same 20 years.

Problems 16–20 modify the cable car program CABLE, given on page 123.

16. Modify the cable car velocity program so that it uses a WHILE loop instead of a DO loop.

17. Modify the cable car velocity program so that it reads the distance increment from a data line.

18. Modify the cable car velocity program so that the report includes a fourth column that gives the distance of the cable car from the nearest tower.

19. Modify the cable car velocity program so that the distance increment is 10 feet unless the cable car is less than 20 feet from a tower, in which case the distance increment should be 5 feet.

20. Modify the cable car velocity program so that there are two supporting towers between the first and last towers: The first supporting tower is 300 feet from the first tower and the second supporting tower is 300 feet from the last tower.

For problems 21–24, write complete FORTRAN programs to print tables showing the values of the input variables and the function shown using DO loops to control the loops.

21. Print a table of values for K where

$$K = 3M$$

for values of $M = 1, 2, 3, 4$.

22. Print a table of values for K where

$$K = I^2 + 2I + 2$$

for values of $I = 0, 1, 2, \ldots , 20$.

23. Print a table of values for Y where

$$Y = \frac{X^2 - 9}{X^2 + 2}$$

for values of $X = 1.5, 2.0, 2.5, \ldots , 9$.

24. Print a table of values for F where

$$F = \frac{X^2 - Y^2}{2XY}$$

for values of $X = 1, 2, \ldots , 9$, and for values of $Y = 0.5, 0.75, 1.0, \ldots , 2.5$.

Develop new programs in problems 25–33. Use the five-phase design process.

25. Write a program to print a table of consecutive even integers and their square values, beginning with 2, until the value of I is greater than 200. Use the following output format:

```
I AND I*I

2         4
4        16
.
.
.
```

26. Write a program to read a value FINAL. Print a table that contains values of X and X*X, starting with X equal to zero and incrementing by 0.5, until X is greater than FINAL. Use the following output format:

```
        X                    X²

      0.0                  0.00
      0.5                  0.25
       .                     
       .                     
       .                     
```

27. Write a program that will read circuit inspection data from the terminal. Each line should contain a circuit ID number and the number of inspections successfully completed. If the number of inspections successfully completed is between 0 and 11, the inspection is in-progress; if the number of inspections successfully completed is 12, the inspection is complete and the circuit passes inspection; and if the number of inspections is -1, the inspection is complete but the circuit has failed inspection. Thus, the classification of a circuit is based on the following table:

CLASSIFICATION	TESTS COMPLETED
In-Progress	0–11
Passed	12
Failed	-1

The program should print a report similar to the following, with a line of output for each circuit:

```
INSPECTION REPORT

CIRCUIT ID AND CLASSIFICATION
XXXXX    -    XXXXXXXXXX
  .
  .
  .
```

An ID of 999 will indicate the end of the data.

28. Modify problem 27 so that a final summary report follows the inspection report and has the following form:

```
INSPECTION SUMMARY

IN-PROGRESS      XXXX
PASSED           XXXX
FAILED           XXXX

TOTAL CIRCUITS        XXXXX
```

29. A rocket is being designed to test a retrorocket that is intended to permit softer landings. The designers have derived the following equations that they believe will predict the performance of the test rocket, where t represents the elapsed time in seconds:

$$\text{ACCELERATION} = 4.25 - 0.015t^2$$
$$\text{VELOCITY} = 4.25t - .005t^3$$
$$\text{DISTANCE} = 90 + 2.125t^2 - .00125t^4$$

The distance equation gives the height above ground level at time t. Thus, the first term (90) is the height in feet above ground level of the nose of the rocket at launch. To check the predicted performance, the rocket will be "flown" on a computer, using the derived equations. Write a program to print the time, height, velocity, and acceleration for the rocket from a time of zero seconds through 50 seconds, in increments of 1 second. Use the following report form:

```
                 ROCKET FLIGHT SIMULATION

  TIME         ACCELERATION      VELOCITY      DISTANCE
  (SEC)        (FT/SEC*SEC)      (FT/SEC)      (FT)

  XXX.XX         XXXX.XX         XXXX.XX       XXXX.XX
    .
    .
    .
```

30. A biologist, after discovering the omega germ, has spent 5 years determining the characteristics of the new virus. She has found that the germ has a constant growth rate. If 10 cells are present with a growth factor of 0.1, the next generation will have $10 + 10(0.1) = 11$ cells. Write a program that will compute and print a report with the following format:

```
                      OMEGA GERM GROWTH

                    NUMBER OF CELLS     PETRI DISH      GROWTH
  CULTURE NUMBER       INITIALLY      DIAMETER (CM)      RATE

     XXXX                 XXXX             XXX          XX.XX

  GENERATION   NUMBER OF CELLS   % AREA OF PETRI DISH COVERED

      1            XXXX.X                 XXX.XX
      .
      .
      .
      5
```

Ten cells occupy 1 square millimeter. Use the following input data for four cultures:

CULTURE NUMBER	NUMBER OF CELLS INITIALLY	PETRI DISH DIAMETER	GROWTH RATE
1984	100	10 cm	0.50
1776	1300	5 cm	0.16
1812	600	15 cm	0.55
1056	700	8 cm	0.80

31. The square of the sine function can be represented by the following:

$$\sin^2 X = X^2 - \frac{2^3 X^4}{4!} + \frac{2^5 X^6}{6!} - \cdots = \sum_{n=1}^{\infty} \frac{(-1)^{n+1} 2^{2n-1} X^{2n}}{(2n)!}$$

Write a program to evaluate this series for an input value X, printing the results after 2, 4, 6, 8, . . . , 14 terms and comparing each sum to the true solution. Note that the term for $n = 1$ is X*X, and that all consecutive terms can be obtained by multiplying the previous term by

$$\frac{-(2X)^2}{2n(2n - 1)}$$

The output should have the following form:

```
          COMPARISON OF VALUES OF SINE SQUARED

   NUMBER          SERIES         INTRINSIC        ABSOLUTE
   OF TERMS       SUMMATION        FUNCTION       DIFFERENCE

      2           XX.XXXX          XX.XXXX          XX.XXXX
      4           XX.XXXX          XX.XXXX          XX.XXXX
      .
      .
      .
     14
```

32. When N is an integer greater than or equal to zero, the expression N! (called N factorial) represents the product of all integers from 1 through N. We define 0! to be equal to 1. The following are a few factorials and their corresponding values:

$$0! = 1$$
$$1! = 1$$
$$2! = 1 \cdot 2 = 2$$
$$3! = 1 \cdot 2 \cdot 3 = 6$$

An approximation to N! can be computed using Stirling's formula

$$N! = \sqrt{2\pi N}\left(\frac{N}{e}\right)^N$$

where $e = 2.718282$. Write a program that reads a value of N from the terminal and then computes an approximation of N! using Stirling's formula. Print the following message before you read the value of N:

          ENTER N WHERE N IS BETWEEN 1 AND 10

Limiting the size of N is necessary to ensure that the value of N! will fit within our limits of integers on most computers. The output of the program should be in this form:

          XX! IS APPROXIMATELY XXXXXXX

(continued)

Continue reading values of N and computing an approximation to $N!$ until a negative value is read. If a value greater than 10 is read, print a message that the input is out of the specified range and ask the user to enter a new value.

33. The current-voltage relationship in an ideal *p-n* junction diode is described by the equation

$$I = I_s(\exp{(QV/kT)} - 1)$$

where I = current through diode, amps
V = voltage across diode, volts
I_s = saturation current, amps
Q = electron charge, 1.6E−19 coulomb
k = Boltzmann's constant, 1.38E−23 joule/degree K
T = junction temperature, K

Write a program that calculates I as V varies from −.250 V to 0.500 V in increments of 0.125 V, for junction temperatures of 32, 100, and 212 degrees Fahrenheit. (Use the following equation to convert degrees Fahrenheit to degrees Kelvin: K = (F − 32) · (5/9) + 273.16.) Saturation current is 1 microamp in all three cases. Your output should be in the following form:

```
JUNCTION TEMPERATURE = XXX.XX F = XXX.XX K

VOLTAGE ACROSS DIODE              CURRENT THROUGH DIODE
     -0.250 V                         ±0.XXXXE±XX  A
     -0.125 V                         ±0.XXXXE±XX  A
       .
       .
       .
      0.500 V                         ±0.XXXXE±XX  A
```

FORTRAN STATEMENT SUMMARY

CONTINUE Statement:

$$k \;\; \texttt{CONTINUE}$$

Example:

$$\texttt{10 CONTINUE}$$

Discussion:

The CONTINUE statement is used to define the end of a DO loop. The statement number of the CONTINUE statement is also referenced in the DO statement.

DO Statement:

$$\texttt{DO } k \;\; index{=}initial, limit, increment$$

Examples:

```
DO 10 I=1,20

DO 20 TIME=1,200,5

DO 30 K=10,0,-1

DO 4C K=1,NUMBER
```

Discussion:

The DO statement defines an iterative loop where k is the statement number of the statement that represents the end of the loop; index is a variable used as the loop counter; initial represents the initial value given to the loop counter; limit represents the value used to determine when the DO loop has been completed; and increment represents the value to be added to the loop counter each time that the loop is executed. If the increment is omitted, an increment of 1 is assumed.

GO TO Statement:

$$\texttt{GO TO } n$$

Example:

$$\texttt{GO TO 25}$$

Discussion:

The GO TO statement is an unconditional branch to the executable statement with label n. It should only be used to implement the WHILE loop.

$$IF \ (condition) \ statement$$

Examples:

```
IF (A.GT.15.5) COUNT = COUNT + 1

IF (X.LE.0.0) PRINT*, 'DATA ERROR'
```

Discussion:
The IF statement is used to execute a single statement if the condition is true. The statement on the same line as the condition may not be another IF statement.

IF-THEN Statement:

```
IF (condition) THEN
    set of statements
ENDIF
```

Example:

```
IF (MIN.GE.60.0) THEN
    HOURS = HOURS + 1
    MIN = MIN - 60.0
    PRINT 5, HOURS
5   FORMAT (1X,I6,' HOURS')
ENDIF
```

Discussion:
If the condition is true, then all the statements between the THEN and the corresponding ENDIF statement are executed. This statement differs from the IF statement in that it can execute more than one statement if the condition is true.

IF-ELSE Statement:

```
IF (condition) THEN
    set of statements
ELSE
    set of statements
ENDIF
```

Example:

```
IF (TIME.GE.LAUNCH) THEN
    VELCTY=ACCEL*TIME
ELSE
    VELCTY=0.0
ENDIF
```

Discussion:
The IF-ELSE statement allows you to execute one set of statements if the condition is true and a different set of statements if the condition is false.

```
        IF (condition 1) THEN
            set of statements
        ELSEIF (condition 2) THEN
            set of statements
        ELSE
            set of statements
        ENDIF
```

Example:

```
    IF (TEMP.GE.65.0.AND.TEMP.LE.70.0) THEN
        PRINT 5
5       FORMAT (1X, 'NORMAL TEMPERATURE')
    ELSEIF (TEMP.LT.65.0) THEN
        PRINT 6
6       FORMAT (1X,'LOW TEMPERATURE')
    ELSE
        PRINT 7
7       FORMAT (1X,'HIGH TEMPERATURE')
    ENDIF
```

Discussion:

The IF-ELSEIF statement includes several conditions. The conditions are tested in the order in which they appear in the statement. When a true condition is encountered, the set of statements following that condition is executed; control then passes to the statement following the ENDIF. If none of the conditions are true, the set of statements following the ELSE statement is executed. The ELSE portion of the IF-ELSEIF statement is optional.

LOGICAL Statement:

```
        LOGICAL   variable list
```

Examples:

```
        LOGICAL   DONE

        LOGICAL   SORTED, ERROR
```

Discussion:

The LOGICAL statement explicitly lists all variables that are to store logical variables. These variables may have values of either true or false.

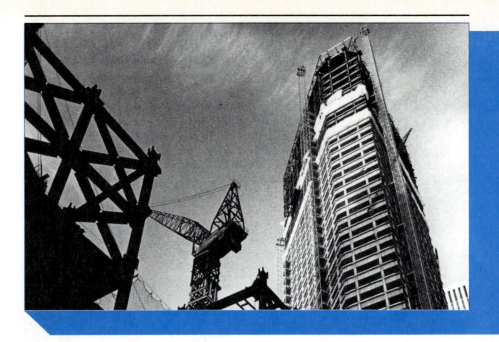

APPLICATION — Critical Path Analysis (Manufacturing Engineering)

The timely use of resources is important to the success of any engineering project. It is often achieved by the use of a critical path analysis of a project. One method for this analysis starts by breaking a project into sequential events, then breaking each event into various tasks. Although one event must be completed before the next one is started, various tasks within an event can occur simultaneously. The time it takes to complete an event therefore depends on the number of days required to finish its longest task. Similarly, the total time it takes to finish a project is the sum of time it takes to finish each event.

Assume that the critical path information for a major construction project has been stored in a data file in the computer. You have been asked to analyze this information so that your company can develop a bid on the project. (See Section 4–2 for the solution.)

4

DATA FILES AND MORE I/O

Introduction

4–1 Data Files

4–2 Application — Critical Path Analysis (Manufacturing Engineering)

4–3 Application — Population Study (Sociology)

4–4 Formatted Input

4–5 Additional FORMAT Features

4–6 Application — Quality Control (Manufacturing Engineering)

Summary

INTRODUCTION

Engineers and scientists must often analyze large amounts of data. It is not reasonable to enter all this data into the computer by hand each time it is needed. We can enter the data once into a data file; then each time that data is needed, we can read it from the data file. Instead of printing the data in a report, we can write it into a data file; other programs then can use the data and it is still available if we decide to print it. In this chapter, we learn how to build and use data files. We also present more I/O features that are available in FORTRAN.

4–1 DATA FILES

Up to this point, we have entered all our data using READ* statements. When our program execution reached a READ* statement, we entered the data at the terminal, usually following a request for information. Every time we reran the program, we reentered the data.

An alternate way to enter data is with a *data file*. Data files are built separately, much as you enter your programs (which are really program files). You can use your computer system's editing capabilities to build, correct, and update the data file. Each line of the file (also called a *record*) corresponds to a line of data, which you enter by hand.

You must enter some special statements in your programs to use data files: We present them in this section, along with discussions of how to detect when you have reached the end of your data file when you did not know how many entries it contained. We also show you how to write information into a data file from your program instead of displaying it on the terminal screen or printing it with a line printer.

To use data files with our programs, we must use some new statements and some extensions of old statements. Each of these statements references the filename of the file that we want to use in our program. You assign a filename when a file is built. If you build a data file with your computer system's editor, you assign the filename before you begin entering the data.

To use data files, we must use new forms of input and output statements. The list-directed input statement that reads information from a data file uses the following general form:

> **READ** *(unit number,*) variable list*

The list-directed output statement that writes information into a data file uses the following general form:

> **WRITE** *(unit number,*) expression list*

The formatted output statement that writes information into a data file uses the following general form:

WRITE *(unit number,k) expression list*

where *k* is the statement number of the corresponding FORMAT statement. In all of these general forms, the unit number is used to specify the number of the file that we wish to read or the number of the file into which we wish to write data. Because a program may use several different data files, this unit number identifies the file that is to be used with a specific statement. The asterisk following the unit number specifies that you are using list-directed input or output.

Most computer systems are attached to several input or output devices. Each device is assigned a unit number. For example, if a laser printer has been assigned unit number 8, then the following statement would direct that the values of X and Y be printed on the laser printer:

$$\text{WRITE (8,*) X, Y}$$

Many systems assign the standard input device (typically the terminal keyboard) to unit number 5 and the standard output device (typically the terminal screen) to unit number 6 — these devices are used when your program executes READ* or PRINT* statements. Avoid using preassigned unit numbers with your data files; if your computer system assigns unit number 5 and 6 as previously defined, do not use these with your data files. Confusion could result if your program assigned a data file to unit 6, and the program then executed a PRINT* statement.

The statement that assigns a unit number to a data file is the OPEN statement. Its general form is

OPEN **(UNIT=***integer expression,* **FILE=***filename,* **STATUS=***literal***)**

The integer expression designates the unit number to be used in READ or WRITE statements. The filename refers to the name given to the file when it was built. The STATUS literal tells the computer whether we are opening an input file to be used with READ statements or an output file to be used with WRITE statements. If the file is an input file, it already has data in it and is specified with STATUS='OLD'; if the file is an output file, it does not contain data yet and is specified with STATUS='NEW'.

The OPEN statement must precede any READ or WRITE statements that use the file. The OPEN statement should be executed only once; therefore, it should not be inside a loop. Some systems require a REWIND statement after opening an input file to position the file at its beginning. The REWIND statement and additional information on building and accessing data files are presented in Chapter 9.

We now look at several examples to illustrate these statements.

EXAMPLE 4-1   **Parallel Resistance**

A data file RES3 contains three data lines, each containing a resistance value from a resistor in an instrumentation circuit. Write a complete program to read the three real resistances and compute their combined resistance *(RC)* for a parallel arrangement, as shown:

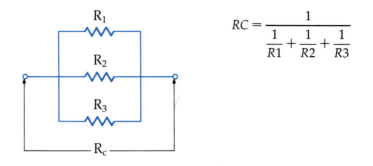

$$RC = \frac{1}{\dfrac{1}{R1} + \dfrac{1}{R2} + \dfrac{1}{R3}}$$

Print the value of *RC*. The resistance is measured in ohms.

Solution

The decomposition of this problem solution is

DECOMPOSITION

| Read *R1*, *R2*, *R3*. |
| Compute *RC*. |
| Print *RC*. |

Adding detail to the computation step gives the following refinement in pseudocode.

REFINEMENT IN PSEUDOCODE

RESIS1: Read *R1, R2, R3*
     Print *R1, R2, R3*
$$RC \leftarrow \frac{1}{\dfrac{1}{R1} + \dfrac{1}{R2} + \dfrac{1}{R3}}$$
     Print *RC*

As we convert these steps into FORTRAN, we must remember that the data is being read from a data file RES3 that has already been built. The name of the file is determined when the file is built, but we may choose any unit number to refer to the file as long as the number is not preassigned by our computer system.

FORTRAN Program

```
*------------------------------------------------------*
      PROGRAM  RESIS1
*
*  This program reads a data file with three resistance
*  values and computes their equivalent parallel value.
*
      REAL  R1, R2, R3, RC
*
      OPEN (UNIT=10,FILE='RES3',STATUS='OLD')
      READ (10,*) R1, R2, R3
      PRINT 5, R1, R2, R3
    5 FORMAT (1X,'INPUT VALUES ARE: ',F7.2,2X,F7.2,2X,F7.2)
      RC = 1.0/(1.0/R1 + 1.0/R2 + 1.0/R3)
      PRINT 10, RC
   10 FORMAT (1X,'COMBINED PARALLEL RESISTANCE = ',
      +           F7.1,' OHMS')
      END
*------------------------------------------------------*
```

Data File RES3

$$1000.0$$
$$1100.0$$
$$2000.0$$

Using data file RES3, the output of this program is

```
INPUT VALUES ARE: 1000.00  1100.00  2000.00
COMBINED PARALLEL RESISTANCE =    415.1 OHMS
```

Example 4–1 used a small data file, but the advantages of a data file become obvious with large amounts of data. Once the data file is built, no matter how many times you run a program that uses the file, you do not have to reenter the data. It is easy to change and update a data file with the editing capabilities available on terminal systems. In addition, data files can be shared by various programs, reducing data redundancy and minimizing the memory requirements.

Data files can be built by a FORTRAN program with WRITE statements; instead of using the terminal screen or line printer as an output device, we can write the information into a data file. This is often done when plotting data; the data to be plotted is first written into a data file, and the plotter then uses the data file.

EXAMPLE 4-2

Parallel Resistance with Output File

Modify the program in Example 4–1 such that the combined resistance (RC) is printed and also stored in a file called RESC.

Solution

Because this solution is so similar to that of Example 4–1, we include only the modified FORTRAN program and the input and output from a sample test run.

FORTRAN Program

```
*-------------------------------------------------------*
      PROGRAM  RESIS2
*
*  This program reads a data file with three resistance
*  values and computes their equivalent parallel value,
*  which is printed and stored in a data file.
*
      REAL  R1, R2, R3, RC
*
      OPEN (UNIT=10,FILE='RES3',STATUS='OLD')
      OPEN (UNIT=11,FILE='RESC',STATUS='NEW')
*
      READ (10,*) R1, R2, R3
      PRINT 5, R1, R2, R3
    5 FORMAT (1X,'INPUT VALUES ARE: ',F7.2,2X,F7.2,2X,F7.2)
      RC = 1.0/(1.0/R1 + 1.0/R2 + 1.0/R3)
      PRINT 10, RC
   10 FORMAT (1X,'COMBINED PARALLEL RESISTANCE = ',
     +          F7.1,' OHMS')
      WRITE (11,*) RC
      END
*-------------------------------------------------------*
```

Data File RES3

```
              1000.0
              1100.0
              2000.0
```

Using data file RES3, the screen and corresponding data file output from this program are

```
INPUT VALUES ARE: 1000.00  1100.00  2000.00
COMBINED PARALLEL RESISTANCE =    415.1 OHMS
```

Data File RESC

```
              415.1
```

TRAILER AND SENTINEL SIGNALS

Many applications require the computer to read a number of data values, such as test scores or experimental results. The DO loop can accomplish these tasks if you know exactly how many data values are in the file. For instance, if 50 data values are to be read, we can use a DO loop of this form:

```
DO 10 COUNT=1,50
   READ (15,*) X
     .
     .
     .
10 CONTINUE
```

If the number of data values to be read is available in another variable, we can use a DO loop of this form:

```
        DO 10 COUNT=1,NUM
          READ (15,*) X
                .
                .
                .
       10 CONTINUE
```

However, you may not always know exactly how many data values need to be read prior to executing your program; you must be careful in handling these situations because if you execute a READ statement for which there is no data line, an execution error will occur and program execution will stop. There are two techniques for handling an unspecified number of input data values: one uses a *trailer*, or *sentinel*, signal and the other uses an end-of-file option in the READ statement.

The first technique uses special data values called trailer, or sentinel, signals to indicate the end of the data. For example, a valid identification number for a student record may be three digits, ranging from 000 to 500. If we were reading student records, we could use an identification number of 999 as a trailer signal. As we read each data line, we test the identification number for the value 999; when we find 999, we then exit the loop. This process can be structured easily in a WHILE loop; but because the condition uses a value from the data, we must read one student record before entering the WHILE loop, as shown:

```
          READ (15,*) ID, GPA
        5 IF (ID.NE.999) THEN
                .
                .
                .
          READ (15,*) ID, GPA
          GO TO 5
        ENDIF
```

If we need to know the number of data values read, a counter can be used in the WHILE loop. Be sure not to count the trailer value as a valid data value. This technique should look familiar because we have already used it in some of our example programs.

EXAMPLE 4-3 **Test Scores with Trailer Signal**

A group of integer test scores have been entered into a data file TESTS1, one score per line. The last line contains a negative value to signal the end of the test scores. Write a complete program to read the data, compute the test average, and print the number of tests and the test average.

Solution

The decomposition of this problem is

DECOMPOSITION

| Read and total test scores. |
| Compute average. |
| Print average. |

In the refinement of this decomposition, we include the WHILE loop, which reads and totals the test scores until we read a negative value.

REFINEMENT IN PSEUDOCODE

AVERG1: number ← 0
          total ← 0
          Read test
          While test ≥ 0 do
              number ← number + 1
              total ← total + test
              Read test
          average ← total/number
          Print number, average

As we convert the pseudocode into FORTRAN statements, remember that we are reading the test scores from a data file — thus we need to use the OPEN statement and the new form of the READ statement.

FORTRAN PROGRAM

```
*----------------------------------------------------------------*
      PROGRAM  AVERG1
*
*   This program computes the average of a group of test
*   scores that are followed by a negative value.
*
      INTEGER  TEST, TOTAL, NUMBER
      REAL   AVERG
*
      OPEN (UNIT=12,FILE='TESTS1',STATUS='OLD')
      NUMBER = 0
      TOTAL = 0
      READ (12,*) TEST
    5 IF (TEST.GE.0) THEN
         NUMBER = NUMBER + 1
         TOTAL = TOTAL + TEST
         READ (12,*) TEST
         GO TO 5
      ENDIF
      AVERG = REAL(TOTAL)/REAL(NUMBER)
      PRINT 10, NUMBER, AVERG
   10 FORMAT (1X,'THE AVERAGE OF ',I4,
     +          ' TEST SCORES IS ',F5.1)
      END
*----------------------------------------------------------------*
```

A sample data file and the corresponding output from this program are

DATA FILE TESTS1

          85
          92
        100
          87
          75
          73
          81
         −1

```
THE AVERAGE OF    7 TEST SCORES IS   84.7
```

END OPTION

If a set of data does not have a trailer signal at the end, and if we do not know the number of data lines in the file, we must use a different technique with the WHILE loop. In pseudocode, we want to perform these steps:

> While more data do
> Read variables
> Process variables

To implement this in FORTRAN, we use an option available with the READ statement that tests for the end of the data. A list-directed READ statement that uses this option has the following general form:

READ (*unit number*,**,END=***n***) *variable list*

As long as there is data to read in the data file, this statement executes exactly like this:

READ (*unit number*,**) *variable list*

However, if the last line of the data file has already been read and we execute the READ statement again, instead of getting an execution error, control is passed to the statement referenced in the END option, statement *n*. If the READ statement were executed a second time after the end of the data, an execution error would occur.

   A READ statement with the END option is actually a special form of the WHILE loop. When using it in your programs, use the same indenting style as used in the WHILE loop. A GO TO statement is also needed to complete the WHILE loop, as shown:

```
   8 READ (13,*,END=10) A, B
        .
        .
        .
     GO TO 8
  10 .
        .
        .
```

   This is a special implementation of the WHILE loop that is used when you do not know the number of data lines to be read and there is no trailer signal at the end of the file. Remember, if you have a trailer value, test for that value to exit the loop instead of using the END option.

   The two techniques presented in this section should not be used together; they are techniques for handling two different data situations.

EXAMPLE 4-4   **Test Scores without Trailer Signal**

A group of integer test scores has been entered into a data file TESTS2, one score per line, with no trailer line. Write a complete program to read the data, compute the test average, and print the number of tests and the test average.

Solution

The decomposition of the problem is the same as in Example 4–3.

DECOMPOSITION

Read and total test scores.
Compute average.
Print average.

As we refine the solution, we indicate which technique we will use for detecting the end of the file. Because there is no trailer signal, we do not need to read the first data line outside the loop. The condition in the WHILE loop determines whether or not there is more data to read. If there is not more data, we exit the WHILE loop.

REFINEMENT IN PSEUDOCODE

AVERG2: number ← 0
            total ← 0
            While more tests do
                Read test
                number ← number + 1
                total ← total + test
            average ← total/number
            Print number, average

In converting the pseudocode to FORTRAN, note that the READ statement with the END option replaces both the WHILE statement and the standard READ statement.

FORTRAN PROGRAM

```
*-------------------------------------------------------------*
      PROGRAM  AVERG2
*
*   This program computes the average of a group of test
*   scores that do not have a trailer line in the file.
*
      INTEGER  TEST, TOTAL, NUMBER
      REAL  AVERG
*
```

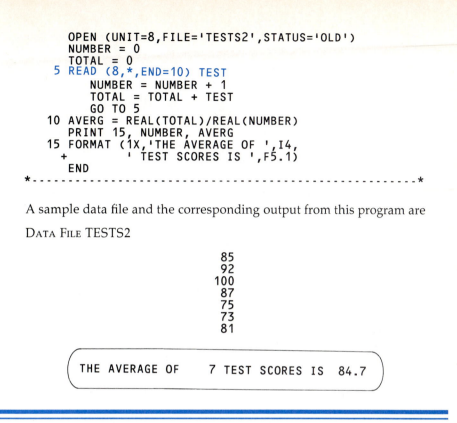

```
      OPEN (UNIT=8,FILE='TESTS2',STATUS='OLD')
      NUMBER = 0
      TOTAL = 0
    5 READ (8,*,END=10) TEST
      NUMBER = NUMBER + 1
      TOTAL = TOTAL + TEST
      GO TO 5
   10 AVERG = REAL(TOTAL)/REAL(NUMBER)
      PRINT 15, NUMBER, AVERG
   15 FORMAT (1X,'THE AVERAGE OF ',I4,
     +          ' TEST SCORES IS ',F5.1)
      END
```

A sample data file and the corresponding output from this program are

DATA FILE TESTS2

```
85
92
100
87
75
73
81
```

```
THE AVERAGE OF      7 TEST SCORES IS  84.7
```

4–2 APPLICATION—CRITICAL PATH ANALYSIS (Manufacturing Engineering)

A critical path analysis is a technique used to determine the time schedule for a project. This information is important in the planning stages before a project is begun, and it is also useful to evaluate the progress of a project that is partially completed. One method for this analysis starts by breaking a project into sequential events, then breaking each event into various tasks. Although one event must be completed before the next one is started, various tasks within an event can occur simultaneously. The time it takes to complete an event, therefore, depends on the number of days required to finish its longest task. Similarly, the total time it takes to finish a project is the sum of time it takes to finish each event.

Assume that the critical path information for a major construction project has been stored in a data file in the computer. You have been asked to analyze this information so that your company can develop a bid on the project. Specifically, the management would like a summary report that lists each event along with the number of days for the shortest task in that event and the number of days for the longest task in that event. In addition they would like the total project length computed in days and converted to weeks (five days per week).

The data file named PROJECT contains three integers per line. The first number is the event number, the second number is the task number, and the third number is the number of days required to complete the task. The data has been stored such that all the task data for event 1 is followed by all the task data for event 2, and so on. The task data for a particular event is also in order. You do not know ahead of time how many entries are in the file, but there is an upper limit of 98 total events, so a trailer signal is used to indicate the last line in the data file. The last line will contain a value of 99 for the event number and zeros for the corresponding task and days.

PROBLEM STATEMENT

Write a program to determine and print a project completion timetable.

INPUT/OUTPUT DESCRIPTION

The input to the program is a data file that contains the critical path information for the events in the project. The information in the file is in order by events, with the event number starting at 1. Within an event, the task information is also in order. Each line of the file contains the event number, task number, and corresponding number of days necessary to complete the task. There is a maximum of 98 events, and the last line in the file will be indicated by a trailer signal with a value of 99 for the event number. The output is to be a summary report with the following format:

```
PROJECT COMPLETION TIMETABLE

EVENT NUMBER      MINIMUM DAYS      MAXIMUM DAYS
X                 X                 X
  .
  .
  .


TOTAL PROJECT LENGTH = XX DAYS
                     = XX WEEKS X DAYS
```

HAND EXAMPLE

Use the following set of project data for the hand example:

Event Number	Task Number	Days
1	1	5
1	2	4
2	1	3
2	2	7
2	3	4
3	1	6
99	0	0

The corresponding report based on this data is shown next:

```
PROJECT COMPLETION TIMETABLE

EVENT NUMBER      MINIMUM DAYS      MAXIMUM DAYS
1                 4                 5
2                 3                 7
3                 6                 6

TOTAL PROJECT LENGTH = 18 DAYS
                     =  3 WEEKS 3 DAYS
```

ALGORITHM DEVELOPMENT

The decomposition of this problem solution is:

DECOMPOSITION

Read project event data and print event information
Print summary information

To develop an algorithm, we look at the way we compiled the data in the hand example. Because all the data for the first event is together, we scan down the list of data for event 1 and keep track of the minimum number of days and maximum number of days. When we reach the first task for event 2, we print the information related to event 1 and then repeat the process for event 2. We continue until we reach event 99, which is a signal that we do not have any more data. We print the information for the last event and then print the summary information using a total in which we accumulated the total maximum number of days for all the events.

INITIAL REFINEMENT IN PSEUDOCODE

PATH: total ← 0
      Read event, task, days
      number ← event
      min ← days
      max ← days
      While not done do
          If same event then
            Update min and max
          Else
            Print number, min, max
            total ← total + max
            number ← event
            min ← days
            max ← days
          Read event, task, days
      Print number, min, max for last event
      Print total

As we refine the pseudocode, we need to be more specific about how we determine if we are done. We also need to add more details to the update for the minimum and maximum days for an event. Finally, when we print the total, we also need to compute and print the number of weeks.

FINAL REFINEMENT IN PSEUDOCODE

```
PATH: total ← 0
      Read event, task, days
      number ← event
      min ← days
      max ← days
      If event = 99 then
         done ← true
      Else
         done ← false
      While not done do
         If event = number then
            If days < min then
               min ← days
            If days > max then
               max ← days
         Else
            Print number, min, max
            total ← total + max
            number ← event
            min ← days
            max ← days
         Read event, task, days
         If event = 99 then
            done ← true
      Print number, min, max for last event
      weeks ← total/5
      plus ←total − weeks*5
      Print total, weeks, plus
```

Note that we will need to do the computation for WEEKS so that the result is an integer instead of a real value. As we convert the final pseudocode into FORTRAN, we must remember to open the data file and use the new form of the READ statement.

```
*------------------------------------------------------------*
      PROGRAM  PATH
* This program determines the critical path
* information for a project.
*
      INTEGER  EVENT, TASK, DAYS, TOTAL, NUMBER, MIN, MAX,
     +         WEEKS, PLUS
      LOGICAL  DONE
*
      OPEN (UNIT=8,FILE='PROJECT',STATUS='OLD')
      TOTAL = 0
      PRINT*, 'PROJECT COMPLETION TIMETABLE'
      PRINT*
      PRINT*, 'EVENT NUMBER    MINIMUM TIME    MAXIMUM TIME'
*
      READ (8,*) EVENT, TASK, DAYS
      NUMBER = EVENT
      MIN = DAYS
      MAX = DAYS
      IF (EVENT.EQ.99) THEN
         DONE = .TRUE.
      ELSE
         DONE = .FALSE.
      ENDIF
*
    5 IF (.NOT.DONE) THEN
         IF (EVENT.EQ.NUMBER) THEN
            IF (DAYS.LT.MIN) THEN
               MIN = DAYS
            ELSEIF  (DAYS.GT.MAX) THEN
               MAX = DAYS
            ENDIF
         ELSE
            PRINT 10, NUMBER, MIN, MAX
   10       FORMAT (1X,I2,14X,I3,13X,I3)
            TOTAL = TOTAL + MAX
            NUMBER = EVENT
            MIN = DAYS
            MAX = DAYS
         ENDIF
         READ (8,*) EVENT, TASK, DAYS
         IF (EVENT.EQ.99) DONE = .TRUE.
         GO TO 5
      ENDIF
      PRINT 10, NUMBER, MIN, MAX
      TOTAL = TOTAL + MAX
*
      WEEKS = TOTAL/5
      PLUS = TOTAL - WEEKS*5
      PRINT*
      PRINT 15, TOTAL
   15 FORMAT (1X,'TOTAL PROJECT LENGTH = ',I2,' DAYS')
      PRINT 20, WEEKS, PLUS
   20 FORMAT (1X,'                        = ',I1,' WEEKS',
     +          I2,' DAYS')
      END
*------------------------------------------------------------*
```

Note that the days remaining after subtracting the number of days in the full weeks could have been computed using the MOD function, as shown here:

$$PLUS = MOD(TOTAL,5)$$

TESTING

If we use the sample set of data from the hand example with this program, the following report is printed:

```
PROJECTION COMPLETION TIMETABLE

EVENT NUMBER       MINIMUM DAYS      MAXIMUM DAYS
1                  4                 5
2                  3                 7
3                  6                 6

TOTAL PROJECT LENGTH = 18 DAYS
                     = 3 WEEKS 3 DAYS
```

4–3 APPLICATION—POPULATION STUDY (Sociology)

The population of Shakespeare, New Mexico (1880–1980) has been stored in a data file called PEOPLE. Each line of the data file contains a year and the corresponding population. The data lines are in ascending order by year. Write a program to read the data and determine the two consecutive years in which the percentage increase in population was the greatest.

PROBLEM STATEMENT

Find the two consecutive years in which the percentage increase in population was the greatest for Shakespeare, New Mexico.

INPUT/OUTPUT DESCRIPTION

The input is a data file with 101 lines. Each line contains a year and corresponding population. The data is in ascending order by year. The output is the two consecutive years with the largest percentage increase in population.

HAND EXAMPLE

First, we look at some typical data and compute the percentage increase in the data each year to be sure that we understand the computations involved.

YEAR	POPULATION	PERCENTAGE INCREASE
1950	82	−32% $[(56 - 82)/82 \cdot 100]$
1951	56	27% $[(71 - 56)/56 \cdot 100]$
1952	71	21% $[(86 - 71)/71 \cdot 100]$
1953	86	19% $[(102 - 86)/86 \cdot 100]$
1954	102	

During the years listed, the largest percentage increase was from 1951 to 1952. Note that this was not the largest increase in actual population. The largest increase in actual population occurred from 1953 to 1954.

ALGORITHM DEVELOPMENT

The decomposition of the steps in this algorithm can be described as

DECOMPOSITION

Read data and determine years with largest percentage increase.
Print result.

To compute the change in population from one year to the next, we need the previous year (old value) and the following year (new value). Thus, as we refine the decomposition, we need to read the first value (old value) outside our loop so that we can read the following year (new value) and compute the change within the loop. We execute the steps within this loop 100 times.

INITIAL REFINEMENT IN PSEUDOCODE

CENSUS: Read first set of data
       year of increase ← first year
       For year=1 to 100 do
         Read next set of data
         Compute percentage increase in population
         If new increase > previous best then
           year of increase ← current year
       Print year of increase and its previous year

Because we need not only the information on the current line but also the information on the previous data line to compute the population increase, we use the following variables:

YRNEW	The year just read from a data line
YROLD	The year from the previous data line
POPNEW	The population just read from a data line
POPOLD	The population from the previous data line
PERC	The current percentage increase in population
GPIYR	The year in which there was the greatest percentage increase
GPI	The percentage that represents the greatest percentage increase

Note that in the final pseudocode we are initially setting the first pair of years as the ones with the greatest percentage increase. Each time through the loop, we compare this increase with the current increase; if the current increase is higher, this value is placed in the variable GPI (greatest percent increase), and the year is placed in GPIYR.

Final Refinement in Pseudocode

CENSUS: Read yrold, popold
      For $i = 1$ to 100 do
         Read yrnew, popnew
         perc ← (popnew − popold) · 100/popold
         If $i = 1$ or perc > gpi then
            gpi ← perc
            gpiyr ← yrnew
         yrold ← ynew
         popold ← popnew
      yr1 ← gpiyr − 1
      yr2 ← gpiyr
      Print yr1, yr2

We now convert our final pseudocode into FORTRAN. Because our data is being read from a data file, we must remember to open the data file and use the new form of the READ statement.

```
*-------------------------------------------------------*
      PROGRAM  CENSUS
*
*  This program reads 101 population values and determines
*  the years of greatest percentage increase in population.
*
      INTEGER  YROLD, YRNEW, POPOLD, POPNEW,
     +         GPIYR, YR1, YR2, I
      REAL  PERC, GPI
*
      OPEN (UNIT=15,FILE='PEOPLE',STATUS='OLD')
      GPI = 0.0
      READ (15,*) YROLD, POPOLD
      DO 50 I=1,100
         READ (15,*) YRNEW, POPNEW
         PERC = (POPNEW - POPOLD)*100.0/POPOLD
         IF (I.EQ.1.OR.PERC.GT.GPI) THEN
            GPI = PERC
            GPIYR = YRNEW
         ENDIF
         YROLD = YRNEW
         POPOLD = POPNEW
   50 CONTINUE
      YR1 = GPIYR - 1
      YR2 = GPIYR
      PRINT 55, YR1, YR2
   55 FORMAT (1X,'GREATEST PERCENT INCREASE OCCURRED',
     +        ' BETWEEN ',I4,' AND ',I4)
      END
*-------------------------------------------------------*
```

TESTING

A sample output from this program is

```
GREATEST PERCENT INCREASE OCCURRED BETWEEN 1890 AND 1891
```

If you want to test this program with a smaller data file, you can easily change the final value in the DO loop statement to a smaller number. For example, if you build a test file with 10 sets of data, change the DO loop statement to

```
DO 50 I=1,9
```

In this program we updated the greatest percentage increase when (I.EQ.1.OR.PERC.GT.GPI). Why is it necessary to include the expression I.EQ.1? For most data sets, the logical expression I.EQ.1 is not necessary because as soon as a percentage increase greater than zero is encountered, it replaces the values of zero used to initialize GPI. However, suppose all increases are negative; without the compound logical expression, our final result would be incorrect.

4–4 FORMATTED INPUT

To specify the columns to be used in reading data from a data line, we use a formatted READ statement. The general form of a formatted READ statement is

> **READ** *k, variable list*

The variable list determines the order in which new values are stored, and *k* is a format reference number that refers to the FORMAT statement that will describe the positions to be read. A typical READ/FORMAT combination is

```
    READ 2, DIST, VEL
  2 FORMAT (F4.1,3X,F4.2)
```

If the FORMAT statement is being used to read information from a data file, a typical READ/FORMAT combination is

```
    READ (10,5) X,Y
  5 FORMAT (F5.1,2X,F6.1)
```

The form of the FORMAT appears the same as that used with PRINT statements; even the specifications look familiar. There are, however, differences between the specifications used for reading data values and those used for writing data values. Also, no carriage control is needed with READ statements. Each READ statement begins reading at column 1 of a new data line. The new values must agree in type (integer or real) with the variables in the list.

We now look at each specification individually, as we did for the PRINT statement specifications.

X SPECIFICATION

The X specification will skip positions on the data line. Its general form is nX, where n represents the number of positions to skip; thus, we can skip over unnecessary values.

I SPECIFICATION

The I specification is required when reading a value into an integer variable. The form of this specification is Iw where w represents the number of positions to use on the data line. Any blanks in the w positions will be interpreted as zeros. Any characters besides numbers, plus or minus signs, and blanks will cause an execution error. Thus, 5.0 cannot be read with an I3 specification; but, $_{bb}5$ will be read correctly with an I3 specification.

EXAMPLE 4-5   **MEAN and NORM**

Read the values of the variables MEAN and NORM from a data line. MEAN is in columns 1–4 and NORM is in columns 10–11.

Correct Solution

FORTRAN STATEMENTS

```
         READ 1, MEAN, NORM
       1 FORMAT (I4,5X,I2)
```

DATA LINE

$$b\,^{123}bbbbb\,^{10}$$

COMPUTER MEMORY

MEAN | 123 |

NORM | 10 |

The first four columns, $_b123$, are used to assign a value to MEAN. The first blank is interpreted as a zero; thus 0123 is stored in MEAN. We then skip the next five columns. From columns 10–11, we pick up the value 10 for NORM.

Incorrect Solution

FORTRAN STATEMENTS

```
         READ 2, MEAN, NORM
       2 FORMAT (1X,I4,5X,I2)
```

DATA LINE

$$b\,^{123}bbbbb\,^{10}b$$

COMPUTER MEMORY

MEAN | 1230 |

NORM | 0 |

If carriage control is used with READ statements, incorrect values may be stored in memory. Using the preceding format, we skip the first columns and use the next four columns for determining the value of MEAN. These columns contain 123_b, which is interpreted as 1230. We then skip five columns, and use the next two columns for determining the value of NORM. The contents 0_b will be interpreted as 0.

F SPECIFICATION

The F specification can be used to read a value for a real variable. The form of this specification is Fw.d, where w represents the total number of positions to use on the data line and d represents the number of decimal positions. As with the I specification, any blanks in the w positions will be interpreted as zeros. If there is a decimal point included in the w positions, the value will be stored as it was entered, regardless of what value has been given to d. Thus, if a real value DIST is read with a F4.1 specification, and the four characters are 1.26, the value of DIST is 1.26. If there is no decimal point within the specified positions, the value of d is used to position a decimal place before storing the value. Thus, if the characters 1246 are read with an F4.1 specification, the value stored is 124.6, a value with one decimal position. Note that printing this value would require an F5.1 specification; the same specification will therefore not always work for both input and output.

EXAMPLE 4-6

TIME and TEMP

Read two variables, TIME and TEMP. TIME will be in columns 10–13, with two decimal positions, and TEMP will be in columns 16–18, with one decimal position.

Solution

FORTRAN STATEMENTS

```
      READ 200, TIME, TEMP
  200 FORMAT (9X,F4.2,2X,F3.1)
```

DATA LINE

$$bbbbbbbbb\,4.66\,bb\,125$$

COMPUTER MEMORY

TIME | 4.66 |

TEMP | 12.5 |

Because there was no decimal point in the TEMP field, which was read with F3.1, one was positioned in the three numbers so that one position was a decimal position.

When running a program in a batch-processing system (as opposed to a time-sharing system), your computer and compiler will require additional information. This *job control information* is unique to your computer system; it consists of information such as your name, the compiler you are using, and other additional data about your program. Your instructor or the computer center documentation will provide you with the job control requirments for your computer system.

The placement of the control lines and a program to calculate the slope of the line between two points are given in Figure 4–1.

```
*--------------------------------------------*
*        PROGRAM  SLOPE1
*
*    This program computes the slope of a
*    straight line through two points.
*
*        REAL  X1, Y1, X2, Y2, SLOPE
*
         READ 10, X1, Y1, X2, Y2
      10 FORMAT (F4.1,F4.1,F4.1,F4.1)
         SLOPE = (Y2 - Y1)/(X2 - X1)
         PRINT 20, X1, Y1, X2, Y2, SLOPE
      20 FORMAT (1X,'THE SLOPE OF THE LINE ',
     +           'THROUGH (',F4.1,',',F4.1,
     +           ') AND (',F4.1,',',F4.1,
     +           ') IS',F4.1)
         END
*--------------------------------------------*
```

FORTRAN Program is indicated to the left of the program listing above.

Job Control
Information { (system dependent)

Data { ᵦ5.5ᵦ3.1ᵦ0.5−1.6

Job Control
Information { (system dependent)

FIGURE 4-1 Job control information placement and FORTRAN program with data.

The output from the program in Figure 4–1 is

```
          1111111111222222222233333333334444444444555555555566666
 12345678901234567890123456789012345678901234567890123456789012334
```

```
THE SLOPE OF THE LINE THROUGH ( 5.5, 3.1) AND ( 0.5,-1.6) IS 0.9
```

E SPECIFICATION

The E specification is used in a READ/FORMAT combination when a variable is entered in an E format, or exponential form. The general form is Ew.d, where w represents the total number of positions that are being considered, and d represents the number of decimal positions when the value is expressed in exponential form. If a decimal point is included, its placement will override the value of d. If no decimal point is included, one is located, according to d, before storing the value. It is not necessary that the width be at least seven positions greater than the number of decimal positions (as is necessary for output with an E format).

For READ statements, the E format will accept many forms of input. The following list shows some of the different ways in which the value 1.26 can be entered in a field read with E9.2. Note that the data can even be in an F specification form.

DATA LINE	VALUE STORED
0.126E$_b$01	1.26
1.26$_b$E$_b$00	1.26
1.26$_{bbbbb}$	1.26
12.60E−01	1.26
$_{bbb}$.126E1	1.26
$_{bbbbbb}$126	1.26

Remember that the system will use two positions for the exponent if they are available. Thus $_{bbb}$.126E1 will be interpreted as 1.26, but $_{bb}$.126E1$_b$ will be interpreted as $_{bb}$.126E10, or 0.126X 10**10.

EXAMPLE 4-7   **Job Number and Computer Time**

Read two values. The first value, in columns 2–6, represents an integer job number assigned to a computer run. The second value, in columns 10–16, represents the number of computer seconds used to run the program. This computer time will be entered in an exponential form, with two decimal places.

Solution

FORTRAN STATEMENTS

```
          READ 10, NUM, CTIME
       10 FORMAT (1X,I5,3X,E7.2)
```

DATA LINE

$_b$13034$_{bbb}$.36E−02

COMPUTER MEMORY

NUM	13034
CTIME	0.0036

EXAMPLE 4-8   **Nutrition Research Results**

A research scientist performed nutrition tests using three animals. Data on each animal includes an identification number, the weight of the animal at the beginning of the experiment, and the weight of the animal at the end of the experiment. This data is stored in a data file called TEST1, and the data values for each animal are on a separate line: the integer identification number in columns 1–5, the initial weight in columns 10–14, and the final weight in columns 15–18. Both weights have one decimal position. Write a complete program to read this information and print a report. The report is to include both the original information and the percentage increase in weight for each test animal.

Solution

The decomposition is only a single step.

DECOMPOSITION

> Generate report.

In the refinement, we break the report generation step into a loop that reads the data for each animal, then computes and prints the corresponding data line.

REFINEMENT IN PSEUDOCODE

RESRCH: Print headers
For $i = 1$ to 3 do
        Read ID, initial weight, final weight
        percent increase $\leftarrow$ (final − initial)/initial $\cdot$ 100
        Print ID, initial, final, percent increase

Converting the pseudocode into a FORTRAN program gives the following:

FORTRAN PROGRAM

```
*------------------------------------------------------------*
      PROGRAM  RESRCH
*
*  This program prints a report on the results of
*  an experiment involving three test animals.
*
      INTEGER  I, ID
      REAL  IWT, FWT, PERC
*
      PRINT 5
    5 FORMAT (1X,'TEST RESULTS')
      PRINT*
      PRINT 10
   10 FORMAT ('NUMBER   INITIAL WT   FINAL WT  ',
     +          'PERCENTAGE INCREASE')
*
      OPEN (UNIT=10,FILE='TEST1',STATUS='OLD')
      DO 25 I=1,3
          READ (10,15) ID,IWT,FWT
   15     FORMAT (I5,4X,F5.1,F5.1)
          PERC = (FWT - IWT)/IWT*100.0
          PRINT 20, ID,IWT,FWT
   20     FORMAT (1X,I4,5X,F5.1,6X,F5.1,6X,F10.5)
   25 CONTINUE
      END
*------------------------------------------------------------*
```

A sample data file and its corresponding output are

DATA FILE

$$bbb^{10}bbbbbb^{5.3}bb^{6.2}$$
$$bbb^{11}bbbbbb^{5.2}bb^{5.2}$$
$$bbb^{12}bbbbbb^{5.3}bb^{5.1}$$

COMPUTER OUTPUT

```
TEST RESULTS

NUMBER   INITIAL WT   FINAL WT   PERCENTAGE INCREASE
  10        5.3         6.2            16.98112
  11        5.2         5.2             0.00000
  12        5.3         5.1            -3.77359
```

4-5 ADDITIONAL FORMAT FEATURES

In this section we present several useful features of FORMAT statements. We illustrate each feature with an example.

REPETITION

If we have two identical specifications in a row, we can use a constant in front of the specification (or sets of specifications) to indicate repetition. For instance, I2,I2,I2 can be replaced by 3I2. Often our FORMAT statements can be made shorter with repetition constants. The following pairs of FORMAT statements illustrate the use of repetition constants:

```
10 FORMAT (3X,I2,3X,I2)
10 FORMAT (2(3X,I2))

20 FORMAT (1X,F4.1,F4.1,1X,I3,1X,I3,1X,I3)
20 FORMAT (1X,2F4.1,3(1X,I3))
```

SLASH

The FORMAT statement may also contain the character slash (/). Commas around the slash in a FORMAT are optional. If the slash is in a READ statement, a new data line is read when the slash is encountered. The slash also can be used with PRINT statements. It is important, however, to interpret the slash as a signal that says "print the current buffer and start a new one"—the carriage control character following the slash will determine whether the spacing between lines is single spacing, double spacing, or some other spacing.

EXAMPLE 4-9   **Real Values**

Read the values HT1 and HT2 from one data line, TIME from a second line, and VEL from a third data line. Each number is entered in four columns, with one decimal position. There are no extra columns between HT1 and HT2.

Solution 1

FORTRAN STATEMENTS

```
        READ 15, HT1, HT2, TIME, VEL
    15 FORMAT (2F4.1/F4.1/F4.1)
```

DATA LINES

```
        16.518.2
        00.5
        -4.6
```

COMPUTER MEMORY

HT1 | 16.5 |

HT2 | 18.2 |

TIME | 0.5 |

VEL | −4.6 |

Solution 2

In this solution, we do not use the slash. Notice the extra READ statements that are required.

FORTRAN STATEMENTS

```
        READ 15, HT1,HT2
    15 FORMAT (2F4.1)
        READ 16, TIME
        READ 16, VEL
    16 FORMAT (F4.1)
```

DATA LINES

```
        16.518.2
        00.5
        -4.6
```

COMPUTER MEMORY

HT1 | 16.5 |

HT2 | 18.2 |

TIME | 0.5 |

VEL | −4.6 |

EXAMPLE 4-10   **Title and Heading**

Print the heading TEST RESULTS followed by column headings TIME and HEIGHT. Separate the column headings by five columns and center the heading over the columns.

Solution 1

```
    PRINT 5
  5 FORMAT (1X,2X,'TEST RESULTS'/1X,'TIME      HEIGHT')
```

BUFFER CONTENTS

bbb TEST RESULTS
b TIME   HEIGHT

COMPUTER OUTPUT

```
      TEST RESULTS
   TIME       HEIGHT
```

When the slash is encountered, we "print the current buffer." The carriage control character is a space; thus, the first line is printed after spacing to the next line. We then "start a new buffer." The 1X specification puts a blank in the first position in the buffer. When we reach the end of the FORMAT, this line will be single spaced from the first line. If the 1X had been omitted and our system used carriage control, the character T would have been used for carriage control; this is an undefined carriage control character, which also causes single spacing. However, the computer output would be

```
      TEST RESULTS
   IME        HEIGHT
```

Solution 2

In this solution, we use the slash to leave a blank line between the main header and the column headings.

FORTRAN STATEMENTS

```
    PRINT 5
  5 FORMAT (1X,2X,'TEST RESULTS'//1X,'TIME      HEIGHT')
```

BUFFER CONTENTS

bbb TEST RESULTS
bbbbbbbbbbbbbbb
b TIME   HEIGHT

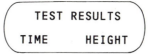

```
TEST RESULTS
TIME      HEIGHT
```

The first slash encountered prints the first buffer and starts a new buffer. Another slash is encountered, which causes the buffer filled with blanks to be printed and starts a new buffer. This buffer is filled and the end of the FORMAT is reached, causing this last buffer to be printed.

TAB SPECIFICATION

The tab specification Tn allows you to shift directly to a specified position, n, in the input or output buffer. The following pairs of FORMAT statements function exactly the same:

```
500 FORMAT (58X,'EXPERIMENT NO. 1')
500 FORMAT (T59,'EXPERIMENT NO. 1')

550 FORMAT (1X,'SALES',10X,'PROFIT',10X,'LOSS')
550 FORMAT (1X,'SALES',T17,'PROFIT',T33,'LOSS')

600 FORMAT (F6.1,15X,I7)
600 FORMAT (F6.1,T22,I7)
```

The TLn and TRn specifications tab left or right for n positions from the current position. The following formats are therefore equivalent:

```
85 FORMAT (1X,25X,'HEIGHT',5X,'WEIGHT')
85 FORMAT (T27,'HEIGHT',TR5,'WEIGHT')
```

The tab specifications are especially useful in aligning column headings and data.

NUMBER OF SPECIFICATIONS

Suppose there are more FORMAT specifications than variables on a READ or PRINT list, as shown:

```
READ 1, SPEED,DIST
1 FORMAT (4F5.2)
```

In these cases, the computer uses as much of the specification list as it needs and ignores the rest. In our example, SPEED and DIST would be matched to the first two specifications; the last two specifications would be ignored. This rule occasionally allows us to use the same FORMAT with several statements.

Suppose there are fewer FORMAT specifications than variables on a READ or PRINT list, as shown:

```
PRINT 20, TEMP, VOL
20 FORMAT (1X,F6.2)
```

In these cases, we match variables and specifications until we reach the end of the FORMAT. Then, two events occur:

1. With a READ statement, we go to the next data line; with a PRINT statement, we print the current buffer and start a new one.
2. We back up in the FORMAT specification list with both READ and PRINT statements until we reach a left parenthesis, and we again begin matching the remaining variables to the specifications at that point. If a repetition constant is in front of this left parenthesis, it applies to the FORMAT specifications being reused.

In the previous statements, TEMP would be matched to the F6.2 specification. Because there is no specification for VOL, we do the following:

1. Print the value of TEMP after single spacing.
2. Back up to the beginning of the FORMAT specification list (first left parenthesis) and match the F6.2 to the value of VOL. We then reach the end of the list and single space to print the value of VOL. TEMP and VOL are thus printed on separate lines.

SELF-TEST 4-1

This self-test allows you to check quickly to see if you have remembered some of the key points from Section 4–5. If you have any problems with the exercises, you should reread this section. The solutions are included at the end of the text.

For problems 1–2, show the values that will be stored in the variables after execution of the following READ statements.

1.   READ 15, ID, HT, WIDTH
    15 FORMAT (I4,2X,2F4.1)

    Data Line:
    1456$_{bb}$14.6$_{bb}$.7

2.   READ 7, ID, HT, WIDTH
     7 FORMAT (I2,F4.1,2X,F4.2)

    Data Line:
    $_{bb}$13.7$_{bb}$.865

In problems 3–6, tell how many data lines are required for the following READ statements to work correctly. Indicate which variables are on each line and which columns must be used.

```
3.     READ 4, TIME, DIST, VEL, ACCEL
     4 FORMAT (4F6.3)

4.     READ 14, TIME, DIST, VEL, ACCEL
    14 FORMAT (F6.2)

5.     READ 2, TIME, DIST, VEL, ACCEL
     2 FORMAT (F3.2/F4.1)

6.     READ 3, TIME, DIST
       READ 3, VEL, ACCEL
     3 FORMAT (4F6.3)
```

In problems 7–9, show the output from the following PRINT statements. Be sure to indicate the vertical as well as the horizontal spacing. Use the following variables and corresponding values:

$$TIME = 4.55, \quad RESP1 = 0.00074, \quad RESP2 = 56.83$$

```
7.    PRINT 5, TIME, RESP1, RESP2
     5 FORMAT (1X,F6.2,5X,2F7.4)

8.    PRINT 4, TIME, RESP1, TIME, RESP2
     4 FORMAT (1X,'TIME = ',F5.2,2X,'RESPONSE 1 = ',F8.5/
     +         1X,'TIME = ',F5.2,2X,'RESPONSE 2 = ',F8.5)

9.    PRINT 1, TIME, RESP1, RESP2
     1 FORMAT (1X,'EXPERIMENT RESULTS'//1X,'TIME',2X,
     +         'RESPONSE 1',2X,'RESPONSE 2'/
     +         1X,F4.2,2E12.3)
```

4–6   APPLICATION—QUALITY CONTROL
(Manufacturing Engineering)

In a manufacturing or assembly plant, quality control receives close attention. One of the key responsibilities of a quality-control engineer is to collect accurate data on the quality of the product being manufactured. This data can be used to identify problem areas in the assembly line or in the materials being used in the product.

In this section, we use information collected over a 1-month period that specifies both the type of defect and the number of defects detected in the assembly of the computer board for a personal computer. These defects have been divided into three categories: broken wires, defective integrated circuit chips (ICs), and defective non-IC components (such as resistors and capacitors). The data has been stored in a file called REPORT. The first line in the data file contains the number of boards assembled in the period of time represented by the data in the file. Each line following contains a board identification number followed by three integers that represent the number of broken wires, defective ICs, and defective non-ICs, respectively, on the board.

At least one of these numbers is greater than zero because the file contains only information on boards with defects.

Our program is to read this set of information and compute the total number of defects in each category and the number of boards with defects. We are also to print the board identification numbers for boards that have three or more defects. This information will allow the quality-control engineer to identify trouble areas by using the identification numbers to determine the date of assembly and the lot of materials used in those computer boards.

PROBLEM STATEMENT

Print a report analyzing the defects in a set of computer boards.

INPUT/OUTPUT DESCRIPTION

The input to the program is to be entered from a data file. The first line in the file contains the total number of boards assembled. Each line following contains a board identification number and three integers representing the three types of defects that may occur in the board: broken wires, defective ICs, and defective non-ICs. The end of the data is indicated by a 99999 in board identification. The output is a report with the following information:

```
               MONTHLY QUALITY ANALYSIS REPORT

    IDENTIFICATION NUMBERS OF BOARDS WITH THREE OR MORE DEFECTS:

        XXX

    TOTAL NUMBER OF BOARDS ASSEMBLED = XXXX

    TOTAL BOARDS WITH DEFECTS = XXXX

        XXXX BOARDS WITH BROKEN WIRES
        XXXX BOARDS WITH DEFECTIVE IC COMPONENTS
        XXXX BOARDS WITH DEFECTIVE NON-IC COMPONENTS

    DEFECT ANALYSIS

        XXX.X% OF DEFECTS ARE BROKEN WIRES
        XXX.X% OF DEFECTS ARE DEFECTIVE IC COMPONENTS
        XXX.X% OF DEFECTS ARE DEFECTIVE NON-IC COMPONENTS
```

HAND EXAMPLE

Assuming that a total of 528 computer boards were assembled during the month, consider the following set of defect data:

IDENTIFICATION	DEFECTS IN THE THREE CATEGORIES
528	
145	0 0 1
188	1 1 0
410	0 1 0
312	2 0 0
366	0 0 1
368	0 0 1
279	1 1 2
407	1 0 0
99999	0 0 0

The analysis of the sample data yields the following quality analysis report:

```
              MONTHLY QUALITY ANALYSIS REPORT

   IDENTIFICATION NUMBERS OF BOARDS WITH THREE OR MORE DEFECTS:

      279

   TOTAL NUMBER OF BOARDS ASSEMBLED =   528

   TOTAL BOARDS WITH DEFECTS =      8

         4 BOARDS WITH BROKEN WIRES
         3 BOARDS WITH DEFECTIVE IC COMPONENTS
         4 BOARDS WITH DEFECTIVE NON-IC COMPONENTS

   DEFECT ANALYSIS

         38.5% OF DEFECTS ARE BROKEN WIRES
         23.1% OF DEFECTS ARE DEFECTIVE IC COMPONENTS
         38.5% OF DEFECTS ARE DEFECTIVE NON-IC COMPONENTS
```

ALGORITHM DEVELOPMENT

Most of the information in the report is based on totals that we need to determine as the data is entered. For example, we need the following:

Total number of boards assembled
Total number of boards with defects
Total number of boards with broken wires
Total number of boards with defective ICs
Total number of boards with defective non-IC components
Total number of broken wires

Total number of defective ICs

Total number of defective non-IC components

Recall that we also want to print the identification number of any board that has three or more defects. Because we do not know in advance how many of these boards there are, we cannot easily keep the identification numbers in memory; therefore, we print the identification numbers as soon as we read them. The WHILE loop for reading this data is executed "while ID is not 99999," so we need to read the first set of defect data before we test this WHILE condition.

Putting these ideas into our decomposition step yields

DECOMPOSITION

Read data and compute totals and print ID for boards with three or more defects.
Compute data for defect summary.
Print report.

Adding more detail to these steps, our refinement in pseudocode becomes

QUALTY: Initialize all totals to zero
   Read number of boards assembled
   Read ID, defects
   While ID not equal to 99999 do
    If number of defects ≥ 3 print ID
    Increment appropriate totals
    Read ID, defects
   Compute additional totals and percentages
   Print report

We are now ready to convert the steps in pseudocode into FORTRAN statements. We again list the totals that we need, along with the FORTRAN names that we are using for them.

BOARDS	Total number of boards assembled
BDDEF	Total number of boards with defects
BDWIRE	Total number of boards with broken wires
BDIC	Total number of boards with defective ICs
BDNON	Total number of boards with defective non-ICs
WIRE	Total number of broken wires
IC	Total number of defective ICs
NON	Total number of defective non-IC components

FORTRAN Program

```
*------------------------------------------------------------*
      PROGRAM  QUALTY
*
* This program uses defect data to print
* a Quality Analysis Report.
*
      INTEGER  BOARDS, BDDEF, BDWIRE, BDIC, BDNON, WIRE,
     +         IC, NON, ID, NWIRE, NIC, NNON, DEFECT
      REAL  PERCW, PERCIC, PERCNO
*
      BDDEF = 0
      BDWIRE = 0
      BDIC = 0
      BDNON = 0
      WIRE = 0
      IC = 0
      NON = 0
      OPEN (UNIT=10,FILE='REPORT',STATUS='OLD')
      READ (10,*) BOARDS
*
      PRINT*, '            MONTHLY QUALITY ANALYSIS REPORT'
      PRINT*
      PRINT*, 'IDENTIFICATION NUMBERS OF BOARDS WITH ',
     +        'THREE OR MORE DEFECTS:'
      PRINT*
*
      READ (10,*) ID, NWIRE, NIC, NNON
   10 IF (ID.NE.99999) THEN
         IF (NWIRE + NIC + NNON.GE.3) PRINT 15, ID
   15    FORMAT (1X,I8)
         BDDEF = BDDEF + 1
         IF (NWIRE.GT.0) BDWIRE = BDWIRE + 1
         IF (NIC.GT.0) BDIC = BDIC + 1
         IF (NNON.GT.0) BDNON = BDNON + 1
         WIRE = WIRE + NWIRE
         IC = IC + NIC
         NON = NON + NNON
         READ (10,*) ID, NWIRE, NIC, NNON
         GO TO 10
      ENDIF
*
      PRINT 20, BOARDS, BDDEF, BDWIRE, BDIC, BDNON
   20 FORMAT ( /,1X,'TOTAL NUMBER OF BOARDS ASSEMBLED = ',I4,//,
     +         1X,'TOTAL  BOARDS WITH DEFECTS = ',I4,//,
     +         1X,5X,I4,' BOARDS WITH BROKEN WIRES',//,
     +         1X,5X,I4,' BOARDS WITH DEFECTIVE IC COMPONENTS',/,
     +         1X,5X,I4,' BOARDS WITH DEFECTIVE NON-IC COMPONENTS')
      DEFECT = WIRE + IC   + NON
      PERCW = REAL(WIRE)*100.0/REAL(DEFECT)
      PERCIC = REAL(IC)*100.00/REAL(DEFECT)
      PERCNO = REAL(NON)*100.0/REAL(DEFECT)
      PRINT 30, PERCW, PERCIC, PERCNO
   30 FORMAT (/,1X,'DEFECT ANALYSIS',//,
     +         1X,5X,F5.1,'% OF DEFECTS ARE BROKEN WIRES',/,
     +         1X,5X,F5.1,'% OF DEFECTS ARE DEFECTIVE ',
     +                    'IC COMPONENTS',/,
     +         1X,5X,F5.1,'% OF DEFECTS ARE DEFECTIVE ',
     +                    'NON-IC COMPONENTS')
      END
*------------------------------------------------------------*
```

Several of the literals in our FORMAT statements were too long to fit on one line and had to be separated into two lines. Instead of continuing the literal to column 72, it is more readable if we split the line between words.

TESTING

If we use our sample data from the program, our output is

```
            MONTHLY QUALITY ANALYSIS REPORT

IDENTIFICATION NUMBERS OF BOARDS WITH THREE OR MORE DEFECTS:

    279

TOTAL NUMBER OF BOARDS ASSEMBLED =   528

TOTAL BOARDS WITH DEFECTS =      8

        4 BOARDS WITH BROKEN WIRES
        3 BOARDS WITH DEFECTIVE IC COMPONENTS
        4 BOARDS WITH DEFECTIVE NON-IC COMPONENTS

DEFECT ANALYSIS

        38.5% OF DEFECTS ARE BROKEN WIRES
        23.1% OF DEFECTS ARE DEFECTIVE IC COMPONENTS
        38.5% OF DEFECTS ARE DEFECTIVE NON-IC COMPONENTS
```

Once our program is working correctly with a typical set of data, we should design data sets that test special conditions. For example, we should test this program with data that does not include one of the defects; if we eliminate all the IC defects in our sample set, the preceding program produces the following report:

```
            MONTHLY QUALITY ANALYSIS REPORT

IDENTIFICATION NUMBERS OF BOARDS WITH THREE OR MORE DEFECTS:

    279

TOTAL NUMBER OF BOARDS ASSEMBLED = 528

TOTAL BOARDS WITH DEFECTS =      7

        4 BOARDS WITH BROKEN WIRES
        0 BOARDS WITH DEFECTIVE IC COMPONENTS
        4 BOARDS WITH DEFECTIVE NON-IC COMPONENTS

DEFECT ANALYSIS

        50.0% OF DEFECTS ARE BROKEN WIRES
         0.0% OF DEFECTS ARE DEFECTIVE IC COMPONENTS
        50.0% OF DEFECTS ARE DEFECTIVE NON-IC COMPONENTS
```

When entering the data in the file REPORT, is it necessary to include three zeros after the identification number 99999? Yes, it is necessary because the corresponding READ statement lists four variables; otherwise, an execution error will occur.

SUMMARY

This chapter presented a number of I/O features available in FORTRAN. The most important feature is the data file. Data files are necessary in engineering and science applications because they often use large amounts of data. We will use data files frequently throughout this text so that you can become comfortable with them.

We also presented details on formatted input and output. The only way to become proficient with formatting is to use it frequently. We suggest that you use list-directed input and output in your testing and debugging phases. Once you get correct answers, use formatted output statements to give a neat and attractive form to your answers.

DEBUGGING AIDS

The following steps will help you correct input and output statements that are not working properly.

1. Check to be sure you have given values to all variables in an output list.
2. Echo values that you read; that is, immediately after reading a value, print it for a comparison check.
3. If any of your output values contains asterisks instead of numbers, enlarge the width of the corresponding specifications or use an E format.
4. Be sure that the order of variables in the input or output list matches the order you used when writing the format.
5. Check every line of output to ensure that you have correctly specified carriage control unless you are using list-directed output. Look for incorrect spacing between lines or missing first letters or numbers in the output.
6. Be sure that you have as many FORMAT specifications as variable names in the READ or PRINT list. In general, do not try to share FORMAT statements.
7. Be sure you do not have the characters I and 1 or the characters O (letter) and 0 (number) interchanged.
8. Be sure that you have not exceeded column 72 on long statements.
9. Do not combine too many lines of output in a single output statement.
10. Use unformatted statements to print values first. After you determine that the values are correct, change to formatted statements, if needed.

11. Check input formats to ensure that you have not included carriage control.
12. Be careful splitting a literal specification when continuing a long format to the next line. Break the literal into two literals so that unexpected blanks do not appear; for example, consider the following FORMAT statement:

```
10 FORMAT (1X,'EXPERIMENTAL RESULTS
   +           FROM PROJECT #1')
```

Any blanks between the word RESULTS and column 72 of the first line and between the continuation character + and the word FROM will be inserted in the literal. Thus, the heading would appear something like:

EXPERIMENTAL RESULTS   FROM PROJECT #1

A better solution is to split the literal into two literals, which is illustrated in the following FORMAT and its corresponding output:

```
10 FORMAT (1X,'EXPERIMENTAL RESULTS ',
   +          'FROM PROJECT #1')
```

EXPERIMENTAL RESULTS FROM PROJECT #1

STYLE/TECHNIQUE GUIDES

1. Develop the habit of echo printing values that you have read.
2. Print the physical units that correspond to the numeric values being printed — this information is vital for proper interpretation of results.
3. Be consistent about your placement of FORMAT statements. Either put the FORMAT immediately after the statement that uses it, or put the FORMAT just before the END statement in your program.
4. Label FORMAT statements so that the numbers are in ascending order and they fit into the order of other statements in your program. Do not, however, number statements sequentially — you may need to insert additional statements later.
5. Make your carriage control evident. For instance, use (1X,F4.1) instead of (F5.1).
6. Label values printed. Use (1X,'X=',F3.1) instead of (1X,F3.1).
7. Use an E format to print values for which you cannot approximate the size. After seeing the answer, you can change the E specification to an F specification that will accommodate the value, if you wish.
8. Do not print more significant digits than you have. For instance, if you compute sums with values that have one decimal position, do not print the result with three decimal positions.
9. Generally, it is best to use the same number of specifications in the FORMAT as there are variable names in the variable list.

10. Do not use extremely long FORMAT statements; use additional statements with separate FORMAT statements.
11. Remember that the slash character must always be followed by carriage control in output statements.

KEY WORDS

data file   record
END option   sentinel signal
job control information   trailer signal

PROBLEMS

We begin our problem set with modifications to programs developed earlier in this chapter. Give the decomposition, refined pseudocode or flowchart, and FORTRAN program for each problem.

Problems 1–5 modify the critical path analysis program PATH, given on page 157.

1. Modify the critical path analysis program so that it prints the event number and task number for the task that requires the maximum amount of time.
2. Modify the critical path analysis program so that it prints the event number for the event that requires the maximum amount of time.
3. Modify the critical path analysis program so that it prints the average amount of time required for the tasks.
4. Modify the critical path analysis program so that it prints the event and task number for all tasks requiring more than five days.
5. Modify the critical path analysis program so that it prints a list of the events and the number of tasks in each event.

Problems 6–10 modify the population growth program CENSUS, given on page 161.

6. Modify the population growth program so that it finds the two consecutive years in which the percentage increase in population was the smallest.
7. Modify the population growth program so that it finds and prints the year and the corresponding population that was the smallest population value. Print all years with this minimum population.
8. Modify the population growth program so that it computes the average increase in population per year for the total period of time represented by the data in the data file.

9. Modify the population growth program so that it finds the two consecutive years in which the actual increase in population was the largest.

10. Modify the population growth program so that it prints the population values for the two consecutive years in which the actual increase in population was the smallest.

Problems 11–15 modify the quality control program QUALITY, given on page 177.

11. Modify the quality control program so that it prints an error message if the identification number is greater than 5000.

12. Modify the quality control program so that it prints the percentage of boards with defects.

13. Modify the quality control program so that it prints the total number of defects.

14. Modify the quality control program so that it prints the identification numbers of boards with a defect in two or more of the categories.

15. Modify the quality control program so that it determines and prints the number of boards with one defect, the number of boards with two defects, the number of boards with three defects, and the number of boards with more than three defects.

In problems 16–30 develop programs using the five-phase design process.

16. As a practicing engineer, you have been collecting data on the performance of a new solar device. You have been measuring the sun's intensity and the voltage produced by a photovoltaic cell exposed to the sun. These measurements have been taken every 30 minutes during daylight hours for 2 months. Because the sun sets at a different time each day, the number of measurements taken each day may vary.

   Each line of valid data contains the sun's intensity (integer), the time (24-hour form where 1430 represents 2:30 PM), and the voltage (real). A trailer signal contains 9999 for the sun's intensity. Write a complete program to read this data and compute and print the total number of measurements, the average intensity of the sun, and the average voltage value.

17. Write a program for a nutrition study that will read the value of N from the first line in a data file called WEIGHTS. If N is zero or negative, stop the program; otherwise, use N to specify the number of data lines remaining in the data file, where each data line contains an identification number (integer), the initial weight, and the final weight of a participant in the study. Print a table containing this original data and the percentage increase in weight for each participant. Number the lines. Use the following report form:

	ID	INITIAL WT	FINAL WT	PERCENT INCREASE
1.	XXX	XXX.X	XXX.X	XXX.XX
2.	XXX	XXX.X	XXX.X	XXX.XX
.	.	.	.	.
.	.	.	.	.
.	.	.	.	.
N.	XXX	XXX.X	XXX.X	XXX.XX

18. Write a program for analyzing pressure data. Read 20 lines of data with three integer numbers per line from a data file called RESULTS. Each line represents pressure measurements made in three different chambers. Find the maximum pressure in each chamber and print the following:

```
MAXIMUM PRESSURE IN CHAMBER 1 = XXXX
MAXIMUM PRESSURE IN CHAMBER 2 = XXXX
MAXIMUM PRESSURE IN CHAMBER 3 = XXXX
```

19. Twenty-four temperature measurements for two compounds have been taken at 20-minute intervals over a period of time. Each pair of temperatures is entered in a data file TEMP in the order in which the measurements were made. Write a program to read the data and print it in the following manner:

```
TEMPERATURE MEASUREMENTS
```

TIME ELAPSED HOURS	AND MINUTES	COMPOUND 1	COMPOUND 2
0	0	XXXXX	XXXXX
0	20	XXXXX	XXXXX
0	40	XXXXX	XXXXX
1	00	XXXXX	XXXXX
1	20	XXXXX	XXXXX
1	40	XXXXX	XXXXX
2	0	XXXXX	XXXXX
.	.	.	.
.	.	.	.
7	40	XXXXX	XXXXX

20. Modify problem 19 so that the following output lines are printed after the temperature measurements:

```
MINIMUM TEMPERATURE AND TIME ELAPSED (HOURS AND MINUTES)
     COMPOUND 1        XXXXX          XX        XX
     COMPOUND 2        XXXXX          XX        XX
```

21. Write a program to compute fuel cost information for an automobile. The input data is stored in a data file called MILES. The first line in the file contains the initial mileage (odometer reading). Each following data line contains information collected as the automobile was refueled and includes the new mileage reading, the cost of the fuel, and the number of gallons of fuel. The last line of the file contains a negative value and two zeros, instead of the refueling information. The output of the program should compute the

cost per mile and the number of miles per gallon for each line of input data. Use the report format shown:

```
                        FUEL COST INFORMATION

      MILES        GALLONS       COST       COST/MILE     MILES/GALLON
      XXX.X         XX.X        XX.XX         X.XX            XX.X
        .
        .
        .
```

22. Add the following summary information at the end of the report printed in problem 21:

```
                        SUMMARY INFORMATION

              TOTAL MILES                XXXX.X
              TOTAL COST                XXXXX.XX
              TOTAL GALLONS              XXXX.X
              AVERAGE COST/MILE            X.XX
              AVERAGE MILES/GALLON         XX.X
```

23. Oil exploration and recovery is an important concern of large petroleum companies. Profitable oil recovery requires careful testing by drilling seismic holes and blasting with specific amounts of dynamite. For optimum seismic readings, a specific ratio between the amount of dynamite and the depth of the hole is required. Assume that each stick of dynamite is $2\frac{1}{2}$ feet long, and weighs 5 pounds. The ideal powder charge requires a ratio of 1:3 for the dynamite to depth-of-hole ratio. Thus, a 60-foot hole would require 20 feet of dynamite, which is equal to 8 sticks, or 40 pounds. The actual powder charge is not always equal to the ideal powder charge because the ideal powder charge may not be in 5-pound increments; in these cases, the actual powder charge should be rounded down to the nearest 5-pound increment. (You cannot cut or break the dynamite into shorter lengths for field operations.)

The following example should clarify this process:

Hole depth = 85 feet
Ideal charge = 85/3 = 28.33333 feet
$\qquad\qquad\qquad$ = 11.33333 sticks
$\qquad\qquad\qquad$ = 56.66666 pounds
Actual charge = 55 pounds
$\qquad\qquad\qquad$ = 11 sticks

Information on the depths of the holes to be tested each day is stored in a data file called DRILL. The first line contains the number of sites to be tested that day. Each following line contains integer information for a specified site that gives the site identification number and the depth of the hole in feet. Write a complete program to read this information and print the following report:

SITE ID	DEPTH (FT)	IDEAL POWDER CHARGE (LBS)	ACTUAL POWDER CHARGE (LBS)	STICKS
12980	85	56.6666	55	11
.	.	.	.	.
.	.	.	.	.
.	.	.	.	.

(*Hint:* The MOD function would be useful in this program.)

24. Modify the program in problem 23 so that a final summary report follows the drilling report and has the form

```
TOTAL POWDER USED = XXXXX LBS   (XXXX STICKS)
TOTAL DRILLING FOOTAGE = XXXXXX FT
```

25. Modify the program in problem 24 so that it takes into consideration a special situation: If the depth of the hole is less than 30 feet, the hole is too shallow for blasting. Instead of printing the charge values for such a hole, print the site identification number, the depth, and the message HOLE TOO SHALLOW FOR BLASTING. The summary report printed at the end of the report should not include data for these shallow holes. Add a line to the summary report that contains the number of holes too shallow for blasting.

26. Beam analysis is an important part of the structural analysis conducted before construction of a building begins. A frequently used type of beam is a cantilever beam, which is fixed on one end and free on the other. The amount of deflection when a load is applied to this type of beam can be computed with the following equation:

$$\text{DEFLECTION} = \frac{(L)(a^2)}{2(E)(I)} \cdot \left(\text{length} - \frac{a}{3.0} \right)$$

where L = applied load in pounds
a = length from fixed end to applied load in feet
E = elasticity of material (wood, steel, . . .)
I = moment of inertia of the beam, which can be computed with the following equation:

$$I = \frac{(\text{base})(\text{height})^3}{12}$$

Assume that we have information on five different beams in a data file BEAM. The data for each beam is given in the following five real values, which are stored in one data line in the proper units for the equations above:

Beam length
Beam base
Beam height
Elasticity constant
Applied load

Write a program to read the information for each beam and print a report that places the applied load at 1-foot intervals starting at one foot from the fixed end and moving down the length of the beam. The output for a beam should contain the following information:

```
BEAM NO. 1    TOTAL LENGTH = XXX.XX FT

      DISTANCE OF LOAD FROM FIXED END        DEFLECTION
                  1.0                          XXX.XX
                  2.0                          XXX.XX
                   .                              .
                   .                              .
                   .                              .
```

27. Modify the program in problem 26 so that the deflections for each beam are printed only as long as they are less than 5 percent of the beam length. When the beam deflection is greater than or equal to 5 percent, the program should stop computing values for that beam and go on to the next. If the deflection distance of 5 percent is never reached, the program should print an appropriate message. The header line for each beam should also contain the 5 percent length computation. An example of this output is

```
BEAM NO. 1    TOTAL LENGTH = 10.00 FT
              5% OF LENGTH =  0.50 FT

      DISTANCE FROM FIXED END          DEFLECTION
                1.00                      0.15
                2.00                      0.38
                3.00                      0.48

BEAM NO. 2    TOTAL LENGTH =  3.00 FT
              5% OF LENGTH =  0.15 FT

      DISTANCE FROM FIXED END          DEFLECTION
                1.00                      0.04
                2.00                      0.09
                3.00                      0.12

        DEFLECTION OF 5% OF LENGTH NOT REACHED
```

28. Assume that a data file called DATAXY contains a set of data coordinates that are to be used by several different programs. The first line of the file contains the number of data coordinates in the file, and each of the rest of the lines contain the x and y coordinates for one of the data points. Some of the programs need to use the coordinates in polar form instead of rectangular form. Rather than have each program that needs polar coordinates convert the data, we will generate a second data file that has each point in polar form, which is a radius and an angle in radians. Then, no matter how many programs use the data, it only has to be converted to polar coordinates once, and each program can then reference the appropriate file. Write a program to generate a new file called POLAR that contains coordinates in polar form instead of rectangular form. The following equations convert a coordinate in

rectangular form to polar form:

$$r = \sqrt{x^2 + y^2}$$
$$theta = \tan^{-1}(y/x)$$

(Be sure that the first line of the new data file specifies the number of data coordinates.)

29. Rewrite the program from problem 28, assuming that the original file is POLAR and that it contains data coordinates in polar form. The new output file should be called DATAXY and should contain data coordinates in rectangular form. The equations for converting polar coordinates to rectangular coordinates are

$$x = r\,\cos(theta)$$
$$y = r\,\sin(theta)$$

30. Rewrite the program from problem 28 such that it creates a new data file called DATA. The first line of data should still contain the number of coordinates in the data file. Each following line of the data file should contain four values. The first two values represent the rectangular coordinates (x and y), and the next two values represent the corresponding polar coordinates (r and theta) for the data point.

FORTRAN STATEMENT SUMMARY

OPEN Statement:

> **OPEN** (**UNIT**=*integer expression*, **FILE**=*filename*, **STATUS**=*literal*)

Examples:

> OPEN (UNIT=15,FILE='EXAMS',STATUS='OLD')
>
> OPEN (UNIT=10,FILE='ACCEL',STATUS='NEW')

Discussion:

The OPEN statement is used to designate that a particular data file will be used for all input or output statements that refer to the unit number in the OPEN statement. If the file is an input file, then its status is 'OLD'; if the file is an output file, then its status is 'NEW'.

READ * Statement:

> **READ** (*unit number,***,END**=*n*) *variable list*

Examples:

> READ (10,*) X, Y
>
> READ (15,*,END=50) TIME, TEMP

Discussion:

This form of the READ statement is used with data files. The specific data file is referenced by the unit number, which must correspond to a unit number assigned to a file by an OPEN statement. The asterisk specifies that the statement is a list-directed input statement. The END clause is optional and will cause control to be passed to the statement with statement number n if the READ statement is executed after the last line of data has been read.

READ k Statement:

> **READ** (*unit number,k,***END**=*n*) *variable list*

Examples:

> READ (15,5) X, Y, Z
>
> READ (15,20,END=50) TIME, DIST

Discussion:

This form of the READ statement is used with data files. The specific data file is referenced by the unit number, which must correspond to a unit number assigned to a file by an OPEN statement. The format statement to be used in reading the data is referenced by the second number in the parentheses. The END clause is optional and will cause control to be passed to the statement with statement number n if the READ statement is executed after the last line of data has been read.

$$\text{WRITE } (unit \;\; number,\text{*}) \;\; variable \;\; list$$

Examples:

```
WRITE (13,*) A, B, C

WRITE (10,*) X
```

Discussion:
This WRITE statement is a list-directed output statement that writes information into a data file specified by the unit number. The unit number must correspond to the unit number of a file that has been assigned in an OPEN statement.

WRITE *k* Statement:

$$\text{WRITE } (unit \;\; number,k) \;\; variable \;\; list$$

Examples:

```
WRITE (10,5) A, B, C

WRITE (15,15) X
```

Discussion:
This WRITE statement is a formatted output statement that writes information into a data file specified by the unit number. The unit number must correspond to the unit number of a file that has been assigned in an OPEN statement. The format statement is referenced by the second number in the parentheses.

APPLICATION—Earthquake Measurements (Civil Engineering)

Engineers and scientists are hopeful that one day they will be able to predict accurately the size and location of major earthquakes. Data from seismometers, instruments that record the earth's motion, is collected from locations around the world. By studying this data that is collected before, during, and after earthquakes, scientists hope to identify changes that will aid in this prediction process.

Write a program that will sort the data collected from one seismometer during recent earthquakes so that the order of the data is from smallest earthquake to largest earthquake. (See Section 5–5 for the solution.)

Photo courtesy of U. S. Dept. of Interior.

5

ARRAY PROCESSING

Introduction

5–1 One-Dimensional Arrays

5–2 DATA Statement

5–3 Application — National Park Snowfall (Meteorology)

5–4 Sorting Algorithms

5–5 Application — Earthquake Measurements (Civil Engineering)

5–6 Two-Dimensional Arrays

5–7 Application — Power Plant Data Analysis (Power Engineering)

5–8 Application — Terrain Navigation (Aeronautical Engineering)

5–9 Multidimensional Arrays

Summary

INTRODUCTION

This chapter develops a method for storing groups of values without explicitly giving each value a different name — each group (called an array) has a common name but individual values have a unique index or subscript. This technique allows us to analyze the data using loops, where the common name remains the same but the index or subscript becomes a variable that changes with each pass through the loop. Because the data values are stored in separate memory locations, we can also access the data as often as needed without rereading it. An array is used to store the earthquake data in the chapter opener application because we need to have all the data available in order to sort it.

5–1   ONE-DIMENSIONAL ARRAYS

An *array* is a group of storage locations that have the same name. Individual members of an array are called *elements* and are distinguished by using the common name followed by a *subscript* or an index in parentheses. Subscripts are represented by consecutive integers, usually beginning with the integer 1. A one-dimensional array can be visualized as either one column of data or one row of data. The storage locations and associated names for a one-dimensional integer array J of 5 elements and a one-dimensional real array DIST with 4 elements are shown:

J(1)	2
J(2)	−5
J(3)	14
J(4)	80
J(5)	−12

1.2	−0.8	36.9	−0.07
DIST(1)	DIST(2)	DIST(3)	DIST(4)

STORAGE AND INITIALIZATION

The DIMENSION statement, a nonexecutable statement, is used to reserve memory space or storage for an array. In its general form, a list of array names and their corresponding sizes follows the word DIMENSION, as shown:

```
DIMENSION   array1(size), array2(size), . . .
```

Array sizes must be specified with constants, not variables. A DIMENSION statement that reserves storage for the two arrays previously mentioned is

```
DIMENSION   J(5), DIST(4)
```

The number in parentheses after the array name gives the total number of values that can be stored in that array. Two separate DIMENSION statements, with one array listed in each statement, would also be valid but not preferable because it would require an extra statement. All DIMENSION statements must be placed before any executable statements in your program because they are specification statements.

The type of values stored in an array can be specified implicitly through the choice of array name or explicitly with a REAL, INTEGER, or LOGICAL statement. The following statement specifies that AREA is an array of 15 elements that contains integer values

`INTEGER   AREA(15)`

The typing of an array, whether implicit or explicit, applies to all elements of the array; hence, an array cannot contain both real values and integer values. Explicitly typed array names do not appear in DIMENSION statements because the array size has also been specified in the type statement. Because explicit typing is desirable, we will use explicit typing statements instead of DIMENSION statements for defining the arrays in our examples.

The range of subscripts associated with an array can be specified with a beginning subscript number and an ending subscript number. Both numbers must be integers separated by a colon and must follow the array name in the DIMENSION statement or the type statement. The following statements reserve storage for a real array TAX whose elements are TAX(0), TAX(1), TAX(2), TAX(3), TAX(4), and TAX(5); and an integer array INCOME whose elements are INCOME(−3), INCOME(−2), INCOME(−1), INCOME(0), INCOME(1), INCOME(2), and INCOME(3):

`REAL   TAX(0:5)`

`INTEGER   INCOME(-3:3)`

Also note that the following declarations are equivalent:

`INTEGER   AREA(1:15)`

`INTEGER   AREA(15)`

Unless otherwise stated, we will assume in our text that all array subscripts begin with the integer 1. However, there are situations in which the range of the subscripts logically starts with an integer other than 1; for instance, in Section 4–3 (Application — Population Study), we discussed a set of population values from the years 1880–1980. If this data were to be stored in an array, it might be convenient to use the year to specify the corresponding population. We could specify such an array with the following statement:

`INTEGER   POPUL(1880:1890)`

Then, if we wish to refer to the population for 1885, we use the reference POPUL(1885).

Values are assigned to array elements in the same way that values are assigned to regular variables. The following are valid assignment statements:

`J(1) = 0`

`J(5) = NUM*COUNT`

`DIST(2) = 46.2 + SIN(X)`

It is not valid to use an array name without a subscript in an assignment statement.

It is also extremely helpful to use variables and expressions, instead of constants, as subscripts. The following loop initializes all elements of the array J to the value 10. Observe that the variable I is used as a subscript and also as the DO loop index:

```
DO 20 I=1,5
   J(I) = 10
20 CONTINUE
```

The next loop initializes the array J to the values shown:

```
DO 30 I=1,5
   J(I) = I
30 CONTINUE
```

1	2	3	4	5

J(1) J(2) J(3) J(4) J(5)

The values of the array DIST are initialized to real values with this set of statements:

```
DO 5 K=1,4
   DIST(K) = REAL(K)*1.5
5 CONTINUE
```

1.5	3.0	4.5	6.0

DIST(1) DIST(2) DIST(3) DIST(4)

The previous examples illustrate that a subscript can be an integer constant or an integer variable. Subscripts can also be integer expressions, as indicated in the following statements:

```
J(2*I) = 3

R(J) = R(J-1)

B = TR(2*I) + TR(2*I+1)
```

Whenever an expression is used as a subscript, be sure the value of the expression is between the starting and ending subscript value. If a subscript is outside the proper range, the program will not work correctly. With some compilers, a logic error message is given if a subscript is out of bounds, other compilers use an incorrect value for the invalid array reference, causing serious errors that are difficult to detect.

INPUT AND OUTPUT

To read data into an array from a terminal or from a data file, we use the READ statement. If we wish to read an entire array, we can use the name of the array without subscripts. We can also specify specific elements in a READ statement. If the array A contains 3 elements, then the following two READ statements are equivalent; if the array A contains 8 elements, then the first READ statement reads values for all 8 elements and the second READ statement reads values for only the first 3 elements:

```
READ*, A

READ*, A(1), A(2), A(3)
```

Array values may also be read using an *implied DO loop*. Implied DO loops use the indexing feature of the DO statement and may be used only in input and output statements and in the DATA statement presented in Section 5–2. For example, if we wish to read the first 10 elements of the array R, we can use the following implied DO loop in the READ statement:

```
READ*, (R(I), I=1,10)
```

Further examples illustrate the use of these techniques for reading data into an array.

EXAMPLE 5-1   **Temperature Measurements**

A set of 50 temperature measurements has been entered into a data file, 1 value per line. The file is accessed with unit number 9. Give a set of statements to read this data into an array:

TEMP(1) ← Line 1 of data file
TEMP(2) ← Line 2 of data file

.

.

.

TEMP(50) ← Line 50 of data file

Solution 1

The READ statement in this solution reads 1 value, but it is in a loop that is executed 50 times and reads the entire array:

```
REAL  TEMP(50)
  .
  .
  .
DO 10 I=1,50
    READ (9,*) TEMP(I)
10 CONTINUE
```

Solution 2

The READ statement in this solution contains no subscript; thus, it reads the entire array:

```
REAL  TEMP(50)
  .
  .
  .
READ (9,*) TEMP
```

Solution 3

The READ statement in this solution contains an implied loop and is equivalent to a READ statement that listed TEMP(1), TEMP(2), . . . , TEMP(50):

```
REAL   TEMP(50)
     .
     .
     .
READ (9,*) (TEMP(I), I=1,50)
```

Note that Solution 2 and Solution 3 are exactly the same as far as the computer is concerned; they both represent one READ statement with 50 variables. Solution 1 is the same as 50 READ statements with 1 variable per READ statement. If the data file contains 50 lines, each with 1 temperature measurement, all three solutions store the same data in the array TEMP.

However, suppose that each of the 50 lines in the data file has two numbers: a temperature measurement and a humidity measurement. Solution 1 will read a new data line for each temperature measurement because it is the equivalent of 50 READ statements. But, because Solutions 2 and 3 are the equivalent of one READ statement with 50 variables listed, they will go to a new line only when they run out of data. Thus, the data is stored as shown:

TEMP(1) ← First temperature
TEMP(2) ← First humidity
TEMP(3) ← Second temperature
TEMP(4) ← Second humidity
.
.
.

This is a subtle, but important, distinction: The computer does not recognize that an error has occurred in the last example shown. It has data for the array and continues processing, assuming it has the correct data.

EXAMPLE 5-2

Rainfall Data

A set of 28 daily rainfall measurements is stored in a data file, with 1 week of data per line. The unit number is again assumed to be 9. Give statements to read this data into an array called RAIN:

RAIN(1)	RAIN(2)	. . .	RAIN(7) ← Line 1 of data file
RAIN(8)	RAIN(9)	. . .	RAIN(14) ← Line 2 of data file
RAIN(15)	RAIN(16)	. . .	RAIN(21) ← Line 3 of data file
RAIN(22)	RAIN(23)	. . .	RAIN(28) ← Line 4 of data file

Correct Solution

The READ statement in this solution contains no subscript and thus reads the entire array. Because each line contains 7 data values, 4 lines of data are required:

```
REAL   RAIN(28)
  .
  .
  .
READ (9,*) RAIN
```

Incorrect Solution

The READ statement in this solution reads 1 value, and the READ statement is in a loop executed 28 times; thus, 28 lines of data are required. Because the data file contains only 4 lines of data, an execution error occurs:

```
REAL   RAIN(28)
   .
   .
   .
DO 10 I=1,28
     READ (9,*) RAIN(I)
10 CONTINUE
```

Techniques to print or write values from an array are similar to those used to read values into an array. The following examples illustrate the use of DO loops and implied loops for arrays in PRINT statements.

EXAMPLE 5-3   **Mass Measurements**

A group of 30 mass measurements are stored in a real array MASS. Print the values in the following tabulation:

```
MASS( 1) = XXX.X  KG
MASS( 2) = XXX.X  KG
  .
  .
  .
MASS(30) = XXX.X  KG
```

Solution

For each output line, we need to reference 1 value in the array. The values of the subscript can be generated with a DO statement that has an index of 1 – 30. The output form of this solution is important; go through it carefully to be sure you understand the placement of the literals in the FORMAT statement:

```
REAL   MASS(30)
   .
   .
   .
DO 20 I=1,30
     PRINT 15, I, MASS(I)
15     FORMAT (1X,'MASS(',I2,') = ',F5.1,'  KG')
20 CONTINUE
```

EXAMPLE 5-4   **Distance, Velocity, Acceleration**

Arrays DIS, VEL, and ACC each contain 50 values: The first value in each array represents the distance, velocity, and acceleration, respectively, of a test rocket at time equal to 1 second. The second set of values represents data for time equal to 2 seconds, and so on. Print the data in the following tabulation:

```
TIME    DISTANCE    VELOCITY    ACCELERATION
(SEC)   (M)         (M/SEC)     (M/(SEC*SEC))
  1     XXX.XX      XXX.XX      XXX.XX
  .       .           .           .
  .       .           .           .
  .       .           .           .
 50     XXX.XX      XXX.XX      XXX.XX
```

Correct Solution

The index of the DO loop is used as a subscript for each array reference. This solution is the equivalent of 50 PRINT statements, each with 4 output variables:

```
      REAL  DIS(50), VEL(50), ACC(50)
      .
      .
      .
      PRINT 5
    5 FORMAT (1X,'TIME    DISTANCE    VELOCITY',
     +        '    ACCELERATION')
      PRINT 6
    6 FORMAT (1X,'(SEC)   (M)         (M/SEC) ',
     +        '   (M/(SEC*SEC))')
      DO 10 I=1,50
         PRINT 7, I, DIS(I), VEL(I), ACC(I)
    7    FORMAT (1X,I3,4X,F6.2,5X,F6.2,5X,F6.2)
   10 CONTINUE
```

Incorrect Solution

This solution is incorrect because each time through the loop, we are printing the index I, the entire DIS array (50 values), the entire VEL array (50 values), and the entire ACC array (50 values)—thus, each time through the loop, we print 151 values.

```
      REAL  DIS(50), VEL(50), ACC(50)
      .
      .
      .
      PRINT 5
    5 FORMAT (1X,'TIME    DISTANCE    VELOCITY',
     +        '    ACCELERATION')
      PRINT 6
    6 FORMAT (1X,'(SEC)   (M)         (M/SEC) ',
     +        '   (M/(SEC*SEC))')
      DO 10 I=1,50
         PRINT 7, I, DIS, VEL, ACC
    7    FORMAT (1X,I3,4X,F6.2,5X,F6.2,5X,F6.2)
   10 CONTINUE
```

This self-test allows you to check quickly to see if you have remembered some of the key points from Section 5-1. If you have any problems with the exercises, you should reread this section. The solutions are included at the end of the text.

Problems 1-3 contain statements that initialize and print one-dimensional arrays. Show the output from each set of statements. Assume that each set of statements is independent of the others.

```
1.     INTEGER  I, M(10)
       DO 5 I=1,10
           M(I) = I + 1
     5 CONTINUE
       PRINT*, 'ARRAY VALUES:'
       DO 15 I=1,10
           PRINT 10, M(I)
    10     FORMAT (1X,I4)
    15 CONTINUE

2.     INTEGER  K, LIST(8)
       DO 5 K=1,8
           LIST(9-K) = K
     5 CONTINUE
       PRINT 10, (LIST(K), K=1,5)
    10 FORMAT (1X,5I5)

3.     INTEGER  J
       REAL  TIME(20)
       DO 5 J=1,20
           TIME(J) = REAL(J-1)*0.5
     5 CONTINUE
       DO 15 J=1,20,4
           PRINT 10, J, TIME(J)
    10     FORMAT (1X,'TIME ',I2,' = ',F4.2)
    15 CONTINUE
```

5-2 DATA STATEMENT

The DATA statement is a specification statement and is therefore nonexecutable; it is useful in initializing both simple variables and arrays. The general form of the DATA statement is

> DATA   *list of variable names /list of constants/*

An example of a DATA statement to initialize simple variables is

```
DATA  SUM, VEL, VOLT, LENGTH /0.0, 32.75, -2.5, 10/
```

The number of data values must match the number of variable names. The data values should also be of the correct type so that the computer does not have to convert them. The preceding DATA statement initializes the following variables:

SUM	0.0
VEL	32.75
VOLT	−2.5
LENGTH	10

Because the DATA statement is a specification statement, it should precede any executable statements; it is therefore located near the beginning of your program, along with the REAL, INTEGER, LOGICAL, and DIMENSION statements. It follows these other statements because the specification of the types of variables or the declaration of an array should precede values given to the corresponding memory locations.

Caution should be exercised when using the DATA statement because it initializes values only at the beginning of program execution; this means that the DATA statement cannot be used in a loop to reinitialize variables. If it is necessary to reinitialize variables, you must use assignment statements.

If a number of values are to be repeated in the list of values, a constant followed by an asterisk indicates a repetition. The following statement initializes all 4 variables to zero:

```
DATA  A, B, C, D /4*0.0/
```

The next two statements initialize the variables I, J, and K to 1, and X, Y, and Z to −0.5. Notice the change in the order of the variable names between the two statements:

```
DATA   I, J, K, X, Y, Z /3*1, 3*-0.5/
```

or

```
DATA   I, X, J, Y, K, Z /3*(1, -0.5)/
```

A DATA statement can also be used to initialize one or more elements of an array:

```
INTEGER   J(5)
REAL   TIME(4)
DATA   J, TIME /5*0, 1.0, 2.0, 3.0, 4.0/
```

J | 0 | 0 | 0 | 0 | 0 |

TIME | 1.0 | 2.0 | 3.0 | 4.0 |

or

```
REAL    HOURS(5)
DATA    HOURS(1) /60.0/
```

HOURS $\boxed{60.0}\boxed{?}\boxed{?}\boxed{?}\boxed{?}$

The question marks indicate that some array elements were not initialized by the DATA statement. A syntax error would have occurred if the subscript were left off the array reference HOURS(1) because the number of variables would then not match the number of data values; that is, HOURS represents 5 variables, but HOURS(1) represents only 1 variable.

An implied loop can also be used in a DATA statement to initialize all or part of an array, as in

```
INTEGER  YEAR(100)
DATA  (YEAR(I), I=1,50) /50*0/
```

The first 50 elements of the array are initialized to zero and the last 50 are not initialized. You must therefore make no assumptions about the contents of the last 50 values in the array.

5–3   APPLICATION—NATIONAL PARK SNOWFALL (Meteorology)

The daily snowfall for the month of January has been stored in a data file called JAN. Each data line contains 1 week of snowfall amounts recorded in inches. Line 1 contains the data for the first week in January; line 2 contains the data for the second week in January; and so on. Determine the average daily snowfall and the number of days with above-average snowfall for January.

PROBLEM STATEMENT

Compute the average snowfall for January and the number of days with above-average snowfall.

INPUT/OUTPUT DESCRIPTION

The input data is contained in a file called JAN that contains the snowfall for each day in January. The output is the average daily snowfall and the number of days with above-average snowfall.

HAND EXAMPLE

For a hand-worked example, we use 1 week's data instead of 1 month's data. The values are:

Day 1	4.2 inches
Day 2	3.1 inches
Day 3	1.5 inches
Day 4	0.2 inches
Day 5	0.0 inches
Day 6	0.0 inches
Day 7	1.8 inches

To determine the average value, we total the amounts and then divide by 7, which yields 10.8/7, or 1.54 inches. We now compare this value to the original data values and find that 3 days had snowfalls above the average. Notice that we had to use the data values twice—thus, we must use an array. The array allows us to read all the data to compute the total and still have all the values accessible for comparing them to the average.

ALGORITHM DEVELOPMENT

After completion of the hand-worked example, the initial decomposition is straightforward.

DECOMPOSITION

Read snowfall data.
Compute average snowfall.
Determine the number of days with above-average snowfall.
Print average, number of days.

In the refinement, we need two loops: one to total the data and the other to compare the data to the average. Note that the loops are independent. We must complete the first loop and calculate the average before we can compare the individual values to the average. Often, we can read a data value and add it to a total in the same loop, as shown:

```
      DO 10 I=1,31
         READ (10,*) SNOW(I)
         TOTAL = TOTAL + SNOW(I)
   10 CONTINUE
```

However, the preceding loop requires that the data be stored 1 value per line in the data file. Since our data file contains 1 week of data per data line, we must read the complete set of data before we can compute the total.

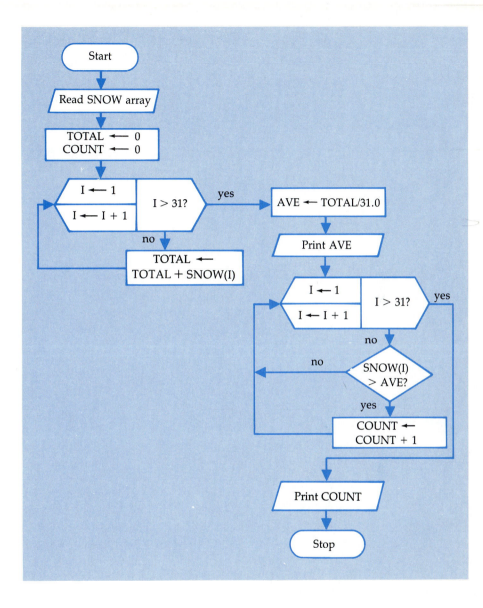

FORTRAN Program

```
*- - - - - - - - - - - - - - - - - - - - - - - - - - - - - - - - - - - - - - - - - - - - - - - - - - - - - - - - *
       PROGRAM  SNOFAL
*
*  This program computes the average snowfall
*  for January and counts the number of days
*  with above-average snowfall.
*
       INTEGER  COUNT
       REAL  SNOW(31), TOTAL, AVE
       DATA  TOTAL, COUNT /0.0, 0/
*
       OPEN (UNIT=10,FILE='JAN',STATUS='OLD')
       READ (10,*) SNOW
       PRINT 5, SNOW
     5 FORMAT (1X,4F8.1)
*
       DO 10 I=1,31
          TOTAL = TOTAL + SNOW(I)
    10 CONTINUE
       AVE = TOTAL/31.0
       PRINT 20, AVE
    20 FORMAT (1X,'AVERAGE SNOWFALL IS ',F5.2,' INCHES')
*
       DO 30 I=1,31
          IF (SNOW(I).GT.AVE) COUNT = COUNT + 1
    30 CONTINUE
       PRINT 40, COUNT
    40 FORMAT (1X,I2,' DAYS WITH ABOVE-AVERAGE SNOWFALL')
*
       END
*- - - - - - - - - - - - - - - - - - - - - - - - - - - - - - - - - - - - - - - - - - - - - - - - - - - - - - - - *
```

TESTING

The program includes a statement to print the original data, which is useful in debugging a program. How is the snowfall data printed? Is it 1 value per line or several values per line? Because the entire array is listed in a single PRINT statement, the number of values printed depends on the corresponding format specification; in this example, the values are printed 4 per line. This PRINT statement can be removed easily after the program has been carefully tested. Sometimes it is convenient to turn a PRINT statement into a comment by placing an asterisk in column 1: The statement is then ignored during compilation. If you make modifications to the program or if it does not seem to be working properly, it is easy to remove the asterisk and reactivate the PRINT statement in the program. The computer output that follows does not include the output from this PRINT statement, but it does show the last two lines of output:

DATA VALUES

```
4.2  3.1  1.5  0.2  0.0  0.0  1.8
1.1  0.9  0.0  0.0  0.0  0.2  0.0
0.9  1.4  1.2  0.3  0.0  0.0  0.0
0.0  0.0  1.5  1.2  0.4  1.6  0.7
0.3  0.0  0.0
```

```
AVERAGE SNOWFALL IS  0.73 INCHES
12 DAYS WITH ABOVE-AVERAGE SNOWFALL
```

5-4 SORTING ALGORITHMS

In this section we develop algorithms to sort a one-dimensional array or list in *ascending*, or low-to-high, order. (With minor alterations, the algorithm can be changed to one that sorts into *descending*, high-to-low, order. We will also see in Chapter 8 that these sort algorithms can be used to alphabetize character data.) The topic of sorting techniques is the subject of entire textbooks and courses; therefore this text will not attempt to present all the important aspects of sorting. Instead, we present three common sorting techniques and develop pseudocode and FORTRAN solutions for all three so that you can compare the different techniques.

Selection Sort This is a simple sort that is based on finding the minimum value and placing it first in the list, finding the next smallest value and placing it second in the list, and so on.

Bubble Sort This is a simple sort that is based on interchanging adjacent values in the array until all the values are in the proper position. This sort is sometimes called a multipass sort.

Insertion Sort This sort begins at the top of the list, comparing adjacent elements. If an element is out of order, it is continually exchanged with the value above it in the list until it is in its proper place. The sort then continues with the next element out of order.

No one sort algorithm is the best to use for all situations. In order to choose a good algorithm, you need to know something about the expected order of the data. For example, if your data is already very close to being in the correct order, both the insertion sort and the version of the bubble sort presented in this section are good choices. If your data is in a random order, or close to the opposite order desired, then the insertion sort or the selection sort are good choices. None of these sorts is efficient if you are sorting a very large set of data. You should consult texts which cover other types of sorts in order to choose a good sort algorithm for a large set of data.

In the three sort algorithms presented in this section we will use only one array. If you need to keep the original order of the data as well as the sorted data, copy the original data into a second array and sort it. Since the actual number of values in the array may be less than the maximum number of values that could be stored in it, we will assume that the variable COUNT specifies the actual number of data values to be sorted.

SELECTION SORT

We begin the discussion of the *selection sort* with a hand example. Consider the list of data values below:

Original List

4.1
7.3
1.7
5.2
1.3

In this algorithm, we first find the minimum value. Scanning down the list, we find that the last value, 1.3, is the minimum. We now want to put the value 1.3 in the first position of the array, but we do not want to lose the value 4.1 that is currently in the first position. Therefore, we will exchange the values.

The switch of two values requires three steps, not two as you might imagine. Consider these statements:

$$X(I) = X(J)$$
$$X(J) = X(I)$$

Suppose X(I) contained the value 3.0 and X(J) contained the value -1.0. The first statement will change the contents of X(I) from the value 3.0 to the value -1.0. The second statement will move the value in X(I) to X(J), so that both locations contain -1.0. These steps are shown next, along with the changes in the corresponding memory locations:

	X(I)	X(J)
	3.0	-1.0
X(I) = X(J)	-1.0	-1.0
X(J) = X(I)	-1.0	-1.0

A correct way to switch the two values is shown here, along with the changes in the corresponding memory locations:

	X(I)	X(J)	HOLD
	3.0	-1.0	?
HOLD = X(I)	3.0	-1.0	3.0
X(I) = X(J)	-1.0	-1.0	3.0
X(J) = HOLD	-1.0	3.0	3.0

Once we have switched the first value in the array with the value that has the minimum value, we search the values in the array from the second value to the last value for the minimum in that list. We then switch the second value with the minimum. We continue this until we are looking at the next-to-last and last values. If they are out of order, we switch them. At this point, the entire array will be sorted into an ascending order, as shown in the diagram below:

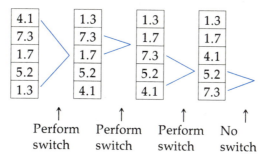

We now develop the pseudocode and FORTRAN statements for this selection sort.

DECOMPOSITION

Sort list of data values into ascending order.

In the refinement below, notice that we do not keep track of the minimum value itself; instead, we are interested in keeping track of the subscript or location of the minimum value. We need the subscript in order to be able to switch positions with another element in the array. Since the portion of the array that we search for the next minimum gets smaller, we use two variables, FIRST and LAST, to keep track of this array portion. FIRST will start at 2 and increment by one each time we do a switch. LAST will always be equal to COUNT since we search to the bottom of the list of valid values each time.

PSEUDOCODE FOR SELECTION SORT

(Assumes: the values are already stored in the array X; and a variable COUNT specifies the number of valid data values in the array.)

```
last ← count
For j = 1 to count − 1 do
    ptr ← j
    first ← j + 1
    For k = first to last do
        If x(k) < x(ptr) then
            ptr ← k
    Switch values in x(j) and x(ptr)
```

The only step that needs more detail is the step to switch values, because we must specify the three different moves that are necessary. We can add this additional detail as we convert the pseudocode to FORTRAN.

```
          .
          .
          .
     LAST = COUNT
     DO 10 J=1,COUNT-1
          PTR = J
          FIRST = J + 1
          DO 5 K=FIRST,LAST
               IF (X(K).LT.X(PTR)) PTR = K
  5       CONTINUE
          HOLD = X(J)
          X(J) = X(PTR)
          X(PTR) = HOLD
 10  CONTINUE
```

BUBBLE SORT

The basic step to the *bubble sort* algorithm is a single pass through the array, comparing adjacent elements. If a pair of adjacent elements is in the correct order (that is, the first value less than or equal to the second value), we go to the next pair. If the pair is out of order, we switch the values and then go to the next pair.

The single pass through the array can be performed in a counting loop with index J. Each pair of adjacent values will be referred to by the subscripts J and J + 1. If the number of valid data elements in the array is stored in COUNT, we will make COUNT − 1 comparisons of adjacent values in a single pass through the array.

A single pass through a one-dimensional array, switching adjacent elements that are out of order, is not guaranteed to sort the values. Consider a single pass through the following array:

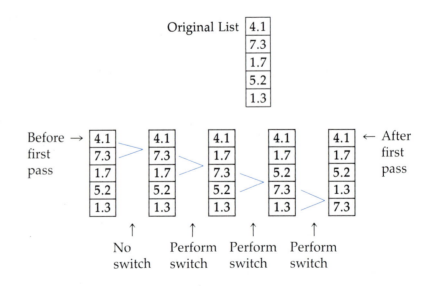

It will take two more complete passes before the array is sorted into ascending order, as shown in the following diagram:

After first pass		After second pass	
4.1		1.7	
1.7		4.1	
5.2		1.3	
1.3		5.2	
7.3		7.3	

After third pass		After fourth pass	
1.7		1.3	
1.3		1.7	
4.1		4.1	
5.2		5.1	
7.3		7.3	

A maximum of COUNT passes may be necessary to sort an array with this technique. If no switches are made during a single pass through the array, however, it is in ascending order. Thus, our algorithm for sorting a one-dimensional array will be to perform single passes through the array making switches until no elements are out of order. In developing the pseudocode we use a logical variable SORTED that is initialized to true at the beginning of each pass through the data array. If any adjacent values are out of order, we switch the values and then change the value of SORTED to false because at least one pair of values was out of order on the pass. At the end of a pass through the data, if the value of SORTED is still true, the array is in ascending order.

We will make one more addition to the algorithm. Observe that during the first pass through the array we switch any adjacent pairs that are out of order. Although this does not necessarily sort the entire array, it is guaranteed to move the largest value to the bottom of the list. During the second pass, the next-largest value will be moved to the next-to-the-last position. Therefore, when we make each pass through the array, we must start at the first position, but we do not need to check values all the way to the end. In fact, with each pass we can reduce the number of positions that we check by one.

We now develop the pseudocode and FORTRAN statements for this bubble sort.

DECOMPOSITION

Sort list of data values into ascending order.

Pseudocode for Bubble Sort

(Assumes: the values are already stored in the array X; and a variable COUNT specifies the number of valid data values in the array.)

```
sorted ← false
first ← 1
last ← count − 1
While not sorted do
    sorted ← true
    For j = first to last do
        If x(j) > x(j + 1) then
            Switch values
                sorted ← false
    last ← last − 1
```

The only step that needs more detail is the step to switch values, because we need to specify the three different moves that are necessary. These moves are specified in the following FORTRAN statements.

FORTRAN Statements

```
       .
       .
       .
       SORTED = .FALSE.
       FIRST = 1
       LAST = COUNT − 1
    5  IF (.NOT.SORTED) THEN
           SORTED = .TRUE.
           DO 10 J=FIRST,LAST
               IF (X(J).GT.X(J+1)) THEN
                   HOLD = X(J)
                   X(J) = X(J+1)
                   X(J+1) = HOLD
                   SORTED = .FALSE.
               ENDIF
   10      CONTINUE
           LAST = LAST − 1
           GO TO 5
       ENDIF
```

INSERTION SORT

The *insertion sort* starts at the beginning of the list, comparing adjacent elements. If an element is out of order, we switch it with the previous element and check to see if it is now in its proper place. If not, we switch it with the new previous element, and again check. We continue moving the element up in the array until it is in its proper position. We then return to the position in the list where we located the element out of order and pick up at that point, comparing the next pair of adjacent elements. When we reach the end of the list, it will be in order because each element that we found out of order was inserted in its proper position before we continued. The following diagram shows these steps with our sample array.

Original List

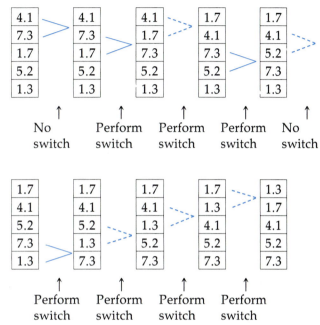

We now develop the pseudocode and FORTRAN statements for this insertion sort.

DECOMPOSITION

Sort list of data values into ascending order.

In the following refinement, notice that we use the subscript *j* of the counting loop to point to our position before we begin backing up in the array to find the proper position for the element out of order. After putting the element in the correct spot, we can jump back to the next pair of elements in the list that we need to compare, since the value of the subscript *j* has not been changed.

Pseudocode for Insertion Sort

(Assumes: the values are already stored in the array X; and a variable COUNT specifies the number of valid data values in the array.)

For j = 1 to count − 1 do
  If x(j) > x(j + 1) then
    done ← false
    k ← j
    While not done do
      Switch x(k) with x(k + 1)
      If (k = 1) or (x(k) ≥ x(k − 1)) then
        done ← true
      Else
        k ← k − 1

Again, the step to switch values will need the three moves necessary to interchange the values of x(k) and x(k+1). The corresponding FORTRAN statements are then the following:

FORTRAN Statements

```
      .
      .
      .
      DO 10 J=1,COUNT-1
         IF (X(J).GT.X(J+1)) THEN
            DONE = .FALSE.
            K = J
    5       IF (.NOT.DONE) THEN
               HOLD = X(K)
               X(K) = X(K+1)
               X(K+1) = HOLD
               IF (K.EQ.1) THEN
                  DONE = .TRUE.
               ELSEIF (X(K).GT.X(K-1)) THEN
                  DONE = .TRUE.
               ELSE
                  K = K - 1
               ENDIF
               GO TO 5
            ENDIF
         ENDIF
   10 CONTINUE
```

The final condition was separated into two separate conditions in the FORTRAN statements because it would be invalid to examine X(K − 1) if K has the value 1.

This self-test allows you to check quickly to see if you have remembered certain key points from Section 5–4. If you have any problems with the exercises, you should reread this section. The solutions are included at the end of the text. Consider the following list with six elements in it:

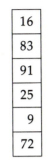

| 16 |
| 83 |
| 91 |
| 25 |
| 9 |
| 72 |

1. Show the sequence of changes that occur in the list if it is sorted using the selection sort algorithm.
2. Show the sequence of changes that occur in the list if it is sorted using the bubble sort algorithm.
3. Show the sequence of changes that occur in the list if it is sorted using the insertion sort algorithm.

5–5 APPLICATION—EARTHQUAKE MEASUREMENTS (Civil Engineering)

In this application we analyze data that might be collected in a field laboratory that monitors seismic (earthquake) activity. This data is collected by instruments called seismometers that are located around the world. Suppose that a location in California has been the site of earthquake activity for a number of years. The magnitude of each event has been recorded using the Richter scale. This data is stored in a data file MOTION in the chronological order in which the earthquakes occurred. Write a program to read this information, sort it into ascending order based on magnitude, and print the data in this new order.

The initial line of the data file contains a five-digit integer that represents the location number for the laboratory. When new earthquakes occur, the information is added to the end of the file. Therefore, you do not know ahead of time how many data values are in the file. You can, however, assume an upper limit of 200 data values.

PROBLEM STATEMENT

Sort a group of earthquake measurements into ascending order and print the values in the new order.

INPUT/OUTPUT DESCRIPTION

The earthquake measurements are stored in a data file, 1 value per line. The first line of the data file contains a location number. The number of entries in the file is not known ahead of time. The output is to be a listing of the same set of data sorted into an ascending order.

HAND EXAMPLE

Using the following example test file data, we sort the data into ascending order and print it.

DATA FILE MOTION

```
17758
2.5810
1.5000
1.6200
3.7800
4.2500
1.7330
```

SORTED OUTPUT LIST

```
1.5000
1.6200
1.7330
2.5810
3.7800
4.2500
```

ALGORITHM DEVELOPMENT

In Section 5–4 we presented three different sort techniques. Any of the three techniques could be used in this example; we have selected the first sort algorithm, the selection sort. You may want to review the selection sort algorithm before continuing with this development.

The decomposition of this problem solution breaks into the following steps:

DECOMPOSITION

| Read location number. |
| Print location number. |
| Read quake values. |
| Sort quake values. |
| Print quake values. |

Initial Refinement in Pseudocode

EARTH: Read location number
    Print location number
    $i \leftarrow 1$
    While more quake data do
        Read quake(i)
        $i \leftarrow i + 1$
    $n \leftarrow i - 1$
    Sort quake array
    Print quake array

We now refine the sort step using the selection sort algorithm. The steps are copied here from the previous section, with the appropriate change in variable names.

Final Refinement in Pseudocode

EARTH: Read location number
    Print location number
    $i \leftarrow 1$
    While more quake data do
        READ quake(i)
        $i \leftarrow i + 1$
    $n \leftarrow i - 1$
    last $\leftarrow n$
    For j = 1 to n − 1 do
        ptr $\leftarrow$ j
        first $\leftarrow$ j + 1
        For k = first to last do
            If x(k) < x(ptr) then
                ptr $\leftarrow$ k
        Switch values in x(j) and x(ptr)
    Print quake array

The only step that needs more detail is the step to switch values, because we must specify the three different moves that are necessary. We can add this additional detail as we convert the pseudocode to FORTRAN.

FORTRAN Program

```
*--------------------------------------------------------------*
       PROGRAM  EARTH
*
*  This program will read a file of earthquake data
*  and sort and print it in ascending order.
*
       INTEGER  LOCATE, I, N, J, PTR, LAST, FIRST, K
       REAL  QUAKE(200), HOLD
*
       OPEN (UNIT=9,FILE='MOTION',STATUS='OLD')
       READ (9,*) LOCATE
       PRINT 5, LOCATE
     5 FORMAT (1X,'LOCATION NUMBER: ',I5)
*
       I = 1
    10 READ (9,*,END=20) QUAKE(I)
          I = I + 1
          GO TO 10
*
    20 N = I - 1
       LAST = N
       DO 40 J=1,N-1
          PTR = J
          FIRST = J + 1
          DO 30 K = FIRST, LAST
             IF (QUAKE(K).LT.QUAKE(PTR)) PTR = K
    30     CONTINUE
          HOLD = QUAKE(J)
          QUAKE(J) = QUAKE(PTR)
          QUAKE(PTR) = HOLD
    40 CONTINUE
*
       DO 60 I=1,N
          PRINT 50  I, QUAKE(I)
    50     FORMAT (1X,I3,'.',3X,F6.4)
    60 CONTINUE
*
       END
*--------------------------------------------------------------*
```

TESTING

As our programs become longer, testing becomes more of a challenge; a good procedure is to test the program in pieces. An easy way to accomplish this is to insert PRINT statements followed by a STOP statement after the portion of the program that you want to check. When you are convinced that this portion is working, remove the PRINT statements and the STOP statement and modify them to check the next portion. For example, to test the input portion of the program just developed, insert the following statements after statement 20:

```
      PRINT 22, LOCATE, N
   22 FORMAT (1X,'LOCATION = ',I5,'; N = ',I4)
      PRINT 23
   23 FORMAT (1X,'QUAKE DATA:')
      PRINT 24, (QUAKE (I), I=1,N)
   24 FORMAT (1X,5F5.2)
      STOP
```

To test the sort portion, use a small data set so that you are not overwhelmed with data. Insert the PRINT statements previously used to print the QUAKE array just after statement 40; this will print the data values after each pass through the array, just as we did in the hand-worked example. If there are problems, move the PRINT statements inside the DO loop, just before statement 40, which will allow you to see the results of each comparison. Notice how these pieces that we test individually correspond to the overall steps in the initial decomposition.

When you have the algorithm working, be sure to use a variety of test data sets. Use sets that are already in order and sets that are in reverse order, in addition to sequences in random order. The output from a sample set of data would be in this form:

DATA FILE MOTION

```
                  17758
                  2.5810
                  1.5000
                  1.6200
                  3.7800
                  4.2500
                  1.7330
```

COMPUTER OUTPUT

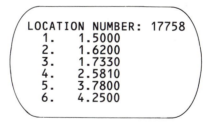

```
LOCATION NUMBER:  17758
   1.     1.5000
   2.     1.6200
   3.     1.7330
   4.     2.5810
   5.     3.7800
   6.     4.2500
```

After sorting the array QUAKE, we changed the order of the values from one that was sequential in time to one that is in ascending order. In so doing, we lost the original order within our program. The data file is still in the original order, but our program has the data only in ascending order. If the program also needed the original data, we could copy the original data into a second array after it was read, but before it was sorted. Then, after sorting, we would have two arrays of data—one in the original order and one in ascending order.

5-6 TWO-DIMENSIONAL ARRAYS

If we visualize a one-dimensional array as a single column of data, we can visualize a two-dimensional array as a group of columns, as illustrated:

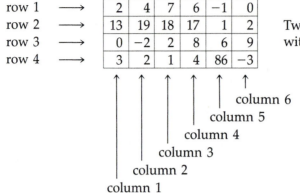

Two-dimensional array with 4 rows and 6 columns

The diagram depicts an integer array with 24 elements. As in one-dimensional arrays, each of the 24 elements has the same array name. However, one subscript is not sufficient to specify an element in a two-dimensional array; for instance, if the array's name is M, it is not clear whether M(3) should be the third element in the first row or the third element in the first column. To avoid ambiguity, elements in a two-dimensional array are referenced with two subscripts: The first subscript references the row and the second subscript references the column. Thus, M(2,3) refers to the number in the second row, third column. In our diagram, M(2,3) contains the value 18.

STORAGE AND INITIALIZATION

Two-dimensional arrays must be specified with a DIMENSION statement or a type statement — but not both. The following type statements reserve storage for a one-dimensional real array B of 10 elements, a two-dimensional real array C with 3 rows and 5 columns, a two-dimensional real array NUM with 5 rows and 2 columns, and a two-dimensional integer array J with 7 rows and 4 columns:

```
REAL   B(10), C(3,5), NUM(5,2)
INTEGER  J(7,4)
```

This next statement reserves storage for a two-dimensional array with three rows and three columns:

```
REAL   R(0:2,-1:1)
```

Two-dimensional arrays can be initialized with assignment statements, with input statements, and with the DATA statement. A two-dimensional array name can be used without subscripts in input statements, DATA statements, and output statements; if the name of the array is used in one of these statements without subscripts, the array is accessed in column order. We will always explicitly use subscripts with two-dimensional arrays in order to be clear whether we are referencing the array elements in row order or in column order. It is common notation to use I for the row subscript and J for the column subscript.

EXAMPLE 5-5   **Array Initialization, AREA**

Define an array AREA with 5 rows and 4 columns. Fill it with the values shown:

1.0	1.0	2.0	2.0
1.0	1.0	2.0	2.0
1.0	1.0	2.0	2.0
1.0	1.0	2.0	2.0
1.0	1.0	2.0	2.0

Solution 1

```
REAL   AREA(5,4)
 .
 .
 .
DO 10 I=1,5
    AREA(I,1) = 1.0
    AREA(I,2) = 1.0
    AREA(I,3) = 2.0
    AREA(I,4) = 2.0
10 CONTINUE
```

Solution 2

```
REAL   AREA(5,4)
DATA   ((AREA(I,J),I=1,5),J=1,4) /10*1.0, 10*2.0/
```

EXAMPLE 5-6   **Array Initialization, SUM**

Define and fill the integer array SUM as shown:

1	1	1
2	2	2
3	3	3
4	4	4

Solution 1

If we observe that each element of the array contains its corresponding row number, then the following solution can be used:

```
INTEGER  SUM(4,3)
 .
 .
 .
DO 10 I=1,4
    DO 5 J=1,3
        SUM(I,J) = I
5     CONTINUE
10 CONTINUE
```

Solution 2

The following DATA statements also initialize the array correctly:

```
INTEGER  SUM(4,3)
DATA  ((SUM(I,J),I=1,4),J=1,3)   /3*(1, 2, 3, 4)/
```

or

```
INTEGER  SUM(4,3)
DATA  ((SUM(I,J),J=1,3),I=1,4)   /3*1, 3*2, 3*3, 3*4/
```

EXAMPLE 5-7   **Identity Matrix**

A *matrix* is another name for a two-dimensional array. When using matrix operations to solve engineering and science problems, we frequently use a matrix called an *identity matrix*. This matrix has the same number of rows as columns, so it is also called a *square matrix*. The identity matrix contains all 0's except for the main diagonal elements, which are 1's. (The main diagonal is composed of elements that have the same value for row number and for column number.) An identity matrix with 5 rows and 5 columns is shown.

1.0	0.0	0.0	0.0	0.0
0.0	1.0	0.0	0.0	0.0
0.0	0.0	1.0	0.0	0.0
0.0	0.0	0.0	1.0	0.0
0.0	0.0	0.0	0.0	1.0

Define and fill an array with these values.

Solution

Because the value 1.0 appears at different positions in each row of the array, we cannot use the same type of solution we used in Example 5–6. If we list the elements that contain the value 1.0, we find that they are positions (1,1), (2,2), (3,3), (4,4), and (5,5); thus, the row and the column number are the same value. Recognizing this pattern, we can initialize the array as follows:

```
REAL   IDEN(5,5)
    .
    .
    .
DO 10 I=1,5
    DO 5 J=1,5
        IF (I.EQ.J) THEN
            IDEN(I,J) = 1.0
        ELSE
            IDEN(I,J) = 0.0
        ENDIF
5       CONTINUE
10 CONTINUE
```

INPUT AND OUTPUT

The main difference between using values from a one-dimensional array and using values from a two-dimensional array is that the latter requires two subscripts. Most loops used in the reading or printing of two-dimensional arrays are therefore nested loops.

EXAMPLE 5-8 **Medical Data**

The analysis of a medical experiment requires the use of a set of data containing the weight of 100 participants at the beginning and at the end of an experiment. The integer data values have been stored in a data file and are accessed using unit number 13. Each line in the file contains the initial weight and the final weight of a participant. Give statements to define a two-dimensional array to store the data and to read the information from the file into the array.

Solution 1

```
      INTEGER  WEIGHT(100,2)
      .
      .
      .
      DO 10 I=1,100
          READ (13,*) WEIGHT(I,1), WEIGHT(I,2)
   10 CONTINUE
```

Solution 2

```
      INTEGER  WEIGHT(100,2)
      .
      .
      .
      READ (13,*) (WEIGHT(I,1), WEIGHT(I,2), I=1,100)
```

EXAMPLE 5-9 **Terminal Inventory**

A large technical firm keeps an inventory of the locations of its computer terminals in a data file. Assume that this data has already been read into a two-dimensional array. There are 4 types of terminals, represented by the 4 columns, and 20 laboratories using the terminals, represented by the 20 rows of the array. Print the data in a form similar to the following:

```
      TERMINAL INVENTORY
      ------------------------
      TYPE       1   2   3   4
      ------------------------
      LAB  1    XX  XX  XX  XX
      LAB  2    XX  XX  XX  XX
      .
      .
      LAB 20    XX  XX  XX  XX
```

Solution

This solution uses the index of a DO loop as the row subscript. The index of an implied loop in the PRINT statement supplies the column subscript. Thus, each time the PRINT statement is executed, one row of data is printed.

```
      INTEGER  INVEN(20,4)
      .
      .
      .
      PRINT 5
    5 FORMAT (1X,'TERMINAL INVENTORY')
      PRINT 10
   10 FORMAT (1X,'---------------------------')
      PRINT 15
   15 FORMAT (1X,'TYPE        1    2    3    4')
      PRINT 20
   20 FORMAT (1X,'---------------------------')
      DO 200 I=1,20
          PRINT 30, I, (INVEN(I,J), J=1,4)
   30     FORMAT (1X,'LAB',I4,3X,I2,3X,I2,3X,I2,3X,I2)
  200 CONTINUE
```

SELF-TEST 5–3

This self-test allows you to check quickly to see if you have remembered some of the key points from Section 5–6. If you have any problems with the exercises, you should reread this section. The solutions are included at the end of the text.

Problems 1–3 contain statements that initialize and print two-dimensional arrays. Draw the array and indicate the contents of each position in the array. Then, show the output from each set of statements. Assume that each set of statements is independent of the others.

```
1.    INTEGER  I, J, CH(5,4)
      DO 10 I=1,5
          DO 5 J=1,4
              CH(I,J) = I*J
    5     CONTINUE
   10 CONTINUE
      PRINT 15, (CH(3,J),J=1,4)
   15 FORMAT (1X,I5)

2.    INTEGER  I, J, K(3,3)
      DO 20 I=1,3
          K(I,1) = 5
          K(I,2) = -5
          K(I,3) = 0
   20 CONTINUE
      PRINT 30 (K(3,J), J=1,3)
   30 FORMAT (1X,I4)
```

```
3.    INTEGER  I, J
      REAL   DIST(4,3), SUM
      SUM = 10.0
      DO 10 J=1,3
         DO 5 I=1,4
            SUM = SUM + 1.5
            DIST(I,J) = SUM
    5    CONTINUE
   10 CONTINUE
      DO 20 I=1,2
         PRINT 15, (DIST(I,J), J=1,3)
   15    FORMAT (1X,3F5.1)
   20 CONTINUE
```

5–7 APPLICATION—POWER PLANT DATA ANALYSIS (Power Engineering)

The following table of data represents typical power outputs in megawatts from a power plant over a period of 8 weeks. Each row represents 1 week's data; each column represents data taken on the same day of the week. The data is stored 1 row per data line in a data file called PLANT.

	Day 1	Day 2	Day 3	Day 4	Day 5	Day 6	Day 7
Week 1	207	301	222	302	22	167	125
Week 2	367	60	120	111	301	400	434
Week 3	211	72	441	102	21	203	317
Week 4	401	340	161	297	441	117	206
Week 5	448	111	370	220	264	444	207
Week 6	21	313	204	222	446	401	337
Week 7	213	208	444	321	320	335	313
Week 8	162	137	265	44	370	315	322

A program is needed to read the data, analyze it, and print the results in the following composite report:

```
              COMPOSITE INFORMATION
AVERAGE DAILY POWER OUTPUT = XXX.X MEGAWATTS
NUMBER OF DAYS WITH GREATER THAN AVERAGE POWER OUTPUT = XX
DAY(S) WITH MINIMUM POWER OUTPUT:
         WEEK X    DAY X
            .
            .
            .
```

Analyze a set of data from a power plant to determine its average daily power output, the number of days with greater-than-average output, and the day or days that had minimum power output.

INPUT/OUTPUT DESCRIPTION

The input is a data file with 1 week's data per line, in an integer form. The file contains data for 8 weeks. The output is to be a report as shown:

```
              COMPOSITE INFORMATION
AVERAGE DAILY POWER OUTPUT = XXX.X MEGAWATTS
NUMBER OF DAYS WITH GREATER THAN AVERAGE POWER OUTPUT = XX
DAY(S) WITH MINIMUM POWER OUTPUT:
          WEEK X    DAY X
          .
          .
          .
```

HAND EXAMPLE

For the hand-worked example, we use a smaller set of data, but one that still maintains the two-dimensional array form. Consider this set of data:

	Day 1	Day 2
Week 1	311	405
Week 2	210	264
Week 3	361	210

First, we must sum all the values and divide by 6 to determine the average, which yields 1761/6, or 293.5 megawatts. Second, we compare each value to the average to determine how many values were greater than the average. In our small set of data, 3 values were greater than the average. Third, we must determine the number of days with minimum power output, which involves two steps: going through the data again to determine the minimum value; and going back through the data to find the day or days with the minimum power value, then printing its/their position(s) in the array. Using the small set of data, we find that the minimum value is 210, and it occurred on two days. Thus, the output from our hand-worked example is

```
              COMPOSITE INFORMATION
AVERAGE DAILY POWER OUTPUT = 293.5 MEGAWATTS
NUMBER OF DAYS WITH GREATER THAN AVERAGE POWER OUTPUT = 3
DAY(S) WITH MINIMUM POWER OUTPUT:
          WEEK 2    DAY 1
          WEEK 3    DAY 2
```

ALGORITHM DEVELOPMENT

Before we decompose the problem solution, it is important to spend some time considering the best way to store the data that we need for the program. Unfortunately, once we become comfortable with arrays, we tend to overuse them. Using an array complicates our programs because of the subscript handling. We should always ask ourselves, "Should we really use an array for this data?"

If the individual data values will be needed more than once, an array is probably required. An array is also necessary if the data is not in the order needed. In general, arrays are helpful when we must read all the data before we can go back and begin processing it. However, if an average of a group of data values is all that is to be computed, we probably do not need an array; as we read the values, we can add them to a total, and read the next value into the same memory location as the previous value. The individual values are not needed again because all the information required is now in the total.

Now, let us look at our specific problem and determine whether or not we need to use an array. First, we need to compute an average daily power output. Then, we need to count the number of days with output greater than average, which requires that we compare each output value to the average. For this application, we need to store all the data in an array, and a two-dimensional array is the best choice of data structure.

When we performed the solution by hand, we made several passes through the data to obtain different pieces of information. As we begin to develop the computer solution, we would like to minimize the number of passes through the data. We can compute the sum of the data points in the same loop in which we determine the minimum data value. However, we must make a separate pass through the data to determine how many values are greater than the average. Because the number of days with greater-than-average output is printed before we print the specific day or days that has/ have minimum output, we need separate loops for these operations. For this solution, we need three loops (passes) through the array.

DECOMPOSITION

Read data.
Compute information.
Print information.

INITIAL REFINEMENT IN PSEUDOCODE

PWRPLT: Read data
          Compute average power and minimum power
          Print average power
          Count days with above-average power
          Print count of days
          Print days with minimum power

FINAL REFINEMENT IN PSEUDOCODE

PWRPLT: Read data
          Compute average and minimum value
          Print heading, average
          count ← 0
          For each data value do
             If data value > average then
                 count ← count + 1
          Print count
          For each data value do
             If data value = minimum then
                 Print row position, column position

FORTRAN Program

```
*-----------------------------------------------------*
      PROGRAM  PWRPLT
*
*  This program computes and prints a composite report
*  summarizing eight weeks of power plant data.
*
      INTEGER  POWER(8,7), MIN, TOTAL, COUNT, I, J
      REAL  AVE
      DATA  TOTAL, COUNT /0, 0/
*
      OPEN (UNIT=12,FILE='PLANT',STATUS='OLD')
      DO 5 I=1,8
         READ (12,*) (POWER(I,J), J=1,7)
    5 CONTINUE
*
      MIN = POWER(1,1)
      DO 15 I=1,8
         DO 10 J=1,7
            TOTAL = TOTAL + POWER(I,J)
            IF (POWER(I,J).LT.MIN) MIN = POWER(I,J)
   10    CONTINUE
   15 CONTINUE
      AVE = REAL(TOTAL)/56.0
*
      DO 25 I=1,8
         DO 20 J=1,7
            IF (POWER(I,J).GT.AVE) COUNT = COUNT + 1
   20    CONTINUE
   25 CONTINUE
*
```

```
      PRINT 30
   30 FORMAT (1X,15X,'COMPOSITE INFORMATION')
      PRINT 35, AVE
   35 FORMAT (1X,'AVERAGE DAILY POWER OUTPUT = ',F5.1,
      +          ' MEGAWATTS')
      PRINT 40, COUNT
   40 FORMAT (1X,'NUMBER OF DAYS WITH GREATER THAN ',
      +          'AVERAGE POWER OUTPUT = ',I2)
      PRINT 45
   45 FORMAT (1X,'DAY(S) WITH MINIMUM POWER OUTPUT:')
      DO 60 I=1,8
         DO 55 J=1,7
            IF (POWER(I,J).EQ.MIN) PRINT 50, I, J
   50       FORMAT (1X,12X,'WEEK ',I2,'   DAY ',I2)
   55    CONTINUE
   60 CONTINUE
*
      END
*- - - - - - - - - - - - - - - - - - - - - - - - - - - - - - - - - - - - - - - - - - - - -*
```

This program should be tested in stages; again, the decomposition gives a good idea of the overall steps involved and can thus be used to identify the steps that should be tested individually. Remember that one of the most useful tools for debugging is the PRINT statement—use it to print the values of key variables in loops that may contain errors.

The output from this program using the data file given at the beginning of this section is

```
               COMPOSITE INFORMATION
AVERAGE DAILY POWER OUTPUT = 254.4 MEGAWATTS
NUMBER OF DAYS WITH GREATER THAN AVERAGE POWER OUTPUT = 29
DAY(S) WITH MINIMUM POWER OUTPUT:
            WEEK  3    DAY  5
            WEEK  6    DAY  1
```

5–8 APPLICATION—TERRAIN NAVIGATION
(Aeronautical Engineering)

The study of terrain navigation has become popular with the advent of remotely-piloted vehicles such as planes, missiles, and tanks. The systems that guide these vehicles must be tested over a variety of land formations and topologies. Elevation information for large grids of land is available in computer databases. One way of measuring the "difficulty" of a land grid with respect to terrain navigation is to determine the number of peaks in the grid (a peak is a point that has lower elevations all around it).

The program we develop in this application will read the elevation information for a set of grids. Then, for each grid, we will determine the number of peaks in that grid according to our definition.

We assume that the file that contains the elevation information is called ELEVTN. The first line for each grid contains an identification number. The second line contains the number of points along the side of the grid and the number of points along the top of the grid. The elevation data for that grid then begins on the next line, with the data for the top row first, then the second row, and so on. If the data for the first row does not fit on one line, as many lines as are needed will be used. However, each new row of data will begin on a new line. The last line in the data file contains an identification number of 99999. You can assume that the maximum size grid will be 100 points by 100 points. For each grid, print the identification number, the total number of points in the grid, and the number of peaks in the grid.

PROBLEM STATEMENT

Determine the number of peaks in a grid of elevation values, where we assume that a peak is defined by a point that is higher than all four of its surrounding points.

INPUT/OUTPUT DESCRIPTION

The input is a data file called ELEVTN that contains information on a number of grids. Each set of information contains the grid identification, the number of points along the side of the grid, the number of points along the top of the grid, and the elevations points in row order. The output is to be a report that lists each grid identification number, the total number of points in the grid, and the number of peaks within the grid.

HAND EXAMPLE

Assume that the following data represents the elevations for a grid that has 6 points along the side and 8 points along the top. We have circled peaks within the data.

```
92547
6   8
25    59    63    23    21    34    21    50
32    45    43    30    37    32    30    27
34    38    38    39    36    28    28    35
40    45    42    48    32    30    27    25
39    39    40    42    48    49    25    30
31    31    31    32    32    33    44    35
99999
```

The output for this grid is

IDENTIFICATION	NUMBER OF POINTS	NUMBER OF PEAKS
92547	48	4

You probably realized that the search for peaks need only consider interior points in the grid. A point along the edge cannot be counted as a peak because we do not know the elevation on one of its sides. If we are considering a point at location MAP(I,J), then the four adjacent points are at positions MAP(I − 1,J), MAP(I + 1,J), MAP(I,J − 1), and MAP(I,J + 1), as shown:

	MAP(I-1,J)	
MAP(I,J-1)	MAP(I,J)	MAP(I,J+1)
	MAP(I+1,J)	

Thus, for MAP(I,J) to be a peak, the following must be true:

```
MAP(I,J-1) < MAP(I,J)
MAP(I,J+1) < MAP(I,J)
MAP(I-1,J) < MAP(I,J)
MAP(I+1,J) < MAP(I,J)
```

If all of these conditions are met for a point MAP(I,J), it represents a peak.

DECOMPOSITION

Print heading.
Read map information and generate report.

REFINEMENT IN PSEUDOCODE

NAVIG: Print heading
     Read ID
     While ID not = 99999 do
       Read NROW, NCOL
       Read array MAP
       count ← 0
       For each interior point do
         If interior point is higher than all four
           adjacent points then increment count
       Print ID, number of peaks
       Read ID

```
*------------------------------------------------------------------*
      PROGRAM  NAVIG
*
*  This program reads the elevation data for a set of land
*  grids and determines the number of peaks in each grid.
*
      INTEGER  MAP(100,100), I, J, ID, NROWS, NCOLS, COUNT
*
      PRINT 5
    5 FORMAT (1X,'SUMMARY OF LAND GRID ANALYSIS')
      PRINT 10
   10 FORMAT (1X,'IDENTIFICATION   NUMBER OF POINTS   ',
      +          'NUMBER OF PEAKS')
*
      OPEN (UNIT=15,FILE='ELEVTN',STATUS='OLD')
      READ (15,*) ID
   15 IF (ID.NE.99999) THEN
         READ (15,*) NROWS, NCOLS
         DO 20 I=1,NROWS
            READ (15,*) (MAP(I,J), J=1,NCOLS)
   20    CONTINUE
         COUNT = 0
         DO 30 I=2,NROWS-1
            DO 25 J=2,NCOLS-1
               IF ((MAP(I-1,J).LT.MAP(I,J)).AND.
      +            (MAP(I+1,J).LT.MAP(I,J)).AND.
      +            (MAP(I,J-1).LT.MAP(I,J)).AND.
      +            (MAP(I,J+1).LT.MAP(I,J))) THEN
                     COUNT = COUNT + 1
               ENDIF
   25       CONTINUE
   30    CONTINUE
         PRINT 35, ID, NROWS*NCOLS, COUNT
   35    FORMAT (1X,I7,10X,I7,10X,I7)
         READ (15,*) ID
         GO TO 15
      ENDIF
*
      END
*------------------------------------------------------------------*
```

TESTING

Using the data from the hand-worked example, our output is

```
SUMMARY OF LAND GRID ANALYSIS
IDENTIFICATION    NUMBER OF POINTS    NUMBER OF PEAKS
  92547                 48                  4
```

As you try to think of any special cases that might cause problems for this program, you can probably think of some unique grid shapes, such as grids with 1 or 2 rows or 1 or 2 columns. If we look at our program, we see that the DO loops used in counting peaks are

```
DO 30 I=2,NROWS-1
   DO 25 J=2,NCOLS-1
```

If we substitute 2 for NROWS and NCOLS, we have the following loops:

```
DO 30 I=2,1
   DO 25 J=2,1
```

These loops would not be executed, and because the number of peaks was initialized to zero, the number of peaks would remain at zero. Thus, the program can handle these unique grid cases correctly. If the values of NROWS and NCOLS were less than 1 or greater than 100, then the program would not work correctly. It might be a good idea to test NROWS and NCOLS after they are read and print an appropriate error message if they are out of bounds.

Note: This program will locate individual peaks; but, it will not locate a ridge where two or more adjacent peaks are at the same elevation. Our algorithm would need to be modified if we were interested in this type of formation.

5–9 MULTIDIMENSIONAL ARRAYS

FORTRAN allows as many as seven dimensions for arrays. We can easily visualize a three-dimensional array, such as a cube. We are also familiar with using three coordinates, X, Y, and Z, to locate points. This idea extends into subscripts. The following three-dimensional array could be defined with this statement:

```
REAL   T(3,4,4)
```

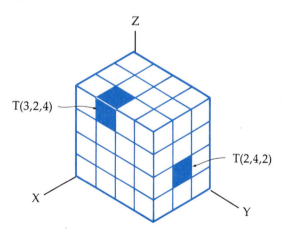

If we use the three-dimensional array name without subscripts, we access the array with the first subscript changing fastest, the second subscript changing second fastest, and the third subscript changing the slowest. Thus, using the array T from the previous diagram, these two statements are equivalent:

```
READ *, T

READ *, (((T(I,J,K), I=1,3), J=1,4), K=1,4)
```

It should be evident that three levels of nesting in DO loops are often needed to access a three-dimensional array.

Most applications do not use arrays with more than three dimensions, probably because visualizing more than three dimensions seems too abstract. However, here is a simple scheme that may help you to picture even a seven-dimensional array.

Four-Dimensional Array Picture a row of three-dimensional arrays. The first subscript specifies a unique three-dimensional array. The other three subscripts specify a unique position in that array.

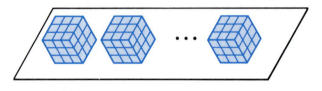

Five-Dimensional Array Picture a block or grid of three-dimensional arrays. The first two subscripts specify a unique three-dimensional array. The other three subscripts specify a unique position in that array.

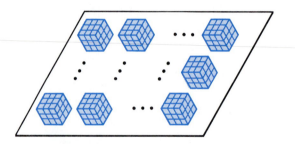

Six-Dimensional Array Picture a row of blocks or grids. One subscript specifies the grid. The other five subscripts specify the unique position in the grid.

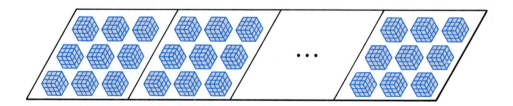

Seven-Dimensional Array Picture a grid of grids or a grid of blocks. Two subscripts specify the grid. The other five subscripts specify the unique position in the grid.

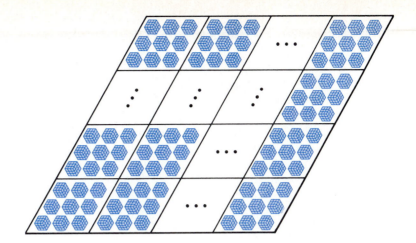

Now that you can visualize multidimensional arrays, a natural question is "What dimension array do I use for solving a problem?" There is no single answer. A problem that can be solved with a two-dimensional array of 4 rows and 3 columns can also be solved with four one-dimensional arrays of 3 elements each. Usually, the data fits one array form better than another; you should choose the form that is the easiest for you to work with in your program. For example, if you have census data from 10 countries over the period 1950–1980, you would probably use an array with 10 rows and 31 columns, or 31 rows and 10 columns. If the data represents the populations of 5 cities from each of 10 countries for the period 1950–1980, a three-dimensional array would be most appropriate: The three subscripts would represent year, country, and city.

SUMMARY

In this chapter we learned how to use an array — a group of storage locations that all have a common name but are distinguished by one or more subscripts. Arrays are one of the most powerful elements in FORTRAN because they allow us to keep large amounts of data easily accessible to our programs. The remaining chapters in this text rely heavily on arrays for storing and manipulating data. Also presented were three sort algorithms.

DEBUGGING AIDS

Because arrays are so convenient for handling large amounts of data, a natural tendency is to overuse them — and, unfortunately, arrays can also introduce new errors. As you debug programs that use arrays, consider the decision to use each array: Ask yourself, "Will I need this data more than once?" and "Must this data be stored before I can use it?" If the answers to both questions are "No," you should eliminate the array and replace it with simple variables. You will also probably be eliminating some loops and statements involving subscripts; these changes may not only reduce the number of errors in your program but will also reduce its overall complexity.

If arrays are necessary, then consider each of the following items if your program is working incorrectly:

Size — The array specification must specify the maximum number of elements that is to be stored in the array. Although you do not have to use all the elements of an array, you can never use more elements than originally specified.

Subscript — Check each subscript to be sure that it represents an integer that falls within the proper range of values. Particularly check for subscript values that are one value too small or one value too large.

DO Loop — If you are using the index of a DO loop as a subscript, be sure you have used the same variable identifier in your statements. That is, if the DO loop index is K, did you use I instead of K as a subscript?

Reverse Subscripts — When you are working with multidimensional arrays, be sure you have the subscripts in the proper order. Do you want B(K,L) or B(L,K)?

STYLE/TECHNIQUE GUIDES

As mentioned in "Debugging Aids," be sure that you really need an array before implementing an algorithm with an array. If you need arrays to solve your problem, take some time to decide the optimum size. Depending on the application, you may find that a two-dimensional array with 10 rows and 2 columns is more direct and understandable than two separate arrays of 10 elements each. Choose the array structure that best suits the data.

Be consistent in your choice of subscript names. Common practice is to use the variable I for the first subscript, J for the second subscript, and K for the third subscript. If you follow the same pattern or a similar pattern, it is much easier to decide the nesting of loops and the values of DO loop indexes that are also used as subscripts.

KEY WORDS

array	multidimensional array
ascending order	multipass sort
bubble sort	one-dimensional array
descending order	selection sort
element	sort
implied DO loop	subscript
insertion sort	two-dimensional array

PROBLEMS

We begin our problem set with modifications to programs developed in this chapter. Give the decomposition, refined pseudocode or flowchart, and FORTRAN program for each problem.

Problems 1–5 modify the average snowfall program SNOFAL, given on page 204.

1. Modify the average snowfall program so that it prints the number of days in the month with no snowfall.
2. Modify the average snowfall program so that it prints the maximum snowfall and the day(s) on which it occurred.
3. Modify the average snowfall program so that it prints the minimum snowfall and the number of days on which it occurred.
4. Modify the average snowfall program so that it prints the longest number of consecutive days for which there was no snowfall.
5. Modify the average snowfall program so that it prints the longest number of consecutive days for which there was measurable snowfall.

Problems 6–10 modify the earthquake measurement program EARTH, given on page 216.

6. Modify the earthquake measurement program so that it sorts the data values into descending order.
7. Modify the earthquake measurement program so that it prints the average earthquake value.
8. Modify the earthquake measurement program so that it prints the maximum earthquake value.
9. Modify the earthquake measurement program so that it prints the median earthquake value.
10. Modify the earthquake measurement program so that it computes and prints the number of earthquake values that are in the same position in the list both before and after the ascending sort.

Problems 11–15 modify the power plant data analysis program PWRPLT, given on page 226.

11. Modify the power plant data analysis program so that it prints the minimum power output, in addition to printing the days on which it occurred.
12. Modify the power plant data analysis program so that it prints both the minimum and the maximum power outputs.
13. Modify the power plant data analysis program so that it reads a value N that determines the number of weeks that will be used for the report. Assume that N will never be more than 20.
14. Modify the power plant data analysis program so that it prints a count of the

number of days with the minimum power output instead of printing the specific days.

15. Modify the power plant data analysis program so that it prints the average daily power output for each week of data.

Problems 16–20 modify the terrain navigation program NAVIG, given on page 230.

16. Modify the terrain navigation program so that it prints a count of the number of land grids analyzed.

17. Modify the terrain navigation program so that it prints the location (row and column subscripts) of the peaks in each land grid.

18. Modify the terrain navigation program so that it computes and prints the percentage of points in each grid that are peaks.

19. Modify the terrain navigation program so that it prints the maximum and minimum elevations for each land grid.

20. Modify the terrain navigation program so that it computes and prints the average elevation for each land grid.

For problems 21–24, assume that K, a one-dimensional array of 50 integer values, has already been filled with data.

21. Give FORTRAN statements to find and print the maximum value of K in the following form:

```
MAXIMUM VALUE IS XXXXX
```

22. Give FORTRAN statements to find and print the minimum value of K and its position or positions in the array in the following form:

```
MINIMUM VALUE OF K IS
K(XX) = XXXXX
```

23. Give FORTRAN statements to count the number of positive values, zero values, and negative values in K. The output form should be

```
XXX POSITIVE VALUES
XXX ZERO VALUES
XXX NEGATIVE VALUES
```

24. Give FORTRAN statements to replace each value of K with its absolute value; then print the array K with two values per line.

Develop these programs and program segments. Use the five-phase design process for all complete programs.

25. An array TIME contains 30 integers. Give statements that will print every other value, beginning with the second value, in this form:

```
TIME( 2) CONTAINS XXXX SECONDS
TIME( 4) CONTAINS XXXX SECONDS
     .
     .
TIME(30) CONTAINS XXXX SECONDS
```

26. An array WIND of 70 integer values represents the average daily wind velocities in Chicago over a 10-week period. Assume the array with 10 rows and 7 columns has been filled. Give FORTRAN statements to print the data so that each week is on a separate line. Use a heading as shown:

```
CHICAGO WIND VELOCITY (MILES/HOUR)
XXX    XXX    XXX    XXX    XXX    XXX    XXX
```

27. Give FORTRAN statements to print the last 10 elements of a real array M of size N. For instance, if M contains 25 elements, the output form is

```
M( 16) = XXX.X
M( 17) = XXX.X
.
.
M( 25) = XXX.X
```

28. Give FORTRAN statements to interchange the first and one-hundredth elements, the second and ninety-ninth elements, and so on, of the array NUM that contains 100 integer values. See the diagram that follows:

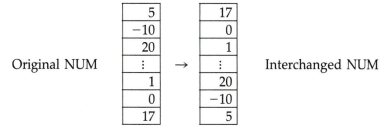

Original NUM → Interchanged NUM

(*Hint:* You will need a temporary storage when you switch values.)

29. An array TREMOR contains integer counts of the number of daily earth tremors detected for 100 days following a major earthquake. Give the FORTRAN statements necessary to find the average of the first 50 days and the second 50 days. Print the following:

```
                AVERAGES
FIRST 50 TREMORS      SECOND 50 TREMORS
     XXX.XX                XXX.XX
```

30. Write a complete program that will read as many as 20 integers from a file NUMBER, one integer per line. The last line will contain 9999. Write the data in the reverse order from which it was read; thus, the value 9999 will be the first value printed.

31. When a plot is made from experimental data, sometimes the scatter of the data points is such that it is difficult to select a "best representative line" for

the plot. In such a case, the data can be adjusted to reduce the scatter by using a "moving average" mathematical method of finding the average of three points in succession and replacing the middle value with this average.

Write a complete program to read an array Y of 20 real values from a file EXPR where the values are entered one per line. Build an array Z of 20 values where Z is the array of adjusted values. That is, Z(2) is the average of Y(1), Y(2), and Y(3); Z(3) is the average of Y(2), Y(3), and Y(4); and so on. Notice that the first and last values of Y cannot be adjusted and should be moved to Z without being changed. Do not destroy the original values in Y. Print the original and the adjusted values next to each other in a table.

32. A truck leasing company owns 12 delivery vans which are leased to several operators. Maintenance hours for each truck are allocated using a maintenance rate multiplied by the total number of hours accumulated by the entire fleet. The maintenance rate for each truck is determined from its percentage of the total fleet hours, and the following table:

PERCENT OF HOURS	MAINTENANCE RATE
0.00 – 9.99	0.02
10.00 – 24.99	0.04
25.00 – 100.00	0.06

A vehicle identification number and the monthly hours of use are entered in a data file HOURS. Write a complete program to read the data, convert each truck's hours to a percentage of the total fleet hours, and compute its maintenance hours using the maintenance rate. Round the calculated maintenance hours to the nearest hour, and ensure that each truck is allotted a minimum of one hour of maintenance each month. Print the following report:

```
MONTHLY MAINTENANCE REPORT
ID               HOURS           PERCENT         MAINTENANCE HOURS
XXX              XXXX            XXX.X           XXX
 .
 .
 .
TOTALS           XXXXX           XXX.X           XXXX
```

Test your program with the following input data:

ID	HOURS
002	61
009	83
012	101
016	55
025	410
036	97
037	66
040	70
043	122
044	136
045	23
046	142

33. Write a complete program that will read a two-dimensional array called RAIN containing 12 rows (one for each month) and 5 columns (one for each year 1978–1982). Each row of real values is entered on a data line in a file WATER. Determine and print the following table of information:

```
        AVERAGE YEARLY RAINFALL
        1978 - XXX.XX
        1979 - XXX.XX
        1980 - XXX.XX
        1981 - XXX.XX
        1982 - XXX.XX

        MAXIMUM RAINFALL
        MONTH XX   YEAR XXXX

        MINIMUM RAINFALL
        MONTH XX   YEAR XXXX
```

34. Assume that the reservations for an airplane flight have been stored in a file called FLIGHT. The plane contains 38 rows with 6 seats in each row. The seats in each row are numbered 1–6 as follows:

   1 Window seat, left side

   2 Center seat, left side

   3 Aisle seat, left side

   4 Aisle seat, right side

   5 Center seat, right side

   6 Window seat, right side

The file FLIGHT contains 38 lines of information corresponding to the 38 rows. Each line contains 6 values corresponding to the 6 seats. The value for any seat is either 0 or 1, representing either an empty or an occupied seat.

   Write a complete program to read the FLIGHT information into a two-dimensional array called SEAT. Find and print all pairs of adjacent seats that are empty. Adjacent aisle seats should not be printed. If all three seats on one side of the plane are empty, then two pairs of adjacent seats should be printed. Print this information in the following manner:

```
        AVAILABLE SEAT PAIRS
           ROW      SEATS
           XX       X,X
            .
            .
            .
           XX       X,X
```

If no pairs of seats are available, print an appropriate message.

35. The horsepower needed to pump water through a nuclear plant's cooling system is a function of the length of the pipe and the volume flowrate of the water. The following table shows the horsepower required for six different flowrates through five different cooling loops.

| | Flowrate | | | | | |
	1	2	3	4	5	6
Loop 1	2.1	4.0	8.7	15.2	21.0	34.8
2	2.7	4.2	9.1	18.0	30.0	41.5
3	4.0	12.9	27.3	52.6	94.4	131.8
4	3.3	10.0	22.7	44.7	80.9	11.2
5	1.8	4.1	8.5	15.3	27.2	46.4

Write a program that uses a DATA statement to initialize an array called POWER for storing the data above for the various combinations of flowrates and pipeline loops. The array's columns represent the six different flowrates in gallons per second and the rows represent the five cooling loops. The horsepower needed to pump J gallons per second through cooling loop I is stored in POWER(I,J). For example, POWER(3,2) contains 12.9, so the horsepower required to pump two gallons per second through cooling loop 3 is 12.9.

The program should ask the user to enter the flowrate in gallons per second for each loop. After rounding the flowrate to the nearest integer, find the corresponding horsepower needed for that cooling loop. If the flowrate is over 6.5 gallons per second or less than 0.5 gallons per second, print an error message. Print the horsepower needed for each loop, and the total horsepower needed for the entire cooling system.

36. Engineering data files often contain the dates on which information was recorded along with the information itself. If the data file is large, the date is often stored in a Julian date form, which is the year followed by the number of the day in the year (1 to 365) since the Julian date will need only five digits, while a Gregorian date (month-day-year) requires six digits. For example, 010982 is a Gregorian date that converts to 82009 in Julian form. Write a complete program to convert a Gregorian date to a Julian date. Be sure to take leap years into account. (*Hint:* Use an array to store the number of days in each month.)

37. In problem 36 we saw that engineering data files sometimes contain Julian dates to minimize storage. However, when the information in the files is printed in reports we want to convert the Julian dates to the more common Gregorian dates. Write a complete program to convert a Julian date to a Gregorian date.

38. A communication system often uses multiple lines, or channels, for sending information. Assume that a communication system has five channels for sending information. There is always a background noise signal on the channel, and the average noise value is monitored because it can indicate the quality of the channel for transmitting information. Assume that background noise for the five channels has been collected in a data file. The data file contains 200 lines of information, with five numbers per line that represent the noise level of the five channels at a specific time. Write a program to read the information into a two-dimensional array. Then compute and print the average noise value for each channel, and the percent of time that the noise is above average for each channel.

FORTRAN STATEMENT SUMMARY

DATA Statement:

> **DATA** *list of variable names /list of values/*

Example:

> **DATA X, Y, COUNTR /1.0, 15.78, 0.0/**

Discussion:

The DATA statement is used to initialize variables at the beginning of your program. It is a specification statement and thus should be positioned before any executable statements.

DIMENSION Statement:

> **DIMENSION** *array1(size), array2(size), . . .*

Example:

> **DIMENSION LIST(50), GRID(5,8)**

Discussion:

The DIMENSION statement is used to define arrays and their corresponding sizes. Elements in an array are referenced using a common name plus a subscript that specifies a unique element of the array. When arrays are defined with the DIMENSION statement, the array type is implicitly specified depending on the first letter of the array name. Because this statement is a specification statement, it should be positioned before any executable statements.

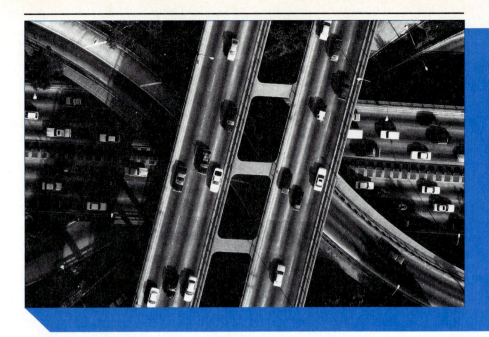

APPLICATION—Traffic Flow
(Transportation Engineering)

The design of transportation systems becomes increasingly important as our population and urban areas increase. Their design must incorporate not only current needs but also projected needs. The data for determining needs and projections includes simple information such as the traffic flow in the current transportation system. Write a program to analyze traffic flow information and determine the average number of cars that pass through an intersection per minute. (See Section 6–7 for the solution.)

6

IMPLEMENTING TOP-DOWN DESIGN WITH FUNCTIONS

Introduction

6–1 Intrinsic Functions

6–2 Statement Functions

6–3 Application — Temperature Conversions (Chemistry)

6–4 Top-Down Design and Structure Charts

6–5 Function Subprograms

6–6 Application — Oil Well Production (Petroleum Engineering)

6–7 Application — Traffic Flow (Transportation Engineering)

6–8 Functions for Search Algorithms

Summary

INTRODUCTION

As our programs become longer and more complicated, we find it harder to maintain program readability and simplicity. We also find that we frequently need to perform the same set of operations at more than one location in our programs. These problems can be solved with *subprograms*, which are groups of statements that are defined separately and then referenced when we need them in our programs. FORTRAN has two types of subprograms: functions and subroutines. In this chapter we review the intrinsic function (such as the square root function and the logarithm function) and learn how to write our own functions to perform computations unique to our applications. The function is quite useful in solving engineering and science problems because many of our solutions involve arithmetic computations.

6-1 INTRINSIC FUNCTIONS

A *function* computes a single value, such as the square root of a number or the average of an array. You have already used functions in the form of intrinsic functions such as SQRT and SIN. These *intrinsic functions* are in the compiler and are accessible directly from your program. The intrinsic functions (or *library functions*) available in FORTRAN 77 are listed in Appendix A. You should read through the list so that you are aware of the types of operations that can be performed with intrinsic functions. When you need to use one of these operations, you can refer to Appendix A for details on how to use that specific function.

Although we introduced intrinsic functions in Chapter 2, we can summarize the main components of these functions:

1. The function name and its input values (or *arguments*) collectively represent a single value.
2. A function can never be used on the left-hand side of an equal sign in an assignment statement.
3. The name of the intrinsic function typically determines the type of output from the function (for example, if the name begins with one of the letters I through N, its value is an integer).
4. The arguments of a function are generally of the same type as the function itself. For a few exceptions, refer to the list of intrinsic functions in Appendix A.
5. The arguments of a function must be enclosed in parentheses.
6. The arguments of a function may be constants, variables, expressions, or other functions.

Generic functions accept arguments of any allowable type and return a value of the same type as the argument. Thus, the generic function ABS will return an integer absolute value if its argument is an integer; but, it will return a real absolute value if its argument is real. The table in Appendix A identifies generic functions.

EXAMPLE 6-1　　　**Odd and Even Values**

Read an integer and then print the word ODD or EVEN, depending on the value read.

Solution

In this solution we use the intrinsic function MOD. This function has two integer arguments, I and J. The function returns the integer remainder in the division of I by J. This operation is also called modulo division — hence, the function is called a MOD function. Some example values for I, J, and MOD(I,J) are

I	J	MOD(I,J)
3	2	1
4	2	0
6	4	2
10	4	2
88	3	1

If a number K is even, it is a multiple of 2, and MOD(K,2) is zero. If K is odd, then MOD(K,2) is 1. The statements that determine if an integer is odd or even using this function are

```
      PRINT*, 'ENTER AN INTEGER'
      READ*, K
      IF (MOD(K,2).EQ.0) THEN
          PRINT 5, K
    5     FORMAT (1X,I5,' IS EVEN')
      ELSE
          PRINT 6, K
    6     FORMAT (1X,I5,' IS ODD')
      ENDIF
```

The MOD function can also be used to determine if a number is a multiple of another number. For instance, if MOD(M,5) is zero, then M is a multiple of 5.

6–2 STATEMENT FUNCTIONS

Engineering and science applications often require a function that is not included in the intrinsic function list. If the computation is needed frequently or requires several steps, we should implement it as a function instead of listing all the computations each time we need them. FORTRAN allows us to write our own functions in two ways: as a statement function or as a function subprogram. If the computation can be written in a single assignment statement we can use the statement function which will be discussed in this section; otherwise we must use the function subprogram that will be discussed in sections 6–4 and 6–5.

The *statement function* is a function defined at the beginning of your program, along with your type statements and array definitions. It is a nonexecutable statement; thus, it should precede any executable statement. The definition of the statement function contains the name of the function, followed by its arguments in parentheses, on the left-hand side of an equal sign; the expression for computing the function value is on the right-hand side of an equal sign. The general form for this statement is

function name (argument list) = expression

The function name can be included in a type statement; otherwise, implicit typing will determine the function type.

Example 6–2 illustrates the use of the statement function in a complete program.

EXAMPLE 6-2   **Triangle Area**

The area of a triangle can be computed from the lengths of two sides and the angle between them:

$$AREA = 0.5*SIDE1*SIDE2*SIN(ANGLE)$$

Write a program that reads the lengths of the three sides of a triangle and the angles opposite each side.

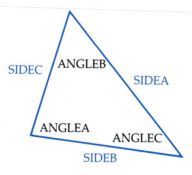

Compute and print the area of the triangle using one pair of sides and its corresponding angle. Then compute and print the area using another pair of sides and its corresponding angle. Finally, compute and print the area using the last pair of sides and its corresponding angle. Use a statement function to compute these areas.

Solution

The solution to this problem contains three steps: read the sides and the angles, compute the area in three ways, and print the areas.

```
+---------------------------------------------+
| Read the sides and angles of a triangle.    |
+---------------------------------------------+
| Compute the area in three ways.             |
+---------------------------------------------+
| Print the three areas.                      |
+---------------------------------------------+
```

REFINEMENT IN PSEUDOCODE

TRIANG: Read sides a, b, c and angles a, b, c
               Compute area using side b, side c, and angle a
               Compute area using side a, side c, and angle b
               Compute area using side a, side b, and angle c
               Print three areas

FORTRAN PROGRAM

```
*-----------------------------------------------------------*
      PROGRAM   TRIANG
*
*     This program reads the lengths of the sides of a triangle
*     along with the corresponding angles in radians. It then
*     computes and prints the area of the triangle using three
*     different sets of information.
*
      REAL  SIDEA, SIDEB, SIDEC, A, B, C, AREA,
     +      AREAA, AREAB, AREAC, SIDE1, SIDE2, ANGLE
      AREA(SIDE1,SIDE2,ANGLE) = 0.5*SIDE1*SIDE2*SIN(ANGLE)
*
      PRINT*, 'ENTER THE LENGTHS OF THE THREE SIDES OF A'
      PRINT*, 'TRIANGLE IN THE FOLLOWING ORDER:'
      PRINT*, 'SIDE A    SIDE B    SIDE C'
      READ*, SIDEA, SIDEB, SIDEC
      PRINT*
      PRINT*, 'ENTER THE ANGLE OPPOSITE SIDE A,'
      PRINT*, 'THEN THE ANGLE OPPOSITE SIDE B,'
      PRINT*, 'AND THEN THE ANGLE OPPOSITE SIDE C.'
      PRINT*, '(IN RADIANS)'
      READ*, A, B, C
      PRINT*
*
      AREAA = AREA(SIDEB,SIDEC,A)
      AREAB = AREA(SIDEC,SIDEA,B)
      AREAC = AREA(SIDEA,SIDEB,C)
      PRINT*, 'THE THREE AREA COMPUTATIONS YIELD:'
      PRINT 5, AREAA, AREAB, AREAC
    5 FORMAT (1X,F6.2,3X,F6.2,3X,F6.2)
*
      END
*-----------------------------------------------------------*
```

The following output represents a typical user interaction with this program:

```
ENTER THE LENGTHS OF THE THREE SIDES OF A
TRIANGLE IN THE FOLLOWING ORDER:
SIDE A     SIDE B     SIDE C
1.0  1.0  1.414

ENTER THE ANGLE OPPOSITE SIDE A,
THEN THE ANGLE OPPOSITE SIDE B,
AND THEN THE ANGLE OPPOSITE SIDE C.
(IN RADIANS)
0.785 0.785 1.571

THE THREE AREA COMPUTATIONS YIELD:
  0.50       0.50       0.50
```

Note that the arguments in the statement function definition are SIDE1, SIDE2, and ANGLE. These arguments do not represent variables used in our program; they tell the compiler that the statement function has three real arguments. When we referenced the function AREA to compute AREAA, note that the variable SIDEB corresponded to the argument SIDE1, the variable SIDEC corresponded to the argument SIDE2, and the variable C corresponded to the argument ANGLE. When we referenced the function AREA to compute AREAB and AREAC, different variables corresponded to the arguments SIDE1, SIDE2, and ANGLE.

Suppose that you forgot to define the statement function AREA. The first statement in your program that uses the function is

```
AREAA = AREA(SIDEB,SIDEC,A)
```

Many compilers assume that AREA is an array that you forgot to define, and they print an error message related to undefined arrays, instead of undefined statement functions. As a result, you may look in the wrong place in your program to correct this error. When you use statement functions, be aware that the compiler may confuse an undefined statement function with an undefined array; similarly, the compiler may diagnose an undefined array as an undefined statement function.

If you want to enter the angles in degrees, you can convert the degrees to radians in an assignment statement such as

```
A = A*(PI/180.0)
```

You can also perform the degree-to-radian conversion within the statement function, as shown:

```
AREA(SIDE1,SIDE2,ANGLE) = 0.5*SIDE1*SIDE2*
+                         SIN(ANGLE*3.14159/180.0)
```

The constant (3.14159/180.0) could be replaced by 0.0175, but leaving it as a division documents the computation for anyone else looking at the program.

This self-test allows you to check quickly to see if you have remembered some of the key points from Section 6–3. If you have any problems with the exercises, you should reread this section. The solutions are included at the end of the text.

For each of the following, give the statement function required to perform the computation.

1. Area of a circle: $A = \pi r^2$

2. Radians from degrees: $radians = \dfrac{180}{\pi} \cdot degrees$

3. Degrees from radians: $degrees = \dfrac{\pi}{180} \cdot radians$

4. Kinetic energy T: $T = \dfrac{mw^2a^2s}{4}$

5. Radius of a circle: $r = \sqrt{x^2 + y^2}$

6–3   APPLICATION—TEMPERATURE CONVERSIONS (Chemistry)

In this application, we develop a program to print a temperature conversion table. To be flexible, we will let the program user specify the type of conversion (Fahrenheit to Centigrade or Centigrade to Fahrenheit), the starting temperature, the change in temperature for each line, and the ending temperature. The output headings should reflect the correct temperature units. The two equations that we need.

$$CENTIGRADE = (FAHRENHEIT - 32) \cdot (5/9)$$
$$FAHRENHEIT = CENTIGRADE \cdot (9/5) + 32$$

Each of these computations requires only a single statement; thus, we can implement them as statement functions.

PROBLEM STATEMENT

Write a program that prints a conversion table for temperatures in Fahrenheit and Centigrade degrees.

INPUT/OUTPUT DESCRIPTION

The input to the program includes the temperature unit for the input values, the initial temperature value, the change in temperature from one line to the next, and the final temperature value. The output is a temperature conversion table.

HAND EXAMPLE

Assume that we want to convert degrees Fahrenheit to degrees Centigrade. Start the table at zero degrees, increment each line by 10 degrees, and stop when the last line in the table is 50 degrees. Using the preceding equation for converting Fahrenheit to Centigrade, we obtain the following table:

```
            TEMPERATURE CONVERSION TABLE
      DEGREES, FAHRENHEIT        DEGREES, CENTIGRADE
           0.00                       -17.78
          10.00                       -12.22
          20.00                        -6.67
          30.00                        -1.11
          40.00                         4.44
          50.00                        10.00
```

ALGORITHM DEVELOPMENT

The overall steps required for this algorithm are shown in the decomposition.

DECOMPOSITION

Read input specifications.
Print table.

As we refine these steps, we see that reading the input specifications is a series of sequential steps that print messages to the user requesting the necessary data and then reading the data. Printing the table involves a WHILE loop that is repeated until we have printed all the lines requested in the table. If we use NEXT to represent the next temperature to be converted, we want to remain in the WHILE loop "while NEXT is less than or equal to the final temperature value." These steps are detailed in the following flowchart:

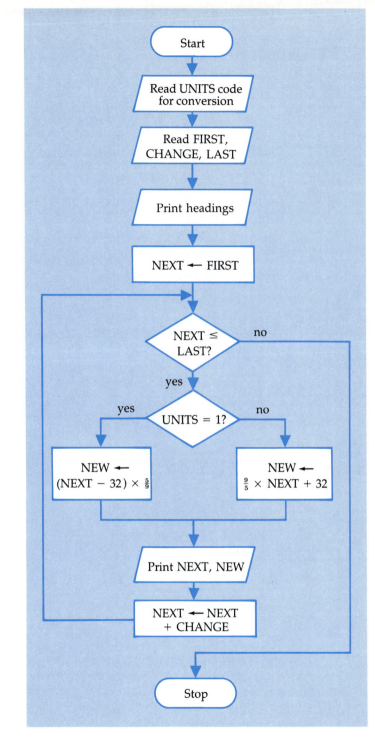

The flowchart is detailed enough to translate the steps into FORTRAN. Note the emphasis in the program on clearly specifying to the user exactly what form to use for entering data.

FORTRAN Program 1

```
*-----------------------------------------------------------------*
      PROGRAM  TABLE1
*
*  This program generates a temperature conversion table.
*
      INTEGER  UNITS
      REAL   CENT, FAHREN, FIRST, CHANGE, LAST, NEXT, NEW, TEMP
      CENT(TEMP) = (TEMP - 32.0)*0.5555556
      FAHREN(TEMP) = 1.8*TEMP + 32.0
*
      PRINT*, 'ENTER 1 TO CONVERT FAHRENHEIT TO CENTIGRADE'
      PRINT*, 'ENTER 2 TO CONVERT CENTIGRADE TO FAHRENHEIT'
      READ*, UNITS
      PRINT*, 'ENTER NUMBER OF DEGREES FOR FIRST LINE'
      READ*, FIRST
      PRINT*, 'ENTER CHANGE IN DEGREES BETWEEN LINES'
      READ*, CHANGE
      PRINT*, 'ENTER NUMBER OF DEGREES FOR LAST LINE'
      READ*, LAST
*
      PRINT 5
   5  FORMAT (1X,10X,'TEMPERATURE CONVERSION TABLE')
      IF (UNITS.EQ.1) THEN
          PRINT 10
  10      FORMAT (1X,'DEGREES, FAHRENHEIT',6X,
     +              'DEGREES, CENTIGRADE')
      ELSE
          PRINT 15
  15      FORMAT (1X,'DEGREES, CENTIGRADE',6X,
     +              'DEGREES, FAHRENHEIT')
      ENDIF
      NEXT = FIRST
  20  IF (NEXT.LE.LAST) THEN
          IF (UNITS.EQ.1) THEN
              NEW = CENT(NEXT)
          ELSE
              NEW = FAHREN(NEXT)
          ENDIF
          PRINT 25, NEXT, NEW
  25      FORMAT (1X,F9.2,18X,F9.2)
          NEXT = NEXT + CHANGE
          GO TO 20
      ENDIF
*
      END
*-----------------------------------------------------------------*
```

Although this solution works correctly and is readable, there are often many ways to solve the same problem. For example, in this solution, we observe that the two equations for converting temperatures are similar. The following steps rewrite the two equations into linear equations with different slopes and different y-intercepts:

$$\text{Centigrade} = (\text{Fahrenheit} - 32) \cdot (5/9)$$
$$= \text{Fahrenheit} \cdot (5/9) - 32 \cdot (5/9)$$
$$= 0.5555556 \cdot \text{Fahrenheit} - 17.77778$$
$$\text{Fahrenheit} = \text{Centigrade} \cdot (9/5) + 32$$
$$= 1.8 \cdot \text{Centigrade} + 32$$

If NEXT contains the temperature that we are going to convert, and NEW is to contain this new value, then both equations can be written in this form:

$$\text{NEW} = \text{SLOPE*NEXT} + \text{INTERC}$$

Thus, instead of using two statement functions, we can use one statement function with three arguments as shown in the following program.

FORTRAN PROGRAM 2

```
*-------------------------------------------------------------*
      PROGRAM  TABLE2
*
* This program generates a temperature conversion table.
*
      INTEGER  UNITS
      REAL  CONV, FIRST, CHANGE, LAST, NEXT, NEW,
     +      SLOPE, INTERC, TEMP, A, B
      CONV(TEMP,A,B) = A*TEMP + B
*
      PRINT*, 'ENTER 1 TO CONVERT FAHRENHEIT TO CENTIGRADE'
      PRINT*, 'ENTER 2 TO CONVERT CENTIGRADE TO FAHRENHEIT'
      READ*, UNITS
      PRINT*, 'ENTER NUMBER OF DEGREES FOR FIRST LINE'
      READ*, FIRST
      PRINT*, 'ENTER CHANGE IN DEGREES BETWEEN LINES'
      READ*, CHANGE
      PRINT*, 'ENTER NUMBER OF DEGREES FOR LAST LINE'
      READ*, LAST
*
      PRINT 5
    5 FORMAT (1X,10X,'TEMPERATURE CONVERSION TABLE')
      IF (UNITS.EQ.1) THEN
          PRINT 10
   10     FORMAT (1X,'DEGREES, FAHRENHEIT',6X,
     +            'DEGREES, CENTIGRADE')
          SLOPE = 0.5555556
          INTERC = -17.77778
      ELSE
          PRINT 15
   15     FORMAT (1X,'DEGREES, CENTIGRADE',6X,
     +            'DEGREES, FAHRENHEIT')
          SLOPE = 1.8
          INTERC = 32.0
      ENDIF
      NEXT = FIRST
   20 IF (NEXT.LE.LAST) THEN
          NEW = CONV(NEXT,SLOPE,INTERC)
          PRINT 25, NEXT, NEW
   25     FORMAT (1X,F9.2,18X,F9.2)
          NEXT = NEXT + CHANGE
          GO TO 20
      ENDIF
*
      END
*-------------------------------------------------------------*
```

If we test either of the programs with our hand-worked example data, the following output is

```
              TEMPERATURE CONVERSION TABLE
  DEGREES, FAHRENHEIT           DEGREES, CENTIGRADE
        0.00                          -17.78
       10.00                          -12.22
       20.00                           -6.67
       30.00                           -1.11
       40.00                            4.44
       50.00                           10.00
```

In this application we did not error check the input values. What would happen if the last temperature value entered was less than the first temperature value entered? The first time that the WHILE condition was executed, it would be false; thus, the WHILE loop would never be executed. The program would end without an error, but only the headings would be printed.

What would happen if the starting temperature and the change were such that the next temperature was never equal to the last temperature? For example, suppose FIRST was specified to be 0.0, CHANGE was specified to be 2.0, and LAST was specified to be 9.0. Output lines would be printed for values 0.0, 2.0, 4.0, 6.0, and 8.0. When the temperature was incremented to 10.0, it would exceed the last value, and we would exit the WHILE loop.

6–4 TOP-DOWN DESIGN AND STRUCTURE CHARTS

In previous chapters we stressed the importance of using top-down design techniques in algorithms and programs. The WHILE loop, DO loop, and IF structures are essential ingredients in structured programming. Another key element in simplifying program logic is the use of modules. These modules, called functions and subroutines in FORTRAN, allow us to write programs composed of nearly independent segments or routines. In fact, when we decompose the problem solution into a series of sequentially executed steps, we are decomposing the problem into steps that could be structured very easily into functions and subroutines. The following are some important advantages to breaking programs into modules:

1. You can write and test each module separately from the rest of the program.
2. Debugging is easier because you are working with smaller sections of the program.

3. Modules can be used in other programs without rewriting or retesting.
4. Programs are more readable and thus more easily understood because of the modular structure.
5. Several programmers can work on different modules of a large program relatively independent of one another.
6. Individual parts of the program become shorter and therefore simpler.
7. A module can be used several times by the same program.

Since modules are so important in writing readable, well-structured programs, we are going to present functions in this chapter and subroutines in the next chapter. The similarities and differences in the two types of modules are easier to see if we study them one at a time.

We have used the decomposition diagram to show the sequential steps necessary to solve a problem. Another type of diagram, the *structure chart*, is also very useful as we decompose our problem solution into smaller problems. While the decomposition diagram outlines the sequential operations needed, the structure chart outlines the modules but does not indicate the order in which they are to be executed.

The diagram below contains a structure chart for a program similar to one that we will be developing in Section 6–6. In the program we are reading oil well production data from a data file. For each oil well we read the daily production in barrels, compute a daily average for the week, and print this information in the report. In addition, we keep summary information for all the wells and print it at the end of the report. A report heading module is used at the beginning of each page to print the header information. The modules shown in this structure chart include both functions and subroutines.

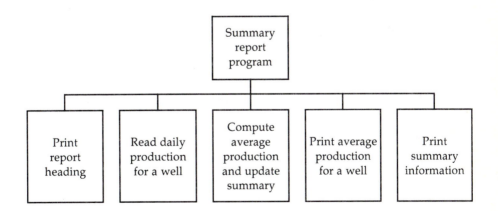

It is important to distinguish between a decomposition diagram and the structure chart. The decomposition diagram for this program shows the sequential order of the steps of the solution.

| Print heading. |
| Read data, accumulate totals, and print report. |
| Print summary information. |

Note that the decomposition does not identify any of the steps as modules. The structure chart, on the other hand, clearly defines the module definitions for the program but does not show the order in which the modules are used. Thus, both charts are useful in describing the algorithm that is being developed for the problem solution because they represent different information about the solution.

The steps to compute an intrinsic function are actually within the compiler and the steps to compute a statement function are within the program itself. Only user-written functions will contain statements that are in a separate module and thus only user-written functions and subroutines will appear in a structure chart.

6-5 FUNCTION SUBPROGRAMS

Because intrinsic functions are contained in a library available to the compiler, you may find that a function in one computer manufacturer's compiler may not be available in another's. For example, a function to generate random numbers is frequently used in computer simulations; but, not all systems include a function to generate random numbers. You may also find that you would like to use a function that is not available in any compiler. These problems can be solved by writing your own function.

A function subprogram, which is a program itself, is separate from the *main program*. It begins with a nonexecutable statement that identifies the function with a name and an argument list, as shown in the general form

FUNCTION *name (argument list)*

Because a function is separate from the main program, it must end with an END statement. The function must also contain a RETURN statement, which returns control to the statement that referenced the function. The general form of the RETURN statement is

RETURN

The rules for choosing a function name are the same as those for choosing a program name. In addition, the first letter of the function name specifies the type of value returned unless it is included in an explicit type specification. The following statements illustrate a simple example with a structure chart, a main program, and the function subprogram:

```
*-------------------------------------------------------------*
         PROGRAM  TEST
      *
      *  This is a sample main program.
      *
         REAL  TEST1, TEST2, TEST3, AVE
      *
         READ*, TEST1, TEST2, TEST3
         PRINT 5, AVE(TEST1,TEST2,TEST3)
       5 FORMAT (1X,'AVERAGE = ',F5.2)
      *
         END
*-------------------------------------------------------------*
      *
         REAL FUNCTION  AVE(X,Y,Z)
      *
      *  This is a sample function.
      *
         REAL  X, Y, Z
         AVE = (X + Y + Z)/3.0
      *
         RETURN
         END
*-------------------------------------------------------------*
```

Main Program

Function Subprogram

Several rules must be observed in writing a function subprogram.

1. The function arguments referenced in the main program must match in type, number, and order, the arguments used in the function statement. In the preceding example, TEST1 corresponds to X, TEST2 corresponds to Y, and TEST3 corresponds to Z.
2. If one of the arguments is an array, its dimensions must be specified in both the main program and in the function subprogram.
3. The value to be returned to the main program is stored in the function name using an assignment statement.
4. When the function is ready to return control to the statement that referenced it, a RETURN statement is used. A function may contain more than one RETURN statement.
5. A function can contain references to other functions, but it cannot contain a reference to itself.

6. A function subprogram is usually placed immediately after the main program, but it also may appear before the main program; in either case, the function is compiled as a separate program. If you have more than one function, the order of the functions does not matter as long as each function is completely separate from the other functions.

7. A main program and its subprograms can be stored in the same program file or in separate files. If they are stored in separate files, it is necessary to link them before the main program can be executed. The statements required to perform the linking depend on the operating system being used (system dependent).

8. The same statement numbers may be used in both a function and in the main program. No confusion occurs as to which statement is referenced because the function and the main program are completely separate. Similarly, a function and a main program can use the same variable name, such as SUM, to store different sums as long as the variable SUM is not an argument to the function.

9. If you wish to define the type of value returned by a function explicitly, the name of the function must appear in a type statement in the main program as well as in the function statement itself. The following statements illustrate the definition of an integer function AVE that computes an integer average. Compare this main program and function to the previous example that computes a real average.

```
*------------------------------------------------------------*
      PROGRAM   TEST
*
*   This is a sample main program.
*
      INTEGER   TEST1, TEST2, TEST3, AVE
*
      READ*, TEST1, TEST2, TEST3
      PRINT 5, AVE(TEST1,TEST2,TEST3)
    5 FORMAT (1X,'AVERAGE =',I5)
      END
*------------------------------------------------------------*
*
      INTEGER FUNCTION   AVE(I,J,K)
*
*   This is a sample function.
*
      INTEGER   I, J, K
*
      AVE = (I + J + K)/3
*
      RETURN
      END
*------------------------------------------------------------*
```

For documentation purposes, our examples explicitly type all function subprograms.

10. Do not try to change the values of the function arguments while inside the function. Some compilers return the new values to the main program; others do not. If you need to return more than the function value itself, use a subroutine (discussed in Chapter 7) instead of a function.

We now present a series of examples to illustrate the use of these rules in writing and using your own functions.

EXAMPLE 6-3

Sales Bonus

A local company has a number of computer programs that are used in maintaining its accounts and preparing payrolls. Several of the programs need to compute the bonus earned by salespeople who work for the company. Instead of recomputing the sales bonus in each program, subprograms are used. This bonus is computed from the total sales of the salesperson, using the following table:

TOTAL SALES	BONUS PERCENT
sales < $1000	1%
$1000 ≤ sales < $2000	2%
$2000 ≤ sales < $2500	3%
$2500 ≤ sales	5%

The function is to be called BONUS and has one argument, the total sales for the salesperson.

Solution 1

Because a function subprogram is a program separate from the main program, you should approach function design and implementation much as you would a complete program. Follow the same guidelines for developing a decomposition diagram, then refine it using pseudocode or flowcharts until it is detailed enough to convert into FORTRAN. Because the function receives values through the argument list, the pseudocode or flowchart should begin with the name of the function and the variables that are arguments to the function.

DECOMPOSITION OF BONUS(SALES)

Compute bonus based on sales.
Return.

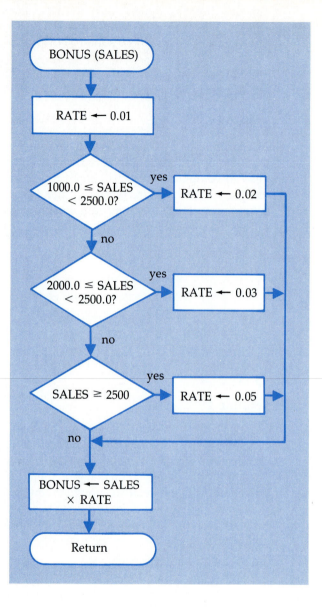

FORTRAN Function

```
*-------------------------------------------------------*
      REAL FUNCTION  BONUS(SALES)
*
*   This function computes a bonus based on sales.
*
      REAL   SALES, RATE
*
      RATE = 0.01
      IF (SALES.GE.1000.0.AND.SALES.LT.2000.0) RATE = 0.02
      IF (SALES.GE.2000.0.AND.SALES.LT.2500.0) RATE = 0.03
      IF (SALES.GE.2500.0) RATE = 0.05
      BONUS = SALES*RATE
*
      RETURN
      END
*-------------------------------------------------------*
```

A main program that uses this function might include a statement such as the following, which reads the sales for one of the salespersons and then prints the sales and bonus:

```
      .
      .
      .
      READ*, ID, SALES
      PRINT 5, ID, SALES, BONUS(SALES)
    5 FORMAT (1X,'SALESPERSON:',I5,3X,'SALES:',F8.2,3X,
   +         'BONUS:',F5.2)
      .
      .
      .
```

Solution 2

This solution uses the IF-ELSEIF statement. The same main program can be used with this function.

FORTRAN Function

```
*-------------------------------------------------------*
      REAL FUNCTION  BONUS(SALES)
*
*   This function computes a bonus based on sales.
*
      REAL   SALES, RATE
*
      IF (SALES.LT.1000.0) THEN
         RATE = 0.01
      ELSEIF (SALES.LT.2000.0) THEN
         RATE = 0.02
      ELSEIF (SALES.LT.2500.0) THEN
         RATE = 0.03
      ELSE
         RATE = 0.05
      ENDIF
      BONUS = SALES*RATE
*
      RETURN
      END
*-------------------------------------------------------*
```

Incorrect Solution

The following function is similar to the function in Solution 2, but this one does not work correctly. See if you can spot the error before reading the explanation.

FORTRAN Function

```
*------------------------------------------------------------*
      REAL FUNCTION  BONUS(SALES)
*
*  This function computes a bonus based on sales.
*
      REAL  SALES, RATE
*
      IF (SALES.GT.2500.0) THEN
         RATE = 0.05
      ELSEIF (SALES.LT.2500.0) THEN
         RATE = 0.03
      ELSEIF (SALES.LT.2000.0) THEN
         RATE = 0.02
      ELSEIF (SALES.LT.1000.0) THEN
         RATE = 0.01
      ENDIF
      BONUS = SALES*RATE
*
      RETURN
      END
*------------------------------------------------------------*
```

The key to understanding the problem with this solution is to remember the manner in which an IF-ELSEIF statement is executed. As soon as a true condition is encountered, the appropriate steps are executed and control passes to the ENDIF at the end of the structure; even if two conditions are true, the first one encountered is the only one tested. Suppose that the SALES amount is $900. The commission rate should be 1%; however, because SALES is less than 2500.0, the rate is computed to be 3% and control is passed to the ENDIF and then to the computation for BONUS.

As stated earlier, when arrays are used as arguments in a function, they must be dimensioned in the function subprogram as well as in the main program. Generally, the array will have the same size in the function as it does in the main program; however, when the size of an array is an argument to the subprogram, we must use a technique called *variable dimensioning*. This technique allows us to specify an array of variable size in the subprogram. The argument value then sets the size of the array when the subprogram is executed. We illustrate the use of an array with a fixed size in Example 6–4 and with a variable size in Example 6–5. (Note that variable dimensioning refers to dimensioning of an array used as an argument to a subprogram. Any array that is not a subprogram argument, but that is defined and used in a subprogram, must be dimensioned in the subprogram with a constant; it is not dimensioned in the main program.)

EXAMPLE 6-4   **Array Average, Fixed Array Size**

Write a function that receives an array of 20 real values. Compute the average of the array and return it as the function value.

Solution

The decomposition and refinement in pseudocode for the function are given.

DECOMPOSITION OF AVE(x)

Compute average of array x.
Return.

REFINEMENT IN PSEUDOCODE

$AVE(x)$: sum $\leftarrow$ 0.0
    For $i = 1$ to 20
        sum $\leftarrow$ sum $+ x(i)$
    ave $\leftarrow$ sum/20.0
    Return

FORTRAN FUNCTION

```
*--------------------------------------------------------------*
      REAL FUNCTION  AVE(X)
*
*  This function computes the average
*  of a real array with twenty values.
*
      INTEGER  I
      REAL  X(20), SUM
*
      SUM = 0.0
      DO 10 I=1,20
         SUM = SUM + X(I)
   10 CONTINUE
      AVE = SUM/20.0
*
      RETURN
      END
*--------------------------------------------------------------*
```

A portion of a main program that might use this function is

```
      PROGRAM  GRADES
*
*  This program computes homework averages.
*
      INTEGER  ID, I
      REAL  SCORES(20), HWAVE
*
      READ*, ID
      READ*, (SCORES(I),I=1,20)
*
      HWAVE = AVE(SCORES)
         .
         .
         .
```

EXAMPLE 6-5   **Median Value, Variable Array Size**

The median of a list of sorted numbers is defined as the number in the middle: In the list −5, 2, 7, 36, and 42, the number 7 is the median. If the list has an even number of values, the median is defined as the average of the 2 middle values: In the list −5, 2, 7, 36, 42, and 82, the median is $(7 + 36)/2$, or 21.5.

Write a function called MEDIAN that has 2 parameters: a real array and an integer that specifies the number of values in the array. The function should assume that the elements of the array have already been sorted. Return the median value of the array as the function value.

Solution

The decomposition of this function is shown.

DECOMPOSITION OF MEDIAN(x,n)

Determine median of array x.
Return.

In Section 6–2, we used the MOD function to determine if an integer was odd or even. We can use the same technique to determine if the number of elements (n) in the array is odd or even. If n is odd, we must decide which subscript refers to the middle value. For example, if n = 5, we want the median to refer to the third value, which is referenced by $(n/2) + 1$. Recall that we are dividing 2 integers, and the result will be truncated to another integer. If n is even, we want to refer to the 2 middle values and compute their average. If $n = 6$, we want to use the third and fourth values, which can be referenced by $(n/2)$ and $(n/2) + 1$.

REFINEMENT IN PSEUDOCODE

MEDIAN(x,n): If n is odd, then
        median ← $x(n/2 + 1)$
    else
        median ← $(x(n/2) + x(n/2 + 1))/2$
    Return

As we convert the pseudocode into FORTRAN, we must remember to specify that the function MEDIAN is a real function (the default will be an integer).

FORTRAN Function

```
*------------------------------------------------------------*
      REAL FUNCTION  MEDIAN(X,N)
*
*  This function determines the median value
*  in a sorted list of real values.
*
      INTEGER  N
      REAL  X(N)
*
      IF (MOD(N,2).NE.0) THEN
         MEDIAN = X(N/2+1)
      ELSE
         MEDIAN = (X(N/2) + X(N/2+1))/2.0
      ENDIF
*
      RETURN
      END
*------------------------------------------------------------*
```

This function could be tested by a program with the following structure chart and statements:

FORTRAN Program

```
*------------------------------------------------------------*
      PROGRAM  TEST
*
*  This program is written to test the median function.
*
      INTEGER  N, I
      REAL  X(10), MEDIAN
*
      PRINT*, 'ENTER NUMBER OF VALUES FOR ARRAY (<11)'
      READ*, N
      PRINT*, 'NOW ENTER SORTED ARRAY VALUES'
      READ*, (X(I), I=1,N)
      PRINT 5, MEDIAN(X,N)
    5 FORMAT (1X,'MEDIAN = ',F7.2)
*
      END
*------------------------------------------------------------*
              MEDIAN function goes here
*------------------------------------------------------------*
```

In Example 6–6, we use a two-dimensional array as an argument in a function.

EXAMPLE 6-6   **Two-Dimensional Array Maximum**

Write a function that will receive an array of integers with 5 rows and 7 columns. The function should return the maximum value in the array.

Solution

DECOMPOSITION OF MAXVAL(K)

To find the maximum value in the array, we initialize the maximum to the first value in the array; then, we compare the rest of the elements in the array to the maximum, replacing the maximum value with any larger value that we find.

REFINEMENT IN PSEUDOCODE

$$MAXVAL(k): maxval \leftarrow k(1,1)$$
$$\text{For } i = 1,5 \text{ do}$$
$$\text{For } j = 1,7 \text{ do}$$
$$\text{If } k(i,j) > maxval \text{ then}$$
$$maxval \leftarrow k(i,j)$$
$$\text{Return}$$

FORTRAN FUNCTION

```
*---------------------------------------------------------*
      INTEGER FUNCTION  MAXVAL(K)
*
*  This function determines the maximum value
*  in an integer array with 5 rows and 7 columns.
*
      INTEGER  K(5,7), I, J
*
      MAXVAL = K(1,1)
      DO 10 I=1,5
         DO 5 J=1,7
            IF (K(I,J).GT.MAXVAL) MAXVAL = K(I,J)
    5    CONTINUE
   10 CONTINUE
*
      RETURN
      END
*---------------------------------------------------------*
```

A statement that might use the function in the main program, after filling an array NUMBER that has 5 rows and 7 columns, is shown in the following group of statements:

```
      INTEGER  NUMBER(5,7), MAXVAL
         .
         .
         .
      PRINT 5, MAXVAL(NUMBER)
    5 FORMAT (1X,'MAXIMUM NUMBER IS ',I5)
```

Problems can arise when you use variable dimensioning with arrays that have more than one dimension. The following is an example: First, we modify the MAXVAL function so that the number of rows and the number of columns are variables.

FORTRAN Function

```
*----------------------------------------------------------*
      INTEGER FUNCTION  MAXVAL(K,M,N)
*
*  This function determines the maximum value
*  in an integer array with M rows and N columns.
*
      INTEGER  K(M,N), M, N, I, J
*
      MAXVAL = K(1,1)
      DO 10 I=1,M
         DO 5 J=1,N
            IF (K(I,J).GT.MAXVAL) MAXVAL = K(I,J)
    5    CONTINUE
   10 CONTINUE
*
      RETURN
      END
*----------------------------------------------------------*
```

If we modify the function reference to the one shown, the correct maximum value is printed:

```
      INTEGER  NUMBER(5,7), MAXVAL
      .
      .
      .
      PRINT 5, MAXVAL(NUMBER,5,7)
    5 FORMAT (1X,'MAXIMUM NUMBER IS ',I5)
```

Suppose we want to determine the maximum value using only the first 2 rows and the first 2 columns of the array NUMBER, as shown in the diagram:

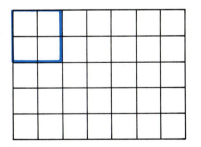

The following statements seem reasonable, but they are incorrect:

```
      INTEGER  NUMBER(5,7), MAXVAL
      .
      .
      .
      PRINT 5, MAXVAL(NUMBER,2,2)
    5 FORMAT (1X,'MAXIMUM NUMBER IS ',I5)
```

These statements are incorrect because FORTRAN stores a two-dimensional array by columns. The array NUMBER is actually stored in memory as shown in the following diagram:

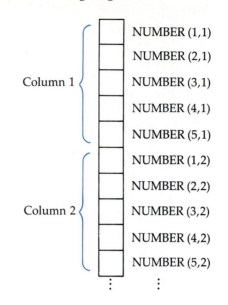

When we reference the array NUMBER in our function and specify that it has 2 rows and 2 columns, FORTRAN assumes that the values in NUMBER are stored in the following order:

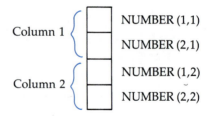

When we put the preceding two diagrams side-by-side, we can see that the array elements do not always match:

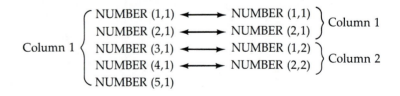

In fact, if we reference an array with 2 rows and 2 columns using the array NUMBER, the elements that we are actually going to use are outlined in the following diagram:

This problem does not result in a compiler error; but, the values used by the function are not those that we expect it to use, which can then present a difficult error to find in a program. In general, you should not use variable dimensions with arrays that have more than one dimension. If you have an application that requires variable dimensioning with two-dimensional arrays, include the declared sizes of the array in the argument list, along with the variable sizes to be used in the function. For example, if an array is defined to have MAXM rows and MAXN columns in the main program, use the array specification illustrated in the following function:

```
*-------------------------------------------------------------*
      INTEGER FUNCTION  MAXVAL(K,M,N,MAXM,MAXN)
*
*   This function determines the maximum value in an integer
*   array with M rows and N columns (original size
*   MAXM by MAXN).
*
      INTEGER  M, N, MAXM, MAXN, K(MAXM,MAXN), I, J
*
      MAXVAL = K(1,1)
      DO 10 I=1,M
         DO 5 J=1,N
            IF (K(I,J).GT.MAXVAL) MAXVAL = K(I,J)
    5    CONTINUE
   10 CONTINUE
*
      RETURN
      END
*-------------------------------------------------------------*
```

This self-test allows you to check quickly to see if you have remembered some of the key points from Section 6–5. If you have any problems with the exercises, you should reread this section. The solutions are included at the end of the text.

For the following problems, give the value of X, assuming that A = −5, B = −6.2, C = 0.1, and D = 16.2. The function TEST is given:

```
*----------------------------------------------------------*
      REAL FUNCTION   TEST(X,Y,Z)
*
*   This function returns either 0.5 or -0.5
*   depending on the values of X, Y, Z.
*
      REAL  X, Y, Z
*
      IF (X.GT.Y.OR.Y.GT.Z) THEN
          TEST = 0.5
      ELSE
          TEST = -0.5
      ENDIF
*
      RETURN
      END
*----------------------------------------------------------*
```

1. X = TEST(5.2,5.3,5.6)

2. X = TEST(B,C,A)

3. X = TEST(ABS(A),C,D)

4. X = TEST(C,C,D*D)

6-6 APPLICATION—OIL WELL PRODUCTION (Petroleum Engineering)

The daily production of oil from a group of wells is entered into a data file each week for analysis. One of the reports that uses this data file computes the average production from each well and prints a summary of the overall production from this group of wells.

Write a FORTRAN program that will read the information from the data file and generate this report. Assume that the first line of the data file contains a date (month, day, and year of the first day of the week that corresponds to the production data). Each following line in the data file contains an integer identification number for the well and 7 real numbers that represent the well's production for the week. The number of wells to be analyzed varies from week to week, so a trailer line is included at the end of the file; this trailer contains the integer 99999, followed by seven zeros. You may assume that no well will have this integer as its identification number.

The report generated should have the following format:

```
OIL WELL PRODUCTION
WEEK OF XX-XX-XX

WELL ID        AVERAGE PRODUCTION
               (IN BARRELS)
XXXXX          XXX.XX
```

Include a final line at the end of the report that gives the total number of oil wells plus their overall average.

Use the following set of data (stored in a file called WELLS) for testing the program:

```
05  06  86
52     87    136   0     54    60    82    51
63     54    73    88    105   20    21    105
24     67    98    177   35    65    98    0
8      23    34    52    67    180   80    3
64     33    55    79    108   118   130   20
66     40    44    63    89    36    54    36
67     20    35    76    87    154   98    80
55     10    13    34    23    43    12    0
3      34    56    187   34    202   23    34
2      98    98    87    34    54    100   20
25     29    43    54    65    12    15    17
18     45    65    202   205   100   99    98
14     36    34    98    34    43    23    9
13     0     9     8     4     3     2     10
36     23    88    99    65    77    45    35
38     23    100   134   122   111   211   0
81     23    34    54    98    5     93    82
89     29    58    39    20    50    30    47
99     100   12    43    98    34    23    9
45     23    93    75    93    2     34    8
88     23    301   23    83    23    9     20
77     28    12    43    43    92    83    98
39     98    43    12    23    54    23    98
12     43    54    92    84    75    72    91
48     83    138   189   73    27    49    10
99999  0     0     0     0     0     0     0
```

PROBLEM STATEMENT

Generate a report on oil well production from daily production data. Give the average production for individual wells and the overall average.

INPUT/OUTPUT DESCRIPTION

The input is a data file with daily production data for a group of oil wells. The first line in the file contains the date of the first day in the week. Each following line contains the identification number of a well and the 7 daily production values for that well. The last line in the file contains 99999, which signals the end of the file. The output is a report in the following form:

```
OIL WELL PRODUCTION
WEEK OF XX-XX-XX

WELL ID          AVERAGE PRODUCTION
                 (IN BARRELS)
XXXXX            XXX.XX
```

HAND EXAMPLE

For the hand-worked example, we use the first 5 lines of the data file given at the beginning of this application, along with the trailer line. Thus, our data file is

```
05 06 86
52     87   136   0    54    60    82    51
63     54   73    88   105   20    21    105
24     67   98    177  35    65    98    0
8      23   34    52   67    180   80    3
99999 0     0     0    0     0     0     0
```

We use the date in the first line of the data file in our heading. Each individual data line in the report contains the well identification (the first value in each line) followed by the average. We compute the average from the 7 daily values that follow the identification. We continue computing the individual averages until we reach the trailer signal 99999. At this point, we average the individual wells and print a final summary line. For this small set of data, our output is

```
OIL WELL PRODUCTION
WEEK OF  5- 6-86

WELL ID          AVERAGE PRODUCTION
                 (IN BARRELS)
     52          67.14
     63          66.57
     24          77.14
      8          62.71

OVERALL AVERAGE FOR    4 WELLS IS   68.39
```

ALGORITHM DEVELOPMENT

Before we consider the steps in the algorithm, we should first decide the best way to store the data. For instance, do we want to store it in a two-dimensional array, or do we want to store the individual oil production amounts in a one-dimensional array, or can we avoid arrays altogether?

We answer these questions by looking at the way in which we need to use the data. To compute the individual well average, we need a sum of the individual production amounts. Because all 7 values are entered in the same data line, we must read them at the same time—we need an array to store the 7 daily production amounts for an individual well. To compute the overall average, we need a sum of the individual averages and a count of the number of wells—we do not need to keep the individual averages from each well.

In summary, we need a one-dimensional array to store the individual production values, and we do not need a two-dimensional array to store all the data.

We now decompose the algorithm into a sequence of steps. At the same time, we need to decide which operations or steps should be written as functions. Experience is the best guide as to selecting which operations to define as functions. By studying how functions are used in the example programs, you will become more proficient at making these decisions. Remember that there are often several ways that functions can be used in a program.

We start by looking at the general decomposition and initial refinement of the algorithm.

DECOMPOSITION

Generate report.
Print summary line.

INITIAL REFINEMENT IN PSEUDOCODE

REPORT: Read date
           Read ID, oil production
           While ID not = 99999 do
              Determine individual average
              Print individual average
              Update overall average and well count
              Read next ID, oil production
           Print summary information

After completing the decomposition and the initial refinement, we can determine if any of the operations should be written as functions. Computations that are repeated in an algorithm and steps that involve long computations are good candidates for functions. Program readability suffers when the details of some of the steps become long and tedious. Even though the steps may be performed only once, placing them in a function may make the program simpler.

For the oil well production problem, a function can be used to compute the individual oil well averages. This operation is needed only once in the main loop; but, it involves several steps—the main program will be more readable if the steps are moved to a function subprogram. The function to compute the individual averages is also one that would be useful in other programs that compute averages. To be flexible, we write the function assuming that the data is in an array whose size is one of the function arguments.

FINAL REFINEMENT IN PSEUDOCODE

REPORT: Read date
          number of wells ← 0
          total oil ← 0.0
          Read ID, oil production
          While ID not = 99999 do
              Compute individual average with function
              Print individual average
              Increment number of wells by 1
              Add individual well average to total oil
              Read next ID, production data
          Print summary information

FUNCTION PSEUDOCODE

AVE(oil, n): sum ← 0.0
          for $i = 1$ to n
              sum ← sum + oil(i)
          ave ← sum$/n$
          return

The structure chart for the solution is shown next, along with the FORTRAN program.

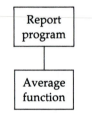

```
*----------------------------------------------------------*
      PROGRAM  REPORT
*
*  This program generates a report from the daily
*  production information for a set of oil wells.
*
      INTEGER  MO, DA, YR, ID, N, I
      REAL  OIL(7), TOTAL, AVE, INDAVE
      DATA  N, TOTAL /0, 0.0/
*
      OPEN (UNIT=12,FILE='WELLS',STATUS='OLD')
      READ (12,*) MO, DA, YR
      PRINT*, 'OIL WELL PRODUCTION'
      PRINT 5, MO, DA, YR
    5 FORMAT (1X,'WEEK OF ',I2,'-',I2,'-',I2)
      PRINT*
      PRINT*, 'WELL ID       AVERAGE PRODUCTION'
      PRINT*, '               (IN BARRELS)'
*
      READ (12,*) ID, (OIL(I), I=1,7)
   10 IF (ID.NE.99999) THEN
         INDAVE = AVE(OIL,7)
         PRINT 15, ID, INDAVE
   15    FORMAT (1X,I5,9X,F6.2)
         N = N + 1
         TOTAL = TOTAL + INDAVE
         READ (12,*) ID, (OIL(I), I=1,7)
         GO TO 10
      ENDIF
*
      PRINT 20, N, TOTAL/REAL(N)
   20 FORMAT (1X,'OVERALL AVERAGE FOR ',I3,
     +         ' WELLS IS ',F6.2)
*
      END
*----------------------------------------------------------*
*
      REAL FUNCTION  AVE(X,N)
*
*  This function computes the average
*  of a real array with N values.
*
      INTEGER  N, I
      REAL  X(N), SUM
*
      SUM = 0.0
      DO 10 I=1,N
         SUM = SUM + X(I)
   10 CONTINUE
      AVE = SUM/REAL(N)
*
      RETURN
      END
*----------------------------------------------------------*
```

Could the variable SUM have been initialized in the function with a DATA statement? (The answer is no. Why?)

Begin testing this program using a small data set such as the one in the hand-worked example. The output from this program using the data file given at the beginning of this application is

```
OIL WELL PRODUCTION
WEEK OF   5- 6-86

WELL ID            AVERAGE PRODUCTION
                   (IN BARRELS)
    52                 67.14
    63                 66.57
    24                 77.14
     8                 62.71
    64                 77.57
    66                 51.71
    67                 78.57
    55                 19.29
     3                 81.43
     2                 70.14
    25                 33.57
    18                116.29
    14                 39.57
    13                  5.14
    36                 61.71
    38                100.14
    81                 55.57
    89                 39.00
    99                 45.57
    45                 46.86
    88                 68.86
    77                 57.00
    39                 50.14
    12                 73.00
    48                 81.29
OVERALL AVERAGE FOR   25 WELLS IS   61.04
```

Could the last line of the data file contain only the trailer identification value 99999 (are the seven zeros necessary in the last line of the data file)? If you try running the program without these last seven zeros, you will find that an execution error occurs because the program has run out of data. Because the identification number and the well production values are on the same line, we must read them with one READ statement. Each time the READ statement is executed, it reads 8 values before control passes to the next statement. When the READ statement reaches the last line in the data file, it needs 7 values in addition to the 99999 value before it can test for the trailer value.

6-7 APPLICATION—TRAFFIC FLOW
(Transportation Engineering)

To study traffic flow at various intersections in large cities, the cars that pass through an intersection during certain time intervals are counted. The data collected can then be analyzed to determine the changes in traffic flow as well as to identify the intersections with the most traffic. In this application, we use traffic flow data to compute the average number of cars that pass through an intersection in 1 minute.

We assume that the data is contained in a file, and that each line of the file contains the intersection identification, the beginning time, the ending time, and the number of cars that passed during that time interval. We assume that the data is added to the file as it is collected; thus, the file is not in order by intersection. We must read all the information in the file to be sure that we have not missed any information. Because there is no special trailer line at the end of the file, we use the END option (a special form of the WHILE loop discussed in Chapter 4) to detect the last line in the file.

PROBLEM STATEMENT

Write a program that will read an intersection identification from the terminal. Compute the average number of cars that passes through the intersection per minute, using the data in a traffic flow data file named CARS.

INPUT/OUTPUT DESCRIPTION

The input to the program comes from two sources: an intersection identification is entered from the terminal and data is read from a traffic flow data file. The output is the average number of cars that passes through the intersection per minute.

HAND EXAMPLE

For our hand-worked example, we assume that the traffic flow data file contains the following information:

INTERSECTION	BEGINNING TIME	ENDING TIME	CARS
23	1330	1338	27
17	1422	1435	52
23	1407	1502	91
23	1507	1512	24

(Note that the time is stored using a 24-hour clock. The first 2 digits represent the hour, and the last 2 digits represent the number of minutes. At midnight, the time begins at 0000 for the new day. The time 0930 represents 9:30 AM and 2130 represents 9:30 PM. This representation assures that the ending time will be an integer larger than the beginning time. We will assume that a single measurement does not extend from one day into the next.)

We are now ready to compute the average number of cars per minute through an intersection. If the intersection number is 23, then the average is computed as shown:

INTERSECTION 23

First measurement   1330 to 1338 = 8 minutes, 27 cars

Next measurement   1407 to 1502 = 55 minutes, 91 cars

Next measurement   1507 to 1512 = 5 minutes, 24 cars

The average is computed by dividing the total number of cars by the total number of minutes, or

$$\frac{(27 + 91 + 24)}{(8 + 55 + 5)} = \frac{142}{68} = 2.09 \text{ cars/minute}$$

Note that the number of minutes in each observation is not simply the difference between the two times. For example, the difference between the integers 1502 and 1407 is 95; but if these integers represent time on a 24-hour clock, the difference is 55 minutes. Thus, we need to be careful about the steps we use to compute the number of minutes in an observation. Because this computation yields a single value, we use a function subprogram. The function converts the beginning and ending time measurements into minutes and then subtracts the two numbers. The MOD function is useful in changing a time based on a 24-hour clock to the number of hours and minutes. For example, consider the time 1330. The number of minutes is 30, which can be computed from the expression MOD(1330,100); the number of hours is 13, which can be computed from the expression 1330/100. (Note that the result of the integer division is 13, not 13.3.) The total number of minutes is then computed by multiplying the number of hours by 60 and adding the number of minutes, or $13 \cdot 60 + 30$. After the function converts both the beginning time and the ending time to minutes, it can return the difference of the 2 values as the number of minutes in the observation.

ALGORITHM DEVELOPMENT

The decomposition for this problem can be defined with the following steps.

DECOMPOSITION

Read intersection number.
Determine total cars and total minutes for this intersection using data file.
Compute and print average cars per minute.

Computing the number of cars and the number of minutes of observation for this intersection can be done in a loop that is executed as long as there is more data. When we exit this loop and print the average, we need to allow for the situation in which there are no observations for the desired intersection. We use these ideas in the refined pseudocode.

REFINEMENT IN PSEUDOCODE

ANALYZ: Read intersection identification
    total cars ← 0
    total minutes ← 0
    While more information in file do
      Read traffic information
      If traffic identification = intersection then
        add minutes to total minutes
        add cars to total cars
    If total minutes = 0 then
      Print 'NO OBSERVATIONS FOR THIS INTERSECTION'
    Else
      average ← total cars/total minutes
      Print average

The structure chart for the solution is shown next, along with the FORTRAN program.

```
*-----------------------------------------------------------*
      PROGRAM  ANALYZ
*
*  This program reads traffic flow information from a
*  data file and computes the average number of cars
*  per minute through a specific intersection.
*
      INTEGER  ID, FILEID, BEGIN, END, FLOW,
     +         MINUTE, TOTMIN, TOTCAR
      DATA  TOTMIN, TOTCAR /0, 0/
*
      PRINT*, 'ENTER INTERSECTION IDENTIFICATION'
      READ*, ID
      OPEN (UNIT=10,FILE='CARS',STATUS='OLD')
    5 READ (10,*,END=50) FILEID, BEGIN, END, FLOW
         IF (FILEID.EQ.ID) THEN
            TOTMIN = TOTMIN + MINUTE(BEGIN,END)
            TOTCAR = TOTCAR + FLOW
         ENDIF
         GO TO 5
   50 IF (TOTMIN.EQ.0) THEN
         PRINT 55, ID
   55    FORMAT (1X,'NO OBSERVATIONS FOR INTERSECTION ',I3)
      ELSE
         PRINT 60, ID
   60    FORMAT (1X,'INTERSECTION ',I3)
         PRINT 65, REAL(TOTCAR)/REAL(TOTMIN)
   65    FORMAT (1X,'AVERAGE CARS PER MINUTE = ',F6.2)
      ENDIF
*
      END
*-----------------------------------------------------------*
*
*
      INTEGER FUNCTION  MINUTE(BEGIN,END)
*
*  This function computes the number of minutes
*  between the beginning time and the ending time.
*
      INTEGER  BEGIN, END, BEGHR, BEGMIN, ENDHR, ENDMIN
*
      BEGHR = BEGIN/100
      BEGMIN = MOD(BEGIN,100)
      ENDHR = END/100
      ENDMIN = MOD(END,100)
      MINUTE = (ENDHR*60 + ENDMIN) - (BEGHR*60 + BEGMIN)
*
      RETURN
      END
*-----------------------------------------------------------*
```

Could we have printed FILEID in place of ID in the statement that prints the intersection number? Printing FILEID instead of ID would be a logic error that might be hard to identify. FILEID contains the last intersection number in the data file; unless this last entry matches the identification that we entered with the terminal, we will print the wrong identification number with the average that was computed.

The following output is the result of three different runs of the program using the data given in the hand-worked example: We entered 23 as the desired intersection number in the first run; we entered 17 as the desired intersection number in the second run; we entered 44 as the desired intersection number in the third run.

```
INTERSECTION   23
AVERAGE CARS PER MINUTE =     2.09
```

```
INTERSECTION   17
AVERAGE CARS PER MINUTE =     4.00
```

```
NO OBSERVATIONS FOR INTERSECTION   44
```

What would happen if there were several observations for an intersection but no cars passed through the intersection during the observations? Because TOTMIN would not be zero, we do not have to worry about division by zero. TOTCAR would be zero, though, and the average value would be zero. The program would print the intersection number and follow that with an average of 0.00.

6-8 FUNCTIONS FOR SEARCH ALGORITHMS

Solutions to different problems often include some of the same steps, such as computing the average of a set of values or finding the maximum of a set of values. Once we have written a function, such as one to compute the average of the values in an array, we can often reuse a function in another program with little or no modification to the function. Another very common operation performed with arrays is searching the array for a specific value. We may want to know if a particular value is in the array, how many times it occurs in the array, or where it first occurs in the array. All these forms of searches determine a single value, and thus are good candidates for functions. In this section we will develop several functions for searching an array; then when you need to perform a search in a program, you can probably use one of these functions with little or no modification to the function.

Searching algorithms fall into two groups: those for searching an unordered list and those for searching an ordered list.

UNORDERED LIST

We first consider searching an unordered list; thus we assume the elements are not necessarily sorted into an ascending numerical order, or any other order that may aid us in searching the array. The algorithm to search an unordered array is just a simple sequential search: check the first element, check the second element, and so on. There are several ways that we could implement this function. We could develop the function as an integer function that returns the position of the desired value in the array or zero if the desired value is not in the array. We could develop the function as an integer function that returns the number of times the element occurs in the array. We could also develop the function as a logical function that returns a value of true if the element is in the array or false if the element is not in the array. All these ideas represent valid functions, and we could think of programs that would use each of these forms. Since we have already written functions that return an integer value and functions that return a real value, we will implement this function as a logical function. We will call the function FOUND in order to make references to the function read smoothly. A reference to the function FOUND, as it might appear in a main program, is shown next.

```
IF (FOUND(X,COUNT,KEY)) THEN
    PRINT*, 'ITEM IS IN STOCK'
ELSE
    PRINT*, 'ITEM IS NOT IN STOCK'
ENDIF
```

Note that the function has three arguments, the array (X), the number of valid data values in the array (COUNT), and the value for which we are searching (KEY).

EXAMPLE 6-7   **Search Function for Unordered List**

Write a logical function to search an unordered list for a specific value. The function should return a value of true if the specific value is found; otherwise the function should return a value of false. The function will need three arguments—the array, the number of valid data entries in the array, and the value for which we are searching. Assume that all these values are integers.

Solution

In the development of the function, we assume that the values are already stored in the array X, a variable COUNT specifies the number of valid data values in the array, and the variable KEY contains the value for which we are searching.

DECOMPOSITION OF FOUND(X,COUNT,KEY)

Search an unordered list for a specific value.

FOUND(x,count,key): If count $>$ 0 then
   done $\leftarrow$ false
   i $\leftarrow$ 1
  Else
   done $\leftarrow$ true
   found $\leftarrow$ false
  While not done do
   If x(i) $=$ key then
    done $\leftarrow$ true
    found $\leftarrow$ true
   Else
    i $\leftarrow$ i $+$ 1
   If i $>$ count then
    done $\leftarrow$ true
    found $\leftarrow$ false
  Return

Converting this to a FORTRAN function yields the following:

FORTRAN Function

```
*------------------------------------------------------------*
      LOGICAL FUNCTION  FOUND(X,COUNT,KEY)
*
*  This function determines whether or not
*  the key value is in an unordered array.
*
      INTEGER  X(COUNT), COUNT, KEY, I
      LOGICAL  DONE
*
      IF (COUNT.GT.0) THEN
         DONE = .FALSE.
         I = 1
      ELSE
         DONE = .TRUE.
         FOUND = .FALSE.
      ENDIF
    5 IF (.NOT.DONE) THEN
         IF (X(I).EQ.KEY) THEN
            DONE = .TRUE.
            FOUND = .TRUE.
         ELSE
            I = I + 1
         ENDIF
         IF (I.GT.COUNT) THEN
            DONE = .TRUE.
            FOUND = .FALSE.
         ENDIF
         GO TO 5
      ENDIF
      RETURN
      END
*------------------------------------------------------------*
```

We now present a program that could be used to test the search function. The program will ask the user to enter a set of data to be stored in the array. It will then ask the user to enter a specific value to be used in searching the array. The program will use the function to do the search; the program will then print a message giving the result of the search. The structure chart for the program is shown next:

FORTRAN Main Program

```
*-------------------------------------------------------------------*
      PROGRAM  TEST
*
*   This program tests the search function.
*
      INTEGER  X(10), COUNT, KEY, J
      LOGICAL   FOUND
*
      PRINT*, 'ENTER COUNT (<11) OF VALUES FOR LIST'
      READ*, COUNT
      PRINT*, 'ENTER VALUES'
      READ*, (X(J),J=1,COUNT)
      PRINT*, 'ENTER VALUE FOR SEARCH'
      READ*, KEY
*
      IF (FOUND(X,COUNT,KEY)) THEN
          PRINT*, KEY,' FOUND IN THE LIST'
      ELSE
          PRINT*, KEY,' NOT FOUND IN THE LIST'
      ENDIF
      END
*-------------------------------------------------------------------*
                    FOUND function goes here
*-------------------------------------------------------------------*
```

An example of a test of the function FOUND using this program is shown below:

```
ENTER COUNT (<11) OF VALUES FOR LIST
3
ENTER VALUES
26    -3    7
ENTER VALUE FOR SEARCH
15
     15 NOT FOUND IN THE LIST
```

ORDERED LIST

We now consider searching an ordered, or sorted, list of values. Consider the list of ordered values below and assume that we are searching for the value 25:

−7
2
14
38
52
77
105

As soon as you reached the value 38, you knew that 25 was not in the list because you knew that the list was ordered. Therefore, we do not have to search the entire list, as we would have to do for an unordered list; we only need to search past the point where the key value should have been located. If the list is in ascending order we search until the current value in the array is larger than the key; if the list is in descending order we search until the current value in the array is smaller than the key value.

We present two common algorithms for searching an ordered list. The first searches sequentially until we either find the item or recognize that we have passed the position where it would have been in the list. The second algorithm first checks the middle of the array and decides if the item for which we are searching is in the first half of the array or the second half of the array. If it is in the first half, we then check the middle of the first half and decide whether the item is in the first fourth of the array or the second fourth of the array. The process of dividing the array into smaller and smaller pieces continues until we find the element or find the position where it should have been. Since this technique continually divides the part of the array that we are searching in half, it is sometimes called a *binary search*.

EXAMPLE 6-8 **Search Function for Ordered List**

Write a logical function to sequentially search an ordered list for a specific value. The function should return a value of true if the specific value is found; otherwise the function should return a value of false. The function will need three arguments — the array, the number of valid data entries in the array, and the value for which we are searching. Assume that all these values are integers.

Solution

In the development of the function, we assume that the sorted values are already stored in the array X, a variable COUNT specifies the number of valid data values in the array, and the variable KEY contains the value for which we are searching.

DECOMPOSITION OF FOUND(X,COUNT,KEY)

Search ordered list for a specific value.

PSEUDOCODE FOR SEQUENTIALLY SEARCHING AN ORDERED LIST

FOUND(x,count,key): If count > 0 then
    done ← false
    i ← 1
Else
    done ← true
    found ← false
While not done do
  If x(i) = key then
    done ← true
    found ← true
  Else if x(i) > key then
    done ← true
    found ← false
  Else
    i ← i + 1
  If i > count then
    done ← true
    found ← false
Return

Converting this to a FORTRAN function yields the following:

FORTRAN Function

```
*--------------------------------------------------*
      LOGICAL FUNCTION  FOUND(X,COUNT,KEY)
*
*  This function determines whether or not
*  the key value is in an ordered array
*  using a sequential search.
*
      INTEGER  X(COUNT), COUNT, KEY, I
      LOGICAL  DONE
*
      IF (COUNT.GT.0) THEN
         DONE = .FALSE.
         I = 1
      ELSE
         DONE = .TRUE.
         FOUND = .FALSE.
      ENDIF
    5 IF (.NOT.DONE) THEN
         IF (X(I).EQ.KEY) THEN
            DONE = .TRUE.
            FOUND = .TRUE.
         ELSEIF (X(I).GT.KEY) THEN
            DONE = .TRUE.
            FOUND = .FALSE.
         ELSE
            I = I + 1
         ENDIF
         IF (I.GT.COUNT) THEN
            DONE = .TRUE.
            FOUND = .FALSE.
         ENDIF
         GO TO 5
      ENDIF
      RETURN
      END
*--------------------------------------------------*
```

EXAMPLE 6-9   **Binary Search Function for Ordered List**

Write a logical function to implement a binary search for a specific value using an ordered list. The function should return a value of true if the specific value is found; otherwise the function should return a value of false. The function will need three arguments — the array, the number of valid data entries in the array, and the value for which we are searching. Assume that all these values are integers.

Solution

In the development of the function, we assume that the values are already stored in the array X, a variable COUNT specifies the number of valid data values in the array, and the variable KEY contains the value for which we are searching.

DECOMPOSITION OF FOUND(X,COUNT,KEY)

Search an ordered list for a specific value using a binary search.

We first illustrate the binary search algorithm with the list used in the previous example in which we were searching sequentially for the value 25.

−7
2
14
38
52
77
105

There are seven values, the first referenced by a subscript value of 1 and the last referenced by a subscript value of 7. In a binary search, we compute the middle position by adding the first position number to the last position number and dividing by two. This should be done as an integer division. In our case, 7 plus 1 equals 8, and 8 divided by 2 is 4. Thus, we check the fourth position and compare its value to the value for which we are searching. The fourth value is 38, which is larger than 25, so we can narrow our search to the top half of the array. Our first position is still 1, and our last position is changed to the position above the middle position, or 3. We now divide that part of the array in half and compute the new midpoint to be $(1 + 3)/2$, or 2. The second value is 2, which is smaller than 25, so we can narrow our search to the second quarter of the array. Our first position is now one past the middle position, or 3, and our last position is 3. When the first and last positions are the same, we have narrowed in on the position where the value should be. Thus, we can exit the search algorithm. This specific example is illustrated in the following diagram. Follow through each step to be sure that you understand the sequence of steps needed.

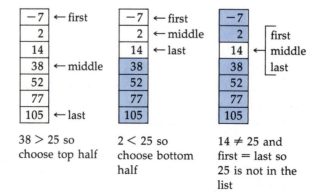

When the number of elements in the array is even, it is possible for the position of the first element to be greater than the position of the last element if the desired value is not in the list. Therefore, if the position of the first element is equal to or greater than the position of the last element, then the key value is not in the list. We now develop the detailed steps for searching an ordered list using a binary search.

PSEUDOCODE FOR A BINARY SEARCH WITH AN ORDERED LIST

FOUND(x,count,key): If count ≤ 0 then
    found ← false
Else
  done ← false
  found ← false
  first ← 1
  last ← count
  While not done do
    middle ← (first + last)/2
    If x(middle) = key then
      found ← true
      done ← true
    If not done then
      If first ≥ last then
        done ← true
      Else if x(middle) > key then
        last ← middle − 1
      Else
        first ← middle + 1
Return

Converting this to a FORTRAN function yields the following:

```
*--------------------------------------------------------*
      LOGICAL FUNCTION  FOUND(X,COUNT,KEY)
*
*  This function determines whether or not
*  the key value is in an ordered array
*  using a binary search.
*
      INTEGER  X(COUNT), COUNT, KEY, FIRST, LAST, MIDDLE
      LOGICAL  DONE
*
      IF (COUNT.LE.0) THEN
          FOUND = .FALSE.
      ELSE
          DONE = .FALSE.
          FOUND = .FALSE.
          FIRST = 1
          LAST = COUNT
    5     IF (.NOT.DONE) THEN
              MIDDLE = (FIRST + LAST)/2
              IF (X(MIDDLE).EQ.KEY) THEN
                  FOUND = .TRUE.
                  DONE = .TRUE.
              ENDIF
              IF (.NOT.DONE) THEN
                  IF (FIRST.GE.LAST) THEN
                      DONE = .TRUE.
                  ELSEIF (X(MIDDLE.GT.KEY) THEN
                      LAST = MIDDLE - 1
                  ELSE
                      FIRST = MIDDLE + 1
                  ENDIF
              ENDIF
              GO TO 5
          ENDIF
      ENDIF
      RETURN
      END
*--------------------------------------------------------*
```

The program presented in Example 6-7 for testing the search function for an unordered list could be used to test the search functions developed in examples 6-8 and 6-9. The only change needed is an additional message to the user to specify that the data values must be in ascending order.

While both the sequential sort and the binary search correctly search for an item in an ordered list, the sequential sort is more efficient for small lists, and the binary search is more efficient for large lists.

SUMMARY

A function is a module that represents a single value. FORTRAN contains many intrinsic functions that compute values such as trigonometric functions and logarithms. We can also write our own functions. The statement function is a specification statement that defines a function within our program. A statement function can only be used when the function can be defined in a single assignment statement. A function subprogram is an independent module that is used to define functions that require more than a single assignment statement. All three forms of functions are useful in engineering and science applications because they simplify the computations in our programs. Several forms of functions for searching an array were also presented.

DEBUGGING AIDS

Testing a function should be approached much like testing a complete program. You will also need a simple program, called a *driver*, to initialize the input to the function that you are testing. This driver program should print the output of the function so that you can determine if it is returning the proper value. If it is not returning the proper value, the following list of checks may help you locate the problem:

1. Be sure that the function is returning the proper type of value. The easiest way to ensure this is to use explicit typing with the function.
2. Be sure that each path to a RETURN provides a value for the function.
3. Be sure that the variables listed in the main program match the arguments listed in the function subprogram. Check the corresponding variables for correct type and order.
4. Print the values of all variables just before using the function and just after returning from the function as you debug it.
5. Include PRINT statements in the function just as you do in a main program to help isolate trouble spots.
6. Remember that variables should not be initialized within the function with a DATA statement because these are not initialized with each use of the function. The DATA statement only initializes variables when the program is first begun.

STYLE/TECHNIQUE GUIDES

Using statement functions and function subprograms to replace computations within a main program greatly improve program structure and readability. The structure of a function subprogram should receive the same attention as the structure of a main program. If a function becomes long and difficult to read, perhaps additional functions should be used. Function subprograms can reference intrinsic functions and even other function subprograms. Once you have decided which operations will be written as functions, follow these three style suggestions:

1. Choose descriptive names for your functions.
2. Use comments in the functions as you would in the main program. In particular, use comments at the beginning of a function to describe its purpose and to define its arguments, if necessary.
3. For clarity, use the same variables in the argument list of the function as those used in the main program, if possible. If the function is needed several times with different arguments, choose completely different function variable names to avoid confusion with main program variables.

KEY WORDS

argument	main program
binary search	module
driver	search algorithm
function	statement function
generic function	structure chart
intrinsic function	subprogram
library function	variable dimensioning

PROBLEMS

We begin our problem set with modifications to programs developed earlier in this chapter. Give the decomposition, refined pseudocode or flowchart, and FORTRAN solution for each problem.

Problems 1–5 modify the temperature conversion program TABLE1, given on page 252.

1. Modify the temperature conversion program so that it reads a variable specifying the number of lines in the table instead of a number of degrees for the last line.
2. Modify the temperature conversion program so that the statement functions convert temperatures using units in Centigrade and in Kelvin. Both conversion equations can be derived from the following equation that converts degrees Kelvin to degrees Centigrade:

$$\text{Centigrade} = \text{Kelvin} - 273.15$$

3. Modify the temperature conversion program so that the statement functions convert temperatures using units in Rankin and in Fahrenheit. Both conversion equations can be derived from the following equation that converts degrees Fahrenheit to degrees Rankin:

$$\text{Rankin} = \text{Fahrenheit} + 459.67$$

4. Modify the temperature conversion program so that the statement functions convert temperatures using units in Rankin and in Kelvin. Both conversion

equations can be derived from the following equation that converts degrees Kelvin to degrees Rankin:

$$\text{Rankin} = 1.8 \times \text{Kelvin}$$

5. Modify the temperature conversion program so that it contains statement functions to convert temperatures from any of the units Fahrenheit, Centigrade, Kelvin, and Rankin, to any of the other units.

Problems 6–10 modify the oil well production program REPORT, given on page 275.

6. Modify the oil production program so that it asks the user to enter the current date and then prints this date in the upper right-hand corner of the first page of the report. Thus, the report will show the date that the report was run in addition to the date of the time period for which the data was collected.

7. Modify the oil production program so that the maximum weekly production is determined and printed after the summary line.

8. Using an additional function, modify the oil production program so that it determines the maximum daily production for each oil well. Print this value in addition to the well average.

9. Using an additional function, modify the oil production program so that it determines the total production for each oil well. Print this value in addition to the well average.

10. Modify the oil production program so that it determines the average oil production for an oil well based on non-zero production days. Thus, if a well produced 0 barrels of oil one day of the week, the average would be based on 6 days instead of 7.

Problems 11–15 modify the traffic flow program ANALYZ, given on page 280.

11. Modify the traffic flow program so that it prints the number of cars passing through the intersection and the total number of minutes of observation.

12. Modify the traffic flow program so that it computes an average of cars per minute for the combined data in the data file.

13. Modify the traffic flow program so that it will reopen the data file after computing the average for an intersection. Continue reading intersections and computing averages until an intersection number of 99999 is reached.

14. Modify the traffic flow program so that it will count the number of different intersections that are represented by the data in the data file.

15. Modify the traffic flow program so that it will allow an observation to extend past midnight. (Thus, the ending time could be smaller than the beginning time: For example, if the beginning time is 2330 and the ending time is 0030, the total time period is 60 minutes.)

For problems 16–20, write the function subprogram whose return value is described. The input to the function is an integer array K of 100 elements.

16. MAXI(K), the maximum value of the array K.

17. MINI(K), the minimum value of the array K.

18. NPOS(K), the number of values greater than or equal to zero in the array K.

19. NNEG(K), the number of values less than zero in the array K.

20. NZERO(K), the number of values equal to zero in the array K.

For problems 21–24, assume that you have a function subprogram DENOM, with input value x, to compute the following expression:

$$x^2 + \sqrt{1 + 2x + 3x^2}$$

Give the main program statements that use this function to compute and print each of the following expressions:

21. $\text{ALPHA} = \dfrac{6.9 + y}{y^2 + \sqrt{1 + 2y + 3y^2}}$

22. $\text{BETA} = \dfrac{\sin y}{y^4 + \sqrt{1 + 2y^2 + 3y^4}}$

23. $\text{GAMMA} = \dfrac{2.3z + z^4}{z^2 + \sqrt{1 + 2z + 3z^2}}$

24. $\text{DELTA} = \dfrac{1}{\sin^2 y + \sqrt{1 + 2 \sin y + 3 \sin^2 y}}$

In problems 25–30, develop these programs and functions. Use the five-phase design process.

25. Write a function whose input is a 2-digit integer. The function is to return a 2-digit number whose digits are reversed from the input number. Thus, if 17 is the input to the function, 71 is the output.

26. Write a function FACT that receives an integer value and returns the factorial of the value. Recall that the definition of a factorial is

$$0! = 1$$
$$n! = n \cdot (n - 1) \cdot (n - 2) \cdot \ldots \cdot 1$$

If $n < 0$, the function should return a value of zero.

27. Write a function TOTAL that will convert three arguments representing hours, minutes, and seconds to all seconds. For example, TOTAL(3,2,5) should return the integer value 10,925.

28. The cosine of an angle may be computed from this series, where x is measured in radians:

$$\cos x = 1 - \frac{x^2}{2!} + \frac{x^4}{4!} - \frac{x^6}{6!} + \cdots$$

Write a function COSX whose input is an angle in radians. The function should compute the first 10 terms of the series and return that approximation of the cosine. Use the factorial function developed in problem 26. (*Hint:* The alternating sign can be obtained by computing $(-1)**K$. When K is even, $(-1)**K$ is equal to $+1$; when K is odd, $(-1)**K$ is equal to -1.)

29. Rewrite the function in problem 28 such that it computes the cosine with only as many terms of the series as are necessary to ensure that the absolute value of the last term is less than 0.000001.

30. Write a main program that will produce a table with three columns. The first column (x) should contain angles from 0.0–3.1 radians in increments of 0.1 radians. The second column should contain the cosines of the angles as computed by the intrinsic function. The third column should contain the cosines as computed by the function in problem 28. Print the cosine values with an F9.7 format.

31. Engineering programs often utilize experimental data which has been collected and then stored in tabular form. The programs read the data and use it to generate plots, displays, or additional data. Examples of such data include wind tunnel force data on a new aircraft design, rocket motor thrust data, or automobile engine horsepower and torque data. The table of data below gives the thrust output of a new rocket motor as a function of time from ignition.

TIME	THRUST
0.0	0.0
1.0	630.0
2.0	915.0
5.0	870.0
8.0	860.0
12.0	885.0
13.0	890.0
15.0	895.0
20.0	888.0
22.0	860.0
23.0	872.0
26.0	810.0
30.0	730.0
32.0	574.0
33.0	217.0
34.0	0.0

Write a function called THRUST which computes the motor thrust for a rocket flight simulation program. The function should estimate the thrust for a specified time value using data from the table above. If the specified time value is not one of the times in the table then the new data value can be determined from the tabulated values by using *linear interpolation*, which is also called linear proportional scaling. For example, the estimated thrust at T = 2.2 seconds would be computed in the following manner:

$$\text{THRUST} = 915.0 + \left(\frac{2.2 - 2.0}{5.0 - 2.0}\right) \cdot (870.0 - 915.0)$$

$$= 912.0$$

Assume that the function has two arguments: the two-dimensional real array with 35 rows and two columns, and the new value of time. If the time matches a time entry in the table, then the function should return the corresponding thrust value. If the time value does not match a time entry in the table, then the function should interpolate for a corresponding thrust value. Assume that the function will not be referenced if the time is less than zero or greater than 34.0.

FORTRAN STATEMENT SUMMARY

FUNCTION Statement:

$$\text{FUNCTION} \quad name \quad (argument \ list)$$

Examples:

```
FUNCTION  SUM(X,N)

REAL FUNCTION  AVE(TESTS)
```

Discussion:

The FUNCTION statement assigns a name to a function and lists the arguments that represent the input to the function. The value returned by the function is assigned to the name of the function. We recommend explicit typing of the function to clearly specify the type of value that is being returned by the function.

Statement Function:

$$name \ (argument \ list) = expression$$

Example:

```
AREA(SIDE) = SIDE*SIDE
```

Discussion:

A statement function is a function that can be computed with a single assignment statement. It is defined at the beginning of the program instead of in a separate subprogram definition.

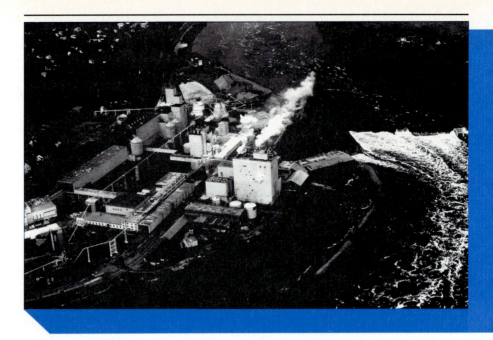

APPLICATION — Waste Water Treatment (Chemical Engineering)

When waste water from industrial plants is released into streams the organic material in the waste water decomposes through chemical and bacterial action. Oxygen is consumed in this process as carbon dioxide and water are produced. As the oxygen is consumed the waste water is deoxygenated. At the same time oxygen is also continuously being absorbed into the stream from the air, and thus the waste water is reoxygenated. These two processes, deoxygenation and reoxygenation, take place at different rates. The rate of each depends on the oxygen level in the combined mixture of waste water and stream water. Write a program to analyze these processes using information from a data file. (See Section 7–3 for the solution.)

7

IMPLEMENTING TOP-DOWN
DESIGN WITH SUBROUTINES

Introduction

7–1 Subroutine Subprograms

7–2 Application — Simulation Data (Computer Science/Engineering)

7–3 Application — Waste Water Treatment (Chemical Engineering)

7–4 Subroutines for Inserting and Deleting

7–5 Application — Computer Security (Computer Science/Engineering)

7–6 Common Blocks

Summary

INTRODUCTION

FORTRAN supports two types of subprograms: functions and subroutines. In Chapter 6 we learned to write our own functions, and we saw a number of applications that used functions. In this chapter we learn to write *subroutines* and how to choose the type of subprogram that best fits a problem solution. Both functions and subroutines are used frequently in our text to illustrate their importance in making our programs simpler and more readable.

7 – 1 SUBROUTINE SUBPROGRAMS

In Chapter 6 we saw that a function subprogram is a module that computes a single value and returns that value through the function reference. FORTRAN contains a number of intrinsic functions that are available to our programs, and we can also write our own functions as either statement functions or as function subprograms. Although these functions are useful when we need to compute a single value, there are applications in which we would like to use a module to return many values or to print a message. In these instances, a subroutine is required. A subroutine differs from a function in the following ways:

1. A subroutine does not represent a value; thus, its name should be chosen for documentation purposes and not to specify a real or integer value.
2. A subroutine is referenced with an executable statement whose general form is

CALL *subroutine name (argument list)*

3. A subroutine uses the argument list not only for subprogram inputs but also for any output. To provide output to the main program, the arguments in the CALL statement must match in type, number, and order those used in the subroutine definition. The argument variable names themselves, though, do not have to match.
4. A subroutine may return one value, many values, or no value.

Writing a subroutine is much like writing a function, except that the first line in a subroutine identifies it as a subroutine. The general form of this statement is

SUBROUTINE *name (argument list)*

Subroutine output is returned by the arguments rather than by the name. (Remember that a function's output is returned by its name.)

Because the subroutine is a separate program, the arguments are the only link between the main program and the subroutine. Thus, the choice of subroutine statement numbers and variable names is independent of the choice of statement numbers and variable names used in the main program. When arrays are used as arguments, it is generally advisable to use the same array sizes in both the main program and the subroutine. Variable dimensioning can also be used in subroutines; you may want to review the discussion on variable dimensioning on page 262 in Chapter 6.

The subroutine, like the function, requires a RETURN statement to return control to the main program or to the subprogram that called it. It also requires an END statement because it is a complete program module.

EXAMPLE 7-1   **Array Statistics**

Information commonly needed from a set of data includes the average, the minimum value, and the maximum value. These values can be computed using three functions; however, if all three are required, it is more efficient to compute them simultaneously. Write a subroutine that is called with the statement

```
CALL STAT(X,N,XAVE,XMIN,XMAX)
```

where N is the number of elements in the real array X.

Solution

A subroutine, like a function, is a complete program that should be developed using the decomposition and refinement process. Because we have already developed solutions for determining averages, minimums, and maximums, these steps are straightforward. Note that we include the name of the subroutine and its parameters in the decomposition and refinement steps, just as we did with functions.

DECOMPOSITION OF STAT(x,n,xave,xmin,xmax)

| Determine xmin, xmax, xsum. |
| Compute xave. |
| Return. |

REFINEMENT IN PSEUDOCODE

```
STAT(x,n,xave,xmin,xmax):
    sum ← x(1)
    xmin ← x(1)
    xmax ← x(1)
    For i = 2 to n do
        sum ← sum + x(i)
        If x(i) < xmin then xmin ← x(i)
        If x(i) > xmax then xmax ← x(i)
    xave ← sum/n
    Return
```

We now present a program that reads a set of exam scores and then calls the subroutine STAT to compute some statistics from the scores.

FORTRAN Program

```
*------------------------------------------------------------*
      PROGRAM  SCORES
*
*   This program reads a set of test scores and
*   then computes their average, minimum, and maximum.
*
      INTEGER  N, I
      REAL   TESTS(100), AVE, MIN, MAX
*
      PRINT*, 'ENTER NUMBER OF TESTS (<101)'
      READ*, N
      PRINT*, 'ENTER TEST SCORES'
      READ*, (TESTS(I), I=1,N)
*
      CALL STAT(TESTS,N,AVE,MIN,MAX)
*
      PRINT 5, AVE
    5 FORMAT (1X,'AVERAGE TEST SCORE = ',F6.2)
      PRINT 10, MIN, MAX
   10 FORMAT (1X,'MINIMUM SCORE = ',F6.2,5X,
     +        'MAXIMUM SCORE = ',F6.2)
*
      END
*------------------------------------------------------------*
*
      SUBROUTINE  STAT(X,N,XAVE,XMIN,XMAX)
*
*   This subroutine computes the average, minimum,
*   and maximum of a real array with N values.
*
      INTEGER  N, I
      REAL   X(N), XAVE, XMIN, XMAX, SUM
*
      SUM = X(1)
      XMIN = X(1)
      XMAX = X(1)
      DO 10 I=2,N
         SUM = SUM + X(I)
         IF (X(I).LT.XMIN) XMIN = X(I)
         IF (X(I).GT.XMAX) XMAX = X(I)
   10 CONTINUE
      XAVE = SUM/REAL(N)
*
      RETURN
      END
*------------------------------------------------------------*
```

EXAMPLE 7-2   **Sort Subroutine**

In Chapter 5, we wrote a program that included the steps to sort a one-dimensional array. This operation is used so frequently that we will rewrite it in the form of a subroutine. To make it flexible, we use a variable in the argument list to specify the number of elements in the array. We suggest that you store this subroutine in your file area so that it can be accessed easily. Note that we copy the input array X into an array Y before sorting Y; this allows us to keep the original order in X and have the ascending order in Y. If you do not wish to use two arrays, use this CALL statement in the following program:

$$\text{CALL SORT(X,X,N)}$$

Solution

We could use any of the three sort algorithms from Chapter 5 in the subroutine. Since we used the selection sort in another program in Chapter 5, we will use the bubble sort here. The structure chart for this program is:

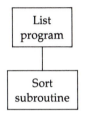

FORTRAN Program

```
*-------------------------------------------------------------*
      PROGRAM  LIST
*
*  This program reads a list of real values,
*  sorts them in ascending order, and prints them.
*
      INTEGER  N, I
      REAL  X(25), Y(25)
*
      PRINT*, 'ENTER THE NUMBER OF VALUES TO SORT'
      PRINT*, '(MAXIMUM 25)'
      READ*, N
      PRINT*, 'ENTER THE VALUES'
      READ*, (X(I), I=1,N)
*
```

continued

```
        CALL SORT(X,Y,N)
*
        PRINT*, 'VALUES IN ASCENDING ORDER:'
        DO 10 I=1,N
           PRINT 5, Y(I)
     5     FORMAT (1X,F5.2)
    10 CONTINUE
*
        END
*------------------------------------------------------------*
*
        SUBROUTINE  SORT(X,Y,N)
*
*  This subroutine sorts an array X into an array Y
*  in ascending order. Both arrays have N values.
*
        INTEGER  N, I, FIRST, LAST
        REAL  X(N), Y(N), TEMP
        LOGICAL  SORTED
*
        DO 10 I=1,N
           Y(I) = X(I)
    10 CONTINUE
*
        SORTED = .FALSE.
        FIRST = 1
        LAST = N - 1
    15 IF (.NOT.SORTED) THEN
           SORTED = .TRUE.
           DO 20 I=FIRST,LAST
              IF (Y(I).GT.Y(I+1)) THEN
                 TEMP = Y(I)
                 Y(I) = Y(I+1)
                 Y(I+1) = TEMP
                 SORTED = .FALSE.
              ENDIF
    20     CONTINUE
           LAST = LAST - 1
           GO TO 15
        ENDIF
*
        RETURN
        END
*------------------------------------------------------------*
```

In the main program, we specified that the list of values to be sorted had a
maximum of 25 values (because we dimensioned our arrays to 25
values). Thus, we can use 25 values or less, but not more than 25. The
subroutine itself does not have any maximum; it can sort any number of
values as long as the values are part of an array that has been properly
defined in the main program.

This self-test allows you to check quickly to see if you have remembered some of the key points from Section 7–1. If you have any problems with these exercises, you should reread this section. The solutions are included at the end of the text.

Questions 1–2 refer to the following program and subroutine. The program generates an array of 10 numbers, containing the integers 1–10. The subroutine modifies these numbers.

FORTRAN PROGRAM

```
*-------------------------------------------------------*
      PROGRAM  QUIZ
*
*  This program tests your understanding of subroutines.
*
      INTEGER  K(10), I
*
      DO 10 I=1,10
         K(I) = I
   10 CONTINUE
*
      CALL MODIFY(K,10)
*
      PRINT*, 'NEW VALUES OF K ARE:'
      PRINT 15, (K(I), I=1,10)
   15 FORMAT (1X,5I5)
*
      END
*-------------------------------------------------------*
*
      SUBROUTINE  MODIFY(K,N)
*
*  This subroutine modifies elements in K.
*
      INTEGER  N, K(N), I
*
      DO 5 I=1,N
         K(I) = K(I)*2
    5 CONTINUE
*
      RETURN
      END
*-------------------------------------------------------*
```

1. What is the program output?
2. What is the program output if the reference to the subroutine is replaced with the following statement?

```
CALL MODIFY(K,5)
```

7–2 APPLICATION—SIMULATION DATA
(Computer Science/Engineering)

A routine to generate random numbers is useful in many engineering and science applications. Most game programs use randomly generated numbers to make the program appear to have a mind of its own—it chooses different actions each time the game is played. Programs that simulate something, such as tosses of a coin or the number of people at the bank window, also use random number generators.

In this application we use a random number generator to simulate (or model) noise that might occur in a piece of instrumentation, such as static. These applications of random events or random numbers use a random number generator routine. The routine that we present generates numbers between 0.0 and 1.0. The numbers are uniformly distributed across the interval between 0.0 and 1.0, which means that we are just as likely to get 0.4455 as we are to get 0.0090. This random number generator requires an argument that is a seed to the computation. When we give the routine a different seed, it returns a different random number. If we want a series of random numbers, we initialize the seed once, and we do not modify it again. The random number generator modifies the seed itself from one call of the routine to the next.

Although the routine computes and returns a single value, it also needs a seed whose value is preserved from one call to the routine to the next. Therefore, we really have two values that are being returned from the routine. You can now see why we use a subroutine instead of a function to implement this random number generator. The details of this random number generator are beyond the scope of this text. It essentially causes the computer to compute integers that are too large to store. The portion of the number that can be stored is a random sequence that is used to determine the random number. If you want more information on this algorithm, see S. D. Stearns, "A Portable Random Number Generator for Use in Signal Processing," Sandia National Laboratories Technical Report.

FORTRAN Subroutine

```
*-------------------------------------------------------------*
      SUBROUTINE  RANDOM(SEED,RANDX)
*
*  This subroutine generates random values
*  between 0.0 and 1.0 using an integer seed.
*
      INTEGER  SEED
      REAL  RANDX
*
      SEED = 2045*SEED + 1
      SEED = SEED - (SEED/1048576)*1048576
      RANDX = REAL(SEED + 1)/1048577.0
*
      RETURN
      END
*-------------------------------------------------------------*
```

The main program that follows allows you to enter a seed; the program then prints the first 10 random numbers generated with that seed. Try the program with different seeds and observe that you get different numbers. An example output is shown for a seed of 12357 so that you can check to see if your subroutine is working properly.

FORTRAN PROGRAM

```
*---------------------------------------------------------------*
      PROGRAM  TEST
*
*  This program tests the random number generator.
*
      INTEGER  I, SEED
      REAL  X
*
      PRINT*, 'ENTER A POSITIVE INTEGER SEED VALUE'
      READ*, SEED
      PRINT*, 'RANDOM NUMBERS:'
      DO 10 I=1,10
         CALL RANDOM(SEED,X)
         PRINT 5, X
    5    FORMAT (1X,F8.6)
   10 CONTINUE
*
      END
*---------------------------------------------------------------*
                    RANDOM subroutine goes here
*---------------------------------------------------------------*
```

SAMPLE OUTPUT

```
ENTER A POSITIVE INTEGER SEED
12357
RANDOM NUMBERS:
0.099414
0.299419
0.310731
0.442812
0.548521
0.725532
0.712078
0.199705
0.395030
0.834445
```

We are now ready to discuss the application problem. We are going to develop an algorithm for a program that generates a data file that simulates a sine wave plus noise. The program uses both the intrinsic sine function and the subroutine to generate random numbers. The data file contains values of the signal

$$f(t) = 2 \sin(2 \cdot pi \cdot t) + noise$$

for $t = 0.0, 0.01, \ldots, 1.00$. Each value of the sine wave is added to a random number produced by the random number generator. Because the sine wave can vary from -2 to $+2$, and the random number generator can vary from 0 to 1, we can expect our experimental signal to vary from -2 to 3. This signal should be stored in a data file called SIGNAL, where each line of the data file should contain the value of t and the corresponding signal value.

PROBLEM STATEMENT

Generate a data file that contains samples of a sine wave $2 \sin(2 \cdot pi \cdot t)$, with uniform random noise between 0.0 and 1.0 added to it. The data points are to be evaluated with $t = 0.0, 0.01, \ldots, 1.00$.

INPUT/OUTPUT DESCRIPTION

The only input to the program is the seed to start the random number generator. The output is a data file called SIGNAL that contains 101 lines of data. Each line of data contains a value of time and the corresponding signal value.

HAND EXAMPLE

In our discussion of the random number generator, we illustrated the first 10 random numbers generated with seed 12357. Using these random numbers, the first 10 data points of the file SIGNAL are

```
f(0.00) = 2*sin(2*pi*0.00) + 0.099414 = 0.0994144
f(0.01) = 2*sin(2*pi*0.01) + 0.299419 = 0.4250000
f(0.02) = 2*sin(2*pi*0.02) + 0.310731 = 0.5613975
f(0.03) = 2*sin(2*pi*0.03) + 0.442812 = 0.8175746
f(0.04) = 2*sin(2*pi*0.04) + 0.548521 = 1.0459008
f(0.05) = 2*sin(2*pi*0.05) + 0.725532 = 1.3435660
f(0.06) = 2*sin(2*pi*0.06) + 0.712078 = 1.4483271
f(0.07) = 2*sin(2*pi*0.07) + 0.199705 = 1.0512636
f(0.08) = 2*sin(2*pi*0.08) + 0.395030 = 1.3585374
f(0.09) = 2*sin(2*pi*0.09) + 0.834445 = 1.9060986
```

ALGORITHM DEVELOPMENT

This program is straightforward. The only input is the random seed. The program then generates the signal values and writes them in a data file. We do not need arrays because each data value is needed only once.

DECOMPOSITION

Read random number seed.
Generate data values and write them to the file.

Refined Flowchart

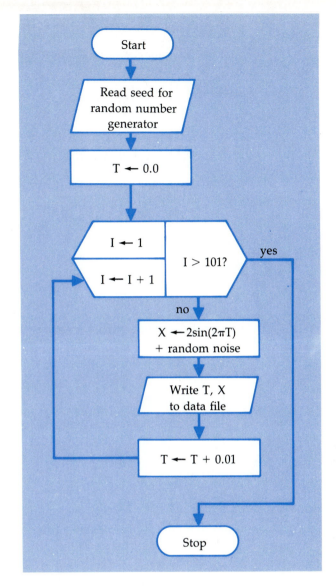

The structure chart for this program is the following:

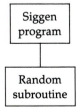

FORTRAN Program

```
*-----------------------------------------------------------------*
      PROGRAM  SIGGEN
*
*  This program generates a signal composed
*  of a sine wave plus random noise.
*
      INTEGER  SEED, I
      REAL  PI, T, NOISE, X
      DATA  PI, T /3.141593, 0.0/
*
      PRINT*, 'ENTER A POSITIVE INTEGER SEED'
      READ*, SEED
      OPEN (UNIT=15,FILE='SIGNAL',STATUS='NEW')
*
      DO 10 I=1,101
         CALL RANDOM(SEED,NOISE)
         X = 2.0*SIN(2.0*PI*T) + NOISE
         WRITE (15,*) T, X
         T = T + 0.01
   10 CONTINUE
*
      END
*-----------------------------------------------------------------*
*
      SUBROUTINE  RANDOM(SEED,RANDX)
*
*  This subroutine generates random values
*  between 0.0 and 1.0 using an integer seed.
*
      INTEGER  SEED
      REAL  RANDX
*
      SEED = 2045*SEED + 1
      SEED = SEED - (SEED/1048576)*1048576
      RANDX = REAL(SEED + 1)/1048577.0
*
      RETURN
      END
*-----------------------------------------------------------------*
```

TESTING

Use the random number generator seed that we used in the hand-worked example. Check the first 10 values of the data signal in the data file; if these match, we can be certain that our random number generator is working. It is difficult to test thoroughly a program with random values because we cannot expect (and should not get) the same values if we change the seed for the random number generator. However, the trend of the data should be the same. For example, in this problem, we should be able to see the sine wave in the data even though we use different random numbers for the noise. A plotting routine is helpful here. (In Chapter 8, problem 33 discusses a simple plot routine that can be used to plot data on your terminal screen.) Some plots of the data from program SIGGEN are shown. The first plot shows the sine wave with no noise; the next two plots are plots of the data file using different random seeds.

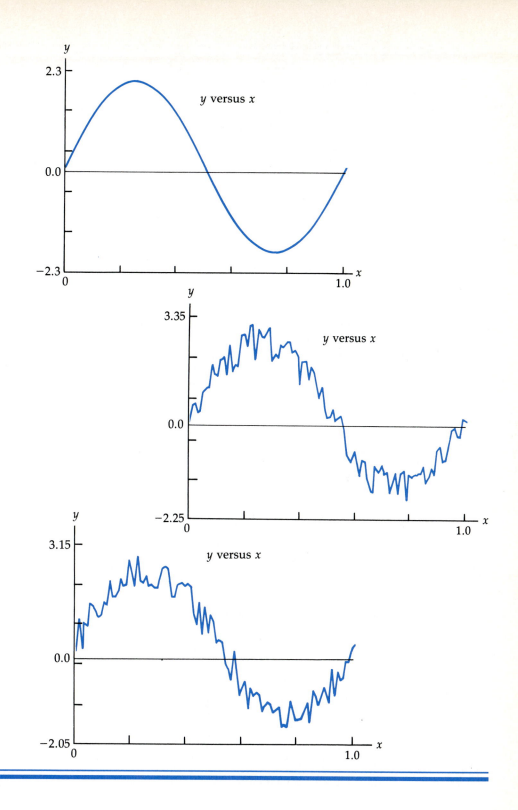

y versus x

y versus x

y versus x

7–3 APPLICATION—WASTE WATER TREATMENT (Chemical Engineering)

Organic material in waste water from industrial plants decomposes through chemical and bacterial action. Oxygen is consumed in this process as carbon dioxide and water are produced. As the oxygen is consumed, the waste water is deoxygenated. A standard procedure for determining the rate of deoxygenation begins by diluting a waste water sample with fresh water containing a known amount of dissolved oxygen. The combined sample is then held at 20° C for 5 days and then checked for the amount of final oxygen. A biological oxygen demand (BOD) is then calculated from the initial and final oxygen levels. The biological oxygen demand for a 20 day test (at 20° C) is called the first-stage demand. It can be calculated using the five day (BOD) measurements.

Although oxygen is consumed from the stream when waste water is discharged, oxygen is also continuously being absorbed into the stream from the air. These two processes, deoxygenation and reoxygenation, take place at different rates. The rate of each depends on the oxygen level in the combined mixture of waste water and stream water. Initially, the rate of deoxygenation is rapid as there is a large amount of oxygen in the mixture. For this same reason the rate of reoxygenation is slow. As oxygen is consumed in decomposing the organic material, the oxygen level of the mixture drops. The lower oxygen level in the mixture causes the deoxygenation rate to decrease. It also causes the reoxygenation rate to increase. Hence, the dissolved oxygen level in the mixture decreases with time, reaches a minimum, and then increases. As the dissolved oxygen level decreases below the normal oxygen level of the stream, an oxygen deficit in the mixture is said to occur. The oxygen deficit of the mixture can be calculated in the following manner:

First, calculate the biological oxygen demand for the mixture of the stream and the waste water discharge:

$$bodmix = \frac{bods \cdot qs + bodd \cdot qd}{qs + qd}$$

where *bods* is the biological oxygen demand of the stream
  bodd is the biological oxygen demand of the discharge
  qs is the stream flow rate in million gallons/day
  qd is the discharge flow rate in million gallons/day

Next, estimate the first stage demand *(fsmix)* at the mixture temperature *(tmix)* in degrees centigrade, using the following formula:

$$f\,smix = \frac{bodmix}{0.68} \cdot [(0.02 \cdot tmix) + 0.6]$$

Finally, calculate the oxygen deficit as a function of time with the equation:

$$defct = \left\{ \frac{kd \cdot f\,smix}{kr - kd} \cdot [10^{-kd \cdot t} - 10^{-kr \cdot t}] \right\} + [doxygn \cdot 10^{-kr \cdot t}]$$

where kd is the coefficient of deoxygenation
kr is the coefficient of reoxygenation
$doxygn$ is the initial oxygen deficit
t is the elapsed time in days

Also, kd can be estimated by:

$$kd = 0.1 \cdot 1.047^{(tmix-20)}$$

Assume that you have been hired as a private consultant to a new water analysis laboratory, Clear View Unlimited. Your contract is to write a FORTRAN program to calculate the oxygen deficit as a function of time for several streams being analyzed. The information for the streams is stored in a file called STREAMS. The value in the first data line contains the number of streams in the file. Then each subsequent data line contains the information for one stream in the following order: qd, qs, $bodd$, $bods$, $tmix$, kr, and $doxygn$. (All these data values are in the units mentioned in the earlier discussion.) Your program should calculate the oxygen deficit for each stream in the file over a time period using 0.1 day increments. It should find the maximum deficit and when it occurred for each stream. The time period for the analysis will be entered by the user when the program is run.

PROBLEM STATEMENT

Write a FORTRAN program to determine the maximum oxygen deficit for each stream in a data file over a time period using 0.1 day increments.

INPUT/OUTPUT DESCRIPTION

The stream information for the program is stored in a data file. The first line of the file specifies how many streams are to be analyzed. Then, for each stream to be analyzed, an additional line in the file gives the values for qd, qs, $bodd$, $bods$, $tmix$, kr, and $doxygn$. The user will enter the time period to use in the analysis.

HAND EXAMPLE

For a hand example, we will use the following values for the equations:

$$qd = 2.5$$
$$qs = 65.0$$
$$bodd = 0.1$$
$$bods = 15.0$$
$$tmix = 17.6$$
$$kr = 0.45$$
$$doxygn = 7.3$$

The following table lists the value for days in increments of 0.1 for one day and the corresponding deficit:

DAYS	DEFICIT
0.1	6.974
0.2	6.671
0.3	6.391
0.4	6.131
0.5	5.888
0.6	5.662
0.7	5.451
0.8	5.254
0.9	5.070
1.0	4.896

If we were analyzing this stream over one day, the maximum deficit of 6.974 occurred at day 0.1.

ALGORITHM DEVELOPMENT

The decomposition for this problem is the following:

DECOMPOSITION

Print header.
Compute and print the maximum deficit and the day that it occurred for each stream.

As we refine the steps in the decomposition, we want to consider steps that might be written as functions and subroutines. In this problem, we read a set of parameters for each stream and then use them to compute two values, the maximum deficit and the day that it occurred. Since the computations involved are rather long, a subroutine would be a good way to implement the computations of these two values. (A function is not appropriate since there are two values that need to be returned to the main program.) We now develop a flowchart for the main program and a separate flowchart for the subroutine to calculate the maximum deficit and the day that it occurred.

The structure chart for this solution and the corresponding FORTRAN program follow:

FORTRAN Program

```
*----------------------------------------------------------------*
      PROGRAM  STREAM
*
* This program computes the maximum oxygen deficit for
* a group of waste water discharge streams.
*
      INTEGER  N, J
      REAL   DAYS, QD, QS, BODD, BODS, TMIX, KR, DOXYGN,
     +       DEFMAX, DEFDAY
*
      OPEN (UNIT=10,FILE='STREAMS',STATUS='OLD')
      PRINT*, 'ENTER TIME PERIOD FOR STREAM ANALYSIS'
      PRINT*, '(USE TIME IN TENTHS OF DAYS XX.X)'
      READ*, DAYS
      PRINT*
      PRINT*, 'OXYGEN DEFICIT ANALYSIS OF ',
     +        'WASTE WATER DISCHARGE STREAMS'
      PRINT*
*
      READ (10,*) N
      DO 30 J=1,N
         READ (10,*) QD, QS, BODD, BODS, TMIX, KR, DOXYGN
         CALL CALC(QD,QS,BODD,BODS,TMIX,KR,DOXYGN,
     +             DAYS,DEFMAX,DEFDAY)
         PRINT 10, J, DEFMAX
   10    FORMAT (1X,'STREAM ',I3,':',' MAXIMUM DEFICIT = ',F6.3)
         PRINT 20, DEFDAY
   20    FORMAT (1X,12X,'OCCURRED AT DAY ',F3.1)
         PRINT*
   30 CONTINUE
*
      END
*----------------------------------------------------------------*
*
      SUBROUTINE  CALC(QD,QS,BODD,BODS,TMIX,KR,DOXYGN,
     +                 DAYS,DEFMAX,DEFDAY)
*
* This subroutine calculates the maximum oxygen deficit for a
* stream along with the day that it occurred.
*
      INTEGER  STEPS, J
      REAL   QD, QS, BODD, BODS, TMIX, KR, DOXYGN,
     +       FSMIX, KD, BODMIX, DEFCT,
     +       DAYS, DEFMAX, DEFDAY, T, TEMP1, TEMP2, TEMP3
*
```

continued

```
                    BODMIX = ((BODS*QS) + (BODD*QD))/(QS + QD)
                    FSMIX = BODMIX*(0.02*TMIX + 0.6)/0.68
                    KD = 0.1*(1.047**(TMIX - 20.0))
        *
                    DEFMAX = 0.0
                    DEFDAY = 0.0
                    STEPS = INT(DAYS*10.0)
        *
                    DO 10 J=1,STEPS
                        T = REAL(J)*0.1
                        TEMP1 = (KD*FSMIX)/(KR - KD)
                        TEMP2 = 10.0**(-KD*T) - 10.0**(-KR*T)
                        TEMP3 = DOXYGN*(10.0**(-KR*T))
                        DEFCT = (TEMP1*TEMP2) + TEMP3
                        IF (J.EQ.1.OR.DEFCT.GT.DEFMAX) THEN
                            DEFMAX = DEFCT
                            DEFDAY = T
                        ENDIF
                10 CONTINUE
        *
                    RETURN
                    END
        *-------------------------------------------------------------*
```

TESTING

A sample data file and its corresponding output are shown below:

Data File STREAMS

```
     4
     2.5    65.0   0.1    15.0   17.6   0.45   7.3
     5.0   108.0   2.5    23.0   12.5   1.85   2.5
    23.9     3.5   0.0   145.0   17.6   0.20   1.3
     5.0   108.0   2.5     0.5   20.5   0.20   2.3
```

```
ENTER TIME PERIOD FOR STREAM ANALYSIS
(USE TIME IN TENTHS OF DAYS XX.X)
4.0

OXYGEN DEFICIT ANALYSIS OF WASTE WATER DISCHARGE STREAMS

STREAM    1: MAXIMUM DEFICIT = 6.974
             OCCURRED AT DAY 0.1

STREAM    2: MAXIMUM DEFICIT = 1.997
             OCCURRED AT DAY 0.1

STREAM    3: MAXIMUM DEFICIT = 6.374
             OCCURRED AT DAY 2.9

STREAM    4: MAXIMUM DEFICIT = 2.216
             OCCURRED AT DAY 0.1
```

When you are testing this program, it would be a good idea to put a PRINT statement inside the loop that is computing the deficit for each increment of a day. By checking the set of values computed each time through the DO loop in the subroutine, you can be sure that the steps to determine the maximum deficit are working properly.

7-4 SUBROUTINES FOR INSERTING AND DELETING

In the previous chapter we presented a number of common techniques that we implemented with functions. In this section we develop subroutines for inserting and deleting elements in a list. These techniques are also commonly used in engineering and scientific programs, and like the functions from Chapter 6, will be useful in a variety of programs. The common techniques discussed in the last couple of chapters are often called *software tools* because they are used so frequently. You may want to store these functions and subroutines so they will be convenient to add to programs as you need them.

We now consider the steps to insert or delete an element in an ordered list. We assume that the list is ordered in an array and that the value of a variable COUNT will specify how many of the elements in the array represent actual data values.

INSERTING IN AN ORDERED LIST

Before we develop the pseudocode for inserting a value in an ordered list of values, we look at a simple hand example:

Original List

123
247
253
496

There are four valid entries in the array, although we assume that the size of the array might be much larger. Suppose we want to insert the value 147. Think through the steps as you perform them. You scan down the array until you find a value larger than 147, you move all the rest of the array elements down one position in the array, and then insert the new value in the position left open after moving the rest of the array down. (We use the terms "up one position in the array" to mean toward the top of the array, or the top of the page. "Down one position in the array" means toward the bottom of the array, or the bottom of the page.) The number of valid elements in the array has now been increased by 1. The new contents of the array are the following:

Modified List

123
147
247
253
496

Suppose we now want to insert the value 512. As we scan down the list, we find that we reach the end and the value to be inserted is greater than the last value in the list. We add the new value at the end of the list, and increment the count.

Modified List

123
147
247
253
496
512

Are there any special cases that can occur when inserting values in an ordered list? What happens if the value to be inserted is already in the list? If the list is updating the list of valid users for a computer system, we don't want to list the identification for a person more than once, so we would not insert the value again if it were already there; on the other hand, if the list represents bank transactions on a specific account, there could be multiple transactions on the same account, so we would want to add the additional information. As another special case, suppose the count equals the defined size of the array; that is, the array is full. To know how to handle this situation requires knowing more about the problem being solved. In some cases we would want to print an error message stating that the array was full and the value could not be added; in other cases we would want to insert the new value and move the rest of the elements down in the array until we reached the end of the array — thus losing the last value in the array.

EXAMPLE 7-3   **Subroutine for Inserting in an Ordered List**

Write a subroutine to insert a value in an ordered list. The arguments of the subroutine include the array X, a variable COUNT that specifies the number of valid data values in the array, the variable LIMIT that contains the defined size of the array, and the variable NEW that contains the value to be inserted in the array. Write the subroutine so that it will add a new value to the array even if it is already in the array. If a new element is added to a full array, the last value in the array will be lost.

Solution

It should be clear that inserting a value in an ordered list requires a subroutine instead of a function because many values in the array may be changed by an insertion. We also need to increment the value of COUNT if the array was not full when we did the insertion. We now derive the detailed steps for the subroutine.

DECOMPOSITION OF INSERT(LIMIT,NEW,COUNT,X)

```
┌─────────────────────────────────────┐
│  Insert new item in ordered list.    │
└─────────────────────────────────────┘
```

INITIAL PSEUDOCODE

INSERT(limit,new,count,x): If count = limit then
  Print message that last
    value will be lost
  done ← false
  j ← 1
  While (j ≤ count) and
      (not done) do
    If x(j) < new value then
      j ← j + 1
    Else
      done ← true
  If j > count then
    Update count
    Add new value at end of list
  Else
    Update count
    Insert new value at this point
  Return

We still need to refine a couple of these steps. When we exit the WHILE loop, the first IF structure tests to see if J is greater than COUNT. If the condition is true, the new element goes at the end of the values. Thus, if the array is not full, we increment the count and add the new value at the end of the list of valid values; however, if the array is already full, we do nothing because the new value would belong at the end of the list of valid values, and there is no room there.

When the new value belongs within the list, we must insert it carefully. First we go to the end of the valid data and move the last value down one position. Then we can move the next-to-the-last value to the position vacated. We continue to move values down until we have moved the value in the position where the new value is to be inserted; we can then insert the new value. If the array is full when we perform the insertion, the value in the last position will be lost. The final pseudocode refinement details these steps.

FINAL REFINEMENT

```
INSERT(limit,new,count,x): If count = limit then
                              Print message that last
                                  value will be lost
                           done ← false
                           j ← 1
                           While (j ≤ count) and
                                  (not done) do
                             If x(j) < new value then
                                 j ← j + 1
                             Else
                                 done ← true
                           If j > count then
                             If count < limit then
                                   count ← count + 1
                             x(count) ← new value
                           Else
                             If count < limit then
                                 count ← count + 1
                             For k = count to j + 1 by −1 do
                                   x(k) ← x(k − 1)
                             x(j) ← new value
                           Return
```

Before we convert this to FORTRAN, consider the situation of inserting a value in an empty list, that is, a list which has no valid data values in it and thus has a count of zero. Look at the pseudocode and see if it will handle this situation. (It does, but be sure that you are convinced.) Converting this final refinement to FORTRAN yields the following:

```
*----------------------------------------------------------------*
      SUBROUTINE  INSERT (LIMIT,NEW,COUNT,X)
*
*  This subroutine inserts an element in an ordered list.
*
      INTEGER  LIMIT, NEW, COUNT, X(LIMIT), J, K
      LOGICAL  DONE
*
      IF (COUNT.EQ.LIMIT) THEN
         PRINT*, 'ARRAY IS FULL'
         PRINT*, 'LAST VALUE WILL BE LOST'
      ENDIF
      DONE = .FALSE.
      J = 1
    5 IF ((J.LE.COUNT).AND.(.NOT.DONE)) THEN
         IF (X(J).LT.NEW) THEN
            J = J + 1
         ELSE
            DONE = .TRUE.
         ENDIF
         GO TO 5
      ENDIF
*
      IF (J.GT.COUNT) THEN
         IF (COUNT.LT.LIMIT) COUNT = COUNT + 1
         X(COUNT) = NEW
      ELSE
         IF (COUNT.LT.LIMIT) COUNT = COUNT + 1
         DO 10 K=COUNT,J+1,-1
            X(K) = X(K-1)
   10    CONTINUE
         X(J) = NEW
      ENDIF
*
      RETURN
      END
*----------------------------------------------------------------*
```

The insertion technique is not trivial. It requires a thorough understanding of arrays and subscript handling. Go through the pseudocode and corresponding FORTRAN statements until you understand the steps. After we develop the subroutine for deleting an element from an ordered list, we present a program for testing both the insertion and the deletion subroutines.

DELETING FROM AN ORDERED LIST

After you master the insertion technique, you will find the deletion technique easier because there are many similarities. We again assume that the list is ordered in an array and that the value of a variable COUNT will specify how many of the elements in the array represent actual data values. Let's begin with a simple hand example:

Original List	123
	247
	253
	496

As before, there are four valid entries in the original array, but we still assume that the actual size of the array could be larger. Suppose we want to delete value 253. Think through the steps as you perform them: you scan down the array until you find the value, you remove the value, and you move the rest of the array values up one position in the array. The number of valid elements in the array has now been decreased by 1. The new contents of the array are the following:

Modified List	123
	247
	496

Are there any special cases that can occur when deleting values in an ordered list? What happens if the value to be deleted is not in the list? In this situation we probably want to print a message to the user. What happens if we delete the only element in the list? In this situation the count will be decremented to the value zero and we will have an empty list.

We are now ready to develop the detailed steps for deleting an item from an ordered list.

EXAMPLE 7-4   **Subroutine for Deleting from an Ordered List**

Write a subroutine to delete a value from an ordered list. The arguments of the subroutine include the array X, a variable COUNT that specifies the number of valid data values in the array, and the variable OLD that contains the value to be deleted from the array.

DECOMPOSITION OF DELETE(OLD,COUNT,X)

Delete item from ordered list.

```
DELETE(old,count,x): done ← false
                     j ← 1
                     While (j ≤ count) and (not done) do
                         If x(j) < old then
                             j ← j + 1
                         Else
                             done ← true
                     If (j > count) or (x(j) > old) then
                             Write message that value
                                     is not in the list
                     Else
                         Update count
                         Delete old value from list
```

Will this pseudocode handle the situation in which the array is empty? Since COUNT will be equal to zero, the condition in the WHILE loop will be false the first time it is tested, because the value of J is 1. A message will be printed that the value is not in the list, which handles the situation properly.

We still need to refine a couple of the steps in the pseudocode. When we exit the WHILE loop, the IF structure tests to see if the element was actually in the loop. If we searched until we reached the end of the loop (j > count) or until we passed the position where the element should have been (x(j) > old), we write a message indicating that the element was not in the list. If the element was in the list, we need to subtract one from the count and "delete old value from list." However, we really do not explicitly delete the old value. Instead, we move the value below the old value up one position in the array, the value below that one up one position in the array, and so on until we have moved all the values below the one to be deleted up one position in the array. The final pseudocode refinement details these steps.

FINAL REFINEMENT

```
DELETE(old,count,x): done ← false
                     j ← 1
                     While (j ≤ count) and (not done) do
                         If x(j) < old then
                             j ← j + 1
                         Else
                             done ← true
                     If (j > count) or (x(j) > old) then
                             Write message that value
                                     is not in the list
                     Else
                         count ← count − 1
                         For k = j to count do
                             x(k) ← x(k + 1)
```

Converting this final pseudocode to FORTRAN yields the following statements:

FORTRAN Subroutine

```
*------------------------------------------------------------*
      SUBROUTINE  DELETE (OLD,COUNT,X)
*
*   This subroutine deletes an element from an ordered list.
*
      INTEGER  OLD, COUNT, X(COUNT), J, K
      LOGICAL  DONE
*
      DONE = .FALSE.
      J = 1
    5 IF ((J.LE.COUNT).AND.(.NOT.DONE)) THEN
         IF (X(J).LT.OLD) THEN
            J = J + 1
         ELSE
            DONE = .TRUE.
         ENDIF
         GO TO 5
      ENDIF
*
      IF ((J.GT.COUNT).OR.(X(J).GT.OLD)) THEN
         PRINT*, 'VALUE TO DELETE IS NOT IN LIST'
      ELSE
         COUNT = COUNT - 1
         DO 10 K=J,COUNT
            X(K) = X(K+1)
   10    CONTINUE
      ENDIF
*
      RETURN
      END
*------------------------------------------------------------*
```

These two subroutines have been developed independently of a specific application to ensure that they will be useful in a number of applications. However, just because these routines are not part of a specific problem, we cannot skip the important step of testing them. Therefore, we will write a special program (called a driver) to test the subroutines. The driver program allows us to test modules independently of a specific program. In the driver program below, the user is asked to enter a list of ordered values. The values are stored; then the user is allowed to perform both deletions and insertions. The driver has the following structure chart:

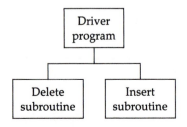

In the program, we indicate the position of the subroutines to show clearly where they would be included. The order of the routines is not important; they could be interchanged with no effect on the program.

FORTRAN Program

```
*-----------------------------------------------------------------*
      PROGRAM  DRIVER
*
*  This driver tests both the insertion and deletion routines.
*
      INTEGER  X(10), COUNT, I, CODE, NEW, OLD, LIMIT
      LOGICAL  DONE
      DATA  LIMIT /10/
*
      PRINT*, 'ENTER COUNT (<11) OF VALUES FOR LIST'
      READ*, COUNT
      PRINT*, 'ENTER VALUES IN ASCENDING ORDER'
      READ*, (X(I),I=1,COUNT)
*
      DONE = .FALSE.
    5 IF (.NOT.DONE) THEN
         PRINT*, 'ENTER -1 FOR DELETE, 1 TO INSERT, ',
     +           '9 TO QUIT'
         READ*, CODE
         IF (CODE.EQ.-1) THEN
            PRINT*, 'ENTER VALUE TO DELETE'
            READ*, OLD
            CALL DELETE(OLD,COUNT,X)
         ELSEIF (CODE.EQ.1) THEN
            PRINT*, 'ENTER VALUE TO INSERT'
            READ*, NEW
            CALL INSERT(LIMIT,NEW,COUNT,X)
         ENDIF
         IF (CODE.EQ.9) THEN
            DONE = .TRUE.
         ELSE
            PRINT*, 'NEW LIST'
            DO 10 I=1,COUNT
               PRINT*, X(I)
   10       CONTINUE
         ENDIF
         GO TO 5
      ENDIF
*
      END
*-----------------------------------------------------------------*
                  DELETE subroutine goes here
*-----------------------------------------------------------------*
                  INSERT subroutine goes here
*-----------------------------------------------------------------*
```

An example of a test of the insert and delete subroutines using this driver follows:

```
ENTER COUNT (<11) OF VALUES FOR LIST
3
ENTER VALUES IN ASCENDING ORDER
5   13   17
ENTER -1 FOR DELETE, 1 TO INSERT, 9 TO QUIT
1
ENTER VALUE TO INSERT
8
NEW LIST:
        5
        8
       13
       17
ENTER -1 FOR DELETE, 1 TO INSERT, 9 TO QUIT
-1
ENTER VALUE TO DELETE
15
VALUE TO DELETE IS NOT IN LIST
NEW LIST:
        5
        8
       13
       17
ENTER -1 FOR DELETE, 1 TO INSERT, 9 TO QUIT
9
```

If you did not want to require that the user enter data that had already been sorted, you could add a sort subroutine such as the one that we developed in Example 7–2 on page 303. The new structure chart for the program would then be the one shown below:

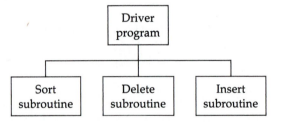

The steps in the driver program that prompt the user to enter the data would then be replaced by the following:

```
PRINT*, 'ENTER COUNT (<11) OF VALUES FOR LIST'
READ*, COUNT
PRINT*, 'ENTER VALUES'
READ*, (X(I),I=1,COUNT)
CALL SORT(X,X,COUNT)
```

This self-test allows you to check quickly to see if you have remembered some of the key points from Section 7–4. If you have any problems with this exercise, reread this section. The solutions are included at the end of the text.

Given below is a FORTRAN program that includes the INSERT subroutine developed in this section. The program reads an array of integers that are entered in a random order. Add statements to the program that will sort the array using the INSERT subroutine. Do not modify the INSERT subroutine and do not add any other modules. (*Hint:* You may want to consider calling the INSERT subroutine from a DO loop.)

FORTRAN Program

```
*-------------------------------------------------------------*
*       PROGRAM  QUIZ
*
*  This program tests your understanding of the insert
*  subroutine.
*
        INTEGER  X(10), COUNT, J
*
        PRINT*, 'ENTER COUNT (<11) OF VALUES FOR LIST'
        READ*, COUNT
        PRINT*, 'ENTER VALUES IN RANDOM ORDER'
        READ*, (X(J),J=1,COUNT)
*
*  Replace this statement with statements to sort the
*  array of values using the INSERT subroutine.
*
        PRINT*, 'ORDERED LIST'
        DO 10 J=1,COUNT
            PRINT*, X(J)
     10 CONTINUE
        END
*-------------------------------------------------------------*
        INSERT subroutine from page 323 goes here
*-------------------------------------------------------------*
```

7-5 APPLICATION—COMPUTER SECURITY
(Computer Science/Engineering)

Computer security is an important issue because so much information is stored in computer systems. Some of this information is confidential. One way to maintain security is to limit access to the computer systems that store this data. A limited access system must keep a list of users that have permission to use the system. New users are added to the list as they are approved; others are deleted from the list when they no longer need access to the system. In this application we assume that such a list uses Social Security numbers for identifying users. This list is kept in ascending order in a data file. A trailer signal of 999999999 is at the end of the file. The number of users varies, but we assume that the actual number of users never exceeds 499. Thus, with the trailer signal, the list never exceeds 500 values.

As we develop a program that allows Social Security numbers to be added and deleted from this list, we must be concerned about the *user interface*—the part of the program that interfaces the user to the steps in the program itself. The user interface needs to be designed to be easy to use so that users will make fewer errors when entering the information. (Programs that are easy to use are also called *user-friendly* programs.) We will assume that the user will be entering Social Security numbers from the keyboard for additions and deletions. Since the input is probably entered from request forms, we will allow the information to be entered in any order; that is, we will not require all deletions before the insertions, and we will not assume that the Social Security numbers to be inserted or deleted are in any particular order.

Because we are inserting and deleting elements in a computer access list, it does not make sense to insert an element already in the list. Therefore, we must modify the insertion subroutine from the previous section so that a message is printed if the element is already in the list. Similarly, if the list is full we do not want to insert another element in the list because we would lose the last element in the list. Therefore, before referencing the insert subroutine we will check to see if the list is full and, if so, print a message to the user.

PROBLEM STATEMENT

Write a program to update a computer access list.

INPUT/OUTPUT DESCRIPTION

The computer access list is stored in ascending order in a data file named ACCESS that has a trailer signal of 999999999. The input to the program is a set of Social Security numbers to be added to the list or deleted from the list. The output is an updated list of information stored in a file named

NEWACCES. Error messages are also printed on the terminal screen if numbers to be added are already in the file or if numbers to be deleted are not in the file.

HAND EXAMPLE

Assume that the current access list contains the following Social Security numbers:

203294433
289129430
319330022
450123452
999999999

The updates to this list include the following insertions and deletions:

additions:	122899823
	244448353
	595959591
deletions:	289129430

After updating the list, the new computer access list is the following:

122899823
203294433
244448353
319330022
450123452
595959591
999999999

ALGORITHM DEVELOPMENT

The decomposition of this problem solution is

DECOMPOSITION

Read access list from file.
Perform insertions and deletions to list.
Write updated list to new file.

We will use the following code to determine whether the user wants to insert a number, delete a number, or quit the program:

Code Value	Operation Desired
-1	deletion
1	addition
0	quit

We now refine the decomposition steps into pseudocode.

REFINEMENT IN PSEUDOCODE

UPDATE: Read ssn list from data file
   done ← false
   While not done do
    Print message asking for code
    Read code
    If code $= -1$ then
     Print message asking for ssn
     Read old
     Delete old from ssn list
    Else if code $= 1$ then
     If count $=$ limit then
      Print message that list is full
     Else
      Print message asking for ssn
      Read new
      Insert new in ssn list
    Else
     done ← true
   Write ssn list to new file

We now present the pseudocode for the insertion routine. (Since the deletion subroutine developed in the previous section does not require any modifications, we do not list it again.) Some modifications are needed in the insertion routine because we do not want to insert a duplicate number in the computer access list. Instead, we will print a message that the number is already in the list. If the list is full, we will not perform an insertion because we would lose a value; instead, before we reference the insertion subroutine, we will check to see if the list is full and print a message if it is full. Also, since the list includes a trailer signal of 999999999, any insertions will be before that value, so we can omit the test for inserting at the end of the list.

The pseudocode assumes that the values are already in an ascending order in the array X, a variable COUNT specifies the number of data values (including the trailer signal) in the array, a variable LIMIT contains the defined size of the array, and the variable NEW contains the value to be inserted in the array.

PSEUDOCODE FOR INSERTION IN AN ORDERED LIST

INSERT(limit,new,count,x): done ← false
    j ← 1
    While (not done) do
        If x(j) < new value then
            j ← j + 1
        Else
            done ← true
    If x(j) = new then
        Print message that item
            is already in list
    Else
        count ← count + 1
        For k = count to j + 1 by −1 do
            x(k) ← x(k − 1)
        x(j) ← new value
    Return

The structure chart for the solution is shown next, along with the FORTRAN program.

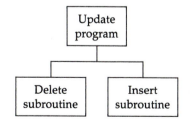

```
*------------------------------------------------------------------*
      PROGRAM  UPDATE
*
*  This program updates a computer access list.
*
      INTEGER  J, CODE, COUNT, OLD, NEW, SSN(500), LIMIT
      LOGICAL  DONE
*
      OPEN (UNIT=8,FILE='ACCESS',STATUS='OLD')
      OPEN (UNIT=9,FILE='NEWACCES',STATUS='NEW')
*
      DONE = .FALSE.
      LIMIT = 500
      J = 1
    5 IF (.NOT.DONE) THEN
         READ (8,*) SSN(J)
         IF (SSN(J).EQ.999999999) THEN
            DONE = .TRUE.
         ELSE
            J = J + 1
         ENDIF
         GO TO 5
      ENDIF
      COUNT = J
      DONE = .FALSE.
*
   10 IF (.NOT.DONE) THEN
         PRINT*, 'ENTER -1 FOR DELETION, 1 FOR INSERTION, ',
     +           '0 TO QUIT'
         READ*, CODE
         IF (CODE.EQ.-1) THEN
            PRINT*, 'ENTER SSN FOR DELETION'
            READ*, OLD
            CALL DELETE(OLD,COUNT,SSN)
         ELSEIF (CODE.EQ.1) THEN
            IF (COUNT.EQ.500) THEN
               PRINT*, 'LIST IS FULL - DO DELETIONS FIRST'
            ELSE
               PRINT*, 'ENTER SSN FOR INSERTION'
               READ*, NEW
               CALL INSERT(LIMIT,NEW,COUNT,SSN)
            ENDIF
         ELSE
            DONE = .TRUE.
         ENDIF
         GO TO 10
      ENDIF
*
      DO 15 J=1,COUNT
         WRITE (9,*) SSN(J)
   15 CONTINUE
*
      END
*------------------------------------------------------------------*
              DELETE subroutine from page 326 goes here
*------------------------------------------------------------------*
```

```
      SUBROUTINE  INSERT (LIMIT,NEW,COUNT,X)
*
* This subroutine inserts an element in an ordered list.
*
      INTEGER  NEW, COUNT, X(LIMIT), J, K, LIMIT
      LOGICAL  DONE
*
      DONE = .FALSE.
      J = 1
    5 IF (.NOT.DONE) THEN
         IF (X(J).LT.NEW) THEN
            J = J + 1
         ELSE
            DONE = .TRUE.
         ENDIF
         GO TO 5
      ENDIF
*
      IF (X(J).EQ.NEW) THEN
         PRINT*, 'SSN ALREADY IN FILE'
      ELSE
         COUNT = COUNT + 1
         DO 10 K=COUNT,J+1,-1
            X(K) = X(K-1)
   10    CONTINUE
         X(J) = NEW
      ENDIF
*
      RETURN
      END
*-------------------------------------------------------------*
```

TESTING

Testing this program is much simpler since we used procedures that have already been tested independently. We know that the procedures work properly by themselves, so we can spend most of our testing time checking the interaction between the modules and the program. Of course, since we modified the insert procedure, it must be carefully tested again.

The terminal screen interaction and the input and output file contents from the hand example follow:

```
ENTER -1 FOR DELETION, 1 FOR INSERTION, 0 TO QUIT
1
ENTER SSN FOR INSERTION
122899823
ENTER -1 FOR DELETION, 1 FOR INSERTION, 0 TO QUIT
1
ENTER SSN FOR INSERTION
244448353
ENTER -1 FOR DELETION, 1 FOR INSERTION, 0 TO QUIT
1
ENTER SSN FOR INSERTION
595959591
ENTER -1 FOR DELETION, 1 FOR INSERTION, 0 TO QUIT
-1
ENTER SSN FOR DELETION
289129430
ENTER -1 FOR DELETION, 1 FOR INSERTION, 0 TO QUIT
0
```

File ACCESS	203294433
	289129430
	319330022
	450123452
	999999999
File NEWACCES	122899823
	203294433
	244448353
	319330022
	450123452
	595959591
	999999999

Note that the trailer signal was kept in the array along with the Social Security numbers. This was convenient because we always are inserting values within the array, instead of at the end of the array, since all values would be less than 999999999. Also, by including it in the list of values, it is automatically written to the data file at the end of the program.

7-6 COMMON BLOCKS

As you modularize your programs, you will find that the argument lists can become lengthy as you pass more and more data to functions and subroutines. FORTRAN allows you to set up a block of memory that is accessible, or common, to the main program and to all its subprograms—a *common block*. The variables in this block of memory do not have to be passed through argument lists and cannot be used as arguments in subprograms.

FORTRAN allows two types of common blocks: *blank common* and *named common*. Blank common is set up with the specification statement shown:

COMMON   *variable list*

Each subprogram that uses data in this common block must also contain a COMMON statement. Although the data names do not have to match in every subprogram, the type and order of the names are important. Consider these COMMON statements from a main program and a subprogram, respectively:

```
PROGRAM    TEST1
INTEGER    J
REAL    A, B, X, Y
COMMON    A, J, B
  .
  .
  .
CALL ANSWR(X,Y)
  .
  .
  .
END
SUBROUTINE    ANSWR(X,Y)
INTEGER    KTOT
REAL    TEMP, SUM, X, Y
COMMON    TEMP, KTOT, SUM
  .
  .
  .
END
```

In these statements, the main program communicates with the subroutine using two arguments, X and Y. In addition, the main program and the subroutine share a memory area. A and TEMP represent the same memory location; J and KTOT represent the same memory location; and B and SUM represent the same memory location, as shown in the following diagram below

Common Memory Area

A	57.63	TEMP
J	−25	KTOT
B	0.007	SUM

Named common, also referred to as *labeled common*, is established if the list of variable names in the COMMON statement is preceded by a name enclosed in slashes:

```
COMMON    /name/ variable list
```

The purpose of establishing different blocks of common with unique names is to allow subprograms to refer to the named common block with which they wish to share data without listing all the other variables in the other common blocks.

For example, one group of variables may be used in a set of computations, and another group of variables may be used in generating graphs to be plotted. The first group of variables could comprise one common area named CALC, and the other group of variables could comprise another common area named GRAPH. Both named COMMON statements appear in the main program; then individual subprograms include either or both named COMMON statements depending on the variables they need to access. The argument lists for the individual subprograms include other input and output variables that are not in the common areas. A variable cannot appear in more than one block of named common, and thus a variable could not appear in both the CALC and GRAPH common blocks; if the variable is needed in the computations and the graphics, it should be passed through the argument list of the subprograms or in a third named common block.

Arrays may be included in the COMMON statement. The COMMON statement can be used to define the storage for these arrays as shown:

```
COMMON  X(50), INCOME(4)
```

An array size can be specified in the COMMON statement, as shown in the previous statement, or it can be specified in an explicit type statement as in

```
INTEGER  SUM
REAL  TIME(25), DIST(25)
COMMON  SUM, TIME, DIST
```

The size of an array cannot be specified in both a type statement and a COMMON statement.

Variables in blank common cannot be initialized with DATA statements. They can be initialized with READ statements or assignment statements. Variables in named common can be initialized with READ statements, assignment statements, or with a special subprogram called a BLOCK DATA subprogram. This subprogram is nonexecutable and serves only to assign initial values to variables in a named common block. An example of a BLOCK DATA subprogram to initialize two named common blocks is

```
BLOCK DATA
COMMON  /EXPER1/ TEMP(100)
COMMON  /EXPER2/ TIME, DIST, VEL(10)
DATA  TEMP, TIME, DIST, VEL /100*0.0, 50.5, 0.5, 10*0.0/
END
```

Both of the COMMON statements must be in the main program. Either or both of the statements also appear in any subprogram that uses variables in these common blocks of memory.

Unless extremely large amounts of data must be passed to subprograms, the use of common blocks is discouraged because they weaken the independence of modules; the module can be affected not only by its arguments but also by variables in common. If you do use common blocks, pay attention to the order of the variables on all COMMON statements. Also look for omitted variables; if a variable is left out of a COMMON statement in a subprogram, incorrect values are used for all variables following it in the COMMON statement. These errors can cause problems that are difficult to locate.

SUMMARY

The subroutine is a subprogram that allows us to return multiple values to the main program, such as when we want to sort an array, or to return no values to the main program, such as when we want to print an error message. Functions and other subroutines can also call a subroutine, in addition to the main program. The subroutine, along with the function, allows us to structure our programs by breaking them into modules that can be written and tested independently of each other. Not only do programs become simpler, but the same module can also be used in other programs without retesting. In this chapter we developed subroutines that are useful in many applications — a sort routine, an insert routine, and a delete routine.

DEBUGGING AIDS

Subroutine testing, like function testing, is the same as program testing: It generally involves writing a special main program or driver to initialize values and call the subroutine. The specific guides that we enumerate refer to the argument list, which is the link between the subroutine and the main program:

1. In general, use the argument list to pass information back and forth between the program and the subroutine, as opposed to using common blocks.
2. Be sure that the variables or expressions listed in the argument list match in type and in order the argument list in the SUBROUTINE statement.
3. Include all variables in the subroutine in type statements to avoid incorrect default typing.
4. Use PRINT statements in the subroutine for debugging, just as you do in the main program.
5. Test each subroutine separately before combining it in a program with other subprograms.
6. Test each of the subroutines with several sets of data to check any special conditions.

STYLE/TECHNIQUE GUIDES

Separating a long program into modules that transfer control smoothly from one to another becomes easier with practice. Although different sets of subprograms may solve the same problem, some choices are more logical and readable than others; these are the solutions that you want to develop. Once you have selected a segment that is to be made into a subroutine, you must decide what arguments are needed. Listed are a few style suggestions to keep in mind as you make these decisions:

1. Choose descriptive names for your subroutines.
2. Use comments in the subroutines as you would in the program. In particular, use comments at the beginning of a subroutine to describe its purpose and to define its arguments, if necessary.
3. For clarity, use the same variables in the argument list of the subroutine as those used in the main program, if possible. If the subroutine is called several times with different arguments, choose completely different variable names in the subroutine to avoid confusion with variables in the main program.
4. List input parameters before output parameters in the argument list.

KEY WORDS

blank common   named common
BLOCK DATA subprogram software tools
common block   subroutine
deletion   user-friendly
insertion   user interface

PROBLEMS

We begin our problem set with modifications to programs developed earlier in this chapter. Give the decomposition, refined pseudocode or flowchart, and FORTRAN solution for each problem.

Problems 1–5 modify the program SIGGEN, given on page 310, which generated a data file composed of a sine wave plus random noise.

1. Modify the signal generating program so that it increments the time by 0.25 instead of 0.01.
2. Modify the signal generating program so that it reads the time increment from the terminal.

3. Modify the signal generating program so that it reads the number of data points that are to be generated from the terminal, instead of generating 101 points.

4. Modify the signal generating program so that it multiplies the noise value generated by the random number generator by a constant that is read from the terminal.

5. Modify the signal generating program so that it adds the noise value to a cosine, instead of a sine wave.

For problems 6–10 modify the program STREAM, given on page 317, which determines the maximum oxygen deficit for each stream in a data file.

6. Modify the oxygen deficit program so that it determines the minimum oxygen deficit for each stream in a data file.

7. Modify the oxygen deficit program so that it determines the maximum oxygen deficit for each stream in a data file using 0.25 day increments.

8. Modify the oxygen deficit program so that it determines the maximum oxygen deficit for each stream in a data file using a daily increment that is entered from the terminal.

9. Modify the oxygen deficit program so that it determines the overall maximum oxygen deficit for the group of streams in a data file, and prints this maximum at the end of the summary.

10. Modify the oxygen deficit program so that it determines the maximum oxygen deficit for each stream in a data file and prints the day on which it occurred as an integer, instead of a real number. Thus, if the maximum deficit occurred at day 2.8, the program would indicate that it occurred on day 2.

For problems 11–15 modify the program UPDATE, given on page 334, which updates a computer access list.

11. Modify the computer access program so that it writes the number of additions and deletions performed by the program on the terminal screen before exiting the program.

12. Modify the computer access program so that it writes the number of valid users in the access file on the terminal screen before exiting the program.

13. Modify the computer access program so that it writes the number of valid users in the original access file on the terminal screen before beginning the update process.

14. Modify the computer access program so that it assumes that the access file is in descending order instead of ascending order and has a trailer value of zero.

15. Modify the computer access program so that it prints a report that lists all the valid access numbers after the access list is updated.

For problems 16–21, assume that TIME, a one-dimensional array of 100 real values, has already been filled with data.

16. Write a subroutine to determine the maximum value in the array TIME and to subtract that value from each value in the array.
17. Write a subroutine to determine the minimum value in the array TIME and to add that value to each value in the array.
18. Write a subroutine to replace each negative value in the array TIME with 0.0.
19. Write a subroutine to determine the average of the values in the array TIME. Add 1.0 to all values above the average; subtract 1.0 from all values below the average.
20. Write a subroutine to replace all values in the array TIME with the absolute value of the corresponding value.
21. Write a subroutine to return a logical value of true if all the values in the array TIME are zero; otherwise, the values returned should be false.

For problems 22–25, assume that Z, a two-dimensional array with 5 rows and 4 columns of real values, has already been filled with data.

22. Write a subroutine that fills an array W (the same size as Z) with the absolute value of the corresponding element in Z.
23. Write a subroutine that fills an array W (the same size as Z) with a value based on the corresponding element in Z, where

$$W(I,J) = 0.0 \qquad \text{if } Z(I,J) = 0$$
$$W(I,J) = -1.0 \qquad \text{if } Z(I,J) < 0$$
$$W(I,J) = 1.0 \qquad \text{if } Z(I,J) > 0$$

24. Write a subroutine that fills an array W (the same size as Z) in the following manner: W should contain the same values of Z unless the corresponding values in Z are greater than the average value of Z. In these cases, the corresponding value of W should contain the average value of Z.
25. Write a subroutine that fills an array W (the same size as Z) with numbers such that each element of W is the corresponding value of Z rounded up to the next multiple of 10. Thus, 10.76 rounds to 20.0; 18.7 rounds to 20.0; 0.05 rounds to 10.0; 10.0 rounds to 10.0; and −5.76 rounds to 0.0.

Develop these programs and subroutines. Use the five-phase design process.

26. Write a subroutine called RANGE that receives an integer array with 50 elements and returns the maximum and minimum values.
27. Write a subroutine that reads a group of test measurements from a data file until it finds a negative measurement. The subroutine should return the number of test measurements read before the negative value was encoun-

tered and the average of those test measurements. Assume that the data file has been opened and assigned to unit 12.

28. Write a subroutine that computes the average, the variance, and the standard deviation of an array X of 100 data values. Use the following formulas:

Average
$$\bar{X} = \frac{\sum\limits_{i=1}^{100} X_i}{100}$$

Variance
$$\sigma^2 = \frac{\sum\limits_{i=1}^{100} (\bar{X} - X_i)^2}{99}$$

Standard
deviation
$$\sigma = \sqrt{\sigma^2}$$

29. Rewrite the subroutine in problem 28 so that it computes the average, variance, and standard deviation for an array with 500 values. Assume that N contains the number of actual values in the array. The denominator of the expression for the variance should then be $N - 1$, instead of 99.

30. Write a subroutine called BIAS that is called with the following statement:

$$\text{CALL BIAS(X,Y,N)}$$

where X is an input array of 200 real values; N is an integer that specifies how many of the values represent actual data values; and Y is an output array the same size as X whose values should be the values of X with the minimum value of the X array subtracted from each one. For example,

if $X =$ | 10 | , then $Y =$ | 8 |
|----|---------------|---|
| 2 | | 0 |
| 36 | | 34 |
| 8 | | 6 |

Thus, the minimum value of Y is always zero. (This operation is referred to as removing the bias in X or adjusting for bias in X.)

FORTRAN STATEMENT SUMMARY

COMMON *variable list*

Example:

COMMON   A, B, X(100)

Discussion:
The blank COMMON statement defines variables that are stored in a block of memory accessible to all subprograms that also contain the COMMON statement, without the variables being listed as arguments in the subprograms.

BLOCK DATA Statement:

BLOCK DATA

Discussion:
The BLOCK DATA statement is the first statement in a BLOCK DATA subprogram. This subprogram contains only DATA statements and is used to initialize variables in common blocks.

CALL Statement:

CALL *subroutine name (argument list)*

Examples:

CALL MERGE(X,Y)

CALL ERROR

Discussion:
The CALL statement is used to transfer control to a subroutine. The inputs and outputs to the subroutine must be listed in the argument list and must match in type and in number those used in the SUBROUTINE statement.

Labeled COMMON Statement:

COMMON */name/ variable list*

Example:

COMMON   /REPORT/ DATE, PAGENO, TOTAL

Discussion:
The labeled COMMON statement allows us to define several blocks of memory available to subprograms. The subprogram must include the labeled COMMON statement that contains the variables to be used in that subprogram. The main program must include all labeled COMMON statements.

$$\textbf{SUBROUTINE} \quad \textit{name} \quad \textit{(argument list)}$$

Examples:

$$\textbf{SUBROUTINE} \quad \textbf{SORT(A,B,N)}$$

$$\textbf{SUBROUTINE} \quad \textbf{HEADING}$$

Discussion:

The SUBROUTINE statement assigns a name to a subroutine and lists the arguments that represent the input and output for the subroutine.

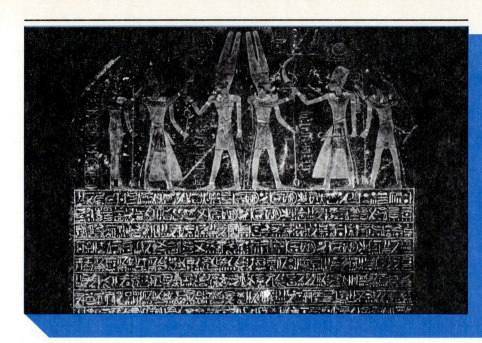

APPLICATION—Cryptography (Computer Science/Engineering)

Computers are widely used in *cryptography*, the encoding and decoding of information to prevent unauthorized use. Codes range from simple codes (one character represents another character) to complicated codes (multiple character substitutions). A key specifies the substitutions being used. This key is generally required to decode the information. Write a program to help decipher an encoded message without the key. (See Section 8–2 for the solution.)

Photo courtesy of Egyptian Museum of Cairo.

8

ADDITIONAL DATA TYPES

Introduction

8–1 Character Data

8–2 Application — Cryptography (Computer Science/Engineering)

8–3 Double-Precision Data

8–4 Application — Temperature Distribution (Mechanical Engineering)

8–5 Complex Data

8–6 Application — Electric Circuit Model (Electrical Engineering)

Summary

INTRODUCTION

This chapter presents three data types: character, double precision, and complex. The character data type allows us to read and analyze character data such as names and addresses. With double-precision data, we can process numeric data more precisely than we could using previously discussed data types. With complex data, we can represent data as numbers that have a real portion and an imaginary portion. Although we don't use these data types routinely, they are special features of FORTRAN that help make it a powerful language for engineering and scientific applications.

8–1 CHARACTER DATA

In Chapter 1 we learned that computers use binary languages, an internal notation composed of 0's and 1's. Integers and real numbers are converted to binary numbers when they are used in a computer. If you study computer hardware or computer architecture, you learn how to convert values such as 56 and −13.25 to binary numbers — to use FORTRAN, however, it is not necessary to learn this conversion.

Characters also must be converted into binary form to be used in the computer; they are converted to *binary strings*, which are also series of 0's and 1's. Several codes convert character information to binary strings, but most computers use EBCDIC (Extended Binary Coded Decimal Interchange Code) or ASCII (American Standard Code for Information Interchange). In these codes, each character is represented by a binary string. Table 8–1 contains a few characters and their EBCDIC and ASCII equivalents.

TABLE 8-1 Binary Character Codes

CHARACTER	ASCII	EBCDIC
A	1000001	11000001
H	1001000	11001000
Y	1011001	11101000
3	0110011	11110011
+	0101011	01001110
$	0100100	01011011
=	0111101	01111110

You do not need to use the character binary codes to use the characters in your FORTRAN programs. However, you must be aware that the computer stores characters differently than the numbers used in arithmetic computations; that is, the integer number 5 and the character 5 are not stored the same. Thus, it is not possible to use arithmetic operations with character data even if the characters represent numbers.

We often refer to character data as character strings because we usually refer to groups or lists of characters that go together. For example, a city is usually given one variable name instead of a variable name for each letter in the city's name. Using character strings in FORTRAN is similar to using numeric data. We can have character string constants that always represent the same information. Character string variables have names and represent character strings that may remain constant or may change. Generally, these character string constants and variables contain characters from the FORTRAN character set, which is composed of the 26 alphabetic letters, the 10 numeric digits, a blank, and the following 12 symbols:

$$+ \ - \ * \ / \ = \ (\ ) \ , \ . \ ' \ \$ \ :$$

If other symbols are used, a program may not execute the same way on one computer as it does on another.

Character constants are always enclosed in apostrophes. These apostrophes are not counted when determining the length or number of characters in a constant. If 2 consecutive apostrophes (not a double quotation mark) are encountered within a character constant, they represent a single apostrophe. For example, the character constant for the word LET'S is 'LET''s'. The following list gives several examples of character constants and their corresponding lengths:

CONSTANT	LENGTH
'SENSOR 23'	9 characters
'TIME AND DISTANCE'	17 characters
' $ AMT.'	7 characters
' '	2 characters
'08:40-13:25'	11 characters
''''''	2 characters

A character string variable must always be defined with a specification statement whose general form is

CHARACTER*n *variable list*

where *n* represents the number of characters in the variable string. For instance, the statement

CHARACTER*8 CODE, NAME

identifies CODE and NAME as variables containing 8 characters each. Unlike numeric variable names, there is no significance to the first letter of a character variable's name. A variation of the CHARACTER statement allows you to specify character strings of different lengths in the same statement, as shown:

$$\text{CHARACTER} \quad \text{TITLE*10, STATE*2}$$

An array that contains characters can be defined as

$$\text{CHARACTER*4} \quad \text{NAME(50)}$$

or

$$\text{CHARACTER} \quad \text{NAME(50)*4}$$

The preceding specifications reserve memory for 50 elements in the array NAME, where each element contains 4 characters. A reference to NAME(18) references the character string that is the eighteenth element of the array, and it contains 4 characters.

Character strings can also be used as arguments in subprograms in which they must be specified in a CHARACTER statement in both the main program and in the subprogram. A subprogram can specify a character string without giving a specific length, as shown:

$$\text{CHARACTER*(*)} \quad \text{STRING}$$

This technique is similar to specifying the length of an array with an integer variable, as in

$$\text{INTEGER} \quad \text{SSN(N)}$$

It is also possible to define in a subprogram an array of N variables, each of which contains a character string. To make the character string more flexible, its length does not have to be specified in the CHARACTER statement. We use the following statement in the subprogram to accomplish this flexibility:

$$\text{CHARACTER*(*)} \quad \text{NAME(N)}$$

We discuss special operations and intrinsic functions for character strings later in this section. First, we illustrate how to use character strings in our input and output statements.

CHARACTER I/O

When a character string is used in a list-directed output statement, the entire character string is printed. Blanks are automatically inserted around the character string to separate it from other output on the same line. When a character string variable is used in a list-directed input statement, the corresponding data value must be enclosed in apostrophes. If the character string within the apostrophes is longer than the defined length of the character string variable, any extra characters to the right are ignored; if the character string within the apostrophes is shorter than the length of the character string variable, the extra positions to the right are automatically filled with blanks. In either instance, the character data is left-justified in the character string variable. To print a character string in a formatted output statement, we use A as the corresponding format specification to print the entire string.

EXAMPLE 8-1   **Character I/O**

Write a complete FORTRAN program to read an item description from the terminal and then print the description. Assume that the length of the description is no more than 20 characters.

Solution

Even though this is a simple program, we still use the decomposition and stepwise refinement method for developing the solution.

DECOMPOSITION

Read description.
Print description.

The following refinement indicates the conversation with the user.

REFINEMENT IN PSEUDOCODE

OUTPUT: Print message to user to enter description
Read description
Print description

Translating these steps into FORTRAN results in the following program:

FORTRAN PROGRAM

```
*------------------------------------------------------------*
      PROGRAM   OUTPUT
*
*  This program reads and prints an item description.
*
      CHARACTER*20   ITEM
*
      PRINT*, 'ENTER ITEM DESCRIPTION IN APOSTROPHES'
      READ*, ITEM
      PRINT 5, ITEM
    5 FORMAT(1X,'ITEM DESCRIPTION IS ',A)
      END
*------------------------------------------------------------*
```

A typical interaction when running this program is

```
ENTER ITEM DESCRIPTION IN APOSTROPHES
'COMPUTER MODEM'
ITEM DESCRIPTION IS COMPUTER MODEM
```

Note that the data entered was not 20 characters long. In this example, the padding of blanks on the end is not noticeable with the output; however, if the output FORMAT had been

```
FORMAT(1X,A,' IS THE ITEM DESCRIPTION')
```

the interaction would have the following appearance:

```
ENTER ITEM DESCRIPTION IN APOSTROPHES
'COMPUTER MODEM'
COMPUTER MODEM      IS THE ITEM DESCRIPTION
```

Another interaction that could come from the original program is

```
ENTER ITEM DESCRIPTION IN APOSTROPHES
'DIGITAL OSCILLOSCOPE WITH MEMORY'
ITEM DESCRIPTION IS DIGITAL OSCILLOSCOPE
```

In this case, the name exceeded the maximum number of characters specified for the description, thus part of the data was lost. To avoid this situation, carefully choose the length of your character variables based on the maximum length that you expect. You can also tell the program user what length you are expecting. In this example, you could use the following pair of PRINT statements:

```
PRINT*, 'ENTER ITEM DESCRIPTION IN APOSTROPHES'
PRINT*, '(MAXIMUM OF 20 CHARACTERS)'
```

CHARACTER OPERATIONS

Although character strings cannot be used in arithmetic computations, we can assign values to character strings, compare two character strings, extract a substring of a character string, and combine two character strings into one longer character string.

Assign Values Values can be assigned to character variables with the assignment statement and a character constant. The following statements initialize a character string array RANK with the 5 abbreviations for freshman, sophomore, junior, senior, and graduate:

```
CHARACTER*2  RANK(5)
RANK(1) = 'FR'
RANK(2) = 'SO'
RANK(3) = 'JR'
RANK(4) = 'SR'
RANK(5) = 'GR'
```

If a character constant in an assignment statement is shorter in length than the character variable, blanks are added to the right of the constant. If the following statement were executed, RANK(1) would contain the letter F followed by a blank:

```
RANK(1) = 'F'
```

That is, an equivalent statement would be

```
RANK(1) = 'F '
```

If a character constant in an assignment statement is longer than the character variable, the excess characters on the right are ignored. Thus, the following statement,

```
RANK(1) = 'FRESHMAN'
```

would store the letters FR in the character array element RANK(1). These examples emphasize the importance of using character strings that are the same length as the variables used to store them; otherwise, the statements can be misleading.

One character string variable can also be used to initialize another character string variable, as shown:

```
CHARACTER*4  GRADE1, GRADE2
GRADE1 = 'GOOD'
GRADE2 = GRADE1
```

Both variables, GRADE1 and GRADE2, contain the character string 'GOOD'.

Character strings can be initialized with DATA statements. The preceding examples can be performed with DATA statements, as shown:

```
CHARACTER  RANK(5)*2, GRADE1*4, GRADE2*4
DATA  RANK, GRADE1, GRADE2 /'FR', 'SO', 'JR', 'SR',
+                           'GR', 2*'GOOD'/
```

Compare Values An IF statement can be used to compare character strings. Assuming that the variable DEPT and the array CH are character strings, the following are valid statements:

```
IF (DEPT.EQ.'EECE') KT = KT + 1

IF (CH(I).GT.CH(I+1)) THEN
   CALL SWITCH(I,CH)
   CALL PRINT(CH)
ENDIF
```

To evaluate a logical expression using character strings, first look at the length of the two strings. If one string is shorter than the other, add blanks to the right of the shorter string so that you can proceed with the evaluation using strings of equal length.

The comparison of two character strings of the same length is made from left to right, one character at a time. Two strings must have exactly the same characters in the same order to be equal.

A *collating sequence* lists characters from the lowest to the highest value. Partial collating sequences for EBCDIC and ASCII are given in Table 8–2. Although the ordering is not exactly the same, some similarities include

1. Capital letters are in order from A to Z.
2. Digits are in order from 0 to 9.
3. Capital letters and digits do not overlap; digits either precede letters or letters precede digits.
4. The blank character is less than any letter or number. When necessary for clarity, we use Ƀ to represent a blank.

TABLE 8-2 Partial Collating Sequences for Characters

ASCII
ƀ " # $ % & ( ) * + , − . /
0 1 2 3 4 5 6 7 8 9
: ; = ? @
A B C D E F G H I J K L M N O P Q R S T U V W X Y Z

EBCDIC
ƀ . (+ & $ *) ; − / , % ? : # @ = "
A B C D E F G H I J K L M N O P Q R S T U V W X Y Z
0 1 2 3 4 5 6 7 8 9

Several pairs of character strings are now listed, along with their correct relationships:

```
'A1'    <  'A2'
'JOHN'  <  'JOHNSTON'
'176'   <  '177'
'THREE' <  'TWO'
'$'     <  'DOLLAR'
```

If character strings contain only letters, their ordering is alphabetical — a *lexicographic* ordering.

Extract Substrings A *substring* of a character string is any string that represents a subset of the original string and maintains the original order. The following list contains all substrings of the string 'FORTRAN':

```
'F'  'FO'  'FOR'  'FORT'  'FORTR'  'FORTRA'  'FORTRAN'
'O'  'OR'  'ORT'  'ORTR'  'ORTRA'  'ORTRAN'
'R'  'RT'  'RTR'  'RTRA'  'RTRAN'
'T'  'TR'  'TRA'  'TRAN'
'R'  'RA'  'RAN'
'A'  'AN'
'N'
```

Substrings are referenced by using the name of the character string, followed by two integer expressions in parentheses, separated by a colon. The first expression in parentheses gives the position in the original string of the beginning of the substring; the second expression gives the position of the end of the substring. If the string 'FORTRAN' is stored in a variable LANG, some of its substring references are as shown:

REFERENCE	SUBSTRING
LANG(1:1)	'F'
LANG(1:7)	'FORTRAN'
LANG(2:3)	'OR'
LANG(7:7)	'N'

If the first expression in parentheses is omitted, the substring begins at the beginning of the string; thus, LANG(:4) refers to the substring 'FORT'. If the second expression in parentheses is omitted, the substring ends at the end of the string; thus, LANG(5:) refers to the substring 'RAN'.

The substring operation cannot operate correctly if the beginning and ending positions are not integers, are negative, or contain values greater than the number of characters in the substring. The ending position must also be greater than or equal to the beginning position of the substring.

The substring operator is a powerful tool, as the next two examples illustrate.

EXAMPLE 8-2   **Propane-Heated Balloons**

All aircraft including hot air balloons are assigned registration numbers by the Federal Aviation Agency. A new registration system for balloons has been proposed in which the registration number is a character string of 7 characters. The fifth character specifies balloon type: P, for propane-heated; S, for solar-heated; and H, for helium- or hydrogen-filled. Write a segment of FORTRAN code that counts the number of propane-heated hot air balloons using a character array of 500 registration numbers.

Solution

We need a loop to step through the array, checking each balloon registration number. We increment our count if the fifth character in the registration number is the letter P:

```
CHARACTER*7  REGNUM(500)
INTEGER  COUNT, I
DATA  COUNT /0/
   .
   .
   .
DO 10 I=1,500
   IF (REGNUM(I)(5:5).EQ.'P') COUNT = COUNT + 1
10 CONTINUE
```

EXAMPLE 8-3   **Character Count**

A string of 50 characters contains encoded information. The number of occurrences of the letter S represents a special piece of information. Write a loop that counts the number of occurrences of the letter S.

Solution

The loop index is used with the substring operator to allow us to test each character in the string:

```
CHARACTER*50  CODE
INTEGER  COUNT, I
DATA  COUNT /0/
   .
   .
   .
DO 20 I=1,50
    IF (CODE(I:I).EQ.'S') COUNT = COUNT + 1
20 CONTINUE
```

A reference to a substring can be used anywhere that a string can be used. For instance, if LANG contains the character string 'FORTRAN', the following statement changes the value of LANG to 'FORMATS':

```
LANG(4:7) = 'MATS'
```

If LANG contains 'FORMATS', the following statement changes the value of LANG to 'FORMASS':

```
LANG(6:6) = LANG(7:7)
```

When modifying a substring of a character string with a substring of the same character string, the substrings must not overlap: that is, do not use LANG(2:4) to replace LANG(3:5). Also, recall that if a substring is being moved into a smaller string, only as many characters as are needed to replace the smaller string are moved from left to right; if the substring is being moved into a larger string, the extra positions on the right are filled with blanks.

Combine Strings *Concatenation* is the operation of combining two or more character strings into one character string. It is indicated by two slashes between the character strings to be combined. The following expression concatenates the constants 'WORK' and 'ED' into one string constant 'WORKED':

```
'WORK'//'ED'
```

The next statement combines the contents of three character string variables MO, DA, and YR into one character string and then moves the combined string into a variable called DATE:

```
DATE = MO//DA//YR
```

If MO = '05', DA = '15', and YR = '86', then DATE = '051586'. Because concatenation represents an operation, it cannot appear on the left-hand side of an equal sign.

CHARACTER INTRINSIC FUNCTIONS

A number of intrinsic functions are designed for use with character strings:

> INDEX locates specific substrings within a given character string.
>
> LEN determines the length of a string and is used primarily in subroutines and functions that have character string arguments.
>
> CHAR and ICHAR determine the position of a character in the collating sequence of the computer.
>
> LGE, LGT, LLE, and LLT allow comparisons to be made based on the ASCII collating sequence, regardless of the collating sequence of the computer.

INDEX The INDEX function has two arguments, both of which are character strings. The function returns an integer value giving the position in the first string of the second string. Thus, if STRGA contains the phrase 'TO BE OR NOT TO BE', INDEX(STRGA,'BE') returns the value 4, which points to the first occurrence of the string 'BE'. To find the second occurrence of the string, we can use the following statements:

```
CHARACTER*18   STRGA
   .
   .
   .
K = INDEX(STRGA,'BE')
J = INDEX(STRGA(K+1:),'BE') + K
```

After execution, K would contain the value 4 and J would contain the value 17. (Note that we had to add K to the second reference of INDEX because the second use referred to the substring 'E OR NOT TO BE'; without K, the second INDEX reference would return a value of 13, not 17. The value of INDEX(STRGA,'AND') would be 0 because the second string 'AND' does not occur in the first string STRGA.)

LEN The input to the function LEN is a character string; the output is an integer that contains the length of the character string. This function is useful in a subprogram that accepts character strings of any length but needs the actual length within the subprogram. The statement in the subprogram that allows a character string to be used with any length is

```
CHARACTER*(*)   A, B, STRGA
```

This form can be used only in subprograms. Example 8–4 uses both the LEN function and the variable string length parameter in a subprogram.

EXAMPLE 8-4   **Frequency of Blanks**

Write a function subprogram that accepts a character string and returns a count of the number of blanks in the string.

Solution

To make this function flexible, we write it so that it can be used with any size character string:

```
*- - - - - - - - - - - - - - - - - - - - - - - - - - - - - - - - - - - - - - - - - - - - - -*
      INTEGER FUNCTION  BLANKS(X)
*
*   This function counts the number
*   of blanks in a character string X.
*
      INTEGER  I
      CHARACTER*(*)  X
*
      BLANKS = 0
      DO 10 I=1,LEN(X)
         IF (X(I:I).EQ.' ') BLANKS = BLANKS + 1
   10 CONTINUE
*
      RETURN
      END
*- - - - - - - - - - - - - - - - - - - - - - - - - - - - - - - - - - - - - - - - - - - - - -*
```

Character strings may also be used in user-written subroutines. In Example 8–5, we write a subroutine that combines input character strings into an output character string.

EXAMPLE 8-5   **Name Editing**

Write a subroutine that receives 3 character strings, FIRST, MIDDLE, and LAST, each containing 15 characters. The output of the subroutine is a character string 35 characters long that contains the first name followed by 1 blank, the middle initial followed by a period and 1 blank, and the last name. Assume that FIRST, MIDDLE, and LAST have no leading blanks and no embedded blanks. Thus, if

```
          FIRST = 'JOSEPH         '
          MIDDLE = 'CHARLES         '
          LAST = 'LAWTON        '
```

then

```
      NAME = 'JOSEPH C. LAWTON                   '
```

Solution

The solution to this problem is simplified by the use of the substring operation that allows us to look at individual characters and the INDEX function that is used to find the end of the first name. We move to NAME the characters in FIRST, then a blank, the middle initial, a period, another blank, and the last name. As you go through the solution, observe the use of the concatenation operation. Also, note that the move of the first name fills the rest of the character string NAME with blanks because FIRST is shorter than the field to which it is moved:

```
*...........................................................*
*          SUBROUTINE  EDIT(FIRST,MIDDLE,LAST,NAME)
*
*    This subroutine edits a name to the form
*    first, middle initial, last.
*
      INTEGER  L
      CHARACTER*15  FIRST, MIDDLE, LAST
      CHARACTER*35  NAME
*
*    MOVE FIRST NAME
*
      NAME = FIRST
*
*    MOVE MIDDLE INITIAL
*
      L = INDEX(NAME,' ')
      NAME(L:L+3) = ' '//MIDDLE(1:1)//'. '
*
*    MOVE LAST NAME
*
      NAME(L+4:) = LAST
*
      RETURN
      END
*...........................................................*
```

CHAR, ICHAR These functions refer to the collating sequence used in the computer. If a computer has 50 characters in its collating sequence, these characters are numbered from 0 to 49. For example, assume that the letter A corresponds to position 12. The function CHAR has an integer argument that specifies the position of a desired character in the collating sequence. The function returns the character in the specified position. The following statements print the character A:

```
N = 12
PRINT*, CHAR(N)
```

The ICHAR function is the inverse of the CHAR function. The argument to the ICHAR function is a character variable that contains one character. The function returns an integer that gives the position of the character in the collating sequence. Thus, the output of the following statements is the number 12:

```
CHARACTER*1  INFO
INFO = 'A'
PRINT*, ICHAR(INFO)
```

Because different computers have different collating sequences, these functions can be used to determine the position of certain characters in the collating sequence.

EXAMPLE 8-6   **Collating Sequence**

Print each character in the FORTRAN character set along with its position in the collating sequence on your computer. The FORTRAN character set is given on page 349.

Solution

Note the use of the substring operator in initializing the character set:

```
*-------------------------------------------------------*
      PROGRAM  SEQNCE
*
*  This program prints the position in the collating
*  sequence of each FORTRAN character.
*
      CHARACTER*49  SET
*
      SET(1:26) = 'ABCDEFGHIJKLMNOPQRSTUVWXYZ'
      SET(27:36) = '0123456789'
      SET(37:49) = ' +-*/=(),.''$:'
*
      DO 10 I=1,49
         PRINT*, SET(I:I), ICHAR(SET(I:I))
   10 CONTINUE
*
      END
*-------------------------------------------------------*
```

Why did we put two apostrophes in the assignment for SET(37:49)? Remember that two apostrophes are converted into a single apostrophe when they are in a literal. If you have several computers available, run this program on each of them to see if they all use the same collating sequence for the FORTRAN character set.

LGE, LGT, LLE, LLT This set of functions allows you to compare character strings based on the ASCII collating sequence. These functions become useful if a program is going to be used on a number of different computers and is using character comparisons or character sorts. The functions represent a logical value, true or false. Each function has two character string arguments, STRG1 and STRG2. The function reference LGE(STRG1,STRG2) is true if STRG1 is lexically greater than or equal to STRG2; thus, if STRG1 comes after STRG2 in an alphabetical sort, this function reference is true. Remember, these functions are based on an ASCII collating sequence regardless of the sequence being used on the computer. The functions LGT, LLE, and LLT perform comparisons "lexically greater than," "lexically less than or equal to," and "lexically less than."

EXAMPLE 8-7   **ASCII Sort**

In a sort based on the collating sequence in a computer, we perform the following steps, where STRG represents a character array:

```
        IF (STRG(I).GT.STRG(I+1)) THEN
            TEMP = STRG(I)
            STRG(I) = STRG(I+1)
            STRG(I+1) = TEMP
            SORTED = .FALSE.
        ENDIF
```

Rewrite this loop so the switch of character strings occurs based on an ASCII collating sequence even if the computer does not use an ASCII code.

Solution

The solution involves replacing the character comparison with the character intrinsic function LGT:

```
IF (LGT(STRG(I),STRG(I+1))) THEN
    TEMP = STRG(I)
    STRG(I) = STRG(I+1)
    STRG(I+1) = TEMP
    SORTED = .FALSE.
ENDIF
```

SELF-TEST 8-1

This self-test allows you to check quickly to see if you have remembered some of the key points from Section 8-1. If you have any problems with the exercises, you should reread this section. The solutions are included at the end of the text.

For problems 1-10, give the substring referred to in each reference. Assume that a character string of length 25 called TITLE has been initialized with the statements:

```
CHARACTER*25  TITLE
TITLE = 'CONSERVATION OF ENERGY'
```

1. TITLE(1:25)
2. TITLE(1:12)
3. TITLE(13:23)
4. TITLE(16:16)
5. TITLE(17:)
6. TITLE(:12)
7. TITLE(:)
8. TITLE//'LAW'
9. TITLE(1:7)//'E'//TITLE(16:)
10. ''''//TITLE(1:4)//'ID'//TITLE(19:20)//'ATE'//''''

In problems 11-16, WORD is a character string of length 6. What is stored in WORD after each of the following statements?

11. WORD = 'DENSITY'
12. WORD = 'AREA'
13. WORD = 'CAN''T'
14. WORD = '''''''!'
15. WORD = 'FT'//'/SEC'
16. WORD = ' VOLUME'

8-2 APPLICATION—CRYPTOGRAPHY (Computer Science/Engineering)

Computers not only can encode and decode messages for a specific code, but they also can attempt to break unknown codes. One simple test used to analyze a code is to count the number of occurrences of each character in a coded message. In English text, the most common letter is the letter "e." If a code simply substitutes one letter for another, then the most frequently used letter is likely to be the letter e. Obviously, more complicated codes are more difficult to analyze.

In this application, we write a program to read a coded message and to count the number of occurrences of each of the vowels, a, e, i, o, and u. We then compare the number of occurrences using a bar graph. This program allows us to use characters for input data and also for printing the bar graph. Before we discuss the solution, we develop a subroutine for generating a bar graph. (The development of this subroutine is the main interest of this section. The program is just an extension of Example 8–4.)

Bar graphs are used frequently to compare a set of data points. For instance, a company with an 8-person sales staff can compare monthly sales in a bar graph, as shown:

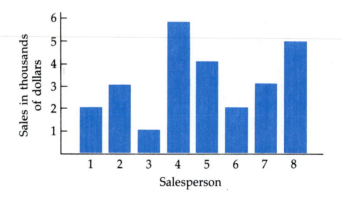

We cannot draw lines such as these on the printer or on the terminal screen (unless the terminal is a graphics terminal), but we can make the bars with characters such as asterisks. We can develop a subroutine to print a bar graph from a set of data. The input to the subroutine is an array of numeric values. The procedure uses these values to generate and print a bar graph.

We begin by looking at a simple case. Suppose the data numbers are 1, 4, 2, and 3. We could then print a bar with 1 asterisk, with 4 asterisks, and so on, generating a pattern that represents a horizontal bar graph:

```
*
****
**
***
```

If the numbers were in an array NUM, this bar graph could be printed with the following statements:

```
          DIMENSION  NUM(4)
          CHARACTER*4  BAR
          DATA  BAR /'****'/
             .
             .
             .
          DO 10 I=1,4
              PRINT*, BAR(1:NUM(I))
       10 CONTINUE
```

The value of NUM(I) is used to specify how many asterisks to print for each bar. Each time through the loop, another value in the NUM array is used to specify the number of asterisks to be printed. This solution works as long as we assume that the array of data values contains integer values greater than zero. Also, the data values cannot be greater than the number of asterisks in BAR or greater than the number of positions in our output line.

Printing bar graphs with large data values can be accomplished by scaling the data values. For instance, suppose that our data values are 20, 8, 40, and 32. We want the maximum bar length to be 20. Because 40 is the maximum value, we would print a bar with 20 asterisks; other bars would be scaled accordingly. The output would be

```
**********
****
********************
****************
```

The code to perform this type of scaling follows. (Note that the scale factor is the length of the maximum bar divided by the maximum data value. If the maximum value is exactly the desired length of the maximum bar, the scale factor is 1, and none of the values are changed. If the maximum data value is less than the desired length of the maximum bar, then the quotient is greater than 1, and all the values increase proportionally. If the maximum data value is greater than the length of the maximum bar, the quotient is less than 1, and all the values decrease proportionally.)

```
*--------------------------------------------------------*
        INTEGER  NUM(4), MAX, I
        REAL  SCALE
        CHARACTER*20  BAR
        DATA  BAR /'********************'/
              .
              .
              .
*
*   Find maximum value in num.
*
        MAX = NUM(1)
        DO 10 I=2,4
            IF (MAX.LT.NUM(I)) MAX = NUM(I)
     10 CONTINUE
*
*   Compute scale factor.
*
        SCALE = 20.0/REAL(MAX)
*
*   Print bar graph.
*
        DO 20 I=1,4
            PRINT*, BAR(1:INT(SCALE*REAL(NUM(I))))
     20 CONTINUE
*--------------------------------------------------------*
```

Note that because SCALE is a real value, we used a real constant 20.0 and the function REAL to avoid an integer division. However, when the scale factor is multiplied by a data value to determine the number of asterisks to print, we want this result to be an integer—therefore, we used the INT function to truncate the result to an integer.

If we add two more modifications to the routine, we have a versatile bar graph routine. First, we allow the data to be real values. If we want to use the procedure with an integer array, we can simply move the values into a real array and then call the bar graph routine with the real array. The other modification involves the line length. The optimum line length for the maximum bar depends on the application and on the output device being used. If the output device is a line printer, we may want to use the entire line of 132 characters; if the output device is a small terminal screen, we may want to use only 30 or so characters.

To accommodate all these possibilities, we let an argument LINE specify the maximum bar length, up to a maximum of 130 characters. The number of asterisks to be printed for a data value is computed with the following expression:

$$VALUE(I)*(REAL(LINE)/MAX)$$

(We look at this expression more closely in the hand-worked example.)

Before we describe the design steps, we want to mention a limitation of this routine: no negative data values are permitted. We must write the routine such that a value of zero causes a bar to be skipped, but a negative value causes the routine to be exited.

PROBLEM STATEMENT

Write a subroutine that prints a bar graph from a real array of N data values. Assume that the values are nonnegative. An argument LINE determines the maximum bar length.

INPUT/OUTPUT DESCRIPTION

The input to the subroutine is the real array of N values, the value of N, and the maximum bar length LINE. No output arguments are passed back through the subroutine.

HAND EXAMPLE

For our hand-worked example, we use the following data values:

```
VALUE(1) = 15.0
VALUE(2) = 26.0
VALUE(3) =  4.0
VALUE(4) =  8.0
VALUE(5) = 15.8
```

Assume that the line length is 30. The first step in computing the scale factor is to find the maximum data value. For our set of data, the maximum value is 26.0. The scale factor can then be computed as the maximum bar length divided by the maximum data value, or 30/26.0, which yields 1.15. We then multiply each data value by the scale factor to determine the number of asterisks to print for each bar. The result must be an integer because we cannot print a part of an asterisk; therefore, we can either truncate (drop) the fractional portion or round the fractional portion to the nearest integer. In this example, we choose rounding. The results are shown in the following table:

DATA VALUE	×	SCALE FACTOR	=	BAR LENGTH	→	ROUNDED
15.0	×	1.15	=	17.25	→	17
26.0	×	1.15	=	29.90	→	30
4.0	×	1.15	=	4.60	→	5
8.0	×	1.15	=	9.20	→	9
15.8	×	1.15	=	18.17	→	18

The corresponding bar graph is

```
*****************
******************************
*****
*********
******************
```

ALGORITHM DEVELOPMENT

Earlier discussions are summarized.

Decomposition

Scale data values to line size.
Print corresponding bars of asterisks.

Refinement in Pseudocode

GRAPH(data values, N, LINE):
  Determine MAX and MIN data values
  If MIN < 0 or LINE < 0 or LINE > 130 then
    Print error message
  else
    Compute scale factor
    For each data value do
      Compute number of asterisks for bar
      Print bar

FORTRAN Subroutine

```
*------------------------------------------------------------*
      SUBROUTINE  GRAPH(VALUE,N,LINE)
*
*  This subroutine prints a bar graph using an array
*  of N elements with a maximum line size.
*
      INTEGER  N, LINE, I, K
      REAL  VALUE(N), MAX, SCALE
      LOGICAL  NEGNUM
      CHARACTER*130  BAR
*
*  Find maximum and check for error conditions.
*
      IF (LINE.GT.130.OR.LINE.LT.1) THEN
         PRINT*, 'LINE LENGTH ERROR ', LINE
      ELSE
         NEGNUM = .FALSE.
         MAX = VALUE(1)
         DO 10 I=1,N
            IF (VALUE(I).LT.0.0) THEN
               NEGNUM = .TRUE.
            ELSE
               IF (VALUE(I).GT.MAX) MAX = VALUE(I)
            ENDIF
10       CONTINUE
```

```
*
*   Fill bar with asterisks.
*
          IF (.NOT.NEGNUM) THEN
             DO 20 I=1,LINE
                BAR(I:I) = '*'
   20        CONTINUE
*
*   Scale data values and print bar.
*
             SCALE = REAL(LINE)/MAX
             DO 30 I=1,N
                K = NINT(VALUE(I)*SCALE)
                PRINT*, BAR(1:K)
   30        CONTINUE
          ENDIF
       ENDIF
*
       RETURN
       END
*-------------------------------------------------------------*
```

Note the use of the intrinsic function NINT to round to the nearest integer.

TESTING

A driver for testing this procedure is

```
*-------------------------------------------------------------*
       PROGRAM  DRIVER
*
*   This program tests the bar graph subroutine.
*
       INTEGER  LINE
       REAL  VALUE(5)
*
       PRINT*, 'ENTER 5 DATA VALUES'
       READ*, VALUE
       PRINT*, 'ENTER LINE SIZE'
       READ*, LINE
       PRINT*
       PRINT*, 'LINE = ',LINE
       CALL GRAPH(VALUE,5,LINE)
*
       END
*-------------------------------------------------------------*
       GRAPH subroutine goes here
*-------------------------------------------------------------*
```

Here are a few examples of output with different line sizes using the data
values in the hand-worked example:

```
LINE = 10
*****
*********
**
***
*****
```

```
LINE = 20
***********
*******************
***
******
************
```

```
LINE = 30
****************
*****************************
*****
*********
******************
```

```
LINE = 40
***********************
*****************************************
******
************
************************
```

```
LINE = 50
****************************
*****************************************************
********
***************
*****************************
```

Can you think of ways to improve the appearance of the bar graph? How about double-row or triple-row bars instead of single-row bars? These bars could be separated by blank lines, and headings and scales on the sides might also help. This bar graph routine is general enough to be used with many types of data but simple enough to be customized for specific uses. Other types of printer plots (ones that do not use a graphics plotter but use the regular keyboard characters) are developed in problems 1–5 and 33 at the end of the chapter.

We now present a program that reads character strings from a data file. Each line in the data file contains a character string of 50 characters. In addition, each line begins and ends with an apostrophe so that we can read the file with list-directed statements. Assume that the first line in the data file specifies how many lines of text follow in the file. As we read the data, we keep track of the number of occurrences of each vowel and print the numbers along with a corresponding bar graph.

The structure chart for this program is:

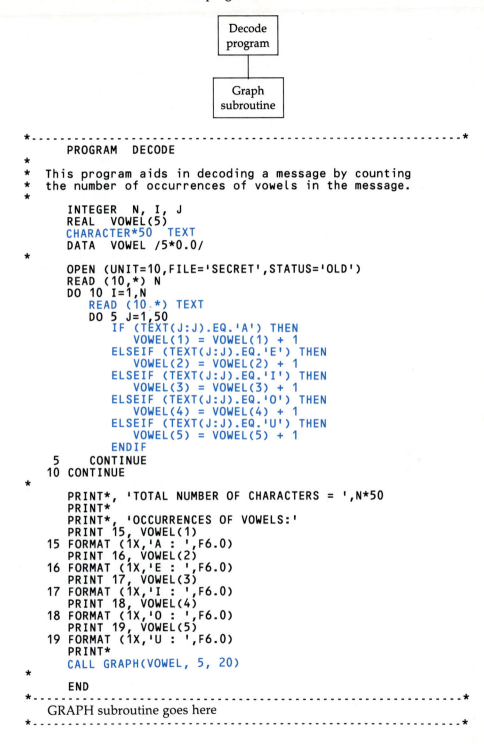

```
*------------------------------------------------------------*
      PROGRAM  DECODE
*
*  This program aids in decoding a message by counting
*  the number of occurrences of vowels in the message.
*
      INTEGER  N, I, J
      REAL   VOWEL(5)
      CHARACTER*50  TEXT
      DATA  VOWEL /5*0.0/
*
      OPEN (UNIT=10,FILE='SECRET',STATUS='OLD')
      READ (10,*) N
      DO 10 I=1,N
         READ (10,*) TEXT
         DO 5 J=1,50
            IF (TEXT(J:J).EQ.'A') THEN
               VOWEL(1) = VOWEL(1) + 1
            ELSEIF (TEXT(J:J).EQ.'E') THEN
               VOWEL(2) = VOWEL(2) + 1
            ELSEIF (TEXT(J:J).EQ.'I') THEN
               VOWEL(3) = VOWEL(3) + 1
            ELSEIF (TEXT(J:J).EQ.'O') THEN
               VOWEL(4) = VOWEL(4) + 1
            ELSEIF (TEXT(J:J).EQ.'U') THEN
               VOWEL(5) = VOWEL(5) + 1
            ENDIF
 5       CONTINUE
10    CONTINUE
*
      PRINT*, 'TOTAL NUMBER OF CHARACTERS = ',N*50
      PRINT*
      PRINT*, 'OCCURRENCES OF VOWELS:'
      PRINT 15, VOWEL(1)
15    FORMAT (1X,'A : ',F6.0)
      PRINT 16, VOWEL(2)
16    FORMAT (1X,'E : ',F6.0)
      PRINT 17, VOWEL(3)
17    FORMAT (1X,'I : ',F6.0)
      PRINT 18, VOWEL(4)
18    FORMAT (1X,'O : ',F6.0)
      PRINT 19, VOWEL(5)
19    FORMAT (1X,'U : ',F6.0)
      PRINT*
      CALL GRAPH(VOWEL, 5, 20)
*
      END
*------------------------------------------------------------*
      GRAPH subroutine goes here
*------------------------------------------------------------*
```

A sample output from this program is

```
TOTAL NUMBER OF CHARACTERS = 250

OCCURRENCES OF VOWELS:
A:     15.
E:     26.
I:      4.
O:      8.
U:     16.
************
********************
***
******
************
```

8-3   DOUBLE-PRECISION DATA

Double-precision variables are necessary any time we want to keep more significant digits than are stored in real variables. Assume that a real variable can store 7 significant digits; this means that the real variable will keep 7 digits of accuracy, beginning with the first nonzero digit, in addition to remembering where the decimal point goes. A double-precision value can store more digits, with the exact number of digits dependent on the computer. For this discussion, assume that double-precision variables store 14 digits. The following table compares values that can be stored in real values (also called single-precision values) and in double-precision values.

Value to Be Stored	Single Precision	Double Precision
37.6892718	37.68927	37.689271800000
−1.60003	−1.600030	−1.6000300000000
820000000487.	820000000000.	820000000487.00
18268296.300405079	18268290.	18268296.300405

Note that we are doubling (or at least increasing) the precision of our values, but we are not doubling the range of numbers that can be stored. The same range of numbers applies to both single- and double-precision values, but double-precision values store those numbers with more digits of precision.

Many science and engineering applications use double-precision values to increase accuracy. For example, the study of solar systems, galaxies, and stars requires storing immense distances with as much precision as possible. Even economic models often need double precision. A model for predicting the gross national debt must handle numbers exceeding $1 trillion. With single precision, you cannot store the values with an accuracy to the nearest dollar. With double precision, amounts up to 10 trillion can be used and still have significant digits for all dollar amounts.

A double-precision constant is written in an exponential form, with a D in place of the E. Some examples of double-precision constants are

```
0.378926542D+04
1.4762D-02
0.25D+00
```

Always use the exponential form with the letter D for double-precision constants, even if the constant uses 7 or fewer digits of accuracy; otherwise, you may lose some accuracy because a fractional value that can be expressed evenly in decimal notation may not be expressed exactly in binary notation.

Double-precision variables are specified with a specification statement, whose general form is

DOUBLE PRECISION   *variable list*

A double-precision array is specified as

```
DOUBLE PRECISION   DTEMP(50)
```

DOUBLE-PRECISION I/O

Double-precision variables can be used in list-directed output in the same manner that we list real values: The only distinction is that more digits of accuracy can be stored in a double-precision value; therefore, more digits of accuracy can be written from a double precision value.

In formatted input and output, double-precision values may be referenced with the F or E format specifications. Another specification, Dw.d, may also be used. Dw.d functions essentially like the E specification, but the D emphasizes that it is being used with a double-precision value. In output, the value in this exponential form is printed with a D, instead of an E. Thus, if the following statements were executed,

```
   DOUBLE PRECISION   DX
     .
     .
     .
   DX = 1.66587514521D+00
   PRINT 10, DX
10 FORMAT (1X,'DX = ',D17.10)
```

the output would be

```
DX =   0.1665875145D+01
```

EXAMPLE 8-8   **Solar Distances**

Assume that a character array has been filled with the names of planets, moons, and other celestial bodies. A corresponding array has been filled with the distances of these objects from the sun in millions of miles. Both arrays have been defined to hold 200 values, and an integer N specifies how many elements are actually stored in the arrays. The array NAME is an array of character strings of length 20 and the array DIST is a double-precision array. Give the statements to print these names and distances.

Solution

Before printing the data in the arrays, we print a heading for the data. Next, a loop is executed N times and is used to print the object name and its corresponding distance from the sun in millions of miles. We use a D format for the output because the set of distances may cover a large range of values. The CHARACTER statement and the DOUBLE PRECISION statement are included with the statements to print the data:

```
      CHARACTER*20  NAME(200)
      DOUBLE PRECISION  DIST(200)
        .
        .
        .
      PRINT*, 'SOLAR OBJECTS AND DISTANCES FROM THE SUN'
      PRINT*, '                   (MILLIONS OF MILES)'
      PRINT*
      DO 10 I=1,N
         PRINT 5, NAME(I), DIST(I)
    5    FORMAT (1X,A,2X,D15.8)
   10 CONTINUE
```

A sample output from these statements is

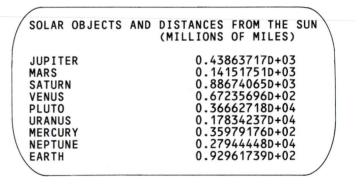

```
SOLAR OBJECTS AND DISTANCES FROM THE SUN
                (MILLIONS OF MILES)

JUPITER                0.43863717D+03
MARS                   0.14151751D+03
SATURN                 0.88674065D+03
VENUS                  0.67235696D+02
PLUTO                  0.36662718D+04
URANUS                 0.17834237D+04
MERCURY                0.35979176D+02
NEPTUNE                0.27944448D+04
EARTH                  0.92961739D+02
```

DOUBLE-PRECISION OPERATIONS

When an arithmetic operation is performed with two double-precision values, the result is double precision. If an operation involves a double-precision value and a single-precision value or an integer, the result is a double-precision result. In such a mixed-mode operation, do not assume that the other value is converted to double precision; instead, think of the other value as being extended in length with zeros. To illustrate, the first two assignment statements that follow yield exactly the same values; the third assignment statement, however, adds a double-precision constant to DX and yields the most accurate result of the three statements:

```
DOUBLE PRECISION  DX, DY1, DY2, DY3
    .
    .
    .
DY1 = DX + 0.3872
DY2 = DX + 0.38720000000000
DY3 = DX + 0.3872D+00
```

The most accurate way to obtain a constant that cannot be written in a fixed number of decimal places is to perform a double-precision operation that yields the desired value. For instance, to obtain the double-precision constant one-third, use the following expression:

$$1.0D+00/3.0D+00$$

Using double-precision values increases the precision of our results, but there is a price for this additional precision — the execution time for computations is longer and more memory is required.

DOUBLE-PRECISION INTRINSIC FUNCTIONS

If a double-precision argument is used in a generic function, the function value is also double precision. Many of the common intrinsic functions for real numbers can be converted to double precision functions by preceding the function name with the letter D: for instance, DSQRT, DABS, DMOD, DSIN, DEXP, DLOG, and DLOG10 all require double-precision arguments and yield double-precision values. Double-precision functions can also be used to compute constants with double-precision accuracy. For instance, the following statements compute pi with double-precision accuracy:

```
DOUBLE PRECISION  DPI
    .
    .
    .
DPI = 4.0D+00*DATAN(1.0D+00)
```

(Recall that $\pi/4$ is equal to the arctangent of 1.0.)

Although Appendix A contains a complete list of the functions that relate to double-precision values, two functions, DBLE and DPROD, are specifically designed for use with double-precision variables. DBLE converts a REAL argument to a double-precision value by adding zeros. DPROD has two real arguments and returns the double-precision product of the two arguments.

EXAMPLE 8-9 **Spherical Mirror Sag**

The alignment of curved mirrors in a laser system is an extremely precise operation. The calculations may include computing the sag of the spherical mirror surface, which is calculated with the following equation, assuming that r is the radius of the spherical mirror and s is the distance from the center of the spherical mirror to its tangent plane:

$$\text{Sag} = \frac{rs^2}{1 + \sqrt{1 - r^2 s^2}}$$

Assume that DR and DS represent double-precision values in the proper units for the radius *(DR)* of a spherical mirror and the distance *(DS)* from the center of the spherical mirror to its tangent plane. These two values have already been computed in a program. Give the statement to compute the sag to at least 10 digits of accuracy (assuming real values have 7 digits of accuracy).

Solution

```
DOUBLE PRECISION  DR, DS, DSAG
  .
  .
  .
DSAG = DR*DS*DS/(1.0D+00 + DSQRT(1.0D+00 - DR*DR*DS*DS))
```

SELF-TEST 8-2

This self-test allows you to check quickly to see if you have remembered some of the key points from Section 8-3. If you have any problems with the exercises, you should reread this section. The solutions are included at the end of the text.

In problems 1-6, show how to represent these constants as double precision constants.

1. 0.25
2. 0.58
3. 1/7
4. 1/13
5. 108.3
6. 2.0

In problems 7-9, show the output of the following PRINT statements if DX = 14.17862459, where DX is a double-precision variable.

```
7.   PRINT 4, DX
   4 FORMAT (1X,D14.6)
8.   PRINT 5, DX
   5 FORMAT (1X,D19.12)
9.   PRINT 6, DX
   6 FORMAT (1X,F10.6)
```

8-4 APPLICATION—TEMPERATURE DISTRIBUTION (Mechanical Engineering)

In this application, we consider the temperature distribution in a thin metal plate as it reaches a point of thermal equilibrium. The plate is constructed so that each edge is isothermal (maintained at a constant temperature). The temperature of an interior point on the plate is a function of the temperature of the surrounding material. If we consider the plate to be similar to a grid, then a two-dimensional array could be used to store the temperatures of the corresponding points on the plate. The following diagram contains an array that is used to store the temperatures of a plate that is being analyzed with 5 temperature measurements along the sides and 10 temperature measurements along the top and botton. A total of 50 temperature values are stored.

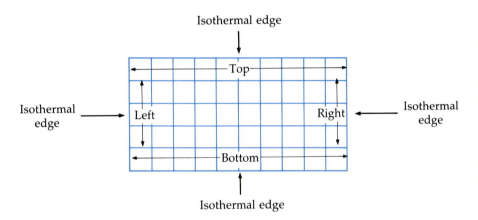

The isothermal temperatures at the top, bottom, left, and right would be given as inputs. The interior points are initially set to some arbitrary temperature, usually zero. The new temperature of each interior point is calculated as the average of its 4 surrounding points, as shown in the diagram:

$$T_0 = \frac{T_1 + T_2 + T_3 + T_4}{4}$$

After computing the new temperature for an interior point, the difference between the old temperature and the new temperature is computed. If the magnitude of a temperature change is greater than some specified tolerance value, the plate is not yet in thermal equilibrium, and the entire process is repeated.

We use two arrays for the temperatures, one for the old temperatures and one for the new temperatures. We need two arrays because we assume that the temperature changes for all the points are occurring simultaneously, even though we compute them one at a time. If we used only one array, we would be updating information before we were through with the old information. For example, suppose that we are computing the new temperature at position (3,3). The new value would be the average of temperatures in positions (2,3), (3,2), (3,4), and (4,3). When we move on to compute the new temperature at position (3,4), we again compute an average, but we want to use the old value in position (3,3), not its updated value.

Thus, we use a two-dimensional array of old temperatures to compute a two-dimensional array of new temperatures and, at the same time, to check if any of the temperature changes exceed the tolerance. We then move the new temperatures to the old array. When none of the temperature changes exceed the tolerance, we assume that equilibrium has been reached, and we print the final temperatures. We use double-precision values so that the equilibrium values can be determined accurately.

PROBLEM STATEMENT

Determine the equilibrium values for a metal plate.

INPUT/OUTPUT DESCRIPTION

The input values to the program include the number of rows and the number of columns in the temperature grid, the top temperature, the bottom temperature, the left temperature, the right temperature, and the tolerance value. The output from the program should be a grid of values representing the final temperature values when they have reached equilibrium.

HAND EXAMPLE

To be sure that we understand the process, we examine a simple case, studying each iteration. Assume that the array contains 4 rows and 4 columns. The isothermal edge temperatures are

$$
\begin{aligned}
\text{Top} &\leftarrow 100.0 \\
\text{Bottom} &\leftarrow 200.0 \\
\text{Left side} &\leftarrow 100.0 \\
\text{Right side} &\leftarrow 200.0
\end{aligned}
$$

The internal points are initialized to zero, and the tolerance value is 5.0.

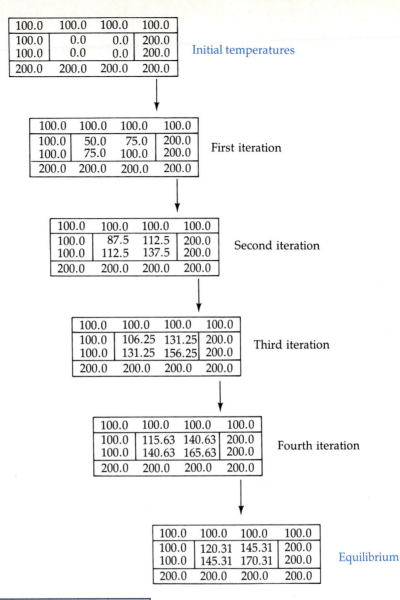

100.0	100.0	100.0	100.0
100.0	0.0	0.0	200.0
100.0	0.0	0.0	200.0
200.0	200.0	200.0	200.0

Initial temperatures

100.0	100.0	100.0	100.0
100.0	50.0	75.0	200.0
100.0	75.0	100.0	200.0
200.0	200.0	200.0	200.0

First iteration

100.0	100.0	100.0	100.0
100.0	87.5	112.5	200.0
100.0	112.5	137.5	200.0
200.0	200.0	200.0	200.0

Second iteration

100.0	100.0	100.0	100.0
100.0	106.25	131.25	200.0
100.0	131.25	156.25	200.0
200.0	200.0	200.0	200.0

Third iteration

100.0	100.0	100.0	100.0
100.0	115.63	140.63	200.0
100.0	140.63	165.63	200.0
200.0	200.0	200.0	200.0

Fourth iteration

100.0	100.0	100.0	100.0
100.0	120.31	145.31	200.0
100.0	145.31	170.31	200.0
200.0	200.0	200.0	200.0

Equilibrium

ALGORITHM DEVELOPMENT

The general decomposition of the steps in solving this problem are given.

DECOMPOSITION

Read isothermal edge temperatures and tolerance.
Update temperatures until equilibrium is reached.
Print equilibrium temperatures.

The first refinement of these steps is illustrated in the following general flowchart:

The portion of this flowchart that needs refinement before we can convert the solution into FORTRAN is the step "perform update of internal temperatures." It is in this step that we must compute the updated temperatures, determine if we have reached equilibrium, and move the new temperatures to the array of old temperatures. The refined portion of the flowchart follows:

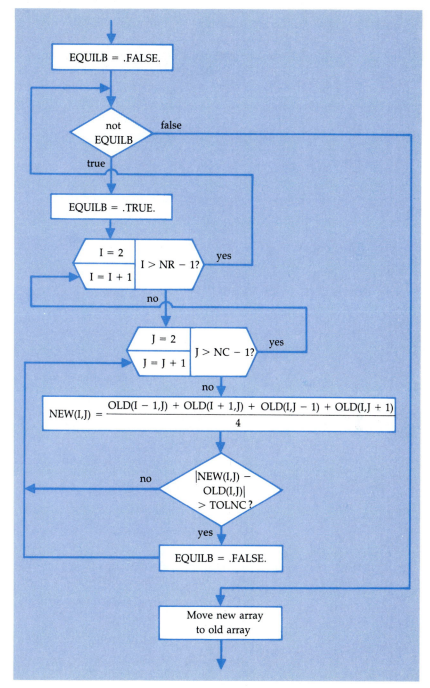

Before we convert the flowchart steps into FORTRAN, we must discuss data structures and subprograms. Clearly, the data that we are using is best represented by a two-dimensional array. We use a double-precision array to be able to work with tolerances that might be much smaller than the actual temperatures themselves. The arrays need to be defined with a maximum size, and we assume that 10 rows and 10 columns represent this maximum size.

The second issue we need to address is subprograms: As we developed the flowchart for this algorithm, there was no set of operations that needed to be performed in several places in the program. However, if we consider the overall program, it is getting lengthy; and long programs are harder to follow, even if they are properly structured. Therefore, you should look for operations that can easily be written in a subprogram, making our main programs more readable. In this program, the loop to move the new temperatures to the old temperature array is written as a subroutine. In addition, we write a subroutine to print the new temperatures. Even though the problem statement specifies that the temperatures are written only once, we definitely want to print them more often in the debugging stages; thus, it is useful to have a subroutine for printing out the temperatures at intermediate stages. In fact, we will print the initial set of temperatures in this program in order to be sure that the proper data was entered by the user.

The structure chart for this program is:

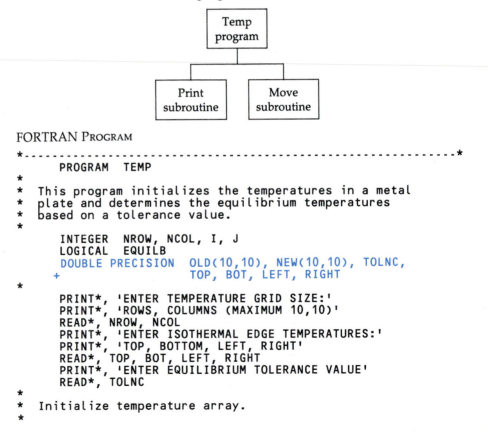

FORTRAN Program

```
*-----------------------------------------------------------------*
      PROGRAM  TEMP
*
*  This program initializes the temperatures in a metal
*  plate and determines the equilibrium temperatures
*  based on a tolerance value.
*
      INTEGER  NROW, NCOL, I, J
      LOGICAL  EQUILB
      DOUBLE PRECISION  OLD(10,10), NEW(10,10), TOLNC,
     +                  TOP, BOT, LEFT, RIGHT
*
      PRINT*, 'ENTER TEMPERATURE GRID SIZE:'
      PRINT*, 'ROWS, COLUMNS (MAXIMUM 10,10)'
      READ*, NROW, NCOL
      PRINT*, 'ENTER ISOTHERMAL EDGE TEMPERATURES:'
      PRINT*, 'TOP, BOTTOM, LEFT, RIGHT'
      READ*, TOP, BOT, LEFT, RIGHT
      PRINT*, 'ENTER EQUILIBRIUM TOLERANCE VALUE'
      READ*, TOLNC
*
*  Initialize temperature array.
*
```

```
          DO 5 J=1,NCOL
              NEW(1,J) = TOP
              NEW(NROW,J) = BOT
      5 CONTINUE
          DO 15 I=2,NROW-1
              NEW(I,1) = LEFT
              DO 10 J=2,NCOL-1
                  NEW(I,J) = O.OD+00
      10    CONTINUE
              NEW(I,NCOL) = RIGHT
      15 CONTINUE
          CALL MOVE(OLD,NEW,NROW,NCOL)
*
*  Print initial temperature array.
*
          PRINT*
          PRINT*, 'INITIAL TEMPERATURES'
          PRINT*
          CALL PRINT(OLD,NROW,NCOL)
*
*  Update temperatures until equilibrium.
*
          EQUILB = .FALSE.
      20 IF (.NOT.EQUILB) THEN
              EQUILB = .TRUE.
              DO 30 I=2,NROW-1
                  DO 25 J=2,NCOL-1
                      NEW(I,J) = (OLD(I-1,J) + OLD(I+1,J) +
     +                          OLD(I,J-1) + OLD(I,J+1))/4.0D+00
                      IF (DABS(NEW(I,J) - OLD(I,J)).GT.TOLNC)
     +                          EQUILB = .FALSE.
      25        CONTINUE
      30    CONTINUE
              CALL MOVE(OLD,NEW,NROW,NCOL)
              GO TO 20
          ENDIF
*
*  Print equilibrium temperature array.
*
          PRINT*
          PRINT*, 'EQUILIBRIUM TEMPERATURES'
          PRINT*
          CALL PRINT(OLD,NROW,NCOL)
*
          END
*--------------------------------------------------------------*
*
*
          SUBROUTINE  PRINT(OLD,NROW,NCOL)
*
*  This subroutine prints a double-precision
*  array with NROW rows and NCOL columns.
*
          INTEGER  NROW, NCOL, I, J
          DOUBLE PRECISION  OLD(10,10)
*
          DO 10 I=1,NROW
              PRINT 5, (OLD(I,J), J=1,NCOL)
      5     FORMAT(1X,10(D12.5,1X))
      10 CONTINUE
*
          RETURN
          END
*--------------------------------------------------------------*
```

```
      *
      *
            SUBROUTINE  MOVE(OLD,NEW,NROW,NCOL)
      *
      *  This subroutine moves the values in the new array
      *  into the old array.
      *
            INTEGER  NROW, NCOL, I, J
            DOUBLE PRECISION  OLD(10,10), NEW(10,10)
      *
            DO 10 I=1,NROW
               DO 5 J=1,NCOL
                  OLD(I,J) = NEW(I,J)
         5     CONTINUE
        10 CONTINUE
      *
            RETURN
            END
      *-----------------------------------------------------------------*
```

TESTING

Testing this program is easier because of the subroutine that prints the values in the OLD array. You can call this subroutine just after the new temperatures are moved to the old temperatures (just before GO TO 20), which allows you to check the values after each update loop.

Note that the two subroutines used the variables NROW and NCOL as DO loop parameters but not as array dimensions. Remember that it is easy to cause problems with two-dimensional arrays when you use variable dimensioning; thus, we recommend that you use the maximum array size in all subprogram array definitions, as we did in this example. Then use variables to control the portion of the array that you actually use.

If we use the data from our hand-worked example in this program, our output is

```
INITIAL TEMPERATURES

0.10000D+03   0.10000D+03   0.10000D+03   0.10000D+03
0.10000D+03   0.00000D+00   0.00000D+00   0.20000D+03
0.10000D+03   0.00000D+00   0.00000D+00   0.20000D+03
0.20000D+03   0.20000D+03   0.20000D+00   0.20000D+03

EQUILIBRIUM TEMPERATURES

0.10000D+03   0.10000D+03   0.10000D+03   0.10000D+03
0.10000D+03   0.12031D+03   0.14531D+03   0.20000D+03
0.10000D+03   0.14531D+03   0.17031D+03   0.20000D+03
0.20000D+03   0.20000D+03   0.20000D+00   0.20000D+03
```

8–5 COMPLEX DATA

Complex numbers are needed to solve many problems in science and engineering, particularly in physics and electrical engineering. To help in their solutions, FORTRAN includes a special data type for complex variables and constants. (Recall that complex numbers have the form $a + bi$, where i is $\sqrt{-1}$ and a and b are real numbers. Thus, the real part of the number is represented by a, and the imaginary part of the number is represented by b.) These complex values are stored as an ordered pair of real values that represents the real and the imaginary portions of the value.

A complex constant is specified by two real constants separated by a comma and enclosed in parentheses. The first constant represents the real part of the complex value; the second constant represents the imaginary part of the complex value. Thus, the complex constant $3.0 + 1.5i$, where i represents the square root of -1, is written in FORTRAN as the complex constant (3.0, 1.5).

Complex variables are specified with a specification statement, whose general form is

COMPLEX   *variable list*

A complex array is specified as

```
COMPLEX   CX(100)
```

COMPLEX I/O

A complex value in list-directed output is printed as two real values separated by a comma and enclosed in parentheses. Two real values are read for each complex value in a list-directed input statement.

In formatted input, a complex value is read with two real specifications. For output, a complex value is printed with two real specifications. The real part of the complex value is read or printed before the imaginary portion. It is good practice to enclose the two parts printed in parentheses and separate them by a comma, or print them in the $a + bi$ form. Both forms are illustrated in the following statements:

```
   COMPLEX  CX, CY
   .
   .
   .
   CX = (1.5, 4.0)
   CY = (0.0, 2.4)
   PRINT 5, CX, CY
 5 FORMAT (1X,'(',F4.1,',',F4.1,')'/1X,F4.1,' + ', F4.1,' I')
```

The output from the PRINT statement is

$$(\ 1.5, \ 4.0)$$
$$0.0 \ + \ \ 2.4 \ I$$

COMPLEX OPERATIONS

When an arithmetic operation is performed between two complex values, the result is also a complex value. In an expression containing a complex value and a real or integer value, the real or integer value is converted to a complex value whose imaginary part is zero. Expressions containing both complex values and double-precision values are not allowed.

The rules for complex arithmetic are not as familiar as those for integers or real values. The following display lists the results of basic operations on two complex numbers C_1 and C_2, where $C_1 = a_1 + b_1 i$ and $C_2 = a_2 + b_2 i$:

$$C_1 + C_2 = (a_1 + a_2) + i(b_1 + b_2)$$
$$C_1 - C_2 = (a_1 - a_2) + i(b_1 - b_2)$$
$$C_1 * C_2 = (a_1 a_2 - b_1 b_2) + i(a_1 b_2 + a_2 b_1)$$
$$\frac{C_1}{C_2} = \frac{a_1 a_2 + b_1 b_2}{a_2{}^2 + b_2{}^2} + i \ \frac{a_2 b_1 - b_2 a_1}{a_2{}^2 + b_2{}^2}$$
$$|C_1| = \sqrt{a_1{}^2 + b_1{}^2}$$
$$e^{C_1} = e^{a_1} \cos b_1 + i e^{a_1} \sin b_1$$
$$\cos C_1 = 1 - \frac{C_1{}^3}{3!} + \frac{C_1{}^5}{5!} - \frac{C_1{}^7}{7!} + \cdots$$

COMPLEX INTRINSIC FUNCTIONS

If a complex value is used in one of the generic functions, such as SQRT, ABS, SIN, COS, EXP, or LOG, the function value is also complex. The functions CSQRT, CABS, CSIN, CCOS, CEXP, and CLOG are all intrinsic functions with complex arguments. These function names begin with the letter C to emphasize that they are complex functions.

Although Appendix A contains a complete list of the functions that relate to complex values, four functions, REAL, AIMAG, CONJG, and CMPLX, are specifically designed for use with complex variables: REAL yields the real part of its complex argument; AIMAG yields the imaginary part of its complex argument; CONJG converts a complex number to its conjugate, where the conjugate of $(a + bi)$ is $(a - bi)$; COMPLX converts two real arguments, a and b, into a complex value $(a + bi)$. Note that while (2.0,1.0) is equal to the complex constant $2.0 + 1.0i$, we must use the expression CMPLX(A,B) to specify the complex variable $A + Bi$; the expression (A,B) by itself does not represent a complex variable in FORTRAN 77.

EXAMPLE 8–10 Quadratic Formula

The roots of a quadratic equation with real coefficients may be complex. Give the statements to compute and print the two roots of a quadratic equation, given the coefficients A, B, and C as shown:

$$AX^2 + BX + C = 0$$

$$X_1 = \frac{-B + \sqrt{B^2 - 4AC}}{2A} \qquad X_2 = \frac{-B - \sqrt{B^2 - 4AC}}{2A}$$

Solution

```
COMPLEX  DISCR, ROOT1, ROOT2
   .
   .
   .
DISCR = CMPLX(B*B - 4.0*A*C,0.0)
ROOT1 = (-B + SQRT(DISCR))/(2.0*A)
ROOT2 = (-B - SQRT(DISCR))/(2.0*A)
PRINT*, 'ROOTS TO THE QUADRATIC EQUATION ARE:'
PRINT 5, ROOT1, ROOT2
5 FORMAT (1X,F5.2,' + ',F5.2,' I',4X, F5.2,' + ',F5.2,' I')
```

Two sets of sample output are shown, one in which both roots are real and one in which both roots are complex:

```
ROOTS TO THE QUADRATIC EQUATION ARE:
 1.56 +  0.00 I     2.00 +  0.00 I
```

```
ROOTS TO THE QUADRATIC EQUATION ARE:
-2.36 +  2.45 I  -2.36 +   -2.45 I
```

This self-test allows you to check quickly to see if you have remembered some of the key points from Section 8–5. If you have any problems with the exercises, you should reread this section. The solutions are included at the end of the text.

In problems 1–6, compute the value stored in CX if $CY = 1.0 + 3.0i$ and $CZ = 0.5 - 1.0i$. Assume CX, CY, and CZ are complex variables.

```
1. CX = CY + CZ
2. CX = CY - CZ
3. CX = CONJG(CZ)
4. CX = REAL(CY) + AIMAG(CZ)
5. CX = CMPLX(5.0,0.2)
6. CX = ABS(CY)
```

In problems 7–8, show the output of the following PRINT statements. Assume that $CX = 2.3 + 0.2i$.

```
7.    PRINT 5, CX
    5 FORMAT (1X,2F8.2)
8.    PRINT 6, CX
    6 FORMAT (1X,'(',F8.2,',',F8.2,')')
```

8–6 APPLICATION—ELECTRIC CIRCUIT MODEL (Electrical Engineering)

In the analysis of an electric circuit, we are often interested in the transfer function of the circuit. This transfer function can be used to determine the effect of the circuit on a sine function, in terms of magnitude changes and phase changes. The magnitude (absolute value) of the transfer function evaluated at the frequency of the sine wave is multiplied by the input magnitude to give the output magnitude. The phase (arctangent of the imaginary part divided by the real part) of the transfer function evaluated at the frequency of the sine wave is added to the input phase to give the output phase. For example, consider the following circuit that contains a capacitor C and a resistor R:

Kirchhoff's voltage law can be used to derive the transfer function for this system:

$$H(w) = \frac{\omega RCi}{1 + \omega RCi}$$

where ω represents frequency in radians per second and i represents the square root of -1. Write a program that determines the magnitude and phase changes caused by this circuit when a sine wave of a given frequency passes through the circuit.

PROBLEM STATEMENT

Write a program that determines the magnitude and phase changes of a sine wave after it passes through the given electric circuit.

INPUT/OUTPUT DESCRIPTION

There are three input values: the resistance R in ohms, the capacitance C in farads, and the frequency of the input sine wave. The output is the magnitude and phase of the transfer function evaluated at the input frequency.

HAND EXAMPLE

Assume that the input to the circuit is sine $100t$. The frequency of this sine wave is 100 radians per second. Also assume that R is equal to 10,000 ohms and that C is equal to 2.0 microfarads (or 0.000002 farads). The transfer function with these parameters is

$$H(100) = \frac{(100)(10000)(0.000002)i}{1 + (100)(10000)(0.000002)i} = \frac{2i}{1 + 2i}$$

$$= \frac{2i(1 - 2i)}{(1 + 2i)(1 - 2i)} = \frac{4 + 2i}{1 + 4} = 0.8 + 0.4i$$

The magnitude of $(0.8 + 0.4i)$ is .89, and the phase is 0.46 radians. Thus, a sine wave with a frequency of 100 radians per second has its magnitude multiplied by 0.89 and its phase changed by 0.46 radians when it passes through the circuit in this example.

ALGORITHM DEVELOPMENT

The decomposition of this problem solution involves reading the input values and then computing the corresponding transfer function magnitude and phase.

DECOMPOSITION

Read R, C, and ω.
Compute magnitude and phase.
Print ω, magnitude, and phase.

The refinement of this algorithm involves substituting the equations in the computation step.

REFINEMENT IN PSEUDOCODE

ELECT1: Read R, C, and ω
        Compute $H(\omega)$
        Determine magnitude of $H(\omega)$
        Determine phase of $H(\omega)$
        Print ω, magnitude, and phase

FORTRAN PROGRAM

```
*---------------------------------------------------------------*
      PROGRAM  ELECT1
*
*  This program determines the magnitude and phase
*  effects of an RC circuit on a sine wave.
*
      REAL  R, C, W, MAGN, PHASE
      COMPLEX  I, HW

      I = (0.0, 1.0)
*
      PRINT*, 'ENTER RESISTANCE IN OHMS'
      READ*, R
      PRINT*, 'ENTER CAPACITANCE IN FARADS'
      READ*, C
      PRINT*, 'ENTER THE SINE FREQUENCY IN RADIANS PER SEC'
      READ*, W
*
      HW = (W*R*C*I)/(1.0 + W*R*C*I)
      MAGN = CABS(HW)
      PHASE = ATAN(AIMAG(HW)/REAL(HW))
*
      PRINT 5, MAGN, PHASE
    5 FORMAT (1X,'MAGNITUDE EFFECT: ',F5.2,3X,
     +             'PHASE EFFECT: ',F5.2)
*
      END
*---------------------------------------------------------------*
```

TESTING

If we use the frequency from our hand-worked example to test this program, our output is

```
ENTER RESISTANCE IN OHMS
10000.
ENTER CAPACITANCE IN FARADS
0.000002
ENTER THE SINE FREQUENCY IN RADIANS PER SEC
100.0
MAGNITUDE EFFECT:  0.89    PHASE EFFECT:  0.46
```

An interesting modification to this program involves looking at the magnitude changes of the circuit over an interval of frequencies as opposed to a specific frequency. For example, some circuits are called low-pass circuits, which means that they pass frequencies below a certain frequency and reject frequencies above a certain frequency. When the magnitude effect is near 1.0, a frequency is being passed; when the magnitude effect is near 0.0, the frequency is being rejected. Other types of circuits are high-pass circuits, band-pass circuits, and band-reject circuits.

If we modify our program to read the starting and ending frequency for an interval of frequencies, we can look at the magnitude effect over that interval and determine the type of circuit being analyzed. In this program, we print 20 values over the frequency interval. The modified program and a sample output are given.

FORTRAN Program

```
*-----------------------------------------------------------------*
      PROGRAM  ELECT2
*
*  This program determines the magnitude
*  effect of an RC circuit over a frequency interval.
*
      INTEGER  K
      REAL  W, R, C, WS, WE, STEP, MAGN
      COMPLEX  I, H, HW
*
      H(W) = (W*R*C*I)/(1.0 + W*R*C*I)
*
      I = (0.0, 1.0)
*
      PRINT*, 'ENTER RESISTANCE IN OHMS'
      READ*, R
      PRINT*, 'ENTER CAPACITANCE IN FARADS'
      READ*, C
      PRINT*, 'ENTER THE STARTING AND ENDING FREQUENCIES'
      PRINT*, '(RADIANS PER SEC)'
      READ*, WS, WE
*
      PRINT*
      PRINT*, 'FREQUENCY AND MAGNITUDE'
      STEP = (WE - WS)/20.0
      DO 20 K=1,20
         W = (K - 1)*STEP + WS
         HW = H(W)
         MAGN = CABS(HW)
         PRINT 10, W, MAGN
   10    FORMAT (1X,F6.2,5X,F5.2)
   20 CONTINUE
*
      END
*-----------------------------------------------------------------*
```

```
ENTER RESISTANCE IN OHMS
10000.
ENTER CAPACITANCE IN FARADS
0.000002
ENTER THE STARTING AND ENDING FREQUENCIES
(IN RADIANS)
0.0 200.0

FREQUENCY AND MAGNITUDE
    0.00         0.00
   10.00         0.20
   20.00         0.37
   30.00         0.51
   40.00         0.62
   50.00         0.71
   60.00         0.77
   70.00         0.81
   80.00         0.85
   90.00         0.87
  100.00         0.89
  110.00         0.91
  120.00         0.92
  130.00         0.93
  140.00         0.94
  150.00         0.95
  160.00         0.95
  170.00         0.96
  180.00         0.96
  190.00         0.97
```

Note that this circuit rejects frequencies near zero and passes frequencies with little magnitude distortion when the frequency is above 150.00 radians per second.

SUMMARY

With the data types presented in this chapter, we now have a number of choices for defining our variables and constants. For numeric data, we can select integers, real values, or double-precision values. We have character data for information that is not going to be used in numeric computations. For special applications, we have complex variables. In addition to being able to choose the proper data type for our data, we also have special intrinsic functions and operations for simplifying our work with the data.

Many errors in character string manipulations occur because the character string is used incorrectly with numeric data. Some typical examples are:

Arithmetic expressions — Even if a character string contains numeric digits, it cannot be used in arithmetic operations.

Comparisons — Character strings should always be compared to other character strings and not to a numeric constant or variable.

Subprogram arguments — A character string used as an argument to a subprogram must be identified in CHARACTER statements in both the main program and in the subprogram.

Another source of errors may be introduced when moving or comparing strings of unequal length. For comparisons, the shorter string will be compared as if it had enough blanks on the right to be equal in length to the longer string. Character strings are always moved character by character from left to right, until the receiving string is filled. If there are too few characters in the sending string, blanks are moved into the right-most characters of the receiving string.

A final caution relative to the substring operation: Invalid results occur if the beginning or ending positions of the substring reference are outside the original string itself.

The primary debugging tool for double-precision and complex values is the PRINT statement. If an error is related to a double-precision value, print it out with an E21.14 format (assumes 14 digits of accuracy) each time it is used to be sure that you are not losing the extra accuracy. Also, be sure that you are not moving the value into a single-precision variable in an intermediate step in the program.

If your program errors relate to complex values, write the values of the complex numbers as soon as they are initialized and after each modification. Remember that if you move a complex value into a real variable, the imaginary portion is lost.

STYLE/TECHNIQUE GUIDES

A programmer who is comfortable and proficient with character string manipulations will find them extremely useful. The ability to display information clearly and simply is valuable in communication, and the use of character strings adds a new dimension to the method of both reading and displaying information.

Some guides for using character strings in your programs are:

1. Use character strings of the same length where possible.
2. Use the function INDEX instead of writing your own routines to find substrings in a string.

3. Become proficient with the substring and concatenation operators; these are powerful tools in manipulating and analyzing character strings.

4. Take advantage of the printer-plotting techniques described in this chapter and in the problems at the end of the chapter.

Finally, when you use a feature of FORTRAN (such as double-precision or complex variables) that is not commonly used, good documentation is important. More comment lines may be necessary to clarify your code. If a computation uses complex numbers, explain the computations in more detail than in regular arithmetic computations. Part of good documentation also includes choosing descriptive names.

KEY WORDS

ASCII code
character string
collating sequence
complex value
concatenation

double-precision value
EBCDIC code
FORTRAN character set
lexicographical order
substring

PROBLEMS

We begin our problem set with modifications to programs developed earlier in this chapter. Give the decomposition, refined pseudocode or flowchart, and FORTRAN solution for each problem.

Problems 1–5 modify the program DECODE, given on page 369, which generated a bar graph to compare the number of occurrences of vowels in a piece of text.

1. Modify the graph subroutine so that it prints two lines of asterisks for each bar.

2. Modify the graph subroutine so that it prints three lines of asterisks for each bar. Separate each group of three lines by a blank line.

3. Modify the decode program so that it includes lowercase or uppercase letters in each vowel count.

4. Modify the decode program so that it reads from the terminal the specific characters that it is going to count. The user first enters the number of specific characters and then the characters themselves. Assume that 30 characters is the upper limit.

5. Modify the graph subroutine so that it computes the average of the data values. In each bar, print asterisks up to the average value and plus signs for any part of the bar that is over the average. Thus, if a data value is below the average, its bar is entirely asterisks; if a data value is above the average, its bar is composed of asterisks and plus signs.

Problems 6–10 modify the program TEMP, given on page 380, which determined an equilibrium temperature distribution in a metal plate.

6. Modify the temperature distribution program so that it counts the number of iterations needed for the plate to reach equilibrium. Print this value after the final grid.
7. Modify the temperature distribution program so that the initialization of the temperature array is performed in a subroutine.
8. Modify the temperature distribution program so that the computation of the new temperature values is performed in a subroutine.
9. Modify the temperature distribution program so that the temperature iteration continues until equilibrium has been reached or until 10 iterations have been performed.
10. Modify the print subroutine so that it also prints the maximum and minimum temperatures and their positions in the temperature array.

Problems 11–15 modify the program ELECT1, given on page 388, which determines the magnitude and phase effects of an *RC* circuit on a sine wave.

11. Modify the program ELECT1 so that it prints the phase effect in degrees instead of in radians.
12. Modify the program ELECT1 so that it reads the resistance in units of thousands of ohms, or kilo-ohms.
13. Modify the program ELECT1 so that it reads the capacitance in units of microfarads. (one microfarad = 0.000001 farad)
14. Modify the program ELECT1 so that it reads the sine frequency in hertz (or cycles per second) instead of in radians per second. (1 hertz = 2*pi radians per second)
15. Add a loop to the program ELECT1 so it continues computing magnitude and phase effects until a negative value is entered for the sine frequency.

In problems 16–35, develop programs and modules using the five-phase design process.

16. Write a complete program that reads a data file ADDR containing 50 names and addresses. The first line for each person contains the first name (10 characters), the middle name (6 characters), and the last name (21 characters). The second line contains the address (25 characters), the city (10 characters), the state abbreviation (2 characters), and the zip code (5 characters). Print the information in the following label form:

```
First Initial. Middle Initial. Last Name
Address
City, State   Zip
```

Skip four lines between labels. The city should not contain any blanks before the comma that follows it. A typical label might be

```
J. D. Doe
117 Main St.
Taos, NM   87166
```

For simplicity, assume there are no embedded blanks in the individual data values. For example, San Jose would be entered as SanJose and printed in the same manner.

17. Write a subroutine CNDNS that receives a character array of 50 characters and returns a character array OUT, also of 50 characters, which has no adjacent blanks except at the end of the string. Thus, if IN was composed of HELLO THERE' followed by blanks, then the output array OUT should contain 'HELLO THERE' followed by blanks.

18. Write a complete program to read a double-precision value from the terminal. Compute the sine of the value using the following series:

$$\sin X = X - \frac{X^3}{3!} + \frac{X^5}{5!} - \frac{X^7}{7!} + \cdots$$

Continue using terms until the absolute value of a term is less than 1.0D−09. Print the computed sine and the value obtained from the function DSIN for comparison.

19. Write a complete program that reads the coefficients A, B, and C of a quadratic equation from a data line. Compute and print the two roots of the equation. If the roots are real values, use an F format to print them. If the roots are complex, use the $a + bi$ form for output. If the value of A is zero, print a message stating that the equation is linear and not quadratic.

20. Write a program that reads the complex coefficients for a general transfer function with the following equation:

$$H(\omega) = \frac{A*\omega*\omega + B*\omega + C}{\omega*\omega + D*\omega + E}$$

Read an input frequency ω and determine the magnitude and phase effects of this transfer function on a sinusoid with frequency ω.

21. Modify the program in problem 20 to read a beginning and ending frequency from the terminal. Compute and print the magnitude effects for 20 frequency points spaced evenly over the interval.

22. Modify the program in problem 20 to read a beginning and ending frequency from the terminal. Also read the number of points desired in the frequency interval. Print the magnitude effects for these frequency points spaced evenly over the interval.

23. Write a program that prints a table of values for exp(x) where x varies from 0.1 to 2.0 in increments of 0.1. Print 3 columns: x, exp(x) using the single-precision intrinsic function, and exp(x) using the double-precision intrinsic function.

24. Write a subroutine DELETE that has an argument list composed of a character array TEXT of 100 characters and a pointer PTR. The subroutine should delete the character in position PTR. The characters in the positions following PTR should be moved one position to the left. A blank should be added at the end of TEXT to keep the length of TEXT at 100 characters.

25. Write a subroutine INSERT that has an argument list composed of a character string TEXT of 100 characters, a pointer PTR, and a single character CHAR1. The subroutine should insert CHAR1 in the position pointed to by PTR. The rest of the characters should be moved one position to the right, with the last character truncated to keep the length of TEXT at 100 characters.

26. A data file called CARS contains the license plate number and the number of gallons of gas that can be put into the car for each car in a certain state. The license plate is composed of 3 characters, followed by a space, and then 3 digits. Each line in the file contains a license number and a real number that gives the corresponding gallons of gas. The last line in the file has a license number of ZZZ 999 and is not a valid data line. Write a complete program that helps analyze the feasibility of gas rationing based on whether the license plate number is odd or even. The data to be computed and printed is the following:

```
SUM OF GAS FOR ODD CARS    XXXXX GALLONS    XX.X%
SUM OF GAS FOR EVEN CARS   XXXXX GALLONS    XX.X%
```

27. A palindrome is a word or piece of text that is spelled the same forward and backward. The word 'RADAR' is an example of a palindrome, but ' RADAR' is not a palindrome because of the unmatched blank. 'ABLE ELBA' is another palindrome. Write a logical function PALIND that receives a character variable X of length 20. The function should be true if the character array is a palindrome; otherwise, it should be false.

28. Write a subroutine ALPHA that receives an array of 50 letters. The subroutine should alphabetize the list of letters.

29. Modify the subroutine in problem 28 to remove duplicate letters and to add blanks at the end of the array for the letters removed.

30. Write a subroutine whose input is a character array of length 50. Change all punctuation marks (commas, periods, exclamation points, and question marks) to blanks. Assume that the program calls the subroutine with the following statement:

```
CALL EDIT(STRING)
```

31. Write a subroutine that receives a piece of text called PROSE that contains 200 characters. The subprogram should print the text in lines of 30 characters each. Do not split words between two lines. Do not print any lines that are completely blank.

32. Write a function CONSNT that receives a character array of 100 alphabetic letters. Count the number of consonants and return that number to the main program. (It might be easiest to count the number of vowels and subtract that number from 100.)

33. Write a subroutine that receives an array of N real values (maximum value of N is 200) and prints a printer plot. Use an output line of 101 characters. Scale the line from the minimum value to the maximum value. The first line of output should be 101 periods representing the Y-axis. All the following lines should contain a period in the column representing $X = 0$ (if this point is included in the graph), and the letter X in the position of each data point, as shown in the following diagram. (In this diagram, the minimum and the maximum values have the same absolute value.)

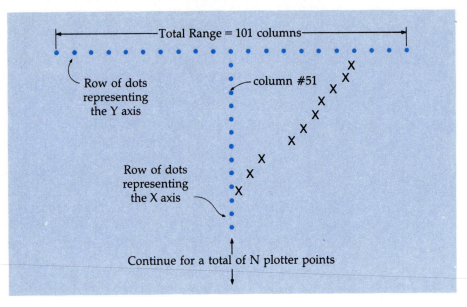

34. Write a complete program that reads and stores the following two-dimensional array of characters:

```
ATIDEB
LENGTH
ECPLOT
DDUEFS
OUTPUT
CGDAER
HIRXJI
KATIMN
BHPARG
```

Now read the 11 strings that follow and find the same strings in the preceding array. Print the positions of characters of these hidden words that may appear forward, backward, up, down, or diagonally. For instance, the word EDIT is located in positions (1,5), (1,4), (1,3), and (1,2).

HIDDEN WORDS

PLOT	STRING
CODE	TEXT
EDIT	READ
LENGTH	GRAPH
INPUT	BAR
OUTPUT	

35. Modify the subprogram of problem 31 such that the length of the output line is an argument of the subroutine. Distribute any blanks between words on a line such that every line begins and ends with a nonblank character. Thus, if the character string PROSE contained a portion of the Gettysburg Address and the line length is 23, then the first three lines of output should be

```
FOUR   SCORE   AND   SEVEN
YEARS AGO   OUR   FATHERS
BROUGHT FORTH UPON THIS
```

36. Text material is sometimes analyzed very carefully to determine quantities such as average word length. Such a quantity can be used to recommend the level of reading ability necessary to read the text. Average word length can even be used to help determine authorship of a literary work; it has been applied to the works of Shakespeare in an attempt to indicate whether Sir Frances Bacon authored some of the plays attributed to Shakespeare. Write a function that receives a character string and returns the average word length of the string. Assume that all words are separated from adjacent words by at least one blank. The first and last characters may or may not be blanks.

37. Write a subroutine that sorts a complex array of N values into a descending order based on the absolute value of the complex values. Assume that the subroutine is called with the statement

```
CALL ORDER(CDATA,N)
```

where CDATA is an array of N complex values.

38. Write a subroutine ENCODE that receives a character string KEY containing 26 characters and a character string MESSGE of an unspecified size. The subroutine should encode MESSGE, using a substitution code where the first letter in KEY is substituted for the letter A in MESSGE, the second letter in KEY is substituted for the letter B in MESSGE, and so on. Thus, if KEY contained the character string

'YXAZKLMBJOCFDVSWTREGHNIPUQ'

and MESSGE contained the character string

'MEET AT AIRPORT SATURDAY'

then the encoded character string would be

'DKKG YG YJRWSRG EYGHRZYU'

The encoded character string should be stored in a character string called SECRET. The subroutine is called with the following statement:

CALL ENCODE(KEY,MESSGE,SECRET)

39. Write a subroutine DECODE that receives a character string KEY containing 26 characters and a character string SECRET of an unspecified size. The subroutine should decode SECRET, which has been encoded with a substitution key where the first letter in KEY was substituted for the letter A, the second letter in KEY was substituted for the letter B, and so on. Blanks were not changed in the coding process. Thus, if KEY contained the character string

'YXAZKLMBJOCFDVSWTREGHNIPUQ'

and SECRET contained the character string

'DKKG YG YJRWSRG EYGHRZYU'

then the decoded character string would be

'MEET AT AIRPORT SATURDAY'

The decoded character string should be stored in a character string called MESSGE. The subroutine is called with the statement

CALL DECODE(KEY,SECRET,MESSGE)

40. Write a subroutine to sort a character string array into alphabetical order. Assume that each character string in the array contains 4 characters. Remove any leading blanks from the character strings before sorting. The input is a character array with N values. The output is the same array, but with the character strings reordered into alphabetical order and the leading blanks removed. Use the following statement to call the subroutine:

CALL ALPHA(NAME,N)

The following example illustrates the reason for removing leading blanks:

Original Order	Alphabetical Order with Blanks	Alphabetical Order without Blanks
SAM$_b$	bb^{ED}	AL$_{bb}$
bb^{ED}	b^{AL}$_b$	AMY$_b$
b^{SUE}	b^{SUE}	BEV$_b$
MARY	AMY$_b$	ED$_{bb}$
JOSE	BEV$_b$	JOHN
JOHN	JOHN	JOSE
AMY$_b$	JOSE	LISA
b^{AL}$_b$	LISA	MARY
LISA	MARY	SAM$_b$
BEV$_b$	SAM$_b$	SUE$_b$

FORTRAN STATEMENT SUMMARY

CHARACTER Statement:

CHARACTER *variable list*

Examples:

```
CHARACTER*5  NAME, DESC(10)

CHARACTER  CITY*20, LOCATION*35
```

Discussion:
The CHARACTER statement defines variables that store character information. It also specifies the number of characters in the variable.

COMPLEX Statement:

COMPLEX *variable list*

Example:

```
COMPLEX  I, CX, Z(10)
```

Discussion:
The COMPLEX statement defines variables that represent complex values. Each complex variable consists of two real values: the first representing the real part of the complex value and the second representing the imaginary part of the complex value. When a COMPLEX value is read or printed, two real values correspond to the COMPLEX value.

DOUBLE PRECISION Statement:

DOUBLE PRECISION *variable list*

Example:

```
DOUBLE PRECISION  X, Y, ACCEL(25)
```

Discussion:
The DOUBLE PRECISION statement defines variables that have more significant digits of accuracy than real variables. The exact number of significant digits of accuracy in a double-precision variable depends on the computer system. Typically, a real value contains 7 digits of accuracy and a double-precision value contains 14 digits of accuracy.

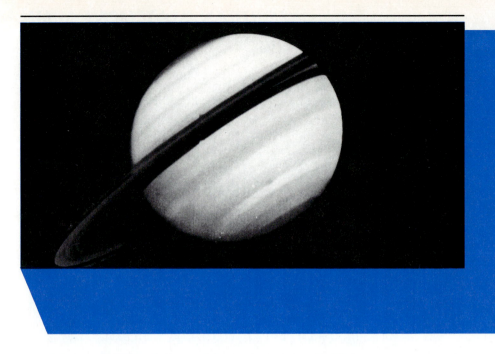

APPLICATION—Voyager Spacecraft Data Analysis (Electrical Engineering)

The pictures of Saturn sent back by Voyager II were spectacular. However, these pictures were initially transmitted as long strings of numbers which represented light intensities detected by the cameras on Voyager II. Sophisticated image processing techniques were used to turn the strings of numbers into recreated images of the surface of Saturn. Write a program to read a data file of light intensities and perform a simple type of digital image processing called edge detection, where an edge detector distinguishes between different surfaces in a two-dimensional image. (See Section 9–3 for the solution.)

Photo courtesy of NASA.

9

ADDITIONAL FILE HANDLING

Introduction

9-1 Internal Files

9-2 Sequential Files

9-3 Application—Voyager Spacecraft Data Analysis (Electrical Engineering)

9-4 Application—Whooping Crane Migration (Biology)

9-5 Direct-Access Files

9-6 Application—Computer Parts Inventory (Computer Science/ Engineering)

9-7 Inquire Statement

Summary

INTRODUCTION

In previous chapters, we used files extensively. For example, READ* and PRINT* statements that referred to input and output on the terminal screen (or a line printer) caused the input and output files to be connected automatically to your program. Using the OPEN statement introduced in Chapter 4, we could also connect other data files. These types of files are called *external files* because they are external to the memory area reserved by our program.

External files can also be read from other devices such as magnetic tape drives or magnetic disk drives; on these devices, these files have special properties that determine the types of statements used to process them. Processing magnetic tape or magnetic disk files also requires some knowledge of sequential access and direct access. In both of these access methods, we use the term *record* to describe a unit of information in the file; in a data file, one line represents a *record*. Each record contains *fields* of information. For instance, a payroll file contains individual payroll records, and each record could contain fields such as a name, hours worked, and hourly rate.

Sequential access of a file involves processing records from the physical beginning of the file. Throughout this text, we have used this type of access. We read the first data line, then the second data line, and so on. In *direct access*, information is not necessarily accessed in its physical order. We may reference the tenth record, then the last record, and then the second record, all without reading the records in between. This type of access is also called random access because we can access the records in a random order.

External files are often used because they are *portable* — they can be used not only on another computer of the same manufacturer, but also on computers made by different manufacturers. For example, a magnetic tape file created on a Digital Equipment Corporation VAX computer can be read on a Control Data Corporation 7600 computer. But for these files to be portable, standard procedures must be observed when creating and using them; for example, because list-directed input and output are system dependent with regard to the formats used, all input and output stored on external devices must use formats to guarantee consistency from one computer to another. You may want to refer to some of the formatting material in Chapter 4 as you study this chapter.

FORTRAN also has a feature called *internal files* that allows us to use a character string as if it were a file to manipulate the data internally.

9-1 INTERNAL FILES

When the unit number in an input or output statement is the name of a character variable, the statement transfers data from one internal storage area to another. These storage areas are called internal files. For instance, we can read data from a character string instead of a data line; the input and output statements function exactly as if the contents of the character string were actually entered in a data line, as shown:

```
       CHARACTER*13  DATA
       DATA = '127 65   42.17'
       READ (DATA,*) I, J, X
```

After execution, the value of I is 127, the value of J is 65, and the value of X is 42.17.

The internal file feature is useful if you want to perform some type of editing on the data before using it. For example, suppose you are reading information from a data file that contains amounts entered with dollar signs to the left of the amounts. If the fields are read directly into real variables, execution errors occur. Using internal files, you can read the data into an internal character file, edit the data by changing all dollar signs to blanks, and then read the number values from the internal file. The following statements read 10 positions from a data line, change any leading dollar sign to a blank, and then read the value into a real variable:

```
       INTEGER  PTR
       REAL   AMOUNT
       CHARACTER*10   TEMP
         .
         .
         .
       READ (12,5) TEMP
     5 FORMAT (A)
       IF (INDEX(TEMP,'$').NE.0) THEN
           PTR = INDEX(TEMP,'$')
           TEMP(PTR:PTR) = ' '
       ENDIF
       READ (TEMP,*) AMOUNT
```

A similar use of internal files is beneficial if you want to edit lines of an output report before printing. For example, you might want to insert dollar signs next to real values to be printed; with internal files, you can insert the dollar sign next to the digits, as in $_{bbb}$\$146.21, instead of next to the output field, as in \$$_{bbb}$146.21.

9-2 SEQUENTIAL FILES

Sequential files are typically built by one program and then accessed by other programs. Once a sequential file is created, individual records cannot be updated. When changes need to be made to the information, the updating is usually done by reading the information in a record, updating it if desired, and then writing the information to an output record. The process is repeated for each record in the file. Sometimes this technique is referred to as *father-son updating*. (The original file is the father file, and the updated file is the son.)

When we use sequential files, the same READ and WRITE statements are used, but other statements may also be needed: an extended form of the OPEN statement; and statements to close the file, to reposition the record pointer to the first record in the file, to backspace one record in the file, and to add an end-of-file indicator to a new file.

OPEN STATEMENT

The OPEN statement connects an external file to a program. The OPEN statement is executable but typically is placed at the beginning of the program because it should generally be executed only once. A simplified form of the OPEN statement was introduced in Chapter 4. The complete form of the OPEN statement is

```
OPEN (UNIT=integer expression,
      FILE=character expression,
      ACCESS=character expression,
      STATUS=character expression,
      FORM=character expression,
      IOSTAT=integer variable,
      RECL=integer expression,
      BLANK=character expression,
      ERR=integer statement reference)
```

UNIT Number The integer expression in this specification is usually a constant. This value is used in READ or WRITE statements to specify the file to be used. The following example illustrates the use of unit number 13 to open the file DIST and write information into it with a WRITE statement:

```
    OPEN (UNIT=13,FILE='DIST',STATUS='NEW')
    WRITE (13,10) X, Y
 10 FORMAT (F8.3,F5.1)
```

FILE The character expression in this file specification is the name of the file; all references to the file must use the same name. Filenames typically consist of 1–6 alphabetic letters or numbers, with an alphabetic letter as the first character.

ACCESS The character string in this specification must be either 'SEQUENTIAL' or 'DIRECT'. If this specification is omitted, 'SEQUENTIAL' is assumed.

STATUS The character string in this specification must be 'NEW', 'OLD', or 'SCRATCH'. 'NEW' specifies that the file is being created through WRITE statements. 'OLD' specifies that the file is already built, and its records are accessed with READ statements. 'SCRATCH' specifies that the file is an output file that is not being used after the program has been executed; hence, it will be deleted.

FORM The character string in this specification must be either 'FORMATTED' or 'UNFORMATTED'. A FORMATTED file uses either formatted READ and WRITE statements or list-directed input/output statements. All examples used in this text have been formatted. UNFORMATTED input/output is used for transfer of data with no data conversion; the data is transferred as binary strings, not as numbers or characters. One of the main uses of UNFORMATTED input/output is to transfer tape or disk data to another tape or disk file. If this specification is omitted, the default is 'FORMATTED' for sequential files and 'UNFORMATTED' for direct files.

IOSTAT The IOSTAT specification is not required but can be used to provide error-recovery. If no errors occur in attaching the specified file to the program, the value of the integer variable is zero. If an error occurs, such as when an input file with the proper name is not found, a value specified by the computer system is stored in the variable. You can test this variable in your program and specify what action is to be taken if it is nonzero. In this next example, an error in opening the file causes IERR to be nonzero. An error message can be printed, and execution then continues. If the IOSTAT specification were not used and an error occurred in opening the file, execution would be terminated with an execution error:

```
      OPEN (UNIT=15,FILE='XYDATA',STATUS='OLD',
     +      IOSTAT=IERR)
      IF (IERR.NE.O) PRINT*, IERR
```

The IOSTAT specification can also be used with READ and WRITE statements.

RECL The RECL specification is required for direct-access files and specifies the record length. It is not used with sequential-access files. This specification is discussed further in Section 9–5.

BLANK The character string in this specification must be either 'NULL' or 'ZERO' and cannot be used with unformatted files. If the specification is 'NULL', blanks are usually ignored in numeric fields, but this is system dependent; if the specification is 'ZERO', blanks are assumed to be zeros in numeric fields. If the specification is omitted, 'NULL' is assumed.

ERR This specification is optional and provides error-recovery. If an error occurs during execution of a statement that contains this ERR specification, control passes to the statement referenced by this specification instead of causing an execution error. The ERR specification can also be used with READ and WRITE statements.

CLOSE STATEMENT

The CLOSE statement is an executable statement that disconnects a file from a program. Its general form is

```
CLOSE (UNIT=integer expression,
       STATUS=character expression,
       IOSTAT=integer variable,
       ERR=integer statement reference)
```

The CLOSE statement is optional because all files are closed automatically upon termination of program execution. The STATUS, IOSTAT, and ERR specifications are also optional. The STATUS specification options for the CLOSE statement are not the same as for the OPEN statement. When a file is closed, the default option is 'KEEP', which indicates that the file is to be kept. The option 'DELETE' may be chosen to indicate that the file is no longer needed and should be deleted.

REWIND STATEMENT

The REWIND statement is an executable statement that repositions a sequential file at the first record of the file. Its general form is

REWIND (UNIT=*integer expression,*
IOSTAT=*integer variable,*
ERR=*integer statement reference*)

Some systems require a REWIND statement before reading an input file.

BACKSPACE STATEMENT

The BACKSPACE statement is an executable statement that repositions a sequential file to the last record read; thus, it backs up one record in the file. Its general form is

BACKSPACE (UNIT=*integer expression,*
IOSTAT=*integer variable,*
ERR=*integer statement reference*)

ENDFILE STATEMENT

When a sequential file is being built, a special end-of-file record must be written to specify the end of the file. This special record is written when the ENDFILE statement is executed. The general form of the executable ENDFILE statement is

ENDFILE (UNIT=*integer expression,*
IOSTAT=*integer variable,*
ERR=*integer statement reference*)

The CLOSE statement automatically performs this function on most systems.

This self-test allows you to check quickly to see if you have remembered some of the key points from Section 9-2. If you have any problems with the exercise, you should reread this section. The solution is included at the end of the text.

1. Write a program to count the number of records in a file called XYDATA. Assume that the file is sequential and each record contains 2 real values in the following format:

   FORMAT (F6.2,1X,F6.2)

   Print the number of records. If an error occurs in opening the file, print an error message.

9-3 APPLICATION—VOYAGER SPACECRAFT DATA ANALYSIS (Electrical Engineering)

The pictures of Saturn sent back by Voyager II were spectacular. However, these pictures were not discernible by the human eye because they were transmitted as a long string of numbers or digital intensities that had to be processed and reassembled to compose the pictures that we saw. In this application we will write a program to perform a simple type of digital image processing called edge detection, where an edge detector distinguishes between the different surfaces in a two-dimensional image.

In the program, we will assume that we have a data file similar to that which might have been sent by Voyager II. Although it takes a very sophisticated procedure to recreate the original image, you can often determine the major features of the image by locating major differences in the digital intensities. If a major difference occurs between the intensities represented by the data points, an edge has been encountered. The actual calculation to determine if an edge has been encountered is performed as follows (assuming that we are trying to determine if point P5 is part of an edge):

P1	P2	P3
P4	P5	P6
P7	P8	P9

$$DIF = \frac{|P5 - P2| + |P5 - P4| + |P5 - P6| + |P5 - P8|}{4}$$

If DIF is greater than some specified threshold, such as 1.25, then you may have detected an edge. The threshold may be changed depending on the amount of detail you wish to have in your reconstructed image.

Assume that the image intensities are represented by integers from 0 to 9, with 0 representing white and 9 representing black, and the integers in between representing shades of gray. Furthermore, assume that the spacecraft camera converts its images into two-dimensional information with a maximum of 50 values per line and a maximum of 40 lines. The number of values per line and the number of lines per image depends on the resolution desired for the particular image. The data is sent back to earth in streams of integers that are stored one row per line in a data file. Each image is preceded by a line that gives an identification number for the image and the number of rows and the number of columns in that image. In order to store the information efficiently, no blanks or commas are used between the integers that represent the intensities, or shades of gray in the image; therefore, this information will need to be read with a formatted READ statement. A trailer line in the file will contain an identification number of 9999 followed by two zero values.

The output from your program is to be a picture of the edges in a specified image. Thus, at each point in the image that corresponds to an edge, print the symbol #; at each point in the image that is not an edge, print a blank. Allow the user to enter the threshold for edge detection.

The program should ask the user for the name of the data file to be used by the program. Since there might be many images stored in the same data file, the program should first scan the file and print the identification and size of all images in the file. Because there might be many images, it is not feasible to store them all in memory as you read them; only print the identification and size of the images. Then, ask the user which image is to be analyzed and the threshold to be used. After reading this information from the terminal, rewind the file and locate the desired image. Read the image data into an array and perform the edge analysis using the threshold specified by the user.

PROBLEM STATEMENT

Write a program to read a two-dimensional image from a data file. The program should determine the location of edges in the file and print the edge image.

INPUT/OUTPUT DESCRIPTION

The user will specify the name of the data file that will be assumed to contain images. The program will list the identification and size of all images in the file, and the user will enter the identification number of the file to be analyzed and the threshold value. The intensity information is represented by integers that are not separated by blanks or commas. The output will be a two-dimensional image of the edges generated using the symbol # and blanks.

We will use a small image for our example. Consider the following two-dimensional array of intensities:

3	7	8	8	8	7
4	5	7	8	8	6
4	5	5	5	5	6
4	4	4	5	6	6

In general, we assume that points on the top, bottom, and sides of the array are not edges because we do not have complete data on these points. Therefore, we consider only "interior" points in our analysis. Call the array P, and then for the point in $P(2,2)$, we compute the difference DIF to be the following:

$$DIF = (|5 - 7| + |5 - 4| + |5 - 7| + |5 - 5|)/4 = 1.25$$

If our threshold is 1.25 or below, then $P(2,2)$ corresponds to an edge; otherwise it is not an edge. If we generate an image with the symbol #, using a threshold of 0.9, our image is the following:

	#	#	#	#	
				#	

ALGORITHM DEVELOPMENT

DECOMPOSITION

Read file name.
Read desired intensity data.
Determine and print edge information.

EDGE: Read filename
　　　　Print a list of all images in file
　　　　Read desired intensity data
　　　　Read threshold
　　　　Determine edge information
　　　　Print edge information

The step to produce the list of images in the file will require reading and printing the identification and size of an image, reading past its image data, reading and printing the identification and size of the next image, and so on until we reach the identification number of 9999. Since we know that each line of an image starts on a new line in the file, we only have to read the first value of the line as we skim through the file looking for the next image. We need the complete data only for the image that we are going to analyze.

As we convert the pseudocode to FORTRAN, we want to ask ourselves if any of the steps involved should be implemented as functions or subroutines. The step to determine the edge information is one that is a good candidate for a subroutine because it involves a number of steps that will make our program longer and harder to read if we include them in the main program. If we use a subroutine, we can reference it in the main program and put the details in the subroutine itself. The structure chart for this program is:

```
*-------------------------------------------------------------------*
      PROGRAM   VOYAGE
*
*  This program detects edges in a two-dimensional image.
*
      INTEGER   I, J, IMAGE(40,50), ID, NR, NC, NEWID
      REAL   LIMIT
      CHARACTER   FILENM*6, EDGE(40)*50
      LOGICAL   DONE
*
      PRINT*, 'ENTER NAME OF IMAGE FILE ENCLOSED IN QUOTES'
      READ*, FILENM
      OPEN (UNIT=8,FILE=FILENM,STATUS='OLD')
```

```
*
      PRINT*
      PRINT*,'IMAGES IN THIS FILE'
      READ(8,*) ID, NR, NC
    5 IF (ID.NE.9999) THEN
         PRINT 10, ID, NR, NC
   10    FORMAT (1X,'ID = ',I4,' SIZE = (',I2,',',I2,')')
         DO 20 I=1,NR
            READ(8,15)IMAGE(I,1)
   15       FORMAT (50I1)
   20    CONTINUE
         READ(8,*)ID, NR, NC
         GO TO 5
      ENDIF
*
      PRINT*
      PRINT*, 'ENTER ID OF IMAGE TO BE ANALYZED'
      READ*, NEWID
      PRINT*, 'ENTER THRESHOLD FOR EDGE DETECTION'
      READ*, LIMIT
*
      REWIND (UNIT=8)
      READ(8,*) ID, NR, NC
      DONE = .FALSE.
   25 IF (.NOT.DONE) THEN
         IF (ID.EQ.NEWID) THEN
            DO 30 I=1,NR
               READ (8,15) (IMAGE(I,J),J=1,NC)
   30       CONTINUE
            CALL CONVERT(LIMIT,IMAGE,EDGE,NR,NC)
            PRINT*
            PRINT 35, LIMIT
   35       FORMAT (1X,'THRESHOLD VALUE = ',F5.2)
            DO 45 I=1,NR
               PRINT 40, EDGE(I)(1:NC)
   40          FORMAT (1X,A)
   45       CONTINUE
            DONE = .TRUE.
         ELSEIF (ID.EQ.9999) THEN
            DONE = .TRUE.
            PRINT*, 'IMAGE NOT FOUND'
         ELSE
            DO 50 I=1,NR
               READ(8,15) IMAGE(I,1)
   50       CONTINUE
            READ(8,*) ID, NR, NC
         ENDIF
         GO TO 25
      ENDIF
      END
*-------------------------------------------------------------*
```

continued

```
      SUBROUTINE  CONVRT (LIMIT,IMAGE,EDGE,NR,NC)
*
*  This subroutine converts a two-dimensional image
*  to a character array containing edge information.
*
      INTEGER  IMAGE(40,50), I, J, NR, NC
      REAL  LIMIT, DIF
      CHARACTER  EDGE(40)*50
*
      DO 5 J=1,NC
         EDGE(1)(J:J) = ' '
    5 CONTINUE
      DO 20 I=2,NR-1
         EDGE(I)(1:1) = ' '
         DO 15 J=2,NC-1
            DIF = (ABS(IMAGE(I-1,J)-IMAGE(I,J)) +
     +              ABS(IMAGE(I,J-1)-IMAGE(I,J)) +
     +              ABS(IMAGE(I,J+1)-IMAGE(I,J)) +
     +              ABS(IMAGE(I+1,J)-IMAGE(I,J)))/4.0
            IF  (DIF.GT.LIMIT) THEN
                EDGE(I)(J:J) = '#'
            ELSE
                EDGE(I)(J:J) = ' '
            ENDIF
   15    CONTINUE
         EDGE(I)(NC:NC) = ' '
   20 CONTINUE
      DO 25 J=1,NC
         EDGE(NR)(J:J) = ' '
   25 CONTINUE
*
      RETURN
      END
*- - - - - - - - - - - - - - - - - - - - - - - - - - - - - - - - - - - - - - -*
```

Note that the first DO loop in the subroutine fills the top row of the image
with blanks, and that the last DO loop in the subroutine fills the bottom row
of the image with blanks. The first statement of the DO 20 loop fills the left
side of the other rows with a blank, and the last statement of the DO 20 loop
fills the right side of the other rows with a blank.

The following data file called IMAGES was used to test the edge detection program:

```
87  4  6
378887
457886
455556
444566
25  12  28
111111111111111311111111331
133311111111111131111111311
111131111111111113311111131
111113111111111111133111113
111113111111111111111311111
111111311111111111111411111
111111411111111111111311111
111111131111111111111131111
111111131111111111111113111
111111113111111111111111311
111111111311111111111113111
111111111311111111111111111
34  5  4
22435
22444
23334
24244
24333
9999  0  0
```

The output from the program is shown below:

```
ENTER NAME OF IMAGE FILE ENCLOSED IN QUOTES
'IMAGES'

IMAGES IN THIS FILE
ID =   87 SIZE = ( 4, 6)
ID =   25 SIZE = (12,28)
ID =   34 SIZE = ( 5, 4)

ENTER ID OF IMAGE TO BE ANALYZED
25
ENTER THRESHOLD FOR EDGE DETECTION
1.0

THRESHOLD VALUE = 1.00


   # #              #        ##
     #            ##         #
      #             ##
      #              #
       #             #
       ##            #
       ##             #
        #             #
         #            ##
          #           #
```

9–4 APPLICATION—WHOOPING CRANE MIGRATION (Biology)

Several operations are commonly encountered as we process data. For instance, we have seen a number of applications that use sorting algorithms. Other operations frequently used include finding the minimum value or maximum value in a set of data, computing the average value in a set of data, inserting or deleting values in a list, and searching for a value in a list.

In this application, we use the merge operation, which is the combining of an ordered list (the current whooping crane migration information) with another list that preserves the same order (the new sightings information). We assume that we are merging only two lists.

Assume that arrays A and B have each been sorted into ascending order, as shown:

Array A
| 1 |
| 5 |
| 8 |
| 25 |
| 92 |

Array B
| 7 |
| 15 |
| 19 |
| 106 |

If these arrays are merged into an array C, the result is

Array C

| 1 |
| 5 |
| 7 |
| 8 |
| 15 |
| 19 |
| 25 |
| 92 |
| 106 |

Note that array C is larger than either array A or B; in fact, if array A contains N elements and array B contains M elements, array C should contain $N + M$ elements.

Data to be merged must have some order, such as ascending or descending. Alphabetical data can also be merged. In either case, what should you do about items that appear in both lists? Should the duplicate item appear once or twice in the merged list?

The answer depends on the application. If the merged data represents an alphabetical mailing list that has been put together from several sources, we would not want to duplicate a name on both lists. However, if we are merging bank transactions that are received in the mail with transactions processed at the teller windows, we would want to keep transactions with the same account number because they represent different transactions. Therefore, a specific requirement on how to handle duplicates must be included in the problem statement for a problem that includes a merging operation.

In this application, recall that the whooping crane migration problem involved printing the sightings information collected by the Wildlife Service. We want to print this information in the order of the sightings, which requires merging the master file with new sightings information received by the Wildlife Service. Assume that each sighting record contains the following information:

Sighting date (month, day, year)
Sighting time (time using a 24-hour clock)
Grid location (2 integer coordinates)
Number of birds

We assume that the data in the master file CRANES is stored as a series of integers (month, day, year, time, grid1, grid2, and birds) with the following format:

FORMAT (3I2,1X,I4,1X,2I2,1X,I4)

The new sightings information in the file SIGHTS is stored in the same format.

Write a program to merge data in two files: the current whooping crane migration information file with the new sightings information file.

INPUT/OUTPUT DESCRIPTION

The migration data is in a data file CRANES that contains the sightings information in ascending order by date and time. The new information is to be merged with this information to generate an updated file, also called CRANES. After updating the data, an ordered listing of the sightings information is to be printed.

HAND EXAMPLE

For a hand-worked example, we use the following data for the master file and the file of new sightings information:

MASTER FILE CRANES

DATE	TIME	GRID	NUMBER OF BIRDS
040386	0920	21 07	5
040886	0830	21 07	4
050186	1805	22 08	4
051086	0915	22 09	4
051586	0730	23 07	5

UPDATE FILE SIGHTS

040586	0815	21 09	4
051086	0800	22 09	4

If we merge these files by the date and time, the migration file CRANES and the corresponding report should contain the following information:

```
WHOOPING CRANE MIGRATION

CURRENT SIGHTINGS

4- 3-86      920
        GRID LOCATION:  21   7
        NUMBER OF BIRDS      5

4- 5-86       815
        GRID LOCATION:  21   9
        NUMBER OF BIRDS      4

4- 8-86       830
        GRID LOCATION:  21   7
        NUMBER OF BIRDS      4

5- 1-86      1805
        GRID LOCATION:  22   8
        NUMBER OF BIRDS      4

5-10-86       800
        GRID LOCATION:  22   9
        NUMBER OF BIRDS      4

5-10-86       915
        GRID LOCATION:  22   9
        NUMBER OF BIRDS      4

5-15-86       730
        GRID LOCATION:  23   7
        NUMBER OF BIRDS      5
```

Note that we may need to use part or all of the values for year, month, day, and time to order the sightings correctly.

ALGORITHM DEVELOPMENT

The general steps in the algorithm are simple to list. We want to merge the two data files, generate a new master file, and print the contents of the master file.

DECOMPOSITION

Merge sightings file and master file into new master file.
Print the data in the new master file.

We now need to develop an algorithm for merging two lists. One algorithm might be to move one list (with M elements) into the first part of a larger array with $M + N$ elements, and then move the other array (with N elements) into the last part of the larger array. We could sort the large array and have the data items in the desired order. This idea could be extended to three or more lists. However, there are two reasons why this is not a good algorithm: It is inefficient because each individual array or list is already sorted; and, it requires that all the data to be merged reside in memory at one time, which is impractical with large files.

If we reexamine the hand-worked example, we see that we need only the next value on each list to determine which record should be moved to the output file: The record with the smaller date is moved to the output file, and the next record of that file is read. A trailer signal simplifies the algorithm's logic development because we do not need to worry about what to do when we reach the end of a data file while there are still records left in the other file. When we read a trailer record with 999999 as the date, it is larger than the other valid dates and thus forces the rest of the records to be moved to the output file until we are positioned at the trailer signal of each file. We then write a trailer signal to the output file.

Let's try some simple data with this algorithm. Assume that we want to merge File 1 and File 2. Both files contain a trailer signal 999. The arrows point to the current record (the one we have just read for the input files or the one we have just written for output files).

File 1	File 2	Output File
→ 5	→ 2	
10	51	
82	999	
107		
999		

File 1	File 2	Output File
→ 5	2	→ 2
10	→ 51	
82	999	
107		
999		

File 1	File 2	Output File
5	2	2
→ 10	→ 51	→ 5
82	999	
107		
999		

File 1	File 2	Output File
5	2	2
10	→ 51	5
→ 82	999	→ 10
107		
999		

File 1	File 2	Output File
5	2	2
10	51	5
→ 82	→ 999	10
107		→ 51
999		

(continued)

File 1	File 2	Output File
5	2	2
10	51	5
82	→ 999	10
→ 107		51
999		→ 82

File 1	File 2	Output File
5	2	2
10	51	5
82	→ 999	10
107		51
→ 999		82
		→ 107

File 1	File 2	Output File
5	2	2
10	51	5
82	→ 999	10
107		51
→ 999		82
		107
		→ 999

We develop the pseudocode for the merge separately, and then add it to the pseudocode for the whooping crane migration algorithm. We assume that a merge of two files is always sufficient: If you have three files to merge, merge two of them, and then merge the combined file with the third file. If you have more than three files, continue merging two at a time until you have combined them all.

MERGE REFINEMENT IN PSEUDOCODE

MERGE: Read first record in both files
       While more data do
          Write information from file with smaller code
          Read new information from file with smaller code
       Write trailer signal

We now return to our whooping crane migration problem and include the steps for the merge.

Refinement in Pseudocode

MIGRAT: Read first master record
Read first update record
While more sightings do
 If update date < master date then
  Write update record
  Read new update record
 else
  Write master record
  Read new master record
Write trailer signal
Copy merged file to master file and print report

Because we are reading data that represents the same types of information from both files, we would like to choose names that indicate which file contained the data. Thus, for the day from the file CRANES, we use the variable CDA; for the day from the file SIGHTS, we use the variable SDA. When we copy the output file back into the file CRANES, we use the variable DA because it is not being compared to other variables.

Before we convert the refined pseudocode into FORTRAN, we need to discuss one more item in the algorithm. We compare the date from one record with the date in another record to determine which date occurred first: This comparison first involves comparing the years. If the years are equal, we compare the months. If the months are equal, we compare the days. If the days are equal, we compare the times. This process is easy to understand, but it is cumbersome to translate into FORTRAN. Thus, we use a statement function to recombine the month, day, year, and time into a number that can make all the comparisons simultaneously; for example, if month = 09, day = 25, year = 86, and time = 0845, we create a number equal to the value 8609250845. If we compare another date in this new form, we need only one comparison to determine which date occurred first. This new number that we compute cannot be an integer because its value is typically greater than the maximum integer in many computers (approximately 2 billion for a VAX computer). We also cannot use a real number because we need 10 digits of precision. Thus, we must use a double precision number to store the number that combines the year, month, day, and time information.

```
*-----------------------------------------------------------*
      PROGRAM  MIGRAT
*
* This program merges new sighting information into the
* master file of migration information on whooping cranes.
*
      INTEGER  M,D,Y,T,MO,DA,YR,TIME,GRID1,GRID2,BIRDS,
     +         SMO,SDA,SYR,STIME,SGRID1,SGRID2,SBIRDS,
     +         CMO,CDA,CYR,CTIME,CGRID1,CGRID2,CBIRDS
      DOUBLE PRECISION  DATE, CDATE, SDATE
      LOGICAL  DONE
*
      DATE(M,D,Y,T) = DBLE(REAL(Y)*1.0D08) +
     +                DBLE(REAL(M)*1.0D06) +
     +                DBLE(REAL(D)*1.0D04) +
     +                DBLE(REAL(T))
*
      OPEN (UNIT=10,FILE='SIGHTS',STATUS='OLD')
      OPEN (UNIT=11,FILE='CRANES',STATUS='OLD')
      OPEN (UNIT=12,FILE='TEMP',STATUS='NEW')

      READ (10,5) SMO,SDA,SYR,STIME,SGRID1,SGRID2,SBIRDS
    5 FORMAT (3I2,1X,I4,1X,2I2,1X,I4)
      READ (11,5) CMO,CDA,CYR,CTIME,CGRID1,CGRID2,CBIRDS
      SDATE = DATE(SMO,SDA,SYR,STIME)
      CDATE = DATE(CMO,CDA,CYR,CTIME)
      IF (SMO.EQ.99.AND.CMO.EQ.99) THEN
         DONE = .TRUE.
      ELSE
         DONE = .FALSE.
      ENDIF
*
   10 IF (.NOT.DONE) THEN
         IF (CDATE.LT.SDATE) THEN
            WRITE (12,5) CMO,CDA,CYR,CTIME,CGRID1,
     +                   CGRID2,CBIRDS
            READ (11,5) CMO,CDA,CYR,CTIME,CGRID1,
     +                  CGRID2,CBIRDS
            CDATE = DATE(CMO,CDA,CYR,CTIME)
         ELSE
            WRITE (12,5) SMO,SDA,SYR,STIME,SGRID1,
     +                   SGRID2,SBIRDS
            READ (10,5) SMO,SDA,SYR,STIME,SGRID1,
     +                  SGRID2,SBIRDS
            SDATE = DATE(SMO,SDA,SYR,STIME)
         ENDIF
         IF (SMO.EQ.99.AND.CMO.EQ.99) DONE = .TRUE.
         GO TO 10
      ENDIF
      WRITE (12,5) SMO,SDA,SYR,STIME,SGRID1,SGRID2,SBIRDS
      CLOSE (UNIT=11,STATUS='DELETE')
      CLOSE (UNIT=12)

      OPEN (UNIT=11,FILE='CRANES',STATUS='NEW')
      OPEN (UNIT=12,FILE='TEMP',STATUS='OLD')
      PRINT*, 'WHOOPING CRANE MIGRATION'
      PRINT*
      PRINT*, 'CURRENT SIGHTINGS'
      PRINT*
*
```

continued

```
15 READ (12,5,END=50) MO,DA,YR,TIME,GRID1,GRID2,BIRDS
   IF (MO.NE.99) THEN
      PRINT 20, MO,DA,YR,TIME
20    FORMAT (1X,I2,'-',I2,'-',I2,4X,I4)
      PRINT 25, GRID1,GRID2
25    FORMAT (1X,5X,'GRID LOCATION: ',2I3)
      PRINT 30, BIRDS
30    FORMAT (1X,5X,'NUMBER OF BIRDS',1X,I5)
      PRINT*
   ENDIF
   WRITE (11,5) MO,DA,YR,TIME,GRID1,GRID2,BIRDS
   GO TO 15
*
50 STOP
   END
*---------------------------------------------------------*
```

TESTING

If we use the data from the hand-worked example in this program, the output
from our program is

```
WHOOPING CRANE MIGRATION

CURRENT SIGHTINGS

4- 3-86    0920
            GRID LOCATION:  21   7
            NUMBER OF BIRDS       5

4- 5-86    0815
            GRID LOCATION:  21   9
            NUMBER OF BIRDS       4

4- 8-86    0830
            GRID LOCATION:  21   7
            NUMBER OF BIRDS       4

5- 1-86    1805
            GRID LOCATION:  22   8
            NUMBER OF BIRDS       4

5-10-86    0800
            GRID LOCATION:  22   9
            NUMBER OF BIRDS       4

5-10-86    0915
            GRID LOCATION:  22   9
            NUMBER OF BIRDS       4

5-15-86    0730
            GRID LOCATION:  23   7
            NUMBER OF BIRDS       5
```

Throughout this text, we have emphasized the importance of carefully
selecting test data. If you look at the updates in this set of test data, you see
that it includes data in an order that causes insertions to be made at two

different points in the file. Also, the program is not thoroughly tested until the test data includes insertions that occur both at the beginning and at the end of the master file. Finally, because the date and time are involved in determining the correct order of the sightings, we include some sightings with the same date but different times to test this part of the program.

9–5 DIRECT-ACCESS FILES

Records in direct-access files are not accessed sequentially; they are accessed in the order specified. You specify that you want to read the tenth record, then the second record, and so forth. (However, you could read them sequentially by specifying that you want to read the first record, then the second record, and so on.)

When a direct file is opened, the ACCESS specification in the OPEN statement must be set to 'DIRECT' and a record length must be given with the RECL specifier. The READ and WRITE statements must include a REC specification to give the record number of the record to be addressed. The general form of a direct-access READ or WRITE is

READ   (*unit number,format reference,*REC=*integer expression*)   *variable list*

WRITE   (*unit number,format reference,*REC=*integer expression*)   *variable list*

The integer expression on the REC specification is evaluated to give the record number to be accessed. The ERR and IOSTAT specifications may also be used with the direct-access READ or WRITE statement. The END option may be used only with the READ statement.

Applications that use direct files usually have an account number or identification number that is part of each record, which can be used as the record number. For example, student identification numbers in a university often start at 00001 and increase in steps of 1; thus, the information for student number 00210 could be stored in record 210. Sometimes a numerical computation is performed on a field in the record to yield its record number: Suppose an inventory file contains records for items with stock numbers 500 through 1000. If 499 is subtracted from the stock number, we have the record number for the record that stores information about that stock item. When the steps to convert a value into a record number for a direct file reference become more complicated, the steps are called a *hash code*, the value computed as the record number is often called a *key*.

A direct file is usually built by loading the information into the file sequentially, with the record number starting at 1 and increasing by 1 each time a new record is written. The file can be accessed in a sequential order by varying the record number from 1 through the total number of records. However, the real power of a direct file is apparent when we want to update information in some of its records. Instead of reading each record sequentially, looking for the one we want to update, we specify the record number and that record is accessed automatically. Once we have updated the information in that record, we can write that new information into the record. Note that this is not father-son updating — we are actually updating information in the direct file itself, which can be considered a master file, because it contains all the updated information. If we specify a record number in a READ statement for a record that does not exist, an error occurs. To recover, the ERR specification can be included in the WRITE statement to provide a controlling branch to an error routine. These concepts are illustrated in Section 9–6.

SELF-TEST 9–2

This self-test allows you to check quickly to see if you have remembered some of the key points from Section 9–5. If you have any problems with the exercise, you should reread this section. The solution is included at the end of the text.

1. A direct-access file called STORES contains 100 records. Each record contains an item number that varies from 1 through 100 and is used as the record key. Each record also contains the number of items in the warehouse. The format of each record is

   FORMAT (I5,2X,I5)

   Write a program to print the item number of all items in which the record indicates that there are fewer than 5 items in the warehouse.

9–6 APPLICATION—COMPUTER PARTS INVENTORY (Computer Science/Engineering)

In this application, we develop a program to update an inventory file for the automated warehouse of a computer manufacturing plant. The inventory file is a direct-access file with the following record format:

Stock number	Item description	Quantity	Unit price

Stock number is a numeric value that can range from 001 to 999. Item description is a 10-character description of the item. The quantity or number of units of that piece of equipment is a 4-digit integer. The unit price of one item is stored in a real value with a format of F6.2. Thus, the total record length is 23 characters and will appear as RECL = 23 in the OPEN statement.

The file that we use to update the inventory file PARTS is a transaction file called TRANS that contains information on items received and shipped out. The order of the transactions is the order in which they occurred. The transaction record consists of a stock number and a quantity: If the quantity is positive, the transaction represents items received; if the quantity is negative, the transaction represents items sent to the assembly lines. The transaction file is a sequential file with the following record format:

| Stock number | Quantity |

The stock number is a 3-digit integer, and the quantity is a 4-digit integer. Two blanks separate the fields. Assume that a trailer line in the transaction file contains 999 in the stock number.

Write a program to update the computer parts inventory file using this transaction file. (Note that we are not adding new records to the inventory file. We are only updating the records currently in the inventory file.)

PROBLEM STATEMENT

Write a program to update the quantity in a direct-access file.

INPUT/OUTPUT DESCRIPTION

The input to the program is two files: the direct-access master inventory file and the sequential transaction file.

HAND EXAMPLE

Assume that the two files contain this computer equipment information:

MASTER INVENTORY FILE

STOCK NUMBER	ITEM DESCRIPTION	QUANTITY	UNIT PRICE
1	microprocessor	10	586.92
2	modem	5	85.00
3	power supply	3	299.50
4	cable	12	24.95

TRANSACTION FILE

STOCK NUMBER	QUANTITY
1	-2
3	-1
2	8
1	15
1	-2
2	-2

After the update, the master inventory file should be updated to contain the following information:

MASTER INVENTORY FILE

STOCK NUMBER	ITEM DESCRIPTION	QUANTITY	UNIT PRICE
1	microprocessor	21	586.92
2	modem	11	85.00
3	power supply	2	299.50
4	cable	12	24.95

ALGORITHM DEVELOPMENT

The steps used to solve this problem are straightforward, as shown in the following decomposition. The primary reason that this solution is simple is because of the power of direct-access file processing.

DECOMPOSITION

Read transaction records and update master file.

In the initial refinement we show the WHILE loop that is executed as long as there are transactions to process.

INITIAL REFINEMENT IN PSEUDOCODE

UPDATE: While more transactions do
        Read transaction record
        Read corresponding inventory record
        Update quantity
        Write updated inventory record

In further refining the solution, we add an error routine to print a message on the terminal screen if a match cannot be found between the inventory stock number and the transaction stock number.

FINAL REFINEMENT IN PSEUDOCODE

UPDATE: Read stock number, update
   If stock number = 999 then
    more ← false
   else
    more ← true
   While more do
    Read corresponding inventory record
    If no match then
     Print error message
    else
     new quantity ← old quantity + update
     Write inventory record
    Read stock number, update
    If stock number = 999 then
     more ← false

The program for performing this update for a direct-access file follows.

FORTRAN PROGRAM

```
*-------------------------------------------------------*
      PROGRAM  UPDATE
*
*  This program updates a direct file
*  using a stock number as the key.
*
      INTEGER  STOCK, CHANGE, QUANT, KEY
      REAL  PRICE
      LOGICAL  MORE
      CHARACTER*10  DESC
*
      DATA  MORE /.TRUE./
*
      OPEN (UNIT=10,FILE='TRANS',ACCESS='SEQUENTIAL',
     +      STATUS='OLD',FORM='FORMATTED')
      OPEN (UNIT=11, FILE='PARTS',ACCESS='DIRECT',
     +      STATUS='OLD',FORM='FORMATTED',RECL=23)
*
      READ (10,5) KEY, CHANGE
    5 FORMAT (I3,2X,I4)
      IF (KEY.EQ.999) MORE = .FALSE.
*
   10 IF (MORE) THEN
         READ (11,15,REC=KEY,ERR=20,END=20)
     +        STOCK, DESC, QUANT, PRICE
   15    FORMAT (I3,A10,I4,F6.2)
         QUANT = QUANT + CHANGE
         WRITE (11,15,REC=KEY) STOCK, DESC, QUANT, PRICE
   20    IF (KEY.NE.STOCK) PRINT*, 'NO MATCH FOR', KEY
         READ (10,5) KEY, CHANGE
         IF (KEY.EQ.999) MORE = .FALSE.
         GO TO 10
      ENDIF
*
      END
*-------------------------------------------------------*
```

Before you can test this program, you must create the direct-access master file. A program to build the direct-access file from data entered from the terminal follows: The program closes the file after it is built, reopens it as an input file, and prints the data. Try this with the initial set of hand-worked data; then, try the update program. After you are comfortable with the steps, develop some new test data. Be sure to try transactions without a match in the master inventory file.

FORTRAN Program

```
*--------------------------------------------------------------*
      PROGRAM   CREATE
*
*  This program creates an inventory direct file
*  from terminal input data.
*
      INTEGER  STOCK, QUANT, N
      CHARACTER*10  DESC
*
      OPEN (UNIT=9,FILE='PARTS',ACCESS='DIRECT',
     +      STATUS='NEW',FORM='FORMATTED',RECL=23)
      PRINT*, 'ENTER NUMBER OF RECORDS FOR MASTER FILE'
      READ*, N
      DO 10 I=1,N
          PRINT*, 'ENTER STOCK NUMBER'
          READ*, STOCK
          PRINT*, 'ENTER DESCRIPTION IN APOSTROPHES'
          READ*, DESC
          PRINT*, 'ENTER INITIAL QUANTITY'
          READ*, QUANT
          PRINT*, 'ENTER PRICE (NO DOLLAR SIGN)'
          READ*, PRICE
          WRITE (9,5,REC=STOCK) STOCK, DESC, QUANT, PRICE
    5     FORMAT (I3,A,I4,F6.2)
   10 CONTINUE
*
      CLOSE (UNIT=9)
      OPEN (UNIT=9,FILE='PARTS',ACCESS='DIRECT',
     +      STATUS='OLD',FORM='FORMATTED',RECL=23)
      DO 15 I=1,N
          READ (9,5,REC=I,ERR=12) STOCK, DESC, QUANT, PRICE
          PRINT*, STOCK, DESC, QUANT, PRICE
   12     IF (I.NE.STOCK) PRINT*, 'NO RECORD NUMBER', I
   15 CONTINUE
*
      END
*--------------------------------------------------------------*
```

9-7 INQUIRE STATEMENT

Our final statement used with files is the INQUIRE statement. It has two general forms:

> INQUIRE (FILE=*character expression,inquiry specifier list*)

> INQUIRE (UNIT=*integer expression,inquiry specifier list*)

This executable statement gains information about a file or a unit number. For example, suppose that we are going to allow a user to enter the name of a data file to be used in a program, as we did in the edge detection program in Section 9-3. If the user enters the name of a file that does not exist, then the program will terminate with an execution error. If we use the INQUIRE statement, we can determine whether the file exists, and if it does not exist, we can ask the user to enter a different file name. The following statements illustrate this type of interaction with the user:

```
  DONE = .FALSE.
  FOUND = .FALSE.
  PRINT*, 'ENTER FILE NAME OF IMAGE FILE IN QUOTES'
  READ*, FILENM
5 IF (.NOT.DONE) THEN
    INQUIRE (FILE=FILENM, EXIST=THERE)
    IF (.NOT.THERE) THEN
       PRINT*, 'FILE DOES NOT EXIST'
       PRINT*, 'ENTER NEW FILE NAME OR QUIT IN QUOTES'
       READ*, FILENM
       IF (FILENM.EQ.'QUIT') DONE = .TRUE.
    ELSE
       DONE = .TRUE.
       FOUND = .TRUE.
    ENDIF
    GO TO 5
  ENDIF
  IF (FOUND) THEN
     OPEN (UNIT=10,FILE=FILENM,STATUS='OLD')
     .
     .
     .
```

These statements assume that FOUND, DONE, and THERE have been specified to be logical variables, and that FILENM has been specified to be a character variable.

The INQUIRE statement is also useful when we are writing a module (function or subroutine) that uses a file, and we don't know whether the file has been opened. We will assume that the main program and the modules using the file all use the value 15 for the unit number. The following pair of statements could then be used in a module to determine whether the file had been opened, and to then open the file if it was not already open:

```
INQUIRE (UNIT=15,OPENED=AVAIL)
IF (.NOT.AVAIL) OPEN(UNIT=15,FILE='FLIGHT',STATUS='OLD')
```

These statements would assume that AVAIL had been specified to be a logical variable.

Table 9–1 contains a complete list of the inquiry specifiers that can be used with the INQUIRE statement.

TABLE 9–1 Inquiry Specifiers

Inquiry Specifier	Variable Type	Value for File Inquiry	Value for Unit Inquiry
ACCESS =	character	'SEQUENTIAL' 'DIRECT'	'SEQUENTIAL' 'DIRECT'
BLANK =	character	'NULL' 'ZERO'	'NULL' 'ZERO'
DIRECT =	character	'YES' 'NO' 'UNKNOWN'	—
ERR =	integer	statement number of error routine	statement number of error routine
EXIST =	logical	.TRUE. .FALSE.	.TRUE. .FALSE.
FORM =	character	'FORMATTED' 'UNFORMATTED'	'FORMATTED' 'UNFORMATTED'
FORMATTED =	character	'YES' 'NO' 'UNKNOWN'	—
IOSTAT =	integer	error code	error code
NAME =	character	—	name of the file if it is not a scratch file
NAMED† =	logical	—	.TRUE. .FALSE.
NEXTREC =	integer	next record number in direct-access file	next record number in direct-access file
NUMBER† =	integer	unit number	—
OPENED =	logical	.TRUE. .FALSE.	.TRUE. .FALSE.
RECL =	integer	record length	record length
SEQUENTIAL =	character	'YES' 'NO' 'UNKNOWN'	—
UNFORMATTED =	character	'YES' 'NO' 'UNKNOWN'	—

† These specifiers do not refer to scratch files.

SUMMARY

In this chapter we presented a complete discussion of file processing with both sequential and direct files. Data is often used by more than one program; thus, the data file makes the same data easily available to many programs. By carefully choosing the type of file (sequential or direct) and the order of the data in the file, we can handle large amounts of data with simple algorithms and programs.

DEBUGGING AIDS

When processing files, a useful subroutine prints the data in the current record in a highly readable form — you might call this routine SNAP because it gives you a snapshot of a record in the file. When you are debugging a program that uses the file, call the routine every time that you want to check the contents of the current record.

Another handy subroutine opens a file and reads through it, printing the key information in each record. This subroutine is useful before and after updating the file to see if the new information has been entered properly.

We also want to emphasize that proper handling of files must occur when one of the files that we are using is empty. Using trailer signals helps this situation because a file without data should still have the trailer signal. If you are concerned that a file may not exist, you can use the INQUIRE statement to determine whether or not it exists without causing a program execution error.

STYLE/TECHNIQUE GUIDES

Good documentation is always important when working with data files. The record format and its field descriptions should have the same names in all programs that use the file; for example, if a file contains a stock number, give it the same name in each program that uses it. It is also good to use all the specifications that relate to the file in the OPEN statement; they do not need to be repeated in the other statements that refer to the file, but they should all be included at the beginning of the OPEN statement.

KEY WORDS

direct-access file   master file
external file   merge
father-son update   random access
field   record
hash code   sequential-access file
internal file   transaction file
key

PROBLEMS

We begin our problem set with modifications to the programs developed earlier in this chapter. Give the decomposition, refined pseudocode or flowchart, and FORTRAN solution for each problem.

Problems 1–5 modify the program VOYAGE, given on page 410, which detects edges in a two-dimensional image.

1. Modify the edge-detection program so that it allows the user to specify the symbol used to indicate the edges when the edge image is printed.
2. Modify the edge-detection program so that asterisks are used to outline the edge image when it is printed.
3. Modify the edge-detection program so that it uses the diagonal elements in the computation for the difference. Then instead of using four elements, the computation will use eight elements.
4. Modify the edge-detection program so that it computes the number of points that are interior points, and prints the percentage of interior points that are also edge points after printing the edge image.
5. Modify the edge-detection program so that it allows points on the top, bottom, or sides to be edges by using the points on two or three sides for computing the difference, and then comparing the difference to one-half or three-fourths of the threshold.

Problems 6–10 modify the program MIGRAT, given on page 421, which merged the new whooping crane sightings information with the master data file.

6. Modify the migration program so that it prints a count of the total number of sightings at the end of the report.
7. Modify the migration program so that it prints the maximum number of birds that have been sighted in the current report.
8. Modify the migration program so that it prints a final list of all grid locations of sightings along with the number of sightings in that grid.

9. Modify the migration program so that it tracks only a certain size sighting group. For example, the program could ask the user to enter the size of group of cranes; if the user enters the number 5, then the program prints a report only for the data that included 5 birds in the sightings data.

10. Modify the migration program so that it prints the most sightings during one day in the file. Print this at the end of the report.

Problems 11–15 modify the computer parts inventory program UPDATE, given on page 427.

11. Write a program to create a direct-access file from a sequential data file.

12. Write a subroutine to print the data in the inventory file in a report form by stock number order.

13. Write a program to change the description for selected stock items in the inventory file, using input from the terminal.

14. Write a program to print a reorder report for items whose quantity has gone below 5 units. Include the number of items to be ordered to bring the total quantity to 10.

15. Write a function to compute the total value of all items in the warehouse.

Problems 16–22 use data in a data file called SENSOR that contains maintenance information on mechanical measurement equipment used in a new chemical plant. Each line in the file contains the following information:

> Work order number
> Identification code for type of measurement device

These values are stored with the following format:

FORMAT (I5,2X,I1)

The identification code is an integer that represents the following measuring devices:

1. Counter
2. Flowmeter
3. Pressure transducer
4. Thermocouple
5. Pyrometer

The order of the lines in the file correspond to the order in which the work orders were issued. If a repair involved more than one sensor, more than one line in the file has the same work order number; these lines are consecutive in the file. The following programs are needed by the plant engineers to analyze the reliability of process equipment.

16. Write a program that reads the data from the file SENSOR and prints a report that gives the total number of work orders for counters, flowmeters, and so on. Use the following report form:

```
WORK ORDER SUMMARY
SENSOR                  NUMBER OF WORK ORDERS
- - - - - - - - - - - - - - - - - - - - - - - - - - - - - - - - - - - -
COUNTER                 XXXX
FLOWMETER               XXXX
PRESSURE TRANSDUCER     XXXX
THERMOCOUPLE            XXXX
PYROMETER               XXXX
```

17. Write a program to print all the work orders for an identification code that is read from the terminal.

18. Write a function called COUNT that reads the data in the file and returns a count of the work orders required for a specified identification code, which is an input argument to the function.

19. Modify the program in problem 16 so that it also prints the total number of work orders.

20. Modify the program in problem 16 so that it includes the following analysis information in the summary report:

```
NUMBER OF SENSORS NEEDING MAINTENANCE           XXXX
NUMBER OF WORK ORDERS WITH ONE SENSOR           XXXX
NUMBER OF WORK ORDERS WITH MULTIPLE SENSORS     XXXX
```

21. Modify the program in problem 16 so that it includes the following summary information in the report:

```
NUMBER OF WORK ORDERS REQUIRING MAINTENANCE
ON BOTH PRESSURE TRANSDUCERS AND PYROMETERS IS    XXXX
```

22. Modify the program in problem 16 so that it prints the work order numbers for all requests of maintenance that includes thermocouples. Print four numbers per line using the following format:

```
WORK ORDER NUMBERS FOR THERMOCOUPLE MAINTENANCE
      XXXX   XXXX    XXXX   XXXX
```

Problems 23–27 use the data in a direct-access file called TEST that contains the status of tests being performed at a materials testing laboratory. The testing lab offers four types of tests: compression, tensile, shear, and fatigue. The codes for these tests are, respectively, C, T, S, and F. Each time a test is completed on a material sample, the information is added to the test status file. The file TEST contains the sample number (integers 1–500); the material identification (30 characters); and four characters, which are initially blanks, but are updated to C, T, S, and F, as the material is tested. The format for each record in the file is

```
FORMAT (I3,1X,A30,1X,A4)
```

23. Write a program that reads the information in this file and prints a list of sample numbers for samples that have had the shear test completed. (The tests can occur in any order; thus, the four codes (C,T,S,F) can appear in any order in the string of characters.)

24. Write a program that reads the information in this file and prints a testing report. First list all samples that have been through the compression test, then all that have been through the tensile test, and so on. (The tests can occur in any order; thus the four codes (C,T,S,F) can appear in any order in the string of characters.) Put appropriate headers at the beginning of each list. If two tests have been completed on a sample, its sample number and identification will appear twice in the report, and so on.

25. Write a program that prints a summary report to give the percentages of materials that have been through each test. Use the following format:

```
SUMMARY OF MATERIAL TESTS
TEST                PERCENTAGE
- - - - - - - - - - - - - - - - - - - - - - - - -
COMPRESSION         XXX.X
TENSILE             XXX.X
SHEAR               XXX.X
FATIGUE             XXX.X
```

26. Modify the program in problem 25 so that it also prints the total number of samples in the test file and the total number of tests that have been completed.

27. Modify the program in problem 25 so that it also prints the number of samples that have had one test completed, the number of samples that have had two tests completed, the number of samples that have had three tests completed, and the number of samples that have had all four tests completed.

FORTRAN STATEMENT SUMMARY

BACKSPACE (UNIT=*integer expression,optional file specifiers*)

Examples:

BACKSPACE (UNIT=10)

BACKSPACE (UNIT=12,IOSTAT=ERROR)

Discussion:

The BACKSPACE statement allows you to back up to the previous record in an input file. When you execute a READ statement following the BACKSPACE statement, you are accessing the same information as the READ statement before the BACKSPACE statement. The file specifiers are discussed in Section 9–2.

CLOSE Statement:

CLOSE (UNIT=*integer expression,optional file specifiers*)

Examples:

CLOSE (UNIT=10)

CLOSE (UNIT=15,ERR=99)

Discussion:

The CLOSE statement closes a file. Files are automatically closed at the end of a program, so this statement is used primarily when the file is to be closed and reopened again in the same program.

ENDFILE Statement:

ENDFILE (UNIT=*integer expression,optional file specifiers*)

Example:

ENDFILE (UNIT=12)

Discussion:

The ENDFILE statement writes an end-of-file record to an output file. The CLOSE and END statements automatically perform this function on most systems.

INQUIRE Statement:

```
INQUIRE (FILE=character expression,inquiry specifier list)
INQUIRE (UNIT=integer expression,inquiry specifier list)
```

Examples:

```
INQUIRE (FILE='XYDATA',SEQUENTIAL=ANSWER)

INQUIRE (UNIT=12,SEQUENTIAL=ANSWER)
```

Discussion:

The INQUIRE statement has two forms: one to obtain information about a file with a specified name and one to obtain information about a file with a specified unit. The INQUIRY specifiers are listed in Table 9–1.

OPEN Statement:

```
OPEN (UNIT=integer expression,FILE=character expression,
      STATUS=character expression,optional file specifiers)
```

Examples:

```
OPEN (UNIT=10,FILE='XYDATA',STATUS='OLD')

OPEN (UNIT=15,FILE='EXPER1',ACCESS='DIRECT',STATUS='OLD')
```

Discussion:

The OPEN statement must be used to connect data files to a program. The UNIT, FILE, and STATUS specifiers must also be used. Other optional file specifiers may be used to emphasize certain characteristics of the file or to change the default characteristics that are assumed when some file specifiers are omitted.

REWIND Statement:

```
REWIND (UNIT=integer expression,file specifiers)
```

Examples:

```
REWIND (UNIT=9)

REWIND (UNIT=13,IOSTAT=ERROR,ERR=500)
```

Discussion:

The REWIND statement repositions a sequential file at the first record of the file. Some systems require a REWIND statement after opening a file to begin reading information at the beginning of the file.

PART II

NUMERICAL METHODS

In Chapters 10–15 we develop a group of numerical methods that represent the most commonly used numerical techniques for solving engineering problems. In addition to presenting the algorithms and computer programs for implementing the methods, we present a large number of *diagrams and graphs* to help you visualize the concepts behind the methods. When you understand the concepts, you are able to select the types of applications that can benefit from the use of numerical methods.

The *numerical methods* presented include five methods for finding roots to equations, including the Newton-Raphson method, which can be used to find both real roots and complex roots. A number of routines are developed for performing operations on matrices, and some of these operations are then used to solve systems of simultaneous equations. Cramer's rule is presented for solving small systems of equations; Gauss elimination and the Gauss-Seidel method are presented for solving larger systems of equations. Techniques developed for estimating unknown values of a function include linear interpolation, cubic spline interpolation, and least-squares methods. Several methods are also discussed for numerical integration and numerical differentiation. Euler's method and the fourth-order Runge-Kutta method are developed for integrating ordinary differential equations.

We have also included a chapter on *digital signal processing* (DSP). Digital filters are used in all areas of engineering to analyze signals and to select (or "filter") the desired information from a signal. We discuss how to generate signals, including signals with noise, and then how to implement a digital filter, which is really another numerical method.

In addition to all the special features included with the earlier chapters, we also include a section on *error analysis* in each chapter in Part II. Understanding the types of errors that can be introduced by computations becomes especially important as you use more advanced techniques and as you need to interpret the results of these techniques.

APPLICATION—Robot Arm Control (Mechanical Engineering)

Robotics involves the use of mechanisms, sensors, actuators, and computers to synthesize some aspects of human functions. The area of robotics is often split into four major areas: mechanical manipulation, locomotion, computer vision, and artificial intelligence. The area of mechanical manipulation involves the movement of objects (parts, tools, the robot itself) in three-dimensional space. The design of a control system for the movement of a robot arm involves a careful analysis of the stability of the design, and one step in this analysis involves finding the roots of a polynomial. Write a program to find the roots of a polynomial. (See Section 10–7 for the solution.)

10

ROOTS OF EQUATIONS

Introduction

10-1 Incremental-Search Method

10-2 Bisection Method

10-3 False-Position Method

10-4 Application—Digital Filter Design (Electrical Engineering)

10-5 Newton-Raphson Method

10-6 Secant Method

10-7 Application—Robot Arm Control (Mechanical Engineering)

Summary

INTRODUCTION

The solutions to many engineering problems involve finding the *roots of an equation* of the form

$$y = f(x)$$

where the roots are the values of x for which y is equal to zero. Examples of applications in which we need to find roots of equations include designing the control system for a robot arm, designing springs and shock absorbers for an automobile, analyzing the response of a motor, and analyzing the stability of an electric circuit.

Suppose that we have a cubic (third-degree) polynomial equation

$$y = f(x)$$
$$= x^3 - 5x^2 + 2x + 8$$

which is plotted below:

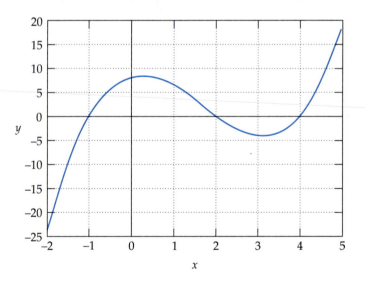

From the plot, we see that at the points $x = -1$, $x = 2$, and $x = 4$, the value of y is zero. Substituting any one of these values of x into the equation gives a value of zero for y, which confirms our observations. Thus, the roots of an equation are found by setting y equal to zero and solving for all the values of x that satisfy the resulting equation. For our cubic polynomial, the equation we need to solve is

$$x^3 - 5x^2 + 2x + 8 = 0$$

This polynomial can be factored as follows:

$$(x + 1)(x - 2)(x - 4) = 0$$

We now see immediately that the values of x which will satisfy this equation, and thus are the roots of the equation, are $-1, 2$, and 4.

In a few special cases, such as this one, we are able to factor an expression or use a formula, such as the quadratic formula, to find the roots. More often, however, no simple algebraic methods are applicable, so we turn to computers and specialized programs that use numerical methods to obtain an estimate of the roots. In this chapter, we discuss numerical methods that use a repetitive technique called *iteration* to find the roots of an equation.

Although the techniques presented in this chapter can be used to determine roots for equations $y = f(x)$ where f(x) is a continuous function, we most often are searching for roots or solutions to polynomial equations, like the cubic equation discussed earlier, which can be written in the following general form:

$$a_0x^n + a_1x^{n-1} + a_2x^{n-2} + \cdots + a_{n-2}x^2 + a_{n-1}x + a_n = 0$$

A polynomial of degree n will always have exactly n roots, some of which may be *multiple roots* or *complex roots*. A complex root is one that is expressed as a complex number, which, as described earlier in Section 8–5, has the form $a + bi$, where i is $\sqrt{-1}$ and a and b are real numbers.

An example of a quadratic equation having a multiple root is the following:

$$x^2 + 4x + 4 = 0$$

Factoring this polynomial gives

$$(x + 2)(x + 2) = 0$$

showing that there is a multiple root at $x = -2$.

Some quadratic equations are not easily factored, so we use the quadratic formula to compute the roots. For example, the equation

$$x^2 - 2x + 2 = 0$$

has complex roots $x = 1 + i$ and $x = 1 - i$. These roots are called a complex conjugate pair because they differ only in the sign of the imaginary term. If a polynomial has only real coefficients, any complex roots it may have will result from quadratic factors such as the one above and will therefore always be conjugate pairs. That is, if $x = a + bi$ is a root, then $x = a - bi$ will also be a root. Polynomial equations that represent the physical systems or processes encountered in engineering and science will have real coefficients.

Thus, if we have a fifth-degree polynomial with real coefficients, the roots could appear in several ways:

1. There could be five distinct *real roots*.
2. There could be five real roots, with some of the roots being multiple roots.
3. There could be three real roots (two of which could be multiple roots) and a complex conjugate pair of roots.

4. There could be one real root and two complex conjugate pairs of roots.
5. There could be one real root and multiple complex conjugate pairs of roots.

We now present examples that illustrate these various ways in which the roots of a fifth-degree polynomial could appear.

The following equation has five distinct real roots:

$$y = (x + 3)(x + 1)(x - 1)(x - 2)(x - 4)$$
$$= x^5 - 3x^4 - 11x^3 + 27x^2 + 10x - 24$$

Note that the function curve crosses the x axis at each root location in the plot of this function:

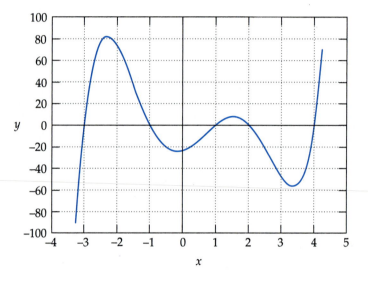

In the following equation, the roots are again all real, but there is now a multiple root at $x = -2$:

$$y = (x + 2)^2(x - 1)(x - 3)(x - 4)$$
$$= x^5 - 4x^4 - 9x^3 + 32x^2 + 28x - 48$$

Note in the next plot that the function touches but does not cross the x axis at the location of the multiple root:

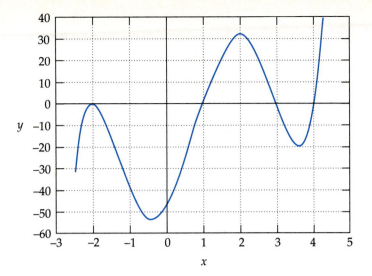

The next equation has one single real root, a real multiple root, and a complex conjugate pair of roots:

$$y = (x + 2)^2(x - 3)(x + (1 + i))(x + (1 - i))$$
$$= x^5 + 3x^4 - 4x^3 - 26x^2 - 40x - 24$$

As before, the single real root occurs where the curve crosses the x axis, and the multiple real roots occur where the curve only touches the x axis:

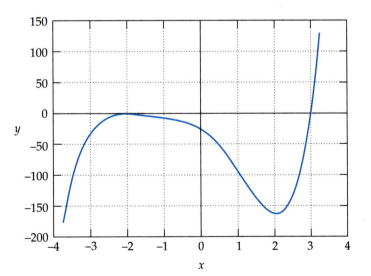

Also note that there are no places where the curve crosses or touches the x axis that may be associated with the complex roots.

The fourth equation has a single real root and two complex conjugate pairs of roots:

$$y = (x - 1)(x - (1 + i))(x - (1 - i))(x - (3 + 2i))(x - (3 - 2i))$$
$$= x^5 - 9x^4 + 35x^3 - 65x^2 + 64x - 26$$

There is now only one place where the curve crosses the x axis:

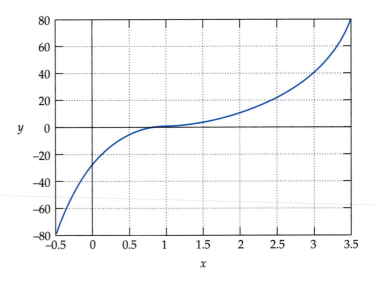

The fifth equation has a single real root and a multiple complex conjugate root:

$$y = (x + 1)(x - (1 + i))^2(x - (1 - i))^2$$
$$= x^5 - 3x^4 + 4x^3 - 4x + 4$$

Again, there is only a single crossing of the x axis:

In these examples we identified the roots of polynomials, but the process of searching for a point where the function crosses the x axis (also called a zero crossing) can also be used to find roots of equations containing other functions, such as trigonometric functions and logarithmic functions.

It should be apparent that using the computer to find the roots of an equation can be an involved process. The preceding observations will help us understand the various methods to be presented, which include the incremental-search method, the bisection method, the false-position method, the Newton-Raphson method, and the secant method. All of these methods can be used to find real roots of an equation, and the Newton-Raphson method can also be used to find complex roots. Specific algorithms and FORTRAN programs are developed for the incremental-search method, the bisection method, and the Newton-Raphson method.

10-1   INCREMENTAL-SEARCH METHOD

One of the simplest yet most reliable methods for finding roots of an equation is the incremental-search method. A search region of x values is first selected and divided into intervals, as shown below:

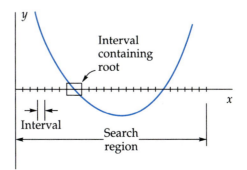

The intervals are chosen to be small enough that it is unlikely there will be more than one root in any interval. Proceeding from left to right, we search for the intervals that contain roots by looking for the places where the function curve crosses the x axis, as it does in the small box drawn in the figure. We identify these intervals containing a root by computing the values of the function at the endpoints of the interval and checking the signs. If the signs of the function values at the endpoints are different, then we know the curve has crossed the x axis and that there is at least one root in the interval.

As shown in the next figure, the interval containing the root has been further divided into subintervals, and the search process begins again from the left end of the interval until the subinterval containing the root is similarly located.

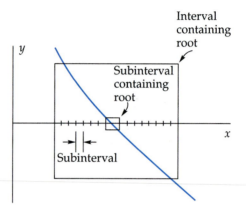

The process of subdividing and searching is repeated until the root has been determined with sufficient accuracy. Once a root has been located, we move to the next interval and continue the search for any remaining roots.

The *incremental-search method* will detect only places where the curve crosses the x axis and the function values change sign. Therefore, as seen in the example plots for the fifth-degree polynomial equations earlier, it will not be able to find complex roots or multiple roots, since the function value does not change signs at those locations. Nevertheless, it is a useful method for finding single real roots. It can also be used to provide a search algorithm for the bisection method, which is discussed in the next section.

This self-test allows you to check quickly to see if you have remembered the key points from Section 10–1. If you have any problems with the exercises, you should reread this section. The solutions are included at the end of the text.

Consider the following equation:

$$y = x^3 - 1.58x^2 - 4.04x + 2.29$$

1. How many roots exist for this equation?
2. Starting at $x = -10$, use the incremental-search method to find all intervals of size 1.0 in the interval $[-10,10]$ that contain roots for this equation.
3. Explain why you might find fewer than three small intervals containing roots for a cubic equation over a given interval.
4. Explain why you should be concerned if you find more than three small intervals containing roots for a cubic equation over a given interval.
5. Use a plot package to graph this function in order to verify your answer to problem 2. (See Appendix C if you have not used a plot package.)

10-2   BISECTION METHOD

The *bisection method* begins with an interval that is already known to contain a root. Unlike the incremental-search method, which divides the interval into many subintervals before searching again, the bisection method simply bisects, or divides the interval in half, and then determines which half contains the root. The bisection process is continued until the root is found to the desired accuracy. In most cases, the bisection method converges to the root much quicker than the incremental-search method.

To explain the bisection method in more detail, we look at a simple curve represented by $y = f(x)$:

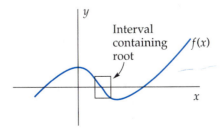

Suppose we evaluated the function at $x = a$ and at $x = b$, and determined that $f(a) \cdot f(b)$ is negative.

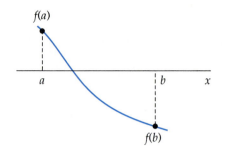

We know from the previous section that there is at least one real root in the interval between a and b because the curve must have crossed the x axis for the product of $f(a)$ and $f(b)$ to be negative. There could also be three roots, or another odd number of roots, in the interval between a and b.

We now want to reduce the size of the interval containing the root. If the function is evaluated at m, the midpoint of the interval, there are three possible outcomes: If $f(a) \cdot f(m)$ is zero, then m is a root; if $f(a) \cdot f(m)$ is negative, then the root falls in the interval between a and m; and if $f(a) \cdot f(m)$ is positive, a root falls in the interval between m and b. Thus, either we have found the root or we have halved (or bisected) the interval within which the root must lie. We now perform the steps again, bisecting the new interval known to contain the root. In the graph below, the new interval containing the root is $[a,m]$.

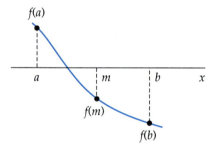

At some point, we need to stop the iterative process because finding the exact root is seldom practical or necessary. Most often, we will iterate until we find a root to within some tolerance or accuracy that we specify. For example, we might want to continue the process until $|f(m)| < 0.01$. We could also stop the process at some maximum number of iterations; for example, once we found an interval containing a root, we could perform a maximum of five iterations and use the estimate of the root at that point.

At the beginning of this section we stated that the bisection method begins with an interval that is already known to contain a root. The same is true of the false-position method, which is discussed in the next section. There are various methods that we can use to find the intervals with roots. One would be to plot enough points of the curve so that intervals containing the x-axis crossings can be determined. Perhaps the easiest way to find the intervals is to use the first part of the incremental-search method discussed in the preceding section. Specifically, we select a search region of x values and divide that region into small intervals. We then search for the intervals where the product of the function values at the endpoints is negative. When we find such an interval, we use the bisection method or the false-position method to find the root.

It is important to remember that the bisection method, like the incremental-search method and the false-position method, can find only single, real roots. Multiple roots and complex roots will not be located because all of these methods rely on the function crossing the x axis.

SELF-TEST 10–2

This self-test allows you to check quickly to see if you have remembered the key points from Section 10–2. If you have any problems with the exercises, you should reread this section. The solutions are included at the end of the text.

The interval [2,3] contains a root of the following equation:

$$y = x^3 - 1.58x^2 - 4.04x + 2.29$$

1. Use two iterations of the bisection method to approximate the root in this interval.
2. Use the bisection method to approximate a root x, in this interval, such that $|f(x)| < 0.1$.

10–3 FALSE-POSITION METHOD

The *false-position method* is essentially the same as the bisection method, except that instead of using the midpoint of the interval to split the interval into two parts, interpolation is used to find the intersection of the x axis and the straight line joining the two function values at the endpoints of the interval. Using the interval [a,b] of a function f(x), as shown in the graph, the next iteration of the bisection method would use the interval [a,m], whereas the method of false position would use the interval [a,c].

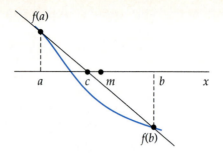

Similar triangles are used to compute the intersection point c on the x axis for each iteration:

$$c = \frac{a \cdot f(b) - b \cdot f(a)}{f(b) - f(a)}$$

The advantage of the false-position method is that, for each iteration, the point c will generally be closer to the root than the midpoint m. As a result, the false-position method usually converges to the root in fewer iterations than the bisection method. Sketching a few example curves, like the one above, will make it easy to see why this is true.

SELF-TEST 10–3

This self-test allows you to check quickly to see if you have remembered the key points from Section 10–3. If you have any problems with the exercises, you should reread this section. The solutions are included at the end of the text.

The interval [2,3] contains a root of the following equation:

$$y = x^3 - 1.58x^2 - 4.04x + 2.29$$

1. Use two iterations of the false-position method to approximate the root in this interval. Compare your answer to that computed in the previous self-test, which used two iterations of the bisection method.
2. Use the false-position method to approximate a root x, in this interval, such that $|f(x)| < 0.1$. Would you expect to get the same value as you did in the previous self-test, which used the bisection method? Why?

```
ROOTS: Read coefficients
        count ← 0
        For left = −5.0 to 4.75 in steps of 0.25 do
            right ← left + 0.25
            If |f(left)| < 0.001 then
                Print left
                count ← count + 1
            Else if f(left)*f(right) < 0.0 then
                Iterate for root
                Print root
                count ← count + 1
        If |f(left)| < 0.001 then
            Print left
            count ← count + 1
        If count = 0 then
            Print 'NO ROOTS IN INTERVAL'
```

We must further refine the iteration step, since it contains the bisection method. We will continue the bisection process until the root is found or until the width of the interval is less than 0.01. We will assume that the root is found when the absolute value of the function is less than or equal to 0.001.

REFINEMENT OF ITERATION IN PSEUDOCODE

```
ITERAT: done ← false
        size ← right − left
        While size > 0.01 and not done do
            mid ← (left + right)/2
            If |f(mid)| < 0.001 then
                done ← true
            Else if f(mid)*f(left) < 0.0 then
                right ← mid
            Else
                left ← mid
            size ← right − left
        If size > 0.01 then
            root ← mid
        Else
            root ← (left + right)/2
```

We are now ready to convert the pseudocode into FORTRAN. To keep the main program reasonably short, we implement the iteration process as a subroutine. The evaluation of the polynomial is implemented as a function; this function is referenced from both the main program and the iteration subroutine. It needs an array A of the coefficients and the value of x for evaluating the polynomial; thus, the reference should be $F(A,X)$.

The structure chart for this program is

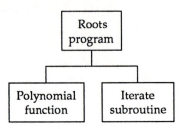

FORTRAN PROGRAM

```
*-------------------------------------------------------------*
      PROGRAM  ROOTS
*
*  This program determines the roots in the interval [-5,5]
*  for a quartic polynomial using incremental search and
*  the bisection method.
*
      INTEGER  COUNT
      REAL  A(0:4), LEFT, RIGHT, P
*
      PRINT*, 'ENTER COEFFICIENTS A0,A1,A2,A3,A4'
      READ*, A
*
      PRINT*
      PRINT*, 'POLYNOMIAL:'
      PRINT 5
    5 FORMAT (1X,9X,'4',11X,'3',11X,'2')
      PRINT 10, A
   10 FORMAT (1X,4(F7.3,' X + '),F7.3)
      PRINT*
*
      COUNT = 0
      DO 20 LEFT=-5,4.75,0.25
         RIGHT = LEFT + 0.25
         IF (ABS(F(A,LEFT)).LT.0.001) THEN
            PRINT 15, LEFT, F(A,LEFT)
   15       FORMAT (1X,'ROOT = ',F7.3,3X,
     +                  'F(ROOT) = ',F7.3)
            COUNT = COUNT + 1
         ELSEIF (F(A,LEFT)*F(A,RIGHT).LT.0.0) THEN
            CALL ITERAT (A,LEFT,RIGHT,ROOT)
            PRINT 15, ROOT, F(A,ROOT)
            COUNT = COUNT + 1
         ENDIF
   20 CONTINUE
*
```

```
            IF (ABS(F(A,LEFT)).LT.0.001) THEN
                PRINT 15, LEFT, F(A,LEFT)
                COUNT = COUNT + 1
            ENDIF
            IF (COUNT.EQ.0) THEN
                PRINT*, 'NO ROOTS IN INTERVAL [-5,5]'
            ENDIF
*
            END
*----------------------------------------------------------------*
            REAL FUNCTION  F(A,X)
*
*   This function evaluates a quartic polynomial at X.
*
            REAL A(0:4), X
*
            F = A(0)*X**4 + A(1)*X**3 + A(2)*X**2 + A(3)*X + A(4)
*
            RETURN
            END
*----------------------------------------------------------------*
            SUBROUTINE  ITERAT(A,LEFT,RIGHT,ROOT)
*
*   This subroutine uses interval halving to find a root.
*
            REAL  A(0:4), LEFT, RIGHT, ROOT, SIZE, MID
            LOGICAL  DONE
*
            DONE = .FALSE.
            SIZE = RIGHT - LEFT
        5   IF (SIZE.GT.0.01.AND..NOT.DONE) THEN
                MID = (LEFT + RIGHT)/2.0
                IF (ABS(F(A,MID)).LT.0.001) THEN
                    DONE = .TRUE.
                ELSEIF (F(A,MID)*F(A,LEFT).LT.0.0) THEN
                    RIGHT = MID
                ELSE
                    LEFT = MID
                ENDIF
                SIZE = RIGHT - LEFT
                GO TO 5
            ENDIF
*
            IF (SIZE.GT.0.01) THEN
                ROOT = MID
            ELSE
                ROOT = (LEFT + RIGHT)/2.0
            ENDIF
*
            RETURN
            END
*----------------------------------------------------------------*
```

TESTING

Five different polynomials were used as test data. These polynomials covered the cases with no real roots, one real root, and three real roots; some of the roots also fell on interval endpoints. The last polynomial is the one we used in the hand-worked example. The output from the program is shown for each polynomial, along with a MATLAB plot (see Appendix C) of the function so that you can see the zero crossings.

```
ENTER COEFFICIENTS A0,A1,A2,A3,A4
0. 1. -2.125 -25. 53.125

POLYNOMIAL:
         4              3              2
  0.000 X +    1.000 X +   -2.125 X + -25.000 X +   53.125

ROOT =  -5.000    F(ROOT) =    0.000
ROOT =   2.125    F(ROOT) =    0.000
ROOT =   5.000    F(ROOT) =    0.000
```

```
ENTER COEFFICIENTS A0,A1,A2,A3,A4
0. 0. 1. 14. 3.

POLYNOMIAL:
         4              3              2
  0.000 X +    0.000 X +    1.000 X +  14.000 X +    3.000

ROOT =  -0.215    F(ROOT) =    0.038
```

```
ENTER COEFFICIENTS A0,A1,A2,A3,A4
3. -12.4 -26.29 29.766 0.

POLYNOMIAL:
      4              3            2
  3.000 X + -12.400 X + -26.290 X +  29.766 X +    0.000

ROOT =  -2.137   F(ROOT) =  -0.131
ROOT =   0.000   F(ROOT) =   0.000
ROOT =   0.855   F(ROOT) =   0.068
```

```
ENTER COEFFICIENTS A0,A1,A2,A3,A4
0. 0. 1.234 -1.2 10.44

POLYNOMIAL:
         4          3          2
  0.000 X +   0.000 X +   1.234 X +  -1.200 X +  10.440

NO ROOTS IN INTERVAL [-5,5]
```

```
ENTER COEFFICIENTS A0,A1,A2,A3,A4
0. 0. 0. 3. -2.5

POLYNOMIAL:
         4          3          2
  0.000 X +   0.000 X +   0.000 X +   3.000 X +  -2.500

ROOT =    0.832    F(ROOT) =  -0.004
```

10-5 NEWTON-RAPHSON METHOD

The bisection method discussed in Sections 10–2 and 10–4 searches for roots by moving across the overall interval in small steps and then iterating when it detects a sign change for the function value between steps. The advantage of this approach is that it will find all the roots within the overall interval, provided the step size is smaller than the distance between roots. The disadvantage of this method is that many steps and many iterations may be required to find just a few roots.

If we have certain information about the equation, there are methods that can be used to find the roots more efficiently than the bisection method. One popular root-finding technique that relies on information about the equation is the *Newton-Raphson method*. It is also known as the tangent method because of the root estimation technique it uses.

The Newton-Raphson method uses both the function $f(x)$ and its derivative $f'(x)$ to compute the slope of a *tangent line*, which is then used as a straight-line approximation of the curve at each iteration point. The intersection of the tangent line and the x axis becomes the next estimate for the root and the next point at which the tangent line is computed. The process is repeated until the root is found. Since the Newton-Raphson method makes a better "guess" for the root at each step than does the bisection method, it typically requires significantly fewer iterations to converge.

Using the next graph, the Newton-Raphson method can be described with the following series of steps. An *initial guess*, x_1, is made for the root of the function $f(x)$. The slope of the curve at x_1 is then computed using $f'(x_1)$, and a tangent line with that slope is then drawn through $f(x_1)$. The point x_2 where the tangent line intersects the x axis becomes the new estimate for the root. The process then repeats using $f'(x_2)$ as the slope of the tangent line drawn through

$f(x_2)$, which intersects the x axis at x_3, and so on until it converges on the root at x_r.

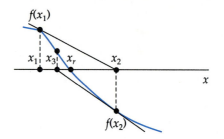

The algorithm for finding the next estimate for the root, x_{k+1}, given the current estimate for the root, x_k, is obtained by noting that the slope of the tangent line at $f(x_k)$ can be computed by dividing the change in y by the change in x:

$$f'(x_k) = \frac{f(x_k) - 0}{x_k - x_{k+1}}$$

Solving this equation for x_{k+1} provides the algorithm we need for the next estimate of the root:

$$x_{k+1} = x_k - \frac{f(x_k)}{f'(x_k)}$$

As stated earlier, an advantage of the Newton-Raphson method is that it generally requires fewer iterations and, therefore, is computationally more efficient than the bisection method. In addition, it can be used to find complex roots when complex variables are used and when the initial guess is a complex value. The method can also be generalized to multiple dimensions for use in solving systems of nonlinear equations.

The algorithm also has some limitations. The most important limitation relates to the initial guess; if the initial guess for the root is not good enough, the algorithm may miss the root entirely, finding instead one of the other roots or not finding a root at all. Therefore, good engineering estimates of the roots may be needed to ensure that all of the roots are located. Other problems can arise, depending on the equation itself. Places where $f'(x)$ is zero or close to zero at peaks or inflection points in the curve can cause difficulties. A root at $x = 0$ will cause both the function and its derivative to be zero and result in the method failing at the origin. But these problems can usually be avoided if the initial guess for a root is close enough. Another problem is that it may not be easy or even possible to compute the derivative of the function. Methods that do not require the derivative, such as the secant method discussed in the next section, can be used in these situations.

If the Newton-Raphson method converges to a root that has already been located, even when you use different starting points, a new function can be obtained by dividing the original function by the factor of the known root. This procedure removes the known root from the original function, so that when you apply the Newton-Raphson method to the new function it should converge to a new root. For example, one of the equations used in the introduction was

$$y = x^5 - 3x^4 - 11x^3 + 27x^2 + 10x - 24$$

This equation has distinct roots at $x = -3, -1, 1, 2,$ and 4. If the root at $x = 4$ is located first, it can be divided out to give

$$y = x^4 + x^3 - 7x^2 - x + 6$$

When we use the Newton-Raphson method on this equation, it will now converge to one of the remaining roots. This technique should be used only when the program keeps converging to the same root for different initial guesses, rather than finding a new root. Since the root that has been found is only an approximation, dividing it out will introduce inaccuracies in the new polynomial, which will cause inaccuracies in subsequent root approximations.

SELF-TEST 10–4

This self-test allows you to check quickly to see if you have remembered the key points from Section 10–5. If you have any problems with the exercises, you should reread this section. The solutions are included at the end of the text.

Use the following equation in problems 1 through 6:

$$y = f(x)$$
$$= x^3 - 1.58x^2 - 4.04x + 2.29$$

1. Give the expression for the derivative $f'(x)$.
2. Evaluate the function $f(x)$ and its derivative $f'(x)$ for $x = 2$.
3. Using $x = 2$ as an initial guess, find the next estimate for a root of the equation.
4. Evaluate the function $f(x)$ and its derivative $f'(x)$ for $x = 3$.
5. Using $x = 3$ as an initial guess, find the next estimate for a root of the equation.
6. Use a plot package to graph this function in order to verify your answers.

10–6 SECANT METHOD

The *secant method* is similar to both the false-position method and the Newton-Raphson method. It begins exactly the same way as the false-position method by drawing a straight line from $f(a)$ to $f(b)$ and locating the point c that intersects the x axis using

$$c = \frac{a \cdot f(b) - b \cdot f(a)}{f(b) - f(a)}$$

It then evaluates the function at c to find $f(c)$ and draws a secant line from $f(b)$, through $f(c)$ until it intersects the x axis at d. The steps are then repeated, using the interval $[d,c]$ as the interval containing the root.

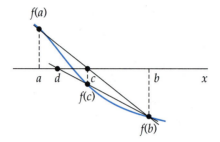

The secant method uses the secant line to approximate the root location, whereas the Newton-Raphson method uses the tangent line. As the interval containing the root gets smaller, the secant line and the tangent line approach the same line. The performance of the secant method is therefore similar to that of the Newton-Raphson method, and it is often used as a replacement for Newton-Raphson when the derivative of the function is difficult or impossible to evaluate. Also, as in the Newton-Raphson method, certain conditions can cause the method to diverge rather than converge to a root. It cannot be used to find complex roots, however, unless it is modified.

SELF-TEST 10–5

This self-test allows you to check quickly to see if you have remembered the key points from Section 10–6. If you have any problems with the exercises, you should reread this section. The solutions are included at the end of the text.

Use the following equation in problems 1 and 2:

$$y = f(x)$$
$$= x^3 - 1.58x^2 - 4.04x + 2.29$$

1. Given that the interval [2,3] contains a root of the equation, use the secant method to compute an estimate of the root after one iteration.

2. Using the results from Problem 1, perform a second iteration of the secant method. Explain how you know that the secant method has failed for an initial interval of [2,3].

10–7   APPLICATION—Robot Arm Control (Mechanical Engineering)

The design of a control system for a robot arm includes a careful analysis of the stability of the system. One step in the stability analysis uses the roots of a polynomial equation called the *characteristic equation*. Often the roots of the characteristic equation are complex, having the form $a + bi$. Write a program which uses the Newton-Raphson method to find the roots of a third-degree polynomial having complex roots. (You may want to review the complex data type and complex arithmetic operations in Section 8–5 before continuing in this section.)

PROBLEM STATEMENT

Write a program to determine the roots of a polynomial $p(x)$ having both real and complex roots, where $p(x)$ has the following form:

$$y = p(x)$$
$$= a_0x^3 + a_1x^2 + a_2x + a_3$$

Assume that a root has been located if the absolute value of $p(x)$ is less than 0.001.

INPUT/OUTPUT DESCRIPTION

The inputs to the program are the polynomial coefficients $a_0, a_1, a_2,$ and a_3 and the initial guess for a root. The output should include the polynomial equation, the initial guess for the root, the root to which the method converges, and the number of iterations required to find the root. If the program does not converge to a root within 100 iterations, print an appropriate message.

For this test case, assume that the polynomial equation is

$$y = p(x)$$
$$= x^2 + 2x + 10$$

This equation is a special case of a cubic polynomial equation with the following coefficients:

$$a_0 = 0, a_1 = 1, a_2 = 2, a_3 = 10$$

We can use the quadratic formula to determine that the roots of this equation are $x = -1 + 3i$ and $x = -1 - 3i$. The Newton-Raphson method also requires the derivative of the polynomial, which in this case is

$$p'(x) = 2x + 2$$

We begin with an initial guess for a complex root and compute the values for the function and its derivative using complex variables. The error measurement is the absolute value of the function. Note that it is not the error made in the estimate of the root. When the error is less than 0.001, the process is terminated; otherwise, the next estimate for the root is determined using the equation derived in Section 10–3 that computes the next estimate of a root (x_{k+1}) given a current estimate (x_k):

$$x_{k+1} = x_k - \frac{p(x_k)}{p'(x_k)}$$

Using the initial guess of $x_1 = -2 + 5i$, or $(-2,5)$, we compute $p(x_1)$ so that we can then compute the initial error, which is the absolute value of the complex number $p(x_1)$:

$$p(x_1) = (-15, -10)$$
$$\text{Error} = \text{sqrt}[(-15)^2 + (-10)^2] = 18.0278$$

Since the error is greater than 0.001, we begin the iterations:

Iteration 1: $p'(x_1) = (-2,10)$
$$x_2 = x_1 - \frac{p(x_1)}{p'(x_1)} = (-1.3269,3.3654)$$
$$p(x_2) = (-2.2189, -2.2004)$$
$$\text{Error} = \text{sqrt}[(-2.2189)^2 + (-2.2004)^2] = 3.1250$$
Iteration 2: $p'(x_2) = (-0.6538,6.7308)$
$$x_3 = x_2 - \frac{p(x_2)}{p'(x_2)} = (-1.0348,3.0073)$$
$$p(x_3) = (-0.0429, -0.2092)$$
$$\text{Error} = 0.2135$$

Iteration 3: $p'(x_3) = (-0.0696, 6.0147)$

$$x_4 = x_3 - \frac{p(x_3)}{p'(x_3)} = (-1.0001, 2.9998)$$

$p(x_4) = (0.0011, -0.0005)$

Error $= 0.0013$

Iteration 4: $p'(x_4) = (-0.0002, 5.9996)$

$$x_5 = x_4 - \frac{p(x_4)}{p'(x_4)} = (-1.0000, 3.0000)$$

$p(x_5) = (0.0000, 0.0000)$

Error $= 0.0000$

Since the error is less than 0.001, we terminate the iterations.

In only four iterations, the procedure has converged to one of the roots of the equation. The second root could be found using another initial guess; however, since polynomials having only real coefficients can have only real roots, or complex conjugate pairs of roots, it is more efficient to find the remaining complex root by just forming the complex conjugate of $x = (-1.0, 3.0)$, which is $(-1.0, -3.0)$.

ALGORITHM DEVELOPMENT

The decomposition of this algorithm involves reading the coefficients, making an initial guess for a root, and finding a root. When a root has been found, another guess is read, and the next root is found. The program will be written so that it can find both real roots and complex roots. An initial guess of (99,99) terminates the program.

DECOMPOSITION

Read coefficients.
Read initial guesses and determine roots.

REFINEMENT IN PSEUDOCODE

NEWTON: Read coefficients
         Print polynomial equation
         Read x

                    While x is not (99,99) do
                        calculate p(x), error
                        k ← 0
                        While error > 0.001 and k < 100 do
                            calculate p'(x)
                            calculate next x
                            calculate p(x), error
                            k ← k + 1
                        If error ≤ 0.001 then
                            If root is complex then
                                generate conjugate
                            Print root(s)
                        Else
                            Print 'DID NOT CONVERGE'
                        Print number of iterations, k
                    Read guess for root

Note that the iteration continues until either the error becomes less than a tolerance value of 0.001 or the number of iteration steps exceeds 100.

Since the program is relatively short and straightforward, no modules are needed, and thus there is no need for a structure chart.

FORTRAN PROGRAM

```
*---------------------------------------------------------------*
         PROGRAM   NEWTON
*
*   This program solves for real and complex roots of a
*   cubic polynomial using the Newton-Raphson method.
*
         INTEGER   K
         REAL   A0, A1, A2, A3
         COMPLEX   X, P, DP
*
         PRINT*, 'ENTER COEFFICIENTS A0, A1, A2, A3'
         READ*, A0,A1,A2,A3
         PRINT*
         PRINT 4
    4 FORMAT (1X,'                        3              2')
         PRINT 5, A0, A1, A2, A3
    5 FORMAT (1X,'P(X) = ',F7.3,' X  + ',F7.3,' X  + ',
      +        F7.3,' X + ',F7.3)
         PRINT*
         PRINT*,'ENTER INITIAL COMPLEX GUESS FOR ROOT AS TWO REAL VALUE
         READ*, X
```

```
10 IF (X.NE.(99.,99.)) THEN
      P = A0*(X**3) + A1*(X**2) + A2*X + A3
      ERROR = CABS(P)
      K = 0
15    IF (ERROR.GT.0.001.AND.K.LT.100) THEN
         DP = 3.0*A0*(X**2) + 2.0*A1*X + A2
         X=X-P/DP
         P = A0*(X**3) + A1*(X**2) + A2*X + A3
         ERROR = CABS(P)
         K = K + 1
         GO TO 15
      ENDIF
      IF (ERROR.LE.0.001) THEN
         IF (ABS(AIMAG(X)).GT.0.001) THEN
            PRINT*,'COMPLEX ROOTS, X = ', X, CONJG(X)
         ELSE
            PRINT*,'REAL ROOT, X = ',REAL(X)
         ENDIF
      ELSE
         PRINT*,'DID NOT CONVERGE'
      ENDIF
      PRINT*, K, ' ITERATIONS'
      PRINT*
      PRINT*, 'ENTER INITIAL COMPLEX GUESS FOR ROOT ',
    +         'AS TWO REAL VALUES'
      PRINT*, '(99,99 TO QUIT)'
      READ*, X
      GO TO 10
   ENDIF
   END
*-------------------------------------------------------*
```

TESTING

The following test used the hand example. When our initial guess is the complex value $-2+5i$, the complex roots are found in 4 iterations. When the real value $10+0i$ is used as the initial guess, the technique cannot find the complex roots because both the function and its derivative are real expressions only.

```
ENTER COEFFICIENTS A0, A1, A2, A3
0 1 2 10

                3            2
P(X) =   0.000 X  +   1.000 X  +   2.000 X +   10.000

ENTER INITIAL COMPLEX GUESS FOR ROOT AS TWO REAL VALUES
-2 5
COMPLEX ROOTS, X =   (-1.00000,3.00000) (-1.00000,-3.00000)
 4 ITERATIONS

ENTER INITIAL COMPLEX GUESS FOR ROOT AS TWO REAL VALUES
(99,99 TO QUIT)
10 0
DID NOT CONVERGE
 100 ITERATIONS

ENTER INITIAL COMPLEX GUESS FOR ROOT AS TWO REAL VALUES
(99,99 TO QUIT)
99 99
```

The rest of the examples used to test the Newton-Raphson method are examples that were also used to test the bisection method. Refer to page 458 to review these equations.

The next example uses a cubic equation. We know that there are three roots, but unless we plot the function, we do not have any additional information. Therefore, an initial guess of $0 + 0i$ is reasonable, and the iterations from there identify one of the roots. Our next guess happened to be one of the roots, and so no iterations were necessary. Since we know two of the three roots are real values, the third root must also be a real value. With two more initial guesses, we are able to identify the third root. We also used a complex guess to show that a complex guess can find a real root.

```
ENTER COEFFICIENTS A0, A1, A2, A3
1 -2.125 -25 53.125

              3              2
P(X) =   1.000 X   +  -2.125 X   + -25.000 X +   53.125

ENTER INITIAL COMPLEX GUESS FOR ROOT AS TWO REAL VALUES
0 0
REAL ROOT, X =   2.12500
  1 ITERATIONS

ENTER INITIAL COMPLEX GUESS FOR ROOT AS TWO REAL VALUES
(99,99 TO QUIT)
5 0
REAL ROOT, X =   5.00000
  0 ITERATIONS

ENTER INITIAL COMPLEX GUESS FOR ROOT AS TWO REAL VALUES
(99,99 TO QUIT)
10 0
REAL ROOT, X =   5.00000
  6 ITERATIONS

ENTER INITIAL COMPLEX GUESS FOR ROOT AS TWO REAL VALUES
(99,99 TO QUIT)
-10 0
REAL ROOT, X =  -5.00000
  5 ITERATIONS

ENTER INITIAL COMPLEX GUESS FOR ROOT AS TWO REAL VALUES
(99,99 TO QUIT)
1 1
REAL ROOT, X =   2.12501
  3 ITERATIONS

ENTER INITIAL COMPLEX GUESS FOR ROOT AS TWO REAL VALUES
(99,99 TO QUIT)
99 99
```

This example uses a quadratic equation. The first root was determined with the initial guess of $0 + 0i$. The next two guesses located the same root, using different initial guesses and different numbers of iterations. The initial guess of $-10 + 0i$ finally located the second root.

```
ENTER COEFFICIENTS A0, A1, A2, A3
0 1 14 3

                  3           2
P(X) =   0.000 X    +   1.000 X   +  14.000 X +    3.000

ENTER INITIAL COMPLEX GUESS FOR ROOT AS TWO REAL VALUES
0 0
REAL ROOT, X =  -0.217669
 2 ITERATIONS

ENTER INITIAL COMPLEX GUESS FOR ROOT AS TWO REAL VALUES
(99,99 TO QUIT)
5 0
REAL ROOT, X =  -0.217670
 4 ITERATIONS

ENTER INITIAL COMPLEX GUESS FOR ROOT AS TWO REAL VALUES
(99,99 TO QUIT)
-5 0
REAL ROOT, X =  -0.217670
 5 ITERATIONS

ENTER INITIAL COMPLEX GUESS FOR ROOT AS TWO REAL VALUES
(99,99 TO QUIT)
-10 0
REAL ROOT, X =  -13.7823
 4 ITERATIONS

ENTER INITIAL COMPLEX GUESS FOR ROOT AS TWO REAL VALUES
(99,99 TO QUIT)
99 99
```

The next example represents another quadratic equation. When the initial guess of $0 + 0i$ did not find a root, we used a complex value as our initial guess and found the two complex roots.

```
ENTER COEFFICIENTS A0, A1, A2, A3
0 1.234 -1.2 10.44

                  3           2
P(X) =   0.000 X    +   1.234 X   +  -1.200 X +   10.440

ENTER INITIAL COMPLEX GUESS FOR ROOT AS TWO REAL VALUES
0 0
DID NOT CONVERGE
 100 ITERATIONS

ENTER INITIAL COMPLEX GUESS FOR ROOT AS TWO REAL VALUES
(99,99 TO QUIT)
1 1
COMPLEX ROOTS, X =  (0.486214,2.86781) (0.486214,-2.86781)
 4 ITERATIONS

ENTER INITIAL COMPLEX GUESS FOR ROOT AS TWO REAL VALUES
(99,99 TO QUIT)
99 99
```

This last example uses a linear equation. We used four different guesses (three real values and one complex value). Each guess gave us the correct root in one iteration. Why? (Review the assumption made when the location of the next estimate of the root is computed.)

```
ENTER COEFFICIENTS A0, A1, A2, A3
0 0 3 -2.5

              3              2
P(X) =   0.000 X  +   0.000 X  +   3.000 X +   -2.500

ENTER INITIAL COMPLEX GUESS FOR ROOT AS TWO REAL VALUES
0 0
REAL ROOT, X =  0.833333
 1 ITERATIONS

ENTER INITIAL COMPLEX GUESS FOR ROOT AS TWO REAL VALUES
(99,99 TO QUIT)
4 0
REAL ROOT, X =  0.833333
 1 ITERATIONS

ENTER INITIAL COMPLEX GUESS FOR ROOT AS TWO REAL VALUES
(99,99 TO QUIT)
-10 0
REAL ROOT, X =  0.833333
 1 ITERATIONS

ENTER INITIAL COMPLEX GUESS FOR ROOT AS TWO REAL VALUES
(99,99 TO QUIT)
-1 1
REAL ROOT, X =  0.833333
 1 ITERATIONS

ENTER INITIAL COMPLEX GUESS FOR ROOT AS TWO REAL VALUES
(99,99 TO QUIT)
99 99
```

SUMMARY

In this chapter we discussed five iterative techniques for finding roots of equations: incremental search, bisection, false position, Newton-Raphson, and secant. The incremental-search method is useful in finding intervals that contain roots; the bisection, false-position, and secant methods begin with an interval that contains a root and then determine smaller subintervals that contain the root. We presented the Newton-Raphson method since many engineering problems require identification of both real and complex roots of an equation. The Newton-Raphson method requires the use of the derivative of the original function.

DEBUGGING AIDS

To debug computer algorithms for finding roots of equations, be sure to have a variety of equations for testing. The examples from the sections in this chapter provide a wide range of polynomials with both real and complex roots; also be sure to use examples other than polynomials. When using an algorithm that requires an initial guess, remember that a complex value is required to find a complex root. Also, since many different guesses can converge to the same root, you may need to divide the polynomial by a factor containing the root to obtain a polynomial with a lower degree and then use the algorithm on that polynomial. The roots of the new polynomial will also be new roots of the original polynomial. When working with numerical methods that evaluate polynomials, you may also want to include some conditions to determine if the absolute value of the polynomial is getting very large (approaching $\pm\infty$) because these values could cause an execution error due to underflow or overflow in the computer. When you detect these very large values, you may want to increase or decrease the value of x so that it has a reasonable polynomial value, or you may want to print an error message and let the user select a new value of x.

STYLE/TECHNIQUE GUIDES

When using an interactive algorithm such as the root-finding algorithms, be sure to repeat information that the user has entered to check that there were no errors in entering the data. For example, when coefficients are entered, print the equation with the specific coefficients included in it. If you are using initial guesses or initial interval values, print these values also. In any iterative technique, it is a good idea to print the number of iterations used to converge to the final answer. This is not only helpful in debugging, but it also allows you to compare different techniques for solving the same problem.

ERROR ANALYSIS

Analysis of the error in a numerical result is important for both hand-computed and computer-calculated results. For engineers and scientists, this analysis is especially important because the results of engineering and scientific computations are often used in designs that could affect safety. The first step in understanding errors is distinguishing between *relative errors* and *absolute errors.* The absolute error is the difference between the true value and the approximation to the true value; the relative error is the absolute error divided by the approximation. For example, in the hand example in Section 10–4, we used the bisection method to approximate the root of a linear equation. After five iterations, the estimate of the root was 0.8321, and the true value of the root was 0.8333 (with both numbers given to four significant digits). Thus, the absolute error is $(0.8333 - 0.8321)$ or 0.0012, whereas the relative error is $\dfrac{0.0012}{0.8321}$, or 0.0014, which is equivalent to 0.14%. The absolute error and the relative error are similar in value for values around 1, but they can be very different if the values are very large or very small. Therefore, when you are discussing errors in computations, be sure that you distinguish between absolute errors and relative errors.

KEY WORDS

absolute error

bisection method

complex roots

false-position method

incremental-search method

initial guess

iteration

multiple roots

Newton-Raphson method

real roots

relative error

roots of equations

secant method

tangent line

PROBLEMS

We begin our problem set with modifications to programs developed earlier in this chapter. Give the decomposition, refined pseudocode or flowchart, and FORTRAN solution for each problem.

Problems 1–5 modify the program ROOTS, given on page 456, which uses the bisection method to find the roots to a quartic polynomial in a given interval.

1. Modify the polynomial program so that it allows the user to enter the interval endpoints instead of using $[-5,5]$.

2. Modify the polynomial program so that it allows the user to enter the size of the small intervals used to search initially for the roots.

3. Modify the polynomial program so that it prints the maximum and minimum polynomial values over the interval.

4. Modify the polynomial program so that it prints the number of iterations performed to find the root.

5. Modify the polynomial program so that it continues halving the interval until the absolute value of the function is less than a user-entered tolerance.

Problems 6–10 modify the program NEWTON, given on page 468, which identifies roots of polynomials using the Newton-Raphson method.

6. Modify the root-finding program so that it allows the user to enter the error tolerance used to stop the iterations.

7. Modify the root-finding program so that it allows the user to enter the maximum number of iterations to use before the program returns a message that it did not converge to a root.

8. Modify the root-finding program so that it keeps track of the roots found

and prints a list of the roots after each new root is found. Be sure to list each root only once.

9. Modify the root-finding program so that it finds the roots of a fifth-degree polynomial.

10. Modify the root-finding program so that it reminds the user to use complex initial guesses each time that the method does not converge.

In problems 11–16, develop programs and modules using the five-phase design process.

11. Write a subroutine that receives the coefficients of a quartic polynomial $q(x)$ and a root of the polynomial. Determine the coefficients of the cubic polynomial $c(x)$ that is a factor of the original quartic polynomial, and return these new coefficients from the subroutine, where

$$c(x) = \frac{q(x)}{(x - \text{root})}$$

This module would be helpful in identifying multiple roots in a polynomial.

12. Write a program to implement the incremental-search algorithm that was discussed in this chapter.

13. Write a program to implement the false-position method that was discussed in this chapter.

14. Write a program that generates polynomials for testing a root-finding algorithm. The program should ask the user for the degree of the polynomial and then ask for the same number of real roots. After multiplying the factors, the program should print the coefficients of the polynomial with the corresponding roots.

15. Modify the program from problem 14 so that it allows the user to enter complex roots. If a complex root is entered, the program should automatically assume that the conjugate root is also to be used.

16. Write functions that could be used by the Newton-Raphson method program to evaluate the polynomial and its derivative. These functions would be useful if the evaluations of the polynomial and its derivative were complicated. Show the changes that would be necessary in the program NEWTON.

17. Use the incremental-search and the bisection method to find the roots of this equation:

$$y = \sin(x)$$

in the interval $[-10,10]$.

18. Use the Newton-Raphson method to find the roots of this equation:

$$y = e^x - 4x$$

19. Use the incremental-search and the secant method to find the roots of this equation:

$$y = \sin(x) \cdot \cos(x/2)$$

in the interval $[-5,5]$. Plot the function using a plotting package to see where the roots are for this interval.

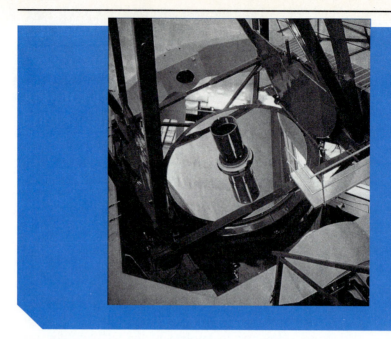

APPLICATION—Deformable Mirrors (Optical Engineering)

One of the most interesting recent advances in the area of optics has been the development of "deformable" mirrors—mirrors whose surfaces can be reshaped by various techniques to correct for distortions in the optical path between the observer and the object being viewed. For example, when used in a telescope, the deformable mirrors, or "adaptive optics," can use information about the atmospheric distortion caused by turbulence and pressure changes, as well as imperfections in the various optical elements of the telescope, to cancel the distortion, thereby presenting the viewer or a sensor with an undistorted image. Write a program to compute the voltage needed for each actuator (movable element) in the mirror, given a system of equations defining the corrections needed to cancel the distortion. (See Section 11–4 for solution.)

11

MATRICES AND SYSTEMS OF SIMULTANEOUS EQUATIONS

Introduction

11–1 Matrix Operations

11–2 Cramer's Rule

11–3 Gauss Elimination

11–4 Application—Deformable Mirrors (Optical Engineering)

11–5 Gauss-Seidel Method

11–6 Application—Electrical Circuits (Electrical Engineering)

Summary

INTRODUCTION

Engineering and science computations often use large amounts of data. In order to handle these data easily, we need a variety of ways to represent them. A *matrix* is a mathematical structure for storing data in a rectangular grid with rows and columns. In FORTRAN, we can easily represent a matrix with a two-dimensional array. In this chapter we define a number of matrix operations and develop FORTRAN routines to implement them.

We also discuss solving a set of *simultaneous equations*. A general set of three simultaneous equations can be written in the following form:

$$a_{1,1}x + a_{1,2}y + a_{1,3}z = b_1$$
$$a_{2,1}x + a_{2,2}y + a_{2,3}z = b_2$$
$$a_{3,1}x + a_{3,2}y + a_{3,3}z = b_3$$

The solution to this set of simultaneous equations is a unique set of values for x, y, and z which satisfy each of the three equations.

Geometrically, each equation of a set of three simultaneous equations with three unknowns represents a plane. If the three planes intersect in a common point, then the solution of the three simultaneous equations is the set of x, y, and z coordinates of the single point that is common to all three planes, as shown in the diagram below:

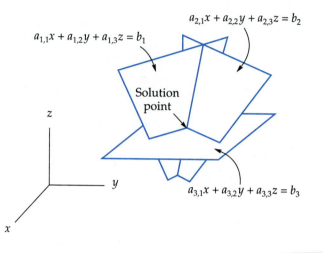

A unique solution does not exist if two or more of the equations represent the same plane. In fact, there are infinitely many solutions to the set of equations in this case:

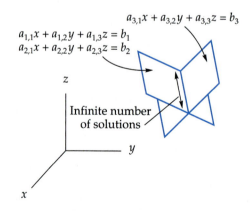

If two or more of the planes are parallel, then the planes do not meet in a single common point, and there is no solution to the system of equations:

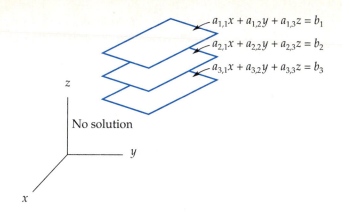

$$a_{1,1}x + a_{1,2}y + a_{1,3}z = b_1$$
$$a_{2,1}x + a_{2,2}y + a_{2,3}z = b_2$$
$$a_{3,1}x + a_{3,2}y + a_{3,3}z = b_3$$

No solution

When there is not a unique solution, the system is called a singular system of equations. Conversely, a nonsingular system is one which has a unique solution. In practice, a third possibility occurs when the planes are very nearly the same plane or are very nearly parallel; these systems are called ill-conditioned systems.

We present several techniques for solving a system of linear equations. These techniques (Cramer's rule, the Gauss elimination method, and the Gauss-Seidel method) use matrices to store the coefficients of the systems of equations and then perform computations using the matrices to find the solutions to the systems of simultaneous equations.

11–1   MATRIX OPERATIONS

Many engineering and science computations use a matrix as a convenient way to represent a set of data. Capital letters in boldface are used to refer to entire matrices, and lowercase letters with subscripts are used to refer to individual elements in the matrix. To refer to the entire matrix, we also use a reference to an individual element in brackets with variable subscripts, as in $[a_{i,j}]$. In FORTRAN, a matrix is easily represented with a two-dimensional array. Operations performed with two-dimensional arrays generally require more than a single statement because the operations must be able to access all elements of the array; thus loops are needed. In this section, we define a number of the common operations performed with matrices and develop subprograms to implement them in FORTRAN. (The next standard, Fortran 90, will implement many two-dimensional array operations with a single statement; until then, however, we need to perform them using the techniques that follow.)

In Chapter 5 (Array Processing), we emphasized the importance of using the same array dimension specification both in the main program and in a subprogram when using two-dimensional arrays. In this chapter we assure correct dimensioning by using an operational size and a dimensional size for two-dimensional arrays. The dimensional size is the number of rows and the number of columns used in the array definition; we use DROWS and DCOLS to specify this dimensional size. The operational size is specified by NR (the number of rows) and NC (the number of columns), and represents the size of the two-dimensional array actually used. (Recall that in FORTRAN 77 we must dimension the array to the maximum size that we want to be able to use.)

EXAMPLE 11–1

Scalar Multiplication

Multiplying each element in a matrix by a scalar is referred to as *scalar multiplication*. Write a subroutine to multiply a matrix **A** by a scalar s and return the result in a matrix **B**, as shown in the following matrix notation:

$$[b_{i,j}] \leftarrow [s \cdot a_{i,j}]$$

To illustrate, the elements of the matrix **A** are multiplied by a scalar value of 4, and the result is a new matrix **B**:

$$\mathbf{A} = \begin{bmatrix} 1.0 & 2.2 \\ 3.0 & 4.0 \\ -1.0 & 0.0 \end{bmatrix} \quad 4\mathbf{A} = \mathbf{B} = \begin{bmatrix} 4.0 & 8.8 \\ 12.0 & 16.0 \\ -4.0 & 0.0 \end{bmatrix}$$

The operational size of the arrays representing **A** and **B** must be the same, and we assume that their dimensional size is also the same. (If the dimensional sizes are different, two additional arguments are needed for the subroutine.)

Solution

The steps in this solution involve defining a pair of nested loops to access each element of the arrays and then multiplying each element of **A** by the scalar:

```
*--------------------------------------------------------------*
      SUBROUTINE  SCALAR(A,S,B,NR,NC,DROWS,DCOLS)
*
*   This subroutine multiplies an array by a scalar.
*
      INTEGER  NR, NC, DROWS, DCOLS, I, J
      REAL  A(DROWS,DCOLS), S, B(DROWS,DCOLS)
*
      DO 10 I=1,NR
         DO 5 J=1,NC
            B(I,J) = S*A(I,J)
    5    CONTINUE
   10 CONTINUE
*
      RETURN
      END
*--------------------------------------------------------------*
```

EXAMPLE 11–2

Matrix Addition

Matrix addition can be performed only with matrices of the same size. The result of the addition is another matrix of the same size in which the elements are the sum of the elements in the corresponding positions of the original matrices, as shown in matrix notation:

$$[c_{i,j}] \leftarrow [a_{i,j} + b_{i,j}]$$

To illustrate, matrix **A** is added to matrix **B**, and the result is a new matrix **C**:

$$\mathbf{A} = \begin{bmatrix} 1.0 & 2.2 \\ 3.0 & 4.0 \\ -1.0 & 0.0 \end{bmatrix} \quad \mathbf{B} = \begin{bmatrix} 4.0 & -3.0 \\ 2.0 & 6.0 \\ -4.0 & 0.5 \end{bmatrix}$$

$$\mathbf{A} + \mathbf{B} = \mathbf{C} = \begin{bmatrix} 5.0 & -0.8 \\ 5.0 & 10.0 \\ -5.0 & 0.5 \end{bmatrix}$$

Write a subroutine called ADDMX with arguments that include the three matrices plus the operational size and dimensional size of the arrays representing the matrices. Again, if the arrays have different dimensional sizes, more subroutine arguments are needed.

Solution

This subroutine is similar to the one for scalar multiplication, but instead of multiplying each element by a number, the corresponding elements of the two input matrices are added:

```
*-----------------------------------------------------------*
      SUBROUTINE  ADDMX(A,B,C,NR,NC,DROWS,DCOLS)
*
*   This subroutine adds matrices A and B and
*   stores the result in matrix C.
*
      INTEGER  NR, NC, DROWS, DCOLS, I, J
      REAL   A(DROWS,DCOLS), B(DROWS,DCOLS), C(DROWS,DCOLS)
*
      DO 10 I=1,NR
         DO 5 J=1,NC
            C(I,J) = A(I,J) + B(I,J)
    5    CONTINUE
   10 CONTINUE
*
      RETURN
      END
*-----------------------------------------------------------*
```

This subroutine is written so that the matrix that represents the sum is a separate matrix; but, if we want to store the sum in one of the original matrices, we can list it also as the output matrix in the CALL statement, as shown:

```
      CALL ADDMX(A,B,B,NR,NC,DROWS,DCOLS)
```

EXAMPLE 11-3 **Matrix Subtraction**

Matrix subtraction can also be performed only with matrices of the same size. The result of the subtraction is another matrix of the same size in which the elements are the difference of the elements in the corresponding positions of the original matrices, as shown in matrix notation:

$$[c_{i,j}] \leftarrow [a_{i,j} - b_{i,j}]$$

To illustrate, matrix **B** is subtracted from matrix **A**, and the result is a new matrix **C**:

$$\mathbf{A} = \begin{bmatrix} 1.0 & 2.2 \\ 3.0 & 4.0 \\ -1.0 & 0.0 \end{bmatrix} \quad \mathbf{B} = \begin{bmatrix} 4.0 & -3.0 \\ 2.0 & 6.0 \\ -4.0 & 0.5 \end{bmatrix}$$

$$\mathbf{A} - \mathbf{B} = \mathbf{C} = \begin{bmatrix} -3.0 & 5.2 \\ 1.0 & -2.0 \\ 3.0 & -0.5 \end{bmatrix}$$

Although the order in adding matrices does not matter, the order in subtracting matrices obviously does matter.

Write a subroutine called SUBMX with arguments that include the three matrices plus the operational size and dimensional size of the arrays representing the matrices. Again, if the arrays have different dimensional sizes, more subroutine arguments are needed.

Solution

This subroutine is very similar to the one to add two matrices:

```
*------------------------------------------------------------*
*       SUBROUTINE  SUBMX(A,B,C,NR,NC,DROWS,DCOLS)
*
*   This subroutine subtracts matrix B from matrix A
*   and stores the result in matrix C.
*
        INTEGER  NR, NC, DROWS, DCOLS, I, J
        REAL   A(DROWS,DCOLS), B(DROWS,DCOLS), C(DROWS,DCOLS)
*
        DO 10 I=1,NR
          DO 5 J=1,NC
            C(I,J) = A(I,J) - B(I,J)
    5     CONTINUE
   10 CONTINUE
*
        RETURN
        END
*------------------------------------------------------------*
```

As before, this subroutine is written so that the matrix that represents the difference is a separate matrix, but if we want to store the difference in one of the original matrices, we can list it also as the output matrix in the CALL statement.

EXAMPLE 11-4   **Dot Product**

The *dot product* is an operation performed with two vectors of the same size. (A *vector* is a matrix with one column and is thus easily implemented in a one-dimensional array.) The dot product between two vectors of size N is a number computed by adding the products of the values in corresponding positions in the vectors, as shown in the summation equation:

$$\text{Dot product} \leftarrow \sum_{i=1}^{N} a_i b_i$$

To illustrate, the dot product of vectors **A** and **B** is computed:

$$\mathbf{A} = \begin{bmatrix} 3.0 \\ 1.5 \\ -0.5 \end{bmatrix} \quad \mathbf{B} = \begin{bmatrix} 1.0 \\ 2.0 \\ 3.0 \end{bmatrix}$$

$$
\begin{aligned}
\text{Dot product of } \mathbf{A} \text{ and } \mathbf{B} &= \mathbf{A} \cdot \mathbf{B} \\
&= (3.0)(1.0) + (1.5)(2.0) + (-0.5)(3.0) \\
&= 3.0 + 3.0 - 1.5 \\
&= 4.5
\end{aligned}
$$

Write a function to compute the dot product of two vectors with a common size N.

Solution

Note that this subprogram is written as a function instead of as a subroutine because it returns a single value to the main program. Also, since we are using one-dimensional arrays, we do not have to distinguish between operational size and dimensional size.

```
*------------------------------------------------------------*
      REAL FUNCTION  DOT(A,B,N)
*
*  This function computes the dot product of A and B.
*
      INTEGER  N, I
      REAL   A(N), B(N)
*
      DOT = 0.0
      DO 10 I=1,N
         DOT = DOT + A(I)*B(I)
   10 CONTINUE
*
      RETURN
      END
*------------------------------------------------------------*
```

EXAMPLE 11–5   **Matrix Multiplication**

Matrix multiplication is not computed by multiplying corresponding elements of the matrices. The value in position (i,j) of the product of two matrices is the dot product of row i of the first matrix and column j of the second matrix, as shown in the summation equation

$$[c_{i,j}] \leftarrow \sum_{k=1}^{N} a_{i,k} b_{k,j}$$

In the equation, i and j are fixed values, and k varies in the summation.

Because dot products require that the vectors have the same number of elements, we must have the same number of elements in each row of the first matrix as we have in each column of the second matrix to compute the product of the two matrices. The product matrix has the same number of rows as the first matrix and the same number of columns as the second matrix. Thus, if **A** and **B** both have 5 rows and 5 columns, their product has 5 rows and 5 columns. If **A** has 3 rows and 2 columns and **B** has 2 rows and 2 columns, their product has 3 rows and 2 columns. To illustrate, consider the following matrices **A** and **B**:

$$\mathbf{A} = \begin{bmatrix} 1.0 & 2.2 \\ 3.0 & 4.0 \\ -1.0 & 0.0 \end{bmatrix} \qquad \mathbf{B} = \begin{bmatrix} 4.0 & -3.0 \\ 2.0 & 6.0 \end{bmatrix}$$

The first element in the product **C** = **AB** is

$$\begin{aligned} c_{1,1} &= \sum_{k=1}^{2} a_{1,k} b_{k,1} \\ &= a_{1,1} b_{1,1} + a_{1,2} b_{2,1} \\ &= (1.0)(4.0) + (2.2)(2.0) \\ &= 8.4 \end{aligned}$$

Similarly, we can compute the rest of the elements in the product of **A** and **B**:

$$\mathbf{AB} = \mathbf{C} = \begin{bmatrix} 8.4 & 10.2 \\ 20.0 & 15.0 \\ -4.0 & 3.0 \end{bmatrix}$$

In this example, we cannot compute **BA** because **B** does not have the same number of elements in each row as **A** has in each column. But, when both **AB** and **BA** can be computed, **AB** is usually not equal to **BA**.

We now develop a subroutine to multiply two matrices. The arguments of the subroutine must include the two input matrices, the output matrix, and the operational sizes and dimensional sizes of the arrays representing the matrices. We will not assume that the dimensional sizes of all the arrays are the same in matrix multiplication.

Solution

In the subroutine, we print an error message if the operational sizes of the arrays are not correct for matrix multiplication.

```
*--------------------------------------------------------*
      SUBROUTINE  MULTMX(A,ANR,ANC,ADROWS,ADCOLS,
     +                   B,BNR,BNC,BDROWS,BDCOLS,
     +                   C,CNR,CNC,CDROWS,CDCOLS)
*
*   This subroutine multiplies arrays A and B
*   and stores the product in array C.
*
      INTEGER  ANR,ANC,ADROWS,ADCOLS,BNR,BNC,BDROWS,BDCOLS,
     +         CNR,CNC,CDROWS,CDCOLS,I,J,K
      REAL  A(ADROWS,ADCOLS),B(BDROWS,BDCOLS),C(CDROWS,CDCOLS)
      LOGICAL  ERROR
*
      ERROR = .FALSE.
      IF (ANC.NE.BNR) ERROR = .TRUE.
      IF (ANR.NE.CNR) ERROR = .TRUE.
      IF (BNC.NE.CNC) ERROR = .TRUE.
*
      IF (ERROR) THEN
         PRINT*, 'ERROR IN ARRAY SIZES'
      ELSE
         DO 30 I=1,CNR
            DO 25 J=1,CNC
               C(I,J) = 0.0
               DO 15 K=1,ANC
                  C(I,J) = C(I,J) + A(I,K)*B(K,J)
   15          CONTINUE
   25       CONTINUE
   30    CONTINUE
      ENDIF
*
      RETURN
      END
*--------------------------------------------------------*
```

In Section 11-2, we use matrix operations in applying Cramer's rule to solve simultaneous linear equations. Systems of simultaneous equations appear in virtually every technical area. They are often used in the stress analysis of mechanical systems, in the analysis of a fluid-flow system, and in the analysis of the current or voltages in an electrical circuit. The design of airplane control systems also requires the solution of systems of simultaneous equations. The data from these analyses are stored in a matrix, and the system of simultaneous equations represented by this matrix is solved to compute the desired result.

This self-test allows you to check quickly to see if you have remembered the key points from Section 11–1. If you have any problems with the exercises, reread this section. The solutions are included at the end of the text.

Compute the following new matrices using **A**, **B**, **C**, and **D**:

$$\mathbf{A} = \begin{bmatrix} 2.0 & 1.0 \\ 0.0 & -1.0 \\ 3.0 & 0.0 \end{bmatrix} \quad \mathbf{B} = \begin{bmatrix} 1.0 & 3.0 \\ -1.0 & 5.0 \end{bmatrix}$$

$$\mathbf{C} = \begin{bmatrix} 3.0 & 2.0 \\ -1.0 & -2.0 \\ 0.0 & 2.0 \end{bmatrix} \quad \mathbf{D} = \begin{bmatrix} 1.0 \\ 2.0 \end{bmatrix}$$

1. $\mathbf{A} + 2\mathbf{C}$
2. $4\mathbf{C} - \mathbf{A}$
3. $4(\mathbf{C} - \mathbf{A})$
4. $\mathbf{D} \cdot \mathbf{D}$
5. $(2\mathbf{D}) \cdot (-3\mathbf{D})$
6. $\mathbf{AB}$
7. $\mathbf{BD}$
8. $\mathbf{CD}$
9. $(\mathbf{CB})\mathbf{D}$
10. $(\mathbf{A} + \mathbf{C})\mathbf{D}$

11–2 CRAMER'S RULE

In this section, we develop a program to solve three simultaneous linear equations. A general set of three simultaneous equations can be written in the following form (which is modified slightly from the notation presented at the beginning of the chapter):

$$a_1 x + b_1 y + c_1 z = d_1$$
$$a_2 x + b_2 y + c_2 z = d_2$$
$$a_3 x + b_3 y + c_3 z = d_3$$

This system of equations can be expressed in matrix form if we define a matrix **K** that contains the coefficients of the unknowns, a matrix **U** that contains the unknown variables, and a matrix **D** that contains the constants of the right side of the equations:

$$\mathbf{K} = \begin{bmatrix} a_1 & b_1 & c_1 \\ a_2 & b_2 & c_2 \\ a_3 & b_3 & c_3 \end{bmatrix} \quad \mathbf{U} = \begin{bmatrix} x \\ y \\ z \end{bmatrix} \quad \mathbf{D} = \begin{bmatrix} d_1 \\ d_2 \\ d_3 \end{bmatrix}$$

Then, we have

$$\mathbf{KU} = \mathbf{D}$$

where **KU** is the product of matrices **K** and **U**. It is instructive to multiply these matrices by hand and see that we obtain the three equations given at the beginning of this paragraph.

There are many ways to solve a system of simultaneous equations. In this section, we use *Cramer's rule*, which is a simple method for solving three simultaneous equations. While this technique can be extended to work with more than three equations, it becomes very inefficient as the number of equations increases. Later sections present other techniques that are better for solving more than three simultaneous equations.

Cramer's rule uses the *determinant* of a matrix, which is a number computed from the elements of the matrix. Using the matrix **K** to represent a general matrix with three rows and three columns, the determinant of **K** is defined to be the following sum:

$$\det \mathbf{K} = a_1 \cdot b_2 \cdot c_3 + b_1 \cdot c_2 \cdot a_3 + c_1 \cdot a_2 \cdot b_3$$
$$- a_3 \cdot b_2 \cdot c_1 - b_3 \cdot c_2 \cdot a_1 - c_3 \cdot a_2 \cdot b_1$$

The determinant of a matrix is represented by the name of the matrix within straight lines or bars; the determinant can also be represented by listing the values of the matrix itself within straight lines:

$$\det \mathbf{K} = |\mathbf{K}|$$

$$= \begin{vmatrix} a_1 & b_1 & c_1 \\ a_2 & b_2 & c_2 \\ a_3 & b_3 & c_3 \end{vmatrix}$$

Thus, using a specific set of values, we have

$$\begin{vmatrix} 2 & 2 & 4 \\ 1 & -2 & 0 \\ 3 & -1 & 5 \end{vmatrix} = (2)(-2)(5) + (2)(0)(3) + (4)(1)(-1)$$
$$- (3)(-2)(4) - (-1)(0)(2) - (5)(1)(2)$$
$$= -20 + 0 - 4 - (-24) - 0 - 10$$
$$= -10$$

General formulas can be used to compute determinants for larger (or smaller) matrices, but in this section we are only concerned with determinants for matrices with three rows and three columns.

When we solve three equations simultaneously, we obtain equations for x, y, and z in terms of the coefficients of the unknown variables (which are also the elements of the matrix **K**) and the constants from the right side of the equations (which are also the elements of the matrix **D**). Cramer's rule expresses these equations for x, y, and z using the quotient of two determinants. The denominator determinant for each equation is the determinant of **K**. The numerator determinant for computing x uses the matrix **K**, with the first column of **K** replaced by the constants of the original set of equations. The numerator determinant for computing y uses the matrix **K**, with the second column of **K** replaced by the constants of the original set of equations. Finally, the numerator determinant for computing z uses the matrix **K**, with the third column of **K** replaced by the constants of the original set of equations. Thus, the values for x, y, and z can be computed, using Cramer's rule, as shown:

$$x = \frac{\begin{vmatrix} d_1 & b_1 & c_1 \\ d_2 & b_2 & c_2 \\ d_3 & b_3 & c_3 \end{vmatrix}}{\det(\mathbf{K})} \qquad y = \frac{\begin{vmatrix} a_1 & d_1 & c_1 \\ a_2 & d_2 & c_2 \\ a_3 & d_3 & c_3 \end{vmatrix}}{\det(\mathbf{K})} \qquad z = \frac{\begin{vmatrix} a_1 & b_1 & d_1 \\ a_2 & b_2 & d_2 \\ a_3 & b_3 & d_3 \end{vmatrix}}{\det(\mathbf{K})}$$

Again, note that all three equations have the same denominator, which is the determinant formed from the coefficients of x, y, and z. When this determinant is equal to zero, a solution does not exist. If the determinant of $\mathbf{K}$ is very close to zero, then the solution is very susceptible to roundoff errors; these systems are called ill-conditioned systems.

Write a program that reads the coefficients of three simultaneous equations with three variables and solves the system of equations using Cramer's rule.

PROBLEM STATEMENT

Use Cramer's rule to find the x, y, and z values that solve a set of three simultaneous equations. Print an appropriate error message if a unique solution does not exist.

INPUT/OUTPUT DESCRIPTION

The input is the set of coefficients and constants for the equations, or a total of 12 values. The output is the set of values for x, y, and z that solve all three equations, or an appropriate error message.

HAND EXAMPLE

Assume that the following set of equations is to be solved using determinants:

$$2x + 3y - z = 1$$
$$3x + 5y + 2z = 8$$
$$x - 2y - 3z = -1$$

We first compute the determinant of the matrix $\mathbf{K}$ formed from the coefficients of x, y, and z to determine if a unique solution exists:

$$\det \mathbf{K} = \begin{vmatrix} 2 & 3 & -1 \\ 3 & 5 & 2 \\ 1 & -2 & -3 \end{vmatrix} = -30 + 6 + 6 + 5 + 8 + 27 = 22$$

Because the determinant is nonzero, a unique solution exists. We now compute the specific values for x, y, and z.

$$x = \frac{\begin{vmatrix} 1 & 3 & -1 \\ 8 & 5 & 2 \\ -1 & -2 & -3 \end{vmatrix}}{22} = \frac{-15 - 6 + 16 - 5 + 4 + 72}{22} = \frac{66}{22} = 3$$

$$y = \frac{\begin{vmatrix} 2 & 1 & -1 \\ 3 & 8 & 2 \\ 1 & -1 & -3 \end{vmatrix}}{22} = \frac{-48 + 2 + 3 + 8 + 4 + 9}{22} = \frac{-22}{22} = -1$$

$$z = \frac{\begin{vmatrix} 2 & 3 & 1 \\ 3 & 5 & 8 \\ 1 & -2 & -1 \end{vmatrix}}{22} = \frac{-10 + 24 - 6 - 5 + 32 + 9}{22} = \frac{44}{22} = 2$$

We can substitute these values in the original equations to verify that they solve all three equations.

ALGORITHM DEVELOPMENT

The decomposition of our solution in general steps is the following:

DECOMPOSITION

Read coefficients and constants.
Compute solution.
Print solution.

As we refine these steps, we realize that we need to compute several determinants in the solution. This computation can be performed in a function that is referenced each time that we need it. We want to think carefully about the arguments to this function—it is cumbersome to list 9 different variables that represent the matrix elements. Because the elements used to compute the determinant vary with each computation, a two-dimensional array is also not a good choice for storing the arguments of the determinant function. If we refer to the hand-worked example, we see that the matrix is composed of 3 columns, and each time the matrix changes, one of these columns changes. Therefore, if we send the 3 columns of the matrix to the determinant function as 3 one-dimensional arrays, we need only 3 arguments; it will also be easy to change arguments because we need to change only one-dimensional array names.

REFINEMENT IN PSEUDOCODE

EQN3: Read coefficients and constants
    If determinant = 0 then
      Print 'NO UNIQUE SOLUTION'
    Else
      Compute x, y, z
      Print x, y, z

As we convert the pseudocode into FORTRAN we want to make it as easy as possible to enter the coefficients—this is important because we have 12 values to enter, and if they are entered out of order, the solution will be incorrect.

The structure chart for this program is

FORTRAN PROGRAM

```
*-----------------------------------------------------------------*
      PROGRAM   EQN3
*
*   This program computes the solution to three simultaneous
*   equations using determinants.
*
      REAL  A(3),B(3),C(3),D(3),DENOM,DET,X,Y,Z
*
      PRINT*, 'EACH EQUATION SHOULD BE IN THIS FORM:'
      PRINT*, 'A*X + B*Y + C*Z = D'
      PRINT*, 'ENTER A,B,C,D FOR EQUATION 1'
      READ*, A(1), B(1), C(1), D(1)
      PRINT*, 'ENTER A,B,C,D FOR EQUATION 2'
      READ*, A(2), B(2), C(2), D(2)
      PRINT*, 'ENTER A,B,C,D FOR EQUATION 3'
      READ*, A(3), B(3), C(3), D(3)
      PRINT*
*
      DENOM = DET(A,B,C)
      IF (ABS(DENOM).LT.0.001) THEN
          PRINT*, 'NO UNIQUE SOLUTION EXISTS'
      ELSE
          X = DET(D,B,C)/DENOM
          Y = DET(A,D,C)/DENOM
          Z = DET(A,B,D)/DENOM
          PRINT 5, X
    5     FORMAT (1X,'SOLUTION: X = ',F7.2)
          PRINT 6, Y
    6     FORMAT (1X,'          Y = ',F7.2)
          PRINT 7, Z
    7     FORMAT (1X,'          Z = ',F7.2)
      ENDIF
*
      END
*-----------------------------------------------------------------*
      REAL FUNCTION  DET(P,Q,R)
*
*   This function computes the determinant of a 3X3 matrix
*   where P,Q,R represent the three columns of the matrix.
```

```
*
      REAL  P(3),Q(3),R(3)
*
      DET = P(1)*Q(2)*R(3) + Q(1)*R(2)*P(3) + R(1)*P(2)*Q(3)
     +        - P(3)*Q(2)*R(1) - Q(3)*R(2)*P(1) - R(3)*P(2)*Q(1)
*
      RETURN
      END
*------------------------------------------------------------*
```

Note that we did not use A, B, and C as variable names in the function. It would be confusing to use A, B, C, or D as variable names in the function because different combinations of those names were used as arguments in the function references in the main program.

TESTING

The output of this program with the data from the hand-worked example is

```
EACH EQUATION SHOULD BE IN THIS FORM:
A*X + B*Y + C*Z = D
ENTER A,B,C,D FOR EQUATION 1
2.0 3.0 -1.0 1.0
ENTER A,B,C,D FOR EQUATION 2
3.0 5.0 2.0 8.0
ENTER A,B,C,D FOR EQUATION 3
1.0 -2.0 -3.0 -1.0

SOLUTION: X =    3.00
          Y =   -1.00
          Z =    2.00
```

This is a simple technique for solving systems of three equations, but it is not generally used for systems with four or more equations because the determinant becomes more complicated to compute. The next section presents the Gauss elimination method, which is commonly used when the number of equations is greater than three. In addition to the Gauss elimination method, the Gauss-Jordan method for solving a system of equations can also be used; it frequently requires a number of row manipulations to solve the system of equations. The Gauss-Seidel method is a multistep technique that is often used for a sparse system (one in which many of the coefficients are zero). The Gauss-Seidel method is discussed in Section 11-5.

This self-test allows you to check quickly to see if you have remembered the key points from Section 11-2. If you have any problems with the exercises, you should reread this section. The solutions are included at the end of the text.

Compute the determinant of the following matrices:

1. $A = \begin{bmatrix} 2.0 & 1.0 & 0.0 \\ -1.0 & 2.0 & 2.0 \\ 3.0 & 3.0 & 0.0 \end{bmatrix}$

2. $B = \begin{bmatrix} -1.0 & 5.0 & 0.0 \\ 2.0 & 2.0 & 1.0 \\ 3.0 & -1.0 & 5.0 \end{bmatrix}$

3. $C = \begin{bmatrix} -4.0 & 0.0 & 4.0 \\ 3.0 & 2.0 & -1.0 \\ -2.0 & 0.0 & 2.0 \end{bmatrix}$

4. Use Cramer's rule to solve the nonsingular systems of equations in problems 1–3, assuming that the constants for the three equations are $2, -1, 3$.

11-3 GAUSS ELIMINATION

The *Gauss elimination* method of solving a system of equations is one in which we solve for the unknowns by combining equations. We will first illustrate this method with an example. Specifically, we use the set of equations that was used to illustrate Cramer's rule in Section 11-2.

$$\begin{aligned} 2x + 3y - z &= 1 \\ 3x + 5y + 2z &= 8 \\ x - 2y - 3z &= -1 \end{aligned}$$

Gauss elimination begins by using the first equation to eliminate the first variable, $3x$, in the second equation. To do this, we multiply the first equation by $\frac{3}{2}$ (or 1.5) and subtract it from the second equation, as shown:

$$\begin{array}{ll} 3x + 5y + 2z = 8 & \text{second equation} \\ \underline{3x + 4.5y - 1.5z = 1.5} & \text{first equation times 1.5} \\ 0x + 0.5y + 3.5z = 6.5 & \text{difference} \end{array}$$

Thus, our new set of equations is

$$\begin{aligned}
2x &+ 3y & -z &= 1 \\
0x &+ 0.5y & +3.5z &= 6.5 \\
x &- 2y & -3z &= -1
\end{aligned}$$

The solution to this new set of equations is also a solution to the original set of equations since the modifications only added equivalent expressions to both sides of an equation or multiplied both sides of an equation by the same value.

We now eliminate the variable x in the third equation by multiplying the first equation by 0.5 and subtracting it from the third equation, as shown:

$$\begin{array}{llll}
x & -2y & -3z = & -1 & \text{third equation} \\
x & +1.5y & -0.5z = & 0.5 & \text{first equation times 0.5} \\
\hline
0x & -3.5y & -2.5z = & -1.5 & \text{difference}
\end{array}$$

Our new set of equations is now

$$\begin{aligned}
2x &+ 3y & -z &= 1 \\
0x &+ 0.5y & +3.5z &= 6.5 \\
0x &- 3.5y & -2.5z &= -1.5
\end{aligned}$$

Note that we have now eliminated all terms with x except in the first equation. We now move to the second variable and eliminate it in all equations after the second equation. We accomplish this by multiplying the second equation by -7 and subtracting it from the third equation, which yields

$$\begin{aligned}
2x &+ 3y & -z &= 1 \\
0x &+ 0.5y & +3.5z &= 6.5 \\
0x &+ 0y & +22z &= 44
\end{aligned}$$

If we have N equations with N unknowns, we eliminate the first unknown from all but the first equation, we eliminate the second unknown from all but the first and second equations, and so on until the last equation has only one variable.

We now begin the back-substitution process to solve for the unknowns. Using our example data, we know from the last equation that $22z = 44$, or that $z = 2$. Substituting the value of z in the second equation, which is $0.5y + 3.5z = 6.5$, gives $0.5y + 3.5(2) = 6.5$, which results in $y = -1$. We now know the value of y and z and can substitute these values in the first equation to determine the value of x. Since $2x + 3y - z = 1$, then $2x + 3(-1) - (2) = 1$, or $2x = 6$, and finally $x = 3$.

In general, we perform the back-substitution by starting with the last equation, and backing up one equation each step, until we reach the first equation. After performing the back-substitution for each variable, we have the final solution.

To improve accuracy, a process known as "pivoting" is frequently used. In this process, we define a pivot equation and a pivot coefficient. Recall that Gauss elimination begins by using the first equation to eliminate the first variable (x) in all equations after the first equation. For this step, the first equation is the pivot equation and the first coefficient in the pivot equation is the pivot coefficient. We then eliminate the second variable (y) from all equations after the second equation, defining the second equation as the pivot equation and the second coefficient in the pivot equation as the pivot coefficient. This continues until the pivot equation is the last equation and the pivot coefficient is the last coefficient in the pivot equation. If the absolute value of the pivot coefficient is small compared to the corresponding coefficients in the rows below it, then we will have to multiply the pivot coefficient by a large value to perform the elimination step. And if there is a small error in the pivot coefficient from earlier steps, multiplying it by a large value and using it to eliminate the coefficients below can result in large errors. These errors can be greatly reduced if we reorder the set of equations such that the first equation (the pivot equation) is the equation with the largest coefficient (in absolute value) for the first variable (the pivot coefficient). We then eliminate the first variable from the remaining equations. Starting with the second equation, we then reorder the equations such that the second equation has the largest coefficient (in absolute value) for the second variable. We then eliminate the second variable from all equations after the second equation. The reordering and elimination continue in this way until we reach the final equation, which contains only one variable. This process is called "partial pivoting" and usually provides good accuracy. If additional accuracy is needed, "complete pivoting" can be done by similarly exchanging columns. If columns are exchanged, it is important to keep track of the changes in the order of the variables.

The back-substitution process then occurs exactly as discussed previously. If at some time in the reordering we find that all the coefficients for a variable are zero, or are very close to zero, then the system of equations is either ill-conditioned or does not have a unique solution.

We now develop a program that uses Gauss elimination to solve a system of simultaneous equations. This program will read a data file that contains the coefficients of the system of equations. Assume that the first line of the data file contains the number of equations, with a maximum of 25. The coefficients for each equation begin on a new line in the data file.

PROBLEM DESCRIPTION

Write a program that solves a system of simultaneous equations using Gauss elimination.

INPUT/OUTPUT DESCRIPTION

The input is contained in a data file. The first line of the file contains the number of equations in the system. The coefficients for each equation begin on a new line in the data file. The output gives the solution to the system of simultaneous equations.

HAND EXAMPLE

Using the example from earlier discussions in this section, the data file would contain the following information:

$$\begin{array}{cccc} 3 & & & \\ 2 & 3 & -1 & 1 \\ 3 & 5 & 2 & 8 \\ 1 & -2 & -3 & -1 \end{array}$$

Using the reorder and elimination process for each variable gives the following steps.

Select the first variable and reorder the equations if necessary:

$$\begin{aligned} 3x + 5y + 2z &= 8 \\ 2x + 3y - z &= 1 \\ x - 2y - 3z &= -1 \end{aligned}$$

We now eliminate the first variable from each of the equations after the first equation:

$$\begin{aligned} 3x + 5y + 2z &= 8 \\ 0x - \tfrac{1}{3}y - \tfrac{7}{3}z &= -\tfrac{13}{3} \\ 0x - \tfrac{11}{3}y - \tfrac{11}{3}z &= -\tfrac{11}{3} \end{aligned}$$

Starting with the second equation, we reorder the equations so that the second equation has the largest absolute value for the second coefficient:

$$\begin{aligned} 3x + 5y + 2z &= 8 \\ 0x - \tfrac{11}{3}y - \tfrac{11}{3}z &= -\tfrac{11}{3} \\ 0x - \tfrac{1}{3}y - \tfrac{7}{3}z &= -\tfrac{13}{3} \end{aligned}$$

We now eliminate the second variable from each equation after the second equation:

$$\begin{aligned} 3x + 5y + 2z &= 8 \\ 0x - \tfrac{11}{3}y - \tfrac{11}{3}z &= -\tfrac{11}{3} \\ 0x + 0y - 2z &= -4 \end{aligned}$$

We are now ready to do the back-substitution. We start with the last equation and solve for z. We then substitute that value in the next-to-last equation. Thus, from the third equation above, we find that z is equal to 2. Then we add $\tfrac{11}{3}z$ (or $\tfrac{11}{3} \cdot 2$) to both sides of the second equation.

$$\begin{aligned} 3x + 5y + 2z &= 8 \\ 0x - \tfrac{11}{3}y + 0z &= \tfrac{11}{3} \\ 0x + 0y + 1z &= 2 \end{aligned}$$

We now solve the second-from-the-bottom equation:

$$\begin{aligned} 3x + 5y + 2z &= 8 \\ 0x + 1y + 0z &= -1 \\ 0x + 0y + 1z &= 2 \end{aligned}$$

We are now at the first equation, which we solve to get our final solution.

$$1x + 0y + 0z = 3$$
$$0x + 1y + 0z = -1$$
$$0x + 0y + 1z = 2$$

Thus, the final results are

$$x = 3$$
$$y = -1$$
$$z = 2$$

ALGORITHM DEVELOPMENT

The decomposition for this problem solution is the following:

DECOMPOSITION

Read coefficient information.
Solve system of equations.
Print solution.

Solving the system of equations requires pivoting, or reordering of the equations, if necessary, before each elimination step. The reordering is done by finding the equation with the maximum absolute value for the coefficient of the first unknown and putting that equation first. This equation becomes the pivot equation, and its first coefficient is the pivot coefficient. We then use the pivot equation to eliminate the first unknown in all equations after the pivot equation. To do this, we determine a special factor. This factor is the value that we multiply the pivot equation by to get a new equation that we then subtract from the current row in order to eliminate the term in the pivot column. (Refer to the hand example again if necessary.) This factor is the coefficient in the pivot column in the current row divided by the pivot coefficient.

Finally, we need to consider the back-substitution. We start with the last equation, which now has only the last variable. We solve for this variable and back-substitute it into the next-to-last equation, which can then be solved for the next-to-last variable. This back-substitution process continues until we have solved for all of the variables.

As we combine these ideas into pseudocode, it is clear that we have several independent operations—the reordering step, the elimination step, and the back-substitution. We implement these as subroutines to make our program more readable and easier to debug.

In the computer program, we can perform the steps in solving this system of equations using a matrix of coefficients. We also need the constants from the right side of the equations, but instead of storing the constants in a separate matrix, we will use an augmented coefficient matrix that contains the coefficients and the constants. Thus, for the hand example, the augmented matrix is

$$\mathbf{A} = \begin{bmatrix} 2 & 3 & -1 & 1 \\ 3 & 5 & 2 & 8 \\ 1 & -2 & -3 & -1 \end{bmatrix}$$

The algorithm then references elements of this matrix to determine when reordering is needed. The elimination and back-substitution processes also use and modify this matrix, which is implemented in a two-dimensional array. Since this two-dimensional array is used in both the main program and subprograms, we use DROWS and DCOLS as subprogram arguments to specify the dimensional size; the number of equations, N, can be used to specify the operational size, which is N rows and $N + 1$ columns.

REFINEMENT IN PSEUDOCODE

```
GAUSS:   drows ← 25
         dcols ← 26
         Read n and the augmented coefficient array, a
         pivot ← 1
         error ← false
         While pivot < n and no error do
             Call order (a,drows,dcols,n,pivot,error)
             If no error then
                 Call elim (a,drows,dcols,n,pivot)
                 pivot ← pivot + 1
         If error then
             Print 'NO UNIQUE SOLUTION'
         Else
             Call backsb (a,drows,dcols,n,soln)
             Print the solution array, soln

ORDER (a,drows,dcols,n,pivot,error):
         rmax ← pivot
         For row = pivot + 1 to n do
             If abs(a(row,pivot)) > abs(a(rmax,pivot)) then
                 rmax ← row
         If abs(a(rmax,pivot)) < 0.00001 then
             error ← true
         Else
             If rmax ≠ pivot then
                 For k = 1 to n + 1 do
                     temp ← a(rmax,k)
                     a(rmax,k) ← a(pivot,k)
                     a(pivot,k) ← temp
         Return
```

ELIM (a,drows,dcols,n,pivot):
    For row = pivot + 1 to n do

$$\text{factor} \leftarrow \frac{a(row,pivot)}{a(pivot,pivot)}$$

        $a(row,pivot) \leftarrow 0.0$
        For col = pivot + 1 to n + 1 do
            $a(row,col) \leftarrow a(row,col) - a(pivot,col)*factor$
    Return
BACKSB (a,drows,dcols,n,soln);
    For row = n to 1 in steps of −1 do
        For col = n to row + 1 in steps of −1 do
            $a(row,n+1) \leftarrow a(row,n+1) - soln(col)*a(row,col)$

$$soln(row) \leftarrow \frac{a(row,n+1)}{a(row,row)}$$

    Return

The structure chart and FORTRAN program for this solution are the following:

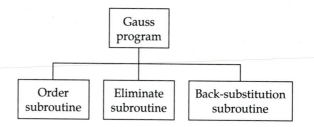

FORTRAN PROGRAM

```
*-----------------------------------------------------------------*
      PROGRAM   GAUSS
*
*   This program uses the Gauss elimination method to
*   solve a set of simultaneous equations.
*
      INTEGER  DROWS, DCOLS, N, I, J, PIVOT
      REAL  A(25,26), SOLN(25)
      LOGICAL  ERROR
*
      DROWS = 25
      DCOLS = 26
      OPEN (UNIT=10,FILE='EQNS',STATUS='OLD')
      READ (10,*) N
      DO 5 I=1,N
         READ (10,*) (A(I,J),J=1,N+1)
    5 CONTINUE
*
      PIVOT = 1
      ERROR = .FALSE.
```

```
      10 IF (PIVOT.LT.N.AND..NOT.ERROR) THEN
             CALL ORDER(A,DROWS,DCOLS,N,PIVOT,ERROR)
             IF (.NOT.ERROR) THEN
                 CALL ELIM(A,DROWS,DCOLS,N,PIVOT)
                 PIVOT = PIVOT + 1
             ENDIF
             GO TO 10
         ENDIF
*
         IF (ERROR) THEN
             PRINT*, 'NO UNIQUE SOLUTION EXISTS'
         ELSE
             CALL BACKSB(A,DROWS,DCOLS,N,SOLN)
             PRINT*, 'SOLUTION TO EQUATIONS'
             PRINT*
             DO 20 I=1,N
                 PRINT 15, I, SOLN(I)
      15         FORMAT (1X,'VARIABLE ',I2,' = ',F7.3)
      20     CONTINUE
         ENDIF
         END
*-------------------------------------------------------------*
         SUBROUTINE  ORDER(A,DROWS,DCOLS,N,PIVOT,ERROR)
*
*     This subroutine reorders the equations so that the pivot
*     position in the pivot equation has the maximum absolute value.
*
         INTEGER  DROWS, DCOLS, N, ROW, RMAX, PIVOT, K
         REAL  A(DROWS,DCOLS), TEMP
         LOGICAL  ERROR
*
         RMAX = PIVOT
         DO 10 ROW=PIVOT+1,N
             IF (ABS(A(ROW,PIVOT)).GT.ABS(A(RMAX,PIVOT))) RMAX = ROW
      10 CONTINUE
         IF (ABS(A(RMAX,PIVOT)).LT.1.0E-05) THEN
             ERROR = .TRUE.
         ELSE
             IF (RMAX.NE.PIVOT) THEN
                 DO 20 K=1,N+1
                     TEMP = A(RMAX,K)
                     A(RMAX,K) = A(PIVOT,K)
                     A(PIVOT,K) = TEMP
      20         CONTINUE
             ENDIF
         ENDIF
         RETURN
         END
*-------------------------------------------------------------*
         SUBROUTINE  ELIM(A,DROWS,DCOLS,N,PIVOT)
*
*     This subroutine eliminates the element in the pivot
*     position from rows following the pivot equation.
*
         INTEGER  DROWS, DCOLS, N, PIVOT, ROW, COL
         REAL  A(DROWS,DCOLS), FACTOR
*
         DO 10 ROW=PIVOT+1,N
             FACTOR = A(ROW,PIVOT)/A(PIVOT,PIVOT)
             A(ROW,PIVOT) = 0.0
             DO 5 COL=PIVOT+1,N+1
                 A(ROW,COL) = A(ROW,COL) - A(PIVOT,COL)*FACTOR
       5     CONTINUE
      10 CONTINUE
```

```
          RETURN
          END
*----------------------------------------------------------*
          SUBROUTINE  BACKSB(A,DROWS,DCOLS,N,SOLN)
     *
     *  This subroutine performs the back-substitution to
     *  determine the solution to the system of equations.
     *
          INTEGER  DROWS, DCOLS, N, ROW, COL
          REAL  A(DROWS,DCOLS), SOLN(DROWS)
     *
          DO 20 ROW=N,1,-1
             DO 10 COL=N,ROW+1,-1
                A(ROW,N+1) = A(ROW,N+1) - SOLN(COL)*A(ROW,COL)
     10      CONTINUE
             SOLN(ROW) = A(ROW,N+1)/A(ROW,ROW)
     20   CONTINUE
          RETURN
          END
*----------------------------------------------------------*
```

TESTING

Using the sample set of data in this program gives the following results:

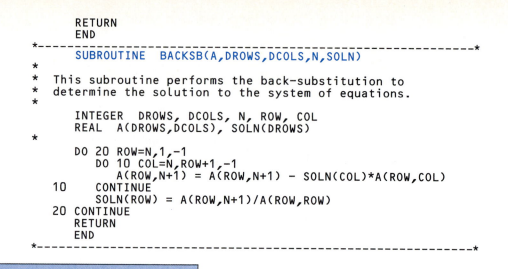

```
SOLUTION TO EQUATIONS

VARIABLE  1 =    3.000
VARIABLE  2 =   -1.000
VARIABLE  3 =    2.000
```

In an algorithm as complicated as this one, you should print the values in the array A as you debug the steps in order to follow the execution of the program. It would be very useful to have a subroutine that would print the values in A in an easily readable form. Then, each time you want to see the values in A, you just insert the following statement in your program:

CALL PRINT (A,N)

In fact, you would probably want to include it in each loop initially. Then, as you verify that certain loops are working properly, you could remove the subroutine reference from those loops. There are ways to combine some of the steps outlined in this algorithm, but we have chosen not to combine them so that the algorithm will be easier to follow.

SELF-TEST 11-3

This self-test allows you to check quickly to see if you have remembered the key points from Section 11–3. If you have any problems with the exercises, you should reread this section. The solutions are included at the end of the text.

Use Gauss elimination to solve the following systems of equations:

1. $2x + y = 4$
   $x - y = -1$

2. $5x + 7y = 12$
   $7x + 10y = 17$

3. $x + y + z = 4$
   $2x + 3y + z = 9$
   $x - y - z = -12$

4. $4x - y + z = 4$
   $x + 6y + 2z = 9$
   $-x - 2y + 5z = 2$

11–4   APPLICATION—DEFORMABLE MIRRORS
(Optical Engineering)

One of the most interesting recent advances in the area of optics has been the development of deformable mirrors—mirrors whose surfaces can be reshaped by various techniques to correct for distortions in the optical path between the observer and the object being viewed. As an example, consider an astronomer who is observing the planet Saturn through a telescope, as shown in the following diagram:

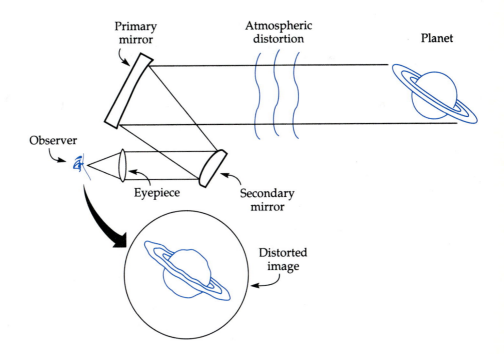

Because of atmospheric distortion caused by turbulence and pressure changes, and imperfections in the various optical elements of the telescope, the light rays are bent to various degrees such that the image of Saturn, as perceived by the astronomer, is distorted. The idea behind deformable mirrors, or "adaptive optics" as they are more generally called, is to somehow detect the distortion present and use that information to recontour one or more of the mirrors in the telescope to cancel the distortion, thereby presenting the viewer with an undistorted image.

One way this technique might be implemented is shown in the following diagram, in which a few new optical elements have been added to the previous diagram:

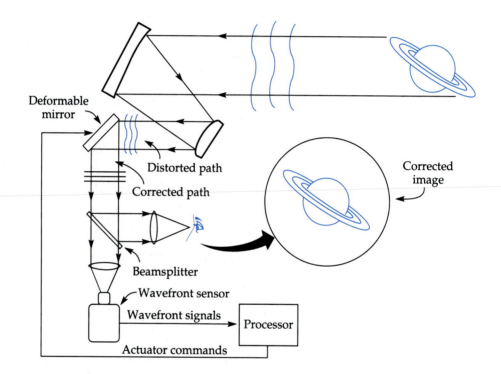

The new elements include a deformable mirror, a beamsplitter that enables a "wavefront sensor" to share the optical path with the observer, and a processor that provides the signals to shape the deformable mirror.

As seen in the diagram, the distorted image is reflected off the deformable mirror and sent to the beamsplitter. The beamsplitter, in turn, sends the image to the observer and the wavefront sensor. The wavefront sensor is a device that measures the distortion in the image. The distortion measurements are sent to a processor which determines the corrections needed to cancel the distortion and then sends the commands to the deformable mirror to reshape it.

The deformable mirror is one of the more interesting elements of the system. A sketch showing a square mirror having 25 actuators (movable elements) is shown in the following diagram:

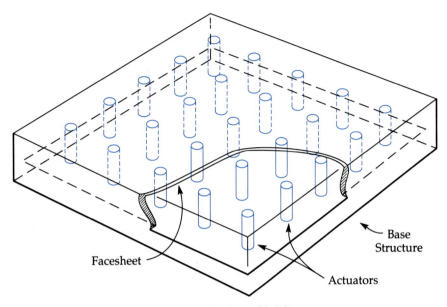

25-Actuator Deformable Mirror

The mirror uses a rigid base structure that supports the actuators. The actuators, along with the mirror's edge, support the relatively thin facesheet, which is a highly polished, extremely flat, metal or glass surface. The actuators can expand or contract slightly when a voltage is applied, thereby moving the facesheet. When the actuators are used in unison, they are capable of producing the optical corrections needed to obtain an undistorted image.

The process used to obtain the correct shape for the facesheet of the deformable mirror involves a number of steps, which can be summarized in a system of equations that need to be solved simultaneously. The coefficients of the system of equations represent the optical corrections that are needed and how the actuators interact with each other. The unknowns of the system of equations represent the voltages that need to be applied simultaneously to the actuators to produce the desired optical correction. Thus, the problem solution involves the solution of N simultaneous equations if there are N actuators in the mirror. The number of actuators in the deformable mirror in the diagram is 25, and thus a system of 25 equations with 25 unknowns would need to be solved in order to deform it properly. Clearly, the determinant method of Section 11−2 does not handle the complexity of this problem, so we use the Gauss elimination method presented in Section 11−3. The solution should be written to a data file because it will be the input to the program that controls the actuators.

PROBLEM STATEMENT

Write a program that solves a system of equations that determine the voltages for the actuators in a deformable mirror.

INPUT/OUTPUT DESCRIPTION

The input is contained in a data file MIRROR. The first line of the file contains the number of actuators for the mirror. The coefficients for each equation begin on a new line in the data file. The output is a data file containing the solution to the set of equations. The first line of the data file contains the number of equations in the system.

HAND EXAMPLE

Since the program is computing a Gauss elimination solution for a set of simultaneous equations, refer to the hand example in Section 11–3, page 494, to review Gauss elimination with a simple set of equations.

ALGORITHM DEVELOPMENT

The decomposition for this problem solution is the following:

DECOMPOSITION

Read mirror equation coefficients.
Solve system of equations.
Write actuator settings to data file.

Since we have already written and tested an algorithm for Gauss elimination, we only need to define the steps in the main program that read the data, reference the Gauss elimination routines developed in the previous section, and then write the answers to a data file.

REFINEMENT IN PSEUDOCODE

DEFORM: drows ← 25
                dcols ← 26
                Read n, the number of equations
                Read a, the augmented coefficients
                pivot ← 1
                error ← false

While pivot < n and no error do
    Call order (a,drows,dcols,n,pivot,error)
    If no error then
        Call elim (a,drows,dcols,n,pivot)
        pivot ← pivot + 1
If error then
    Print 'NO UNIQUE SOLUTION'
Else
    Call backsb (a,drows,dcols,n,soln)
    Print 'SOLUTION WRITTEN TO DATA FILE'
    Write n to data file
    Write soln values to data file

Routines ORDER, ELIM, and BACKSB are from Section 11–3. The structure chart and FORTRAN program are the following:

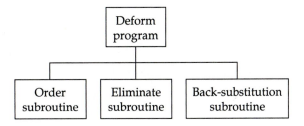

FORTRAN PROGRAM

```
*----------------------------------------------------------------*
      PROGRAM  DEFORM
*
*  This program uses the Gauss elimination method to
*  solve a set of simultaneous equations.
*
      INTEGER  DROWS, DCOLS, N, I, J, PIVOT
      REAL  A(25,26), SOLN(25)
      LOGICAL  ERROR
*
      DROWS = 25
      DCOLS = 26
      OPEN (UNIT=10,FILE='MIRROR',STATUS='OLD')
      READ (10,*) N
      DO 5 I=1,N
         READ (10,*) (A(I,J),J=1,N+1)
    5 CONTINUE
*
      PIVOT = 1
      ERROR = .FALSE.
   10 IF (PIVOT.LT.N.AND..NOT.ERROR) THEN
         CALL ORDER(A,DROWS,DCOLS,N,PIVOT,ERROR)
         IF (.NOT.ERROR) THEN
            CALL ELIM(A,DROWS,DCOLS,N,PIVOT)
            PIVOT = PIVOT + 1
         ENDIF
         GO TO 10
      ENDIF
*
```

```
            IF (ERROR) THEN
                PRINT*, 'NO UNIQUE SOLUTION EXISTS'
            ELSE
                CALL BACKSB(A,DROWS,DCOLS,N,SOLN)
                PRINT*, 'SOLUTION WRITTEN TO DATA FILE'
                OPEN (UNIT=11,FILE='ACTUATOR',STATUS='NEW')
                WRITE (11,*) N
                DO 20 I=1,N
                    WRITE (11,*) SOLN(I)
     20         CONTINUE
            ENDIF
            END
```

--

　　　(no changes in subroutine ORDER)

--

　　　(no changes in subroutine ELIM)

--

　　　(no changes in subroutine BACKSB)

--

TESTING

The following values represent data for a 25-actuator deformable mirror, and thus there are 25 equations in the system of equations:

```
25
20.00   1.69 -0.49   0.00   0.00   1.69   0.40 -0.10   0.00   0.00
-0.48 -0.10 -0.05   0.00   0.00   0.00   0.01   0.00   0.00   0.00
 0.00   0.00   0.00   0.00   0.00 -20.
 1.81 20.00   1.93 -0.47   0.00   0.28   1.76   0.66 -0.13   0.00
-0.48 -0.17 -0.18 -0.03   0.00   0.00   0.00   0.00   0.00   0.00
 0.00   0.00   0.00   0.00   0.00 -10.
-0.49   2.00 20.00   1.98 -0.48 -0.30   0.70   1.78   0.71 -0.31
-0.03 -0.21 -0.20 -0.19 -0.06   0.02   0.00 -0.01   0.00   0.00
 0.00   0.00   0.00   0.00   0.01   0.0
 0.01 -0.50   1.90 20.00   2.00   0.00 -0.16   0.72   1.77   0.29
 0.00 -0.05 -0.21 -0.19 -0.50   0.00   0.00 -0.01 -0.01   0.00
 0.00   0.00   0.00   0.01   0.00  10.
 0.00   0.01 -0.47   1.72 20.00   0.00   0.00 -0.11   0.39   1.70
 0.00   0.00 -0.04 -0.10 -0.52   0.00   0.00   0.00 -0.01 -0.02
 0.00   0.00   0.00   0.01   0.00  20.
 2.00   0.32 -0.48   0.00   0.00 20.00   1.78 -0.21 -0.01   0.00
 2.04   0.67 -0.22   0.00   0.00 -0.52 -0.15 -0.05   0.00   0.00
-0.01 -0.01   0.00   0.00   0.00 -20.
 0.79   3.52   1.00 -0.42   0.00   3.49 20.00   2.97 -0.23   0.01
 1.07   3.13   1.10 -0.18   0.00 -0.40 -0.18 -0.20 -0.04 -0.01
-0.01 -0.01 -0.02 -0.01   0.00 -10.
-0.37   0.75   3.40   0.77 -0.38 -0.58   3.02 20.00   2.99 -0.56
-0.47   0.97   2.85   0.96 -0.46 -0.02 -0.18 -0.21 -0.17 -0.03
 0.00   0.00 -0.01 -0.01   0.00   0.0
```

```
 0.00 -0.44   1.10   3.55   0.82   0.03 -0.22   3.13 20.00   3.57
 0.03 -0.23   1.21   3.21   0.96 -0.01 -0.08 -0.22 -0.21 -0.42
 0.00 -0.01 -0.03 -0.02 -0.02 10.
 0.00   0.01 -0.50   2.97   2.02   0.00   0.00 -0.20   1.84 20.00
 0.00   0.00 -0.20   0.67   1.99   0.00 -0.01 -0.05 -0.15 -0.50
 0.00   0.00   0.00 -0.01 -0.01 20.
-0.51 -0.30 -0.05   0.00   0.00   2.01   0.72 -0.20   0.00   0.00
20.00   1.76 -0.19   0.00   0.00   2.09   0.70 -0.21   0.00   0.00
-0.48 -0.30 -0.05   0.00   0.00 -20.
-0.43 -0.63 -0.52 -0.07   0.01   0.84   3.27   1.13 -0.24   0.00
 3.72 20.00   3.20 -0.23 -0.02   0.87   3.25   1.06 -0.20   0.02
-0.42 -0.62 -0.53 -0.07   0.00 -10.
-0.10 -0.50 -0.45 -0.47 -0.10 -0.49   1.20   3.19   1.20 -0.50
-0.45   3.16 20.00   3.18 -0.44 -0.48   1.22   3.21   1.23 -0.48
-0.10 -0.48 -0.45 -0.50 -0.08   0.0
 0.00 -0.04 -0.46 -0.57 -0.36   0.00 -0.18   0.99   3.03   0.77
 0.00 -0.16   2.70 20.00   3.55   0.00 -0.20   0.97   3.07   0.76
 0.00 -0.03 -0.47 -0.57 -0.38 10.
 0.00   0.00 -0.03 -0.26 -0.48   0.00   0.00 -0.17   0.66   1.88
 0.00   0.00 -0.18   1.80 20.00   0.00   0.00 -0.18   0.67   1.97
 0.00   0.00 -0.04 -0.28 -0.50 20.
-0.01   0.00   0.01   0.00   0.00 -0.50 -0.15 -0.04   0.00   0.00
 1.88   0.70 -0.20   0.00   0.00 20.00   1.77 -0.19 -0.01   0.00
 2.03   0.30 -0.51   0.00   0.00 -20.
 0.00 -0.02   0.00   0.00   0.00 -0.40 -0.20 -0.21 -0.05   0.00
 1.11   3.04   1.10 -0.19   0.00   3.46 20.00   3.00 -0.18   0.00
 0.78   3.51   1.05 -0.41   0.00 -10.
 0.00   0.01 -0.01   0.00   0.02 -0.04 -0.21 -0.18 -0.18 -0.06
-0.52   0.97   3.00   1.00 -0.47 -0.61   3.08 20.00   3.21 -0.61
-0.39   0.80   3.70   0.81 -0.41   0.0
 0.01   0.00   0.00   0.02   0.00   0.01 -0.08 -0.23 -0.21 -0.42
 0.03 -0.22   1.30   3.22   1.21 -0.02 -0.24   3.14 20.00   3.56
-0.02 -0.42   1.06   3.52   0.80 10.
 0.00   0.00   0.01   0.00   0.01   0.00   0.00 -0.06 -0.15 -0.50
 0.01   0.00 -0.20   0.71   2.10   0.00 -0.03 -0.21   1.82 20.00
 0.00   0.00 -0.50   0.32   2.03 20.
-0.01   0.00   0.02   0.00   0.01   0.00   0.00   0.00   0.00   0.00
-0.58 -0.13 -0.06   0.00   0.00   1.77   0.42 -0.12 -0.04   0.00
20.00   1.71 -0.52   0.00   0.00 -20.
 0.00   0.01   0.00   0.01   0.00   0.01   0.02   0.00   0.00   0.00
-0.50 -0.19 -0.20 -0.05   0.00   0.30   1.81   0.70 -0.16   0.00
 1.97 20.00   2.00 -0.48   0.00 -10.
 0.00   0.00   0.00   0.00   0.00   0.00   0.00   0.01   0.00   0.00
-0.03 -0.17 -0.18 -0.17 -0.03 -0.26   0.70   1.75   0.66 -0.27
-0.48   1.97 20.00   1.94 -0.46   0.0
 0.00   0.00   0.00   0.00   0.00   0.00   0.00   0.01 -0.01   0.00
 0.00 -0.04 -0.21 -0.20 -0.46   0.00 -0.16   0.69   1.80   0.30
-0.02 -0.51   1.91 20.00   2.02 10.
```

```
0.00   0.00   0.00   0.00   0.00   0.00   0.00   0.00  -0.01   0.01
0.00   0.00  -0.05  -0.11  -0.48   0.00   0.00  -0.11   0.39   1.70
0.00  -0.01  -0.51   1.70  20.00  20.
```

After running the program, the data file ACTUATOR is generated, which contains the solution to this set of simultaneous equations:

```
25
-.915546
-.403108
1.971845E-03
.393537
.923172
-.814070
-.167461
-3.078443E-03
.177356
.758083
-.854364
-.269669
-4.713885E-03
.285722
.868225
-.818150
-.170535
-1.285186E-03
.156909
.805012
-.917450
-.394034
1.204488E-03
.391093
.917205
```

11-5 GAUSS-SEIDEL METHOD

The Gauss elimination method presented in the previous two sections is a direct solution method which uses "triangularization" of the coefficient matrix and then back-substitution to solve for the unknowns. This method has the advantage of being a finite method that works, at least theoretically, for any nonsingular set of equations. In fact, for some sets of equations, Gauss elimination is the only practical available method. In practice, however, many systems of equations are sparse; that is, they contain a large proportion of zeros for the coefficients. If Gauss elimination is used on such a system, it usually produces a triangular matrix that is no longer sparse, and in the process of triangularizing the coefficient matrix, the computer introduces roundoff errors which may lead to significant errors in the final solution. Often, the accuracy of the solution can be improved significantly if we use an iterative method, such as the *Gauss-*

Seidel method. Unlike the Gauss elimination method, iterative methods do not produce any new nonzero elements in a sparse matrix and thus do not increase the computational burden. And, in general, the roundoff error for iterative methods is smaller than it is for Gauss elimination.

For iterative solutions to work, the set of equations to be solved must meet certain requirements. As was the case for Gauss elimination, the set of equations must be *nonsingular,* but it must also satisfy more complicated requirements for an iterative solution to converge. Determining whether the convergence requirements are met by a system of equations can be difficult, but, in general, the Gauss-Seidel method will converge if the diagonal terms are significantly larger than the off-diagonal terms for each row of the coefficient matrix. It will always converge if the absolute value of the diagonal term is greater than the sum of the absolute values of the off-diagonal terms for at least one row of the coefficient matrix and greater than or equal for the remaining rows. It will occasionally converge when these conditions are not met. Note that it may be possible to rearrange the rows and columns of the matrix to satisfy the convergence criteria.

To illustrate the Gauss-Seidel method, we begin with our familiar set of three simultaneous equations with three unknowns:

$$a_{11}x + a_{12}y + a_{13}z = b_1$$
$$a_{21}x + a_{22}y + a_{23}z = b_2$$
$$a_{31}x + a_{32}y + a_{33}z = b_3$$

We then solve the first equation for x in terms of y and z:

$$x = \frac{b_1 - a_{12}y - a_{13}z}{a_{11}} \tag{11--1}$$

Next, we solve the second equation for y in terms of x and z:

$$y = \frac{b_2 - a_{21}x - a_{23}z}{a_{22}} \tag{11--2}$$

We then solve the third equation for z in terms of x and y:

$$z = \frac{b_3 - a_{31}x - a_{32}y}{a_{33}} \tag{11--3}$$

Next, we make a first approximation to the solution, which we call x_1, y_1, and z_1. (Usually, we select zeros for the first approximation to the solution.) These first approximations are then used in Eq. (11--1) to compute a new approximation for x, which we call x_2:

$$x_2 = \frac{b_1 - a_{12}y_1 - a_{13}z_1}{a_{11}}$$

This second approximation of x, together with our first approximation of z, is used in Eq. (11–2) to compute the second approximation of y:

$$y_2 = \frac{b_2 - a_{21}x_2 - a_{23}z_1}{a_{22}}$$

The second approximation of z is similarly computed using the second approximations for x and y in Eq. (11–3):

$$z_2 = \frac{b_3 - a_{31}x_2 - a_{32}y_2}{a_{33}}$$

This completes the first iteration.

The next iteration begins with our new estimates: x_2, y_2, z_2. We proceed exactly as before, continuing until the technique has converged to a solution. In the technique we also specify an iteration tolerance and assume that convergence has occurred when the differences between the new estimates and the previous estimates for each variable are less than the iteration tolerance. The general equations for the Gauss-Seidel iterations are

$$x_{n+1} = \frac{b_1 - a_{12}y_n - a_{13}z_n}{a_{11}}$$

$$y_{n+1} = \frac{b_2 - a_{21}x_{n+1} - a_{23}z_n}{a_{22}}$$

$$z_{n+1} = \frac{b_3 - a_{31}x_{n+1} - a_{32}y_{n+1}}{a_{33}}$$

We now perform several iterations with a set of two equations to illustrate the steps:

$$\begin{aligned} 2x + y &= 4 \\ x - y &= -1 \end{aligned}$$

We rewrite these equations as

$$x = \frac{4 - y}{2}$$

$$y = \frac{-1 - x}{-1}$$

Our initial estimate of the solution is $x_1 = 0$ and $y_1 = 0$.

Iteration 1:

$$x_2 = \frac{4 - y_1}{2} = 2$$

$$y_2 = \frac{-1 - x_2}{-1} = 3$$

Iteration 2:

$$x_3 = \frac{4 - y_2}{2} = 0.5$$

$$y_3 = \frac{-1 - x_3}{-1} = 1.5$$

Iteration 3:

$$x_4 = \frac{4 - y_3}{2} = 1.25$$

$$y_4 = \frac{-1 - x_4}{-1} = 2.25$$

Thus, after 3 iterations, the solution has converged to $x = 1.25$, $y = 2.25$. After 23 iterations, the process converges to the exact solution of $x = 1$, $y = 2$, within a tolerance of 0.000001. In the next section we develop a program to perform the Gauss-Seidel technique.

SELF-TEST 11-4

This self-test allows you to check quickly to see if you have remembered the key points from Section 11–5. If you have any problems with the exercises, you should reread this section. The solutions are included at the end of the text.

Use the Gauss-Seidel method to compute the solution after 3 iterations for the following systems of equations, assuming that the first estimate is $x = 0$, $y = 0$.

1. $2x + y = 4$
    $x - y = -1$
2. $5x + 2y = 12$
    $7x + 10y = 17$

11–6   APPLICATION—ELECTRICAL CIRCUITS (Electrical Engineering)

A technique often used in the analysis of complex electrical circuit structures is the mesh-current method. It can be used to calculate the current in each window or "mesh" of a circuit such as the one shown below:

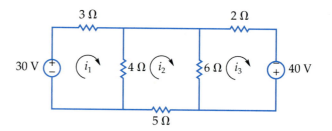

The voltage drops (or increases) across each element in a mesh are summed and set equal to zero to form an equation for each mesh. The resulting set of simultaneous equations is then solved for the currents within each mesh. For the circuit above, the mesh equations are

$$-30 + 3i_1 \qquad\quad +4(i_1 - i_2) = 0$$
$$4(i_2 - i_1) + 6(i_2 - i_3) + 5i_2 \qquad = 0$$
$$6(i_3 - i_2) + 2i_3 \qquad -40 \qquad = 0$$

Combining and rearranging the mesh equations results in a set of equations which meet the convergence properties described in the previous section for the Gauss-Seidel method:

$$7i_1 - 4i_2 + 0i_3 = 30$$
$$-4i_1 + 15i_2 - 6i_3 = 0$$
$$0i_1 - 6i_2 + 8i_3 = 40$$

Write a program which uses the Gauss-Seidel iterative method to solve this set of three simultaneous equations:

$$a_{11}i_1 + a_{12}i_2 + a_{13}i_3 = b_1$$
$$a_{21}i_1 + a_{22}i_2 + a_{23}i_3 = b_2$$
$$a_{31}i_1 + a_{32}i_2 + a_{33}i_3 = b_3$$

These equations can also be expressed in the following matrix form:

$$\mathbf{AX} = \mathbf{B}$$

where

$$\mathbf{A} = \begin{bmatrix} a_{11} & a_{12} & a_{13} \\ a_{21} & a_{22} & a_{23} \\ a_{31} & a_{32} & a_{33} \end{bmatrix} \qquad \mathbf{X} = \begin{bmatrix} i_1 \\ i_2 \\ i_3 \end{bmatrix} \qquad \mathbf{B} = \begin{bmatrix} b_1 \\ b_2 \\ b_3 \end{bmatrix}$$

Write a program which uses the Gauss-Seidel iterative method to solve a set of linear, simultaneous equations.

INPUT/OUTPUT DESCRIPTION

The inputs to the program are the number of equations and the coefficients for the equations. (We will write the program so that it can solve N simultaneous equations instead of just three equations.) In addition, the user enters the tolerance level to be used in testing for convergence and the maximum number of iterations to perform before assuming that the system is not converging. The output is the solution to the set of equations and the number of iterations required for the solution to converge. If the technique does not converge in the specified number of iterations, an appropriate message is printed.

HAND EXAMPLE

We perform the first two iterations for the set of data given at the beginning of this section, assuming that the initial solution contains all zeros. Starting with the three equations:

$$7i_1 - 4i_2 + 0i_3 = 30$$
$$-4i_1 + 15i_2 - 6i_3 = 0$$
$$0i_1 - 6i_2 + 8i_3 = 40$$

we rewrite them in the following form:

$$i_1 = \frac{30 + 4i_2}{7}$$

$$i_2 = \frac{4i_1 + 6i_3}{15}$$

$$i_3 = \frac{40 + 6i_2}{8}$$

Our initial estimate of the solution is $i_1 = i_2 = i_3 = 0$.

Iteration 1:

$$i_1 = \frac{(30 + 4 \cdot 0)}{7} = 4.29$$

$$i_2 = \frac{(4 \cdot 4.29 + 6 \cdot 0)}{15} = 1.14$$

$$i_3 = \frac{(40 + 6 \cdot 1.14)}{8} = 5.86$$

Iteration 2:

$$i_1 = \frac{(30 + 4 \cdot 1.14)}{7} = 4.94$$

$$i_2 = \frac{(4 \cdot 4.94 + 6 \cdot 5.86)}{15} = 3.66$$

$$i_3 = \frac{(40 + 6 \cdot 3.66)}{8} = 7.75$$

ALGORITHM DEVELOPMENT

The decomposition for this problem solution is the following:

DECOMPOSITION

Read coefficients, tolerance, maximum iterations.
Solve system and print solution.

Since reading the input information and printing the coefficient values takes a number of statements, we will use a subroutine to perform these steps. A separate subroutine will be used to read the tolerance and maximum iterations, because we want to use these steps at two places in our algorithm—once at the beginning of the program, and again after iterations are completed. (By calling this routine to read the tolerance and maximum iterations after we finish solving the system, we have an option to rerun the convergence using a smaller tolerance or more iterations if we want to obtain a more accurate solution.) We will use a two-dimensional array A to store the coefficient matrix and a one-dimensional array B to store the constant matrix. The variable N will contain the number of equations in the set, and the array X will represent the solution matrix.

REFINEMENT IN PSEUDOCODE

GS: drows ← 100
     dcols ← 100
     Read and print N and coefficient arrays A and B
     Read tolerance and max number of iterations

While tolerance > 0.0 do
 errormax ← tolerance + 1.0
 count ← 0
 Set values of array X to zero
 While count < max iterations and errormax > tolerance do
  errormax ← 0.0
  For i = 1 to N do
   sum ← 0.0
   For j = 1 to N do
    If j ≠ i then sum ← sum + A(i,j)·X(j)
   xnew ← (B(i)-sum)/A(i,i)
   error ← |xnew-X(i)|
   If error > errormax then errormax ← error
   X(i) ← xnew
  count ← count + 1
 If count ≥ max iterations then
  Print appropriate message
 Else
  Print solution
  Print count
 Read tolerance and max iterations

The structure chart and FORTRAN program for this solution are the following:

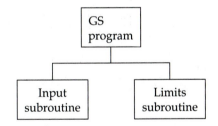

FORTRAN Program

```
*-----------------------------------------------------------*
      PROGRAM  GS
*
*  This program solves a set of N simultaneous equations
*  using the Gauss-Seidel method.
*
      INTEGER  DROWS, DCOLS, N, MAXIT, COUNT, I, J
      REAL  A(100,100), B(100), TOL, ERRMAX, X(100), SUM, XNEW, ERROR
*
      DROWS = 100
      DCOLS = 100
      CALL INPUT (N,A,B,DROWS,DCOLS)
      CALL LIMITS (TOL,MAXIT)
*
```

```
   20 IF (TOL.GT.0.0) THEN
          ERRMAX = TOL + 1.0
          COUNT = 0
          DO 25 I=1,N
             X(I) = 0.0
   25     CONTINUE
   30     IF (COUNT.LT.MAXIT.AND.ERRMAX.GT.TOL) THEN
             ERRMAX = 0.0
             DO 40 I=1,N
                SUM = 0.0
                DO 35 J=1,N
                   IF (J.NE.I) SUM = SUM + A(I,J)*X(J)
   35           CONTINUE
                XNEW = (B(I) - SUM)/A(I,I)
                ERROR = ABS(XNEW - X(I))
                IF (ERROR.GT.ERRMAX) ERRMAX = ERROR
                X(I) = XNEW
   40        CONTINUE
             COUNT = COUNT + 1
             GO TO 30
          ENDIF
          IF (COUNT.GE.MAXIT) THEN
             PRINT*
             PRINT*, 'NUMBER OF ITERATIONS EXCEEDED LIMIT'
          ELSE
             PRINT*
             PRINT*,'SOLUTION IS:'
             DO 45 I=1,N
                PRINT*, 'X(',I,') = ',X(I)
   45        CONTINUE
             PRINT*
             PRINT*, 'NUMBER OF ITERATIONS = ', COUNT
          ENDIF
          CALL LIMITS (TOL, MAXIT)
          GO TO 20
      ENDIF
      END
*-------------------------------------------------------------*
      SUBROUTINE  INPUT (N,A,B,DROWS,DCOLS)
*
*  This subroutine asks the user for the equation information.
*
      INTEGER  DROWS, DCOLS, N, I, J
      REAL  A(DROWS,DCOLS), B(DROWS)
*
      PRINT*, 'ENTER NUMBER OF EQUATIONS'
      READ*, N
      DO 5 I=1,N
         PRINT*
         PRINT*, 'ENTER',N+1,' COEFFICIENTS FOR EQUATION ',I
         READ*, (A(I,J),J=1,N), B(I)
    5 CONTINUE
      PRINT*
      PRINT*, 'COEFFICIENTS ARE:'
      DO 15 I=1,N
         PRINT*, 'ROW ',I,':'
         PRINT 10, (A(I,J),J=1,N), B(I)
   10    FORMAT(1X,7F10.2)
   15 CONTINUE
*
```

```
        RETURN
        END
*----------------------------------------------------------------*
        SUBROUTINE  LIMITS (TOL,MAXIT)
*
*  This subroutine asks the user for tolerance and maximum iterations.
*
        INTEGER  MAXIT
        REAL   TOL
*
        PRINT*
        PRINT*, 'ENTER ERROR TOLERANCE AND MAXIMUM NUMBER OF ITERATIONS'
        PRINT*, '(ENTER ZEROS TO QUIT)'
        READ*, TOL, MAXIT
*
        RETURN
        END
*----------------------------------------------------------------*
```

TESTING

Using the set of data from the electrical circuit in this program gives the
following results:

```
ENTER NUMBER OF EQUATIONS
3

ENTER  4 COEFFICIENTS FOR EQUATION 1
7 -4 0 30

ENTER  4 COEFFICIENTS FOR EQUATION 2
-4 15 -6 0

ENTER  4 COEFFICIENTS FOR EQUATION 3
0 -6 8 40

COEFFICIENTS ARE:
ROW  1:
      7.00      -4.00       0.00      30.00
ROW  2:
     -4.00      15.00      -6.00       0.00
ROW  3:
      0.00      -6.00       8.00      40.00

ENTER ERROR TOLERANCE AND MAXIMUM NUMBER OF ITERATIONS
(ENTER ZEROS TO QUIT)
0.1 100

SOLUTION IS:
X( 1) =   7.51546
X( 2) =   5.69974
X( 3) =   9.27480

NUMBER OF ITERATIONS = 7

ENTER ERROR TOLERANCE AND MAXIMUM NUMBER OF ITERATIONS
(ENTER ZEROS TO QUIT)
0.0 0.0
```

Since we used list-directed output statements, the output will vary somewhat from computer to computer.

If we use the set of equations presented at the beginning of Section 11–3 (Gauss Elimination), we find that the Gauss-Seidel method does not converge if the tolerance is a small number. This is not surprising since the matrix of coefficients does not meet the conditions that were given for determining whether the Gauss-Seidel method would converge.

SUMMARY

Matrices are structures used in many engineering applications to store data. In this chapter we saw that a two-dimensional array can be used to represent a matrix, and we developed a number of modules to perform operations with matrices. A common engineering problem that uses matrices in its solution is the problem of finding the solution to a system of simultaneous equations. We presented three techniques in this chapter for solving simultaneous equations. The first, and simplest method, uses Cramer's rule and is simple to apply when we have three simultaneous equations. If we have more than three simultaneous equations, there are better methods to use. The Gauss elimination method is a method that works for any nonsingular set of equations. The process performs a number of operations on the matrix that contains the coefficients from the simultaneous equations and arrives at a solution. We also presented another method, Gauss-Seidel, which is an iterative solution that converges only for special systems of equations; however, when the Gauss-Seidel method can be applied, the solution typically requires fewer computations.

DEBUGGING AIDS

When debugging programs with matrices, it is imperative to have a routine that prints the matrices in an easy-to-read format. Then, as we are debugging, we can use statements to call the print routine each time that we need to check the contents of the array. Once the program is debugged, the calls to the print routine can be removed. These types of routines are often called snapshot routines, because they give us a snapshot of the situation at the time that the routine is referenced. Both the Gauss elimination method and the Gauss-Seidel method are multistep methods, and debugging multistep methods can be very difficult. Start by using a very simple example that you have worked out ahead of time, and compare your hand solution to the output from the snapshot routine to slowly and carefully debug the iterative process.

STYLE/TECHNIQUE GUIDES

When working with large amounts of data (as in the solution of simultaneous equations), it is important that the data be handled carefully. The style and technique that one uses for handling the data can make working with the data easier or harder. A simple style with good documentation helps avoid problems such as those caused by entering data in the wrong order. Once you decide on a simple and straightforward way of dealing with matrices (or other data structures), use the method each time you work with matrices. Do not change your style each time you write a new program; it will be easier for you to write programs using the same techniques, and it will be easier for others to use your programs if the user interactions are similar.

ERROR ANALYSIS

When using the computer, our computations with real numbers almost always incorporate *roundoff errors,* which occur when we truncate an arithmetic result to a fixed number of digits of accuracy or precision. These roundoff errors, which are dependent on the number of digits of accuracy, contribute to the absolute and relative errors discussed in the previous chapter. We present four guidelines for reducing roundoff errors in computations. To illustrate these guidelines, we use examples with three-digit precision. Recall that real numbers are stored in exponential form, and we begin counting digits of precision with the first nonzero digit.

Our first guideline relates to adding (or subtracting) long lists of numbers. To reduce roundoff errors, work with smaller numbers first. You may even want to sort the numbers and then begin adding with the smallest values. To illustrate, consider the following set of numbers:

$$0.0336$$
$$0.0356$$
$$0.3290$$
$$0.5190$$

If we add these values by hand, the sum is 0.9172. If we add these numbers as the computer would, we add them two at a time, with each partial sum being truncated to three digits of precision. This process is illlustrated in two ways: with the addition starting with the smallest numbers on the left side and the addition starting with the largest numbers on the right side. As you can see, the more accurate sum started with the smaller numbers:

ADDING FROM TOP	ADDING FROM BOTTOM
0.0336	0.519
+0.0356	+0.329
0.0692	0.848
+0.329	+0.0356
0.398	0.883
+0.519	+0.0336
0.917	0.916

The second guideline relates to numbers of nearly equal value. If possible, avoid subtracting numbers with nearly equal values. Sometimes, expressions can be written to avoid this subtraction; for example, consider the expression

$$a + b + (c - d)$$

If c and d are nearly equal in value, we can rewrite the expression as

$$(a + c) + (b - d)$$

As a specific example, assume again that we are working with three-digit precision and that the variables have the following values:

$$a = 0.919, b = 0.829, c = 0.0356, d = 0.0330$$

We now substitute these values in both expressions and truncate all intermediate steps to three digits. The correct value is 1.7506, but only one of the computations gives this result accurate to three-digit precision:

$$
\begin{array}{ll}
a + b + (c - d) & 0.919 + 0.829 \;\;= 1.74 \\
& 0.0356 - 0.0330 = 0.00260 \\
& \qquad\qquad\qquad = 1.74 \\
(a + c) + (b - d) & 0.919 + 0.0356 = 0.954 \\
& 0.829 - 0.0330 = 0.796 \\
& \qquad\qquad\qquad = 1.75
\end{array}
$$

The third guideline relates to minimizing the number of arithmetic operations. Because precision errors can occur with each operation, we minimize these effects when we minimize the number of operations. For example, the following expressions are equivalent, but the one on the left uses two operations and the one on the right uses three operations:

$$3 \cdot X \cdot Y \qquad (X + X + X) \cdot Y$$

The final guideline for reducing roundoff errors is to use double-precision variables for all computations and then display the final results to the desired accuracy.

KEY WORDS

Cramer's rule
determinant
dot product
Gauss elimination
Gauss-Seidel method
matrix

matrix multiplication
nonsingular
roundoff error
scalar multiplication
simultaneous equations
vector

PROBLEMS

We begin our problem set with modifications to programs developed earlier in this chapter. Give the decomposition, refined pseudocode or flowchart, and FORTRAN solution for each problem.

Problems 1–5 modify the program EQN3, given on page 490, which uses Cramer's rule to solve a system of three simultaneous equations.

1. Modify the solution program so that the data are read from a data file instead of from the terminal.

2. Modify the solution program so that the set of equations is printed after the user has entered all the coefficients.

3. Modify the solution program so that the solution to the equations is substituted in each equation and the results are printed to verify that the solution is correct.

4. Modify the solution program so that it will allow the user to specify that one or more of the coefficients was entered incorrectly and then accept corrections.

5. Modify the solution program so that it determines whether two of the equations represent the same plane when the determinant is equal to zero. In these cases, print an additional message that specifies which of the planes are the same. Recall that a plane can be represented by two different equations if one equation is simply the other equation multiplied by a constant. Thus, the following equations represent the same plane:

$$3x + 2y - z = 5$$
$$6x + 4y - 2z = 10$$

Problems 6–10 modify the program DEFORM, given on page 505, which uses Gauss elimination to solve a set of simultaneous equations.

6. Modify the Gauss elimination program so that the reorder subroutine prints a message specifying which rows were switched.

7. Modify the Gauss elimination program so that it includes a debugging subroutine PRINT that will print the values in the A array in an easily readable form.

8. Modify the Gauss elimination program so that the steps to print the solution are printed in a subroutine rather than in the main program.

9. Modify the Gauss elimination program so that the data are read by a subroutine instead of the main program. The subroutine should ask the user to enter the name of the file and then open the file, read the data, and close the file from the subroutine.

10. Modify the Gauss elimination program so that it writes the solution to the set of simultaneous equations to a data file. The first line of the data file should contain the number of actuators, and each actuator number and its corresponding setting should be on a separate line in the file.

Problems 11–15 modify the program GS, given on page 515, which uses the Gauss-Seidel method to solve a set of simultaneous equations.

11. Modify the Gauss-Seidel program so that it reads the input from a data file and writes the output to a data file.

12. Modify the Gauss-Seidel program so that it allows the user to specify the initial values used for the variables.

13. Modify the Gauss-Seidel program so that it calls a subroutine to determine whether or not the coefficients meet the conditions to guarantee convergence. Print a message to the user that the set of equations may not converge if the conditions are not met.

14. Modify the Gauss-Seidel program so that it prints the results at the end of every iteration.

15. Modify the Gauss-Seidel program so that it prints the maximum error value (the maximum change in variable value) for each iteration.

In problems 16–18, develop programs and modules using the five-phase design process. Use the modules developed in this chapter for matrix operations as much as possible in your designs.

16. Write a subroutine to compute the transpose of an integer matrix, where a transpose is defined as another matrix that is generated by exchanging the rows and columns of the original matrix. An example of a matrix **A** and its transpose is

$$
A = \begin{bmatrix} 2 & 5 & 1 & 1 \\ 3 & 1 & 0 & 5 \\ 8 & 9 & 9 & 4 \end{bmatrix}
\quad \text{Transpose of } A = \begin{bmatrix} 2 & 3 & 8 \\ 5 & 1 & 9 \\ 1 & 0 & 9 \\ 1 & 5 & 4 \end{bmatrix}
$$

The subroutine would be called with the following statement, where **T** is the transpose of **A**; ANR, ANC, TNR, TNC represent the operational sizes of **A** and **T**; and AROW, ACOLS, TROWS, TCOLS represent the dimensional sizes of **A** and **T**:

```
CALL TRANSP (A,ANR,ANC,AROWS,ACOLS,
             T,TNR,TNC,TROWS,TCOLS)
```

17. Write a subroutine that normalizes the values in a matrix **A** to values between 0 and 1 by replacing each value with the following:

$$
a_{i,j} \leftarrow \frac{a_{i,j} - \text{minimum}}{\text{maximum} - \text{minimum}}
$$

where the minimum is the minimum value in the matrix and the maximum is the maximum value in the matrix. Thus, the maximum value is scaled to 1, the minimum value is scaled to 0, and all values in between are scaled accordingly. Assume that the subroutine is called with the following statement, where **NA** represents the normalized matrix:

```
CALL NORM(A,NA,NR,NC,DROWS,DCOLS)
```

Also assume that NR and NC represent the operational sizes of both matrices and that DROWS and DCOLS represent the dimensional sizes of both matrices.

18. Write a subroutine that multiplies a coefficient matrix **A** by a solution matrix **X**. The result should be equivalent to the constant matrix **B**. Hence, this subroutine could be used in debugging a program to solve a system of simultaneous equations. Use the following statement to reference the subroutine:

```
CALL CALCB (A,NR,NC,DROWS,DCOLS,X,B)
```

Assume that NR and NC represent the operational size of **A** and that DROWS and DCOLS represent the dimensional size of **A**. NR represents the operational size of both **X** and **B**.

APPLICATION—Wind Tunnel Data (Aerospace Engineering)

Wind tunnel data typically consist of very accurate measurements of the lift and drag forces generated by a moving air stream on an aerodynamic body. For example, to measure aerodynamic data for a new aircraft shape, an accurate scale model of the aircraft is mounted on a force-measuring support in the wind tunnel test chamber. The wind tunnel is then operated to generate a certain wind speed, or Mach number (which is the wind speed divided by the speed of sound), and measurements of the forces on the model are then made at many different angles of the model relative to the wind direction. The Mach number is then adjusted to a new value, and another data set is collected. At the end of the tests, many sets of data have been collected and can be used to determine the lift, drag, and other aerodynamic performance characteristics of the new aircraft at its various operating speeds and positions. Write a program using linear interpolation to estimate data values between the measured data points. (See Section 12–2 for the solution.)

Photo courtesy of NASA.

12

CURVE FITTING AND INTERPOLATION

Introduction

12–1 Linear Interpolation

12–2 Application—Wind Tunnel Data (Aerospace Engineering)

12–3 Cubic Spline Interpolation

12–4 Application—Robot Path Generation (Robotic Engineering)

12–5 Discussion of Single Polynomial Interpolation

12–6 Least-Squares Methods

12–7 Application—Accelerometer Model (Mechanical Engineering)

Summary

INTRODUCTION

Curve fitting and *interpolation* are two numerical techniques which are used together to enable us to estimate unknown values of a function by using known values of the function at specific points. The many methods which are available for curve fitting and interpolation differ only in the way they utilize the known values of the function, but the success with which they are able to estimate missing values of the function can vary greatly. As a result, the interpolation function selected for use should be the one that best represents the function. For example, if the known points of the function appear to fall close to a straight line, as depicted in the figure below, then a linear interpolation function would be a good choice.

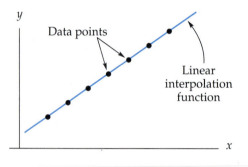

If the known points do not appear to be close to a straight line, then a polynomial function or another nonlinear function may be a better choice for an interpolation function, as shown in the next diagram:

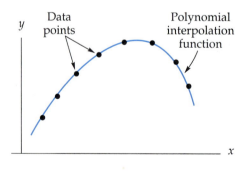

There are two basic categories of curve-fitting methods: those where the curves pass through the data points and those where, in general, the curves do not pass through the data points. The reason for the two categories lies in the nature of the data. If the data points represent accurate values of the function, and we believe that the function should be represented by a curve that passes through those points, then certain curve-fitting methods are applicable. If, on the other hand, we believe that because of noise, measurement error, etc., the data points only approximate the function, then we should use other types of curve-fitting methods. Thus, determining which method to use often requires some knowledge of the physical process that generated the known values of the function.

The first methods discussed are linear interpolation and cubic spline interpolation, which are the most popular methods employing curves which pass through the data points. For curves which do not pass through the data points, least-squares curve-fitting methods are discussed.

12–1   LINEAR INTERPOLATION

The easiest and probably the most popular interpolation method is *linear interpolation*. Essentially, all that is involved is connecting the data points with straight line segments and then interpolating for unknown values of the function on the straight line segments which connect adjacent data points. For example, consider the following graph, which contains two values of a function at $x = 1$ and at $x = 3$. These two points have been connected with a straight line:

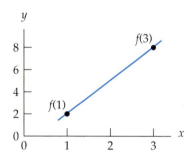

We can use linear interpolation to estimate the value of the function at $x = 1.5$ using similar triangles, as shown in the following graph:

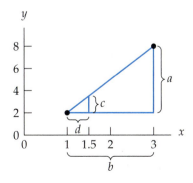

Thus,

$$\frac{a}{b} = \frac{c}{d}$$

or

$$\frac{f(3) - f(1)}{3 - 1} = \frac{f(1.5) - f(1)}{1.5 - 1}$$

If we solve this equation for $f(1.5)$, we have

$$f(1.5) - f(1) = \frac{(1.5 - 1) \cdot (f(3) - f(1))}{3 - 1}$$

or

$$f(1.5) = f(1) + \frac{(1.5 - 1) \cdot (f(3) - f(1))}{3 - 1}$$

$$= 2 + \frac{(0.5) \cdot (8 - 2)}{2}$$

$$= 3.5$$

We can develop a general linear interpolation formula for finding a function value $f(x)$ when x is between a and b and when the values of $f(a)$ and $f(b)$ are known. This formula is essentially the formula used in the previous example. It calculates the portion of the difference between the values on the x axis and then adds the corresponding portion of the difference between the values on the y axis to the leftmost function value:

$$f(x) = f(a) + \frac{(x - a)}{(b - a)} (f(b) - f(a))$$

This general formula works for linear interpolation of straight lines with either positive or negative slopes.

The application in the next section provides an example of the use of linear interpolation to find additional values from wind tunnel test data.

SELF-TEST 12–1

This self-test allows you to check quickly to see if you have remembered the key points from Section 12–1. If you have any problems with the exercises, you should reread this section. The solutions are included at the end of the text.

The following set of data was collected from an experiment:

TIME	TEMPERATURE (DEGREES F)
8:00	56
8:15	62
8:45	73
9:12	79
9:50	83
10:15	80

We assume that the temperature function with respect to time is approximately linear between individual measurements. Use linear interpolation to estimate the temperatures at the following times:

1. 8:10
2. 9:00
3. 9:15
4. 9:30

If the temperature function with respect to time is approximately linear between individual measurements, then the time function with respect to temperature is also approximately linear between individual measurements. Use linear interpolation to estimate the time values associated with the following temperatures:

5. 60 degrees
6. 75 degrees
7. 76 degrees
8. 81 degrees

(There are two answers to problem 8.)

12–2 APPLICATION—WIND TUNNEL DATA (Aerospace Engineering)

Wind tunnel data typically consist of numerous very accurate measurements of the lift and drag forces generated by a moving air stream on an aerodynamic body. For example, to measure aerodynamic data for a new aircraft shape, an accurate scale model of the aircraft is mounted on a force-measuring support in the wind tunnel test chamber. The wind tunnel is then operated to generate a certain wind speed, or Mach number (which is the wind speed divided by the speed of sound), and measurements of the forces on the model are then made at many different angles of the model relative to the wind direction. The Mach number is then adjusted to a new value, and another data set is collected. At the end of the tests, many sets of data have been collected and can be used to determine the lift, drag, and other aerodynamic performance characteristics of the new aircraft at its various operating speeds and positions.

When the data are subsequently used in engineering analyses, linear interpolation is frequently a good method for estimating values between the measured data points. In this section, we use a set of lift data on an aircraft wing. The 17 points in the data file are tabulated and plotted below to show the "coefficient of lift," C_L, at various flight path angles of the wing for a Mach number of 0.3. It is easy to judge from the appearance of the data that linear interpolation provides a reasonably accurate method of estimating the lift coefficient at points between the data points, even in the region where the function is curved.

WIND TUNNEL DATA

FLIGHT PATH ANGLE	COEFFICIENT OF LIFT
−4	−0.202
−2	−0.050
0	0.108
2	0.264
4	0.421
6	0.573
8	0.727
10	0.880
12	1.027
14	1.150
15	1.195
16	1.225
17	1.244
18	1.250
19	1.245
20	1.221
21	1.177

Flight Path Angle (Degrees)

Write a program to read the data from a data file called LIFT. The first line in the data file contains the number of data pairs. Each successive line in the data file contains two numbers, where the first value represents alpha, the flight path angle in degrees, and the second value contains C_L, the coefficient of lift measured during the wind tunnel test for the corresponding angle. Assume that the data pairs contained in the data file are in ascending order based on alpha, with the smallest value of alpha first and the largest value of alpha last.

The program should then read a value of alpha entered from the keyboard for which we need to know the interpolated value of C_L. Using the algorithm shown in the previous section, the program should interpolate for the lift coefficient, print the value of alpha and the corresponding estimate of C_L, and then prompt us for a new value of alpha. If we enter a value of alpha which is outside the range of the data, the program should print a message that the requested value is not within the interpolation region. The program terminates when we enter a value of 999.0 for alpha.

PROBLEM STATEMENT

Using linear interpolation with a wind tunnel data file, compute the lift coefficients which correspond to specified flight path angles.

INPUT/OUTPUT DESCRIPTION

The inputs to the program are the wind tunnel data file and the values of alpha for which we need the interpolated value of C_L. The output is a list of the input values of alpha and the corresponding values of C_L.

The data file that we use for testing contains the 17 data points given at the beginning of this section. Assume that we want to estimate the value of C_L which corresponds to alpha $= 6.3$. Using this data file and the linear interpolation formula from the previous section, the estimated value of C_L is

$$C_L = 0.573 + \frac{6.3 - 6}{8 - 6}(0.727 - 0.573)$$
$$= 0.573 + 0.15(0.154)$$
$$= 0.596$$

ALGORITHM DEVELOPMENT

The decomposition of our solution in general steps is the following:

DECOMPOSITION

Read data file.
Read angles and interpolate coefficients.

As we refine these steps, remember that we need to determine whether the input value of alpha is within the interpolation region. We can do this by checking to see if alpha is between the first flight path angle and the last flight path angle in the data file. If the input value of alpha is not within this allowable interpolation region, we print a message. We also need to check for an input alpha value of 999 so that we can terminate the program.

REFINEMENT IN PSEUDOCODE

WIND: Read N, the number of data pairs
      Read data file into arrays A and C
      Read input angle alpha
      While alpha $\neq$ 999 do
          If A(1) $\leq$ alpha $\leq$ A(N) then
              Find k such that A(k-1) $\leq$ alpha $\leq$ A(k)
              Interpolate for C_L

$$C_L \leftarrow C(k\text{-}1) + \frac{alpha - A(k - 1)}{A(k) - A(k - 1)} \cdot (C(k) - C(k - 1))$$

              Print alpha, C_L
          Else
              Print message that alpha is out of range
          Read new input angle alpha

We now convert the refined pseudocode into FORTRAN.

FORTRAN Program

```
*-------------------------------------------------------------*
      PROGRAM  WIND
*
*  This program reads a file of wind tunnel test data and then
*  uses linear interpolation to compute lift coefficients for
*  additional flight angles.
*
      INTEGER  N, K
      REAL  A(500), C(500), ALPHA, CL
*
      OPEN (UNIT=10,FILE='LIFT',STATUS='OLD')
      READ (10,*) N
      DO 5 K=1,N
         READ (10,*) A(K), C(K)
    5 CONTINUE
*
      PRINT*, 'ENTER FLIGHT PATH ANGLE IN DEGREES'
      READ*, ALPHA
   10 IF (ALPHA.NE.999.0) THEN
         IF (A(1).LE.ALPHA.AND.ALPHA.LE.A(N)) THEN
            K = 1
   15       IF (A(K).LT.ALPHA) THEN
               K = K+1
               GO TO 15
            ENDIF
            CL = C(K-1) + (ALPHA - A(K-1))/(A(K) - A(K-1))
     +                    *(C(K) - C(K-1))
            PRINT 20, ALPHA, CL
   20       FORMAT (1X,'FLIGHT ANGLE = ',F7.2/
     +              1X,'CORRESPONDING COEFFICIENT OF LIFT = ',F7.3)
         ELSE
            PRINT*,'ANGLE OUT OF RANGE FOR DATA FILE'
         ENDIF
         PRINT*
         PRINT*, 'ENTER FLIGHT PATH ANGLE IN DEGREES'
         PRINT*, '(999.0 TO QUIT)'
         READ*, ALPHA
         GO TO 10
      ENDIF
*
      END
*-------------------------------------------------------------*
```

We have specified 500 values for arrays A and C, but these can be increased if we expect to need more values.

TESTING

Using the data file given at the beginning of this section, we tested the program with several values of alpha, including values outside the range of the data file. The interaction with the program is shown below:

```
ENTER FLIGHT PATH ANGLE IN DEGREES
6.3
FLIGHT ANGLE =      6.30
CORRESPONDING COEFFICIENT OF LIFT =    0.596

ENTER FLIGHT PATH ANGLE IN DEGREES
(999.0 TO QUIT)
20.5
FLIGHT ANGLE =     20.50
CORRESPONDING COEFFICIENT OF LIFT =    1.199

ENTER FLIGHT PATH ANGLE IN DEGREES
(999.0 TO QUIT)
-5
ANGLE OUT OF RANGE FOR DATA FILE

ENTER FLIGHT PATH ANGLE IN DEGREES
(999.0 TO QUIT)
22.5
ANGLE OUT OF RANGE FOR DATA FILE

ENTER FLIGHT PATH ANGLE IN DEGREES
(999.0 TO QUIT)
-4
FLIGHT ANGLE =     -4.00
CORRESPONDING COEFFICIENT OF LIFT =   -0.202

ENTER FLIGHT PATH ANGLE IN DEGREES
(999.0 TO QUIT)
21
FLIGHT ANGLE =     21.00
CORRESPONDING COEFFICIENT OF LIFT =    1.177

ENTER FLIGHT PATH ANGLE IN DEGREES
(999.0 TO QUIT)
10
FLIGHT ANGLE =     10.00
CORRESPONDING COEFFICIENT OF LIFT =    0.880

ENTER FLIGHT PATH ANGLE IN DEGREES
(999.0 TO QUIT)
999.0
```

Note that the first value computed by the program is the same value that we computed in the hand example. Also note that we tested all the special cases, including values of alpha that are out of range, values at the endpoints, and values at a data point.

12-3 CUBIC SPLINE INTERPOLATION

In the figure below, a set of data is shown from an unknown function $f(x)$ that is drawn as a solid line. If we used the linear interpolation method of the previous section to approximate $f(x)$, as shown by the dashed line segments connecting the data points in the figure, the estimates we would obtain for $f(x)$ would not be very accurate for many values of x. The problem with using linear interpolation on this set of data is that the function curves too much between the data points, and as a result straight line segments do not adequately represent the shape of the function.

Polynomial functions can be used to generate smooth curves, and as a result they are the most commonly used functions for interpolation methods. In fact, the straight lines used for linear interpolation are actually first-degree polynomials. If we want the interpolation function to curve between the data points, higher-degree polynomials are needed.

To illustrate the use of a polynomial interpolation function, we will construct a curve called a *"cubic spline,"* which consists of a group of third-degree *(cubic) polynomials*—one for each of the intervals between data points. The equations of these cubic polynomials are developed such that when they are drawn between the data points the resulting curve has a smooth continuous appearance from the first point to the last point. To understand the steps involved, a brief discussion of the origin of the cubic spline method is helpful.

Cubic splines are a relatively new mathematical implementation of a drafting procedure known as lofting, which has long been used to draw the smooth curved lines of such things as the surfaces of airplanes and ships. An example of lofting is shown in the historical photograph below:

Reference points are marked on the surface, and flexible wood or plastic strips, called splines, are then held in place at the reference points using lead or cast iron weights, called ducks, to form curved guides for drawing. The spline is actually a very uniform, slender beam which bends when forces are placed on it by the ducks. The equations used for a cubic spline approximate the equations that describe the curve of an actual spline. Therefore, cubic splines and data points mathematically represent the plastic splines and ducks.

To better understand the process of designing a cubic spline for a set of data, we look more closely at a curve which was drawn using a plastic spine:

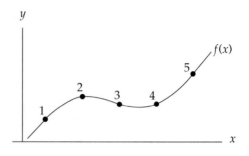

The equations for the cubic spline, which approximates the curve drawn using the plastic spline, are determined by the five data points shown on the curve. These points are used to calculate the parameters of four cubic polynomials (one for each of the four intervals) whose form is

$$y = Ax^3 + Bx^2 + Cx + D$$

One polynomial describes the curve between points 1 and 2; another describes the curve between points 2 and 3; another describes the curve between points 3 and 4; and another describes the curve between points 4 and 5. Looking closely at the curve, we see that these cubic polynomials have to satisfy the following set of requirements:

1. The curves must meet each other exactly at the data points in order to have a continuous cubic spline.
2. The *slopes* of the curves must match at the data points to avoid sharp corners in the spline. This requires the first derivatives of the spline to match at the data points.
3. The *curvature*, or bending in each curve, varies between the data points but must match the curvature of the adjacent curves at the data points. This requires the second derivatives of the spline to match at the data points.
4. The second derivative of the spline at the first and last data points must be zero. This requirement generates a "natural" spline, which corresponds to the plastic or wood spline, which becomes a straight line when it reaches the end ducks. The second derivative of a straight line is equal to zero.

These simple but important requirements are used to derive the equations for the polynomials that will be used to construct the cubic spline. We will not present a complete derivation of the final equations here; instead, we summarize the final equations for constructing the cubic spline.

Assume that we have n data points and that these n data points define $n - 1$ intervals. In the sketch below, the kth interval is bounded by data points (x_k, y_k) and (x_{k+1}, y_{k+1}). The interval width is h_k, which is $x_{k+1} - x_k$.

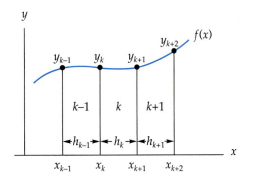

We first generate a set of slopes S_k, for $k = 1$ to $n - 1$, where

$$S_k = \frac{y_{k+1} - y_k}{x_{k+1} - x_k}$$

$$= \frac{y_{k+1} - y_k}{h_k}$$

These slopes are used along with the four requirements specified for the cubic spline to generate a set of $n - 2$ equations of the form

$$R_{k-1}h_{k-1} + 2R_k(h_{k-1} + h_k) + R_{k+1}h_k = 6(S_k - S_{k-1})$$

where R_k is the second derivative or "curvature" of the spline at point k. These equations represent a set of $n - 2$ simultaneous equations which can be solved for the $n - 2$ unknowns R_2 through R_{n-1}. This system of equations can be written in the following matrix form:

$$
\begin{bmatrix}
2(h_1 + h_2) & h_2 & 0 & 0 & 0 & 0 \\
h_2 & 2(h_2 + h_3) & h_3 & \cdot & \cdot & \cdot \\
0 & h_3 & 2(h_3 + h_4) & \cdot & \cdot & \cdot \\
0 & 0 & h_4 & \cdot & \cdot & \cdot \\
0 & 0 & 0 & \cdots & 0 & 0 & 0 \\
\cdot & \cdot & \cdot & h_{n-4} & 0 & 0 \\
\cdot & \cdot & \cdot & 2(h_{n-4} + h_{n-3}) & h_{n-3} & 0 \\
\cdot & \cdot & \cdot & h_{n-3} & 2(h_{n-3} + h_{n-2}) & h_2 \\
0 & 0 & 0 & 0 & h_{n-2} & 2(h_{n-2} + h_{n-1})
\end{bmatrix}
\begin{bmatrix}
R_2 \\
R_3 \\
R_4 \\
\cdot \\
\cdot \\
\cdot \\
R_{n-3} \\
R_{n-2} \\
R_{n-1}
\end{bmatrix}
= 6
\begin{bmatrix}
S_2 - S_1 \\
S_3 - S_2 \\
S_4 - S_3 \\
\cdot \\
\cdot \\
\cdot \\
S_{n-3} - S_{n-4} \\
S_{n-2} - S_{n-3} \\
S_{n-1} - S_{n-2}
\end{bmatrix}
$$

$$(12-1)$$

A set of equations like this, having coefficients arranged in a band along the main diagonal and zeros outside this band, is called a *tridiagonal system*. These systems appear frequently in many types of engineering problems. Gauss elimination is a good way to solve these systems, even though they are sparse, because their structure causes them to remain sparse as they are solved.

Once we solve the system of equations, we have values for the curvatures R_2 through R_{n-1}. Since we are generating a natural spline, the curvature values for R_1 and R_n are zero. Other assumptions can be made for determining the values of R_1 and R_n, but zero is probably the most common assumption used.

We now use these curvature values to calculate the coefficients for the cubic polynomial for the kth interval using the following equations:

$$y = A_k(x - x_k)^3 + B_k(x - x_k)^2 + C_k(x - x_k) + D_k \qquad (12-2)$$

where

$$A_k = \frac{1}{6h_k}(R_{k+1} - R_k)$$

$$B_k = \frac{1}{2}R_k$$

$$C_k = \frac{1}{h_k}(y_{k+1} - y_k) - \frac{1}{6}h_k(R_{k+1} + 2R_k)$$

$$D_k = y_k$$

We can then use the cubic polynomials to construct the spline and to interpolate for additional values of the function between the data points.

We now illustrate this process with the set of five data points shown in the figure below:

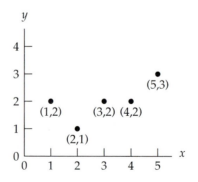

We first compute values for h_1 through h_4:

$$h_1 = x_2 - x_1 = 1$$
$$h_2 = x_3 - x_2 = 1$$
$$h_3 = x_4 - x_3 = 1$$
$$h_4 = x_5 - x_4 = 1$$

We next compute values for the slopes, S_1 through S_4:

$$S_1 = \frac{y_2 - y_1}{h_1} = -1$$

$$S_2 = \frac{y_3 - y_2}{h_2} = 1$$

$$S_3 = \frac{y_4 - y_3}{h_3} = 0$$

$$S_4 = \frac{y_5 - y_4}{h_4} = 1$$

We are now ready to compute the curvature values. First we set R_1 and R_5 equal to zero as described earlier. Then we use Eq. (12–1) to generate three simultaneous equations to solve for the curvatures at the second, third, and fourth data points:

$$2(1 + 1)R_2 \qquad + R_3 \qquad + 0R_4 = 6(1 + 1)$$
$$R_2 + 2(1 + 1)R_3 \qquad + R_4 = 6(0 - 1)$$
$$0R_2 \qquad R_3 + 2(1 + 1)R_4 = 6(1 - 0)$$

These equations can now be expressed in tridiagonal matrix form:

$$\begin{bmatrix} 4 & 1 & 0 \\ 1 & 4 & 1 \\ 0 & 1 & 4 \end{bmatrix} \begin{bmatrix} R_2 \\ R_3 \\ R_4 \end{bmatrix} = \begin{bmatrix} 12 \\ -6 \\ 6 \end{bmatrix}$$

After solving these equations (Cramer's rule provides a quick solution), the values for the curvatures are:

$$R_1 = 0$$
$$R_2 = 3.75$$
$$R_3 = -3$$
$$R_4 = 2.25$$
$$R_5 = 0$$

The curvatures are then used to solve for the coefficients of the four cubic polynomials using Eq. (12–2):

$A_1 = 0.625$	$B_1 = 0$	$C_1 = -1.625$	$D_1 = 2$
$A_2 = -1.125$	$B_2 = 1.875$	$C_2 = 0.25$	$D_2 = 1$
$A_3 = 0.875$	$B_3 = -1.5$	$C_3 = 0.625$	$D_3 = 2$
$A_4 = -0.375$	$B_4 = 1.125$	$C_4 = 0.25$	$D_4 = 2$

Thus, the equations of the four cubic polynomials are

$$y_1 = 0.625(x-1)^3 + 0(x-1)^2 - 1.625(x-1) + 2$$
$$y_2 = -1.125(x-2)^3 + 1.875(x-2)^2 + 0.25(x-2) + 1$$
$$y_3 = 0.875(x-3)^3 - 1.5(x-3)^2 + 0.625(x-3) + 2$$
$$y_4 = -0.375(x-4)^3 + 1.125(x-4)^2 + 0.25(x-4) + 2$$

These equations are shown plotted together in the following two figures. In the first figure, the four separate cubic functions are emphasized; in the second figure, the combined sections that represent the cubic spline are emphasized. The dashed lines show the shape of each cubic polynomial beyond their respective intervals. The cubic spline is shown as the solid line. Notice how the slopes and curvatures of the separate curves, which make up the spline, are the same at data points 2, 3, and 4 and how the curves at each end become straight lines as they approach points 1 and 5.

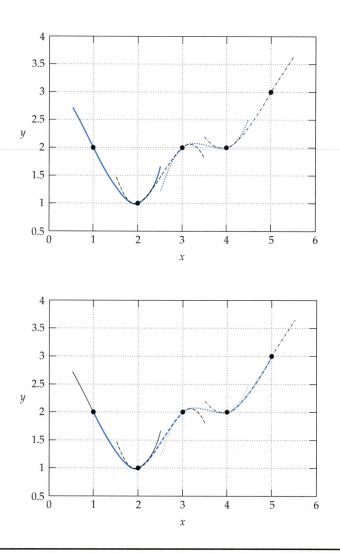

In the next section, we use cubic spline interpolation to compute the path of a robot arm.

SELF-TEST 12–2

This self-test allows you to check quickly to see if you have remembered the key points from Section 12–3. If you have any problems with the exercises, you should reread this section. The solutions are included at the end of the text.

Assume that the following four data points have been collected from a test of a small rocket motor.

TIME (SECONDS)	ALTITUDE (METERS)
1	150
2	350
3	500
4	420

We want to interpolate for other values of the altitude using a cubic spline to approximate the function between values.

1. Determine the two unknown curvatures using the tridiagonal matrix form from Eq. (12–1).
2. Use the curvature values to find the equations of the three cubic polynomials joining these four points. Sketch the cubic spline approximating this set of data.
3. Use the cubic spline to approximate the altitude at 1.5, 2.3, and 3.7 seconds.

12–4 APPLICATION—ROBOT PATH GENERATION (Robotic Engineering)

A robot is to be used to inspect the machining accuracy of a high-speed turbine part. At the end of the robot's arm is a device called an end-effector, which corresponds to our hand. A laser measuring instrument is attached to the end–effector and is capable of making very precise, virtually instantaneous measurements of the sizes of the holes that have been machined into the turbine part. The robot is to be programmed to pass rapidly over the location of each hole, allowing the measuring instrument to collect and record the machining data.

The following figure plots the locations of the centers of eight holes over which the robot must pass. If the robot were to move rapidly from hole to hole using straight line segments, the sudden changes of direction at the holes could damage the measuring instrument as well as the robot arm. Therefore, the robot's high speed and the pattern of the holes dictate that a cubic spline be used to generate path commands that move the measuring instrument along a continuous curve which passes over each hole.

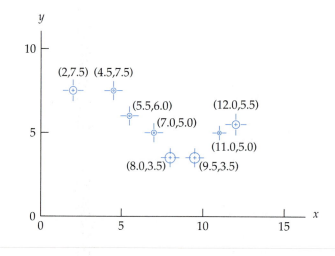

Write a program SPLINE that computes the path for the robot arm using a cubic spline. The program should calculate the coefficients of the tridiagonal system of equations using Eq. (12–1). Then, incorporate a subroutine to solve the resulting set of equations for the curvatures using Gauss elimination. Using Eq. (12–2), together with the curvatures, calculate the coefficients of the cubic polynomials that produce the cubic spline. Print the equation of the cubic polynomial for each interval, and generate a table of interpolated values for the spline that are evenly spaced along the x-axis and that begin at the first hole and end at the last hole. This table will be used to specify the path for the robot arm.

In order to make the program flexible, the input data points are stored in a data file named INPATH. A message is printed asking the user to select the number of points to be interpolated with a cubic spline between the first and last points in the data file. The user is also asked to give an output file name for the interpolated data points. This interaction allows the user to generate additional paths for the robot arm without recompiling the program.

PROBLEM STATEMENT

Write a program that computes a cubic spline for a set of data points and interpolates for points along the spline.

INPUT/OUTPUT DESCRIPTION

The inputs to the program are the set of data points in the file INPATH, which has the number of points as the first value in the file. The number of equally spaced interpolation intervals and the name of the output file are entered by the user. The output is a data file containing the interpolated points for the cubic spline.

HAND EXAMPLE

Refer to the previous section for a hand example of the development of a cubic spline for a set of five data points.

ALGORITHM DEVELOPMENT

The decomposition of this problem involves reading the data points, determining the cubic polynomial equations, and interpolating for the additional values of the function y.

DECOMPOSITION

Read data points.
Compute coefficients of cubic polynomials.
Interpolate for additional values of y.

The program first reads the information in the data file which contains the data points through which the cubic spline will pass. It then computes the entries for the tridiagonal matrix and calls the Gauss elimination subroutine that solves for the curvatures. The cubic polynomial coefficients are computed next. Finally, the interpolated points on the cubic spline are computed and stored in an output data file.

A number of steps are involved, so we will plan to perform some of the steps in modules. Since the computation of the cubic spline is an operation that we might want to include in other programs, we will write it as a subroutine that calls a Gauss elimination subroutine. The main program reads the data file and obtains the information from the user. The cubic spline subroutine computes the equations for the spline and then computes the interpolated values. We write the interpolated values to the data file as we compute them so that we do not have to store them in an array. If we were to store them in an array, we would have to give an upper limit to the number of points that can be interpolated, thus making the program less flexible. The use of an array would also cause the program to run much slower. Since the Gauss elimination routine has already been written and tested as a program in Chapter 11, we need only convert it to a subroutine; in the conversion, we can omit the subroutine ORDER since the structure of the tridiagonal matrix is such that it does not need to be reordered.

The refined pseudocode for the main program and for the cubic spline subroutine is:

REFINEMENT IN PSEUDOCODE

PATH: Read number of data points, ndata
    For k = 1 to ndata do
        Read data points x(k), y(k)
    Read number of interpolation points, npts
    Read output file name
    Call spline subroutine

SPLINE: Compute coefficients for tridiagonal matrix
    Call Gauss elimination to compute curvatures
    Use curvatures to calculate coefficients
        of cubic polynomials
    Compute x increment for interpolated points
    For k = 1 to npts do
        Compute interpolated x value
        Determine cubic polynomial
        Compute interpolated y value
        Print x value, y value

The structure chart for this solution is shown below:

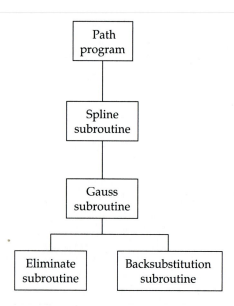

We then convert the pseudocode into the following program.

```
*--------------------------------------------------------------*
      PROGRAM   PATH
*
*  This program uses a cubic spline to interpolate values
*  between given points for a robot arm path.
*
      INTEGER NDATA, K, NPTS
      REAL X(25), Y(25)
      CHARACTER*8 FILENM
*
      OPEN (UNIT=12,FILE='INPATH',STATUS='OLD')
      READ (12,*) NDATA
      DO 5 K=1,NDATA
         READ (12,*) X(K), Y(K)
    5 CONTINUE
*
      PRINT*, 'ENTER NUMBER OF INTERPOLATED OUTPUT VALUES DESIRED'
      READ*, NPTS
      PRINT*, 'ENTER FILE NAME FOR OUTPUT PATH'
      READ*, FILENM
      CALL SPLINE (X, Y, NDATA, NPTS, FILENM)
*
      END
*--------------------------------------------------------------*
      SUBROUTINE   SPLINE (X, Y, NDATA, NPTS, FILENM)
*
*  This subroutine computes the cubic spline equations
*  from a set of input data points.  It then uses the results
*  to interpolate for new points.  The output values are
*  written to a data file.
*
      INTEGER NDATA, NPTS, K, J, DROWS, DCOLS
      REAL X(NDATA), Y(NDATA), H(24), Q(23,24), S(24), TEMP(23), R(25
     +    A(24), B(24), C(24), D(24), DELTA, XINT, YINT
      CHARACTER*8 FILENM
*
      DATA  Q, DROWS, DCOLS /552*0.0,23,24/
*
*  Compute interval width matrix H
*
      DO 10 K=1,NDATA-1
         H(K) = X(K+1) - X(K)
   10 CONTINUE
*
*  Compute tridiagonal matrix Q
*
      Q(1,1) = 2.0*(H(1)+H(2))
      Q(1,2) = H(2)
      DO 15 K=2,NDATA-3
         Q(K,K-1) = H(K)
         Q(K,K) = 2.0*(H(K)+H(K+1))
         Q(K,K+1) = H(K+1)
   15 CONTINUE
      Q(NDATA-2,NDATA-3) = H(NDATA-2)
      Q(NDATA-2,NDATA-2) = 2.0*(H(NDATA-2)+H(NDATA-1))
```

```
*
*   Compute slope matrix S
*
      DO 20 K=1,NDATA-1
          S(K) = (Y(K+1) - Y(K))/H(K)
20 CONTINUE
*
*   Augment tridiagonal matrix Q
*
      DO 25 K=1,NDATA-2
          Q(K,NDATA-1) = 6.0*(S(K+1) - S(K))
25 CONTINUE
*
*   Call Gauss elimination and store curvature values in matrix R
*
      CALL GAUSS (Q,DROWS,DCOLS,NDATA-2,TEMP)
      R(1) = 0.0
      DO 30 K=2,NDATA-1
          R(K) = TEMP(K-1)
30 CONTINUE
      R(NDATA) = 0.0
*
*   Compute cubic equation coefficients
*
      DO 35 K=1,NDATA-1
          A(K) = (1.0/(6.0*H(K)))*(R(K+1)-R(K))
          B(K) = R(K)/2.0
          C(K) = (Y(K+1)-Y(K))/H(K) - H(K)*(R(K+1)+2.0*R(K))/6.0
          D(K) = Y(K)
35 CONTINUE
*
*   Generate file of interpolated values
*
      OPEN (UNIT=14,FILE=FILENM,STATUS='NEW')
      WRITE (14,*) NPTS
      WRITE (14,*) X(1), Y(1)
      DELTA = (X(NDATA)-X(1))/(NPTS-1)
      J = 1
      DO 40 K=1,NPTS-2
          XINT = X(1) + K*DELTA
          IF (XINT.GT.X(J+1)) THEN
              IF (J.LT.NDATA-1) J = J + 1
          ENDIF
          YINT = A(J)*(XINT-X(J))**3 + B(J)*(XINT-X(J))**2
     +            + C(J)*(XINT-X(J)) + D(J)
          WRITE (14,*) XINT, YINT
40 CONTINUE
      WRITE (14,*) X(NDATA), Y(NDATA)
*
      END
```

```
*----------------------------------------------------------------*
      SUBROUTINE  GAUSS  (A,DROWS,DCOLS,NROWS,SOLN)
*
*  This program uses the Gauss elimination method to
*  solve a set of simultaneous equations.
*
      INTEGER  DROWS, DCOLS, NROWS, N, I, J, PIVOT
      REAL  A(DROWS,DCOLS), SOLN(DROWS)
      LOGICAL  ERROR
*
      N = NROWS
      PIVOT = 1
      ERROR = .FALSE.
   10 IF (PIVOT.LT.N.AND..NOT.ERROR) THEN
         IF (.NOT.ERROR) THEN
            CALL ELIM(A,DROWS,DCOLS,N,PIVOT)
            PIVOT = PIVOT + 1
         ENDIF
         GO TO 10
      ENDIF
*
      IF (ERROR) THEN
         PRINT*, 'NO UNIQUE SOLUTION EXISTS'
      ELSE
         CALL BACKSB(A,DROWS,DCOLS,N,SOLN)
      ENDIF
      END
*----------------------------------------------------------------*
                 (no changes in subroutine ELIM)
*----------------------------------------------------------------*
                 (no changes in subroutine BACKSB)
*----------------------------------------------------------------*
```

A few comments related to the arrays used in this program are instructive at this point. The only arrays defined in the main program are X and Y; therefore, any other temporary arrays needed in the subprograms must be defined with specific sizes. For example, the array Q which contains the augmented tridiagonal matrix is defined in the SPLINE subroutine with 23 rows and 24 columns. The dimensional size of Q is passed through arguments DROWS and DCOLS to the GAUSS subroutine, which then uses the variables DROWS and DCOLS in the specification statement.

TESTING

The next plot was drawn using 101 interpolated values for the cubic spline joining the five points in the hand example.

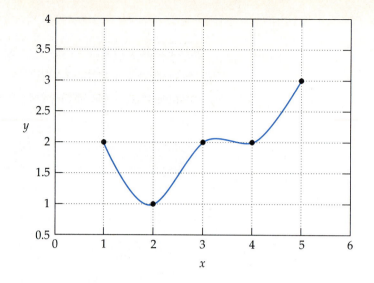

This plot was also drawn using 101 interpolated values for the cubic spline joining the eight points in the robot path generation.

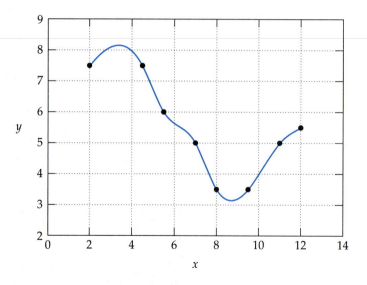

When testing this program with different data sets, be sure that the data are ordered such that the x coordinates are in ascending order; this ensures that the points go from left to right when we connect them. Also, note that this algorithm will not handle the case where two data points have the same x value but different y values. If two points have the same x value, one of the interval width values will be zero, and this will cause a divide by zero when we compute the slopes. If you are concerned that some of your data might include points with the same x value, you should revise the program to check for this possibility and then exit the program with an error message instead of getting an execution error.

You might also want to print some intermediate values in this program to verify some of the properties of a cubic spline. For example, the data point at the intersection of two cubic equations should have the same value from both equations. If you print the equations for the splines, it is easy to verify that the slopes (first derivatives) and the curvatures (second derivatives) of the two equations are the same at the point where they meet. In addition, the second derivative at the first and last points should be zero.

12-5 DISCUSSION OF SINGLE POLYNOMIAL INTERPOLATION

In principle, for any set of n data points, it is possible to find a single polynomial of degree $n - 1$ that will pass exactly through each data point. For example, the following fourth-degree polynomial passes through the five data points used in the example from the cubic spline section:

$$y = 0.208333x^4 - 2.583333x^3 + 11.291666x^2 - 19.916666x + 13.0$$

This curve is shown as the dotted line, along with the cubic spline solution developed in Section 12-3:

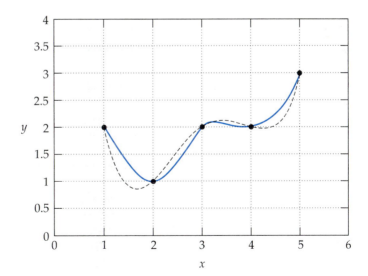

Note that while the two curves are not exactly the same, they are very similar. Thus, it appears in this example that the single fourth-degree polynomial provides a satisfactory interpolation method.

The following seventh-degree polynomial passes through all eight data points from the robot path in Section 12–6:

$$y = 0.00081866x^7 - 0.04336986x^6 + 0.95108768x^5$$
$$- 11.13853436x^4 + 74.80429101x^3$$
$$- 285.7909368x^2 + 567.02273599x - 431.36342564$$

This curve is plotted as a dotted line, together with the cubic spline solution:

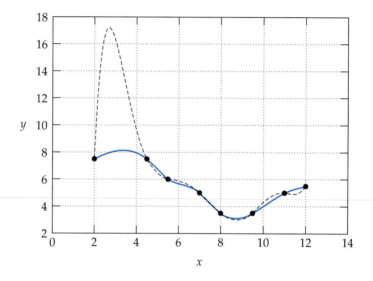

Note that this time the results are not as satisfactory as they were earlier for the fourth-degree polynomial example. This comparison demonstrates a general problem with using single polynomial interpolation. As the degree of the polynomial gets higher, two things usually happen: first, the coefficients of the polynomial need to be determined with increasing precision; and second, the curve begins to "oscillate," exhibiting large excursions, or "wiggles," between the data points as we observed in this example.

The importance of the accuracy of the coefficients in a high-degree interpolating polynomial is illustrated in the next graph, which uses the seventh-degree polynomial for the robot path, but with seven decimal digits of accuracy instead of eight. This very small change in the values of the coefficients generates a polynomial that passes through the first five data points, but not the last three data points:

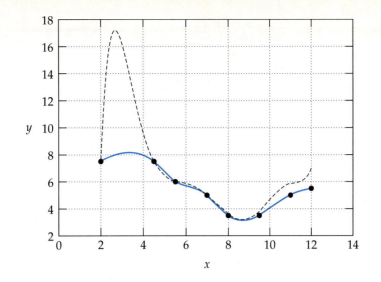

Applications occasionally arise where a single, high-degree interpolating polynomial function is indicated or preferred. But because of the problems discussed earlier, high-degree polynomial interpolation is not used very often. As a result, we will not discuss the various methods in detail.

There are numerous interpolating polynomial formulas. Some of the better-known methods include Lagrange's formula, Newton's formula, Newton-Gregory formulas, Gauss's formulas, and Stirling's formula. All of these methods involve the use of "difference expressions" which are similar to the expressions used earlier in the linear interpolation formula in Section 12–1. These formulas are used, together with a set of n data points, to compute the coefficients of an interpolating polynomial of degree $n - 1$. The resulting polynomial equation is then used to interpolate for additional values of the function.

12–6   LEAST-SQUARES METHODS

We often encounter situations in science and engineering when our understanding of a physical process, or our ability to observe or measure it, is limited. The data that we are able to obtain do not occur at points on the curve where we expect them to because of errors in the data, in the theoretical model, or, most often, both. The curve-fitting methods discussed in the previous sections assume that the data are correct and the function curve must pass through all the data points. These methods may not be appropriate for data that only approximate the function. In these situations, techniques are needed which are directed more at fitting a particular function to the data in some optimum manner. Therefore, in this section, we assume that the data represent approximate values of a specific function whose form we believe will best fit the data.

The task of selecting a function may or may not be straightforward. Often, we understand the physical process that the data represent, and we have a theoretical equation for that process. At other times, the appearance of the plotted data may suggest a certain functional form such as a straight line or a parabola. There may also be times when we must try several different equations before we decide which one best represents the data.

The process of fitting an approximating function to a set of data, such that the resulting curve represents a "best fit," is called *regression* analysis. We first select an equation whose form we know, but whose coefficients we do not know. Regression is then used to find the combination of coefficients that will minimize some measurement of the errors made in fitting the curve to the data. The most popular means of measuring those errors is the *least-squares method*. When fitting a curve to a set of data using the least-squares method, the coefficients of the curve are selected such that the sum of the squared distances between the curve and the data points is minimized. The first least-squares method we discuss uses linear regression to fit a linear equation (a straight line) to a set of data. We then generalize the method for fitting higher-order polynomials to data.

LINEAR MODELS

A *linear model* has the following equation:

$$y = f(x)$$
$$= ax + b$$

Linear regression is used to fit a straight line to a set of data by finding the slope of the line, a, and the y-intercept of the line, b, such that the sum of the squares of the y distances between the line and the data points is minimized. Two simultaneous equations for a and b are obtained using derivatives to minimize the error, and the solutions of those equations are the values of a and b for the straight line which best fits the data. Before we derive the regression equations, we need to define some summation symbols which we will need. The symbol Σ represents a summation of values. Given a set of data points with coordinates $\{(x_1,y_1),(x_2,y_2),...,(x_n,y_n)\}$, we can represent the sum of the x coordinates with the following notation:

$$\sum_{k=1}^{n} x_k = x_1 + x_2 + \cdots + x_n$$

This summation is read as "the sum of x_k as k goes from 1 to n." Similarly, we can express other sums using the notation:

$$\sum_{k=1}^{n} y_k = y_1 + y_2 + \cdots + y_n$$

$$\sum_{k=1}^{n} x_k y_k = x_1 y_1 + x_2 y_2 + \cdots + x_n y_n$$

$$\sum_{k=1}^{n} x_k^2 = x_1^2 + x_2^2 + \cdots + x_n^2$$

$$\sum_{k=1}^{n} b = b + b + \cdots + b = b{\cdot}n$$

To derive the regression equations, we start by computing the vertical distances between the linear function $f(x)$ and the actual data points. These distances are often referred to as residuals of the data points. Using the figure below, the residuals for each data point are seen to be:

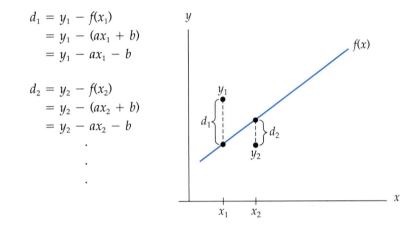

$$d_1 = y_1 - f(x_1)$$
$$ = y_1 - (ax_1 + b)$$
$$ = y_1 - ax_1 - b$$

$$d_2 = y_2 - f(x_2)$$
$$ = y_2 - (ax_2 + b)$$
$$ = y_2 - ax_2 - b$$

We now wish to minimize the sum of these distances, which represents the total error in fitting the curve to the data points. If we were simply to sum the distances, the positive and negative values would tend to cancel and give us an incorrect measurement of the sum of the errors. To avoid this problem, we first square the distances, or *residuals*, before summing them. This sum, which is called the error sum, gives us a way to measure the total error, since all the squared distances are positive quantities. The equation for the summation of the squares of the errors, which we shall call E, is then

$$E = \sum_{k=1}^{n} d_k^2$$
$$ = \sum_{k=1}^{n} (y_k - ax_k - b)^2$$

We now apply differential calculus to find the partial derivatives of E with respect to the two unknown coefficients a and b. Since the minimum of a function occurs when its derivative is equal to zero, we set these partial derivatives equal to zero to give us these two equations:

$$\frac{\partial E}{\partial a} = -2 \sum_{k=1}^{n} x_k(y_k - ax_k - b) = 0$$

$$\frac{\partial E}{\partial b} = -2 \sum_{k=1}^{n} (y_k - ax_k - b) = 0$$

These equations are now rearranged to yield two simultaneous equations in the variables a and b:

$$a \sum_{k=1}^{n} x_k^2 + b \sum_{k=1}^{n} x_k = \sum_{k=1}^{n} x_k y_k$$

$$a \sum_{k=1}^{n} x_k + b \cdot n = \sum_{k=1}^{n} y_k$$

Finally, solving these equations for a and b gives

$$a = \frac{\sum\limits_{k=1}^{n} x_k \sum\limits_{k=1}^{n} y_k - n \sum\limits_{k=1}^{n} x_k y_k}{(\sum\limits_{k=1}^{n} x_k)^2 - n \sum\limits_{k=1}^{n} x_k^2} \qquad (12\text{--}3)$$

$$b = \frac{\sum\limits_{k=1}^{n} x_k \sum\limits_{k=1}^{n} x_k y_k - \sum\limits_{k=1}^{n} x_k^2 \sum\limits_{k=1}^{n} y_k}{(\sum\limits_{k=1}^{n} x_k)^2 - n \sum\limits_{k=1}^{n} x_k^2} \qquad (12\text{--}4)$$

Once the slope a and y-intercept b have been calculated, the equation of the straight line which best fits the data has been determined. If we were to compute the error sum, E, for this line, it would be less than or equal to the error sum for any other line we could draw through the data. The error sum, E, also provides a relative measurement of how close the data points are to the line. For example, assume that we have two sets of data which have the same number of data points. Further assume that we have determined that the same line provides the best fit, in the least-squares sense, to both sets of data. The set of data which has the smaller error sum will generally lie closer to the line and have less "scatter" in it than the set of data which has the larger error sum. Thus, the error sum can be used to provide a measurement of how well the line fits the data, or possibly how accurately the data were measured.

Another form of the equation for computing b is

$$b = \frac{\sum\limits_{k=1}^{n} y_k - a \sum\limits_{k=1}^{n} x_k}{n} \qquad (12\text{--}5)$$

At first glance, this equation would seem to be preferable to Eq. (12–4) since it is shorter. However, there is a disadvantage to using Eq. (12–5) because it can be less accurate. For example, suppose that we are using only a few digits of accuracy to compute the values of a and b. If we use Eq. (12–5) to compute b, we have already rounded or truncated the answer for a, and we then use that value in the computation of b. If we use Eq. (12–4) to compute b, we are using only the values of the various summations and are likely to get a more accurate answer. When we compute b using a computer, both equations give accurate answers because the computer is using its full accuracy for all the intermediate steps. In the next section, we illustrate an example in which the two equations for b give different answers if a small number of digits of accuracy is used.

POLYNOMIAL MODELS

The least-squares method described above can easily be extended to *polynomial models* of the form

$$f(x) = a_0 + a_1 x + a_2 x^2 + \cdots + a_n x^n$$

For example, suppose the appearance of the data suggests that a good fit can be obtained using a quadratic equation:

$$f(x) = a_0 + a_1 x + a_2 x^2$$

The equation for the sum of the squares of the errors, E, is now

$$E = \sum_{i=1}^{n} (y_i - a_0 - a_1 x_i - a_2 x_i^2)^2$$

Differentiating this equation with respect to a_0, a_1, and a_2 gives us three expressions which can be set to zero in order to find the minimum value of E:

$$\frac{\partial E}{\partial a_0} = -2 \sum_{i=1}^{n} (y_i - a_0 - a_1 x_i - a_2 x_i^2) = 0$$

$$\frac{\partial E}{\partial a_1} = -2 \sum_{i=1}^{n} x_i (y_i - a_0 - a_1 x_i - a_2 x_i^2) = 0$$

$$\frac{\partial E}{\partial a_2} = -2 \sum_{i=1}^{n} x_i^2 (y_i - a_0 - a_1 x_i - a_2 x_i^2) = 0$$

When these equations are rearranged, we have the following set of simultaneous equations in a_0, a_1, and a_2, which we can solve to obtain the coefficients of the best-fit quadratic equation.

$$a_2 \sum_{k=1}^{n} x_k^2 + a_1 \sum_{k=1}^{n} x_k + a_0 n = \sum_{k=1}^{n} y_k$$

$$a_2 \sum_{k=1}^{n} x_k^3 + a_1 \sum_{k=1}^{n} x_k^2 + a_0 \sum_{k=1}^{n} x_k = \sum_{k=1}^{n} x_k y_k$$

$$a_2 \sum_{k=1}^{n} x_k^4 + a_1 \sum_{k=1}^{n} x_k^3 + a_0 \sum_{k=1}^{n} x_k^2 = \sum_{k=1}^{n} x_k^2 y_k$$

In principle, we can use this approach to find the equation of a polynomial of any degree we desire which is the best fit in a least-squares sense. In practice, however, the method becomes unstable as the degree of the polynomial gets larger, because of rounding errors in the computer. If it is necessary to use a high-degree polynomial to fit a set of data, a technique known as orthogonal polynomials can be used, but such techniques are beyond the scope of this book. Also keep in mind that the use of high-degree polynomials may lead to oscillation problems as seen in the previous section.

If the data points are approximated by sums of sine functions, the approximation is called a Fourier series approximation. This technique is commonly used in engineering, but it is also beyond the scope of this text.

NONLINEAR MODELS

Least-squares curve-fitting methods can be applied to virtually any function, but the resulting equations for solving for the coefficients of the function may be nonlinear and, as a result, cannot be solved using the methods for linear simultaneous equations. Occasionally, however, a *nonlinear* function can be transformed to a linear function which we can solve using our earlier methods. For example, it may be possible to perform an operation on the original nonlinear function which transforms it into a new function that can be plotted as a straight line. Linear regression is then applied to the new function and the similarly transformed data, exactly as was done earlier, to find a least-squares straight line fit. The slope and y-intercept for this line are then used in the transformation equations for the original function to obtain the nonlinear equation that best fits the original data. An example of a function which can be linearized is

$$f(x) = bx^a \qquad (12-6)$$

where a and b are constants. If we take the natural logarithm of both sides of this equation, we have

$$\ln f(x) = a \ln x + \ln b \qquad (12-7)$$

We now define the following transformation equations:

$$y = f(x) \qquad (12-8)$$
$$\tilde{b} = \ln b \qquad (12-9)$$
$$\tilde{x} = \ln x \qquad (12-10)$$
$$\tilde{y} = \ln y \qquad (12-11)$$

These transformations, when applied to Eq. (12–7), give

$$\tilde{y} = a\tilde{x} + \tilde{b} \qquad (12-12)$$

which is exactly the linear equation form we saw earlier. We then proceed exactly as we did earlier to obtain the equations for the slope and y-intercept of the least-squares line, which are

$$a = \frac{\sum\limits_{k=1}^{n} \tilde{x}_k \sum\limits_{k=1}^{n} \tilde{y}_k - n \sum\limits_{k=1}^{n} \tilde{x}_k \tilde{y}_k}{\left(\sum\limits_{k=1}^{n} \tilde{x}_k \right)^2 - n \sum\limits_{k=1}^{n} \tilde{x}_k^2} \qquad (12\text{--}13)$$

$$\tilde{b} = \frac{\sum\limits_{k=1}^{n} \tilde{x}_k \sum\limits_{k=1}^{n} \tilde{x}_k \tilde{y}_k - \sum\limits_{k=1}^{n} \tilde{x}_k^2 \sum\limits_{k=1}^{n} \tilde{y}_k}{\left(\sum\limits_{k=1}^{n} \tilde{x}_k \right)^2 - n \sum\limits_{k=1}^{n} \tilde{x}_k^2} \qquad (12\text{--}14)$$

The data values x_i, and y_i are then transformed using Eqs. (12–10) and (12–11), the various sums are computed, and the results are substituted into Eqs. (12–13) and (12–14) to find a and $\tilde{b}$. All that remains is to solve Eq. (12–9) for b and substitute into Eq. (12–6) to obtain the final nonlinear equation. A final word of caution is necessary if some of the x and y values are negative, since the logarithm function does not exist for negative values. In this case, additional transformations are used to shift the data so that there will be no negative values.

SELF-TEST 12–3

This self-test allows you to check quickly to see if you have remembered the key points from Section 12–6. If you have any problems with the exercises, you should reread this section. The solutions are included at the end of the text.

Assume that we have the following three data points collected from an experiment:

X	Y
1.0	2.0
3.0	3.0
4.0	6.0

1. The following two equations have been suggested as good linear approximations:

$$y = x$$
$$y = 1.5x - 1$$

Sketch the two lines on the same graph and show the locations of the three points relative to the two lines.
2. Using the error sum, determine which line is the better approximation in terms of least squares.
3. Compute the best linear approximation to these three points using least squares.

4. Consider the nonlinear function

$$y = be^{ax}$$

How would you tranform it to a linear function?

12-7   APPLICATION—ACCELEROMETER MODEL (Mechanical Engineering)

One of the most exciting applications of science and engineering is space exploration. Sophisticated sensors and computer equipment aboard manned and unmanned spacecraft have provided a wealth of scientific data as well as the information needed to make decisions during the flights. Collecting data and then using it to develop an equation or model is an important step in analyzing the complex sensor systems.

The guidance and control system for a spacecraft often utilizes a sensor called an accelerometer, which is an electromechanical device that produces an output voltage proportional to the applied acceleration. An accurate model of the response of an accelerometer to known accelerations is needed for system performance studies. Careful tests are performed in an inertial measurement laboratory to obtain data on the accelerometer at several different acceleration levels. The accelerometer test data given in the hand example on the next page clearly show the linear relationship between the input acceleration and the output voltage that is characteristic of an accelerometer. The x-axis units are multiples of the acceleration of gravity, which is approximately 32.2 ft/sec^2 or 9.8 m/sec^2. The y-axis units are the measured output voltages of the accelerometer for the various input accelerations. The slope of the straight line that has been drawn through the data is referred to as the scale factor, and the y-intercept of the line is referred to as the null bias. Write a program to determine an accelerometer's scale factor and null bias from a set of data stored in a data file XYDATA. Also tabulate the residuals and compute the error sum.

PROBLEM STATEMENT

Find the linear equation that best fits a set of data values. Print a report that gives the linear equation, residuals, and error sum.

INPUT/OUTPUT DESCRIPTION

The input is contained in a data file XYDATA. We do not know how many values are in the file, and it does not contain a trailer signal. Each line of the file contains an experimentally measured x and y value. The output should be a report in the following form:

```
THE LINEAR EQUATION IS
Y = xxx.xxx X + xxx.xxx

ORIGINAL    ORIGINAL    ESTIMATED    RESIDUAL
   X           Y           Y

xxx.xxx     xxx.xxx     xxx.xxx      xxx.xxx
  .
  .
  .

ERROR SUM = xxx.xxx
```

HAND EXAMPLE

A set of eight data values is shown below, along with a graph of the data values and a hand-drawn linear model.

ACCELERATION (A)	VOLTAGE (V)
−4	−0.593
−2	−0.436
0	0.061
2	0.425
4	0.980
6	1.213
8	1.646
10	2.158

Using linear regression, we now compute by hand the best linear model using only the first three data points. The corresponding sums are

$$\sum_{k=1}^{3} x_k = -4 + -2 + 0 = -6$$

$$\sum_{k=1}^{3} y_k = -0.593 + -0.436 + 0.061 = -0.968$$

$$\sum_{k=1}^{3} x_k y_k = -4(-0.593) + -2(-0.436) + 0(0.061) = 3.244$$

$$\sum_{k=1}^{3} x_k^2 = (-4)^2 + (-2)^2 + (0)^2 = 20$$

Using the equations to compute a and b (the slope and y-intercept) from the previous section, we determine the following equation:

$$y = 0.164\,x + 0.004$$

Recall that we presented two equations for computing b in the previous section. Using the first equation, the value of b is 0.00433, which we rounded to three decimal places for the computations in this hand example. However, if we use the second equation for b, the value computed is 0.00533. This difference is a result of the extra operations involved when b is computed using a, instead of being computed directly from the various sums. As we mentioned, this difference is generally not significant when using the full accuracy of a computer, but it can be significant in computations that are limited to a few digits of accuracy as in our hand example. Generally speaking, we should use maximum precision for all intermediate calculations and not round off results until the end of the calculation, whether we do them by hand or computer.

We now use the linear equation to compute the estimated y values and the residuals:

```
THE LINEAR EQUATION IS
Y =    0.164 X +    0.004

ORIGINAL    ORIGINAL    ESTIMATED    RESIDUAL
   X           Y           Y

 -4.000      -0.593      -0.652       0.059
 -2.000      -0.436      -0.324      -0.112
  0.000       0.061       0.004       0.057

ERROR SUM =    0.019
```

ALGORITHM DEVELOPMENT

The decomposition of this problem solution into general steps is:

DECOMPOSITION

Read x and y data.
Compute slope and y-intercept.
Compute y estimates and residuals.
Print report.

As we refine the decomposition, we recognize that we need a loop to read the x and y data. Because we are reading each pair of data values from a single line, we can also add the values as we read them, to the sums that we are going to need for the calculations. We need to use arrays for the x and y data because the data are needed for the report. If we only wanted the values for the slope and *y*-intercept of the linear model, we would not need arrays for the *x* and *y* data. The individual residuals are used for computing the error sum and are also printed in the report. However, we can compute and print the residual and then square and add it to the sum in the same loop—thus, we do not need an array for the residual values.

REFINEMENT IN PSEUDOCODE

```
LINEAR: k ← 1
        sumx ← 0
        sumy ← 0
        sumxy ← 0
        sumxx ← 0
        While more data do
           Read x(k), y(k)
           sumx ← sumx + x(k)
           sumy ← sumy + y(k)
           sumxy ← sumxy + x(k)y(k)
           sumxx ← sumxx + x(k)x(k)
           k ← k + 1
        n ← k − 1
        Compute slope and y-intercept
        Print slope, y-intercept
        error ← 0
        For k = 1 to n do
           ynew ← slope·x(k) + y-intercept
           res ← y(k) − ynew
           error ← error + res·res
           Print x(k), y(k), ynew, res
        Print error
```

We now convert the refined pseudocode into FORTRAN.

FORTRAN Program

```
*------------------------------------------------------------------*
*        PROGRAM LINEAR
*
*   This program computes a linear model for a set of data
*   and then computes the residual sum to evaluate the model.
*
         INTEGER K, N
         REAL X(500), Y(500), SLOPE, YINT, YNEW, RES,
      +       SUMX, SUMY, SUMXY, SUMXX, ERROR
*
         DATA K,SUMX,SUMY,SUMXY,SUMXX,ERROR /1,5*0.0/
*
         OPEN (UNIT=10,FILE='XYDATA',STATUS='OLD')
*
       5 READ (10,*,END=50) X(K), Y(K)
         SUMX = SUMX + X(K)
         SUMY = SUMY + Y(K)
         SUMXY = SUMXY + X(K)*Y(K)
         SUMXX = SUMXX + X(K)*X(K)
         K = K + 1
         GO TO 5
*
      50 N = K - 1
         SLOPE = (SUMX*SUMY - REAL(N)*SUMXY)/
      +          (SUMX*SUMX - REAL(N)*SUMXX)
         YINT = (SUMX*SUMXY - SUMXX*SUMY)/
      +          (SUMX*SUMX - REAL(N)*SUMXX)
*
         PRINT*, 'THE LINEAR EQUATION IS'
         PRINT 55, SLOPE, YINT
      55 FORMAT (1X,'Y = ',F7.3,' X + ',F7.3)
         PRINT*
         PRINT*,'ORIGINAL   ORIGINAL   ESTIMATED   RESIDUAL'
         PRINT*,'   X          Y           Y              '
         PRINT*
*
         DO 65 K=1,N
         YNEW = SLOPE*X(K) + YINT
         RES = Y(K) - YNEW
         ERROR = ERROR + RES*RES
         PRINT 60, X(K), Y(K), YNEW, RES
      60    FORMAT (1X,F7.3,4X,F7.3,4X,F7.3,5X,F7.3)
      65 CONTINUE
*
         PRINT*
         PRINT 70, ERROR
      70 FORMAT (1X,'ERROR SUM = ',F7.3)
*
         END
*------------------------------------------------------------------*
```

TESTING

If we test this program with the data set given earlier in this section, the
following report is printed:

```
THE LINEAR EQUATION IS
Y =   0.200 X +   0.080

ORIGINAL   ORIGINAL   ESTIMATED   RESIDUAL
   X          Y           Y

 -4.000    -0.593     -0.722       0.129
 -2.000    -0.436     -0.321      -0.115
  0.000     0.061      0.080      -0.019
  2.000     0.425      0.481      -0.056
  4.000     0.980      0.882       0.098
  6.000     1.213      1.283      -0.070
  8.000     1.646      1.684      -0.038
 10.000     2.158      2.085       0.073

ERROR SUM =   0.055
```

We can check this using hand calculations. Performing the various summations, we get

$$\sum_{k=1}^{8} x_k = 24$$

$$\sum_{k=1}^{8} y_k = 5.454$$

$$\sum_{k=1}^{8} x_k y_k = 50.040$$

$$\sum_{k=1}^{8} x_k^2 = 240$$

We now use Eqs. (12−3) and (12−4) to compute a and b:

$$a = \frac{(24)(5.454) - (8)(50.040)}{(24)^2 - (8)(240)} = 0.2004643$$

$$b = \frac{(24)(50.040) - (240)(5.454)}{(24)^2 - (8)(240)} = 0.0803571$$

Rounding these results to three places and substituting them into the linear equation form gives

$$y = 0.200x + 0.080$$

The error sum is similarly computed by hand using:

$$E = \sum_{k=1}^{8} (y_k - ax_k - b)^2$$
$$= 0.0546393$$

which rounds to

$$E = 0.055$$

The following graph contains the original data points plus the linear equation determined by our program to be the best fit for the data.

SUMMARY

In this chapter we presented three methods of curve fitting and interpolation. The first method was linear interpolation, which used equations for straight lines between the data points to estimate unknown values of the function. The second method, cubic spline interpolation, connected the data points with matched cubic functions whose coefficients were found by solving a tridiagonal set of simultaneous equations. Cubic spline interpolation is more complicated than linear interpolation, but it is likely to be more accurate if the function has significant curvature between the data points. Both methods assume the data points are accurate since they use interpolating functions that pass exactly through each data point. Examples of single polynomial interpolation were presented and potential problems with their use was discussed. The third interpolation method discussed was the least-squares technique. Least-squares methods assume the data points only approximate a function whose form we think we know. The coefficients of the function are then determined such that the sum of the squared distances between the data points and the function curve is minimized. Polynomial and nonlinear functions were considered for the least-squares method.

DEBUGGING AIDS

To debug computer algorithms for curve fitting and interpolation, it is very useful to plot the original points, the approximating function, and the interpolated points. If you are using linear interpolation or cubic spline interpolation, both the original points and interpolated points should fall on the approximating functions. If you are using a least-squares method, the original points may not fall on the approximating function, but the interpolated points should fall on it. Also, since the accuracy of the coefficients of the various techniques is important, you may want to initially test your program using double precision. After the program is running correctly, you can change to single precision to see if the solution changes significantly. After this check, you may decide to retain the double-precision statement to avoid potential accuracy problems. When testing your program, you should also test "special cases" to ensure that it will work in all situations. Such tests might include zero values, endpoints, out-of-range values, or other cases that might cause the algorithm to fail.

STYLE/TECHNIQUE GUIDES

Curve fitting and interpolation techniques are good candidates for subroutines and functions. By incorporating these techniques as modules, it is also easier to use them in other programs. Be sure to document the modules carefully because these techniques often are not familiar to programmers. The documentation does not have to repeat the details, but it should document the key steps and give a reference to a more complete description of the technique. Extensive use of comments to identify the modules and outline the steps involved will make it much easier for you and others to understand, use, or modify the code. These techniques are especially valuable when you need to refer to a program that you have not used in a long time.

ERROR ANALYSIS

At the end of the previous chapter, we discussed roundoff errors that occur when we perform computations using a fixed number of digits of accuracy. Roundoff errors contribute to the absolute and relative errors that we discussed earlier. We now discuss the propagation of errors when we perform arithmetic operations using estimates of values. Let $\hat{x}$ be an estimate to x, and let $\hat{y}$ be an estimate to y. Then, if e_x and e_y are the absolute errors in the two measurements, we have

$$x + y = (\hat{x} + e_x) + (\hat{y} + e_y)$$
$$= (\hat{x} + \hat{y}) + (e_x + e_y)$$

or

$$(x + y) - (\hat{x} + \hat{y}) = e_x + e_y$$

Thus, the absolute error in the sum of $\hat{x}$ and $\hat{y}$ is $e_x + e_y$. Similarly, we can show that the absolute error in $\hat{x} - \hat{y}$ is $e_x - e_y$. Now consider the product of x and y:

$$\begin{aligned} xy &= (\hat{x} + e_x)(\hat{y} + e_y) \\ &= \hat{x}\hat{y} + e_x\hat{y} + e_y\hat{x} + e_x e_y \end{aligned}$$

If we assume that the absolute errors e_x and e_y are small, then their product is also small and can be ignored. Thus, an approximation to the absolute error in the product of $\hat{x}$ and $\hat{y}$ is the following:

$$e_{xy} \approx e_x\hat{y} + e_y\hat{x}$$

It can also be shown that an approximation to the absolute error in the quotient $\hat{x}/\hat{y}$ is the following:

$$e_{x/y} \approx \frac{1}{\hat{y}}e_x - \frac{\hat{x}}{\hat{y}^2}e_y$$

Recall that the relative error is computed by dividing the absolute error by the approximation. Thus, the following table summarizes the *error propagation* for both absolute errors and relative errors.

ERROR PROPAGATION

	ABSOLUTE ERROR	RELATIVE ERROR
Addition, $x+y$	$e_x + e_y$	$\dfrac{e_x + e_y}{\hat{x} + \hat{y}}$
Subtraction, $x-y$	$e_x - e_y$	$\dfrac{e_x - e_y}{\hat{x} - \hat{y}}$
Multiplication, xy	$e_x\hat{y} + e_y\hat{x}$	$\dfrac{e_x}{\hat{x}} + \dfrac{e_y}{\hat{y}}$
Division, x/y	$\dfrac{1}{\hat{y}}e_x - \dfrac{\hat{x}}{\hat{y}^2}e_y$	$\dfrac{e_x}{\hat{x}} - \dfrac{e_y}{\hat{y}}$

KEY WORDS

cubic polynomial
cubic spline
curvature
curve fitting
error propagation
interpolation
least-squares methods
linear interpolation

linear models
nonlinear models
polynomial models
regression
residual
slope
tridiagonal system

PROBLEMS

We begin our problem set with modifications to programs developed earlier in this chapter. Give the decomposition, refined pseudocode or flowchart, and FORTRAN solution for each problem.

Problems 1–5 modify the program WIND, given on page 533, which uses linear interpolation with data from wind tunnel tests.

1. Modify the linear interpolation program so that it prints a message to the user giving the range of angles that are covered in the data file.
2. Modify the linear interpolation program so that it prints the two flight path angles between which the maximum coefficient of lift occurs.
3. Modify the linear interpolation program so that it computes the range of angles that are covered in the data file and prints this range in both degrees and radians.
4. Modify the linear interpolation program so that it asks the user to enter the flight path angle in radians and then converts the angle to degrees to match the data file in the computations.
5. Modify the linear interpolation program so that it asks the user to enter the flight path angle in degrees, but assume that the data file contains the angle in radians.

Problems 6–10 modify the program PATH, given on page 545, which uses cubic spline interpolation to determine a robot arm path.

6. Modify the cubic spline interpolation program so that it prints the curvature at the points in the given path.
7. Modify the cubic spline interpolation program so that it prints the cubic equations computed for the cubic spline.
8. Modify the cubic spline interpolation program so that it asks the user to enter the increment in the x axis that is to be used for interpolating the points.

9. Modify the cubic spline interpolation program so that it asks the user to enter an x value and then computes the corresponding function value using the cubic spline.

10. Modify the cubic spline interpolation program so that it reads a set of x coordinates from an additional data file XSTEPS. Use the cubic spline to compute the corresponding y values, and write the new set of x and y coordinates to a new data file XYSTEPS.

Problems 11–15 modify the program LINEAR, given on page 562, which computes a linear model for a set of data.

11. Modify the linear model program so that it prints the point that has the largest residual in absolute value (the point that deviates the most from the approximate linear model).

12. Modify the linear model program so that it computes the error sum as the sum of the absolute value of the difference between the actual data value for y and its estimated value.

13. Modify the linear model program so that it computes the slope and y-intercept in a subroutine.

14. Modify the linear model program so that it reads a data file that has a trailer record containing -999, -999 as the coordinates of the data point.

15. Modify the linear model program so that it asks the user to enter an x value and then uses the linear equation that has been computed to estimate the corresponding y value.

In problems 16–23, develop programs and modules using the five-phase design process.

16. Write a program for linear interpolation that reads a file containing x and y coordinates. Assume that the values for x and for y are monotonically increasing; that is, $x(n + 1) > x(n)$ and $y(n + 1) > y(n)$. Allow the user to enter a value for either x or y, and then interpolate for the corresponding value. (In this problem, you are interpolating for a function value that can be a function of x or a function of y. Be careful to adjust the interpolation function appropriately.)

17. The program in problem 16 should work correctly for values of x and y where x and y are monotonically decreasing. Develop a data file and test it with the program from problem 16.

18. The program in problem 16 should work correctly if the values for x are monotonically increasing and the values for y are monotonically decreasing, or vice versa. Develop two data files and test them with the program from problem 16.

19. Assume that we have a data file containing 20 pairs of x and y coordinates, such that all the values of x and y are positive. Compute the best power equation ($y = bx^a$) that fits the data in terms of least squares.

20. Modify the program in problem 19 such that it also computes the best linear model for the data. Determine whether the linear model or the power model is better by comparing the error sums in the two cases.

21. Develop equations to use the linear modeling technique with the exponential equation $y = be^{ax}$. Use the development of Eqs. (12–6)–(12–12) as a guide.

22. Write a program that computes the best exponential model for a set of data, using the equations developed in problem 21. If the set of data contains y coordinates that are negative, print an error message indicating that the model cannot be computed using data with negative y coordinates.

23. Write a program that generates the best linear model, the best power model, and the best exponential model for a set of data. Then determine which model is the best match to the data by comparing the error sums. If the set of data contains x or y coordinates that are negative, print an error message indicating that the power model cannot be computed using data with negative x or y coordinates. If the set of data contains y coordinates that are negative, print an error message indicating that the exponential model cannot be computed using data with negative y coordinates.

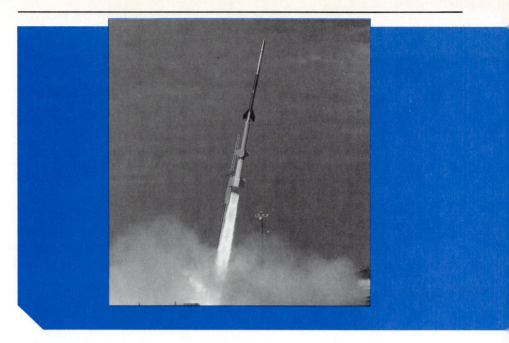

APPLICATION—Sounding Rocket Trajectory (Aerospace Engineering)

Sounding rockets are often used by scientists to study the upper regions of the Earth's atmosphere. A telemetry system, mounted in the nose of the rocket, transmits scientific data to a receiver at the launch site as the rocket passes through the different levels of the atmosphere. In addition to the scientific data, performance measurements on the rocket itself are also transmitted to be monitored by test range safety personnel and to be analyzed later by engineers. One of those measurements is the rocket's altitude from the time of launch until the test is completed. Write a program to compute the velocity and acceleration of the rocket using numerical differentiation of the altitude data. (See Section 13–5 for the solution.)

Photo courtesy of NASA Wallops Flight Facility.

13

NUMERICAL INTEGRATION AND DIFFERENTIATION

Introduction

13–1 Integration Using the Trapezoidal Rule

13–2 Application—Frequency Bands (Electrical Engineering)

13–3 Integration Using Simpson's Rule

13–4 Numerical Differentiation

13–5 Application—Sounding Rocket Trajectory (Aerospace Engineering)

Summary

INTRODUCTION

The operations of integration and differentiation give engineers and scientists important information about functions or data sets. For example, distance, velocity, and acceleration all relate to each other through integrals (*integration*) and derivatives (*differentiation*). Velocity is the integral of acceleration and the derivative of distance with respect to time. The topics of integration and differentiation are covered in detail in calculus courses, but the underlying principles can be explained simply in terms of areas and slopes. The integral of a function over an interval represents the area under the graph of the function; differentiation corresponds to computing the tangents or slopes to the function at specified points. Both of these computations can be numerically approximated using FORTRAN. In this chapter we present several techniques for performing *numerical integration* and *numerical differentiation*.

13–1   INTEGRATION USING THE TRAPEZOIDAL RULE

In order to use the analytical techniques of calculus to obtain the integral of a function over an interval, we must have an equation for the function. In many engineering and scientific applications, we have data points or measurements from the function, but we do not have an explicit equation. Therefore, we need a method that requires only points of the function to numerically compute the integral. In other applications, we may have an equation that defines the function, but it is difficult or impossible to determine the integral analytically. In this case we would also like to have a method that allows us to compute points or values of the function and then numerically evaluate the integral. The technique that we present in this section is a simple way to numerically estimate the area under a curve, given points on the curve. The technique uses the areas of trapezoids and thus is called integration using the *trapezoidal rule*.

The integral of the function $f(x)$, evaluated from a to b, is expressed as $\int_a^b f(x)\,dx$ and represents the area under the function $f(x)$ from $x = a$ to $x = b$, as shown in this diagram:

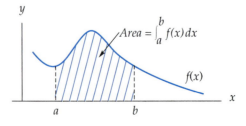

If we are given the function that represents the curve, we can evaluate the function at points spaced along the interval of interest, as shown:

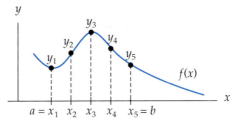

Note that since $y = f(x)$, we can represent $f(x_1)$ as y_1, $f(x_2)$ as y_2, and so on.

If we join the points on the curve with straight line segments, we form a group of trapezoids whose combined areas approximate the area under the curve. The closer the points are together on the curve, the more trapezoids there are in the interval, and thus the more accurate will be our approximation to the integral. In the diagram below, we use five points on the curve to generate four trapezoids, and the sum of the areas of the four trapezoids is then an approximation to the integral of the function between a and b.

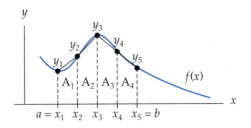

Recall that the equation for computing the area of a trapezoid is equal to one-half times the base times the sum of the two heights (or sides):

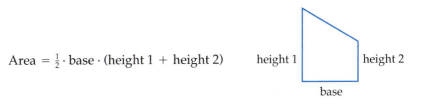

Area $= \frac{1}{2} \cdot \text{base} \cdot (\text{height 1} + \text{height 2})$

Thus, the area of the first trapezoid, A_1, is computed using the pair of points (x_1,y_1) and (x_2,y_2):

$$A_1 = \tfrac{1}{2} \cdot (x_2 - x_1) \cdot (y_1 + y_2)$$

Since the points on the curve are equally spaced along the x axis in this example, the base of each of the trapezoids is the same value. We can then compute the individual areas of the trapezoids as

$$A_1 = \tfrac{1}{2} \cdot \text{base} \cdot (y_1 + y_2)$$
$$A_2 = \tfrac{1}{2} \cdot \text{base} \cdot (y_2 + y_3)$$
$$A_3 = \tfrac{1}{2} \cdot \text{base} \cdot (y_3 + y_4)$$
$$A_4 = \tfrac{1}{2} \cdot \text{base} \cdot (y_4 + y_5)$$

Thus, the total area between a and b can be approximated by the sum of the areas of the four trapezoids:

$$\int_a^b f(x)\, dx \approx \frac{\text{base}}{2} ((y_1 + y_2) + (y_2 + y_3) + (y_3 + y_4) + (y_4 + y_5))$$

$$\approx \frac{\text{base}}{2} (y_1 + 2y_2 + 2y_3 + 2y_4 + y_5)$$

In general, if the area under a curve is divided into N trapezoids with equal bases, the area can be approximated by the following equation:

$$\int_a^b f(x)\, dx \approx \frac{\text{base}}{2} (y_1 + 2 \sum_{k=2}^{N} y_k + y_{N+1})$$

This equation is referred to as the trapezoidal rule.

When computing an integral with this numerical technique, we need to remember that the data points on the curve could come from different sources. If we have the equation for the curve, the program can compute the data points that we then use as the heights of the trapezoids; in this case, we can choose the data points to be as close together or as far apart as we wish. Another possibility is that the points are experimentally collected data; in this case, we have a set of x coordinates that represent the trapezoid base values and the y coordinates that represent the heights of the trapezoids. We can still use the trapezoid areas to estimate the integral, but we cannot choose data points that are closer together or farther apart because we do not have a function to evaluate; we only have the available data to use. If the bases of the trapezoids determined by the data points are not of equal value, we have to add the areas of the trapezoids individually instead of using the equation that assumes that the bases are equal.

This self-test allows you to check quickly to see if you have remembered the key points from Section 13–1. If you have any problems with the exercises, you should reread this section. The solutions are included at the end of the text.

Let the function $f(x)$ be defined by the following equation:

$$f(x) = 3x - 2x^2$$

1. Sketch the function over the interval $[-1, 2]$.
2. Use the trapezoidal rule to compute the integral of $f(x)$ from $x = 0$ to $x = 1$, using two trapezoids.
3. Use the trapezoidal rule to compute the integral of $f(x)$ from $x = 0$ to $x = 1$, using five trapezoids.
4. The exact value of the integral is $\frac{5}{6}$. Compare your answers in problems 2 and 3 to this exact value. Explain the difference between the answers for problems 2 and 3.

13-2 APPLICATION—FREQUENCY BANDS (Electrical Engineering)

When we transmit communication signals, we are concerned about the power in the signal because the more powerful the signal, the better the transmission that occurs. However, for efficient transmission, we do not want to transmit more signal power than is necessary. Hence, when we have a signal to transmit, we often compute the function that describes the power of the signal with respect to the frequencies within the signal. Before transmitting the signal, the power of the signal contained in an interval or band between two frequencies is computed; this computation is the integral of the power function between the two frequencies, or the area under the power function curve between the two frequencies. For some signals we can derive an equation that represents the power in the signal. For other signals, we do not have an equation that defines the power in the signal; instead, we have only points on the power function that are computed using digital signal processing techniques.

Write a program to compute the power in a specified frequency band given the following equation which describes the power in a signal with respect to frequency:

$$y = f(x)$$
$$= 4e^{-x}$$

where the units of x are Hz (Hertz, or cycles per second) and the units of y are power per Hz. Use the trapezoidal rule to approximate the power in a band of frequencies, and allow the user to choose both the band of frequencies and the number of trapezoids.

PROBLEM STATEMENT

Determine an estimate of the integral (between two specified points) of the following equation:

$$y = f(x)$$
$$= 4e^{-x}$$

INPUT/OUTPUT DESCRIPTION

The input values specify the endpoints of the interval and the number of trapezoids to use. The output is the estimate of the area under the function curve.

HAND EXAMPLE

For a hand-worked example, assume that we are interested in the area under $f(x)$ in the interval [0.0,1.0] and that we plan to use five trapezoids.

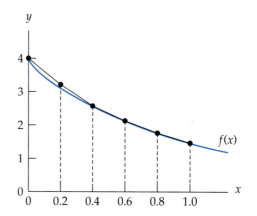

The following table shows the x and y coordinates and the computations for the areas of the five trapezoids:

X	Y	
0.0	4.0	
		$(0.5)(0.2)(4.0 + 3.27) = 0.73$
0.2	3.27	
		$(0.5)(0.2)(3.27 + 2.68) = 0.60$
0.4	2.68	
		$(0.5)(0.2)(2.68 + 2.20) = 0.49$
0.6	2.20	
		$(0.5)(0.2)(2.20 + 1.80) = 0.40$
0.8	1.80	
		$(0.5)(0.2)(1.80 + 1.47) = 0.33$
1.0	1.47	
	Sum of trapezoids	$= 2.55$

(The exact value of the integral is 2.528482 units of power, using seven digits of accuracy.)

ALGORITHM DEVELOPMENT

In the solution that we develop, we allow the user to experiment with the number of trapezoids within the program, rather than having to rerun the program to try a new number of trapezoids. The decomposition of the solution into general steps is the following:

DECOMPOSITION

```
For each estimate,
    Read interval endpoints and number of trapezoids
    Compute and print estimate of area
```

The length of the entire interval is determined by subtracting the left endpoint from the right endpoint. This length is then divided by the number of trapezoids, giving us the size of each base. Since the trapezoids have equal bases, we can use the summation equation presented in the previous section for computing the sum of the areas of the trapezoids. We now develop the pseudocode for this integration technique:

$$\text{AREA1: done} \leftarrow \text{false}$$

While not done do
    Read endpoints a, b
    Read number of trapezoids, N
    If N = 0 then
        done ← true
    Else
        sum ← 0

$$\text{base} \leftarrow \frac{b-a}{N}$$

$$\text{area} \leftarrow \frac{\text{base}}{2}\left(f(a) + 2\sum_{i=2}^{N} f(x_k) + f(b)\right)$$

        Print N, area

Converting the pseudocode into FORTRAN gives the following program:

FORTRAN PROGRAM

```
*-------------------------------------------------------------*
      PROGRAM   AREA1
*
*  This program estimates the area under a given curve
*  using trapezoids with equal bases.
*
      INTEGER  N, K
      REAL   F, X, A, B, SUM, BASE, XK, AREA
      LOGICAL   DONE
*
      F(X) = 4.0*EXP(-X)
*
      DONE = .FALSE.
*
    5 IF (.NOT.DONE) THEN
         PRINT*, 'ENTER THE INTERVAL ENDPOINTS'
         READ*, A, B
         PRINT*, 'ENTER THE NUMBER OF TRAPEZOIDS'
         PRINT*, '(ZERO TO QUIT)'
         READ*, N
         IF (N.EQ.0) THEN
            DONE = .TRUE.
         ELSE
            SUM = 0.0
            BASE = (B-A)/REAL(N)
            DO 10 K=2,N
               XK = A + BASE*(K-1)
               SUM = SUM + F(XK)
   10       CONTINUE
            AREA = 0.5*BASE*(F(A) + 2.0*SUM + F(B))
            PRINT 15, N, AREA
   15       FORMAT (1X,'USING ',I3,' TRAPEZOIDS,'
     +              ' THE ESTIMATED AREA IS ',F7.3)
            PRINT*
         ENDIF
         GO TO 5
      ENDIF
*
      END
*-------------------------------------------------------------*
```

Note that the function $f(x)$ is written as a statement function. If the function could not have been expressed in a single assignment statement, we would have used a regular function subprogram.

TESTING

The following output represents estimates of the function over the interval [0,1], using 5, 10, 50, and 100 trapezoids.

```
ENTER THE INTERVAL ENDPOINTS
0.0 1.0
ENTER THE NUMBER OF TRAPEZOIDS
(ZERO TO QUIT)
5
USING    5 TRAPEZOIDS, THE ESTIMATED AREA IS   2.537

ENTER THE INTERVAL ENDPOINTS
0.0 1.0
ENTER THE NUMBER OF TRAPEZOIDS
(ZERO TO QUIT)
10
USING   10 TRAPEZOIDS, THE ESTIMATED AREA IS   2.531

ENTER THE INTERVAL ENDPOINTS
0.0 1.0
ENTER THE NUMBER OF TRAPEZOIDS
(ZERO TO QUIT)
50
USING   50 TRAPEZOIDS, THE ESTIMATED AREA IS   2.529

ENTER THE INTERVAL ENDPOINTS
0.0 1.0
ENTER THE NUMBER OF TRAPEZOIDS
(ZERO TO QUIT)
100
USING  100 TRAPEZOIDS, THE ESTIMATED AREA IS   2.529

ENTER THE INTERVAL ENDPOINTS
0.0 1.0
ENTER THE NUMBER OF TRAPEZOIDS
(ZERO TO QUIT)
0
```

If we use calculus to integrate the specified function over the interval [0,1], the theoretical answer to seven digits of accuracy is 2.528482. Although we did not see the answer improve when we increased the number of trapezoids from 50 to 100, the answer may have changed in decimal positions that were not printed. If we want to print more than three decimal digits of accuracy, we can increase the number of decimal digits in the corresponding format specification.

We also present a program that reads the data from a file instead of computing it from an equation. Note that the number of data points determines the number of trapezoids. We recalculate the base of the trapezoid for each new pair of data points because we cannot assume that all of the x coordinates are equally spaced across the interval. We do not need the data points after we have determined the area of the corresponding trapezoid; thus, no array is needed to store the data. However, we do need to use the coordinates for two points at a time in order to compute the area of the corresponding trapezoid. We represent these points by a left point and a right point for a trapezoid. Note that the right point becomes the left point for the next trapezoid.

FORTRAN Program

```
*-------------------------------------------------------------*
*      PROGRAM  AREA2
*
*  This program estimates the area under a given curve
*  using a set of data points in a data file.
*
       INTEGER  N
       REAL  SUM, XL, YL, XR, YR, BASE, AREA
*
       DATA  N, SUM /0, 0.0/
*
       OPEN (UNIT=12,FILE='POINTS',STATUS='OLD')
*
       READ (12,*,END=5) XL, YL
*
     1 READ (12,*,END=5) XR,YR
          BASE = XR - XL
          AREA = 0.5*BASE*(YL + YR)
          SUM = SUM + AREA
          XL = XR
          YL = YR
          N = N + 1
          GO TO 1
*
     5 PRINT 15, N, SUM
    15 FORMAT (1X,'USING ',I3,' TRAPEZOIDS,'
       +             ' THE ESTIMATED AREA IS ',F7.3)
*
       END
*-------------------------------------------------------------*
```

13–3 INTEGRATION USING SIMPSON'S RULE

Trapezoidal integration uses straight line segments between the data points to approximate the function being integrated. The error that is made in calculating the integral between any two data points is equal to the area between the function curve and the straight line segment. This error can be reduced if a curve that more closely matches the function curve can be drawn through the data points and then integrated. *Simpson's rule* uses parabolas (second-degree polynomials) between sets of three data points at a time, integrates the area under the parabolas, and then sums those integrals to approximate the integral of the function. This method usually provides a more accurate estimate of the integral than is obtained using the trapezoidal rule.

To use Simpson's rule to approximate an integral, we begin by dividing the area to be integrated into an even number of equally spaced intervals of width h. For the following figure, assume that there are six intervals. We then estimate the integral by summing areas under the function curve using two intervals at a time. Thus, we will calculate the areas A_1, A_2, and A_3 and sum those areas to estimate the area under the curve from x_1 to x_7.

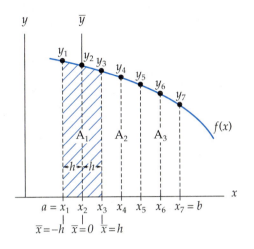

Beginning with the first area, A_1, which is shown as the shaded region in the diagram, we will now find the equation of the parabola that passes through points y_1, y_2, and y_3. For mathematical simplicity, a temporary y axis, $\bar{y}$, is drawn at x_2 by defining

$$\bar{x} = x - x_2 \tag{13-1}$$

A parabola, whose form is

$$\bar{y} = a\bar{x}^2 + b\bar{x} + c \tag{13-2}$$

is then constructed through y_1, y_2, and y_3. The area under this curve, which is the area of the first two intervals, is shown as the shaded region, A_1. We can integrate Eq. (13-2) from x_1 to x_3 to find the area A_1:

$$A_1 = \int_{-h}^{h} (a\bar{x}^2 + b\bar{x} + c)\, d\bar{x}$$

$$= \left[\frac{a}{3}\bar{x}^3 + \frac{b}{2}\bar{x}^2 + c\bar{x} \right] \Bigg|_{-h}^{h}$$

$$= \left[\frac{a}{3}h^3 + \frac{b}{2}h^2 + ch \right] - \left[\frac{a}{3}(-h)^3 + \frac{b}{2}(-h)^2 + c(-h) \right]$$

$$= \tfrac{2}{3}ah^3 + 2ch \tag{13-3}$$

The next step is to determine the constants a and c for the parabola which passes through y_1, y_2, and y_3. This can be done by first writing Eq. (13–2) for each of the three data points:

$$y_1 = a(-h)^2 + b(-h) + c \tag{13–4}$$
$$= ah^2 - bh + c$$
$$y_2 = a(0)^2 + b(0) + c$$
$$= c \tag{13–5}$$
$$y_3 = ah^2 + bh + c \tag{13–6}$$

We then add Eqs. (13–4) and (13–6) to eliminate b:

$$y_1 + y_3 = 2ah^2 + 2c \tag{13–7}$$

Next, we substitute Eq. (13–5) into Eq. (13–7) and solve for a:

$$a = \frac{y_1 - 2y_2 + y_3}{2h^2} \tag{13–8}$$

Finally, we substitute Eqs. (13–5) and (13–8) into Eq. (13–3) and rearrange to find the area A_1:

$$A_1 = \frac{h}{3}(y_1 + 4y_2 + y_3) \tag{13–9}$$

We can then use the same approach to find the areas of A_2 and A_3:

$$A_2 = \frac{h}{3}(y_3 + 4y_4 + y_5) \tag{13–10}$$

$$A_3 = \frac{h}{3}(y_5 + 4y_6 + y_7) \tag{13–11}$$

The integral of the function, $f(x)$, from a to b is then approximated by summing the areas A_1, A_2, and A_3:

$$\int_a^b f(x)\,dx \approx A_1 + A_2 + A_3$$

$$= \frac{h}{3}(y_1 + 4y_2 + 2y_3 + 4y_4 + 2y_5 + 4y_6 + y_7) \tag{13–12}$$

The form of Eq. (13–12) can be expanded to give us a general equation for integrating a function, $f(x)$, by dividing the region to be integrated into an even number of N equally spaced intervals and computing the sum of the terms:

$$\int_{x_1}^{x_{N+1}} f(x)\,dx \approx \frac{h}{3}\left(y_1 + 4\sum_{j\ even}^{N} y_j + 2\sum_{k\ odd}^{N-1} y_k + y_{N+1}\right) \tag{13–13}$$

where j begins with the value 2 and k begins with the value 3. This formula is referred to as Simpson's rule or, occasionally, as Simpson's one-third rule.

Although we have discussed only the trapezoidal rule and Simpson's rule, there are many other numerical integration methods, such as Gauss quadrature formulas. Most of these other methods are more complicated, however, and the accuracy improvement they may offer is seldom needed. Therefore, the relative simplicity and applicability of the trapezoidal rule and Simpson's rule cause them to be used much more often in engineering applications than other numerical integration methods.

SELF-TEST 13–2

This self-test allows you to check quickly to see if you have remembered the key points from Section 13–3. If you have any problems with the exercises, you should reread this section. The solutions are included at the end of the text.

Let the function f be defined by the following equation:

$$f(x) = 4e^{-x}$$

This function was used with trapezoidal integration in Section 13–2.

1. Sketch the function over the interval [0,1].
2. Use Simpson's rule with two intervals to estimate the integral of this function over the interval [0,1]. Keep three decimal digits of accuracy in your answer.
3. When using five trapezoids, this area is estimated to be 2.537. The exact answer to three decimal digits is 2.528. Compare your answer in problem 2 to the trapezoidal estimate and explain the differences.

13–4 NUMERICAL DIFFERENTIATION

Much of the field of calculus is concerned with the concepts of derivatives and integrals of functions. Derivatives and integrals are closely related because they reverse, or "undo," each other. If we take the *derivative* of a function, we get a new function. If we then integrate that new function, we get the original function back again, to within a constant. Reversing the order (integral, then derivative) also gives us back the original function to within a constant.

We saw in the previous sections that the integral of a function could be described graphically—it was the area under the function curve. The derivative of a function is the rate of change of the function. Like the integral, it can also be described graphically as shown in the next plot, which contains a function curve $y = f(x)$ and a line L which is tangent to the curve at the point (x_1, y_1). The first derivative of $f(x)$, with respect to x at x_1, is equal to the slope of the tangent line at x_1, which is dy/dx.

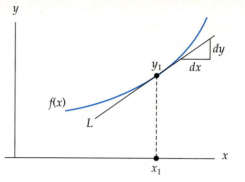

If we calculated the slopes of the tangent lines at many points along the function curve and plotted the resulting values, we would get a new curve which would be the first derivative of $y = f(x)$. Tangent lines to this new curve would represent the derivative of the first derivative, or the second derivative of $y = f(x)$. Third and higher derivatives can be obtained by continuing this process of calculating the slopes of tangent lines to the curve and plotting those values to get the next curve.

When the derivative of a function is difficult or impossible to find mathematically, we can estimate it graphically, and thus numerically, by constructing secant lines between data points for the function and computing their slopes. In the figure below, we show three of the data points from a larger set of data for a function $y = f(x)$.

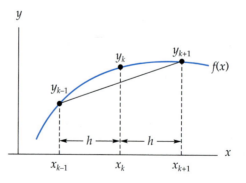

As illustrated in the figure, the first derivative y_k' at x_k can be estimated by computing the slope of the secant line connecting points y_{k-1} and y_{k+1}:

$$y_k' = \frac{y_{k+1} - y_{k-1}}{2h} \tag{13–14}$$

Note that as the data points get closer together, our estimate for the derivative at y_k should become increasingly accurate because, in the limit as h approaches zero, the slope of the secant line connecting the data points approaches the slope of the tangent line at y_k.

To compute the second derivative y_k'', which is the rate of change of the slope or of the first derivative at x_k, we apply this method again. In the following figure, we draw secant lines between the adjacent points and compute the slopes of these two lines. We then compute the difference in the slopes of the two lines and divide by the distance between their midpoints. The result is the rate of change of the slope, which is also an estimate of the second derivative of the function at x_k.

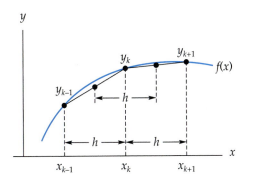

Thus our formula for estimating the second derivative is:

$$y_k'' = \frac{\dfrac{y_{k+1} - y_k}{h} - \dfrac{y_k - y_{k-1}}{h}}{h}$$

$$= \frac{y_{k+1} - 2y_k + y_{k-1}}{h^2} \tag{13-15}$$

The equations for the first derivative and for the second derivative are examples of "central difference" expressions, because they compute differences using data values on both sides of the point at which we are estimating the derivative. Similar *difference expressions* can be derived using only points to the left or only points to the right of the point at which we are estimating the derivative; these formulas are called backward difference and forward difference expressions, respectively. The central difference expressions are recommended over the backward and forward difference expressions because they are more accurate. Note that we cannot compute derivatives for the first and last points of a set of data using central difference equations because we do not have function values on both sides of the endpoints. For these points we would use forward or backward difference expressions.

If we use additional data points to the left and right in the difference expressions above (that is, use more than one point to the left and more than one point to the right), the estimation accuracy for the derivatives can be improved. In fact, derivatives beyond the first derivative and second derivative require us to use additional points. Since most differentiation problems can be solved using the two equations presented in this section, we do not derive any additional difference expressions here; however, some of these equations are provided in the problems at the end of the chapter, and most numerical methods texts contain tables of the various difference expressions.

Caution should be exercised when using numerical differentiation because it should be used only with accurate data sets. Noise or other sources of inaccuracy in the data can cause large inaccuracies in the estimates of the derivatives. This problem can be seen clearly in the figures below. Each graph shows a set of data which represent the same unknown function $f(x)$. In the left figure, the data points are accurate and closely spaced, but in the right figure they are noisy and widely spaced. In the left figure, we see that we can get a reasonably good estimate of the slope of the curve at point B by computing the slope of the secant line which connects points A and C. On the other hand, we see that the same technique applied to the figure on the right does not provide an accurate estimate of the slope at point B. And computing the second derivative, which is the rate of change of the slope of the curve, can introduce even larger errors.

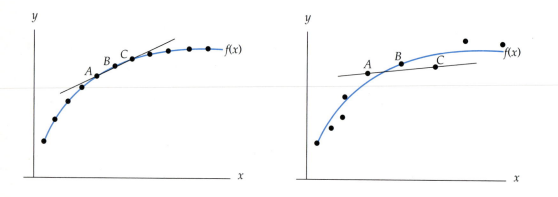

We see, therefore, that numerical differentiation should be used only for data sets that represent the function accurately and that even then the results should be used with care.

Another technique for estimating derivatives, especially when the data are inaccurate, would be to use the curve-fitting techniques of Chapter 12. If you fit a least-squares polynomial model to the data, you can then take the derivative of the polynomial using calculus and solve for the derivatives at specific points. This method may give more accurate results, but it requires more computations.

This self-test allows you to check quickly to see if you have remembered the key points from Section 13–4. If you have any problems with the exercises, you should reread this section. The solutions are included at the end of the text.

The following data represent time data and altitude data from the launch of a weather balloon:

TIME (SECONDS)	ALTITUDE (FEET)
0.0	0.0
0.5	50.0
1.0	75.0
1.5	125.0
2.0	175.0

1. Plot the altitude data and sketch the curve they represent.
2. Compute first derivative values using the central difference equation derived in this section. Sketch these velocity data.
3. Compute second derivative values using the central difference equation derived in this section. Sketch these acceleration data.

13–5 APPLICATION—SOUNDING ROCKET TRAJECTORY (Aerospace Engineering)

A two-stage sounding rocket is launched to perform high-altitude atmospheric research on the ionosphere. (Sounding rockets probe different levels of the atmosphere.) The first stage of the rocket burns for approximately 35 seconds and accelerates the rocket to a velocity of 1250 meters per second. It then coasts for almost 2 minutes before reaching the lower region of the ionosphere at about 100 kilometers. By then, gravity has slowed the rocket's ascent to about 100 meters per second. The second stage then ignites and accelerates the rocket through the ionosphere and into space.

The rocket carries a scientific package for conducting several measurements on the upper atmosphere. A telemetry system in the rocket's payload section (in the nose of the rocket) transmits the data to a receiver at the launch site. In addition to the scientific data, performance measurements on the rocket itself are also transmitted to be monitored by range safety personnel and to be analyzed later by engineers. One of those measurements is the rocket's altitude from the time of launch until the test is completed. The altitude measurements are plotted versus the time of flight in the graph below, which contains data points collected at 10-second intervals along the actual altitude curve.

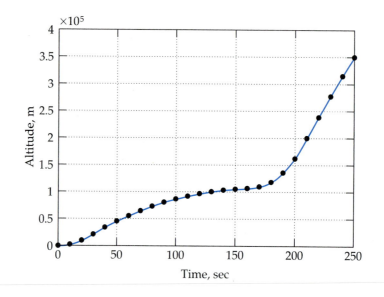

Before the rocket is flown, a simulation program is used to predict the acceleration, velocity, and altitude of the rocket as a function of time. After the actual flight of the rocket, a separate program is needed to differentiate the recorded altitude data in order to obtain estimates for (or to reconstruct) the velocity and acceleration for comparison with the simulation results.

Write the program that reads the recorded altitude data from a data file and estimates the corresponding velocity and acceleration information using numerical differentiation. Assume that the first line in the data file contains an integer which specifies the number of data points in the file; a data point consists of a time value and its corresponding altitude value in meters. Use numerical differentiation to compute and store the velocity and acceleration information in data files.

PROBLEM STATEMENT

Use numerical differentiation to compute velocity and acceleration data for a sounding rocket using the altitude and time data.

The input is a data file containing the altitude data. The output is two data files; one contains the estimated velocity information and the other contains the estimated acceleration information. The first line of each of the three files contains the number of data points in the file.

HAND EXAMPLE

Assume that the first six values of altitude data are the following:

TIME	ALTITUDE
0.0	0.0
1.0	100.
2.0	250.
3.0	430.
4.0	680.
5.0	980.

The derivative with respect to time of altitude data in meters gives the velocity in units of meters per second. Since the data are collected at equally spaced intervals in time, we can use Eq. (13–14) from the previous section to perform the computation of the first derivative, with the increment between data points equal to 1.0 second. Thus, the equation for computing the first derivative is

$$y'_k = \frac{y_{k+1} - y_{k-1}}{2h}$$
$$= \frac{y_{k+1} - y_{k-1}}{2.0}$$

The velocity values are:

$$\text{Velocity at 1.0 sec} = \frac{250 - 0.0}{2.0}$$
$$= 125 \text{ m/sec}$$
$$\text{Velocity at 2.0 sec} = 165 \text{ m/sec}$$
$$\text{Velocity at 3.0 sec} = 215 \text{ m/sec}$$
$$\text{Velocity at 4.0 sec} = 275 \text{ m/sec}$$

We now use Eq. (13–15) to compute the second derivative from the altitude data. This equation is

$$y''_k = \frac{y_{k+1} - 2y_k + y_{k-1}}{h^2}$$
$$= \frac{y_{k+1} - 2y_k + y_{k-1}}{1.0}$$

The acceleration values are:

$$\text{Acceleration at 1.0 sec} = \frac{250 - (2)(100) + 0}{1.0}$$
$$= 50 \text{ m/sec}^2$$

Acceleration at 2.0 sec $= 30 \text{ m/sec}^2$

Acceleration at 3.0 sec $= 70 \text{ m/sec}^2$

Acceleration at 4.0 sec $= 50 \text{ m/sec}^2$

ALGORITHM DEVELOPMENT

The decomposition of the solution into general steps is the following:

DECOMPOSITION

Read altitude data.
Compute and store velocity data.
Compute and store acceleration data.

The most straightforward way to implement the numerical differentiation technique is to store the time and altitude data from the data file in arrays. Then we use the equations for computing the first and second derivatives to calculate values of velocity and acceleration and store these values in additional arrays. When we write the information in the two output data files, we write the number of points in the first line and follow that with the data points.

We now develop the pseudocode to implement this differentiation technique.

NUMDIF: Read the number of altitude points, N
   Read the time and altitude data into arrays
   $h \leftarrow \text{time}(2) - \text{time}(1)$
   For $k = 2$ to $N-1$ do
     $\text{vel}(k) \leftarrow \dfrac{\text{alt}(k + 1) - \text{alt}(k - 1)}{2h}$
     Write time(k), vel(k) to data file
     $\text{acc}(k) \leftarrow \dfrac{\text{alt}(k + 1) - 2 \cdot \text{alt}(k) + \text{alt}(k - 1)}{h^2}$
     Write time(k), acc(k) to data file

The next step is to convert the pseudocode to FORTRAN.

```
*----------------------------------------------------------*
      PROGRAM  NUMDIF
*
*  This program uses numerical differentiation to compute the
*  velocity and acceleration data for a sounding rocket.
*
      INTEGER  N, K
      REAL  TIME(512), ALT(512), H, VEL(512), ACC(512)
*
      OPEN (UNIT=15,FILE='ALTITUDE',STATUS='OLD')
      OPEN (UNIT=16,FILE='VELOCITY',STATUS='NEW')
      OPEN (UNIT=17,FILE='ACCEL',STATUS='NEW')
*
*  Read time and altitude data.
*
      READ (15,*) N
      DO 10 K=1,N
          READ (15,*) TIME(K), ALT(K)
  10 CONTINUE
*
*  Compute and store velocities and accelerations.
*
      H = TIME(2) - TIME(1)
      WRITE (16,*) N-2
      WRITE (17,*) N-2

      DO 20 K=2,N-1
          VEL(K) = (ALT(K+1) - ALT(K-1))/(2.0*H)
          WRITE (16,*) TIME(K), VEL(K)
          ACC(K) = (ALT(K+1) - 2*ALT(K) + ALT(K-1))/(H*H)
          WRITE (17,*) TIME(K), ACC(K)
  20 CONTINUE
*
      END
*----------------------------------------------------------*
```

TESTING

The following data represent time and altitude above sea level for the two-stage rocket discussed at the beginning of this section:

Time	Altitude
0.0	$6.000000E+01$
10.0	$2.926538E+03$
20.0	$1.017024E+04$
30.0	$2.148626E+04$
40.0	$3.383508E+04$
50.0	$4.525083E+04$
60.0	$5.563449E+04$

70.0	6.503796E+04
80.0	7.346143E+04
90.0	8.090491E+04
100.0	8.736838E+04
110.0	9.285185E+04
120.0	9.735532E+04
130.0	1.008788E+05
140.0	1.034222E+05
150.0	1.049857E+05
160.0	1.061926E+05
170.0	1.102465E+05
180.0	1.196263E+05
190.0	1.361064E+05
200.0	1.620957E+05
210.0	1.995064E+05
220.0	2.387758E+05
230.0	2.770653E+05
240.0	3.143748E+05
250.0	3.507043E+05

The next pair of plots contain the actual velocity and acceleration functions along with circles that represent the values computed from the altitude data using numerical differentiation. Note that numerical differentiation does a good job of estimating the velocity and acceleration functions, except at points where the function changes rapidly. Also, from observing the velocity data we can see the rocket's velocity increasing, and then slowly decreasing after the first stage of the rocket burns out. When the second stage is fired, the velocity begins to increase again. From the acceleration plot, you can easily see the accelerations caused by the firing of the first stage and of the second stage. In the intervals after the firings, the acceleration is -9.8 m/sec^2, which is the downward acceleration due to gravity.

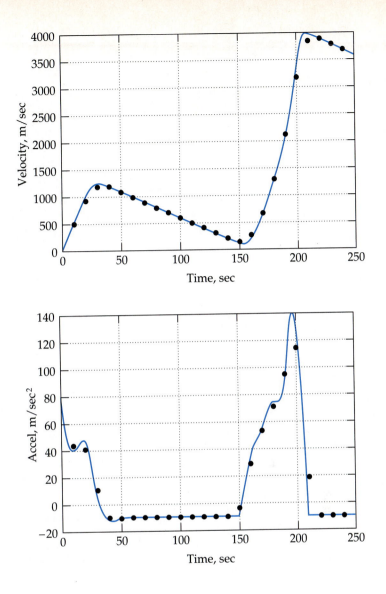

The data in the following two plots provide an interesting comparison to the previous plots. For these plots, the data points are 1 second apart, rather than 10 seconds apart. As you can see, when we use smaller time increments, our numerical estimates for velocity and acceleration become more accurate in the regions where the functions are changing rapidly.

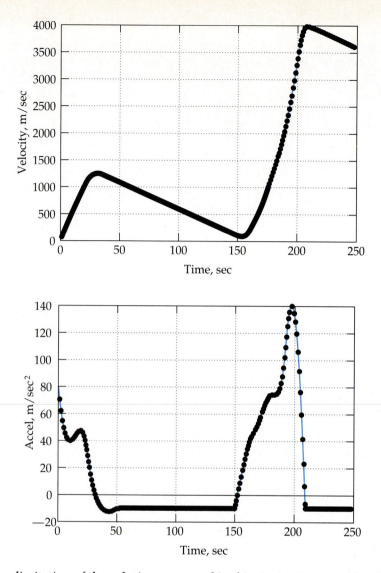

One limitation of the solution presented in this section is caused by the fact that we stored the data in arrays. The program specifies a maximum of 512 points; if more altitude points are needed, the array sizes need to be larger. It is also possible to develop a solution to this problem without using arrays. Since three altitude data points are needed to compute the corresponding velocity and acceleration, we could develop an algorithm that stores three altitude values in memory. After computing the corresponding velocity and acceleration values and writing the new values to data files, we then read a new altitude value to replace one of the three altitude values and repeat the process. This solution is more complicated to develop, but it is not limited by array sizes and is thus a more flexible solution.

SUMMARY

In this chapter we presented techniques for numerical integration and differentiation. The most common numerical integration technique uses areas of trapezoids to estimate the area under a curve. We developed programs that use this technique to estimate integrals using functions to compute points on the curve and also using data files containing experimentally measured points on the curve. We also presented Simpson's rule, which uses parabolic functions to estimate the area under a curve. Simpson's rule is more complicated than the trapezoidal rule but generally gives more accurate results. Numerical differentiation equations were developed using difference expressions for estimating both the first derivative and the second derivative of a function at a given point. Accuracy issues were discussed for both numerical integration and differentiation. The necessity for using accurate data when estimating derivatives was explained.

DEBUGGING AIDS

The equations for most numerical integration and differentiation techniques are simple, and therefore debugging these routines is usually straightforward. However, some caution must be taken in determining the step size of the small intervals used in these techniques. If the step size is too large in numerical integration, then trapezoids may not provide good approximations to the area under the curve. If the step size is too large in numerical differentiation, then the slope is computed using data points that are not close to the point at which we are estimating the derivative, and thus the result may not be accurate. If the step size is too small in numerical integration or differentiation, truncation and roundoff within the computer can cause errors. Therefore, selecting the proper step size can be an important part of numerical integration or differentiation.

STYLE/TECHNIQUE GUIDES

As we have mentioned before, when using a numerical technique, it is important to remember to add more documentation to your program. The documentation should include either specific references to more extensive documentation or some of the details of the technique used. For example, since there are a number of numerical differentiation techniques, the documentation should specify whether the routine is using a central difference approximation to the derivative or whether it is using a backward difference or a forward difference. Since the techniques are sensitive to the selection of the step size, it is convenient to allow the user to experiment with different step sizes. Therefore, you may want to write the routines such that the user can choose the step size. Be sure to include the step size when printing results from a numerical integration or differentiation routine.

ERROR ANALYSIS

At the end of the previous chapter we discussed roundoff errors which occur when we perform computations using a fixed number of digits of accuracy. Roundoff errors propagate as we perform more and more operations. Another type of error propagation is caused by errors in the data measurements themselves, called *inherent errors*. These errors come from a variety of sources. For example, if we measure a temperature by reading the mercury level on the thermometer, we are approximating the temperature. If we use a digital thermometer that shows a temperature of 100.3 degrees, this measurement is unlikely to be exactly 100.3 degrees, but may be accurate to the nearest tenth of a degree. To multiply a number by $\frac{1}{3}$, we can use 0.33, or 0.3333, or 0.3333333 to represent one-third, but an inherent error occurs in each representation. These examples of inherent errors occur when the measurement is made, and they become part of the absolute errors in the original estimates. These errors are also propagated by arithmetic operations. For instance, if $\hat{x}$ and $\hat{y}$ are data measurements with inherent errors i_x and i_y, and if r is the roundoff error, then the absolute error in adding $\hat{x}$ to $\hat{y}$ is

$$e_{x+y} = (x + y) - (x + y)\hat{}$$

But $(x + y)$ is equal to the estimates plus the inherent errors, and $(x + y)\hat{}$ is equal to the sum of the estimates. Therefore, the absolute error is equal to the difference in $(x + y)$ and $(x + y)\hat{}$, plus the roundoff error:

$$= (\hat{x} + i_x + \hat{y} + i_y) - (\hat{x} + \hat{y}) + r$$
$$= i_x + i_y + r$$

This error, e_{x+y}, is the error that is propagated when the sum $(\hat{x} + \hat{y})$ is used in another arithmetic operation.

KEY WORDS

derivative	numerical differentiation
difference expression	numerical integration
differentiation	Simpson's rule
inherent error	trapezoidal rule
integration	

PROBLEMS

We begin our problem set with modifications to programs developed earlier in this chapter. Give the decomposition, refined pseudocode or flowchart, and FORTRAN solution for each problem.

Problems 1–5 modify the program AREA1, given on page 578, which estimates the area under a curve.

1. Modify the area program so that the user specifies the interval only once, instead of entering it every time the number of trapezoids is changed. (Note that this restricts the program because if a different interval is desired, the program must be rerun.)

2. Modify the area program so that the number of trapezoids is initially set to 10 and the corresponding area is computed. Then, the number of trapezoids is doubled and the area is recomputed. This process continues until the change in the area is less than 0.01.

3. Modify the area program so that the number of trapezoids is initially set to 10 and the corresponding area is computed. Then, the number of trapezoids is doubled and the area is recomputed. This process continues until the change in the area is less than a user-entered tolerance.

4. Modify the area program so that the function value is computed in a function subprogram instead of a statement function.

5. Modify the area program so that it stores the x and y coordinates of the endpoints of the trapezoids in a data file so that they can be plotted later.

Problems 6–10 modify the program NUMDIF, given on page 591, which computes the velocity and acceleration for a sounding rocket.

6. Modify the differentiation program so that it uses the following forward difference approximation for the slope:

$$y'_k = \frac{y_{k+1} - y_k}{h}$$

(You will need to modify the equations for both derivatives.)

7. Modify the differentiation program so that it uses the following backward difference approximation for the slope:

$$y'_k = \frac{y_k - y_{k-1}}{h}$$

(You will need to modify the equations for both derivatives.)

8. Modify the differentiation program so that it uses the following central difference approximation, which does not assume that the step size between points is always the same value:

$$y'_k = \frac{y_{k+1} - y_{k-1}}{x_{k+1} - x_{k-1}}$$

(You will need to modify the equations for both derivatives.)

9. Modify the differentiation program so that it does not use arrays and thus is more flexible. (See the comments at the end of Section 13–5.)

10. Modify the differentiation program so that the output is one file that contains both the velocity and acceleration data. The first line of the file contains the number of data points. The following lines contain three values, the time, the corresponding velocity, and the corresponding acceleration.

In problems 11–15, develop programs and modules using the five-phase design process.

11. Modify the numerical integration program AREA1 on page 578 so that it uses Simpson's rule instead of the trapezoidal rule to compute the integral. Specify that the number of intervals must be an even number.

12. Modify the program developed in problem 11 so that it allows the user to specify any number of intervals. If the number of intervals is odd, use the trapezoidal rule for the first interval, and then use Simpson's rule for the rest of the intervals.

13. Write a program to read a set of (x,y) coordinates and compute slope values using the central difference equation developed in the text. Print the x coordinates and corresponding slopes.

14. Modify the program developed in problem 13 so that instead of printing a table of values, it prints the following message:

```
POINT OF MAXIMUM OR MINIMUM IN CURVE MAY OCCUR
NEAR X COORDINATE VALUE XXX.XX
```

This message should be printed when the sign of the slope changes.

15. When the first derivative of a function is zero, we can compute the second derivative to determine whether the point represents a maximum (second derivative is negative), a minimum (second derivative is positive), or an inflection point (second derivative equal to zero). Modify the program in problem 14 so that it specifies whether a point is a maximum, a minimum, or an inflection point when the first derivative is zero. (Assume that a value is zero if its absolute value is less than 0.001.)

Problems 16–18 refer to the following algorithm for computing pi. The area of a circle with radius 1 is equal to pi, and thus the area of a quarter circle with radius 1 is equal to pi/4. If we compute an estimate of the area of this quarter circle and multiply that value by 4, we have an estimate for the value of pi. To compute the area of the quarter circle, we sum the area of the subsections of the circle that are approximated by trapezoids, as shown in the following diagram. The values for y_i and y_{i+1} can be computed using the sine and cosine functions. If we assume that the areas of the subsections are added, starting with the subsections on the right, the appropriate equations are

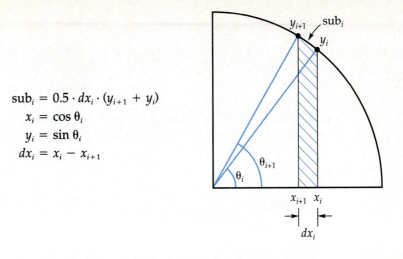

$$sub_i = 0.5 \cdot dx_i \cdot (y_{i+1} + y_i)$$
$$x_i = \cos \theta_i$$
$$y_i = \sin \theta_i$$
$$dx_i = x_i - x_{i+1}$$

16. Write a program to compute pi using the technique just described. Let the number of subsections be entered by the user.

17. Modify the program developed in problem 16 so that the variables and all computations are performed in double precision.

18. Modify the program developed in problem 16 so that the number of subsections is initialized to 100. Print the number of subsections and the estimate of pi, then repeat the process increasing the number of subsections by 100. Continue until the number of subsections is equal to 1000.

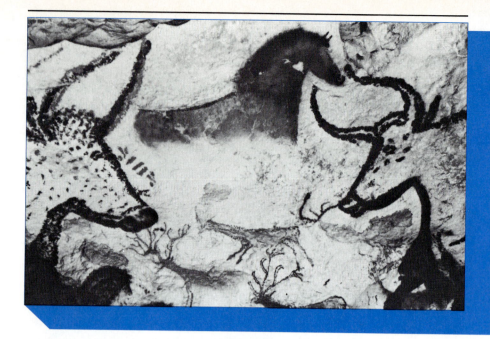

APPLICATION—Radioactive Decay and Carbon Dating (Archeology)

Carbon dating, a technique for estimating the age of organic substances, compares the amount of a radioactive carbon, carbon-14 or ^{14}C, that is contained in the remains of a substance with the amount that would have been in the object at the time it was alive. A specimen of charcoal found at Stonehenge contained 63% as much ^{14}C as a sample of present-day charcoal, and thus, using carbon dating, the sample of charcoal is about 3800 years old. The age of the cave paintings at Lascaux, France, has been estimated at 15,500 years using carbon dating. Radioactive decay can be expressed in terms of an ordinary differential equation. Write a program to numerically integrate this differential equation for use in carbon dating analysis. (See Section 14–2 for the solution.)

14

INTEGRATION OF ORDINARY DIFFERENTIAL EQUATIONS

Introduction

14–1 Euler's Method

14–2 Application—Radioactive Decay and Carbon Dating (Archeology)

14–3 Runge-Kutta Method

14–4 Application—Air Pollution Control (Environmental Engineering)

14–5 Discussion of Advanced Techniques

Summary

INTRODUCTION

Many engineering and scientific applications involve processes or systems that can be described in terms of the rate of change of one variable with respect to another. The equations which describe these relationships are called differential equations. The analysis of differential equations and their solutions is an important area in the field of mathematics. Unfortunately for the scientist or engineer, however, many differential equations of practical importance have very complicated analytical solutions or no analytical solutions at all. Numerical integration techniques have been developed for these instances. We are concerned here with the solution of ordinary differential equations, as opposed to partial differential equations, and more specifically, with first-order differential equations. Examples of first-order differential equations are

$$\frac{dy}{dx} = ky$$

$$\frac{dy}{dx} = \sin x$$

First-order differential equations such as these involve the first derivative of a function y with respect to x. As seen above, they may involve y as well. We should note that both of these differential equations have analytical solutions, which, when available, are always preferable to numerical solutions because they are exact. For those instances where analytical solutions are difficult or impossible to obtain, we present two common numerical techniques for solving ordinary first-order differential equations—Euler's method and the Runge-Kutta method.

14–1   EULER'S METHOD

When we solve a first-order *ordinary differential equation*, our objective is to find an unknown function of x whose first derivative with respect to x is some known function of x and/or y. That is, we are given

$$y' = \frac{d}{dx} f(x) = g(x,y) \tag{14–1}$$

and we wish to find

$$y = f(x) \tag{14–2}$$

If we know the derivative of a function, we should be able to integrate that derivative to find the function itself. That, in fact, is what *Euler's method* does. It is also the reason why the numerical solution is referred to as the "integration of ordinary differential equations."

To explain how Euler's method is applied we will use the next figure, which shows the unknown function curve $y = f(x)$:

We start our numerical approximation to the actual curve at the point (x_0, y_0). Euler's method, as well as other numerical integration solutions of differential equations, requires such starting points or values. As a result, problems which are solved using these methods are frequently referred to as *"initial value"* or "boundary value" problems. Using Eq. (14–1) to calculate the derivative, and thus the slope of the curve at (x_0, y_0), we can construct the tangent line shown in the figure. If we then proceed along this tangent line a small distance h in the x direction, to the point x_1, we can estimate the corresponding point on the function curve using the equation of a straight line. Thus, the estimate for y_1 is equal to y_0 plus the slope of the curve at y_0 times h (where the slope is $y' = dy / dx$):

$$y_1 = y_0 + h \cdot y_0' \qquad (14–3)$$

The current values of x and y are used together with the derivative to approximate the next value of y. With the new values (x_1, y_1), we can proceed to find the next estimates of the curve at (x_2, y_2), and so on, until we have approximated the function at all desired points. Therefore, Eq. (14–3) can be generalized to the following:

$$y_k = y_{k-1} + h \cdot y_{k-1}' \qquad (14–4)$$

If the horizontal distance, h, is reasonably small, the estimates that we compute using the slope (or derivative) are likely to be close to those we would get using the actual function $y = f(x)$. You may notice some similarities between Euler's method and the trapezoidal rule integration discussed in Chapter 13. For the trapezoidal rule, we used known values of the function connected with straight lines to find the integral of the function. For Euler's method, we use initial values of the function and its derivative and extrapolate using straight lines to obtain new estimates of the function and its derivative.

Because of its simplicity, Euler's method can be used to solve differential equations, even though it has the obvious shortcoming of approximating a curved line with a series of short, straight line segments. Nevertheless, it will usually provide a reasonably accurate estimate of the true value of the function if the *step size* is small enough and if the slope of the function curve does not change too rapidly. There are occasions, however, when the estimates diverge from the true values and the error becomes excessive. The reason for this divergence is shown in this figure:

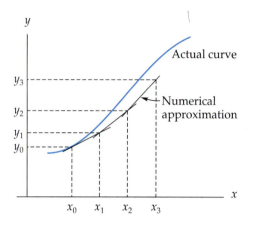

For the function curve shown, each new estimate falls farther away from the actual function value as x gets larger. Eventually, the error accumulates to the point that the estimated value of y may no longer be accurate enough. These errors arise from truncation, which will be discussed further in the section on the Runge-Kutta method. Combined with rounding errors in the computer, Euler's method has limited practical value, and caution should therefore always be exercised when using it. One easy way to check the accuracy of a solution is to compare solution results for different step sizes. For example, if the function value at a specific point changes significantly when the step size is cut in half, the results should be considered inaccurate. In these cases, it is often better to use a more accurate method, such as the improved Euler method, which is discussed in many numerical methods textbooks. There are also routines for adjusting the step size to improve accuracy. But a more accurate method yet would be the Runge-Kutta method, which is described in Section 14–3.

This self-test allows you to check quickly to see if you have remembered the key points from Section 14–1. If you have any problems with the exercises, you should reread this section. The solutions are included at the end of the text.

The following differential equation:

$$\frac{dy}{dx} = -y$$

has a family of solutions which are represented by the following equation:

$$y = f(x)$$
$$= -ke^{-x}$$

Let $k = 3$ in the exercises below.

1. Use the function $y = f(x)$ to compute $y_0 = f(0)$. This data point represents an initial condition.
2. Use the function $y = f(x)$ to compute $y = f(0.1)$ and $y = f(0.5)$. These are the theoretical values of y at $x = 0.1$ and at $x = 0.5$.
3. Use Eq. (14–3) to compute an estimate of y at $x = 0.1$. This is the approximation of the function at $x = 0.1$ using Euler's method. Compare the value to the theoretical value.
4. Use Eq. (14–4) to compute an estimate of y at $x = 0.5$ in two steps. This is the approximation of the function at $x = 0.5$ using Euler's method. Compare the value to the theoretical value. How could you increase the accuracy of the estimate?

14–2 APPLICATION—Radioactive Decay and Carbon Dating (Archeology)

Only about one-fourth of all known elements are stable. The rest of the elements have isotopes of different masses that undergo radioactive decay in which they give off radioactive particles or rays until they eventually become the stable isotope of the element. Carbon dating, a technique for estimating the age of organic substances, compares the amount of a radioactive carbon, carbon-14 or ^{14}C, that is contained in the remains of a substance with the amount that would have been in the object at the time it was alive. The age of the cave paintings at Lascaux, France, has been estimated at 15,500 years using carbon dating. A specimen of charcoal found at Stonehenge contained 63% as much ^{14}C as a sample of present-day charcoal, and thus, using carbon dating, the sample of charcoal is about 3800 years old.*

The rate of decay varies with the type of radioactive material and is directly proportional to the amount of the material that is currently present.

If we let m represent the mass of the radioactive material and λ the decay constant, the decay process can be modeled by the differential equation

$$\frac{dm}{dt} = -\lambda m \qquad (14-5)$$

The value of the decay constant depends on the material; if λ is large, the material decays rapidly; if λ is near zero, the material decays very slowly. It is easily verified that Eq. (14–6) is the solution to the differential equation in Eq. (14–5):

$$\begin{aligned} m &= f(t) \\ &= m_0 e^{-\lambda t} \end{aligned} \qquad (14-6)$$

where m_0 is the initial mass of the radioactive material. Since we know the original differential equation and the solution to the differential equation, we can compare the numerical results of using Euler's method to integrate Eq. (14–5) to the theoretical results using Eq. (14–6).

The decay constant of a radioactive material is often expressed in terms of its half-life, which is the time it takes for the amount of the radioactive material to decrease to one-half of the beginning amount. Half-lives can range from practically instantaneous decay to billions of years. Using Eq. (14–6), we can relate the half-life t_h to the value of the decay constant:

$$0.5 m_0 = m_0 e^{-\lambda t_h}$$

Dividing both sides by m_0, we have

$$0.5 = e^{-\lambda t_h}$$

Solving for t_h gives

$$\begin{aligned} t_h &= \frac{\ln(0.5)}{-\lambda} \\ &= \frac{\ln 2}{\lambda} \end{aligned}$$

Thus, given the half-life t_h, we can easily solve for the decay constant:

$$\begin{aligned} \lambda &= \frac{\ln(0.5)}{-t_h} \\ &= \frac{\ln 2}{t_h} \end{aligned} \qquad (14-7)$$

*From *Calculus and Analytic Geometry*, 3rd Edition, C. H. Edwards, Jr. and D. E. Penney, Prentice Hall, Englewood Cliffs, NJ, 1990.

This equation is useful because most references do not give the decay constants for radioactive materials; instead, they give the half-life values.

Write a program which uses Euler's method to solve the differential equation in Eq. (14–5) for determining the estimated amount of radioactive material remaining after a given number of years. The inputs to the program are the initial amount of the material, the half-life of the material, the number of years that the material will decay, and the step size to use in Euler's method. Compare the results obtained from the numerical method to those obtained from the theoretical solution in Eq. (14–6) by printing the input information, the decay constant, and the theoretical and estimated amounts of material remaining.

PROBLEM STATEMENT

Estimate the remaining amount of radioactive material after a specified number of years by solving numerically the differential equation in Eq. (14–5).

INPUT/OUTPUT DESCRIPTION

The input includes the initial amount of the material, the half-life of the material, the number of years that the material will decay, and the step size to use in Euler's method. The output includes the input parameters plus the decay constant and the theoretical and estimated amounts of material remaining.

HAND EXAMPLE

One of the radioactive materials widely used in nuclear medicine is an isotope of cobalt, ^{60}Co, which has a half-life of 5.3 years. The decay constant for ^{60}Co can be calculated from its half-life, using Eq. (14–7):

$$\lambda = \frac{\ln(0.5)}{-5.3}$$
$$= 0.131$$

Thus, the differential equation that describes the radioactive decay of ^{60}Co is

$$\frac{dm}{dt} = -0.131m$$

Then the solution to the differential equation is

$$m = f(t) = m_0 e^{-0.131t}$$

where m_0 represents the initial mass.

Recall that we need an initial condition in order to start Euler's method; at time zero, the amount remaining is the initial amount, so we have the necessary initial condition. Assume that the initial amount is 4.0, that the step size is 0.5 years, and that we want to estimate the amount remaining after 1 year. From Eq. (14–5), we have the following:

$$m' = \frac{dm}{dt} = -0.131m$$

We repeat here the generalized Euler's formula, with the variables changed to match our variables:

$$m_k = m_{k-1} + m'_{k-1} \cdot h$$

Our initial condition is $t_0 = 0$, $m = 4$. The steps in the computations are

$$m_1 = 4.0 + m'_0 \cdot 0.5$$
$$= 4.0 + (-0.131 \cdot 4.0) \cdot (0.5)$$
$$= 3.7380$$

$$m_2 = 3.7380 + m'_1 \cdot 0.5$$
$$= 3.7380 + (-0.131 \cdot 3.7380) \cdot (0.5)$$
$$= 3.4932$$

Thus, using Euler's method to solve the differential equation, we have that after 1 year, a mass of 3.4932 is left from the initial mass of 4.0. Using the equation that represents the theoretical solution to the differential equation, we find that $f(1.0)$ is

$$f(1.0) = 4.0e^{-0.131(1.0)}$$
$$= 3.5089$$

The theoretical and estimated values of the function are very close, and thus Euler's method does a good job of solving this differential equation. The graph below contains plots of both the function (solid line) and its slope (dotted line) which is the differential equation; both functions change gradually so the errors are relatively small:

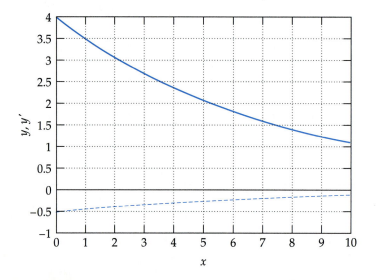

The decomposition of our solution in general steps is the following:

DECOMPOSITION

Read initial amount, half-life, decay time, step size.
Compute decay constant.
Perform steps in Euler's method.
Compute theoretical amount left.
Print decay constant, estimated amount left, and theoretical amount left.

At each iteration in the algorithm, we need only the previous value of the mass in order to compute the next value. However, since the number of iterations in the algorithm is not large, we choose to use an array to store the mass values. By using an array, the equations in our program match exactly the equations in Euler's method, and thus we are less likely to make a mistake in coding the equations and the program will be easier to read and understand.

REFINEMENT IN PSEUDOCODE

DECAY: Read initial, half, time, step

$$dc \leftarrow \frac{\ln 0.5}{-\text{half}}$$

$n \leftarrow \text{round(time/step)}$

$m(0) \leftarrow \text{initial}$

For $k = 1$ to n do

   $\text{slope} \leftarrow -dc \cdot m(k-1)$

   $m(k) \leftarrow m(k-1) + \text{slope·step}$

$\text{approx} \leftarrow m(n)$

$\text{exact} \leftarrow m(0) \cdot \exp(-dc \cdot \text{time})$

Print dc, initial, time, exact, step · n, approx

We now convert the refined pseudocode into FORTRAN:

FORTRAN Program

```
*----------------------------------------------------------*
        PROGRAM  DECAY
*
*   This program uses Euler's method to solve a
*   differential equation.
*
        INTEGER  N, K
        REAL   INIT, HALF, TIME, STEP, DC, SLOPE, M(0:25), APPROX, EXACT
*
        PRINT*, 'ENTER INITIAL MASS, HALF-LIFE, DECAY TIME, STEP SIZE'
        PRINT*, '(MASS IN GRAMS, TIME IN YEARS)
        READ*, INIT, HALF, TIME, STEP
*
*   Compute decay constant and number of steps needed.
*
        DC = LOG(0.5)/(-HALF)
        N = NINT(TIME/STEP)
        M(0) = INIT
*
*   Perform Euler's method and then compute exact value for comparison.
*
        DO 10 K=1,N
            SLOPE = (-DC)*M(K-1)
            M(K) = M(K-1) + SLOPE*STEP
     10 CONTINUE
        APPROX = M(N)
        EXACT = M(0)*EXP((-DC)*TIME)
*
        PRINT 15, DC, INIT, TIME, EXACT, N*STEP, APPROX
     15 FORMAT (1X,'DECAY CONSTANT: ',F8.4/
       +         1X,'INITIAL MASS: ',F8.4/
       +         1X,'EXACT MASS LEFT AT TIME = ',F7.1,' IS ',F9.3/
       +         1X,'APPROXIMATE MASS LEFT AT TIME = ',F7.1,' IS ',F9.3)
*
        END
*----------------------------------------------------------*
```

TESTING

When we test this program with the hand example, the output from the program is the following:

```
ENTER INITIAL MASS, HALF-LIFE, DECAY TIME, STEP SIZE
(MASS IN GRAMS, TIME IN YEARS)
4.0  5.3  1.0  0.5
DECAY CONSTANT:    0.1308
INITIAL MASS:    4.0000
EXACT MASS LEFT AT TIME =      1.0 IS     3.510
APPROXIMATE MASS LEFT AT TIME =      1.0 IS     3.494
```

If we test the program with the same input except that we ask for a smaller step size, we see in the following output that the approximation is more accurate:

```
ENTER INITIAL MASS, HALF-LIFE, DECAY TIME, STEP SIZE
(MASS IN GRAMS, TIME IN YEARS)
4.0   5.3   1.0   0.2
DECAY CONSTANT:     0.1308
INITIAL MASS:     4.0000
EXACT MASS LEFT AT TIME =       1.0 IS        3.510
APPROXIMATE MASS LEFT AT TIME =      1.0 IS        3.504
```

If we test the program with the same input except that we ask for a larger step size, we see in the following output that the approximation is not as accurate:

```
ENTER INITIAL MASS, HALF-LIFE, DECAY TIME, STEP SIZE
(MASS IN GRAMS, TIME IN YEARS)
4.0   5.3   1.0   1.0
DECAY CONSTANT:     0.1308
INITIAL MASS:     4.0000
EXACT MASS LEFT AT TIME =       1.0 IS        3.510
APPROXIMATE MASS LEFT AT TIME =      1.0 IS        3.477
```

14-3 RUNGE-KUTTA METHOD

One of the most popular methods for numerically integrating ordinary differential equations is the *Runge-Kutta method*. This method has several forms, but they all are based on the same technique. In fact, the Euler method discussed in the previous sections is actually a first-order Runge-Kutta method. The other Runge-Kutta methods are second-order, third-order, fourth-order, and even higher-order methods which provide increasing accuracy as the order increases.

To fully explain what is meant by the "order" of a Runge-Kutta method, we first need to describe the theory of Taylor series approximations. Without going into excessive detail and complexity, we will say that a *Taylor series* is an expression which can generally be used to approximate any function to any desired degree of accuracy. The accuracy obtained is dependent on the number of terms that are used in the Taylor series—the more terms, the more accuracy. The following equation is the Taylor series for approximating the value of the function y at x_1, given its value at x_0 and the values of its derivatives (y_0', y_0'', y_0''', ...) at x_0, with a step size h equal to $x_1 - x_0$:

$$y_1 = y_0 + hy_0' + \frac{h^2}{2!}y_0'' + \frac{h^3}{3!}y_0''' + \cdots \tag{14-8}$$

The dots, or "ellipsis," at the end of the equation mean that the equation continues on with additional similar terms which involve higher derivatives of the function. In fact, an infinite number of additional terms may be used in the series if desired. Obviously, it is not practical, nor is it necessary, to use an infinitely long Taylor series to estimate a function accurately. In practice, the Taylor series is "truncated" to the number of terms that are needed to achieve the accuracy required. The point at which the series is terminated determines the "order" of the accuracy.

A Runge-Kutta integration equation is equivalent to a truncated Taylor series. The order of the equation is equal to the highest order of h that appears. For example, to develop a second-order Runge-Kutta method, we would need to retain the first three terms shown in the Taylor series in Eq. (14–8). A fourth-order Runge-Kutta method would need to retain all the terms through h^4. We return to the equation for Euler's method which we developed earlier in Section 14–1:

$$y_1 = y_0 + hy_0' \tag{14–9}$$

We immediately see that Euler's method is a Taylor series that has been truncated after the term containing h and is therefore a first-order Runge-Kutta method.

To continue with the development of higher-order Runge-Kutta methods, as well as their relationship to Taylor series, let's look at what we might be able to do to improve on Euler's method. In Section 14–1, we stated that one of the problems with Euler's method is that it can diverge from the true function curve to the point that it no longer provides accurate estimates of the function. In the figure below, we have drawn the tangent line at (x_0, y_0), just as we did to begin Euler's method. Even though we do not yet know the values of y_1 and y_1', assume for now that we can also draw the tangent line at (x_1, y_1), as shown.

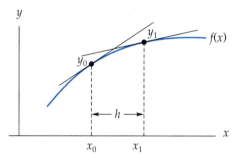

It appears that if we were to average the slopes of these two tangent lines, and use the result to integrate from x_0 to x_1, we would obtain a better estimate for y_1. The average of the slopes is

$$\text{Average slope} = \frac{y_0' + y_1'}{2}$$

Using this expression in place of the slope y_0' in Eq. (14–9), we get

$$y_1 = y_0 + h \frac{y_0' + y_1'}{2} \qquad (14-10)$$

It is interesting to note the functional similarities of this equation and the trapezoidal rule integration equation in Chapter 13.

We now rearrange Eq. (14–10), as follows:

$$y_1 = y_0 + h \frac{2y_0' + y_1' - y_0'}{2}$$

$$= y_0 + hy_0' + \frac{h}{2}(y_1' - y_0')$$

$$= y_0 + hy_0' + \frac{h^2}{2}\left(\frac{y_1' - y_0'}{h}\right)$$

Next, we approximate the second derivative of the function at y_0 using a forward difference expression, which was mentioned in Chapter 13:

$$y_0'' = \frac{y_1' - y_0'}{h}$$

This enables us to write the previous equation for y, as

$$y_1 = y_0 + hy_0' + \frac{h^2}{2} y_0'' \qquad (14-11)$$

We immediately see that Eq. (14–11) is exactly the same as the Taylor series equation, Eq. (14–8), truncated after the term containing h^2. Thus, we have derived a second-order Runge-Kutta method using the first-order Euler's method and the average of the slopes at the beginning and the end of the interval. Also note that Eq. (14–11) does not require that we know y_1 or y_1', as we had assumed earlier.

This discussion has served to illustrate the method for deriving higher-order Runge-Kutta methods. Instead of proceeding with an example using the second-order Runge-Kutta formula, we will move on to the development of the fourth-order Runge-Kutta method since it is used much more often.

The fourth-order Runge-Kutta formula is one of the most commonly used numerical integration methods for ordinary differential equations. We begin by stating the formula and then explain the terms in it. The fourth-order Runge-Kutta formula is expressed as follows:

$$y_1 = y_0 + h\left(\frac{K_1 + 2K_2 + 2K_3 + K_4}{6}\right) \qquad (14-12)$$

where

$$K_1 = y'(x_0, y_0)$$

$$K_2 = y'\left(x_0 + \frac{h}{2}, y_0 + \frac{h}{2}K_1\right)$$

$$K_3 = y'\left(x_0 + \frac{h}{2}, y_0 + \frac{h}{2}K_2\right)$$

$$K_4 = y'(x_0 + h, y_0 + hK_3)$$

Again, it is interesting to note the similarities between the fourth-order Runge-Kutta formula and Simpson's formula for integration in Chapter 13. We see that K_1, K_2, K_3, and K_4 are slopes of the function computed at four different places in the interval from x_0 to x_1. Equation (14–12) is just a weighted average of those slopes multiplied by the step size h and added to the initial value of the function. Thus, the fourth-order Runge-Kutta method is functionally similar to the first-order Euler's method and the second-order Runge-Kutta method developed earlier.

The steps involved in finding the K's are shown in the next figure. The value of K_1 is found first by computing the slope y_0' at (x_0, y_0) using the differential equation, just as we did before for the first- and second-order Runge-Kutta methods. In the upper left graph, the tangent line L_1 with slope K_1 is drawn at (x_0, y_0).

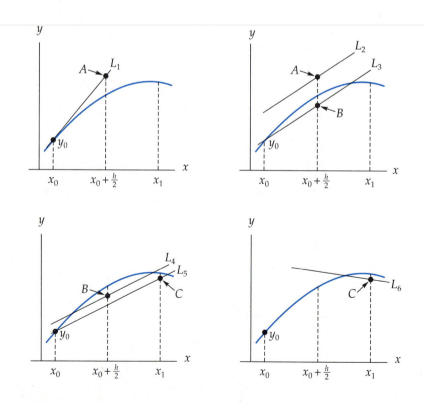

A vertical line is then drawn at the halfway point in the interval until it intersects L_1 at point A. The slope of the function is computed a second time now at point A, using the differential equation, to obtain K_2. Line L_2, with slope K_2, is drawn through A as shown in the upper right graph. We now translate line L_2 to where it will pass through (x_0, y_0) and draw line L_3 with slope K_2.

Line L_3 now intersects the midpoint vertical line at point B. The slope of the function is computed for a third time at point B to obtain K_3. We should note that we have now evaluated the slope of the function twice at the midpoint of the interval—once for point A and once for point B. It might seem that we would get the same result, but since the value of y is different at A and B, we will usually get different values for K_2 and K_3.

In the lower left graph, we have drawn line L_4 with slope K_3 through point B and translated it to (x_0, y_0), where we draw line L_5 with slope K_3, just as we did earlier for lines L_2 and L_3. Line L_5 is now extended to where it intersects the vertical line at the end of the interval at point C.

Finally, K_4 is obtained by computing the slope of the function at point C. In the final graph in the lower right corner, line L_6 has been drawn through point C with slope K_4. Thus, we see that K_1 through K_4 are simply slopes calculated at the left end, at the midpoint, and at the right end of the interval. These slopes are then combined in the weighted average shown in Eq. (14–12) and multiplied by h and added to y_0, just as we did for Euler's method.

There are many different forms of Runge-Kutta equations, but they are all similar to the ones described above. One important feature of all Runge-Kutta formulas is that they are equivalent to a Taylor's series to the order of the method. Similar to what we saw earlier in the case of the second-order method, the fourth-order method we just derived will now duplicate a Taylor's series through the terms containing h^4. As a result, it is considerably more accurate than either Euler's method or the second-order Runge-Kutta method described earlier.

Accuracy is still an issue to be considered in this as well as any approximation method. As discussed previously, the total error is determined by rounding errors, truncation errors, and cumulative (or additive) errors. Simple checks, such as changing the interval width or the order of the method, should always be made before relying on the results obtained. More sophisticated methods which estimate the truncation error at each step can also be incorporated to adjust the step size adaptively as the solution proceeds.

This self-test allows you to check quickly to see if you have remembered the key points from Section 14–3. If you have any problems with the exercises, you should reread this section. The solutions are included at the end of the text.

We are given the following differential equation:

$$\frac{dy}{dx} = x + \frac{3y}{x}$$

with the following initial condition:

$$(x_0, y_0) = (1,0)$$

Use the fourth-order Runge-Kutta method to estimate the function y when $x = 1.1$.

1. If we perform the estimation in one step, then the step size is equal to 0.1. Compute the corresponding values for the slopes K_1, K_2, K_3, and K_4.

2. Use the values for the slopes to estimate the value of y when x is equal to 1.1. Note that this value represents the integral of the differential equation at x equal to 1.1.

3. The actual value of y_1 is 0.121. Compare this answer to your approximation from problem 2.

14–4 APPLICATION—AIR POLLUTION CONTROL (Environmental Engineering)

Many metropolitan areas are implementing air pollution control programs which utilize computer models to predict pollution levels so that control measures, such as driving or fireplace restrictions, can be implemented early enough to avoid potential problems. An example of such a model is one that predicts the concentration of carbon monoxide in a congested region of a city during the morning and evening rush-hours. The figure below shows the "air-quality control volume" as an imaginary box that encloses the region of the city where the pollution levels are often high.

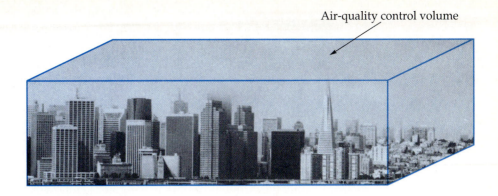

Air-quality control volume

The model that is to be used is an ordinary differential equation which expresses the rate of change of carbon monoxide concentration as a function of the rates at which the carbon monoxide is entering and leaving the control volume:

$$\frac{dC}{dt} = \frac{R}{V} - (K_w + K_c)C$$

In this equation, C is the present concentration of carbon monoxide in kilograms per cubic meter, R is the rate at which carbon monoxide is entering the control volume from vehicle emissions in kilograms per minute, V is the control volume in cubic meters, and K_w and K_c are constants that determine the rate at which wind and chemical reactions remove carbon monoxide from the control volume.

Write a program which uses the fourth-order Runge-Kutta formula to solve the differential equation above and determine the concentration of carbon monoxide within a certain region of the city at 10-minute intervals during the rush-hour period of 7 to 9 am. The inputs to the program are the initial concentration of carbon monoxide, the rate at which carbon monoxide is being added, the wind and chemical reaction constants, and the size of the control volume.

PROBLEM STATEMENT

Use the fourth-order Runge-Kutta formula to solve the following differential equation and estimate the concentration of carbon monoxide at specified times:

$$C' = \frac{dC}{dt} = \frac{R}{V} - (K_w + K_c)C$$

The input includes the initial concentration of carbon monoxide, C_0, the rate R at which it is being added, the size V of the control volume, and the wind and chemical reaction constants K_w and K_c. The output includes the input parameters and a table which shows the concentration of carbon monoxide every 10 minutes beginning at 7:00 am and ending at 9:00 am.

HAND EXAMPLE

Using measurements from the evening before, and other air pollution models, the Air Quality Department has predicted that the following conditions will exist at 7:00 am:

$$C_0 = 0.0022 \text{ kgm/m}^3$$
$$R = 15{,}500 \text{ kgm/min}$$
$$V = 4.5 \text{ E}+08 \text{ m}^3$$
$$K_w = 0.0012/\text{min}$$
$$K_c = 0.0003/\text{min}$$

Thus, the initial concentration of carbon monoxide at 7:00 am has been estimated to be approximately 0.0022 kgm/m^3, and the differential equation which determines the rate at which it will change as a function of time is found by substituting the other parameters into the differential equation:

$$C' = \frac{dC}{dt} = \frac{15{,}500}{4.5\text{E}+08} - (0.0012 + 0.0003)C$$

Thus,

$$C' = 3.4444\text{E}-05 - 0.0015C$$

To estimate the concentration of carbon monoxide at 7:10 am using our fourth-order Runge-Kutta formula, we first compute the slopes K_1 through K_4:

$$\begin{aligned}
K_1 &= C'(t_0, C_0) \\
&= 3.4444\text{E}-05 - (0.0015)C_0 \\
&= 3.4444\text{E}-05 - (0.0015)(0.0022) \\
&= 3.1144\text{E}-05
\end{aligned}$$

$$\begin{aligned}
K_2 &= C'\left(t_0 + \frac{h}{2}, C_0 + \frac{h}{2}K_1\right) \\
&= 3.4444\text{E}-05 - (0.0015)\left[C_0 + \left(\frac{10}{2}\right)K_1\right] \\
&= 3.4444\text{E}-05 - (0.0015)\left[0.0022 + \left(\frac{10}{2}\right)(3.1144\text{E}-05)\right] \\
&= 3.0910\text{E}-05
\end{aligned}$$

$$K_3 = C'\left(t_0 + \frac{h}{2}, C_0 + \frac{h}{2}K_2\right)$$

$$= 3.4444\text{E}{-}05 - (0.0015)\left[C_0 + \left(\frac{10}{2}\right)K_2\right]$$

$$= 3.4444\text{E}{-}05 - (0.0015)\left[0.0022 + \left(\frac{10}{2}\right)(3.0910\text{E}{-}05)\right]$$

$$= 3.0912\text{E}{-}05$$

$$K_4 = C'(t_0 + h, C_0 + hK_3)$$
$$= 3.4444\text{E}{-}05 - (0.0015)[C_0 + 10K_3]$$
$$= 3.4444\text{E}{-}05 - (0.0015)[0.0022 + 10(3.0912\text{E}{-}05)]$$
$$= 3.0680\text{E}{-}05$$

We then combine the slopes in the Runge-Kutta formula as shown in Eq. (14–12) from the previous section to get the estimate of carbon monoxide at 7:10 am:

$$C_{10} = C_0 + \frac{h}{6}(K_1 + 2K_2 + 2K_3 + K_4)$$

$$= 0.0022 + \frac{10}{6}(3.1144 + 6.1820 + 6.1824 + 3.0680)\text{E}{-}05$$

$$= 0.002509$$

Our differential equation is one that can be solved analytically. We can therefore use the analytical solution to check the results we obtain from the numerical solution. The solution of the differential equation is

$$C(t) = 0.022963 - 0.020763e^{-0.0015t}$$

At $t = 10$ minutes, the theoretical value for C would be

$$C_{10} = 0.002509$$

This result is exactly the same as the estimate obtained above in the hand example for the number of digits of accuracy used in the calculations.

ALGORITHM DEVELOPMENT

The decomposition of the solution in general steps is:

DECOMPOSITION

Read input parameters.
Compute and print carbon monoxide concentrations.

The program must ask the user to enter values for the initial carbon monoxide, the vehicle emissions rate, the control volume, and the wind and chemical reaction constants. Since the report is to cover the period from 7:10 to

9:00, we know that the time increment is 10 minutes, starting with the initial carbon monoxide value at zero minutes, and stopping with the final carbon monoxide value at 120 minutes. We perform the fourth-order Runga-Kutta computations to estimate the concentrations in steps of 10 minutes. Since each new computation needs only the past value, we do not need to use arrays. We need to evaluate four slopes using the differential equation that defines the rate of change, so this is a good candidate for a function. We also need to change the time value that goes from 10 to 120 minutes to an hour and minute form for the report; we use a subroutine for these computations.

REFINEMENT IN PSEUDOCODE

CO: Read parameters C_0, r, v, $k_w k_C$
    Print report header
    $x_n \leftarrow 0.0$
    $y_n \leftarrow C_0$
    $h \leftarrow 10.0$
    For n = 1 to 12 do
        $k_1 \leftarrow$ slope computed at $y = y_n$
        $k_2 \leftarrow$ slope computed at $y = y_n + \dfrac{h}{2} k_1$
        $k_3 \leftarrow$ slope computed at $y = y_n + \dfrac{h}{2} k_2$
        $k_4 \leftarrow$ slope computed at $y = y_n + h k_3$
        $x_{new} \leftarrow x_n + h$
        $y_{new} \leftarrow y_n + \dfrac{h}{6} (k_1 + 2k_2 + 2k_3 + k_4)$
        Convert $n \cdot h$ to hour and minute
        Print hour, minute, y_{new}
        $x_n \leftarrow x_{new}$
        $y_n \leftarrow y_{new}$

The structure chart for this program is:

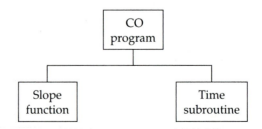

We now convert the refined pseudocode into FORTRAN:

```
*---------------------------------------------------------*
      PROGRAM  CO
*
*  This program computes the concentration of carbon monoxide in
*  a metropolitan area using a differential equation.
*
      INTEGER  N,HOUR,MINUTE
      REAL  CZERO,R,KW,KC,V,XN,YN,H,K1,K2,K3,K4,SLOPE,XNEW,YNEW
*
      PRINT*, 'ENTER INITIAL CARBON MONOXIDE IN KG/CUBIC METER'
      READ*, CZERO
      PRINT*, 'ENTER VEHICLE EMISSIONS RATE IN KG/MINUTE'
      READ*, R
      PRINT*, 'ENTER CONTROL VOLUME IN CUBIC METERS'
      READ*, V
      PRINT*, 'ENTER WIND AND CHEMICAL REACTION CONSTANTS (PER MINUTE)'
      READ*, KW, KC
*
      PRINT*
      PRINT*
      PRINT*, 'DAILY CARBON MONOXIDE CONCENTRATION REPORT'
      PRINT*
      PRINT 1, CZERO
   1  FORMAT (1X,'INITIAL CARBON MONOXIDE IN KG/CUBIC METER = ',F8.4)
      PRINT 2, R
   2  FORMAT (1X,'VEHICLE EMISSIONS RATE IN KG/MINUTE      = ',F10.1)
      PRINT 3, V
   3  FORMAT (1X,'CONTROL VOLUME IN CUBIC METERS           = ',E9.2)
      PRINT 4, KW, KC
   4  FORMAT (1X,'WIND CONSTANT     = ',F8.4,'/MINUTE'/
     +        1X,'CHEMICAL CONSTANT = ',F8.4,'/MINUTE')
      PRINT*
      PRINT*, 'TIME     CARBON MONOXIDE CONCENTRATION'
*
      XN = 0.0
      YN = CZERO
      H = 10.0
      DO 10 N=1,12
         K1 = SLOPE (YN,R,V,KW,KC)
         K2 = SLOPE (YN+(H/2.0)*K1,R,V,KW,KC)
         K3 = SLOPE (YN+(H/2.0)*K2,R,V,KW,KC)
         K4 = SLOPE (YN+H*K3,R,V,KW,KC)
         XNEW = XN + H
         YNEW = YN + H*(K1 + 2.0*K2 + 2.0*K3 + K4)/6.0
         CALL TIME (N,HOUR,MINUTE)
         PRINT 5, HOUR, MINUTE, YNEW
   5     FORMAT(1X,I1,':',I2,5X,F8.4)
         XN = XNEW
         YN = YNEW
  10  CONTINUE
*
      END
```

```
*-----------------------------------------------------------------*
      FUNCTION   SLOPE (Y,R,V,KW,KC)
*
*   This function evaluates the differential equation
*   for the input values of y and constants r,v,kw,kc.
*
      REAL   Y,R,V,KW,KC,SLOPE
*
      SLOPE = R/V - (KW + KC)*Y
*
      RETURN
      END
*-----------------------------------------------------------------*
      SUBROUTINE   TIME (N,HOUR,MINUTE)
*
*   This function determines the hour and minute values for the report.
*
      INTEGER   N,HOUR,MINUTE
*
      IF (N.LT.6) THEN
         HOUR = 7
      ELSEIF (N.LT.12) THEN
         HOUR = 8
      ELSE
         HOUR = 9
      ENDIF
      MINUTE = N*10
      MINUTE = MOD(MINUTE,60)
*
      RETURN
      END
*-----------------------------------------------------------------*
```

TESTING

In order for this program to work properly, it is critical that the input parameters be entered using the correct units. Therefore, when we print the prompts to the user to enter values, we include the units. In the hand example, we also gave the exact solution to this differential equation so that we could use it to check the answers we computed using the fourth-order Runge-Kutta method. When we performed this comparison, we found that the answer was extremely accurate. Using the parameter values given in the hand example, the program prints the following interaction and report:

```
ENTER INITIAL CARBON MONOXIDE IN KG/CUBIC METER
0.0022
ENTER VEHICLE EMISSIONS RATE IN KG/MINUTE
15500
ENTER CONTROL VOLUME IN CUBIC METERS
4.5E+08
ENTER WIND AND CHEMICAL REACTION CONSTANTS (PER MINUTE)
0.0012  0.0003


DAILY CARBON MONOXIDE CONCENTRATION REPORT

INITIAL CARBON MONOXIDE IN KG/CUBIC METER =   0.0022
VEHICLE EMISSIONS RATE IN KG/MINUTE       =   15500.0
CONTROL VOLUME IN CUBIC METERS            = 0.45E+09
WIND CONSTANT     =   0.0012/MINUTE
CHEMICAL CONSTANT =   0.0003/MINUTE

TIME      CARBON MONOXIDE CONCENTRATION
7:10       0.0025
7:20       0.0028
7:30       0.0031
7:40       0.0034
7:50       0.0037
8: 0       0.0040
8:10       0.0043
8:20       0.0045
8:30       0.0048
8:40       0.0051
8:50       0.0054
9: 0       0.0056
```

14–5 DISCUSSION OF ADVANCED TECHNIQUES

Some of the more advanced techniques for solutions to differential equations use numerical methods that we have already discussed in Chapters 10 through 13. We mention two problems related to differential equations that use these techniques.

HIGHER-ORDER ORDINARY DIFFERENTIAL EQUATIONS

We often encounter problems that involve ordinary differential equations of second or higher order. For example, suppose we are analyzing the ability of a packing container to withstand a fall from a platform, as shown in the next figure:

In the analysis, assume we have determined that when the container strikes the ground, its motion can be represented by two second-order differential equations involving the location, k, of the center of the container above the ground, and the angle, θ, of the side of the container relative to the ground:

$$\frac{d^2\theta}{dt^2} = f_1\left(\theta, \frac{d\theta}{dt}, k\right)$$

$$\frac{d^2k}{dt^2} = f_2\left(\theta, \frac{dk}{dt}, k\right)$$

We can use our first-order integration methods to solve a problem such as this by first reducing the two second-order equations above to a set of four simultaneous first-order equations. The same technique can be extended to higher-order differential equations so that we can solve third-, fourth-, or even higher-order systems using the numerical methods we developed for first-order equations.

To illustrate, we express our earlier variables θ, $d\theta/dt$, k, and dk/dt in terms of a more general set of variables w, x, y, and z such that:

$$w = \theta$$
$$x = \frac{d\theta}{dt}$$
$$y = k$$
$$z = \frac{dk}{dt}$$

With these equations, and the two original equations, we can write the following system of simultaneous first-order ordinary differential equations:

$$\frac{dw}{dt} = x$$

$$\frac{dx}{dt} = f_1(w,x,y)$$

$$\frac{dy}{dt} = z$$

$$\frac{dz}{dt} = f_2(x,y,z)$$

We can then integrate these four equations simultaneously using the Euler method or the Runge-Kutta method developed previously to obtain a solution to the two second-order equations.

The initial values for θ, $d\theta/dt$, k, and dk/dt provide the initial values of w, x, y, and z, which we use to compute the four differential equations dw/dt, dx/dt, dy/dt, and dz/dt. We integrate these equations simultaneously to obtain the estimates for w, x, y, and z at the next time step. This process is repeated for the number of time steps needed to analyze the motion of the container.

PARTIAL DIFFERENTIAL EQUATIONS

Sometimes the mathematical formulation of an engineering or science problem involves the rates of change of a variable with respect to two or more independent variables. These equations are called *"partial differential equations."* An example of such an equation is

$$\frac{\partial^2 y}{\partial t^2} = -\frac{\partial^4 y}{\partial x^4}$$

where $\partial^2 y/\partial t^2$ is the second partial derivative of y with respect to t.

The methods we have developed in this chapter deal with the solution of ordinary differential equations. There are also numerical techniques that are useful for solving partial differential equations. The solutions to partial differential equations use techniques that are similar to ones discussed in previous chapters. The methods usually involve systems of simultaneous equations that are made up of finite-difference expressions or similar expressions called finite element equations. The set of simultaneous equations is then solved using the techniques developed previously for that purpose, such as Gauss elimination or Gauss-Seidel. The numerical solution of partial differential equations is an important but vast area of applied mathematics that is too extensive to attempt to address in this book, but most numerical methods textbooks discuss solution techniques for this class of differential equations. There are even books that deal exclusively with the numerical solution of partial differential equations.

SUMMARY

In this chapter we presented two techniques for computing numerical solutions to first-order ordinary differential equations—Euler's method and the fourth-order Runge-Kutta method. Since solving a differential equation is equivalent to computing its integral, these methods are also referred to as integration of ordinary differential equations. Both techniques use the differential equation to compute slopes at various points; the slopes are then used to approximate the next value of the function y by integrating the differential equation. The Euler method, which is really a first-order Runge-Kutta method, uses one slope computation, and the fourth-order Runge-Kutta method uses four slope computations. An initial point (x_0, y_0) is needed to start both methods; this initial point is also called a boundary point. These methods use a step (h) to move from x_0 to $x_1 = x_0 + h$ and to make each new approximation of the function y. In general, the smaller the step size, the more accurate are the results from these methods; however, the fourth-order Runge-Kutta method is more accurate than Euler's method for the same step size. Techniques for solving higher-order ordinary differential equations and partial differential equations were also mentioned.

DEBUGGING AIDS

The numerical computations used in solving differential equations involve evaluating the differential equation for different sets of input values. Therefore, to avoid confusion, it is important that the differential equation be written the same way, and with the same variables, each time it is used in the program or in modules. Another frequent error occurs when the parameters are entered out of order. Therefore, choose the most logical order for the parameters, and be sure to prompt the user with information regarding the order of the parameters as well as the units of measure for the parameters. When we use these techniques, we generally do not have analytical answers for comparison. Therefore, it is important to do our initial testing with differential equations for which we know the solution so that we can determine whether our estimates are reasonable. We should include changing the step size in our testing. Increasing the step size means taking fewer steps to get to the point we want, but the answer is likely to be less accurate; decreasing the step size means taking more steps to get to the point we want, but the answer should be more accurate. Rounding, truncation, and additive errors can also be affected by step size. Choosing a step size which gives accurate results is also application dependent, and thus step size should be a parameter that is easy to change. Finally, during debugging, be sure to print the variable name as well as the variable values so that there is no confusion.

STYLE/TECHNIQUE GUIDES

Since solving differential equations is a complicated mathematical process, it is important to document not only the equations of the technique but also the notation. Use notation in your program to match as carefully as possible the equations of the techniques. For example, if the equation is defined using variables x_i and x_{i+1}, then use variables $x(i)$ and $x(i + 1)$ in your program. Also, if an equation is written in terms of several variables that are computed separately, use the same form for your FORTRAN statements, even though they could easily be combined into a single statement. The closer your FORTRAN statements match the mathematical equations that define the process, the fewer errors are likely to occur in the initial programming of the technique.

ERROR ANALYSIS

In the two previous error analysis sections, we discussed roundoff errors and inherent errors. An inherent error occurs when the initial data representation is not exactly accurate; inherent errors can occur because of imprecise measurements or because the value does not exactly fit in the number of digits allotted to a value in the computer. Roundoff errors occur as we perform operations using a fixed number of digits of accuracy. A third type of error, *truncation error*, also occurs in numerical computations. Truncation errors occur when an infinite process is replaced by a finite process or, equivalently, is truncated to a finite process. For example, consider the following summation:

$$e^x = 1 + x + \frac{x^2}{2!} + \frac{x^3}{3!} + \cdots + \frac{x^n}{n!} + \cdots$$

To estimate e^x using this infinite series requires that we truncate the series to some finite number of terms. The error caused by replacing this infinite sum by a finite sum is called truncation error. (Note that the truncation that was discussed in Chapter 2 is related to storing a real value in an integer variable and is not the same as the truncation error discussed here.) It is important to note that the truncation error is not always reduced by adding more terms; in fact, for the example series above, as n becomes large, other numerical errors are introduced. Euler's method and the Runge-Kutta method, along with some of the methods introduced in earlier chapters, are examples of methods with truncation error because they use truncated processes. Bounds for truncation error can often be computed for numerical methods that replace an infinite process by a finite process.

KEY WORDS

Euler's method
initial value
ordinary differential equation
partial differential equation

Runge-Kutta method
step size
Taylor series
truncation error

PROBLEMS

We begin our problem set with modifications to programs developed earlier in this chapter. Give the decomposition, refined pseudocode or flowchart, and FORTRAN solution for each problem.

Problems 1–5 modify the program DECAY, given on page 610, which estimates radioactive mass left after a specified period of time has passed.

1. Modify the decay program so that the user specifies the number of iterations instead of the step size.

2. Modify the decay program so that the output uses units of centuries if the decay time is greater than 100 years.

3. Modify the decay program so that the output uses units of days if the decay time is less than one year. (Assume that 356 days comprise a year.)

4. Modify the decay program so that the output rounds the number of grams of the mass left to the nearest gram.

5. Modify the decay program so that the output contains a line containing the percent error in the approximation, where the percent error is computed by subtracting the approximate mass from the exact mass, dividing by the exact mass, and then converting to a percent.

Problems 6–10 modify the program CO, given on page 621, which computes the carbon monoxide concentration.

6. Modify the concentration program so that the user can enter the increment in time (h).

7. Modify the concentration program so that the user can enter the period of time covered in minutes, assuming that the starting time is 7:00 am.

8. Modify the concentration program so that the user can enter the starting time, ending time, and increment in time for the report.

9. Modify the concentration program so that the rate is a linear equation instead of a constant. The a and b constants for the linear equation ($R = at + b$) need to be entered. Note that this changes the differential equation. (Assume that the units of time are minutes and range from 0 to 120.)

10. Modify the concentration program so that the parameter values R, V, KW, and KC are stored in a named COMMON area and thus do not need to be listed in the function parameter list.

In problems 11–16, develop programs and modules using the five-phase design process.

11. A differential equation that describes the rate of change with respect to time in the current in a series RL circuit is

$$\frac{dI}{dt} = \frac{E - RI}{L}$$

where E represents the voltage between two points in the circuit, R represents the resistance, and L represents the inductance. Write a program to compute the current at specified values of time using Euler's method. The user should be prompted to enter E (in volts), R (in ohms), L (in henries), and the time t (in seconds), along with the number of steps to use in the computations. Use the initial condition that the current is zero at time zero.

12. Modify problem 11 so that the user specifies the step size instead of the number of steps to use in the computations.

13. Modify problem 11 so that the output is a report giving the current every 0.1 second for 10 seconds, using a step size of 0.05. The user should still enter values for E, R, and L.

14. Modify problem 11 so that it uses the fourth-order Runge-Kutta method instead of Euler's method.

15. Modify problem 14 so that the user specifies the step size instead of the number of steps to use in the computations.

16. Modify problem 14 so that the output is a report giving the current every 0.1 second for 10 seconds, using a step size of 0.05. The user should still enter values for E, R, and L.

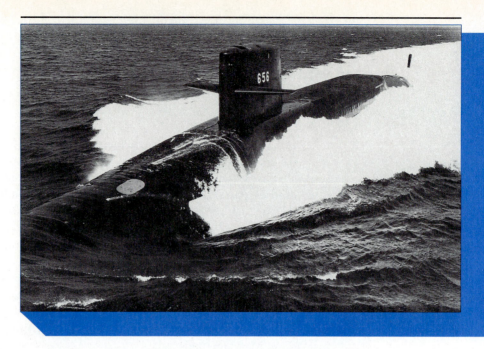

APPLICATION—Sonar Signals (Acoustical Engineering)

The study of sonar (SOund NAvigation and Ranging) includes the generation, transmission, and reception of sound energy in water. Oceanological applications include ocean topography, geological mapping, and biological signal measurements; industrial sonar applications include fish finding, oil and mineral exploration, and acoustic beacon navigation; naval sonar applications include submarine navigation and submarine tracking. An active sonar system transmits a signal that often is a sinusoid with a known frequency. The reflections or echoes of the signal are then received and analyzed to provide information about the surroundings. A passive sonar system does not transmit signals but collects signals from sensors and analyzes them based on their frequency content. Write a program to generate a sinusoidal signal with a specified frequency. (See Section 15–3 for the solution.)

Photo courtesy of USS Bowfin Submarine Museum and Park, Pearl Harbor, Hawaii.

15

INTRODUCTION TO DIGITAL SIGNAL PROCESSING

Introduction

15–1 Sampling a Continuous Signal

15–2 Sinusoid Generation

15–3 Application—Sonar Signals (Acoustical Engineering)

15–4 Random Signal Generation

15–5 Application—Communication Channels (Electrical Engineering)

15–6 Application—Digital Filtering (Electrical Engineering)

Summary

INTRODUCTION

Digital signal processing (DSP) is a field that is becoming more and more important as the computer enables us to easily handle large volumes of data and as new DSP techniques are developed to work with signals from applications that include speech processing, sonar, radar, communications, and biomedical areas. As the area of digital signal processing matures, it becomes more important for engineers in all disciplines to learn the principles and techniques of DSP that apply to their own areas. In this chapter, we focus on digital signals themselves by developing an understanding of signals and the information that they represent. The signals that we use are typically signals that are functions of time, such as temperature measurements, velocity measurements, voltages, blood pressures, earth motion, and speech signals. Most of these signals are initially continuous, or analog, signals that are then sampled to obtain digital signals. We discuss sampling of a continuous signal to obtain a digital signal and we develop techniques for generating sinusoids and random signals. We then generate sinusoids with noise using a specified signal-to-noise ratio. We also discuss digital filtering, which is a numerical technique for removing, or filtering, information from a digital signal.

15–1   SAMPLING A CONTINUOUS SIGNAL

A *signal* is a function (usually with respect to time) that represents information. Continuous signals (also called *analog signals*) are signals represented by continuous functions. For example, consider a temperature sensor that is measuring the temperature within a jet engine. The temperature measurement with respect to time is a continuous function $x(t)$. To analyze the temperature signal with the computer, we use temperature measurements taken at fixed or discrete intervals of time. For example, we can collect temperature measurements every one-hundredth of a second and generate a sequence of temperature values that correspond to times 0.00, 0.01, 0.02, and so on, where 0.00 is assumed to be the time at which we begin taking measurements. We refer to these measurements, taken at multiples of a time interval T, as a digital signal and reference the individual values as x_0, x_1, x_2, and so on, where

$$x_k = x(kT)$$

Thus, using our temperature example, x_3 represents the temperature measured at time equal to 0.03 second. If we want to refer to the entire digital signal (all of the measurements taken at multiples of a time interval T), we put brackets around the individual value reference and use a variable as a subscript, as in $[x_k]$. The plots below illustrate the difference between a continuous signal $x(t)$ and a corresponding digital signal $[x_k]$:

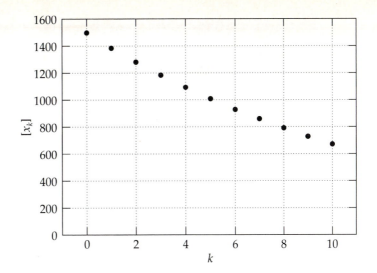

Many different types of *sensors* are used to collect data. Some of the more common types are microphones which measure acoustic or sound data, seismometers which measure earth motion, photocells which measure light intensity, thermistors which measure temperature, and oscilloscopes which measure voltage. When we work with signals collected from sensors, the data are often sampled and stored in data files on computer disks. The hardware that performs the sampling is called an analog-to-digital (A/D) converter. After the DSP techniques are performed on the digital signals, we can also convert the digital signals back to continuous or analog signals with a digital-to-analog (D/A) converter.

Some of the signals that we use come from equations instead of sensors. For example, we might want to generate a signal $x(t)$ using this equation:

$$x(t) = t^2 + t - 1.25$$

To generate a digital sequence from this equation, we evaluate the function at $t = 0, T, 2T, 3T, ...,$ and so on, where T is the interval of time used to take samples of the continuous function. In the next section, we generate signals using sine functions.

Digital signal processing consists of performing operations on digital signals to extract certain information. For example, we might want to compute information about a signal, such as its average value. Or, we might want to remove noise that distorted a signal as it was sent through a communication system. DSP operations such as these are usually performed with a computer, and the techniques are tested in simulations before being used with real signals. Therefore, generating signals to use in testing DSP techniques is an important step in the development of new DSP algorithms.

15-2 SINUSOID GENERATION

One of the most commonly used functions in digital signal processing is the *sinusoid*. Before defining a sinusoid, we first review the properties of the sine function. The sine function is a function of an angle θ in radians or degrees:

$$x(\theta) = \sin\theta$$

The function varies between +1 and −1 and is periodic with a period of 2π radians (or 360 degrees):

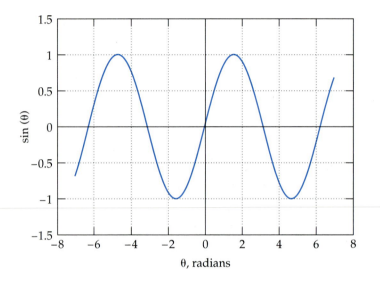

We can multiply the sine function by a constant A, which we call the amplitude of the sine function. We can also let θ be a function of time with the following form:

$$\theta = \omega t + \phi$$

where ω represents a frequency in radians per second and ϕ represents a phase shift in radians. Thus, the general form of a sinusoid, which is now a function of time, is

$$x(t) = A\sin(\omega t + \phi)$$

To show the relationship between the sine function and the sinusoid, we let $A = 1$, $\omega = 1$, and $\phi = 0.0$. The graph of this sinusoid, which is shown next, is exactly the same as the previous graph of the sine function, except that the *x*-axis variable is time in seconds instead of θ in radians.

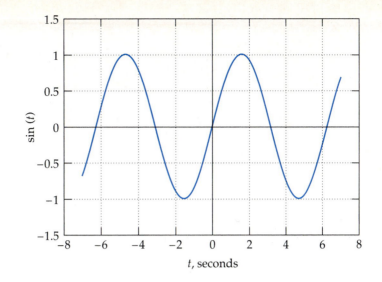

One of the important characteristics of a sinusoid is its frequency, which is the number of periods, or cycles, of the signal that occur in 1 second. The standard unit of measurement for the *frequency* is a Hertz (abbreviated Hz), which is a cycle per second. The frequency and the period of a sinusoid are the inverse of each other:

$$f = \frac{1}{P}, \qquad P = \frac{1}{f}$$

where f represents the frequency in Hz and P represents the period in seconds. The period of the sinusoid in the previous graph is 2π seconds (or approximately 6.28 seconds), and the frequency is $1/2\pi$, or approximately 0.16 Hz (cycles per second).

Sometimes it is convenient to refer to the frequency of a sinusoid in angular frequency (radians per second) rather than Hz (cycles per second). Since one cycle per second corresponds to 2π radians per second, we multiply the frequency in Hz by 2π to determine the frequency in radians per second. Thus,

$$\omega = 2\pi f, \qquad f = \frac{\omega}{2\pi}$$

where ω is the angular frequency in radians per second and f is the frequency in Hz.

The last parameter in the general formula for a sinusoid is a phase shift ϕ. The phase shift is assumed to be in radians unless otherwise specified. Consider the functions $x_1(t)$ and $x_2(t)$, which have the same amplitudes, same frequencies, and different phase shifts:

$$x_1(t) = 2\sin(10\pi t)$$

$$x_2(t) = 2 \sin\left(10\pi t + \frac{\pi}{2}\right)$$

In the following graph, the function $x_1(t)$ is shown as a solid line and the function $x_2(t)$ is shown as a dotted line. We see that the phase shift of $\pi/2$ caused a shift to the left of one-fourth of the cycle, which corresponds to the fact that $\pi/2$ radians is one-fourth of 2π. A negative phase shift causes a shift to the right.

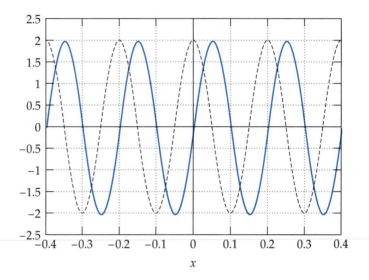

A phase shift can also be expressed as a time shift in seconds using the following notation:

$$\begin{aligned} x(t) &= A \sin(\omega t + \phi) \\ &= A \sin(\omega t + \omega D) \\ &= A \sin(\omega(t + D)) \end{aligned}$$

where ϕ represents a phase shift in radians while D represents a time delay in seconds. The time delay can be positive or negative, just as the phase shift can be positive or negative. A negative time delay shifts the signal to the right; a positive time delay shifts the signal to the left. If we convert the phase shift for $x_2(t)$ to a time delay, we have

$$\begin{aligned} x_2(t) &= 2 \sin\left(10\pi t + \frac{\pi}{2}\right) \\ &= 2 \sin\left(10\pi t + 10\pi\frac{1}{20}\right) \\ &= 2 \sin(10\pi(t + 0.05)) \end{aligned}$$

Thus, the time delay in seconds is 0.05, and that corresponds to the shift (to the left) of 0.05 second in the previous plot.

When generating points from a sinusoid, it is very important always to sample the sinusoid with a sampling time or *sampling interval* that yields more than two samples per period. The signal $x_2(t)$ has a frequency of 5 Hz and a period of 1/5 or 0.2 second. With a sampling interval of 0.01, we are generating 20 samples per period. However, if we sampled the sinusoid with a sampling interval of 0.1 or larger, we would not be generating more than two samples per period. This undersampling causes a problem called aliasing which prevents us from obtaining a valid digital representation of the continuous signal. (For further discussions of sampling and aliasing, refer to a signal processing reference.)

We have used a time interval T to specify the sampling interval used in generating a *digital signal*. Another way to specify the sampling time is by specifying the sampling rate. For example, if we are sampling with a sampling interval of 0.1 second, we are sampling 10 times per second or using 10 sampling cycles per second, which is a sampling rate of 10 Hz. Thus, to determine the sampling points, we need to know either the sampling interval T or the *sampling frequency f_s*. The relationship between the two values is given below:

$$T = \frac{1}{f_s}, \quad f_s = \frac{1}{T}$$

where the units of T are seconds, and the units for the sampling frequency are Hz. (This relationship is similar to the previous one between the period of a periodic function and its frequency.) Remember, to avoid the problems caused by aliasing, the sampling frequency should be more than twice the frequency of any sinusoid contained in the continuous function.

The general form of a sinusoid is a sine function with an amplitude and a phase shift. However, since a sine function becomes a cosine function when it is shifted one-fourth of a period to the left, we can also think of a cosine as a sinusoid. Many of the signals that we use in digital signal processing applications are sums of sinusoids, with different amplitudes, frequencies, and phase shifts. The following example generates a digital signal that is the sum of two sinusoids.

EXAMPLE 15–1

Generating a Sum of Two Sinusoids

Generate a data file containing 200 samples of the following signal, using a sampling frequency of 100 Hz:

$$x(t) = 5 \sin 20\pi t + 5 \sin 22\pi t$$

Solution

The solution to this problem is a simple program with a loop to compute the signal and write the corresponding time and signal values to a data file. Since we are using a sampling frequency of 100 Hz, the sampling time T is 0.01 second.

FORTRAN Program

```
*-----------------------------------------------------------------*
      PROGRAM  SUM
*
*  This program generates a signal formed by the sum
*  of two sinusoidal signals.  The result is stored in SINES.
*
      INTEGER  K
      REAL  PI, T, TIME, X
*
      OPEN (UNIT=10,FILE='SINES',STATUS='NEW')
*
      PI = 3.141593
      T = 0.01
      DO 10 K=0,199
         TIME = REAL(K)*T
         X = 5.0*SIN(20.0*PI*TIME) + 5.0*SIN(22.0*PI*TIME)
         WRITE (10,*) TIME, X
   10 CONTINUE
*
      END
*-----------------------------------------------------------------*
```

A plot of the data file generated is shown below:

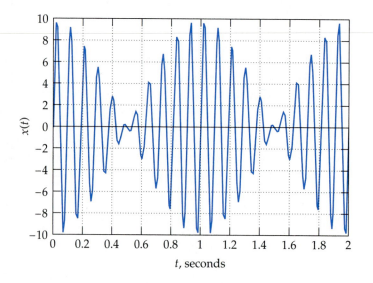

This self-test allows you to check quickly to see if you have remembered the key points from Section 15–2. If you have any problems with the exercises, you should reread this section. The solutions are included at the end of the text.

Sketch the following continuous sinusoids:

1. $2.5 \sin 3\pi t$
2. $2.5 \sin(3\pi t + 0.25\pi)$
3. $-2.5 \sin(3\pi t - 0.25\pi)$
4. $\sin(2t)$
5. $\sin(2t + 0.5)$
6. $\sin(2(t + 0.5))$

15–3 APPLICATION—SONAR SIGNALS (Acoustical Engineering)

Signal processing is one of the most important components in modern sonar (SOund NAvigation and Ranging). An active sonar system transmits a signal of a specified frequency. The reflections or echoes of that signal are then received and analyzed to provide information about the surroundings. A passive sonar system does not transmit signals but collects signals from sensors and analyzes them based on their frequency content. One of the types of signals used in sonar systems is the sinusoid. These sinusoids can be represented by the following equation:*

$$x(t) = \begin{cases} \sqrt{\dfrac{2E}{PD}} \cos(2\pi f_c t), & 0 \leq t \leq PD \\ 0, & \text{elsewhere} \end{cases}$$

where E is the transmitted energy, PD is the pulse duration in seconds, and f_c is the frequency in Hz.

Durations of a sonar signal can range from a fraction of a millisecond to several seconds, and frequencies can range from a few hundred Hz to tens of kHz (kilohertz) depending on the system and its desired operating range.

*"Sonar Signal Processing," by A. B. Baggeroer, Chapter 6 of *Applications of Digital Signal Processing*, Prentice-Hall, A. V. Oppenheim, Editor, Englewood Cliffs, NJ, 1978.

Write an interactive program in which the user inputs the values for E, PD, and f_c. Then generate a data file called SONAR that contains a digital signal $[x(k)]$. The sampling of the digital signal should cover the pulse duration and be such that there are ten samples for every period of $x(t)$. The data file should contain two values for every line: a time value (starting at zero) and the corresponding value of the sonar signal.

PROBLEM STATEMENT

Write a program to generate a sonar signal that contains ten samples from each period of a specified sinusoid, covering a specified time duration.

INPUT/OUTPUT DESCRIPTION

The values of E (transmitted energy in joules), PD (pulse duration in seconds) and f_c (frequency in Hz) are entered by the user when the program is executed. The output is a data file named SONAR which contains time and signal values for the sonar pulse duration.

HAND EXAMPLE

For a hand example, we use the following values:

$$E = 500 \text{ joules}$$
$$PD = 5 \text{ milliseconds (ms)}$$
$$f_c = 3.5 \text{ kHz}$$

The period of the sinusoid is 1/3500, or approximately 0.3 ms. Thus, to have ten samples per period, the sampling interval needs to be approximately 0.03 ms. The pulse duration is 5 ms, and thus we need 167 samples of the following signal:

$$x(t) = \sqrt{\frac{2E}{PD}} \cos(2\pi f_c t)$$

$$= \sqrt{\frac{1000}{0.005}} \cos(2\pi(3500)t)$$

$$= 447.2 \cos(2\pi 3500 t)$$

The first few values for the sonar signal are:

t (ms)	$x(t)$
0.0	447.2
0.03	353.4
0.06	111.2
0.09	-177.6
0.12	-391.9
0.15	-441.7

0.18	-306.1
0.21	-42.1
0.24	239.6
0.27	420.8
0.30	425.3
0.33	251.4

ALGORITHM DEVELOPMENT

The decomposition of the computer solution is:

DECOMPOSITION

Read energy, pulse duration, frequency.
Compute amplitude, sampling time, number of points.
Generate file containing time values and sinusoid values.

We now describe these steps in pseudocode.

REFINEMENT IN PSEUDOCODE

PULSE: Read energy (E), pulse duration (PD) , frequency

$$A \leftarrow \sqrt{\frac{2E}{PD}}$$

$$period \leftarrow \frac{1}{frequency}$$

$$sample\ interval \leftarrow \frac{period}{10}$$

$$number\ of\ samples \leftarrow \frac{PD}{sample\ interval}$$

For k = 0 to (number of samples $-$ 1) do
    time $\leftarrow$ k(sample interval)
    signal $\leftarrow$ A cos (2π frequency $\cdot$ time)
    Write time and signal to data file

We now convert the pseudocode to FORTRAN.

FORTRAN Program

```
*----------------------------------------------------------------*
        PROGRAM  PULSE
*
*   This program generates a sonar signal.
*
        INTEGER  NUMBER, K
        REAL  E, PD, FREQ, A, PERIOD, T, PI, TIME, SIGNAL
*
        OPEN (UNIT=10,FILE='SONAR',STATUS='NEW')
        PRINT*, 'ENTER TRANSMITTED ENERGY IN JOULES'
        READ*, E
        PRINT*, 'ENTER PULSE DURATION IN SECONDS'
        READ*, PD
        PRINT*, 'ENTER SINUSOID FREQUENCY IN HERTZ'
        READ*, FREQ
*
        A = SQRT(2.0*E/PD)
        PERIOD = 1.0/FREQ
        T = PERIOD/10.0
        NUMBER = NINT(PD/T)
        PI = 3.141593
*
        DO 10 K=0,NUMBER-1
            TIME = REAL(K)*T
            SIGNAL = A*COS(2.0*PI*FREQ*TIME)
            WRITE (10,*) TIME, SIGNAL
     10 CONTINUE
*
        END
*----------------------------------------------------------------*
```

The nearest integer function (NINT) was used in the computation of the number of samples to round the answer. We did not need to use an array to store the signal. In fact, using an array would cause the program to be less flexible because we would have to give the array an upper limit in size.

TESTING

The terminal screen interaction and a plot of the SONAR file follow for a sample interaction:

COMPUTER OUTPUT

```
ENTER  TRANSMITTED  ENERGY  IN  JOULES
500.0
ENTER  PULSE  DURATION  IN  SECONDS
0.005
ENTER  SINUSOID  FREQUENCY  IN  HERTZ
3500.0
```

Plot of the file SONAR

t, seconds

When plotting the sonar pulse, we specified that the *x* axis should cover from 0.0 to 0.01 to emphasize the fact that the pulse has a specified duration of 0.005 second. Since the period of the 3.5-kHz sinusoid is approximately 0.0003 second, and the pulse has a duration of 0.005 second, the pulse should contain approximately 17 periods; this is also confirmed by the plot.

15–4 RANDOM SIGNAL GENERATION

Signals which are defined by an equation are called "deterministic" signals; if we wish to know the value of the signal at a specific time, we substitute the time value in the equation to determine the signal value. *Random signals* (sequences of random numbers) are signals which are not defined by an equation but have certain characteristics that define them. For example, noise on a communication line (such as static on a radio channel) can be modeled as a random signal. The random signals used in testing DSP techniques are often generated from uniform random numbers. We now discuss this type of random number and present a routine for generating a uniform random signal.

UNIFORM RANDOM NUMBERS

Random numbers can be characterized by a density function (also called a probability density function, or pdf). This function shows the range of values of the random number and indicates the likelihood of the occurrence of particular values. For example, the subroutine RANDOM presented in Chapter 7 generates numbers equally likely to occur between 0.0 and 1.0; the density function for the random numbers generated by this subroutine can be described by this density function:

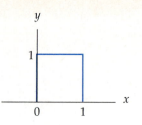

The density function shows the upper and lower bounds (0 and 1) of the random number on the abscissa; the rectangular nature of the function indicates that all values between 0 and 1 are equally likely to occur. The area of a density function is always unity, and since the width of this uniform density function is 1.0, its height must also be 1. (You may want to review Section 7–2, page 306, before proceeding with this material.)

Random signals which range between values other than 0.0 and 1.0 are often needed. For example, the next plot contains a density function for random numbers which are uniformly distributed between −5.0 and 5.0. Again, the area of the density function is unity.

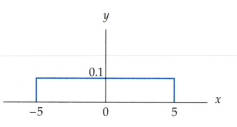

We can generate a random number that is uniformly distributed between a lower bound and an upper bound by modifying the number generated by the RANDOM subroutine used in Chapter 7. We first multiply (or scale) the number generated by RANDOM by the width of the density function of the desired random number. This width is computed by subtracting the lower bound from the upper bound. Then, the scaled value is added to the lower limit to adjust the new value to the proper range. For example, suppose that we want to generate values between 2 and 5. We use the RANDOM subroutine to generate a number between 0 and 1 and then multiply it by 3, which is the difference between the upper and lower bounds (5 − 2). We then add the lower bound (2), giving a result that is equally likely to be any value between 2 and 5.

If two random signals are generated with the same number of samples and the same lower and upper bounds, but with different seed values, the two signals will be different. This is illustrated in the two plots below, which each connect 20 random values and were generated with a lower bound of −5.0 and an upper bound of 5.0 but with different seed values. When we test a DSP technique, we may want to generate the same random signal for several test runs; using the same seed allows us to do that.

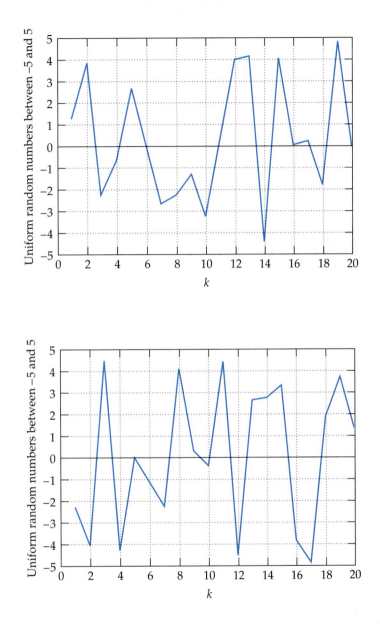

In addition to needing a single random number between two specified limits, we may also want to generate a signal containing a sequence of random numbers from a specified density function. We present next a subroutine that generates a signal containing uniform random values between two specified values. This subroutine is called with the following statement:

CALL UNIF *(signal name, number of samples, lower bound, upper bound, seed value)*

The statements in this routine perform the steps that we described for generating *uniform random numbers* between two bounds:

```
*-------------------------------------------------------------*
       SUBROUTINE  UNIF (X,N,LOWER,UPPER,SEED)
*
*   This subroutine generates a uniform random signal
*   with values between a lower bound and an upper bound.
*
       INTEGER  N, SEED, K
       REAL  X(0:N-1), LOWER, UPPER, RN
*
       DO 10 K=0,N-1
          CALL RANDOM (SEED,RN)
          X(K) = RN*(UPPER-LOWER) + LOWER
   10 CONTINUE
*
       RETURN
       END
*-------------------------------------------------------------*
```

When working with random signals, we are often interested in the average value of the signal. The average value can be computed by summing the signal values and dividing by the number of signal values. Thus, if the signal $[x_k]$ contains N values (referenced by subscripts 0 through $N - 1$), the following summation notation represents the average value, which we indicate with the symbol μ, or μ_x to indicate that the average is for the signal $[x_k]$:

$$\mu_x = \frac{\sum\limits_{k=0}^{N-1} x_k}{N}$$

The average value is also called the *mean*. Theoretically, the average value for a uniform random signal is the midpoint of the density function, or

$$\mu = \frac{\text{upper bound} + \text{lower bound}}{2}$$

Another value that we often compute for a random signal is the *variance*. The variance is the average squared deviation from the mean and is computed using the following equation:

$$\sigma_x^2 = \frac{\sum\limits_{k=0}^{N-1} (x_k - \mu)^2}{N}$$

(For some applications the equation for the variance is written with a denominator of $N - 1$, instead of a denominator of N.) Thus, the wider the density function, the larger will be the value of the variance because the random values can deviate further from the mean. The *standard deviation* (σ) is the square root of the variance:

$$\sigma = \sqrt{\sigma^2}$$

Note that the standard deviation is always a positive value.

Using results from probability theory, it can be shown that the variance can also be expressed as the average squared value minus the square of the average, or

$$\sigma^2 = \frac{\displaystyle\sum_{k=0}^{N-1} x_k^2}{N} - \mu^2$$

The variance of a uniform distribution can also be expressed (again using results from probability theory) in terms of the upper and lower bounds:

$$\sigma^2 = \frac{(\text{upper bound} - \text{lower bound})^2}{12} \tag{15-1}$$

With actual data, the average and variance do not match exactly the theoretical values; however, as we use more and more points from a random distribution, the computed mean and variance should approach the theoretical values. To illustrate, the next example generates uniform random numbers and computes the corresponding mean and variance.

EXAMPLE 15–2   **Computing Signal Statistics**

Write a program to generate 10,000 uniform values, and then compare mean and variance values for the first 10 samples, the first 100 samples, the first 1000 samples, and finally, all 10,000 samples:

Solution

We first generate the uniform random signal. Since the computations for the average and variance are performed for N values, where each N is ten times more than the previous N, we can use a loop with the index representing the power of 10 for the number of random numbers to use in the calculations.

FORTRAN PROGRAM

```
*-------------------------------------------------------------*
      PROGRAM  STATS
*
*   This program calculates the mean and variance
*   for uniform random variables.
*
      INTEGER  SEED, K, N
      REAL  UPPER, LOWER, MEAN, VAR, X(10000), AVE, VARNC
*
      PRINT*, 'ENTER LOWER BOUND, UPPER BOUND, AND INTEGER SEED'
      READ*, LOWER, UPPER, SEED
      PRINT*, 'THEORETICAL MEAN = ',(UPPER+LOWER)/2.0
      PRINT*, 'THEORETICAL VARIANCE = ',(UPPER-LOWER)**2/12.0
      PRINT*
```

```
*
      CALL UNIF (X,10000,LOWER,UPPER,SEED)
      DO 10 K=1,4
         N = 10**K
         CALL CALC (X,N,AVE,VARNC)
    5    PRINT 8, N, AVE, VARNC
    8    FORMAT (1X,I7,' SAMPLES:',5X,'AVE =',F7.4,5X,
   +             'VAR =',F7.4)
 10 CONTINUE
*
      END
*-------------------------------------------------------------*
      SUBROUTINE  CALC (X,N,AVE,VARNC)
*
* This subroutine computes the average and variance for the
* first N values in the array X.
*
      INTEGER  N, K
      REAL  X(N), AVE, VARNC, SUM, SUM2
*
      SUM = 0.0
      SUM2 = 0.0
      DO 10 K=1,N
         SUM = SUM + X(K)
         SUM2 = SUM2 + X(K)*X(K)
 10 CONTINUE
      AVE = SUM/REAL(N)
      VARNC = SUM2/REAL(N) - AVE*AVE
*
      RETURN
      END
*-------------------------------------------------------------*
            UNIF subroutine from page 646 goes here
*-------------------------------------------------------------*
            RANDOM subroutine from page 310 goes here
*-------------------------------------------------------------*
```

Computer Output

```
ENTER LOWER BOUND, UPPER BOUND, AND INTEGER SEED
0 5 82
THEORETICAL MEAN =  2.500000
THEORETICAL VARIANCE =  2.083333

    10 SAMPLES:      AVE = 2.1043      VAR = 2.8062
   100 SAMPLES:      AVE = 2.3967      VAR = 2.1216
  1000 SAMPLES:      AVE = 2.5157      VAR = 2.1037
 10000 SAMPLES:      AVE = 2.5138      VAR = 2.0766
```

If a different seed value is used, slight changes occur in the values computed for the means and variances, but the computed values should still approach the theoretical values entered by the user as the number of samples in the signal increases.

SIGNAL-TO-NOISE RATIOS

We now have subroutines to generate random signals (often called noise signals) with specified characteristics. In generating signals to use in testing our DSP techniques, we often want to generate signals such as the one below, which contains a sinusoid with noise added to it:

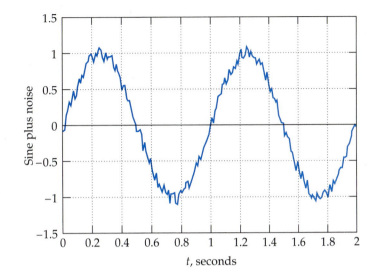

In many situations, we want to generate a signal plus noise with a specification of a *signal-to-noise ratio*, or SNR. For example, an SNR of 1 specifies that the ratio of *signal power* to noise power is 1:1. The power of a digital signal is the average squared value of the signal. It can be shown that the signal power in a sinusoid is one-half its squared amplitude and that the power in a random signal with zero mean is its variance. Therefore, we can generate a sinusoid with noise with an SNR of 1 by generating a sinusoid with amplitude A and adding to it a uniform random signal with a mean of zero and a variance of $A^2/2$. However, when we generate a uniform random signal, we specify only the lower limit and the upper limit for the signal values, so we can use Eq. (15–1) to relate the bounds to the variance.

Suppose that we want to add noise to a signal that has already been collected and stored in a data file. If we want to add noise that maintains a specified SNR, we need to estimate the power of the signal so that we can determine the appropriate power for the noise signal. A good estimate of the power of a signal is the average squared signal value:

$$\text{Power} = \frac{\sum_{k=0}^{N-1} x_k^2}{N}$$

The power in a signal can also be computed from the mean and variance of the signal:

$$\text{Power} = \sigma^2 + \mu^2$$

This equation is very useful because we can employ it several ways. For example, if we know the mean and variance of a signal, we can compute the power of the signal. If the mean value of a signal is zero, we see that the power of the signal is the same value as the variance of the signal. These relationships allow us to determine the proper noise signal to generate to maintain a specified SNR.

SELF-TEST 15–2

This self-test allows you to check quickly to see if you have remembered the key points from Section 15–4. If you have any problems with the exercises, you should reread this section. The solutions are included at the end of the text.

Give the statements that call the subroutine UNIF to generate 100 values of a random signal NOISE which has the following characteristics:

1. Uniform values between 0 and 10.
2. Uniform values between -2 and 4.
3. Uniform values with mean of zero and variance of 1.0.
4. Uniform values with mean of -0.5 and variance of 4.0.

15–5 APPLICATION—COMMUNICATION CHANNELS (Electrical Engineering)

Digital signals are widely used in communications. For example, when we use the telephone our voice signal is sampled to form a digital signal, which is transmitted and then converted back to an analog or continuous signal before it reaches the receiving telephone. Computers communicate over networks using digital signals. These are just a couple of examples of digital signal processing in communications. In many communications applications, continuous signals are sent through a telephone wire, or air, or water, or another medium which propagates the signal. (This medium is also called the communication channel.) As the signal passes through a communication channel, it is often altered by noise in the channel. The signal that is received after passing through the communication channel is considered to be the original signal plus the noise. Digital signal processing techniques can often be used to separate the original signal from the channel noise. In order to test these DSP techniques, we need to generate digital signals that contain an original signal plus added noise. After running the DSP technique, we can compare the resulting signal to the original signal to measure the performance of our noise-canceling technique.

Write a program that generates a signal containing 200 points of a 10-Hz sinusoid with zero-mean uniform noise that has a signal-to-noise ratio of 20. Use a sampling rate of 500 Hz and store the signal in a data file called SNR20.

PROBLEM STATEMENT

Write a program to generate a sinusoid with added noise.

INPUT/OUTPUT DESCRIPTION

No input is needed for the program. The output is a data file named SNR20 that contains 200 points of a digital signal.

HAND EXAMPLE

Since the problem does not specify the amplitude or phase of the sinusoid, we use $A^2/2$ in our analysis for the signal power. Since the phase does not affect the power, we could use any value, so we choose a phase of zero radians. For the SNR to be 20, the ratio $(A^2/2) : \sigma^2$ should be

$$\frac{A^2}{2} : \frac{A^2}{40}$$

where σ^2 is the variance of the noise signal. (Recall that if the mean is zero, the power is equal to the variance.) If we choose an amplitude of 1.0, the noise variance should be 1/40 or 0.025; if we choose an amplitude of 2.0, the noise variance should be 0.1. For this example, we choose an amplitude of 1.0 for the sinusoid. Since the variance of uniform noise is equal to $\text{width}^2/12$ (where width is the width of the uniform density function), we have

$$0.025 = \frac{\text{width}^2}{12}$$

or

$$\text{width}^2 = 0.3$$

Then the width of the uniform density function is 0.5477226 (to seven significant places for computer calculations). Since the uniform random variable is specified to have a mean of zero, the midpoint of the density function is zero, so the lower and upper limits are -0.2738613 and 0.2738613. Thus, a few samples of the signal $[x_k]$ are

k	t_k	x_k
0	0.000	$\sin(2\pi 10 t_0) + \text{noise}_0 = 0.000 + \text{noise}_0$
1	0.002	$\sin(2\pi 10 t_1) + \text{noise}_1 = 0.125 + \text{noise}_1$
2	0.004	$\sin(2\pi 10 t_2) + \text{noise}_2 = 0.249 + \text{noise}_2$
3	0.006	$\sin(2\pi 10 t_3) + \text{noise}_3 = 0.368 + \text{noise}_3$
4	0.008	$\sin(2\pi 10 t_4) + \text{noise}_4 = 0.482 + \text{noise}_4$
5	0.010	$\sin(2\pi 10 t_5) + \text{noise}_5 = 0.588 + \text{noise}_5$

where the values in [noise_k] are uniformly distributed between -0.2738613 and 0.2738613.

ALGORITHM DEVELOPMENT

The decomposition of the computer solution is:

DECOMPOSITION

Generate signal plus noise values.
Write signal plus noise values to data file.

The steps are straightforward, so we can go directly to the refinement in pseudocode, in which we use the module presented in the previous section to generate a uniform noise signal.

REFINEMENT IN PSEUDOCODE

CHANNL: Generate sinusoid
Generate noise signal
Add noise to sinusoid
Write sinusoid + noise to data file

The structure chart for this solution is:

```
*-------------------------------------------------------------------*
        PROGRAM   CHANNL
*
*   This program generates a signal plus
*   uniform noise using a specified SNR.
*
        INTEGER   K
        REAL  NOISE(0:199), PI, T, TIME, X
*
        OPEN (UNIT=10, FILE='SNR20', STATUS='NEW')
        CALL UNIF (NOISE,200,-0.2738613,0.2738613,123)
        PI = 3.141593
        T = 0.002
        DO 10 K=0,199
           TIME = REAL(K)*T
           X = SIN(2.0*PI*10.0*TIME) + NOISE(K)
           WRITE (10,*) TIME, X
    10 CONTINUE
*
        END
*-------------------------------------------------------------------*
```

------------ UNIF subroutine from page 646 goes here ------------

----------- RANDOM subroutine from page 310 goes here -----------

---

TESTING

A plot of the file SNR20 is shown below.

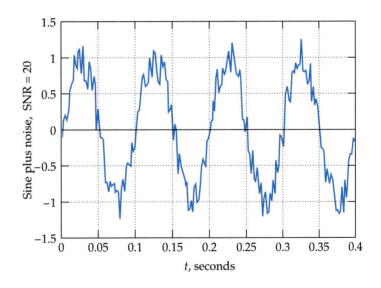

By changing the seed in the UNIF module, a different noise signal will be
generated, but the SNR will still be 20.

15-6 APPLICATION—DIGITAL FILTERING
(Electrical Engineering)

Digital signals are often composed of several signals that have been added together, such as a sinusoid plus noise or a sum of two sinusoids with different frequencies. A digital filter is a special type of equation called a difference equation that describes how to generate a new digital signal from an existing digital signal. By carefully designing this difference equation, we can use the digital filter to separate (or "filter") the components in a signal. A digital filter can also be explained in terms of its effect on a sinusoid: a digital filter will multiply the amplitude of a sinusoid by a scale factor, and it will add a phase shift to the sinusoid, but it will not change the frequency. This definition is related to the concept of a transfer function, which will be defined in this section.

A digital filter is often described in terms of the following diagram, which shows an input signal $[x_k]$, the digital filter which modifies $[x_k]$, and the output sequence $[y_k]$.

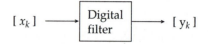

The first value in the signal is usually represented by x_0, and it represents the function $x(t)$ evaluated at time equal to zero; if the values represent experimentally collected information, we assume that the first sample is collected at time equal to zero.

A digital filter is defined with a *difference equation* that specifies the computations to be performed on the input signal. The digital filter that we are going to use in this example is defined by the following difference equation:

$$y_k = \tfrac{1}{3}x_{k-1} + \tfrac{1}{3}x_k + \tfrac{1}{3}x_{k+1} \tag{15-2}$$

If we look closely at this difference equation, we see that it is performing a familiar operation—an average. Using this equation, each output value is generated by averaging three input values. If we write the equation for computing the first four values of the output sequence, we have

$$y_0 = \tfrac{1}{3}x_{-1} + \tfrac{1}{3}x_0 + \tfrac{1}{3}x_1$$

$$y_1 = \tfrac{1}{3}x_0 + \tfrac{1}{3}x_1 + \tfrac{1}{3}x_2$$

$$y_2 = \tfrac{1}{3}x_1 + \tfrac{1}{3}x_2 + \tfrac{1}{3}x_3$$

$$y_3 = \tfrac{1}{3}x_2 + \tfrac{1}{3}x_3 + \tfrac{1}{3}x_4$$

If we assume that we have the values for the input sequence, then it is straightforward to compute these four values in the output sequence, except for the value of y_0. The equation for y_0 is the only equation that has a term with a negative subscript. Since we usually assume that the first value of the digital signal is x_0, we do not have a value for x_{-1}; therefore, we usually assume that these values are zero. If we have 100 samples of an input signal, the values are referenced by x_0 to x_{99}. Similarly, we will have 100 samples of the output signal, referenced by y_0 to y_{99}. If we use the difference equation to compute the value for y_{99}, we have

$$y_{99} = \tfrac{1}{3} x_{98} + \tfrac{1}{3} x_{99} + \tfrac{1}{3} x_{100}$$

Since we do not have a value for x_{100}, we also assume that this value is zero. A difference equation computes output values based on input values; thus, it should be clear that these computations can easily be performed with a FORTRAN program.

Before we develop the program to apply this digital filter to an input signal, we discuss the function of this specific filter. Since this filter averages three values in a row, it is sometimes called a smoothing filter because it will smooth the input signal. It is also called a lowpass filter, which means that it passes low-frequency components with little change and rejects or stops components with high frequencies. This is consistent with the idea of a smoothing filter because we are smoothing the more rapid variations in the input signal. A *transfer function* defines the effect of the filter in terms of amplitude change and phase change, relative to the frequency of the input signal. The plot below contains the magnitude of the transfer function for this filter, and it shows the amplitude modification for inputs at different frequencies as they pass through the filter.

The transfer function is close to 1 for frequencies near zero. For frequencies between 0 and 1500 Hz, the magnitude of the output is at least 0.7 of the input magnitude. Between 1500 and 3000 Hz the magnitude attenuation goes from 0.7 to 0.1. For frequencies between 3000 and 3500 Hz, the signals are essentially eliminated. Between 3500 and 4800 Hz, the magnitude change increases somewhat but is always less than 0.4. This filter is considered to be a lowpass filter because it passes low frequencies with little attenuation but significantly reduces the magnitude of the higher frequencies.

This filter was designed to be used with a sampling frequency of 9.6 kHz. Recall that a sinusoid should always be sampled more than two times per period. Thus, for a sampling rate of 9.6 kHz, we should consider only input sinusoids with frequencies less than 4.8 kHz; hence, the transfer function is valid only for frequencies between 0 and 4.8 kHz, as shown in the magnitude plot. (A sampling frequency of 9.6 kHz is commonly used to collect voice signals because a human voice typically is in the range of 300 to 4000 Hz.)

In addition to changing the amplitude of a sinusoid, a digital filter may also change its phase shift. The next plot shows the phase shift of this specific digital filter as a function of frequency. If the input to the filter is a sinusoid with a frequency of less than 3225 Hz, the output of the filter will have zero phase shift. If the output of the filter is above 3225 Hz, the output of the filter will be shifted by π radians.

We are now ready to develop a program to implement the digital filter defined by the difference equation (15–2). The input should be a sinusoid, with the user selecting the amplitude, frequency, and phase shift. The sampling frequency is 9.6 kHz, and 100 samples of the sinusoid should be generated.

PROBLEM STATEMENT

Implement the digital filter defined by the following difference equation:

$$y_k = \tfrac{1}{3} x_{k-1} + \tfrac{1}{3} x_k + \tfrac{1}{3} x_{k+1}$$

INPUT/OUTPUT DESCRIPTION

The inputs to the program are user-entered values for the amplitude, frequency, and phase shift of a sinusoid. The output is the signal (containing 100 points) generated by applying the filter to the sinusoid specified by the user. A sampling frequency of 9.6 kHz is assumed.

HAND EXAMPLE

For a hand example, we assume that the input is the following:

$$x_k = 2 \sin(2\pi 1500 kT)$$

where $T = 1/9600$. The first four values of this signal are

$$x_0 = 0.0$$
$$x_1 = 1.6629$$
$$x_2 = 1.8478$$
$$x_3 = 0.3902$$

The difference equation that defines the digital filter is

$$y_k = \tfrac{1}{3} x_{k-1} + \tfrac{1}{3} x_k + \tfrac{1}{3} x_{k+1}$$

Therefore, the first three values of the output signal are

$$y_0 = \tfrac{1}{3} x_{-1} + \tfrac{1}{3} x_0 + \tfrac{1}{3} x_1$$
$$= \tfrac{1}{3}(0) + \tfrac{1}{3}(0) + \tfrac{1}{3}(1.6629)$$
$$= 0.5543$$

$$y_1 = \tfrac{1}{3} x_0 + \tfrac{1}{3} x_1 + \tfrac{1}{3} x_2$$
$$= \tfrac{1}{3}(0) + \tfrac{1}{3}(1.6629) + \tfrac{1}{3}(1.8478)$$
$$= 1.1702$$

$$y_2 = \tfrac{1}{3} x_1 + \tfrac{1}{3} x_2 + \tfrac{1}{3} x_3$$
$$= \tfrac{1}{3}(1.6629) + \tfrac{1}{3}(1.8478) + \tfrac{1}{3}(0.3902)$$
$$= 1.3003$$

Note that a special case occurred for the first value because we do not have an input signal value for x_{-1}; we assume a value of zero for x_{-1}. Similarly, a special case occurs when we compute y_{99} because we do not have an input signal value for x_{100}; we again use a value of zero for x_{100} in the difference equation.

The decomposition of the computer solution is:

DECOMPOSITION

Read parameters for sinusoid.
Generate sinusoidal signal.
Apply filter to the sinusoidal signal.
Write input and output signals to data file.

From the hand example, and from examining the difference equation, we see that there are special cases in implementing the filter for the first signal value and for the last signal value. These special cases occur because the difference equation specifies input signal values that are not available.

We are now ready to describe the steps in pseudocode.

REFINEMENT IN PSEUDOCODE

FILTER: Read amplitude (A), frequency (F), phase (PHASE)
$T \leftarrow 1/9600$
For k = 0 to 99 do
$x_k \leftarrow A \sin (2\pi FkT + PHASE)$
$y_0 \leftarrow \dfrac{x_0 + x_1}{3}$
For k = 1 to 98 do
$y_k \leftarrow \dfrac{x_{k-1} + x_k + x_{k+1}}{3}$
$y_{99} \leftarrow \dfrac{x_{98} + x_{99}}{3}$
For k = 0 to 99 do
Write x_k and y_k to data file

We now convert the pseudocode to FORTRAN.

FORTRAN PROGRAM

```
*-------------------------------------------------------------*
      PROGRAM  FILTER
*
*  This program filters a sinusoid sampled at 9.6 kHz
*  using a filter designed to reduce high frequency components.
*
      INTEGER  K
      REAL  PI, T, A, F, PHASE, X(0:99), Y(0:99)
*
      PI = 3.141593
      T = 1/9600.0
*
      PRINT*, 'ENTER AMPLITUDE, FREQUENCY (HZ), PHASE (RADIANS)'
      READ*, A, F, PHASE
```

```
*
        DO 10 K=0,99
            X(K) = A*SIN(2.0*PI*F*K*T+PHASE)
     10 CONTINUE
*
        Y(0) = (X(0) + X(1))/3.0
        DO 20 K=1,98
            Y(K) = (X(K-1) + X(K) + X(K+1))/3.0
     20 CONTINUE
        Y(99) = (X(98) + X(99))/3.0
*
        OPEN (UNIT=10,FILE='FILTER1',STATUS='NEW')
        DO 30 K=0,99
            TIME = K*T
            WRITE (10,*) TIME, X(K), Y(K)
     30 CONTINUE
*
        END
*-------------------------------------------------------*
```

TESTING

We first test the filter using the signal from the hand example, which is a 1.5-kHz sinusoid. If we print the first few values of the data file, we see that they are the same as the values that we computed by hand.

We can also estimate the effect of the filter using the magnitude plot and the phase plot. The filter should multiply the amplitude of the 1.5-kHz sinusoid by approximately 0.7, and it should cause a zero phase shift. If you look at the data file, you will see that the maximum input value is 1.9616 and the maximum output is 1.3804 (which is approximately 0.7 times 1.9021). The maximum output value occurs at the same time sample as the maximum input value, so there has not been a phase shift. The following figure contains a plot of the first part of this filter input and output, showing graphically the magnitude change of 0.7 and the zero phase shift.

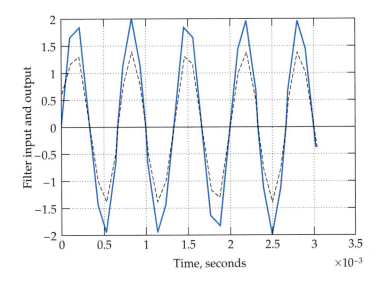

The next plot contains the first part of the input and output of the filter for a frequency of 3.2 kHz. From the magnitude plot of the filter, we would expect the filter to essentially remove or eliminate this signal from the output, as the plot below confirms.

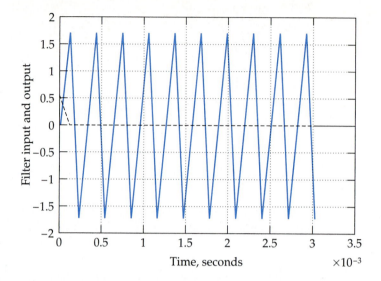

The next plot contains the first part of the input and output of the filter for a frequency of 4.5 kHz. From the magnitude and phase plots of the filter, we would expect the filter to multiply the amplitude by a little over 0.3 and to shift the output by π radians; the plot below confirms both of these changes in the output signal. Also, note that as the frequency of the sinusoid increases (with a constant sampling interval), we have fewer samples per period and thus the appearance of the sinusoid changes when we connect the points with straight lines.

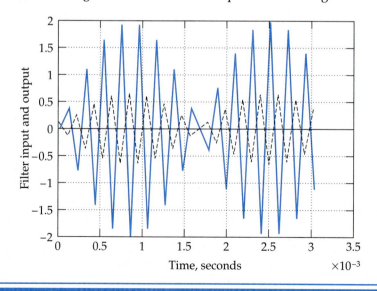

SUMMARY

Sinusoids are special functions that we commonly use in digital signal processing. We can generate them with any specified amplitude, frequency, and phase shift. We can also generate uniform random signals having specified means and variances. These random signals can be added to other signals to generate new signals with a desired signal-to-noise ratio. Digital filters are used to remove or separate components within a digital signal.

DEBUGGING AIDS

When working with digital signals, it is very important to scan the signal visually using a plot of the data points. Refer to Appendix C for a discussion of plotting using some of the commonly available software. It is also important to be careful with units when generating digital signals. Make sure that your program interaction with the user specifies units (radians or degrees, radians per second or Hz, second, or milliseconds, etc.).

STYLE/TECHNIQUE GUIDES

Having a set of modules available to generate random signals is very helpful in developing computer algorithms using digital signals. However, be sure that the modules fit the problem that you are trying to solve. If the modules do not easily fit your solution, add some of your own modifications to maintain a simple solution to the problem. Forcing a program to use prewritten modules often makes the code difficult to follow and to debug.

ERROR ANALYSIS

When a continuous signal, such as an electrical voltage, is sampled to generate a digital signal, a special type of inherent error called a quantizing error occurs. This error is introduced in the A/D converter that converts the analog or continuous signal to a digital signal. The A/D converter is a piece of hardware that uses a finite number of binary digits to represent or encode the continuous value; therefore, there is a fixed number of values that can be represented by the A/D converter. When a continuous value falls between two of these values, the closest value is used for the digital value; the *quantization error* is the difference between the closest value and the actual value.

Quantization errors and roundoff errors are similar because they both occur as a result of storing a value using a fixed number of digits. However, they are different because they occur at different points in a numerical process. Quantization errors occur each time that a continuous signal is sampled to generate a value for the digital signal. Roundoff errors can potentially occur each time that a computation is performed with the computer. Also, the numbers of digits used by the A/D converter and by the computer are often different, thus increasing the possible error that occurs when the output of the A/D converter is stored in a computer.

KEY WORDS

analog signal   sensor
difference equation   signal
digital signal   signal power
frequency   signal-to-noise ratio
mean   sinusoid
random signal   standard deviation
quantization error   transfer function
sampling frequency   uniform random number
sampling interval   variance

PROBLEMS

We begin our problem set with modifications to programs developed earlier in this chapter. Give the decomposition, refined pseudocode or flowchart, and FORTRAN solution for each problem.

Problems 1–4 modify the program PULSE, given on page 642, which generates a sonar signal.

1. Modify the sonar program so that the pulse duration is entered in milliseconds.

2. Modify the sonar program so that the frequency is entered in radians per second.

3. Modify the sonar program so that the user can specify the number of samples per period for sampling the sinusoid.

4. Modify the sonar program so that the user can specify a sampling frequency in Hz.

Problems 5–8 modify the program CHANNL, given on page 653, which generates a signal with noise.

5. Modify the channel signal program so that the user can specify the sampling time.

6. Modify the channel signal program so that it uses uniform noise with an SNR ratio of 30.

7. Modify the channel signal program so that the user can specify the amplitude of the sinusoid. (Remember that the amplitude is related to the bounds for the noise signal.)

8. Modify the channel signal program so that it allows the user to specify the SNR ratio.

Problems 9–13 modify the program FILTER, given on page 658, which filters a sinusoid.

9. Modify the digital filter program so that the user enters the phase in degrees instead of radians.

10. Modify the digital filter program so the user can enter the number of data points, with a maximum of 500.

11. Modify the digital filter program so that the user enters a data file, and the program reads the input times and signal values instead of computing the time and input sinusoid values. Assume that the first line of the data file contains the number of signal values in the file, with a maximum of 500 values.

12. Modify the digital filter program so that the user enters a data file, and the program reads the input times and signal values instead of computing the time and input sinusoid values. Assume that the first line in the data file contains the first time and signal value and that the last line in the file contains the values -99, -99. Remove the arrays from the program so that the data file could have any number of signal values in it. (Hint—perform the filtering and the writing to the output data file in the same loop.)

13. Modify the digital filter program so that the input is a sinusoid sampled at 9.6 kHz with uniform noise added to it to give an SNR of 20. Allow the user to specify the frequency of the sinusoid. The output should be a data file of the input and output to the filter. For low-frequency sinusoids, the filter should remove much of the noise. Demonstrate this by plotting the input and output using an input signal with a frequency of 1.5 kHz.

Problems 14–17 refer to an array of four seismometers (sensors that measure ground motion) that have been positioned as shown:

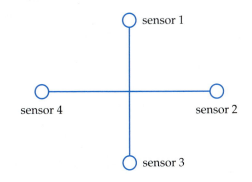

Data are collected from these seismometers at a sampling rate of 200 Hz. Assume that the signal from sensor 1 has been stored in a file called SENSOR1, the signal from sensor 2 has been stored in a file called SENSOR2, and so on. Assume that the signals contain data from a 5-minute period.

14. To test the sensitivity of the seismometers, we might drive a large truck near the array and then evaluate the signals collected. We would expect that the means and variances of the signals from sensors near the truck should be larger than those farther away. Develop a program to compute the means, variances, and power for signals from each sensor and print the output in an easy-to-read report.

15. In our signal processing techniques, we often like to work with signals that are zero mean. In practice, however, many signals are not zero mean. Develop a program to compute the mean for the signal from sensor 1 and then subtract the mean from each sample in the signal. Store the new zero-mean signal in a file called SENS1ZM.

16. We often normalize signals before comparing them. One form of normalization requires scaling the signal so that the maximum value in the signal is 1.0 and then all the rest of the values are scaled by the same value. Develop a program to normalize the signal from sensor 3 and store it in SENS3N.

17. To find seismic events (such as earthquakes, underground blasts, and nuclear explosions) in the signal, we look for regions where the signal values are larger than those in other regions. Larger signal values can also be detected by searching for larger power values. Develop a program to find the 2-second region with the largest power (with respect to other 2-second regions) in the signal from sensor 4, and store it in EVENT4. (Note that this could be done by initially dividing the time data into 2-second regions or by sliding the 2-second region one sample to the right for each computation. The latter technique requires more computation but is more accurate.)

Problems 18–20 refer to a telephone signal in a telephone network:

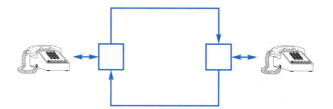

Assume that the signals are collected at 9600 Hz, or 9.6 kHz.

18. For testing purposes, we have collected 1 second of a speech signal and stored it in a data file SPEECH. This speech signal was collected in a sound studio and has no noise added to it. To test the quality of the telephone

network, we want to experiment with the amount of noise that can be added to the signal and still have the speech be understandable. Develop a program to generate noisy speech data files SPEECH1, SPEECH2, and SPEECH10, where the speech signal plus zero-mean uniform noise has an SNR of 1, 2, and 10, respectively.

19. Assume that the original telephone signal contained a 500-Hz sinusoid. Echoes generated by the network appear as shifted and scaled versions of the original signal that have been added to it. We want to generate a signal with 800 samples where the signal contains the original signal plus an echo at one-half amplitude and a shift to the right of 40 samples, and a rolled echo at one-tenth amplitude (a rolled echo is one with a negative amplitude) and a shift to the right of 150 samples. Develop the program for generating this signal.

20. Echoes in a signal can be detected using some of the same techniques used to detect events in a seismic signal. Develop a program for generating a signal containing the power value for a region of 10 samples (also called a moving window). The first value should be the power of the first sample, the second value should be the power of the first two samples, the third value should be the power of the first three samples, and so on, until we get to the 11th sample. The 11th power value should represent the power computed from the 2nd through the 11th samples, the 12th power value should represent the power computed from the 3rd through the 12th samples, and so on. Test your program using the signal generated in problem 16, and see if this method identifies the echoes by generating larger power values at the positions of the echoes.

In problems 21–24, develop programs and modules using the five-phase design process.

21. Develop a program to implement the digital filter defined by the following difference equation:

$$y_k = -0.15x_k - 0.25x_{k-1} + 0.7x_{k-2} - 0.25x_{k-3} - 0.15x_{k-4}$$

Assume that a sampling rate of 2 kHz is used for the input signal, which is a user-specified sinusoid. This is a highpass filter; it will tend to reject low frequencies and pass high frequencies. Remember that the maximum frequency that should be used with this filter is one-half the sampling frequency, or 1 kHz.

22. The following difference equation defines a digital filter that passes frequencies between 500 and 1500 Hz, assuming that the input signal is sampled at 5 kHz:

$$y_k = 0.42x_k - 0.42x_{k-2} + 0.443y_{k-1} - 0.159y_{k-2}$$

Develop a program to implement this filter, with a user-specified sinusoid as input. (Be careful—the output of this filter is based on previous filter outputs in addition to filter inputs.)

23. The following difference equation defines a digital filter that removes a 60-Hz frequency, assuming that the input signal is sampled at 960 Hz:

$$y_k = 0.8394x_k - 1.5509x_{k-1} + 0.8394x_{k-2}$$
$$+ 1.5509y_{k-1} - 0.6788y_{k-2}$$

Develop a program to implement this filter, with a user-specified sinusoid as input. (Be careful—the output of this filter is also based on previous filter outputs in addition to filter inputs.)

24. Generate a 1-kHz sinusoid with an amplitude of 1 that is sampled at 9.6 kHz and with additive uniform noise that varies from −0.5 to 0.5. This noise should make it difficult to see the sinusoid when you plot the signal plus noise. Use this signal as the input to a modified FILTER program, and plot the output. The noise should be reduced but still be significant. Use the output signal values as new input signal values. (This essentially runs the output back through the filter.) Replot the output. Continue this process until the noise in the signal becomes insignificant.

APPENDIX A

FORTRAN 77 INTRINSIC FUNCTIONS

In the following table of intrinsic functions, the names of the arguments specify their type as indicated below:

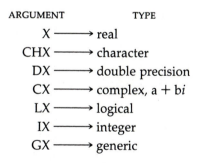

ARGUMENT		TYPE
X	⟶	real
CHX	⟶	character
DX	⟶	double precision
CX	⟶	complex, a + bi
LX	⟶	logical
IX	⟶	integer
GX	⟶	generic

Function type, the second column of the table of intrinsic functions, specifies the type of value returned by the function.

Generic function names are printed in maroon. Any type argument that is applicable can be used with generic functions, and the function value returned will be the same type as the input arguments, except for type conversion functions such as REAL and INT.

Function Name	Function Type	Definition
SQRT(X)	Real	$\sqrt{X}$
DSQRT(DX)	Double precision	$\sqrt{DX}$
CSQRT(CX)	Complex	$\sqrt{CX}$
ABS(X)	Real	$\lvert X \rvert$
IABS(IX)	Integer	$\lvert IX \rvert$
DABS(DX)	Double precision	$\lvert DX \rvert$
CABS(CX)	Complex	$\lvert CX \rvert$
EXP(X)	Real	e^X
DEXP(DX)	Double precision	e^{DX}
CEXP(CX)	Complex	e^{CX}
LOG(GX)	Same as GX	$\log_e GX$
ALOG(X)	Real	$\log_e X$
DLOG(DX)	Double precision	$\log_e DX$
CLOG(CX)	Complex	$\log_e CX$
LOG10(GX)	Same as GX	$\log_{10} GX$
ALOG10(X)	Real	$\log_{10} X$
DLOG10(DX)	Double precision	$\log_{10} DX$
REAL(GX)	Real	Convert GX to real value
FLOAT(IX)	Real	Convert IX to real value
SNGL(DX)	Real	Convert DX to single precision
ANINT(X)	Real	Round to nearest whole number
DNINT(DX)	Double precision	Round to nearest whole number
NINT(X)	Integer	Round to nearest integer
IDNINT(DX)	Integer	Round to nearest integer
AINT(X)	Real	Truncate X to whole number
DINT(DX)	Double precision	Truncate DX to whole number
INT(GX)	Integer	Truncate GX to an integer
IFIX(X)	Integer	Truncate X to an integer
IDINT(DX)	Integer	Truncate DX to an integer
SIGN(X, Y)	Real	Transfer sign of Y to $\lvert X \rvert$
ISIGN(IX, IY)	Integer	Transfer sign of IY to $\lvert IX \rvert$
DSIGN(DX, DY)	Double precision	Transfer sign of DY to $\lvert DX \rvert$
MOD(IX, IY)	Integer	Remainder from IX/IY
AMOD(X, Y)	Real	Remainder from X/Y
DMOD(DX, DY)	Double precision	Remainder from DX/DY
DIM(X, Y)	Real	X − (minimum of X and Y)
IDIM(IX, IY)	Integer	IX − (minimum of IX and IY)
DDIM(DX, DY)	Double precision	DX − (minimum of DX and DY)
MAX(GX,GY, . . .)	Same as GX, GY, . . .	Maximum of (GX,GY, . . .)
MAX0(IX,IY, . . .)	Integer	Maximum of (IX,IY, . . .)
AMAX1(X,Y, . . .)	Real	Maximum of (X,Y, . . .)
DMAX1(DX,DY, . . .)	Double precision	Maximum of (DX,DY, . . .)
AMAX0(IX,IY, . . .)	Real	Maximum of (IX,IY, . . .)
MAX1(X,Y, . . .)	Integer	Maximum of (X,Y, . . .)

Function Name	Function Type	Definition
MIN(GX,GY, . . .)	Same as GX, GY, . . .	Minimum of (GX,GY, . . .)
MIN0(IX,IY, . . .)	Integer	Minimum of (IX,IY, . . .)
AMIN1(X,Y, . . .)	Real	Minimum of (X,Y, . . .)
DMIN1(DX,DY, . . .)	Double precision	Minimum of (DX,DY, . . .)
AMIN0(IX,IY, . . .)	Real	Minimum of (IX,IY, . . .)
MIN1(X,Y, . . .)	Integer	Minimum of (X,Y, . . .)
SIN(X)	Real	Sine of X, assumes radians
DSIN(DX)	Double precision	Sine of DX, assumes radians
CSIN(CX)	Complex	Sine of CX
COS(X)	Real	Cosine of X, assumes radians
DCOS(DX)	Double precision	Cosine of DX, assumes radians
CCOS(CX)	Complex	Cosine of CX
TAN(X)	Real	Tangent of X, assumes radians
DTAN(DX)	Double precision	Tangent of DX, assumes radians
ASIN(X)	Real	Arcsine of X
DASIN(DX)	Double precision	Arcsine of DX
ACOS(X)	Real	Arccosine of X
DACOS(DX)	Double precision	Arccosine of DX
ATAN(X)	Real	Arctangent of X
DATAN(DX)	Double precision	Arctangent of DX
ATAN2(X,Y)	Real	Arctangent of X/Y
DATAN2(DX,DY)	Double precision	Arctangent of DX/DY
SINH(X)	Real	Hyperbolic sine of X
DSINH(DX)	Double precision	Hyperbolic sine of DX
COSH(X)	Real	Hyperbolic cosine of X
DCOSH(DX)	Double precision	Hyperbolic cosine of DX
TANH(X)	Real	Hyperbolic tangent of X
DTANH(DX)	Double precision	Hyperbolic tangent of DX
DPROD(X,Y)	Double precision	Product of X and Y
DBLE(X)	Double precision	Convert X to double precision
CMPLX(X)	Complex	$X + 0i$
CMPLX(X,Y)	Complex	$X + Yi$
AIMAG(CX)	Real	Imaginary part of CX
REAL(CX)	Real	Real part of CX
CONJG(CX)	Complex	Conjugate of CX, $a - bi$
LEN(CHX)	Integer	Length of character string CHX
INDEX(CHX,CHY)	Integer	Position of substring CHY in string CHX
CHAR(IX)	Character string	Character in the IXth position of collating sequence
ICHAR(CHX)	Integer	Position of the character CHX in the collating sequence
LGE(CHX,CHY)	Logical	Value of (CHX is lexically greater than or equal to CHY)

Function Name	Function Type	Definition
LGT(CHX,CHY)	Logical	Value of (CHX is lexically greater than CHY)
LLE(CHX,CHY)	Logical	Value of (CHX is lexically less than or equal to CHY)
LLT(CHX,CHY)	Logical	Value of (CHX is lexically less than CHY)

APPENDIX B

ADDITIONAL FORTRAN 77 TOPICS

This appendix summarizes a number of features of FORTRAN that were not introduced in earlier chapters but that should be included for completeness. We have divided these additional features into specification statements, control statements, subprogram features and formatting features. Most of these features are from older versions of FORTRAN. In general, the use of these features is discouraged because they make programs more difficult to debug and to understand. For example, the control structures discussed employ multiple branches from a single statement and thus no longer yield structures with one entrance and one exit.

SPECIFICATION STATEMENTS

Three specification statements, and thus nonexecutable statements, are included here. The IMPLICIT statement is used to specify the beginning letters of variable names that are to be associated with a particular type, such as REAL or CHARACTER. The PARAMETER statement is used to assign names to constants. The EQUIVALENCE statement allows the sharing of data storage.

IMPLICIT STATEMENT

We have discussed six different specification statements: INTEGER, REAL, LOGICAL, CHARACTER, DOUBLE PRECISION, and COMPLEX. Only two of these statements, INTEGER and REAL, have default values. That is, variable names beginning with letters I–N specify integer variables by default, and all other variable names specify real variables by default. The IMPLICIT statement allows us to specify defaults for variables of all types. Its general form is

> **IMPLICIT** *type 1 (default), type 2 (default), . . .*

For instance, if a program contained only integers, you could specify that any variable is an integer with this statement:

```
IMPLICIT   INTEGER(A-Z)
```

Or you might want to specify that the first half of the alphabet represents beginning letters of integer names and the last half represents real names:

```
IMPLICIT   INTEGER(A-M), REAL(N-Z)
```

If you are following the convention of beginning all double-precision variable names with the letter D instead of listing all the names in a DOUBLE PRECISION statement, you could use the following:

```
IMPLICIT   DOUBLE PRECISION(D)
```

An implicit declaration can be overridden with a specification statement, as shown here:

```
IMPLICIT   COMPLEX(C), LOGICAL(L)
CHARACTER*10   CHAR
```

The variable CHAR should be a complex variable according to the IMPLICIT statement, but instead it is defined as a character string by the CHARACTER statement.

If you type all variables used in your programs, as we have recommended and as we have done in our sample programs, the IMPLICIT statement is unnecessary.

PARAMETER STATEMENT

The PARAMETER statement is a specification statement used to assign names to constants, with the following general form:

> **PARAMETER** *(name 1 = expression, name 2 = expression, . . .)*

The expression after the equal sign typically is a constant, although it can be an expression consisting of other constants and operations. A specific example of the PARAMETER statement is

```
PARAMETER   (PI = 3.141593, N = 75)
```

Type statements should precede the PARAMETER statement in order to assign the proper type to the constant name. Thus, the previous statement should be used with type statements as shown:

```
INTEGER   N
REAL   PI
PARAMETER   (PI = 3.141593, N = 75)
```

The DATA and PARAMETER statements are similar, but there are some significant differences. A DATA statement assigns an initial value to a variable, and the value may or may not be changed by other statements when the program is executed. The PARAMETER statement assigns a name to a constant, and the value of a constant cannot be changed by other statements within the program. A name assigned to a constant by a PARAMETER statement can be used anywhere in a program that a constant is used except in FORMAT statements. For example, the following statements are valid at the beginning of a main program. Although it is not valid to use a variable to specify the dimension of an array in the main program, these statements are correct because N is a constant and not a variable:

```
INTEGER   N
REAL   PI
PARAMETER   (PI = 3.141593, N = 75)
REAL   TEMP(N,N)
```

Note that we needed two REAL statements. The first statement was necessary in order to specify that PI represented a real constant. This statement had to be listed before the constant PI was given a value. Because the array TEMP used the constant N in its specification, it could not be specified before the PARAMETER statement.

A PARAMETER statement can be used to assign names to constants of any type, as shown in the next pair of statements:

```
CHARACTER*6   DATE
PARAMETER   (DATE = '090287')
```

Because the PARAMETER statement must be included at the beginning of a program (or a subprogram), it is easy to locate if we want to change the value of the constant. For example, in the statements above we can change the date used in all references to DATE simply by changing the constant value in the PARAMETER statement.

EQUIVALENCE STATEMENT

The EQUIVALENCE statement, a specification statement that permits data storage to be shared by several variables, has the following general form:

> EQUIVALENCE *(variable list 1), (variable list 2), . . .*

The variable list may contain variable names, array names, and character substring names. The EQUIVALENCE statement causes all the names enclosed in a set of parentheses to reference the same storage location. Character variables cannot be equivalenced with noncharacter variables. In fact, it is best to use the same type in all equivalence lists. The entire arrays are involved when array elements are equivalenced, as shown in the next example, because an array is always stored sequentially in memory. Two variables in a common block or in two different common blocks cannot be made equivalent, and two variables in the same array cannot be made equivalent.

Consider the following EQUIVALENCE statement:

```
INTEGER  HEIGHT, DIST
REAL  A(5), B(9), C(2,2)
EQUIVALENCE  (HEIGHT,DIST), (A(1),B(4),C(1,1))
```

The first variable list specifies that HEIGHT and DIST are to occupy the same location that can be referenced by either variable name. The equivalence of storage locations specified by the second variable list is best explained using the following diagram of computer memory:

By specifying that A(1) and B(4) share the same location, we also have implicitly specified that A(2) and B(5) share the same location, and so on through A(5) and B(8). Furthermore, we have equated the location that stores A(1) and B(4) with C(1,1), and hence other implicit equivalences have been specified as shown in the diagram. When using two-dimensional arrays in equivalence statements, it is important to remember that they are stored by columns.

CONTROL STATEMENTS

The control structures mentioned in this section contain multiple branches and therefore have multiple exits. Because these statements do not follow a one-entrance, one-exit path of execution, we discourage their use. The main reason that multiple branch statements are included in the language is so that programs written in earlier versions can still be used without modifications. (Older versions of FORTRAN did not include all forms of the IF statements that were presented in Chapter 3, and thus multiple branching could not always be avoided.)

ARITHMETIC IF STATEMENT

The general form of the arithmetic IF statement is

> **IF** *(arithmetic expression) label 1, label 2, label 3*

Labels 1, 2, and 3 must be references to executable statements in the program. The arithmetic expression is evaluated, and if it represents a negative value, control passes to the statement referenced by label 1. If the expression represents zero, then control passes to the statement referenced by label 2. Finally, if the expression represents a positive value, control passes to the statement referenced by label 3. In the following arithmetic IF statement, control will pass to statement 10 if A is greater than B, to statement 15 if A is equal to B, and to statement 20 if A is less than B.

$$\text{IF (B - A) 10, 15, 20}$$

Thus, the arithmetic IF statement is a three-way branch, equivalent to the following statements:

```
IF (arithmetic expression.LT.0.0) GO TO label 1
IF (arithmetic expression.EQ.0.0) GO TO label 2
GO TO label 3
```

Early versions of FORTRAN did not include even the simple IF statement presented in Chapter 3. Hence, all IF statements were written in the form of arithmetic IF statements at that time.

COMPUTED GO TO STATEMENT

The general form of the computed GO TO statement is

> **GO TO** *(label 1, label 2, . . . , label n), integer expression*

Labels 1, 2, . . . , and *n* must be references to executable statements in your program. The computed GO TO statement is used for a multi-way branch of control. For example, if we wish to execute a different set of statements dependent on the rank of a student, we could use the following computed GO TO statement, where RANK = 1 for freshman, 2 for sophomore, 3 for junior, 4 for senior, and 5 for graduate. Assume RANK is an integer variable.

```
INTEGER  RANK
   .
   .
   .
GO TO (11, 15, 20, 17, 17), RANK
PRINT*, 'RANK VALUE IN ERROR'
```

If RANK = 1 (representing a freshman), then the computed GO TO statement will be executed as if it were

GO TO 11

Similar branches would occur for RANK = 2 and RANK = 3. For seniors and graduate students (RANK = 4 and RANK = 5), control will transfer to statement 17, thus illustrating the fact that the statement labels do not have to be unique. If the value of RANK is such that it does not cause a branch (in this case, less than 1 or greater than 5), control passes to the next statement, which we have used to print an error message.

This type of multi-way branch is also sometimes called a CASE statement, because it tests a number of cases and then branches depending on the results of the tests. The IF-ELSEIF statement provides a structured way of implementing an algorithm that performs different steps depending on a series of tests.

ASSIGNED GO TO STATEMENT

The ASSIGN statement and the assigned GO TO statement work together to yield a multi-branch structure. The general forms of these two statements are

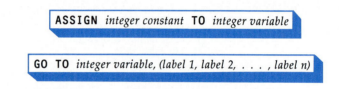

ASSIGN *integer constant* TO *integer variable*

GO TO *integer variable, (label 1, label 2, . . . , label n)*

The assigned GO TO statement looks very similar to the computed GO TO statement, but there are some significant differences.

1. The integer variable referenced in the assigned GO TO must have been initialized with the ASSIGN statement.
2. The integer variable can be used only to store statement references.
3. If the value of the integer variable is not in the list of labels, an execution error occurs.

In the next example, the value 3 has been initially assigned to K. The IF statements may change the value stored in K to either 11 or 20. When the assigned GO TO statement is executed, control will transfer to statement 11 if K = 11, statement 20 if K = 20, or statement 3 if K = 3. Otherwise, an execution error occurs.

```
ASSIGN 3 TO K
.
.
.
IF (A.LT.B) ASSIGN 20 TO K
IF (A.GE.C) ASSIGN 11 TO K
.
.
.
GO TO K, (3, 11, 20)
```

Again, the IF-ELSEIF statement provides a structured alternative to this multi-way branch statement.

SUBPROGRAM FEATURES

This section discusses additional features of FORTRAN that relate to subprograms. The SAVE, INTRINSIC, and EXTERNAL statements are not frequently used but can be very useful, as pointed out in the following discussions. The ENTRY statement and alternate return point from a subprogram are covered so that the coverage of FORTRAN 77 is complete, but their use is discouraged, again because they do not support a one-entrance, one-exit path of execution that is simple to follow.

SAVE

Local variables are those used in a subprogram that are not arguments; thus, they tend to be totals, loop indexes, and counters. The values of these local variables are generally lost when a RETURN statement is executed. A SAVE specification statement will, however, save the values of local variables so they will contain the same values as they did at the end of the previous reference. This nonexecutable statement appears only in the subprogram. The general form of the SAVE statement is

| SAVE | *variable list* |

The values of all local variables will be saved if the list of variables is omitted.

To illustrate the use of the SAVE statement, suppose you wanted to know how many times a subprogram was accessed. The following statements would initialize the counter COUNTR to zero at the beginning of the program and increment COUNTR each time the subprogram was used. Recall that the DATA statement does not reinitialize COUNTR each time the function is used.

```
*-------------------------------------------*
          REAL FUNCTION  AVE(X,Y)
            .
            .
            .
          INTEGER  COUNTR
          SAVE  COUNTR
          DATA  COUNTR /0/
            .
            .
            .
          COUNTR = COUNTR + 1
            .
            .
            .
          RETURN
          END
*-------------------------------------------*
```

INTRINSIC, EXTERNAL

The INTRINSIC and EXTERNAL statements are specification statements used when subprogram names are to be used as arguments in another subprogram. The general forms of these nonexecutable statements are

> **INTRINSIC** *subprogram list*

> **EXTERNAL** *subprogram list*

These statements appear only in the module that sends the arguments representing the subprogram names. If the argument is an intrinsic function, use the INTRINSIC statement. If the argument is a user-written function or a subroutine, use the EXTERNAL statement.

We reference a subroutine twice in the following statements. In one reference, the subroutine replaces each value in an array with its natural logarithm. The other reference replaces each value in an array with its logarithm, using base 10.

```
*-------------------------------------------*
       PROGRAM   TEST1
       .
       .
       .
       REAL   X(10), TIME(10)
       INTRINSIC   ALOG, ALOG10
       .
       .
       .
       CALL COMPUT(X,ALOG)
       .
       .
       .
       CALL COMPUT(TIME,ALOG10)
       .
       .
       .
       END
*-------------------------------------------*
*
       SUBROUTINE   COMPUT(R,F)
*
*  This subroutine applies a function
*  to the real array R.
*
       INTEGER   I
       REAL   R(10)
*
       DO 10 I=1,10
           R(I) = F(R(I))
    10 CONTINUE
*
       RETURN
       END
*-------------------------------------------*
```

ENTRY

The ENTRY statement is used to define entry points into a subprogram other than the entry point at the beginning of the subprogram. The general form of the statement is

> **ENTRY** *entry name (argument list)*

The ENTRY statement is placed at the point in the subprogram that is to be an alternative entry. The argument list does not have to be the same as that for the original entry point. The ENTRY statement is nonexecutable and will not affect execution of the subprogram if it is in the statements being executed from a previous entry point.

The following statements illustrate references to a subroutine through two different entry points:

```
*- - - - - - - - - - - - - - - - - - - - - - - - - - - - - - - - -*
       PROGRAM   TEST2
       .
       .
       .
       CALL SUBAA(X)
       .
       .
       .
       CALL SUBAB(X,K)
       .
       .
       .
       END
*- - - - - - - - - - - - - - - - - - - - - - - - - - - - - - - - -*
*
       SUBROUTINE   SUBAA(T)
       .
       .
       .
       ENTRY   SUBAB(T,J)
       .
       .
       .
*
       RETURN
       END
*- - - - - - - - - - - - - - - - - - - - - - - - - - - - - - - - -*
```

One of the fundamental advantages of structured programming lies in the simplicity of the interface between modules. The use of multiple entry points to a subprogram complicates that linkage; their usage is therefore not generally recommended. If you want to use a portion of a subprogram, define that portion as a subprogram itself. It can then be referenced by other subprograms in addition to the main program, and the simple interface between modules is maintained.

ALTERNATE RETURNS

Normally, the execution of a RETURN statement in a subroutine returns control to the first statement following the CALL statement; however, a return point can be specified with an argument in the subroutine. The argument list in the SUBROUTINE statement contains asterisks in the locations of arguments that are the alternate return points. The RETURN statement has this expanded general form:

RETURN   *integer expression*

If the value of the integer expression is 1, the return point is the statement number that corresponds to the first asterisk in the argument list. If the value of the integer expression is 2, the return point is the statement nunber that corresponds to the second asterisk, and so on. The following statements will help clarify this process:

```
*-------------------------------------------------*
            PROGRAM   TEST3
            .
            .
            .
            CALL SUB1(A,B,*20,*50)
            .
            .
            .
   20 PRINT 25, A
            .
            .
            .
   50 COUNT = COUNT + 1
            .
            .
            .
            END
*-------------------------------------------------*
*
            SUBROUTINE   SUB1(X,Y,*,*)
            .
            .
            .
*
            RETURN I
            END
*-------------------------------------------------*
```

If the value of I is 1 in the subroutine, then control will return to statement 20. If the value of I is 2, then control returns to statement 50. An execution error occurs if the value of I is not 1 or 2.

Again, multiple return points also complicate the linkage between modules and generally should be avoided. Structured alternatives can be developed using the IF structures.

FORMATTING FEATURES

The formatting features discussed here are rarely used. If you do use them or work with programs that use them, be sure to document their use carefully.

ADDITIONAL FORMAT SPECIFICATIONS

The following FORMAT specifications are not routinely used but occassionally simplify the input and output steps in a program.

Gw.d The G format code is a generalized code to transmit real data. The width w specifies the number of positions in the input or output that are used. Input data can be entered in an F or E format. The real advantage of the G format is in output formats. If the exponent of the data value is negative or larger than d, the output is performed with an Ew.d specification; if the exponent is between 0 and d, the output is performed with an F specification that will print d significant digits followed by 4 spaces. Thus, very large or small values are automatically printed with an E format, and values of reasonable size are printed with an F format. For example, if the G specification is G10.3, then the value 26.8 is printed as $_{bb}26.8_{bbbb}$, and the value 1248.1 is printed as $_b0.125E_b04$.

wH Literal data can be specified in an output format with an H, or Hollerith, specification. The width w specifies that total number of positions in the literal. The literal itself immediately follows the H. The following two formats are equivalent:

```
10 FORMAT (1X,'EXPERIMENT NO. 1')
10 FORMAT (1X,16HEXPERIMENT NO. 1)
```

Specifying literals with apostrophes is easier than using an H format because we do not need to count the characters in the literal; hence, H formats are rarely used.

Lw Logical variables can be read or printed with an L specification. In an input specification, the first non-blank character (in the w characters read) must be T or F; the variable receives the corresponding true or false value. In an output specification, the letter T or F is printed, again corresponding to whether the variable is true or false.

FORMAT EXTENSIONS

The following FORMAT extensions are not specifications that correspond to a variable; they are modifiers that affect the performance of the specifications already presented.

Ew.dEe and Gw.dEe The addition of Ee to an exponential or generalized format specifies that e positions are to be printed in the exponent. The Ee affects only output specifications.

nP The addition of nP to an F, E, or G format code specifies a scale factor n that is applied to subsequent specifications until another scale factor is encountered. The actual value stored is multiplied by 10**n to give the number read or printed when the scale factor n is in effect. For instance, if the following READ statement is

```
READ 5, A, B
5 FORMAT (2PF4.1,F5.1)
```

and the data line read is

```
12.1362.4
```

then the value stored in A is 0.121 and the value stored in B is 3.624. Any computations with A and B use the values 0.121 and 3.624.

The output statement

```
PRINT 10, A,B
10 FORMAT (1X,F4.1,1X,F5.1)
```

generates the following data line:

$$00.1_{bbb}3.6$$

The scale factor might be useful in applications that use percentages — the input could be in the form XX.X; but, the internal values used in calculations and the output would use the form .XXX.

S, SP, and SS These options affect I, F, E, and G specifications during execution of output statements. If a numeric value is negative, the minus sign is printed in the first position to the left of the data value. If the numeric value is positive, the printing of the plus sign is system dependent. If SP precedes a specification, in the value to be printed and in all subsequent values, a sign is printed, whether the value is positive or negative. If SS precedes a specification, in the value to be printed and all subsequent values, only a minus sign is printed. If S precedes a specification, the system designation of producing signs is restored. The following example illustrates the use of the SP modifier. If these statements are executed

```
A = 36.2
PRINT 5, A, A, A
5 FORMAT (1X,F5.1,1X,SPF5.1,1X,F5.1)
```

the output line is

$$_{b}36.2_{b}+36.2_{b}+36.2$$

BN and BZ The BN and BZ modifiers specify the interpretation of nonleading blanks in numeric data fields during execution of input statements. Normally, leading and nonleading blanks are converted to zeros in numeric input fields. The modifier BN, however, specifies that blanks be considered null characters or ignored in the current and all succeeding specifications. The BZ modifier restores the interpretation of all blanks as zeros in numeric fields. If the data line

$$_{b}21_{bb}21_{b}$$

is read with the statement

```
     READ 15, I, J
15 FORMAT (I4,BNI4)
```

the value stored in I is 210 and the value stored in J is 21.

Colon A colon terminates the format if there are no more items in the input or output list. The following statements and their corresponding output illustrate the usefulness of this feature:

```
     MAX = 20
     MIN = -5
     PRINT 10, MAX
     PRINT 10, MAX, MIN
10 FORMAT (1X,'MAX =',I3,:,2X,'MIN =',I3)
```

The output from the first PRINT statement is

```
MAX = 20
```

The output from the second PRINT statement is

```
MAX = 20  MIN = -5
```

Without the colon, the output from the first PRINT statement would be

```
MAX = 20  MIN =
```

VARIABLE FORMATTING

In input and output statements up to this point, the format identifier has always been a statement number reference. However, this format identifier can also be an integer variable that has been initialized by an ASSIGN statement (defined earlier in this appendix) with the number of the desired FORMAT statement. The format identifier can also be a character constant, character array element, character array, or character expression.

APPENDIX C

PLOTTING DATA FILES WITH MATLAB AND LOTUS 1-2-3

In solving engineering problems, it can be very helpful to view a plot of data values related to the problem. These data values may represent the input values that are used by a program, or they may represent the output values computed by a program. In either case, we will assume that the data values have been stored in a data file and that we would like to generate a plot of them. We also assume that it is an ASCII file; ASCII (American Standard Code for Information Interchange) files are written in a standard format that can be read by most software programs and packages. When you generate a data file with a FORTRAN 77 program, the file is automatically written as an ASCII file. If you generate a data file using a word processor, you must specify that you want the data stored in an ASCII file (also called a text file); otherwise, the data is stored with special characters that are unique to the word processor, and thus you may have difficulty reading the file with other software.

We now present the steps for plotting a data file using MATLAB and Lotus 1-2-3. In both cases, we are interested in obtaining a simple set of steps for easily generating a graph so that we can visualize the information represented by the data values.

GENERATING A DATA FILE WITH A FORTRAN PROGRAM

The program listed below is a simple FORTRAN 77 program that generates 101 points of the function

$$f(t) = 2 \sin(2\pi t)$$

where t ranges from 0.0 to 1.0 in increments of 0.01 seconds.

```
*----------------------------------------------------------*
      PROGRAM SIGGEN
*
*  This program generates a signal using the sine function.
*
      INTEGER  K
      REAL  PI, T, F
*
      OPEN (UNIT=15,FILE='SIGNAL',STATUS='NEW')
*
      PI = 3.141593
      DO 10 K=1,101
         T = (K-1)*0.01
         F = 2.0*SIN(2.0*PI*T)
         WRITE (15,*) T, F
   10 CONTINUE
*
      END
*----------------------------------------------------------*
```

This program generates a data file containing 101 lines, with each line containing two values. The first value represents the time value and the second value represents the corresponding value of the sine function. The first five function values are

$$f(0.00) = 2*\sin(2*pi*0.00) = 0.0000000$$
$$f(0.01) = 2*\sin(2*pi*0.01) = 0.1255810$$
$$f(0.02) = 2*\sin(2*pi*0.02) = 0.2506665$$
$$f(0.03) = 2*\sin(2*pi*0.03) = 0.3747626$$
$$f(0.04) = 2*\sin(2*pi*0.04) = 0.4973798$$

The first five lines of the data file then contain the following values:

```
0.00 0.0000000
0.01 0.1255810
0.02 0.2506665
0.03 0.3747626
0.04 0.4973798
```

PLOTTING THE DATA FILE WITH MATLAB

MATLAB requires that the name of a data file have a file extension; therefore, assume that we have copied the data file SIGNAL to a file named SIGNAL.DAT. The load command can now be used to load the data values from the file into a matrix, or two-dimensional array, with each line in the data file stored as one row in the array:

```
>>load signal.dat;
```

The name of the array containing the data is the same as the name of the data file, but without the extension. If the data file is not in the same directory as the MATLAB program, the full path name should be used with the load command.

The plot command can be used with one or two arguments. To plot the data in the signal array, we specify that the first variable is the first column and that the second variable is the second column:

```
>>plot(signal(:,1),signal(:,2))
```

The plot command should then generate the following graph.

The plot command generates a linear x-y graph. There are also options that allow you to plot with log-log scales and semi-log scales and to generate polar plots, contour plots, 3-D plots, and bar graphs. MATLAB commands can also be used to label or title the graph and to add grid lines.

The easiest way to print the graph on many computers is to generate a screen dump by holding the Shift key down and then pressing the PrtSC key. If you are using a Macintosh, select the print command from the File menu.

PLOTTING THE DATA FILE WITH LOTUS 1–2–3

To plot data values using Lotus 1–2–3, you must first copy (or import) the values into a worksheet. If you have not used a worksheet, refer to a Lotus 1–2–3 manual for more information on using and accessing a worksheet before proceeding with these steps.

Step 1 Use the arrow keys to position the cell pointer to the cell in which you want to store the first data value from the file. Generally, this will be the upper left corner of the worksheet, or address A1.

Step 2 Select the **File Import Numbers** command, using /FIN. At this point you will be prompted to enter the file name of the ASCII file, with the full path name if the file is not stored in the same directory as the 1–2–3 software. If the file name does not have an extension, 1–2–3 requires that you enter the file name followed by a period. After entering the file name, the data should automatically be stored in the worksheet, as shown in the following worksheet containing the values from the SIGNAL data file.

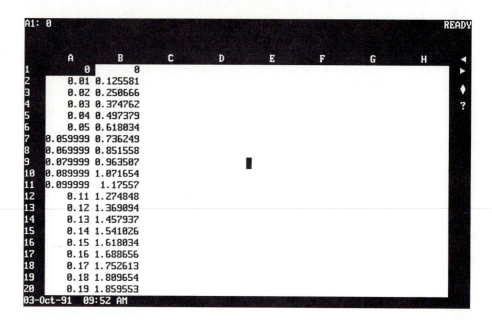

Step 3 To plot the data, select the **Graph** command using /G. Select the F2 (Edit) function key to edit the Graph Settings dialog box. Select an *x-y* plot and give an X range for the *x* values and an A range for the *y* values. Using the worksheet containing the SIGNAL data values, the specific keystrokes are

/G	Selects the graph command.
F2(Edit) function key	Allows you to edit settings.
TX	Selects *x-y* graph type.
RX A1..A101 enter	Selects *x* data range.
RA B1..B101 enter	Selects *y* data range.
enter	Saves graph settings.

The dialog box should now contain the following information:

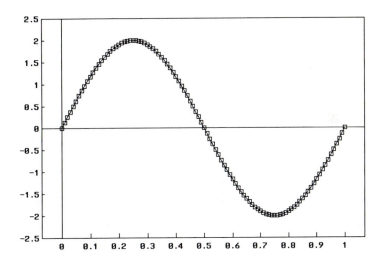

Step 4 Select the **View** command. The corresponding graph should now be displayed on your screen. Press the Enter key to return to the graph menu. If you want to add further enhancements such as titles and grid lines, use the various options available in the dialog boxes. A graph of the data from the SIG-NAL file is shown next.

To print a graph, you must first save it as a graph file. The graph file is then printed using the PrintGraph program. Not all printers can print graphics, so you may need to check the printer manual to be sure that the printer connected to your computer can be used to print graphics.

Step 5 Select the **S**ave command to save the file with a .PIC file extension. Select the **Q**uit command to return to the worksheet, and then select the **Q**uit Yes Yes command to exit the 1–2–3 program.

Step 6 To start the PrintGraph program, enter the word *lotus* after the system prompt. An access menu will be displayed. Choose PrintGraph, and then select **S**ettings **H**ardware **P**rinter to list the printers installed with your system. Choose the desired printer and press the Enter key. Select the **Q**uit command twice to return to the first menu. Then select Image-select to list the graph files available and to highlight the graph that you want to print. (If the graph file is not in the same directory as the 1–2–3 program, you will need to use the **S**ettings **H**ardware menu to specify the directory containing the graph file.) At this point you can use the F10(GRAPH) function key to view the file to be sure that it is the one you want to print. Press the Enter key once to return to the graph menu, and again to return to the main menu. Then select the **A**lign **G**o **P**age command to print the graph.

APPENDIX D

AN INTRODUCTION TO FORTRAN 90

A new Fortran standard called Fortran 90 has expanded the capabilities of FORTRAN 77 in a number of important areas. (Note that only the first letter of the language name is now capitalized.) This new standard is "upward compatible," which means that programs written in standard FORTRAN 77 will compile and execute properly using a Fortran 90 compiler. Even though a new standard has been accepted, it often takes several years before the new compilers are readily available; in fact, even after Fortran 90 compilers are available, some computer centers will maintain both FORTRAN 77 compilers and Fortran 90 compilers on the same system. However, because the additions to the language are substantial, writing programs using the new standard will provide more options and more flexibility.

The official document describing Fortran 90 contains over 350 pages; the few pages presented here are only an introduction to some of the new features.

VARIABLE NAMES

Variable names can contain up to a maximum of 31 characters, and the valid characters list has been expanded to include the underscore (_). Thus, valid variable names now include

```
INITIAL_TEMPERATURE
ERROR_SUM
END_OF_DATA
```

FREE-SOURCE FORM

A compiler option is available that allows a program to be written in free-source form. In this form, the source code statements can start in any column, and multiple statements can be included on a line as long as they are separated by semicolons. Comments can also follow a Fortran statement and are indicated by an exclamation point. Thus, the following statements are valid free-source forms:

```
SUM = SUM + X;     COUNT = COUNT + 1
READ*, N           ! Read number of data points
```

EXPANDED DO LOOP

The DO statement has been expanded so that, in addition to specifying that a set of statements should be executed a specific number of times, it can also specify that a set of statements should be executed until a condition is true. Therefore, this extension allows the DO statement to implement WHILE loops. Because the condition can be tested anywhere in the DO loop, this extension is even more flexible than the WHILE loop (which tests the condition only at the beginning of the loop). An example of this new DO statement is

```
DO
    READ(10,*) X, Y
    IF (X.LT.0.0) EXIT
    SUM = SUM + Y
END DO
```

DYNAMIC STORAGE ALLOCATION

In Fortran 90, array sizes can be specified during the execution of the program, and the memory reserved for arrays can also be released during the execution of the program. This dynamic storage allocation allows memory needed for a large array to be reused later in the program for other arrays.

POINTERS

Pointers, a new variable type, are associated with a data object. They can be used to implement data structures such as linked lists, tree structures, and stacks. These data structures greatly enhance the types of solutions that we can develop using Fortran 90.

NEW ARRAY AND MATRIX OPERATIONS

A number of array and matrix operations have been implemented with a single statement, instead of requiring loops to implement them. There are also a number of new intrinsic functions that have array arguments. Some of these new functions are:

MATMUL	Multiplies two matrices.
DOT_PRODUCT	Computes the dot product of two vectors.
SUM	Computes the sum of the elements of an array.
PRODUCT	Computes the product of the elements of an array.
MAXVAL	Determines the maximum value in an array.
MINVAL	Determines the minimum value in an array.
MAXLOC	Determines the location of a maximum value in an array.
MINLOC	Determines the location of a minimum value in an array.

Some array functions can also include a MASK argument that specifies a "mask" that can be used to select only part of the array for the function evaluation. For example, a MASK argument could specify that only array elements with negative values are to be used in evaluating the function.

Other functions generate new arrays from the elements of existing arrays. These functions include merging arrays, transposing arrays, performing circular shifts on arrays, and performing end-off shifts on arrays.

RECURSIVE SUBPROGRAMS

A recursive function refers to itself in the function, and a recursive subroutine calls itself in the subroutine. Special types of problems can be solved much more efficiently with recursive routines, but previous FORTRAN standards did not allow recursive subprograms.

We have discussed only a few of the important new features of Fortran 90. The document that describes the complete language is entitled *American National Standard Programming Language Fortran 90, ANSI X3.198–1991*. It is identical to *ISO/IEC 1539:1991*, which is the International Fortran Standard. Another reference to this new standard is *Programmer's Guide to Fortran 90* by Brainerd, Goldberg, and Adams, McGraw-Hill, 1990.

GLOSSARY OF KEY WORDS

absolute error   The difference between the true value and the approximation to the true value.

algorithm   A stepwise procedure for solving a problem.

analog signal   A continuous signal that is represented by a continuous function.

approximation   An estimate of a value that is used instead of the actual value.

argument   An expression used in a function or subroutine reference.

arithmetic expression   An expression of variables, constants, and arithmetic operations that can be evaluated as a single numerical value.

arithmetic logic unit (ALU)   A fundamental computer component that performs all the arithmetic and logic operations.

array   A group of variables that share a common name and are specified individually with subscripts.

ascending order   An order from lowest to highest.

ASCII code   A binary code (American Standard Code for Information Interchange) commonly used by computers to store information.

assembler   A program that converts an assembly language program into machine language.

assembly language   A programming language that is unique to an individual computer system.

assignment statement   A FORTRAN statement that assigns a value to a variable.

batch processing A method of interacting with the computer in which programs are executed in generally the same order in which they are submitted.

binary A term used to describe something that has two values, such as a binary digit that can be 0 or 1.

binary search An algorithm that searches an ordered list by continually dividing the array in half as it looks for a specific value.

binary string A string or group of binary values, such as 11011000.

bisection method A method for finding roots of an equation that bisects an interval containing a root and then determines which half contains the root.

blank common A single group of storage locations that is accessible to subprograms without being specified as subprogram arguments.

BLOCK DATA subprogram A subprogram that is used to assign initial values to variables in named common using DATA statements.

branch A change in the flow of a program such that the steps are not executed in the sequential order in which they are written.

bubble sort Another name for a multipass sort algorithm that generally requires more than one pass through the list in order to guarantee that the list is sorted into the desired order.

buffer An internal storage area used to store input and output information.

bug An error in a computer program.

carriage control A character used at the beginning of a buffer of printed output that specifies the page spacing desired before the line is printed.

cathode ray tube (CRT) terminal A terminal that uses a video screen for its input and output.

central processing unit (CPU) The combination of the processor unit, the ALU, and the internal memory that forms the basis of a computer.

character string A string or group of characters that contains numerical digits, alphabetical letters, or special characters.

collating sequence The ascending order of characters specified by a particular code.

comment line A statement that is included in FORTRAN programs to document the program; it is not translated into machine language.

common block A block or group of storage locations that is accessible to subprograms without being specified as subprogram arguments.

compilation The process of converting a program written in a high-level language into machine language.

compiler The program that converts a program written in a high-level language into machine language.

complex root A complex value that is a root of an equation.

complex value A numerical value that is of the form $a + bi$, where $i = \sqrt{-1}$.

compound logical expression   A logical expression formed by combining two single logical expressions with the connectors .AND. or .OR.

computer network   A network that links computers so they can communicate with each other.

concatenation   An operation that connects two strings together to form one string.

condition   An expression that can be evaluated to be true or false.

constant   A specific value used in arithmetic or logical expressions.

continuation line   A statement used to continue a FORTRAN statement that extends past column 72; the continuation statement must contain a non-blank character in column 6 to signify that it is a continuation line.

control structure   A structure that controls the order of execution of a series of steps.

conversational computing   A method of interacting with the computer in which the computer seems to converse with the user in an English-like manner.

counting loop A loop that is repeated a specific number of times.

Cramer's rule   A method for solving simultaneous equations using determinants.

cubic polynomial   A third-degree polynomial.

cubic spline   A curve consisting of third-degree polynomials between data points.

curvature   The second derivative of a curve.

curve fitting   A numerical technique used to estimate unknown values of a function.

data   The information used by a program or generated by a program.

data file   A file used to store information used by a program or generated by a program.

debug   The process of eliminating bugs or errors from a program.

decomposition   The process of dividing a problem solution into a series of smaller problems.

deletion   A technique for removing an element from an ordered list.

derivative   The rate of change or slope of a function.

descending order   An order from highest to lowest.

design phases   A procedure for solving a problem by dividing the solution into a series of phases that begin with the problem description and end with the problem solution.

determinant   A number computed from the elements of a square matrix.

diagnostic   A message that describes an error in a program that has been located in either the compilation or execution step.

difference equation   An equation that specifies the computations to be performed on an input signal.

difference expression   An expression containing differences between data values used to estimate a derivative.

differentiation   The process of computing the derivative of a function at a point.

digital signal   A sequence of values determined by evaluating a signal at a specified set of times.

direct-access file   A file whose information can be accessed in nonsequential order.

DO loop   An iterative loop specified in FORTRAN with the DO statement.

dot product   A number computed from two vectors of the same size.

double-precision value   A real value with more precision than the standard real value.

driver   A main program written specifically to test a subprogram.

EBCDIC code   A binary code (Extended Binary-Coded-Decimal Interchange Code) commonly used by computers to store information.

echo   A debugging aid in which the values of variables are printed immediately after they are read.

editor   A program in a time-sharing system that allows the user to modify programs entered into the system.

element   A specific storage location in an array.

END option   An option that can be used in a READ statement to generate a branch to a specified program statement if the end of the data (or data file) is reached.

error propagation   The transmission of an error from one step to the next in a series of arithmetic operations.

Euler's method   A numerical technique for solving ordinary first-order differential equations.

executable statement   A statement specifying action to be taken in a program that is translated into machine language by the compiler.

execution   The process of executing the steps specified by a program.

explicit typing   A specification of the type of information to be stored in a variable with a specification statement.

exponential notation   A notation for real values that uses the letter E to separate the mantissa and the exponent.

external file   A file that is available to a program through an external device such as a disk drive or a tape drive.

false-position method   A method for finding roots of an equation in which interpolation is used to find the intersection of the x-axis and the straight line joining the two function values at the endpoints of an interval containing a root.

father-son update A type of file updating that uses a transaction (son) file to update information on the master (father) file.

field A unit of information in a record.

flowchart A graphical diagram used to describe the steps in an algorithm.

formatted I/O The input or output statements that use FORMAT statements to describe the spacing.

FORTRAN character set The set of characters accepted by FORTRAN compilers.

FORTRAN 77 The version of FORTRAN established in 1977.

frequency The number of periods, or cycles, of a periodic signal that occur in 1 second.

function A subprogram that returns a single value to the main program.

Gauss elimination A technique for solving a system of equations.

Gauss-Seidel method An iterative method for solving a system of equations.

generic function A function that returns a value of the same type as its input argument.

hardware The physical components of a computer.

hash code A code used to compute a record number for accessing a direct-access file.

high-level language An English-like language that must be converted into machine language before it can be executed.

IF-ELSEIF structure A structure that tests one condition and executes a set of steps if the condition is true; if the condition is false, another condition is tested, and if it is true, a different set of steps is executed.

IF-ELSE structure A structure that tests a condition and executes one set of steps if the condition is true and another set of steps if the condition is false.

IF structure A structure that tests a condition and executes a set of steps if the condition is true.

implicit typing The specification of the type of information (real or integer) to be stored in a variable by the beginning letter of the variable name.

implied DO loop A DO loop that can be specified completely on an I/O statement or a DATA statement.

incremental-search method A method for finding roots of an equation by detecting places where the curve crosses the x-axis.

increment value The parameter in a DO loop that specifies the increment to be added to the index each time the loop is executed.

index   The variable used as a loop counter in a DO loop.

inherent error   A type of error caused by errors in the data measurements themselves.

initial guess   A value used to initiate the Newton-Raphson method for finding the root of a function $f(x)$.

initial value   The parameter in a DO loop that specifies the initial value of the index. Also, the "starting point" for numerical integration solutions of differential equations.

initialize   To give an initial value to a variable.

input/output (I/O)   The information that a program reads or writes.

insertion   A technique for adding an element to an ordered list.

insertion sort   A sort that begins at the top of the list, comparing adjacent elements. If an element is out of order, it is continually exchanged with the value above it in the list until it is in its proper place.

integer value   A value that contains no fractional portion.

integration   The process of computing the integral of a function between two points.

interactive computing   Computing in which the user interacts with the program by answering questions and entering data.

intermediate result   A result used in evaluating an expression to get the final result.

internal file   A file defined on information stored in the internal memory of the computer.

interpolation   A numerical technique used to estimate unknown values of a function.

intrinsic function   A function used so frequently that its code is included in a library available to the compiler.

iteration   A technique that is repeated to give better and better approximations to a value that usually cannot be computed through a direct computation.

iterative loop   A loop that is controlled by the value of a variable called the index of the loop or the loop counter.

job control information   The information that must accompany a program submitted to a batch-processing system.

key   An integer used to specify the record number for accessing records in a direct-access file.

least-squares method   A method that computes an approximation to a function by minimizing the squared distance between the points and the approximating function.

left-justified No blanks on the left side.

lexicographic order Dictionary order.

library function A function used so frequently that its code is available in a library available to the compiler.

limit value The parameter in a DO loop that specifies the value used to determine completion of the DO loop.

linear interpolation An interpolation method that uses straight line segments to estimate unknown values of a function.

linear model An equation of the form $y = ax + b$ that approximates the relationship between two variables.

list-directed I/O The input or output statements that do not use FORMAT statements to describe the spacing.

literal A character string.

logic error An error in the logic used to define an algorithm.

logical expression An expression of variables, constants, and operations that can be evaluated as a single logical value.

logical operator One of the operators .NOT., .AND., and .OR. that is used with logical expressions.

logical value A value that is either true or false.

loop A group of statements that are executed repeatedly.

machine language The binary language understood by computers.

magnitude limitation A limitation on the size of value that can be used in a specific computer.

main program A complete program that may access functions and subroutines.

master file A file that contains the master information or most accurate information.

matrix A mathematical structure for storing information in a rectangular grid with rows and columns.

matrix multiplication An operation between two matrices that yields another matrix.

mean Another term for the average value.

memory The storage available for the variables and constants needed in a program.

merge An operation that combines two ordered lists into one ordered list.

mixed-mode operation An operation between values that are not of the same type.

module A function or a subroutine.

multidimensional array A group of variables that share the same name and whose elements are specified by more than one subscript.

multipass sort   A sort algorithm that generally requires more than one pass through the list in order to guarantee that the list is sorted into the desired order.

multiple root   A value that represents two or more roots to an equation.

named common   A group of storage locations that is accessible to subprograms by name without being specified as subprogram arguments.

nested function   A function reference that is the argument of another function.

nested loop   A loop that is completely contained within another loop.

Newton-Raphson method   A method that uses both the function $f(x)$ and its derivative $f'(x)$ to find the roots of an equation.

nonexecutable statement   A statement that affects the way memory is used by a program, though it is not converted into machine language by the compiler.

nonlinear model   A model that is not of the form $y = ax + b$.

nonsingular   A set of equations with a unique solution.

numerical differentiation   The use of numerical techniques for estimating the derivative (or slope) of a function at a specified point.

numerical integration   The use of numerical techniques for estimating the integral of a function (or the area under the graph of the function) over a specified interval.

object program   A program in machine-language form.

one-dimensional array   A group of variables that share the same name and whose elements are specified by one subscript.

ordinary differential equation   An equation containing the derivative of an unknown function.

overflow   An error condition that occurs when the result of an arithmetic operation yields a result that is too large to be stored in the computer's memory.

parameter   A value or variable used in the DO statement to specify the DO loop.

partial differential equation   An equation that involves the rates of change of a variable with respect to two or more independent variables.

polynomial model   A model of the form $y = f(x)$ where $f(x)$ is a polynomial.

problem solving   The process of determining a solution to a problem.

processor   A fundamental computer component that controls the operation of the other parts of the computer.

program   A set of statements that specify a complete algorithm in a computer language.

pseudocode   The English-like statements used to describe the steps in an algorithm.

quantization error   The difference between the value determined by an analog-to-digital converter and the actual value.

random access   A file-access technique in which records can be accessed in any order.

random signal   A sequence of random values or random numbers.

real root   A real value that is a root of an equation.

real value   A value that may contain a fractional or decimal portion.

record   The basic unit of information related to a data file.

regression   The process of fitting an approximating function to a set of data, such that the resulting curve represents a "best fit."

relational operator   An operator used to compare two arithmetic expressions.

relative error   The absolute error divided by the approximation.

repetition   A structure in which steps are repeated, such as in a WHILE loop or a counting loop.

residual   The vertical distance between the approximating function $f(x)$ and the actual data point.

right-justified   No blanks on the right side.

roots of an equation   The values of x for which $y = f(x) = 0$.

rounding   A technique that approximates a value.

roundoff error   Error due to truncation of an arithmetic result to a fixed number of digits of accuracy.

Runge-Kutta method   A method for numerically integrating ordinary differential equations.

sampling frequency   The frequency at which a signal is sampled; computed as $1/T$ Hz, where T is the sampling interval.

sampling interval   The interval of time used between signal samples.

scalar multiplication   The multiplication of each element in a matrix by a scalar.

scientific notation   A notation for real values that expresses the value as a number between 1 and 10 multiplied by a power of 10.

search algorithm   An algorithm that searches a list looking for a specific value.

secant method   A method for finding roots of an equation that uses a secant line to approximate the root location.

selection   A structure that tests a condition to determine which steps are to be performed next.

selection sort   A sort that is based on finding the minimum value and placing it first in the list, finding the next smallest value and placing it second in the list, and so on.

sensor   A piece of hardware or equipment used to collect data.

sentinel signal   A signal at the end of a data file that indicates that no more data follows.

sequence   A structure in which steps are performed one after another, or sequentially.

sequential-access file   A file whose information can be accessed only in a sequential order.

signal   A function (usually with respect to time) that represents information.

signal power   The average squared value of the signal.

signal-to-noise ratio (SNR)   The ratio of the signal power to the noise power.

Simpson's rule   An integration that uses parabolas between sets of three data points at a time.

simultaneous equations   A set of equations with a common solution.

sinusoid   A sine function expressed as a function of time.

slope   The ratio of the vertical distance and the horizontal distance between two data points.

software   The programs used to specify the operations in a computer.

software tool   A module that implements a technique commonly used in solving problems.

sort   To put in a specific order.

source program   A program in a high-level language form.

specification statement   A statement that specifies the type of values to be stored in a variable.

standard deviation   The square root of the variance.

statement function   A function that can be defined in a single assignment statement placed before any executable statement in a program.

statement label   A number that appears in columns 1–5 of a FORTRAN statement and that can be used by other statements to reference the statement.

step size   The increment between the current estimate and the next estimate in an iterative technique such as Euler's method.

stepwise refinement   A process for converting a general algorithm to one that is detailed enough to be converted into a computer language.

structure chart   A diagram that outlines the module structure of a program.

structured programming   Programming with a top-down flow that is easy to follow and modify because of its structure.

subprogram   A function or subroutine.

subroutine   A subprogram that may return many values, a single value, or no value to the main program.

subscript   An integer variable or constant used to specify a unique element in an array.

substring   A string that is a subset of another string and that maintains the original order of characters.

syntax error   An error in a FORTRAN statement.

tangent line   A straight line through a point on a curve having the same direction as the curve at the point.

Taylor series   An expression that defines a function in terms of its derivatives.

time-sharing   A method of interacting with the computer in which a number of programs are being executed at the same time, though the user appears to have the complete attention of the computer.

top-down design   A technique for problem solving in which the solution is first decomposed into a set of smaller steps, which are then refined individually in more and more detail until the problem is solved.

trailer signal   A signal at the end of a data file that indicates that no more data follows.

transaction file   A file that contains information to update a master file.

transfer function   A function that defines the effect of a filter in terms of amplitude change and phase change, relative to the frequency of the input signal.

trapezoidal rule   An integration technique that uses the areas of trapezoids.

tridiagonal system   A set of equations represented by a matrix with coefficients arranged in a band along the main diagonal and with zeros outside this band.

truncation   A technique that approximates a value by dropping its fractional value and using only the integer portion.

truncation error   An error that occurs when an infinite process is replaced by a finite process or, equivalently, is truncated to a finite process.

two-dimensional array   A group of variables that share the same name and whose elements are specified by two subscripts.

underflow   An error condition that occurs when the result of an arithmetic operation yields a result that is too small to be stored in the computer's memory.

uniform random numbers   Random numbers that are equally likely to be any value between two specified values.

user-friendly   A term used to describe a program that is easy to use.

user interface   The part of the program that interfaces the user to the steps in the program itself. The user interface usually consists of the input and output portions of the program.

variable   A memory location referenced with a name whose value can be changed within a program.

variable dimensioning　A technique that permits the size of an array in a subprogram to be specified by an argument to the subprogram.

variance　The average squared deviation of a signal from its average value.

vector　A matrix with one column.

WHILE loop　A loop that is executed as long as a specified condition is true.

workstation　A computer that can function as a computer itself or that functions as a terminal to other computers through a computer network.

ANSWERS TO SELF-TESTS

Self-test 2-1, page 18

1. valid
2. invalid (too long)
3. valid
4. valid
5. invalid character (−)
6. invalid character (−)
7. invalid characters (parentheses)
8. invalid (starts with a digit)
9. valid
10. invalid character ($)
11. not the same (2300, 23000)
12. not the same (0.000007, 7000.0)
13. same
14. not the same (110.0, 110.1)
15. not the same (−34.7, −34.0)
16. not the same (−0.76, 0.76)

Self-test 2-2, page 25

1. $Y = -4.0$
2. $A = 2.0, K = 2$
3. $T = 4.25$

Self-test 2-3, page 28

1. `SLOPE = (Y2-Y1)/(X2-X1)`
2. `FACTOR = 1 + B/V + C/V**2`
3. `FRICTN = V*V/(30.0*S)`
4. `CENTER = 38.1972*(R**3 - S**3)*SIN(A)/((R*R - S*S)*A)`
5. `LOSS = F*P*(L/D)*(V*V/2.0)`
6. `REQ = 1.0/(1.0/X1 + 1.0/X2 + 1.0/X3 + 1.0/X4)`
7. $\text{MOTION} = \sqrt{VI^2 + 2AX}$
8. $\text{FREQ} = \dfrac{1.0}{\sqrt{2\pi \cdot \frac{1}{XL} \cdot C}}$
9. $\text{RANGE} = \dfrac{2VI^2 \sin(B)\cos(B)}{G}$
10. $\text{LENGTH} = LI\,\sqrt{1-(V/C)^2}$
11. $\text{ENERGY} = 1.6747 \times 10^{-24}\,(2.99 \times 10^{10})^2$
12. $\text{VOLUME} = 2\pi X^2\,((1-\pi/4)Y - (0.8333-\pi/4)X)$

Self-test 2-4, page 44

1. `57.8290bbb23`
2. `DISTANCEb=b15.6832`
   `VELOCITYb=bbb0.27E-01`

Self-test 3-1, page 90

1. true
2. true
3. true
4. false
5. true
6. true
7. true
8. false
9. `IF (TIME.GT.15.0) TIME = TIME + 1.0`
10. `IF (SQRT(POLY).LT.0.5) PRINT*, POLY`
11. `IF (ABS(VOLT1 - VOLT2).GT.10.0) PRINT*, VOLT1, VOLT2`
12. `IF (DEN.LT.0.005) PRINT*, 'DENOMINATOR IS TOO SMALL'`
13.
```
IF (ALOG(X).GE.3.0) THEN
    TIME = 0.0
    COUNT = COUNT + 1
ENDIF
```
14.
```
IF (DIST.LT.50.0.AND.TIME.GT.10.0) THEN
    TIME = TIME + 2.0
ELSE
    TIME = TIME + 2.5
ENDIF
```

```
15. IF (DIST.GE.100.0) THEN
        TIME = TIME + 2.0
    ELSEIF (DIST.GT.50.0) THEN
        TIME = TIME + 1.0
    ELSE
        TIME = TIME + 0.5
    ENDIF
```

Self-test 3-2, page 114

1. 18 times
2. 17 times
3. 9 times
4. 11 times
5. 0 times
6. 0 times
7. COUNT = 10
8. COUNT = 55
9. COUNT = 0
10. COUNT = −15
11. COUNT = 0

Self-test 3-3, page 129

1. COUNT = 100
2. COUNT = 16
3. COUNT = 12

Self-test 4-1, page 172

1. ID = 1456
   HT = 14.6
   WIDTH = 0.7
2. ID = 0
   HT = 13.7
   WIDTH = 0.865
3. one data line: col 1–6   TIME
                   col 7–12   DIST
                   col 13–18 VEL
                   col 19–24 ACCEL
4. four data lines: line 1: col 1–6 TIME
                    line 2: col 1–6 DIST
                    line 3: col 1–6 VEL
                    line 4: col 1–6 ACCEL
5. four data lines: line 1: col 1–3 TIME
                    line 2: col 1–4 DIST
                    line 3: col 1–3 VEL
                    line 4: col 1–4 ACCEL

6. two data lines: line 1: col 1–6   TIME
       col 7–12 DIST
    line 2: col 1–6   VEL
       col 7–12 ACCEL

7. single space: $_{bb}$4.55$_{bbbbbb}$0.000756.8300

8. single space:TIME$_b$=$_{bb}$4.55$_{bb}$RESPONSE$_b$1$_b$=$_{bb}$0.00074

   single space:TIME$_b$=$_{bb}$4.55$_{bb}$RESPONSE$_b$2$_b$=$_b$56.83000

9. single space:EXPERIMENT RESULTS
   single space:
   single space:TIME$_{bb}$RESPONSE$_b$1$_{bb}$RESPONSE$_b$2
   single space:4.55$_{bbb}$0.740E-03$_{bbb}$0.568E+02

Self-test 5-1, page 199

1. ARRAY VALUES:
```
    2
    3
    4
    5
    6
    7
    8
    9
   10
   11
```

2. bbbb^{8}bbbb^{7}bbbb^{6}bbbb^{5}bbbb^4

3.
```
TIME    1 = 0.00
TIME    5 = 2.00
TIME    9 = 4.00
TIME   13 = 6.00
TIME   17 = 8.00
```

Self-test 5-2, page 213

1. Array contents after each switch:

16	9	9	9	9
83	83	16	16	16
91	91	91	25	25
25	25	25	91	72
9	16	83	83	83
72	72	72	72	91

2. Array contents after each switch:

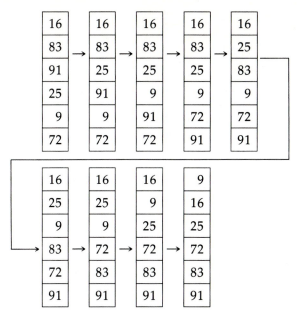

3. Array contents after each switch:

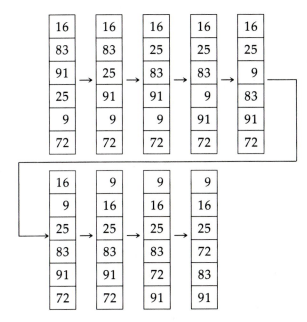

Self-test 5-3, page 222

1.

1	2	3	4
2	4	6	8
3	6	9	12
4	8	12	16
5	10	15	20

bbbb^{3}bbbb^{6}bbbb^{9}bbb^{12}

2.

5	−5	0
5	−5	0
5	−5	0

bbb^5
bb^{-5}
bbb^0

3.

11.5	17.5	23.5
13.0	19.0	25.0
14.5	20.5	26.5
16.0	22.0	28.0

b$^{11.5}$b$^{17.5}$b$^{23.5}$
b$^{13.0}$b$^{19.0}$b$^{25.0}$
b b b

Self-test 6-1, page 249

1. `AREA(R) = 3.14159*R*R`
2. `RADIAN(DEGREE) = (180.0/3.14159)*DEGREE`
3. `DEGREE(RADIAN) = (3.14159/180.0)*RADIAN`
4. `T(M,W,A,S) = M*W*W*A*A*S/4.0`
5. `RADIUS(X,Y) = SQRT(X*X+Y*Y)`

Self-test 6-2, page 270

1. $X = -0.5$
2. $X = 0.5$
3. $X = 0.5$
4. $X = -0.5$

Self-test 7-1, page 305

1. `NEW VALUES OF K ARE:`
bbbb^{2}bbbb^{4}bbbb^{6}bbbb^{8}bbb^{10}
bbb^{12}bbb^{14}bbb^{16}bbb^{18}bbb^{20}

---

2. NEW VALUES OF K ARE:

$$bbbb^2bbbb^4bbbb^6bbbb^8bbb^{10}$$
$$bbbb^6bbbb^7bbbb^8bbbb^9bbb^{10}$$

Self-test 7-2, page 329

```
*
      INTEGER X(10), COUNT, J, HOLD(10)
*
.
.
.
*
      DO 1 J=1,COUNT
         HOLD(J) = X(J)
    1 CONTINUE
      DO 5 J=2,10
         CALL INSERT (10,HOLD(J),J-1,X)
    5 CONTINUE
*
```

Self-test 8-1, page 361

1. CONSERVATION OF ENERGY$_{bbb}$

2. CONSERVATION

3. $_b$OF$_b$ENERGY$_b$

4. $_b$

5. ENERGY$_{bbb}$

6. CONSERVATION

7. CONSERVATION$_b$ OF$_b$ ENERGY$_{bbb}$

8. CONSERVATION$_b$ OF$_b$ ENERGY$_{bbb}$LAW

9. CONSERVE$_b$ ENERGY$_{bbb}$

10. 'CONSIDERATE'

11. DENSIT

12. AREA$_{bb}$

13. CAN'T$_b$

14. '''!$_{bb}$

15. FT/SEC

16. $_{bb}$VOLU

Self-test 8-2, page 374

1. 1.0D+00/4.0D+00
2. 0.58D+00
3. 1.0D+00/7.0D+00
4. 1.0D+00/13.0D+00
5. 108.3D+00
6. 2.0D+00
7. single space: $_{bb}$0.141786D+02
8. single space: $_{b}$0.141786245900D+02
9. single space:14.178625

Self-test 8-3, page 386

1. CX = 1.5 + 2.0i
2. CX = 0.5 + 4.0i
3. CX = 0.5 + 1.0i
4. CX = 1.0 − 1.0i
5. CX = 5.0 + 0.2i
6. CX = 3.162278 + 0.0i
7. single space: $_{bbbb}$2.30$_{bbbb}$0.20
8. single space:($_{bbbb}$2.30,$_{bbbb}$0.20)

Self-test 9-1, page 407

```
*-------------------------------------------------------------------*
      PROGRAM   COUNT
*
*  This program counts the number of records
*  in a data file called XYDATA.
*
      INTEGER   N
      DATA   N /0/
*
      OPEN (UNIT=10,FILE='XYDATA',STATUS='OLD',ERR=100)
*
    1 READ (10,5,END=98) X, Y
    5     FORMAT (F6.2,1X,F6.2)
          N = N + 1
          GO TO 1
*
   98 PRINT 99, N
   99 FORMAT (1X,'FILE CONTAINS',I5,' RECORDS')
      STOP
*
```

```
*--------------------------------------------------------*
     100 PRINT*, 'ERROR IN OPENING DATA FILE'
         STOP
         END
*--------------------------------------------------------*
```

Self-test 9-2, page 242

```
*--------------------------------------------------------*
       PROGRAM  ORDER
*
*  This program prints the item numbers for items that
*  have less than 5 items in the warehouse.
*
       INTEGER  I, ITEM, INVEN
*
       OPEN (UNIT=10,FILE='STORES',ACCESS='DIRECT',
      +      STATUS='OLD',FORM=FORMATTED,RECL=12)
*
       DO 15 I=1,100
          READ (10,5,REC=1) ITEM, INVEN
    5     FORMAT (I5,2X,I5)
          IF (INVEN.LT.5) THEN
             PRINT 10, ITEM
   10        FORMAT ('ITEM NUMBER ',I5,' HAS LESS THAN 5 ',
      +             'ITEMS IN THE WAREHOUSE.')
          ENDIF
   15  CONTINUE
       END
*--------------------------------------------------------*
```

Self-test 10-1, page 449

1. 3
2. $[-2,-1]$, $[0,1]$, $[2,3]$
3. There could be complex roots, multiple roots, or roots outside the specified interval.
4. A third-degree polynomial has exactly three roots.
5.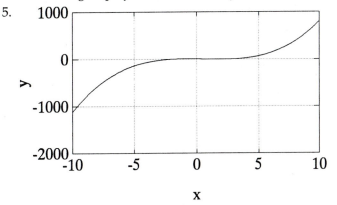

Self-test 10-2, page 451

1. 2.625
2. 2.75

Self-test 10-3, page 452

1. 2.72 (compared with 2.625 using the bisection method)
2. 2.74 (We would not expect to get the same estimate of the root because we are computing the subinterval endpoints differently.)

Self-test 10-4, page 463

1. $f'(x) = 3x^2 - 3.16x - 4.04$
2. $f(2) = -4.11, f'(2) = 1.64$
3. $x_2 = 4.506$
4. $f(3) = 2.95, f'(3) = 13.48$
5. $x_2 = 2.781$
6.

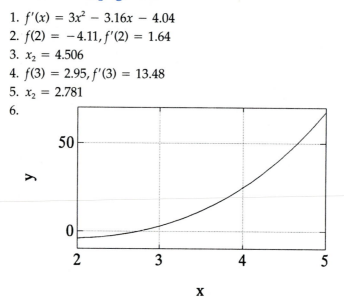

Self-test 10-5, page 464

1. 2.72
2. The secant method has failed because the new internal [2.58,2.72] does not contain a root since the function values at both endpoints are negative.

Self-test 11-1, page 486

1. $\begin{bmatrix} 8 & 5 \\ -2 & -5 \\ 3 & 4 \end{bmatrix}$

2. $\begin{bmatrix} 10 & 7 \\ -4 & -7 \\ -3 & 8 \end{bmatrix}$

3. $\begin{bmatrix} 4 & 4 \\ -4 & -4 \\ -12 & 8 \end{bmatrix}$

4. 5

5. -30

6. $\begin{bmatrix} 1 & 11 \\ 1 & -5 \\ 3 & 9 \end{bmatrix}$

7. $\begin{bmatrix} 7 \\ 9 \end{bmatrix}$

8. $\begin{bmatrix} 7 \\ -5 \\ 4 \end{bmatrix}$

9. $\begin{bmatrix} 39 \\ -25 \\ 18 \end{bmatrix}$

10. $\begin{bmatrix} 11 \\ -7 \\ 7 \end{bmatrix}$

Self-test 11-2, page 492

1. -6
2. -46
3. 0
4. 1. $x = 1, y = 0, z = 0$
   2. $x = -1.3478, y = 0.1304, z = 1.4348$
   3. no unique solution

Self-test 11-3, page 500

1. $x = 1, y = 2$
2. $x = 1, y = 1$
3. $x = -4, y = 4.5, z = 3.5$
4. $x = 1, y = 1, z = 1$

Self-test 11-4, page 511

1. $x = 1.25, y = 2.25$
2. $x = 2.3898, y = 0.0272$

Self-test 12-1, page 528

1. 60 degrees
2. 76.33 degrees
3. 79.32 degrees
4. 80.89 degrees
5. 8:10
6. 8:54

7. 8:59

8. 9:31 and 10:07

Self-test 12-2, page 541

1. $R_2 = 12$, $R_3 = -348$
2. $y_1 = 2(x - 1)^3 + 0(x - 1)^2 + 198(x - 1) + 150$
   $y_2 = -60(x - 2)^3 + 6(x - 2)^2 + 204(x - 2) + 350$
   $y_3 = 58(x - 3)^3 - 174(x - 3)^2 + 36(x - 3) + 500$

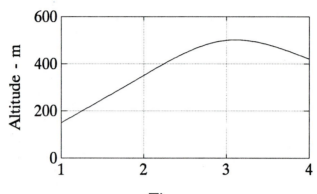

3. $y(1.5) = 249.25$, $y(2.3) = 410.12$, $y(3.7) = 459.83$

Self-test 12-3, page 557

1.
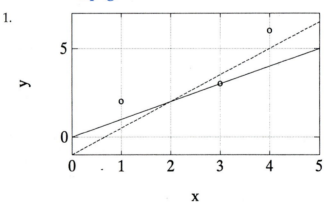

2. Error sum for the first model is 5.0
   Error sum for the second model is 3.5.
   Therefore, the second model is the better model.
3. $y = 1.2143x + 0.4286$
4. Take the natural logarithm of both sides of the equation:

$$ln\ y = ln\ b + ax$$

Let $\tilde{y} = \ln y$, and let $\tilde{b} = \ln b$
Then, $\tilde{y} = ax + \tilde{b}$

Self-test 13-1, page 575

1.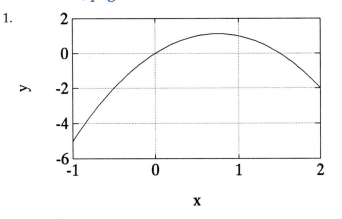

2. 0.75

3. 0.82

4. The exact value is 0.83, to two decimal places. The answer with five trapezoids is more accurate because five trapezoids approximate the area better than two trapezoids.

Self-test 13-2, page 583

1.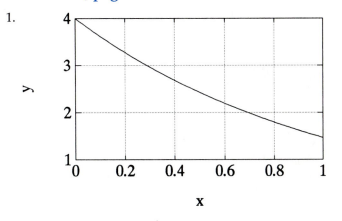

2. 2.529

3. Simpson's rule with two intervals is closer to the exact answer than the trapezoidal rule with five intervals because the function is closer to a parabola than to a straight line.

Self-test 13-3, page 587

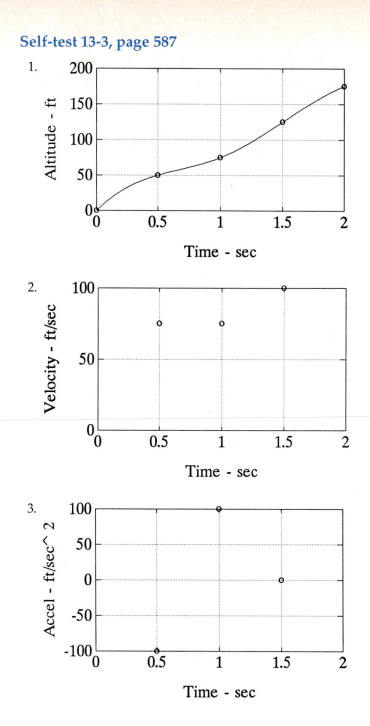

Self-test 14-1, page 605

1. $y_0 = -3$
2. $f(0.1) = -2.715, f(0.5) = -1.820$
3. $y_1 = -2.7$ (compared to -2.715)
4. $y_2 = -1.666$ (compared to -1.820)
   Take smaller steps to improve accuracy.

Self-test 14-2, page 616

1. $K_1 = 1, K_2 = 1.193, K_3 = 1.220, K_4 = 1.433$
2. $y_1 = 0.121$
3. The approximation is equal to the exact answer.

Self-test 15-1, page 639

1.

2.

3.

4.

5.

6.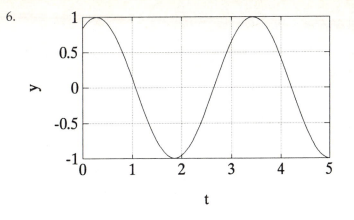

Self-test 15-2, page 650

1. CALL UNIF (NOISE,100,0,10,123)
2. CALL UNIF (NOISE,100,-2,4,123)
3. CALL UNIF (NOISE,100,-1.732,1.732,123)
4. CALL UNIF (NOISE,100,-3.964,2.964,123)

ANSWERS TO SELECTED PROBLEMS

Answers that contain FORTRAN statements are not usually unique. Although these answers represent good solutions to the problems, they are not necessarily the only valid solutions.

Chapter 2

5.
```
*------------------------------------------------------------*
      PROGRAM  CONVRT
*
*  This program converts kilowatt-hours to calories.
*
      REAL  KWH, JOULES, CALRS
*
      PRINT*, 'ENTER ENERGY IN KILOWATT HOURS'
      READ*, KWH
      JOULES = 3.6E+06*KWH
      CALRS = JOULES/4.19
      PRINT 5, KWH, CALRS
    5 FORMAT (1X,F6.2,' KILOWATT-HOURS = ',E9.2,' CALORIES')
      END
*------------------------------------------------------------*
```

9.
```
*------------------------------------------------------------*
      PROGRAM  GROWTH
*
*  This program predicts bacteria growth.
```

```
*
      REAL  TIME1, TIME2, POP1, POP2, CHANGE
*
      PRINT*, 'ENTER TIME1 (HOURS)'
      READ*, TIME1
      PRINT*, 'ENTER TIME2 (>TIME1)'
      READ*, TIME2
      POP1 = EXP(1.386*TIME1)
      POP2 = EXP(1.386*TIME2)
      CHANGE = POP2 - POP1
      PRINT 5, CHANGE
    5 FORMAT (1X,'AMOUNT OF GROWTH = ',F8.2)
      END
*-------------------------------------------------------------*
```

13.
```
*-------------------------------------------------------------*
      PROGRAM  DATE
*
*  This program estimates the age of an artifact from
*  the proportion of carbon remaining in the artifact.
*
      REAL  CARBON, AGE, CENTRY
*
      PRINT*, 'ENTER PROPORTION REMAINING FOR CARBON DATING'
      READ*, CARBON
      AGE = (-LOG(CARBON))/0.0001216
      CENTRY = AGE/100.0
      PRINT 5, CENTRY
    5 FORMAT (1X,'ESTIMATED AGE OF ARTIFACT IS ',F6.2,
     +          ' CENTURIES')
      END
*-------------------------------------------------------------*
```

19.
```
*-------------------------------------------------------------*
      PROGRAM  TRAIN
*
*  This program computes the horizontal force
*  generated by a train on a level curve.
*
      INTEGER  FORCE
      REAL  WEIGHT, MPH, RADIUS
*
      PRINT*, 'ENTER WEIGHT OF TRAIN IN TONS'
      READ*, WEIGHT
      PRINT*, 'ENTER SPEED OF TRAIN IN MILES PER HOUR'
      READ*, MPH
      PRINT*, 'ENTER RADIUS OF CURVE IN FEET'
      READ*, RADIUS
*
      FORCE = NINT((WEIGHT*2000.0/32.0)*
     +          ((MPH*1.4667)**2/RADIUS))
*
      PRINT 10, WEIGHT
   10 FORMAT (1X,'TRAIN WEIGHT - ',F8.2,' TONS')
      PRINT 20, MPH
   20 FORMAT (1X,'TRAIN SPEED - ',F8.2,' MPH')
      PRINT 30, RADIUS
   30 FORMAT (1X,'CURVE RADIUS - ',F8.2,' FEET')
      PRINT*
      PRINT 40, FORCE
```

```
      40 FORMAT (1X,'RESULTING HORIZONTAL FORCE - ',
        +          I8,' POUNDS')
         END
```

23.

```
         PROGRAM   RELY
      *
      *  This program computes the reliability of
      *  instrumentation using a Bernoulli equation.
      *
         INTEGER  N
         REAL   P1, P2, P3, PARALL, SERIES
      *
         PRINT*, 'ENTER RELIABILITY OF COMPONENTS 1, 2, 3'
         PRINT*, '(USE PERCENTAGE BETWEEN 0.0 and 100.0)'
         READ*, P1, P2, P3
      *
         PARALL = (P2/100.0 + P3/100.0 -
        +          (P2/100.0)*(P3/100.0))*100.0
         SERIES = (P1/100.0)*(PARALL/100.0)*100.0
      *
         PRINT*, 'PERCENT OF THE TIME THAT THE EQUIPMENT'
         PRINT 5, SERIES
       5 FORMAT (1X,'SHOULD WORK WITHOUT FAILURE IS ',
        +          F6.2,'%')
         END
```

29.

```
         PROGRAM   CONVRT
      *
      *  This program converts meters to kilometers to miles.
      *
         REAL   METERS, KMETER, MILES
      *
         PRINT*, 'ENTER METERS'
         READ*, METERS
         KMETER = METERS/1000.0
         MILES = KMETER/1.609
         PRINT 5, METERS
       5 FORMAT (1X,F8.2,' METERS')
         PRINT 10, KMETER
      10 FORMAT (1X,F8.2,' KILOMETERS')
         PRINT 15, MILES
      15 FORMAT (1X,F8.2,' MILES')
         END
```

Chapter 3

5.

```
         PROGRAM   ROCKET
      *
      *  This program simulates a rocket flight.
      *
         REAL   TIME, HEIGHT, NEWHT
      *
         TIME = 0.0
         HEIGHT = 60.0
         PRINT 5
```

```
    5 FORMAT (1X,'TIME (SEC.)        HEIGHT (FT.)')
      PRINT*
*
   10 IF (HEIGHT.GT.0.0.AND.TIME.LE.100.0) THEN
         NEWHT = 60.0 + 2.13*TIME**2 - 0.0013*TIME**4
     +           + 0.000034*TIME**4.751
         IF (NEWHT.LT.HEIGHT) THEN
            PRINT 15, TIME
   15       FORMAT (1X,'ROCKET BEGINS RETURNING AT '
     +              F5.1,' SECONDS')
         ENDIF
         HEIGHT = NEWHT
         TIME = TIME + 0.01
         GO TO 10
      ENDIF
      IF (TIME.LE.100.0) THEN
         PRINT 20, TIME
   20    FORMAT (1X,'ROCKET IMPACTED AT ',F5.1,' SECONDS')
      ELSE
         PRINT*, 'TIME LIMIT OF 100 SECS EXCEEDED'
      ENDIF
      END
*------------------------------------------------------------*
 7.
*------------------------------------------------------------*
      PROGRAM  SEALS
*
* This program analyzes data on batches of sutures that have
* not been properly sealed, and then prints a report.
*
      INTEGER  BATCH, COUNT, REJCTT, REJCTP, REJCTD
      REAL  TEMP, PRESSR, DWELL, PERCT, PERCP, PERCD
*
      COUNT = 0
      REJCTT = 0
      REJCTP = 0
      REJCTD = 0
*
      PRINT*, 'ENTER BATCH NUMBER, TEMPERATURE, PRESSURE, DWELL'
      PRINT*, 'FOR BATCHES THAT HAVE BEEN REJECTED'
      PRINT*, '(NEGATIVE BATCH NUMBER TO STOP)'
      READ*, BATCH, TEMP, PRESSR, DWELL
*
    5 IF (BATCH.GE.0)  THEN
         IF (TEMP.LT.150.0.OR.TEMP.GT.170.0) REJCTT = REJCTT + 1
         IF (PRESSR.LT.60.0.OR.PRESSR.GT.70.0) REJCTP = REJCTP + 1
         IF (DWELL.LT.2.0.OR.DWELL.GT.2.5) REJCTD = REJCTD + 1
         COUNT = COUNT + 1
         PRINT*, 'ENTER NEXT SET OF DATA'
         READ*, BATCH, TEMP, PRESSR, DWELL
         GO TO 5
      ENDIF
      PERCT = REAL(REJCTT)/REAL(COUNT)*100.0
      PERCP = REAL(REJCTP)/REAL(COUNT)*100.0
      PERCD = REAL(REJCTD)/REAL(COUNT)*100.0
*
      PRINT*
      PRINT*, 'SUMMARY OF BATCH REJECT INFORMATION'
      PRINT*
      PRINT 10, REJCTT, PERCT
   10 FORMAT (1X,I4,' BATCHES OR ',F6.2,
     +         ' % REJECTED DUE TO TEMPERATURE')
```

```
          PRINT 15, REJCTP, PERCP
   15 FORMAT (1X,I4,' BATCHES OR ',F6.2,
             ' % REJECTED DUE TO PRESSURE')
          PRINT 20, REJCTD, PERCD
   20 FORMAT (1X,I4,' BATCHES OR ',F6.2,
             ' % REJECTED DUE TO DWELL')
          END
```

12.

```
          PROGRAM  TIMBER
*
*  This program computes a reforestation summary
*  for an area which has not been completely harvested.
*
          INTEGER  ID, YEAR
          REAL  TOTAL, UNCUT, RATE, REFOR
*
          PRINT*, 'ENTER LAND IDENTIFICATION (INTEGER)'
          READ*, ID
          PRINT*, 'ENTER TOTAL NUMBER OF ACRES'
          READ*, TOTAL
          PRINT*, 'ENTER NUMBER OF ACRES UNCUT'
          READ*, UNCUT
          PRINT*, 'ENTER REFORESTATION RATE'
          READ*, RATE
*
          IF (UNCUT.GT.TOTAL) THEN
              PRINT*, 'UNCUT AREA LARGER THAN ENTIRE AREA'
          ELSE
              PRINT*
              PRINT*, 'REFORESTATION SUMMARY'
              PRINT*
              PRINT 5, ID
    5         FORMAT (1X,'IDENTIFICATION NUMBER ',I5)
              PRINT 10, TOTAL
   10         FORMAT (1X,'TOTAL ACRES = ',F10.2)
              PRINT 20, UNCUT
   20         FORMAT (1X,'UNCUT ACRES = ',F10.2)
              PRINT 30, RATE
   30         FORMAT (1X,'REFORESTATION RATE = ',F5.3)
              PRINT*
              PRINT*, 'YEAR  REFORESTED  TOTAL REFORESTED'
              DO 50 YEAR=1,20
                  REFOR = UNCUT*RATE
                  UNCUT = UNCUT + REFOR
                  IF (MOD(YEAR,2).EQ.0) THEN
                      PRINT 40, YEAR, REFOR, UNCUT
   40                 FORMAT (1X,I3,F11.3,F17.3)
                  ENDIF
   50         CONTINUE
          ENDIF
          END
```

20.

```
          PROGRAM  CABLE
*
*  This program computes the velocity of a cable car
*  on a thousand-foot cable with three towers.
*
```

```
          INTEGER TOTDIS, DIST, TOWER
          REAL   VEL
    *
          PRINT 1
        1 FORMAT (1X,9X,'CABLE CAR REPORT')
          PRINT*
          PRINT 2
        2 FORMAT (1X,'DISTANCE  NEAREST TOWER  VELOCITY')
          PRINT 3
        3 FORMAT (1X,'  (FT)',19X,'(FT/SEC)')
          PRINT*
    *
          DO 50 TOTDIS=0,1000,10
             IF (TOTDIS.LE.150) THEN
                TOWER = 1
                DIST = TOTDIS
             ELSEIF (TOTDIS.LE.500) THEN
                TOWER = 2
                DIST = ABS(TOTDIS - 300)
             ELSEIF (TOTDIS.LE.850) THEN
                TOWER = 3
                DIST = ABS(TOTDIS - 700)
             ELSE
                TOWER = 4
                DIST = 1000 - TOTDIS
             ENDIF
             IF (DIST.LE.30) THEN
                VEL = 2.425 + 0.00175*DIST*DIST
             ELSE
                VEL = 0.625 + 0.12*DIST - 0.00025*DIST*DIST
             ENDIF
             PRINT 30, TOTDIS, TOWER, VEL
       30    FORMAT (1X,I4,11X,I1,9X,F7.2)
       50 CONTINUE
          END
    *-------------------------------------------------------------*


24.
    *-------------------------------------------------------------*
          PROGRAM  TABLE
    *
    *  This program prints a table of function values.
    *
          INTEGER  I, J
          REAL   X, Y, F
    *
          PRINT*, 'TABLE OF FUNCTION VALUES'
          PRINT*
          PRINT*, 'X          Y          F'
          PRINT*
          DO 15 I = 1,9
             DO 10 J = 1,9
                X = REAL(I)
                Y = (J + 1)*0.25
                F = (X*X - Y*Y)/(2.0*X*Y)
                PRINT 5, X, Y, F
        5       FORMAT (1X,F3.1,5X,F5.2,5X,F5.2)
       10    CONTINUE
       15 CONTINUE
          END
    *-------------------------------------------------------------*
```

Chapter 4

3.
```
*------------------------------------------------------------------------*
      PROGRAM  PATH
*  This program determines the critical path
*  information for a project.
*
      INTEGER  EVENT, TASK, DAYS, TOTAL, NUMBER, MIN, MAX,
     +         WEEKS, PLUS, SUMTSK, NUMTSK
      LOGICAL  DONE
*
      OPEN (UNIT=8,FILE='PROJECT',STATUS='OLD')
      TOTAL = 0
      SUMTSK = 0
      NUMTSK = 0
      PRINT*, 'PROJECT COMPLETION TIMETABLE'
      PRINT*
      PRINT*, 'EVENT NUMBER     MINIMUM TIME     MAXIMUM TIME'
*
      READ (8,*) EVENT, TASK, DAYS
      NUMBER = EVENT
      MIN = DAYS
      MAX = DAYS
      IF (EVENT.EQ.99) THEN
         DONE = .TRUE.
      ELSE
         DONE = .FALSE.
      ENDIF
*
    5 IF (.NOT.DONE) THEN
         IF (EVENT.EQ.NUMBER)  THEN
            IF (DAYS.LT.MIN)  THEN
               MIN = DAYS
            ELSE IF (DAYS.GT.MAX) THEN
               MAX = DAYS
            ENDIF
         ELSE
            PRINT 10, NUMBER, MIN, MAX
   10       FORMAT (1X,I2,14X,I3,13X,I3)
            TOTAL = TOTAL + MAX
            NUMBER = EVENT
            MIN = DAYS
            MAX = DAYS
         ENDIF
         SUMTSK = SUMTSK + DAYS
         NUMTSK = NUMTSK + 1
         READ (8,*) EVENT, TASK, DAYS
         IF (EVENT.EQ.99) DONE = .TRUE.
         GO TO 5
      ENDIF
      PRINT 10, NUMBER, MIN, MAX
      TOTAL = TOTAL + MAX
*
      WEEKS = TOTAL/5
      PLUS = TOTAL - WEEKS*5
      PRINT*
      PRINT 15, TOTAL
   15 FORMAT (1X,'TOTAL PROJECT LENGTH = ',I3,' DAYS')
      PRINT 20, WEEKS, PLUS
   20 FORMAT (1X,'                        = ',I3,' WEEKS',
     +         I2,' DAYS')
```

```
          PRINT*
          PRINT 25, REAL(SUMTSK)/REAL(NUMTSK)
       25 FORMAT (1X,'AVERAGE NUMBER OF DAYS PER TASK = ',F5.1)
          END
*-----------------------------------------------------------------*
```

7.
```
*-----------------------------------------------------------------*
      PROGRAM  CENSUS
*
*  This program reads 101 population values and determines
*  the years of greatest percentage increase in population.
*
      INTEGER  YROLD, YRNEW, POPOLD, POPNEW,
     +         GPIYR, YR1, YR2, MINPOP, I
      REAL  PERC, GPI
*
      OPEN (UNIT=15,FILE='PEOPLE',STATUS='OLD')
      GPI = 0.0
      READ (15,*) YROLD, POPOLD
      MINPOP = POPOLD
      DO 50 I=1,100
         READ (15,*) YRNEW, POPNEW
         IF (POPNEW.LT.MINPOP) MINPOP = POPNEW
         PERC = (POPNEW - POPOLD)*100.0/POPOLD
         IF (I.EQ.1.OR.PERC.GT.GPI) THEN
            GPI = PERC
            GPIYR = YRNEW
         ENDIF
         YROLD = YRNEW
         POPOLD = POPNEW
   50 CONTINUE
      YR1 = GPIYR - 1
      YR2 = GPIYR
      PRINT 55, YR1, YR2
   55 FORMAT (1X,'GREATEST PERCENT INCREASE OCCURRED',
     +        ' BETWEEN ',I4,' AND ',I4)
      CLOSE (UNIT=15)
      OPEN (UNIT=15,FILE='PEOPLE',STATUS='OLD')
      DO 70 I=1,101
         READ(15,*) YROLD, POPOLD
         IF (POPOLD.EQ.MINPOP) THEN
            PRINT 65, YROLD
   65       FORMAT(1X,I4,' HAS MINIMUM POPULATION')
         ENDIF
   70 CONTINUE
      END
*-----------------------------------------------------------------*
```

13.
```
*-----------------------------------------------------------------*
      PROGRAM  QUALTY
*
*  This program uses defect data to print
*  a Quality Analysis Report.
*
      INTEGER  BOARDS, BDDEF, BDWIRE, BDIC, BDNON, WIRE,
     +         IC, NON, ID, NWIRE, NIC, NNON, DEFECT
      REAL  PERCW, PERCIC, PERCNO
*
```

```
                BDDEF = 0
                BDWIRE = 0
                BDIC = 0
                BDNON = 0
                WIRE = 0
                IC = 0
                NON = 0
                OPEN (UNIT=10,FILE='REPORT',STATUS='OLD')
                READ (10,*) BOARDS
      *
                PRINT*, '           MONTHLY QUALITY ANALYSIS REPORT'
                PRINT*
                PRINT*, 'IDENTIFICATION NUMBERS OF BOARDS WITH ',
               +        'THREE OR MORE DEFECTS:'
                PRINT*
      *
                READ (10,*) ID, NWIRE, NIC, NNON
         10  IF (ID.NE.99999)  THEN
                   IF (NWIRE + NIC + NNON.GE.3) PRINT 15, ID
         15     FORMAT (1X,I8)
                   BDDEF = BDDEF + 1
                   IF (NWIRE.GT.0) BDWIRE = BDWIRE + 1
                   IF (NIC.GT.0) BDIC = BDIC + 1
                   IF (NNON.GT.0) BDNON = BDNON + 1
                   WIRE = WIRE + NWIRE
                   IC = IC + NIC
                   NON = NON + NNON
                   READ (10,*) ID, NWIRE, NIC, NNON
                   GO TO 10
                ENDIF
      *
                PRINT 20, BOARDS, BDDEF, BDWIRE, BDIC, BDNON
         20  FORMAT (/,1X,'TOTAL NUMBER OF BOARDS ASSEMBLED = ',I4,//,
               +        1X,'TOTAL BOARDS WITH DEFECTS = ',I4,//,
               +        1X,5X,I4,' BOARDS WITH BROKEN WIRES',/,
               +        1X,5X,I4,' BOARDS WITH DEFECTIVE IC COMPONENTS',/,
               +        1X,5X,I4,' BOARDS WITH DEFECTIVE NON-IC COMPONENTS')
                DEFECT = WIRE + IC + NON
                PERCW = REAL(WIRE)*100.0/REAL(DEFECT)
                PERCIC = REAL(IC)*100.00/REAL(DEFECT)
                PERCNO = REAL(NON)*100.0/REAL(DEFECT)
                PRINT 30, DEFECT, PERCW, PERCIC, PERCNO
         30  FORMAT (/,1X,'DEFECT ANALYSIS',//,
               +        1X,5X,'TOTAL NUMBER OF DEFECTS = ',I5,/,
               +        1X,5X,F5.1,'% OF DEFECTS ARE BROKEN WIRES',/,
               +        1X,5X,F5.1,'% OF DEFECTS ARE DEFECTIVE ',
               +                  'IC COMPONENTS',/,
               +        1X,5X,F5.1,'% OF DEFECTS ARE DEFECTIVE ',
               +                  'NON-IC COMPONENTS')
                END
      *------------------------------------------------------------*


18.
*------------------------------------------------------------*
          PROGRAM  TESTS
      *
      *  This program analyzes pressure data from three chambers.
      *
          INTEGER  PRESS1, PRESS2, PRESS3, MAX1, MAX2, MAX3, I
      *
          OPEN (UNIT=10,FILE='RESULTS',STATUS='OLD')
          READ (10,*) MAX1, MAX2, MAX3
```

```
            DO 5 I=1,19
                READ (10,*) PRESS1, PRESS2, PRESS3
                IF (PRESS1.GT.MAX1) MAX1 = PRESS1
                IF (PRESS2.GT.MAX2) MAX2 = PRESS2
                IF (PRESS3.GT.MAX3) MAX3 = PRESS3
          5 CONTINUE
*
            PRINT 10, 1, MAX1
            PRINT 10, 2, MAX2
            PRINT 10, 3, MAX3
         10 FORMAT (1X,'MAXIMUM PRESSURE IN CHAMBER ',I1,' = ',I4)
*
            END
*-------------------------------------------------------------------*
```

Chapter 5

1.
```
*-------------------------------------------------------------------*
            PROGRAM  SNOFAL
*
*     This program computes the average snowfall
*     for January and counts the number of days
*     with above-average snowfall.
*
            INTEGER  COUNT, NOSNOW, I
            REAL  SNOW(31), TOTAL, AVE
            DATA  TOTAL, COUNT, NOSNOW /0.0, 0, 0/
*
            OPEN (UNIT=10,FILE='JAN',STATUS='OLD')
            READ (10,*) SNOW
            PRINT 5, SNOW
          5 FORMAT (1X,4F8.1)
*
            DO 10 I=1,31
                TOTAL = TOTAL + SNOW(I)
                IF (SNOW(I).EQ.0.0) NOSNOW = NOSNOW + 1
         10 CONTINUE
            AVE = TOTAL/31.0
            PRINT 20, AVE
         20 FORMAT (1X,'AVERAGE SNOWFALL IS ',F5.2,' INCHES')
*
            DO 30 I=1,31
                IF (SNOW(I).GT.AVE) COUNT = COUNT + 1
         30 CONTINUE
            PRINT 40, COUNT
         40 FORMAT (1X,I2,' DAYS WITH ABOVE-AVERAGE SNOWFALL')
            PRINT 45, NOSNOW
         45 FORMAT (1X,I2,' DAYS WITH NO SNOWFALL')
*
            END
*-------------------------------------------------------------------*
```

9.
```
*-------------------------------------------------------------------*
            PROGRAM  EARTH
*
*     This program will read a file of earthquake data
*     and sort and print it in ascending order.
*
            INTEGER  LOCATE, I, N, J, PTR, LAST, FIRST, K
            REAL  QUAKE(200), HOLD, MEDIAN
*
```

```
          OPEN (UNIT=9,FILE='MOTION',STATUS='OLD')
          READ (9,*) LOCATE
          PRINT 5, LOCATE
        5 FORMAT (1X,'LOCATION NUMBER: ',I5)
*
          I = 1
       10 READ (9,*,END=20) QUAKE(I)
             I = I + 1
             GO TO 10
*
       20 N = I - 1
          LAST = N
          DO 40 J=1,N-1
             PTR = J
             FIRST = J + 1
             DO 30 K = FIRST, LAST
                IF (QUAKE(K).LT.QUAKE(PTR)) PTR = K
       30    CONTINUE
             HOLD = QUAKE(J)
             QUAKE(J) = QUAKE(PTR)
             QUAKE(PTR) = HOLD
       40 CONTINUE
*
          DO 60 I=1,N
             PRINT 50, I, QUAKE(I)
       50    FORMAT (1X,I3,'.',3X,F6.4)
       60 CONTINUE
          IF (MOD(N,2).EQ.1) THEN
             MEDIAN = QUAKE(N/2+1)
          ELSE
             MEDIAN = (QUAKE(N/2) + QUAKE(N/2+1))/2.0
          ENDIF
          PRINT 65, MEDIAN
       65 FORMAT (1X,'MEDIAN EARTHQUAKE VALUE IS ',F6.4)
*
          END
*-----------------------------------------------------------*
```

13.
```
*-----------------------------------------------------------*
      PROGRAM  PWRPLT
*
*  This program computes and prints a composite report
*  summarizing several weeks of power plant data.
*
      INTEGER  POWER(20,7), MIN, TOTAL, COUNT, I, J, N
      REAL   AVE
      DATA   TOTAL, COUNT /0, 0/
*
      PRINT*, 'ENTER NUMBER OF WEEKS FOR ANALYSIS'
      READ*, N
      OPEN (UNIT=12,FILE='PLANT',STATUS='OLD')
      DO 5 I=1,N
         READ (12,*) (POWER(I,J), J=1,7)
    5 CONTINUE
*
      MIN = POWER(1,1)
      DO 15 I=1,N
         DO 10 J=1,7
```

```
                   TOTAL = TOTAL + POWER(I,J)
                   IF (POWER(I,J).LT.MIN) MIN = POWER(I,J)
     10      CONTINUE
     15 CONTINUE
        AVE = REAL(TOTAL)/REAL(N*7)
*
        DO 25 I=1,N
           DO 20 J=1,7
                   IF (POWER(I,J).GT.AVE) COUNT = COUNT + 1
     20      CONTINUE
     25 CONTINUE
*
        PRINT 30
     30 FORMAT (1X,15X,'COMPOSITE INFORMATION')
        PRINT 35, AVE
     35 FORMAT (1X,'AVERAGE DAILY POWER OUTPUT = ',F5.1,
       +          ' MEGAWATTS')
        PRINT 40, COUNT
     40 FORMAT (1X,'NUMBER OF DAYS WITH GREATER THAN ',
       +          'AVERAGE POWER OUTPUT = ',I2)
        PRINT 45
     45 FORMAT (1X,'DAY(S) WITH MINIMUM POWER OUTPUT:')
        DO 60 I=1,N
           DO 55 J=1,7
                   IF (POWER(I,J).EQ.MIN) PRINT 50, I, J
     50        FORMAT (1X,12X,'WEEK ',I2,'   DAY ',I2)
     55      CONTINUE
     60 CONTINUE
*
        END
```

--

19.

--

```
        PROGRAM  NAVIG
*
*  This program reads the elevation data for a set of land
*  grids and determines the number of peaks in each grid.
*
        INTEGER  MAP(100,100), I, J, ID, NROWS, NCOLS, COUNT,
       +         MAX, MIN
*
        PRINT 5
      5 FORMAT (1X,'SUMMARY OF LAND GRID ANALYSIS')
        PRINT 10
     10 FORMAT (1X,'IDENTIFICATION    NUMBER OF POINTS   ',
       +          'NUMBER OF PEAKS')
*
        OPEN (UNIT=15,FILE='ELEVTN',STATUS='OLD')
        READ (15,*) ID
     15 IF (ID.NE.99999) THEN
           READ (15,*) NROWS, NCOLS
           DO 20 I=1,NROWS
              READ (15,*) (MAP(I,J), J=1,NCOLS)
     20      CONTINUE
           COUNT = 0
           DO 30 I=2,NROWS-1
              DO 25 J=2,NCOLS-1
                   IF ((MAP(I-1,J).LT.MAP(I,J)).AND.
       +              (MAP(I+1,J).LT.MAP(I,J)).AND.
       +              (MAP(I,J-1).LT.MAP(I,J)).AND.
       +              (MAP(I,J+1).LT.MAP(I,J))) THEN
```

```
                    COUNT = COUNT + 1
                ENDIF
     25        CONTINUE
     30     CONTINUE
           PRINT 35, ID, NROWS*NCOLS, COUNT
     35     FORMAT (1X,I7,10X,I7,10X,I7)
           READ (15,*) ID
           GO TO 15
         ENDIF
*
         MAX = MAP(1,1)
         MIN = MAP(1,1)
         DO 45 I=1,NROWS
            DO 40 J=1,NCOLS
               IF (MAP(I,J).GT.MAX) MAX = MAP(I,J)
               IF (MAP(I,J).LT.MIN) MIN = MAP(I,J)
     40     CONTINUE
     45 CONTINUE
         PRINT 50, MAX, MIN
     50 FORMAT (1X,'MAXIMUM ELEVATION = ',I6,5X,
        +          'MINIMUM ELEVATION = ',I6)
*
         END
*--------------------------------------------------------------*
```

25.

```
         INTEGER  TIME(30)

            .
            .
            .
         DO 50 I=2,30,2
            PRINT 45, I, TIME(I)
     45     FORMAT (1X,'TIME(',I2,') CONTAINS ',I4,' SECONDS')
     50 CONTINUE
```

Chapter 6

5.
```
*--------------------------------------------------------------*
         PROGRAM  TABLE1
*
*  This program generates a temperature conversion table.
*
         INTEGER  IN, OUT
         REAL   FIRST, CHANGE, LAST, NEXT, NEW, TEMP,
        +       CTOF, KTOF, RTOF, FTOC, FTOK, FTOR, HOLD
*
*  Conversion functions use Fahrenheit
*  as the base temperature unit.
*
         CTOF(TEMP) = 1.8*TEMP + 32.0
         KTOF(TEMP) = CTOF(TEMP - 273.15)
         RTOF(TEMP) = TEMP - 459.67
         FTOC(TEMP) = (TEMP - 32.0)*0.5555556
         FTOK(TEMP) = FTOC(TEMP) + 273.15
         FTOR(TEMP) = TEMP + 459.67
*
         PRINT*, 'CODE TEMPERATURE AS FOLLOWS:'
         PRINT*, '1-FAHRENHEIT'
         PRINT*, '2-CENTIGRADE'
         PRINT*, '3-KELVIN'
```

```
               PRINT*, '4- RANKIN'
               PRINT*, 'ENTER CODE FOR TABLE INPUT'
               READ*, IN
               PRINT*, 'ENTER CODE FOR TABLE OUTPUT'
               READ*, OUT
               PRINT*, 'ENTER NUMBER OF DEGREES FOR FIRST LINE: '
               READ*, FIRST
               PRINT*, 'ENTER CHANGE IN DEGREES BETWEEN LINES: '
               READ*, CHANGE
               PRINT*, 'ENTER NUMBER OF DEGREES FOR LAST LINE: '
               READ*, LAST
      *
               PRINT 5
         5     FORMAT (1X,5X,'TEMPERATURE CONVERSION TABLE')
               PRINT 10
        10     FORMAT (1X,'DEGREES, INPUT',10X,
              +        'DEGREES, OUTPUT')
               NEXT = FIRST
        20     IF (NEXT.LE.LAST) THEN
                   IF (IN.EQ.1) THEN
                       HOLD = NEXT
                   ELSEIF (IN.EQ.2) THEN
                       HOLD = CTOF(NEXT)
                   ELSEIF (IN.EQ.3) THEN
                       HOLD = KTOF(NEXT)
                   ELSE
                       HOLD = RTOF(NEXT)
                   ENDIF
                   IF (OUT.EQ.1) THEN
                       NEW = HOLD
                   ELSEIF (OUT.EQ.2) THEN
                       NEW = FTOC(HOLD)
                   ELSEIF (OUT.EQ.3) THEN
                       NEW = FTOK(HOLD)
                   ELSE
                       NEW = FTOR(HOLD)
                   ENDIF
                   PRINT 25, NEXT, NEW
        25         FORMAT (1X,F9.2,18X,F9.2)
                   NEXT = NEXT + CHANGE
                   GO TO 20
               ENDIF
      *
               END
      *------------------------------------------------------------*

       7.
      *------------------------------------------------------------*
               PROGRAM  REPORT
      *
      *  This program generates a report from the daily
      *  production information for a set of oil wells.
      *
               INTEGER  MO, DA, YR, ID, N, I
               REAL  OIL(7), TOTAL, AVE, INDAVE, MAX
               DATA  N, TOTAL, MAX /0, 0.0, 0/
      *
               OPEN (UNIT=12,FILE='WELLS',STATUS='OLD')
               READ (12,*) MO, DA, YR
               PRINT*, 'OIL WELL PRODUCTION'
               PRINT 5, MO, DA, YR
         5     FORMAT (1X,'WEEK OF ',I2,'-',I2,'-',I2)
```

```
      PRINT*
      PRINT*, 'WELL ID        AVERAGE PRODUCTION'
      PRINT*, '                  (IN BARRELS)'
*
      READ (12,*) ID, (OIL(I), I=1,7)
   10 IF (ID.NE.99999) THEN
         INDAVE = AVE(OIL,7)
         PRINT 15, ID, INDAVE
   15    FORMAT (1X,I5,9X,F6.2)
         N = N + 1
         TOTAL = TOTAL + INDAVE
         IF (INDAVE.GT.MAX) MAX = INDAVE
         READ (12,*) ID, (OIL(I), I=1,7)
         GO TO 10
      ENDIF
*
      PRINT*
      PRINT 20, N, TOTAL/REAL(N)
   20 FORMAT (1X,'OVERALL AVERAGE FOR ',I3,
     +        ' WELLS IS ',F6.2)
      PRINT 25, MAX*7.0
   25 FORMAT (1X,'MAXIMUM WEEKLY PRODUCTION IS ',F8.2)
*
      END
*---------------------------------------------------------*
                (no changes in function AVE)
*---------------------------------------------------------*
```

15.
```
*---------------------------------------------------------*
             (no changes in main program ANALYZ)
*---------------------------------------------------------*
*
      INTEGER FUNCTION  MINUTE(BEGIN,END)
*
*  This function computes the number of minutes
*  between the beginning time and the ending time.
*
      INTEGER  BEGIN, END, BEGHR, BEGMIN, ENDHR, ENDMIN
*
      BEGHR = BEGIN/100
      BEGMIN = MOD(BEGIN,100)
      ENDHR = END/100
      ENDMIN = MOD(END,100)
      IF (BEGIN.LT.END) THEN
         MINUTE = (ENDHR*60 + ENDMIN) - (BEGHR*60 + BEGMIN)
      ELSE
         MINUTE = (ENDHR*60+ENDMIN)+1440 - (BEGHR*60+BEGMIN)
      ENDIF
*
      RETURN
      END
*---------------------------------------------------------*
```

25.
```
*---------------------------------------------------------*
      INTEGER FUNCTION  INVERT(NUM)
*
*  This function  reverses the
*  digits in a two-digit number.
*
```

```
          INTEGER  NUM, DIGIT1, DIGIT2
*
      DIGIT1 = NUM/10
      DIGIT2 = MOD(NUM,10)
      INVERT = DIGIT2*10 + DIGIT1
*
      RETURN
      END
*-----------------------------------------------------------------*
```

Chapter 7

3.
```
*-----------------------------------------------------------------*
      PROGRAM  SIGGEN
*
*  This program generates a signal composed
*  of a sine wave plus random noise.
*
      INTEGER  SEED, I, N
      REAL  PI, T, NOISE, X
      DATA  PI, T /3.141593, 0.0/
*
      PRINT*, 'ENTER A POSITIVE INTEGER SEED: '
      READ*, SEED
      OPEN (UNIT=15,FILE='SIGNAL',STATUS='NEW')
*
      PRINT*, 'ENTER NUMBER OF DATA POINTS TO GENERATE'
      READ*, N
      DO 10 I=1,N
         CALL RANDOM (SEED, NOISE)
         X = 2*SIN(2*PI*T) + NOISE
         WRITE (15,*) T, X
         T = T + 0.01
   10 CONTINUE
*
      END
*-----------------------------------------------------------------*
               (no changes in subroutine RANDOM)
*-----------------------------------------------------------------*
```

8.
```
*-----------------------------------------------------------------*
      PROGRAM  STREAM
*
*  This program computes the maximum oxygen deficit for
*  a group of waste water discharge streams.
*
      INTEGER  N, J, NUM
      REAL  DAYS, QD, QS, BODD, BODS, TMIX, KR, DOXYGN,
     +      DEFMAX, DEFDAY
*
      OPEN (UNIT=10,FILE='STREAMS',STATUS='OLD')
      PRINT*, 'ENTER TIME PERIOD FOR STREAM ANALYSIS IN DAYS'
      READ*, DAYS
      PRINT*, 'ENTER NUMBER OF ANALYSES PER DAY (INTEGER)'
      READ*, NUM
      PRINT*
      PRINT*, 'OXYGEN DEFICIT ANALYSIS OF ',
     +        'WASTE WATER DISCHARGE STREAMS'
      PRINT*
*
```

```
          READ (10,*) N
          DO 30 J=1,N
             READ (10,*) QD, QS, BODD, BODS, TMIX, KR, DOXYGN
             CALL CALC(NUM,QD,QS,BODD,BODS,TMIX,KR,DOXYGN,
        +             DAYS,DEFMAX,DEFDAY)
             PRINT 10, J, DEFMAX
   10        FORMAT (1X,'STREAM ',I3,':',' MAXIMUM DEFICIT = ',F6.3)
             PRINT 20, DEFDAY
   20        FORMAT (1X,12X,'OCCURRED AT DAY ',F3.1)
             PRINT*
   30     CONTINUE
*
          END
*-------------------------------------------------------------*
          SUBROUTINE CALC(NUM,QD,QS,BODD,BODS,TMIX,KR,DOXYGN,
        +             DAYS,DEFMAX,DEFDAY)
*
*    This subroutine calculates the maximum oxygen deficit for a
*    stream along with the day that it occurred.
*
          INTEGER  STEPS, J, NUM
          REAL   QD, QS, BODD, BODS, TMIX, KR, DOXYGN,
        +        FSMIX, KD, BODMIX, DEFCT, INCR,
        +        DAYS, DEFMAX, DEFDAY, T, TEMP1, TEMP2, TEMP3
*
          BODMIX = ((BODS*QS) + (BODD*QD))/(QS + QD)
          FSMIX = BODMIX*(0.02*TMIX + 0.6)/0.68
          KD = 0.1*(1.047**(TMIX  - 20.0))
*
          DEFMAX = 0.0
          DEFDAY = 0.0
          STEPS = INT(DAYS)*NUM
          INCR = 1.0/REAL(NUM)
*
          DO 10 J=1,STEPS
             T = REAL(J)*INCR
             TEMP1 = (KD*FSMIX)/(KR -  KD)
             TEMP2 = 10.0**(-KD*T)  - 10.0**(-KR*T)
             TEMP3 = DOXYGN*(10.0**(-KR*T))
             DEFCT = (TEMP1*TEMP2)  + TEMP3
             IF (J.EQ.1.OR.DEFCT.GT.DEFMAX)  THEN
                DEFMAX = DEFCT
                DEFDAY = T
             ENDIF
   10     CONTINUE
*
          RETURN
          END
*-------------------------------------------------------------*


12.
*-------------------------------------------------------------*
          PROGRAM  UPDATE
*
*    This program updates a computer access list.
*
          INTEGER  J, CODE, COUNT, OLD, NEW, SSN(500)
          LOGICAL  DONE
*
          OPEN (UNIT=8,FILE='ACCESS',STATUS='OLD')
          OPEN (UNIT=9,FILE='NEWACCES',STATUS='NEW')
*
```

```
                    DONE = .FALSE.
                   J = 1
              5 IF (.NOT.DONE) THEN
                   READ (8,*) SSN(J)
                   IF (SSN(J).EQ.999999999)  THEN
                       DONE = .TRUE.
                   ELSE
                       J = J + 1
                   ENDIF
                   GO TO 5
                ENDIF
                COUNT = J
                DONE = .FALSE.
*
             10 IF (.NOT.DONE) THEN
                   PRINT*, 'ENTER -1 FOR DELETION, 1 FOR INSERTION, ',
             +               '0 TO QUIT'
                   READ*, CODE
                   IF (CODE.EQ.-1)   THEN
                       PRINT*, 'ENTER SSN FOR DELETION'
                       READ*, OLD
                       CALL DELETE(OLD,COUNT,SSN)
                   ELSE IF (CODE.EQ.1) THEN
                       IF (COUNT.EQ.500) THEN
                           PRINT*, 'LIST IS FULL - DO DELETIONS FIRST'
                       ELSE
                           PRINT*, 'ENTER SSN FOR INSERTION'
                           READ*, NEW
                           CALL INSERT(LIMIT,NEW,COUNT,SSN)
                       ENDIF
                   ELSE
                       DONE = .TRUE.
                   ENDIF
                   GO TO 10
                ENDIF
*
                DO 15 J=1,COUNT
                   WRITE (9,*) SSN(J)
             15 CONTINUE
                PRINT 20, COUNT-1
             20 FORMAT (1X,'NUMBER OF VALID USERS = ',I4)
*
                END
*-----------------------------------------------------------------*
                    (no changes in subroutine DELETE)
*-----------------------------------------------------------------*
                    (no changes in subroutine INSERT)
*-----------------------------------------------------------------*


24.
*-----------------------------------------------------------------*
         SUBROUTINE  GREAT(Z,W)
*
*  This subroutine moves corresponding values of
*  Z into W unless the value is less than
*  the average of all values in Z.  In these
*  cases the average value of Z is used in W.
*
         INTEGER  I, J
         REAL  Z(5,4) W(5,4), SUM, AVE
*
```

```
                SUM = 0.0
                DO 10 I=1,5
                    DO 5 J=1,4
                        SUM = SUM + Z(I,J)
        5       CONTINUE
       10 CONTINUE
                AVE = SUM/20.0
                DO 20 I=1,5
                    DO 15 J=1,4
                        IF (Z(I,J).LE.AVE) THEN
                            W(I,J) = Z(I,J)
                        ELSE
                            W(I,J) = AVE
                        ENDIF
       15       CONTINUE
       20 CONTINUE
    *
                RETURN
                END
    *-------------------------------------------------------------*
```

Chapter 8

3.
```
    *-------------------------------------------------------------*
          PROGRAM   DECODE
    *
    *  This program aids in decoding a message by counting
    *  the number of occurrences of vowels in the message.
    *
          INTEGER  N, I, J
          REAL   VOWEL(5)
          CHARACTER*50  TEXT
          DATA  VOWEL /5*0.0/
    *
          OPEN (UNIT=10,FILE='SECRET',STATUS='OLD')
          READ (10,*) N
          DO 10 I=1,N
              READ (10,*) TEXT
              DO 5 J=1,50
                  IF (TEXT(J:J).EQ.'A'.OR.TEXT(J:J).EQ.'a') THEN
                      VOWEL(1) = VOWEL(1) + 1
                  ELSEIF (TEXT(J:J).EQ.'E'.OR.TEXT(J:J).EQ.'e') THEN
                      VOWEL(2) = VOWEL(2) + 1
                  ELSEIF (TEXT(J:J).EQ.'I'.OR.TEXT(J:J).EQ.'i') THEN
                      VOWEL(3) = VOWEL(3) + 1
                  ELSEIF (TEXT(J:J).EQ.'O'.OR.TEXT(J:J).EQ.'o') THEN
                      VOWEL(4) = VOWEL(4) + 1
                  ELSEIF (TEXT(J:J).EQ.'U'.OR.TEXT(J:J).EQ.'u') THEN
                      VOWEL(5) = VOWEL(5) + 1
                  ENDIF
        5     CONTINUE
       10 CONTINUE
    *
          PRINT*, 'TOTAL NUMBER OF CHARACTERS = ',N*50
          PRINT*
          PRINT*, 'OCCURRENCES OF VOWELS:'
          PRINT 15, VOWEL(1)
       15 FORMAT (1X,'A: = ',F6.0)
          PRINT 16, VOWEL(2)
       16 FORMAT (1X,'E: = ',F6.0)
```

```
                PRINT 17, VOWEL(3)
            17 FORMAT (1X,'I: = ',F6.0)
                PRINT 18, VOWEL(4)
            18 FORMAT (1X,'O: = ',F6.0)
                PRINT 19, VOWEL(5)
            19 FORMAT (1X,'U: = ',F6.0)
                PRINT*
                CALL GRAPH (VOWEL,5,20)
*
                END
*----------------------------------------------------------*
                      (no changes in subroutine GRAPH)
*----------------------------------------------------------*


   7.
*----------------------------------------------------------*
          PROGRAM   TEMP
*
*   This program initializes the temperatures in a metal
*   plate and determines the equilibrium temperatures
*   based on a tolerance value.
*
          INTEGER  NROW, NCOL, I, J
          LOGICAL  EQUILB
          DOUBLE PRECISION  OLD(10,10), NEW(10,10), TOLNC,
         +                  TOP, BOT, LEFT, RIGHT
*
          PRINT*, 'ENTER TEMPERATURE GRID SIZE:'
          PRINT*, 'ROWS, COLUMNS  (MAXIMUM 10,10) '
          READ*, NROW, NCOL
          PRINT*, 'ENTER ISOTHERMAL EDGE TEMPERATURES:'
          PRINT*, 'TOP, BOTTOM, LEFT, RIGHT '
          READ*, TOP, BOT, LEFT, RIGHT
          PRINT*, 'ENTER EQUILIBRIUM TOLERANCE VALUE: '
          READ*, TOLNC
*
*   INITIALIZE TEMPERATURE ARRAY
*
          CALL FIRST(NEW,NROW,NCOL,TOP,BOT,LEFT,RIGHT)
          CALL MOVE(OLD,NEW,NROW,NCOL)
*
*   PRINT INITIAL TEMPERATURE ARRAY
*
          PRINT*
          PRINT*, 'INITIAL TEMPERATURES'
          PRINT*
          CALL PRINT(OLD,NROW,NCOL)
*
*   UPDATE TEMPERATURES UNTIL EQUILIBRIUM
*
          EQUILB = .FALSE.
        20 IF (.NOT.EQUILB) THEN
              EQUILB = .TRUE.
              DO 30 I=2,NROW-1
                 DO 25 J=2,NCOL-1
                    NEW(I,J) = (OLD(I-1,J) + OLD(I+1,J) +
         +                      OLD(I,J-1) + OLD(I,J+1))/4.0+00
                    IF (DABS(NEW(I,J) - OLD(I,J)).GT.TOLNC)
         +                      EQUILB = .FALSE.
        25       CONTINUE
        30    CONTINUE
```

```
               CALL MOVE(OLD,NEW,NROW,NCOL)
               GO TO 20
         ENDIF
*
*    PRINT EQUILIBRIUM TEMPERATURE ARRAY
*
         PRINT*
         PRINT*, 'EQUILBRIUM TEMPERATURES'
         PRINT*
         CALL PRINT(OLD,NROW,NCOL)
*
         END
*-------------------------------------------------------------------*
                   (no changes in subroutine PRINT)
*-------------------------------------------------------------------*
                   (no changes in subroutine MOVE)
*-------------------------------------------------------------------*
*
         SUBROUTINE  FIRST(NEW,NROW,NCOL,TOP,BOT,LEFT,RIGHT)
*
*    This subroutine initializes the temperature array.
*
         INTEGER  NROW, NCOL, I, J
         DOUBLE PRECISION  NEW(10,10), TOP, BOT, LEFT, RIGHT
*
         DO 5 J=1,NCOL
            NEW(1,J) = TOP
            NEW(NROW,J) = BOT
    5    CONTINUE
         DO 15 I=2,NROW-1
            NEW(I,1) = LEFT
            DO 10 J=2,NCOL-1
               NEW(I,J) = 0.0D+00
   10       CONTINUE
            NEW(I,NCOL) = RIGHT
   15    CONTINUE
*
         RETURN
         END
*-------------------------------------------------------------------*
```

13.
```
*-------------------------------------------------------------------*
         PROGRAM  ELECT1
*
*    This program determines the magnitude and phase
*    of an RC circuit on a sine wave.
*
         REAL  R, MC, C, W, MAGN, PHASE
         COMPLEX  I, HW
*
         I = (0.0, 1.0)
*
         PRINT*, 'ENTER RESISTANCE IN OHMS'
         READ*, R
         PRINT*, 'ENTER CAPACITANCE IN MICROFARADS'
         READ*, MC
         PRINT*, 'ENTER THE SINE FREQUENCY IN RADIANS PER SEC'
         READ*, W
*
         C = MC*1.0E-06
         HW = (I*W*R*C)/(1.0 + I*W*R*C)
```

```
          MAGN = CABS(HW)
          PHASE = ATAN(AIMAG(HW)/REAL(HW))
*
          PRINT 5, MAGN, PHASE
        5 FORMAT (1X,'MAGNITUDE EFFECT:',F5.2,3X,
       +            'PHASE EFFECT:', F5.2)
*
          END
*----------------------------------------------------------------*
```

17.
```
*----------------------------------------------------------------*
          SUBROUTINE  CNDNS(IN,OUT)
*
*  This subroutine removes all groups
*  of multiple blanks from IN and
*  stores in OUT.
*
          INTEGER  I, K
          CHARACTER*50  IN, OUT
*
          OUT = ' '
          K = 1
          DO 10 I=1,49
             IF (IN(I:I).NE.' ') THEN
                OUT(K:K) = IN(I:I)
                K = K + 1
             ELSE
                IF (IN(I+1:I+1).NE.' ') THEN
                   OUT(K:K) = IN(I:I)
                   K = K + 1
                ENDIF
             ENDIF
       10 CONTINUE
          OUT(K:K) = IN(50:50)
*
          RETURN
          END
*----------------------------------------------------------------*
```

Chapter 9

2.
```
*----------------------------------------------------------------*
          PROGRAM  VOYAGE
*
*  This program detects edges in a two-dimensional image.
*
          INTEGER  I, J, IMAGE(40,50), ID, NR, NC, NEWID
          REAL   LIMIT
          CHARACTER  FILENM*6, EDGE(40)*50, LINE*50
          LOGICAL   DONE
*
          DO 3 I=1,50
             LINE(I:I) = '*'
        3 CONTINUE
          PRINT*, 'ENTER NAME OF IMAGE FILE ENCLOSED IN QUOTES'
          READ*, FILENM
          OPEN (UNIT=8,FILE=FILENM,STATUS='OLD')
*
```

```
      PRINT*
      PRINT*,'IMAGES IN THIS FILE'
      READ(8,*) ID, NR, NC
    5 IF (ID.NE.9999)  THEN
      PRINT 10, ID,NR,NC
   10     FORMAT (1X,'ID = ',I4,' SIZE = (',I2,',',I2,')')
          DO 20 I=1,NR
              READ(8,15)  IMAGE(I,1)
   15         FORMAT (50I1)
   20     CONTINUE
          READ(8,*) ID, NR, NC
          GO TO 5
      ENDIF
*
      PRINT*
      PRINT*, 'ENTER ID OF IMAGE TO BE ANALYZED'
      READ*, NEWID
      PRINT*, 'ENTER THRESHOLD FOR EDGE DETECTION'
      READ*, LIMIT
*
      REWIND (UNIT=8)
      READ(8,*) ID, NR, NC
      DONE = .FALSE.
   25 IF (.NOT.DONE)  THEN
          IF (ID.EQ.NEWID)  THEN
              DO 30 I=1,NR
                  READ (8,15) (IMAGE(I,J),J=1,NC)
   30         CONTINUE
              CALL CONVERT(LIMIT,IMAGE,EDGE,NR,NC)
              PRINT*
              PRINT 35, LIMIT
   35         FORMAT (1X,'THRESHOLD VALUE = ',F5.2)
              PRINT 40, LINE(1:NC)
              DO 45 I=1,NR
                  PRINT 40, EDGE(I)(1:NC)
   40             FORMAT (1X,'*',A,'*')
   45         CONTINUE
              PRINT 40, LINE(1:NC)
              DONE = .TRUE.
          ELSEIF (ID.EQ.9999)  THEN
              DONE = .TRUE.
              PRINT*, 'IMAGE NOT FOUND'
          ELSE
              DO 50 I=1,NR
                  READ(8,15) IMAGE(I,1)
   50         CONTINUE
              READ(8,*) ID, NR, NC
          ENDIF
          GO TO 25
      ENDIF
      END
*---------------------------------------------------------*
             (no changes in subroutine CONVRT)
*---------------------------------------------------------*


10.
*---------------------------------------------------------*
      PROGRAM  MIGRAT
*
* This program merges new sighting information into the
* master file of migration information on whooping cranes.
*
```

```
                INTEGER   M,D,Y,T,MO,DA,YR,TIME,GRID1,GRID2,BIRDS,
              +           SMO,SDA,SYR,STIME,SGRID1,SGRID2,SBIRDS,
              +           CMO,CDA,CYR,CTIME,CGRID1,CGRID2,CBIRDS,COUNT,
              +           MAXCT,HOLDM,HOLDD
                DOUBLE PRECISION  DATE, CDATE, SDATE
                LOGICAL   DONE
      *
                DATE(M,D,Y,T) = DBLE(REAL(Y)*1.0D08) +
              +                 DBLE(REAL(M)*1.0D06) +
              +                 DBLE(REAL(D)*1.0D04) +
              +                 DBLE(REAL(T))
      *
                OPEN (UNIT=10,FILE='SIGHTS',STATUS='OLD')
                OPEN (UNIT=11,FILE='CRANES',STATUS='OLD')
                OPEN (UNIT=12,FILE='TEMP',STATUS='NEW')
      *
                READ (10,5) SMO,SDA,SYR,STIME,SGRID1,SGRID2,SBIRDS
            5   FORMAT (3I2,1X,I4,1X,2I2,1X,I4)
                READ (11,5) CMO,CDA,CYR,CTIME,CGRID1,CGRID2,CBIRDS
                SDATE = DATE(SMO,SDA,SYR,STIME)
                CDATE = DATE(CMO,CDA,CYR,CTIME)
                IF (SMO.EQ.99.AND.CMO.EQ.99) THEN
                   DONE = .TRUE.
                ELSE
                   DONE = .FALSE.
                ENDIF
      *
           10   IF (.NOT.DONE) THEN
                   IF (CDATE.LT.SDATE) THEN
                      WRITE (12,5) CMO,CDA,CYR,CTIME,CGRID1,
              +                    CGRID2,CBIRDS
                      READ (11,5) CMO,CDA,CYR,CTIME,CGRID1,
              +                   CGRID2,CBIRDS
                      CDATE = DATE(CMO,CDA,CYR,CTIME)
                   ELSE
                      WRITE (12,5) SMO,SDA,SYR,STIME,SGRID1,
              +                    SGRID2,SBIRDS
                      READ (10,5) SMO,SDA,SYR,STIME,SGRID1,
              +                   SGRID2,SBIRDS
                      SDATE = DATE(SMO,SDA,SYR,STIME)
                   ENDIF
                   IF (SMO.EQ.99.AND.CMO.EQ.99) DONE = .TRUE.
                   GO TO 10
                ENDIF
                WRITE (12,5) SMO,SDA,SYR,STIME,SGRID1,SGRID2,SBIRDS
                CLOSE (UNIT=11,STATUS='DELETE')
                CLOSE (UNIT=12)
      *
                OPEN (UNIT=11,FILE='CRANES',STATUS='NEW')
                OPEN (UNIT=12,FILE='TEMP',STATUS='OLD')
                PRINT*, 'WHOOPING CRANE MIGRATION'
                PRINT*
                PRINT*, 'CURRENT SIGHTINGS'
                PRINT*
      *
                HOLDM = 0
                HOLDD = 0
                COUNT = 0
                MAXCT = 0
           15   READ (12,5,END=35) MO,DA,YR,TIME,GRID1,GRID2,BIRDS
                   IF (MO.NE.99) THEN
                      PRINT 20, MO,DA,YR,TIME
```

```
20          FORMAT (1X,I2,'-',I2,'-',I2,4X,I4)
            PRINT 25, GRID1,GRID2
25          FORMAT (1X,5X,'GRID LOCATION: ',2I3)
            PRINT 30, BIRDS
30          FORMAT (1X,5X,'NUMBER OF BIRDS',1X,I5)
            IF (MO.EQ.HOLDM.AND.DA.EQ.HOLDD) THEN
                COUNT = COUNT + 1
            ELSE
                IF (COUNT.GT.MAXCT) MAXCT = COUNT
                COUNT = 1
                HOLDM = MO
                HOLDD = DA
            ENDIF
        ENDIF
        WRITE (11,5) MO,DA,YR,TIME,GRID1,GRID2,BIRDS
        GO TO 15
35 PRINT 40, MAXCT
40 FORMAT (1X,'MAXIMUM NUMBER OF SIGHTINGS IN ONE DAY = ',I4)
*
   50 STOP
      END
*-------------------------------------------------------------*

12.
*-------------------------------------------------------------*
      SUBROUTINE   REPORT
*
*  This subroutine prints the inventory file
*  in stock number order.
*
      INTEGER  KEY, STOCK, QUANT
      REAL   PRICE
      CHARACTER*10   DESC
*
      CLOSE (UNIT=11)
      OPEN (UNIT=11,FILE='PARTS',ACCESS ='DIRECT',
     +      STATUS='OLD',FORM ='FORMATTED',RECL=23)
      PRINT*, 'INVENTORY REPORT'
      PRINT*
      PRINT*, 'NUMBER  DESCRIPTION  QUANTITY  PRICE'
      KEY = 1
   10 READ (11,15,REC=KEY,ERR=25,END=25) STOCK,DESC,QUANT,PRICE
   15    FORMAT (I3,A10,I4,F6.2)
         PRINT 20, STOCK, DESC, QUANT, PRICE
   20    FORMAT (1X,I3,5X,A10,5X,I4,5X,F6.2)
         KEY = KEY + 1
         GO TO 10
   25 CLOSE (UNIT=11)
*
      RETURN
      END
*-------------------------------------------------------------*

17.
*-------------------------------------------------------------*
      PROGRAM   PLANT
*
*  This program prints the work orders
*  for specified pieces of equipment.
*
      INTEGER  TYPE, ORDER, CODE
      LOGICAL   DONE
*
```

```
*--------------------------------------------------------------*
          OPEN (UNIT=8,FILE='SENSOR',STATUS='OLD')
          DONE = .FALSE.
        5 IF (.NOT.DONE)  THEN
              PRINT*, 'ENTER SENSOR TYPE (1 THROUGH 5)'
              PRINT*, 'OR ENTER 9 TO QUIT'
              READ*, TYPE
              IF (TYPE.NE.9) THEN
                  PRINT*
                  PRINT*, 'WORK ORDERS:'
                  REWIND (UNIT=8)
       10         READ (8,15,END=20) ORDER, CODE
       15         FORMAT (15,2X,I1)
                      IF (CODE.EQ.TYPE) PRINT*, ORDER
                      GO TO 10
       20         PRINT*,'END OF FILE REACHED'
              ELSE
                  DONE = .TRUE.
              ENDIF
              GO TO 5
          ENDIF
*
          END
*--------------------------------------------------------------*
```

Chapter 10

4.
```
*--------------------------------------------------------------*
      PROGRAM  ROOTS
*
* This program determines the roots in the interval [-5,5]
* for a quartic polynomial using incremental search and
* the bisection method.
*
      INTEGER  COUNT, STEPS
      REAL  A(0:4), LEFT, RIGHT, P
*
      PRINT*, 'ENTER COEFFICIENTS A0,A1,A2,A3,A4'
      READ*, A
*
      PRINT*
      PRINT*, 'POLYNOMIAL:'
      PRINT 5
    5 FORMAT (1X,9X,'4',11X,'3',11X,'2')
      PRINT 10, A
   10 FORMAT (1X,4(F7.3,' X + '),F7.3)
      PRINT*
*
      COUNT = 0
      DO 20 LEFT=-5,4.75,0.25
          STEPS = 0
          RIGHT = LEFT + 0.25
          IF (ABS(F(A,LEFT)).LT.0.001) THEN
              PRINT 15, LEFT, F(A,LEFT), STEPS
   15         FORMAT (1X,'ROOT = ',F7.3,3X,
     +                'F(ROOT) = ',F7.3,3X,I3,' ITERATIONS')
              COUNT = COUNT + 1
          ELSEIF (F(A,LEFT)*F(A,RIGHT).LT.0.0) THEN
              CALL ITERAT (A,LEFT,RIGHT,ROOT,STEPS)
```

```
                  PRINT 15, ROOT, F(A,ROOT), STEPS
                  COUNT = COUNT + 1
              ENDIF
        20 CONTINUE
      *
              IF (ABS(F(A,LEFT)).LT.0.001) THEN
                  STEPS = 0
                  PRINT 15, LEFT, F(A,LEFT), STEPS
                  COUNT = COUNT + 1
              ENDIF
              IF (COUNT.EQ.0) THEN
                  PRINT*, 'NO ROOTS IN INTERVAL [-5,5]'
              ENDIF
      *
              END
      *-------------------------------------------------------------*
                        (no changes in function F)
      *-------------------------------------------------------------*
              SUBROUTINE   ITERAT(A,LEFT,RIGHT,ROOT,STEPS)
      *
      * This subroutine uses interval halving to find a root.
      *
              REAL  A(0:4), LEFT, RIGHT, ROOT, STEPS, SIZE, MID
              LOGICAL   DONE
      *
              DONE = .FALSE.
              STEPS = 1
              SIZE = RIGHT - LEFT
          5 IF (SIZE.GT.0.01.AND..NOT.DONE) THEN
                  MID = (LEFT + RIGHT)/2.0
                  IF (ABS(F(A,MID)).LT.0.001) THEN
                      DONE = .TRUE.
                  ELSEIF (F(A,MID)*F(A,LEFT).LT.0.0) THEN
                      RIGHT = MID
                  ELSE
                      LEFT = MID
                  ENDIF
                  SIZE = RIGHT - LEFT
                  STEPS = STEPS + 1
                  GO TO 5
              ENDIF
      *
              IF (SIZE.GT.0.01) THEN
                  ROOT = MID
              ELSE
                  ROOT = (LEFT + RIGHT)/2.0
              ENDIF
      *
              RETURN
              END
      *-------------------------------------------------------------*
      6.
      *-------------------------------------------------------------*
              PROGRAM   NEWTON
      *
      * This program solves for real and complex roots of a
      * cubic polynomial using the Newton-Raphson method.
      *
              INTEGER   K
              REAL  A0, A1, A2, A3, TOLNC
              COMPLEX   X, P, DP
      *
```

```
              PRINT*, 'ENTER COEFFICIENTS A0, A1, A2, A3'
              READ*, A0,A1,A2,A3
              PRINT*
              PRINT 4
      4 FORMAT (1X,'                  3          2')
              PRINT 5, A0, A1, A2, A3
      5 FORMAT (1X,'P(X) = ',F7.3,' X  + ',F7.3,' X  + ',
       +        F7.3,' X + ',F7.3)
              PRINT*, 'ENTER ERROR TOLERANCE'
              READ*, TOLNC
              PRINT*
              PRINT*,'ENTER INITIAL COMPLEX GUESS FOR ROOT AS TWO REAL VALUES
              READ*, X
     10 IF (X.NE.(99.,99.)) THEN
              P = A0*(X**3) + A1*(X**2) + A2*X + A3
              ERROR = CABS(P)
              K = 0
     15     IF (ERROR.GT.TOLNC.AND.K.LT.100) THEN
              DP = 3.0*A0*(X**2) + 2.0*A1*X + A2
              X=X-P/DP
              P = A0*(X**3) + A1*(X**2) + A2*X + A3
              ERROR = CABS(P)
              K = K + 1
              GO TO 15
           ENDIF
           IF (ERROR.LE.TOLNC) THEN
              IF (ABS(AIMAG(X)).GT.0.001) THEN
                 PRINT*,'COMPLEX ROOTS, X = ', X, CONJG(X)
              ELSE
                 PRINT*,'REAL ROOT, X = ',REAL(x)
              ENDIF
           ELSE
              PRINT*,'DID NOT CONVERGE'
           ENDIF
           PRINT*, K, ' ITERATIONS'
           PRINT*
           PRINT*, 'ENTER INITIAL COMPLEX GUESS FOR ROOT ',
       +           'AS TWO REAL VALUES'
           PRINT*, '(99,99 TO QUIT)'
           READ*, X
           GO TO 10
        ENDIF
*
        END
*-----------------------------------------------------------*
13.
*-----------------------------------------------------------*
        (no changes in main program ROOTS or function F)
*-----------------------------------------------------------*
        SUBROUTINE  ITERAT(A,LEFT,RIGHT,ROOT)
*
*  This subroutine uses false positioning to find a root.
*
        REAL  A(0:4), LEFT, RIGHT, ROOT, SIZE, C
        LOGICAL   DONE
*
        DONE = .FALSE.
        SIZE = RIGHT - LEFT
      5 IF (SIZE.GT.0.01.AND..NOT.DONE) THEN
           C = (LEFT*F(A,RIGHT)-RIGHT*F(A,LEFT))/(F(A,RIGHT)-F(A,LEFT))
           IF (ABS(F(A,C)).LT.0.001) THEN
              DONE = .TRUE.
```

```
             ELSEIF (F(A,C)*F(A,LEFT).LT.0.0) THEN
                 RIGHT = C
             ELSE
                 LEFT = C
             ENDIF
             SIZE = RIGHT - LEFT
             GO TO 5
         ENDIF
         ROOT = C
*
         RETURN
         END
*- - - - - - - - - - - - - - - - - - - - - - - - - - - - - - - - - - - - - - - - - - - *
```

Chapter 11

3.
```
*- - - - - - - - - - - - - - - - - - - - - - - - - - - - - - - - - - - - - - - - - - - *
         PROGRAM  EQN3
*
*  This program computes the solution to three simultaneous
*  equations using determinants.
*
         REAL  A(3),B(3),C(3),D(3),DENOM,DET,X,Y,Z
*
         PRINT*, 'EACH EQUATION SHOULD BE IN THIS FORM:'
         PRINT*, 'A*X + B*Y + C*Z = D'
         PRINT*, 'ENTER A,B,C,D FOR EQUATION 1'
         READ*, A(1), B(1), C(1), D(1)
         PRINT*, 'ENTER A,B,C,D FOR EQUATION 2'
         READ*, A(2), B(2), C(2), D(2)
         PRINT*, 'ENTER A,B,C,D FOR EQUATION 3'
         READ*, A(3), B(3), C(3), D(3)
         PRINT*
*
         DENOM = DET(A,B,C)
         IF (DENOM.EQ.0.0) THEN
             PRINT*, 'NO UNIQUE SOLUTION EXISTS'
         ELSE
             X = DET(D,B,C)/DENOM
             Y = DET(A,D,C)/DENOM
             Z = DET(A,B,D)/DENOM
             PRINT 5, X
   5         FORMAT (1X,'SOLUTION: X = ',F7.2)
             PRINT 6, Y
   6         FORMAT (1X,'          Y = ',F7.2)
             PRINT 7, Z
   7         FORMAT (1X,'          Z = ',F7.2)
         ENDIF
*
         PRINT*, 'SOLUTION VERIFICATION'
         PRINT*, A(1)*X+B(1)*Y+C(1)*Z, '=', D(1)
         PRINT*, A(2)*X+B(2)*Y+C(2)*Z, '=', D(2)
         PRINT*, A(3)*X+B(3)*Y+C(3)*Z, '=', D(3)
*
         END
*- - - - - - - - - - - - - - - - - - - - - - - - - - - - - - - - - - - - - - - - - - - *
                       (no change in function DET)
*- - - - - - - - - - - - - - - - - - - - - - - - - - - - - - - - - - - - - - - - - - - *
```

8.
```
*------------------------------------------------------------*
      PROGRAM  DEFORM
*
*  This program uses the Gauss elimination method to
*  solve a set of simultaneous equations.
*
      INTEGER  DROWS, DCOLS, N, I, J, PIVOT
      REAL  A(25,26), SOLN(25)
      LOGICAL  ERROR
*
      DROWS = 25
      DCOLS = 26
      OPEN (UNIT=10,FILE='MIRROR',STATUS='OLD')
      READ (10,*) N
      DO 5 I=1,N
         READ (10,*) (A(I,J),J=1,N+1)
    5 CONTINUE
*
      PIVOT = 1
      ERROR = .FALSE.
   10 IF (PIVOT.LT.N.AND..NOT.ERROR) THEN
         CALL ORDER(A,DROWS,DCOLS,N,PIVOT,ERROR)
         IF (.NOT.ERROR) THEN
            CALL ELIM(A,DROWS,DCOLS,N,PIVOT)
            PIVOT = PIVOT + 1
         ENDIF
         GO TO 10
      ENDIF
*
      IF (ERROR) THEN
         PRINT*, 'NO UNIQUE SOLUTION EXISTS'
      ELSE
         CALL BACKSB(A,DROWS,DCOLS,N,SOLN)
         CALL OUTPUT(N,SOLN)
      ENDIF
      END
*------------------------------------------------------------*
      (no changes to subroutines ORDER, ELIM, and BACKSB)
*------------------------------------------------------------*
      SUBROUTINE  OUTPUT(N,SOLN)
*
*  This subroutine writes the solution to a data file.
*
      INTEGER  N, I
      REAL  SOLN(N)
*
      PRINT*, 'SOLUTION WRITTEN TO DATA FILE'
      OPEN (UNIT=11,FILE='ACTUATOR',STATUS='NEW')
      WRITE (11,*) N
      DO 20 I=1,N
         WRITE (11,*) SOLN(I)
   20 CONTINUE
*
      RETURN
      END
*------------------------------------------------------------*
```
13.
```
*------------------------------------------------------------*
      PROGRAM  GS
*
*  This program solves a set of N simultaneous equations
*  using the Gauss-Seidel method.
```

```
*
       INTEGER   DROWS, DCOLS, N, MAXIT, COUNT, I, J
       REAL  A(100,100), B(100), TOL, ERRMAX, X(100), SUM, XNEW, ERROR
*
       DROWS = 100
       DCOLS = 100
       CALL INPUT (N,A,B,DROWS,DCOLS)
       CALL CONVRG (N,A,DROWS,DCOLS)
       CALL LIMITS (TOL,MAXIT)
*
   20 IF (TOL.GT.0.0) THEN
          ERRMAX = TOL + 1.0
          COUNT = 0
          DO 25 I=1,N
             X(I) = 0.0
   25     CONTINUE
   30     IF (COUNT.LT.MAXIT.AND.ERRMAX.GT.TOL) THEN
             ERRMAX = 0.0
             DO 40 I=1,N
                SUM = 0.0
                DO 35 J=1,N
                   IF (J.NE.I) SUM = SUM + A(I,J)*X(J)
   35           CONTINUE
                XNEW = (B(I) - SUM)/A(I,I)
                ERROR = ABS(XNEW - X(I))
                IF (ERROR.GT.ERRMAX) ERRMAX = ERROR
                X(I) = XNEW
   40        CONTINUE
             COUNT = COUNT + 1
             GO TO 30
          ENDIF
          IF (COUNT.GE.MAXIT) THEN
             PRINT*
             PRINT*, 'NUMBER OF ITERATIONS EXCEEDED LIMIT'
          ELSE
             PRINT*
             PRINT*,'SOLUTION IS:'
             DO 45 I=1,N
                PRINT*, 'X(',I,') = ',X(I)
   45        CONTINUE
             PRINT*
             PRINT*, 'NUMBER OF ITERATIONS = ', COUNT
          ENDIF
          CALL LIMITS (TOL, MAXIT)
          GO TO 20
       ENDIF
       END
*------------------------------------------------------------*
          (no changes to subroutines INPUT and LIMITS)
*------------------------------------------------------------*
       SUBROUTINE  CONVRG(N,A,DROWS,DCOLS)
*
* This subroutine determines if the convergence can be guaranteed.
*
       INTEGER   N, DROWS, DCOLS, I, J, GTSUM, GESUM
       REAL  A(DROWS,DCOLS), SUM
*
       DO 10 I=1,N
          SUM = 0.0
          GTSUM = 0.0
          GESUM = 0.0
          DO 5 J=1,N
             IF (I.NE.J) SUM = SUM + ABS(A(I,J))
```

```
      5    CONTINUE
           IF (A(I,I).GT.SUM) GTSUM = GTSUM + 1
           IF (A(I,I).GE.SUM) GESUM = GESUM + 1
     10 CONTINUE
        IF (GESUM.EQ.N.AND.GTSUM.GT.GESUM) THEN
           PRINT*, 'CONVERGENCE GUARANTEED FOR THIS DATA'
        ELSE
           PRINT*, 'CONVERGENCE NOT GUARANTEED FOR THIS DATA'
        ENDIF
  *
        RETURN
        END
  *-------------------------------------------------------------*
17.
  *-------------------------------------------------------------*
        SUBROUTINE  NORM(A,NA,NR,NC,DROWS,DCOLS)
  *
  *  This subroutine normalizes the values in a matrix
  *  to values between 0 and 1.
  *
        INTEGER  NR, NC, DROWS, DCOLS, I, J
        REAL  A(DROWS,DCOLS), NA(DROWS,DCOLS), AMIN, AMAX
  *
        AMIN = A(1,1)
        AMAX = A(1,1)
        DO 10 I=1,NR
           DO 5 J=1,NC
              IF (A(I,J).LT.AMIN) AMIN = A(I,J)
              IF (A(I,J).GT.AMAX) AMAX = A(I,J)
      5    CONTINUE
     10 CONTINUE
  *
        DO 20 I=1,NR
           DO 15 J=1,NC
              NA(I,J) = (A(I,J)-AMIN)/(AMAX-AMIN)
     15    CONTINUE
     20 CONTINUE
  *
        RETURN
        END
  *-------------------------------------------------------------*
```

Chapter 12

1.
```
  *-------------------------------------------------------------*
        PROGRAM WIND
  *
  *  This program reads a file of wind tunnel test data and then
  *  uses linear interpolation to compute lift coefficients for
  *  additional flight angles.
  *
        INTEGER N, K
        REAL A(500), C(500), ALPHA, CL
  *
        OPEN (UNIT=10,FILE='LIFT',STATUS='OLD')
        READ (10,*) N
        DO 5 K=1,N
           READ (10,*) A(K), C(K)
      5 CONTINUE
        PRINT*, 'DATA COVERS ANGLES FROM ',A(1),' TO ',A(N)
  *
```

```
              PRINT*, 'ENTER FLIGHT PATH ANGLE IN DEGREES'
              READ*, ALPHA
          10 IF (ALPHA.NE.999.0) THEN
                  IF (A(1).LE.ALPHA.AND.ALPHA.LE.A(N)) THEN
                      K = 1
          15         IF (A(K).LT.ALPHA) THEN
                          K = K+1
                          GO TO 15
                      ENDIF
                      CL = C(K-1) + (ALPHA - A(K-1))/(A(K) - A(K-1))
        +                           *(C(K) - C(K-1))
                      PRINT 20, ALPHA, CL
          20         FORMAT (1X,'FLIGHT ANGLE = ',F7.2/
        +                   1X,'CORRESPONDING COEFFICIENT OF LIFT = ',F7.3)
                  ELSE
                      PRINT*,'ANGLE OUT OF RANGE FOR DATA FILE'
                  ENDIF
                  PRINT*
                  PRINT*, 'ENTER FLIGHT PATH ANGLE IN DEGREES'
                  PRINT*, '(999.0 TO QUIT)'
                  READ*, ALPHA
                  GO TO 10
              ENDIF
      *
              END
      *-------------------------------------------------------------*

      7.
      *-------------------------------------------------------------*
                      (no change in main program PATH)
      *-------------------------------------------------------------*
              SUBROUTINE  SPLINE (X, Y, NDATA, NPTS, FILENM)
      *
      * This subroutine computes the cubic spline equations
      * from a set of input data points.  It then uses the results
      * to interpolate for new points.  The output values are
      * written to a data file.
      *
              INTEGER NDATA, NPTS, K, J, DROWS, DCOLS
              REAL X(NDATA), Y(NDATA), H(24), Q(23,24), S(24), TEMP(23), R(25),
        +          A(24), B(24), C(24), D(24), DELTA, XINT, YINT
              CHARACTER*8 FILENM
      *
              DATA  Q, DROWS, DCOLS /552*0.0,23,24/
      *
      * Compute interval width matrix H
      *
              DO 10 K=1,NDATA-1
                  H(K) = X(K+1) - X(K)
          10 CONTINUE
      *
      * Compute tridiagonal matrix Q
      *
              Q(1,1) = 2.0*(H(1)+H(2))
              Q(1,2) = H(2)
              DO 15 K=2,NDATA-3
                  Q(K,K-1) = H(K)
                  Q(K,K) = 2.0*(H(K)+H(K+1))
                  Q(K,K+1) = H(K+1)
          15 CONTINUE
              Q(NDATA-2,NDATA-3) = H(NDATA-2)
              Q(NDATA-2,NDATA-2) = 2.0*(H(NDATA-2)+H(NDATA-1))
      *
```

```
*    Compute slope matrix S
*
     DO 20 K=1,NDATA-1
        S(K) = (Y(K+1) - Y(K))/H(K)
  20 CONTINUE
*
*    Augment tridiagonal matrix Q
*
     DO 25 K=1,NDATA-2
        Q(K,NDATA-1) = 6.0*(S(K+1) - S(K))
  25 CONTINUE
*
*    Call Gauss elimination and store curvature values in matrix R
*
     CALL GAUSS (Q,DROWS,DCOLS,NDATA-2,TEMP)
     R(1) = 0.0
     DO 30 K=2,NDATA-1
        R(K) = TEMP(K-1)
  30 CONTINUE
     R(NDATA) = 0.0
*
*    Compute cubic equation coefficients
*
     DO 35 K=1,NDATA-1
        A(K) = (1.0/(6.0*H(K)))*(R(K+1)-R(K))
        B(K) = R(K)/2.0
        C(K) = (Y(K+1)-Y(K))/H(K) - H(K)*(R(K+1)+2.0*R(K))/6.0
        D(K) = Y(K)
  35 CONTINUE
*
*    Generate file of interpolated values
*
     OPEN (UNIT=14,FILE=FILENM,STATUS='NEW')
     WRITE (14,*) NPTS
     WRITE (14,*) X(1), Y(1)
     DELTA = (X(NDATA)-X(1))/(NPTS-1)
     J = 1
     CALL EQNS (NDATA,A,B,C,D,X)
     DO 40 K=1,NPTS-2
        XINT = X(1) + K*DELTA
        IF (XINT.GT.X(J+1)) THEN
           IF (J.LT.NDATA-1) J = J + 1
        ENDIF
        YINT = A(J)*(XINT-X(J))**3 + B(J)*(XINT-X(J))**2
    +          + C(J)*(XINT-X(J)) + D(J)
        WRITE (14,*) XINT, YINT
  40 CONTINUE
     WRITE (14,*) X(NDATA), Y(NDATA)
*
     END
*-------------------------------------------------------------*
    (no changes in subroutines GAUSS, ELIM, and BACKSB)
*-------------------------------------------------------------*
     SUBROUTINE  EQNS(NDATA,A,B,C,D,X)
*
*    This subroutine prints the equations that comprise the spline.
*
     INTEGER  NDATA, J
     REAL  A(NDATA), B(NDATA), C(NDATA), D(NDATA), X(NDATA)
*
     DO 10 J=1,NDATA
        PRINT 5, A(J),X(J),B(J),X(J),C(J),X(J),D(J)
```

```
      5    FORMAT (1X,F7.3,' (X-',F7.3,')^3 + ',
     +                F7.3,' (X-',F7.3,')^2 + ',
     +                F7.3,' (X-',F7.3,') + ',F7.3)
      10 CONTINUE
*
      RETURN
      END
*--------------------------------------------------------*

11.
*--------------------------------------------------------*
      PROGRAM  LINEAR
*
*   This program computes a linear model for a set of data
*   and then computes the residual sum to evaluate the model.
*
      INTEGER  K, N, MAXSUB
      REAL  X(500), Y(500), SLOPE, YINT, YNEW, RES,
     +      SUMX, SUMY, SUMXY, SUMXX, ERROR, MAXRES
*
      DATA  K,SUMX,SUMY,SUMXY,SUMXX,ERROR /1,5*0.0/
*
      OPEN (UNIT=10,FILE='XYDATA',STATUS='OLD')
*
      5 READ (10,*,END=50) X(K), Y(K)
         SUMX = SUMX + X(K)
         SUMY = SUMY + Y(K)
         SUMXY = SUMXY + X(K)*Y(K)
         SUMXX = SUMXX + X(K)*X(K)
         K = K + 1
         GO TO 5
*
      50 N = K - 1
         SLOPE = (SUMX*SUMY - REAL(N)*SUMXY)/
     +           (SUMX*SUMX - REAL(N)*SUMXX)
         YINT = (SUMX*SUMXY - SUMXX*SUMY)/
     +          (SUMX*SUMX - REAL(N)*SUMXX)
*
         PRINT*, 'THE LINEAR EQUATION IS'
         PRINT 55, SLOPE, YINT
      55 FORMAT (1X,'Y = ',F7.3,' X + ',F7.3)
         PRINT*
         PRINT*,'ORIGINAL    ORIGINAL    ESTIMATED    RESIDUAL'
         PRINT*,'   X            Y            Y              '
         PRINT*
*
         DO 65 K=1,N
            YNEW = SLOPE*X(K) + YINT
            RES = Y(K) - YNEW
            IF (K.EQ.1) THEN
               MAXSUB = 1
               MAXRES = ABS(RES)
            ELSE
               IF (ABS(RES).GT.MAXRES) THEN
                  MAXSUB = K
                  MAXRES = ABS(RES)
               ENDIF
            ENDIF
            ERROR = ERROR + RES*RES
            PRINT 60, X(K), Y(K), YNEW, RES
      60    FORMAT (1X,F7.3,4X,F7.3,4X,F7.3,5X,F7.3)
      65 CONTINUE
*
```

```
      PRINT*
      PRINT 68, X(MAXSUB), Y(MAXSUB)
   68 FORMAT (1X,'MAXIMUM DEVIATION FROM THE LINEAR MODEL OCCURS AT',
     +          '(',F7.3,',',F7.3,')')
      PRINT 70, ERROR
   70 FORMAT (1X,'RESIDUAL SUM = ',F7.3)
*
      END
*-----------------------------------------------------------*
```

19.
```
*-----------------------------------------------------------*
      PROGRAM  LINEAR
*
*  This program computes a linear model for a set of data
*  and then computes the residual sum to evaluate the model.
*
      INTEGER  K, N
      REAL  X(20), Y(20), SLOPE, YINT
     +      SUMX, SUMY, SUMXY, SUMXX
*
      DATA  K,SUMX,SUMY,SUMXY,SUMXX /1,4*0.0/
*
      OPEN (UNIT=10,FILE='XYDATA',STATUS='OLD')
*
      DO 5 K=1,20
         READ (10,*) X(K), Y(K)
         SUMX = SUMX + LOG(X(K))
         SUMY = SUMY + LOG(Y(K))
         SUMXY = SUMXY + LOG(X(K))*LOG(Y(K))
         SUMXX = SUMXX + LOG(X(K))*LOG(X(K))
    5 CONTINUE
*
   50 N = 20
      SLOPE = (SUMX*SUMY - REAL(N)*SUMXY)/
     +        (SUMX*SUMX - REAL(N)*SUMXX)
      YINT = (SUMX*SUMXY - SUMXX*SUMY)/
     +        (SUMX*SUMX - REAL(N)*SUMXX)
*
      PRINT*, 'THE LINEAR EQUATION IS'
      PRINT 55, SLOPE, YINT
   55 FORMAT (1X,'LOG Y = ',F7.3,'* LOG X + ',F7.3)
      PRINT*, 'THE POWER EQUATION IS'
      PRINT 60, EXP(YINT), SLOPE
   60 FORMAT (1X,'Y = ',F7.3,'*X^',F7.3)
*
      END
*-----------------------------------------------------------*
```

Chapter 13

4.
```
*-----------------------------------------------------------*
      PROGRAM  AREA1
*
*  This program estimates the area under a given curve
*  using trapezoids with equal bases.
*
      INTEGER  N, K
      REAL  F, X, A, B, SUM, BASE, XK, AREA
      LOGICAL DONE
*
      DONE = .FALSE.
```

```
      5 IF (.NOT.DONE) THEN
           PRINT*, 'ENTER THE INTERVAL ENDPOINTS'
           READ*, A, B
replace    PRINT*, 'ENTER THE NUMBER OF TRAPEZOIDS'
           PRINT*, '(ZERO TO QUIT)'
           READ*, N
           IF (N.EQ.0) THEN
                DONE = .TRUE.
           ELSE
                SUM = 0.0
                BASE = (B-A)/REAL(N)
                DO 10 K=2,N
                    XK = A + BASE*(K-1)
                    SUM = SUM + F(XK)
     10         CONTINUE
                AREA = 0.5*BASE*(F(A) + 2.0*SUM + F(B))
                PRINT 15, N, AREA
     15         FORMAT (1X,'USING ',I3,' TRAPEZOIDS,'
          +            ' THE ESTIMATED AREA IS ',F7.3)
                PRINT*
           ENDIF
           GO TO 5
      ENDIF
*
      END
*-------------------------------------------------------*
      REAL  FUNCTION F(X)
*
*  This function computes a value for f(x).
*
      REAL  X
*
      F = 4.0*EXP(-X)
*
      RETURN
      END
*-------------------------------------------------------*
```

7.
```
*-------------------------------------------------------*
      PROGRAM  NUMDIF
*
*  This program uses numerical differentiation to compute the
*  velocity and acceleration data for a sounding rocket.
*
      INTEGER  N, K
      REAL  TIME(512), ALT(512), H, VEL(512), ACC(512)
*
      OPEN (UNIT=15,FILE='ALTITUDE',STATUS='OLD')
      OPEN (UNIT=16,FILE='VELOCITY',STATUS='NEW')
      OPEN (UNIT=17,FILE='ACCEL',STATUS='NEW')
*
*  Read time and altitude data.
*
      READ (15,*) N
      DO 10 K=1,N
          READ (15,*) TIME(K), ALT(K)
   10 CONTINUE
*
*  Compute and store velocities and accelerations.
*
      H = TIME(2) - TIME(1)
      WRITE (16,*) N-1
      WRITE (17,*) N-2
```

```
*
          DO 20 K=2,N
              VEL(K) = (ALT(K) - ALT(K-1))/H
              WRITE (16,*) TIME(K), VEL(K)
              IF (K.NE.2) THEN
                  ACC(K) = (ALT(K) - 2*ALT(K-1) + ALT(K-2))/(H*H)
                  WRITE (17,*) TIME(K), ACC(K)
              ENDIF
       20 CONTINUE
*
          END
*------------------------------------------------------------*

11.
*------------------------------------------------------------*
          PROGRAM  AREA3
*
*   This program estimates the area under a given curve
*   using Simpson's rule.
*
          INTEGER  N, K
          REAL  F, X, A, B, SUM, BASE, XK, Y(100), AREA, EVEN, ODD
          LOGICAL DONE
*
          F(X) = 4.0*EXP(-X)
*
          DONE = .FALSE.
        5 IF (.NOT.DONE) THEN
              PRINT*, 'ENTER THE INTERVAL ENDPOINTS'
              READ*, A, B
              PRINT*, 'ENTER AN EVEN NUMBER OF INTERVALS'
              PRINT*, '(ZERO TO QUIT)'
              READ*, N
              IF (N.EQ.0) THEN
                  DONE = .TRUE.
              ELSE
                  SUM = 0.0
                  BASE = (B-A)/REAL(N)
                  DO 10 K=1,N+1
                      X = A + BASE*(K-1)
                      Y(K) = F(X)
       10         CONTINUE
                  EVEN = 0
                  DO 20 K=2,N,2
                      EVEN = EVEN + Y(K)
       20         CONTINUE
                  ODD = 0
                  DO 30 K=3,N-1,2
                      ODD = ODD + Y(K)
       30         CONTINUE
                  AREA = (BASE/3.0)*(Y(1) + 4.0*EVEN + 2.0*ODD + Y(N+1))
                  PRINT 15, N, AREA
       15         FORMAT (1X,'USING ',I3,' INTERVALS,'
          +               ' THE ESTIMATED AREA IS ',F7.3)
                  PRINT*
              ENDIF
              GO TO 5
          ENDIF
*
          END
*------------------------------------------------------------*
```

Chapter 14

4.
```
*--------------------------------------------------------------*
      PROGRAM  DECAY
*
*  This program uses Euler's method to solve a
*  differential equation.
*
      INTEGER  N, K, APPROX
      REAL   INIT, HALF, TIME, STEP, DC, SLOPE, M(0:25), EXACT
*
      PRINT*, 'ENTER INITIAL MASS, HALF-LIFE, DECAY TIME, STEP SIZE'
      PRINT*, '(MASS IN GRAMS, TIME IN YEARS)
      READ*, INIT, HALF, TIME, STEP
*
*  Compute decay constant and number of steps needed.
*
      DC = LOG(0.5)/(-HALF)
      N = NINT(TIME/STEP)
      M(0) = INIT
*
*  Perform Euler's method and then compute exact value for comparison.
*
      DO 10 K=1,N
         SLOPE = (-DC)*M(K-1)
         M(K) = M(K-1) + SLOPE*STEP
   10 CONTINUE
      APPROX = NINT(M(N))
      EXACT = M(0)*EXP((-DC)*TIME)
*
      PRINT 15, DC, INIT, TIME, EXACT, N*STEP, APPROX
   15 FORMAT (1X,'DECAY CONSTANT: ',F8.4/
     +         1X,'INITIAL MASS: ',F8.4/
     +         1X,'EXACT MASS LEFT AT TIME = ',F7.1,' IS ',F9.3/
     +         1X,'APPROXIMATE MASS LEFT AT TIME = ',F7.1,' IS ',I9)
*
      END
*--------------------------------------------------------------*
```

7.
```
*--------------------------------------------------------------*
      PROGRAM  CO
*
*  This program computes the concentration of carbon monoxide in
*  a metropolitan area using a differential equation.
*
      INTEGER  N,HOUR,MINUTE,MINITS,STEPS
      REAL   CZERO,R,KW,KC,V,XN,YN,H,K1,K2,K3,K4,SLOPE,XNEW,YNEW
*
      PRINT*, 'ENTER INITIAL CARBON MONOXIDE IN KG/CUBIC METER'
      READ*, CZERO
      PRINT*, 'ENTER VEHICLE EMISSIONS RATE IN KG/MINUTE'
      READ*, R
      PRINT*, 'ENTER CONTROL VOLUME IN CUBIC METERS'
      READ*, V
      PRINT*, 'ENTER WIND AND CHEMICAL REACTION CONSTANTS (PER MINUTE
      READ*, KW, KC
      PRINT*, 'ENTER TOTAL NUMBER OF MINUTES TO BE COVERED'
      PRINT*, '(IN MULTIPLES OF 10 MINUTES)
      READ*, MINITS
```

```
      *
            PRINT*
            PRINT*
            PRINT*, 'DAILY CARBON MONOXIDE CONCENTRATION REPORT'
            PRINT*
            PRINT 1, CZERO
         1 FORMAT (1X,'INITIAL CARBON MONOXIDE IN KG/CUBIC METER = ',F8.4
            PRINT 2, R
         2 FORMAT (1X,'VEHICLE EMISSIONS RATE IN KG/MINUTE      = ',F10.1
            PRINT 3, V
         3 FORMAT (1X,'CONTROL VOLUME IN CUBIC METERS           = ',E9.2)
            PRINT 4, KW, KC
         4 FORMAT (1X,'WIND CONSTANT     = ',F8.4,'/MINUTE'/
           +          1X,'CHEMICAL CONSTANT = ',F8.4,'/MINUTE')
            PRINT*
            PRINT*, 'TIME      CARBON MONOXIDE CONCENTRATION'
      *
            XN = 0.0
            YN = CZERO
            H = 10.0
            STEPS = MINITS/10
            DO 10 N=1,STEPS
               K1 = SLOPE (YN,R,V,KW,KC)
               K2 = SLOPE (YN+(H/2.0)*K1,R,V,KW,KC)
               K3 = SLOPE (YN+(H/2.0)*K2,R,V,KW,KC)
               K4 = SLOPE (YN+H*K3,R,V,KW,KC)
               XNEW = XN + H
               YNEW = YN + H*(K1 + 2.0*K2 + 2.0*K3 + K4)/6.0
               CALL TIME (N,HOUR,MINUTE)
               PRINT 5, HOUR, MINUTE, YNEW
         5     FORMAT(1X,I1,':',I2,5X,F8.4)
               XN = XNEW
               YN = YNEW
        10 CONTINUE
      *
            END
      *-------------------------------------------------------------*
                        (no changes in function SLOPE)
      *-------------------------------------------------------------*
            SUBROUTINE  TIME (N,HOUR,MINUTE)
      *
      * This function determines the hour and minute values for the report
      *
            INTEGER  N,HOUR,MINUTE
      *
            HOUR = N/6 + 7
            MINUTE = N*10
            MINUTE = MOD(MINUTE,60)
      *
            RETURN
            END
      *-------------------------------------------------------------*
     11.
      *-------------------------------------------------------------*
            PROGRAM  CIRCUIT
      *
      * This program uses Euler's method to solve a
      * differential equation.
      *
```

```
      INTEGER  STEPS, K
      REAL  E, R, L, TIME, SIZE, C(0:25), SLOPE
*
      PRINT*, 'ENTER E (VOLTS), R (OHMS), L (HENRIES), TIME (SECONDS)'
      READ*, E, R, L, TIME
      PRINT*, 'ENTER NUMBER OF STEPS'
      READ*, STEPS
*
*  Compute step size.
*
      SIZE = TIME/REAL(STEPS)
      C(0) = 0.0
*
*  Perform Euler's method.
*
      DO 10 K=1,STEPS
         SLOPE = (E - R*C(K-1))/L
         C(K) = C(K-1) + SLOPE*SIZE
   10 CONTINUE
*
      PRINT*, 'TIME = ',TIME,'  CURRENT = ',C(K)
*
      END
*-------------------------------------------------------------*
```

Chapter 15

2.
```
*-------------------------------------------------------------*
      PROGRAM  PULSE
*
*  This program generates a sonar signal.
*
      INTEGER  NUMBER, K
      REAL  E, PD, RPS, FREQ, A, PERIOD, T, PI, TIME, SIGNAL
*
      OPEN (UNIT=10,FILE='SONAR',STATUS='NEW')
      PRINT*, 'ENTER TRANSMITTED ENERGY IN JOULES'
      READ*, E
      PRINT*, 'ENTER PULSE DURATION IN SECONDS'
      READ*, PD
      PRINT*, 'ENTER SINUSOID FREQUENCY IN RADIANS PER SECOND'
      READ*, RPS
*
      PI = 3.141593
      FREQ = RPS/(2.0*PI)
      A = SQRT(2.0*E/PD)
      PERIOD = 1.0/FREQ
      T = PERIOD/10.0
      NUMBER = NINT(PD/T)
*
      DO 10 K=0,NUMBER-1
         TIME = REAL(K)*T
         SIGNAL = A*COS(2.0*PI*FREQ*TIME)
         WRITE (10,*) TIME, SIGNAL
   10 CONTINUE
*
      END
*-------------------------------------------------------------*
```

7.

```
*------------------------------------------------------------*
      PROGRAM   CHANNL
*
*  This program generates a signal plus
*  uniform noise using a specified SNR.
*
      INTEGER  K
      REAL   A, WIDTH, NOISE(0:199), PI, T, TIME, X
*
      PRINT*, 'ENTER AMPLITUDE OF SINUSOID'
      READ*, A
      WIDTH = SQRT(0.3)*A
      OPEN (UNIT=10, FILE='SNR20', STATUS='NEW')
      CALL UNIF (NOISE,200,-WIDTH/2.0,WIDTH/2.0,123)
      PI = 3.141593
      T = 0.002
      DO 10 K=0,199
         TIME = REAL(K)*T
         X = A*SIN(2.0*PI*10.0*TIME) + NOISE(K)
         WRITE (10,*) TIME, X
   10 CONTINUE
*
      END
*------------------------------------------------------------*
        (no changes in subroutines UNIF and RANDOM)
*------------------------------------------------------------*
```

11.

```
*------------------------------------------------------------*
      PROGRAM   FILTER
*
*  This program filters a signal stored in a data file
*  using a filter designed to reduce high frequency components.
*
      INTEGER   N, K
      REAL   TIME(0:499), X(0:499), Y(0:499)
      CHARACTER*8   FILENM
*
      PRINT*, 'ENTER INPUT SIGNAL FILENAME (IN QUOTES)'
      READ*, FILENM
      OPEN (UNIT=9, FILE=FILENM, STATUS='OLD')
      READ (9,*) N
      DO 10 K=0,N-1
         READ (9,*) TIME(K), X(K)
   10 CONTINUE
*
      Y(0) = (X(0) + X(1))/3.0
      DO 20 K=1,N-2
         Y(K) = (X(K-1) + X(K) + X(K+1))/3.0
   20 CONTINUE
      Y(N-1) = (X(N-2) + X(N-1))/3.0
*
      OPEN (UNIT=10,FILE='FILTER1',STATUS='NEW')
      DO 30 K=0,N-1
         WRITE (10,*) TIME(K), X(K), Y(K)
   30 CONTINUE
*
      END
*------------------------------------------------------------*
```

15.
```
*-------------------------------------------------------------*
        PROGRAM  MODIFY
*
*  This program subtracts the mean value from a signal and
*  stores the new zero-mean signal in a data file.
*
        INTEGER  COUNT
        REAL  SUM, TIME, X, AVE
*
        OPEN (UNIT=10,FILE='SENSOR1',STATUS='OLD')
        SUM = 0.0
        COUNT = 0
    5   READ (10,*,END=10) TIME, X
            SUM = SUM + X
            COUNT = COUNT + 1
            GO TO 5
   10 AVE = SUM/REAL(COUNT)
        CLOSE (UNIT=10)
*
        OPEN (UNIT=10,FILE='SENSOR1',STATUS='OLD')
        OPEN (UNIF=11,FILE='SENS1ZM',STATUS='NEW')
   15 READ (10,*,END=20) TIME, X
        WRITE (11,*) TIME, X-AVE
        GO TO 15
   20 CLOSE (UNIT=10)
        CLOSE (UNIT=11)
*
        END
*-------------------------------------------------------------*
```

INDEX

A

.AND., 83
A format specification, 350
Absolute error, 473
ACCESS specifier, 404
Algorithm, 8
Alternate
  entry, 679
  return, 680
ALU. *See* Arithmetic logic unit
Analog signal, 632
Apostrophe format specification, 35
Approximation, 473
Argument
  function, 26, 244, 257
  subroutine, 300
Arithmetic
  expression, 19
  IF statement, 675
  logic unit, 2
  operator, 19
Array
  definition, 192
  dimension, 192
  element, 192
  initialization, 192, 218
  I/O, 194, 221
  multidimensional, 231
  one-dimensional, 192
  specification, 192, 218
  storage, 192, 218
  subscript, 192, 218
  two-dimensional, 218
ASCII code, 348
Assembler, 4
Assembly language, 4
ASSIGN statement, 676
Assigned GO TO statement, 676
Assignment statement, 18

B

BACKSPACE statement, 406
Batch processing, 7
Bernoulli equation, 56
Binary, 4
  code, 348
  search, 285
  string, 4
Bisection method, 449
Blank COMMON statement, 337
BLANK specifier, 405
BLOCK DATA
  statement, 338
  subprogram, 338
BN format modifier, 682
Branch, 91

Bubble sort, 205
Buffer, 34
Bug, 6
BZ format modifier, 682

C

CALL statement, 300
Carriage control, 34
Cathode ray tube terminal, 7
Central procession unit, 3
Character
  codes, 348
  comparison, 353
  constant, 349
  functions, 357
  I/O, 350
  set, 349
  specification, 349
  string, 349
  substring, 354
  variable, 349
CHARACTER statement, 349
Checkpoint, 130
CLOSE statement, 405
Collating sequence, 353
Colon format modifier, 683
Comment line, 14
Common block, 337
COMMON statement, 337
Compilation, 4
Compiler, 4
  errors, 6
Complex
  constant, 383
  functions, 384
  I/O, 383
  roots, 443
  specification, 383
  variable, 383
COMPLEX statement, 383
Compound logical expression, 83
Computed GO TO statement, 675
Computer, 2
  languages, 4
  network, 7
  programs, 3
  terminals, 7
Concatenation, 356
Condition, 74
Constant, 15
  character, 349
  complex, 383
  double-precision, 371
  exponential, 17

integer, 15
logical, 84
named, 672
real, 15
Continuation line, 14
CONTINUE statement, 105
Control structure, 72
Conversational computing, 47
Counter, 22
Counting loop. See Iterative loop
CPU. See Central processing unit
Cramer's rule, 487
CRT terminal. See Cathode ray tube
  terminal
Cubic polynomial, 535
Cubic spline, 535
Curvature, 536
Curve fitting, 526

D

D format specification, 371
Data, 8
  file, 144, 402, 403, 423
DATA statement, 199
Debugging, 6
  aids, 58, 130, 179, 233, 291, 339, 391,
    431, 473, 518, 565, 595, 626, 661
Decomposition, 8
Default typing, 672
Derivative, 583
Design phases, 8
Determinant, 487
Diagnostics, 6
Difference equation, 654
Difference expression, 585
Differentiation, 572
Digital signal, 637
DIMENSION statement, 192
Direct access file, 423
DIRECT specifier, 404
Divide and conquer, 8
DO loop, 104
  implied, 195
  nested, 124
DO statement, 104
Documentation. See Style/technique
  guides
Dot product, 483
Double-precision
  constant, 371
  functions, 373
  I/O, 371
  specification, 371
  variable, 371

DOUBLE PRECISION statement, 371
Double space, 35
Driver, 291

E

.EQ., 83
.EQV., 99
E format specification, 43
EBCDIC code, 348
Echo, 58
Edit, 7
Editor, 7
Element, 192
ELSE statement, 87
ELSEIF statement, 88
END
    specifier, 151
    statement, 45
ENDFILE statement, 406
ENDIF statement, 85
End-of-data signals, 148
End-of-file record, 406
Entry point, 679
ENTRY statement, 679
EQUIVALENCE statement, 673
ERR specifier, 405
Error analysis, 473, 519, 565, 596, 627, 661
Error propagation, 566
Errors
    compiler, 6
    execution, 6
    logic, 6
    run-time, 6
    syntax, 6
Euler's Method, 602
Evaluation order
    arithmetic expressions, 20
    combined expressions, 99
    logic expressions, 83
Executable statement, 16
Execution, 6
EXIST specifier, 430
Explicit typing, 15
Exponent
    overflow, 25
    underflow, 25
Exponential notation, 17
Expression
    arithmetic, 19
    logical, 83
External file, 402
EXTERNAL statement, 678

F

.FALSE., 83
F format specification, 40
False-position method, 451
Father-son update, 403
Field, 402
File
    direct access, 423
    external, 402
    formatted, 404
    internal, 402
    sequential access, 402, 403
    unformatted, 404
FILE specifier, 404
Fixed point, 15
Floating point, 15
Flowchart, 9
    symbols, 73, 74, 106
FORM specifier, 404
Format reference number, 34
FORMAT specifications
    A, 350
    apostrophe, 35
    BN, 682
    BZ, 682
    colon, 683
    Dw.d, 371
    Ee, 681
    Ew.d, 43
    Fw.d, 40
    Gw.d, 681
    Iw, 38
    Lw, 681
    nP, 681
    nX, 37
    repetition, 168
    S, 682
    slash, 168
    SP, 682
    SS, 682
    TLn, 171
    Tn, 171
    TRn, 171
    wH, 681
FORMAT statement, 34
Formatted
    file, 404
    input, 162
    output, 33
FORMATTED specifier, 404
FORTRAN character set, 349
FORTRAN 77, 2, 4
Fortran 90, 691
Frequency, 635

Function
    argument, 26, 244, 257
    generic, 28, 244, 667
    intrinsic, 26, 244, 667
    library, 244
    name, 244, 256
    reference, 244, 256
    statement, 256
    table, 667
    user-written, 245, 256
FUNCTION statement, 256

G

.GE., 83
.GT., 83
G format specification, 681
Gauss elimination, 492
Gauss-Seidel method, 508
Generic function, 28, 244
GO TO statement
    assigned, 676
    computed, 675
    unconditional, 91

H

H format specification, 681
Hardcopy terminal, 7
Hardware, 3
Hash code, 423
Hierarchy
    arithmetic operations, 20
    combined operations, 99
    logical operations, 83
High-level language, 4
Hollerith format specification, 681
Horizontal spacing, 34

I

I format specification, 38
IF statement
    arithmetic, 675
    logical, 84, 87, 88
IF structure, 74
IF-ELSE structure, 75
IF-ELSEIF structure, 75
IMPLICIT statement, 671
Implicit typing, 15
Implied DO loop, 195
Increment value, 104
Incremental-search method, 448

Index of a DO loop, 104
Inherent error, 596
Initial guess, 461
Initial value, 603
Initial value of index, 104
Initialize, 18
Input
    formatted, 162
    list-directed, 32
Input/output, 8
INQUIRE statement, 429
Inquiry specifier
    ACCESS, 430
    BLANK, 430
    DIRECT, 430
    ERR, 430
    EXIST, 430
    FORM, 430
    FORMATTED, 430
    IOSTAT, 430
    NAME, 430
    NEXTREC, 430
    NUMBER, 430
    OPENED, 430
    RECL, 430
    SEQUENTIAL, 430
    UNFORMATTED, 430
Insertion sort, 205
Integer
    constant, 15
    specification, 16
    variable, 15
INTEGER statement, 16
Interface, 3
Integration, 572
Intermediate result, 23
Internal file, 402
Interpolation, 526
Internal halving, 457
Intrinsic function, 26, 244, 667
INTRINSIC statement, 678
I/O. *See* Input/output
IOSTAT specifier, 430
Iteration, 443
Iterative loop, 78

J

Job control information, 32, 164

K

Key, 423

L

.LE., 83
.LT., 83
L format specification, 681
Labeled COMMON statement, 338
Language
 assembly, 4
 high-level, 4
 low-level, 4
 machine, 4
Least-squares method, 552
Left-justified, 35
Lexicographic order, 354
Library function, 244
Limit value, 104
Line printer, 34
Linear interpolation, 527
Linear models, 552
Linkage editor, 6
List-directed
 input, 32
 output, 30
Literal, 31
Literal format specification
 apostrophe, 35
 H, 681
Local variable, 677
Logic error, 6
Logical
 constant, 84
 expression, 83
 IF statement, 84, 87, 88
 variable, 84
Logical operator
 .AND., 83
 .NOT., 83
 .OR., 83
 hierarchy, 83
LOGICAL statement, 84
Loop
 counting, 78
 DO, 104
 implied, 195
 iterative, 78
 nested, 124
 WHILE, 76, 91
Lotus 1-2-3, 685
Low-level language, 4

M

Machine language, 6
Magnetic

disk, 402
 tape, 402
Magnitude, 17
Main program, 256
Mantissa, 16
Master file, 424
MATLAB, 685
Matrix, 220, 447
Matrix multiplication, 484
Mean, 646
Memory, 2
 external, 3
 internal, 3
Merge, 414
Method of least squares, 552
Microprocessor, 2, 3
Minicomputer, 2, 3
Mixed-mode, 23
Module, 254
Multidimensional array, 231
Multiple entry, 679
Multiple roots, 443

N

.NE., 83
.NEQV., 99
.NOT., 83
Name
 array, 192
 constant, 672
 entry, 679
 file, 144
 function, 256
 program, 45
 statement function, 245
 subroutine, 300
 variable, 15
NAME specifier, 430
Named COMMON, 338
NAMED specifier, 430
Nested
 DO loops, 124
 functions, 27
 IF structures, 86
 Newton-Raphson method, 461
NEXTREC specifier, 430
Nonexecutable statement, 16
Nonlinear models, 556
Nonsingular, 509
NUMBER specifier, 430
Numerical
 differentiation, 572
 integration, 572
 methods, 438

O

.OR., 83
Object program, 6
One-dimensional arrays
   initialization, 192
   I/O, 194
   specification, 192
   storage, 192
OPEN statement, 145, 404
OPENED specifier, 430
Operators
   arithmetic, 19
   character, 356
   relational, 83
Ordinary differential equation, 602
Output
   buffer, 34
   formatted, 33
   list-directed, 30
Overflow, 25
Overprint, 35, 41

P

P format specification, 681
PARAMETER statement, 672
Parameters of DO loop, 104
Parentheses precedence, 20
Partial differential equation, 625
Path, 72
Permanent workspace, 7
Plotting
   Lotus 1-2-3, 687
   MATLAB, 686
Precedence
   arithmetic operations, 20
   combined operations, 99
   logical operations, 83
Precision
   double, 370
   single, 17, 370
Print buffer, 34
PRINT statement, 30, 33
Printed output
   formatted, 33
   list directed, 30
Printer plot, 362, 396
Priority of operations. *See* Precedence
Problem solving, 2
Problem statement, 8
Processor, 2
Program
   complete, 45

computer, 2
   main, 256
   name, 45
PROGRAM statement, 45
Pseudocode, 9

Q

Quantization error, 661

R

Random-access file, 402, 423
Random numbers, 306
Random signal, 643
READ statement
   file, 144, 423
   formatted, 162
   list-directed, 32
Real
   constant, 15
   specification, 16
   variable, 15
   roots, 443
REAL statement, 16
REC specifier, 423
RECL specifier, 430
Record, 144
Refinement, 8
Regression, 552
Relational operator, 83
Relative error, 473
Repeat format modifier, 168
Repetition structure, 73
Residual, 553
RETURN statement, 256
REWIND statement, 406
Right-justified, 38
Roots of equations, 442
Roots of polynomials, 443
Round off error, 519
Rounding, 23
Run-time error, 6
Runge-Kutta method, 611

S

S format specification, 682
Sampling frequency, 637
Sampling interval, 637

SAVE statement, 677
Scalar multiplication, 480
Scale factor, 681
Scientific notation, 16
Scratch file, 404
Search
    binary, 285
    sequential, 282, 285
Secant method, 464
Selection structure, 72, 74
Sensor, 633
Sentinel signal, 148
Sequence structure, 72, 73
Sequential access, 402, 403
SEQUENTIAL specifier, 430
Signal, 632
Signal power, 649
Signal-to-noise-ratio, 649
Significant digits, 17
Simpson's rule, 580
Simultaneous equations, 488
Single
    precision, 17, 370
    space, 35
Sinusoid, 634
Slash format specification, 168
Slope, 536
Software, 3
Software tool, 319
Sort
    ascending, 205
    bubble, 205
    descending, 205
    insertion, 205
    multi-pass, 205
    selection, 205
Source program, 6
SP format specification, 682
Specification statement
    CHARACTER, 349
    COMPLEX, 383
    DIMENSION, 192
    DOUBLE PRECISION, 371
    INTEGER, 16
    LOGICAL, 84
    REAL, 16
SS format specification, 682
Standard deviation, 647
Statement
    executable, 16
    function, 245
    nonexecutable, 16
    number, 14
STATUS specifier, 145, 404
Step size, 603
Stepwise refinement, 8

STOP statement, 45
String
    binary, 4
    character, 349
Structure chart, 255
Structured
    algorithm, 72
    program, 72
Style/technique guides, 59, 131, 180,
        234, 291, 340, 391, 431, 473, 519, 565,
        595, 627, 661
Subprogram
    block data, 338
    function, 256
    subroutine, 300
Subroutine
    alternate entry, 679
    alternate return, 680
    argument, 300
    call, 300
    name, 300
    user-written, 245, 256
SUBROUTINE statement, 300
Subscript, 192, 218
Substring, 354
Syntax error, 6

T

.TRUE., 83
Tab specification, 171
Tangent line, 461
Taylor series, 611
Temporary workspace, 7
Technique. *See* Style/technique guides
Terminals, 7
Testing, 10
THEN, 85
Time-sharing, 7
TLn format specification, 171
Tn format specification, 171
Top-down design, 8, 254
Trailer signal, 148
Transaction file, 425
Transfer function, 655
Transfer statement, 91
Tapezoidial rule, 572
Tridiagonal system, 538
TRn format specification, 171
Truncation, 23
Truncation error, 627
Two-dimensional array
    initialization, 218
    I/O, 221

Two-dimensional array *(continued)*
  specification, 218
  storage, 218
Type statement
  character, 349
  complex, 383
  double-precision, 371
  explicit, 15
  implicit, 15
  integer, 16
  logical, 84
  real, 16

U

Unconditional GO TO statement, 430
Underflow, 25
Unformatted file, 404
UNFORMATTED specifier, 430
Uniform random number, 646
Unit number, 145
UNIT specifier, 145, 404
User-written function, 245, 256

V

Variable, 15

  character, 349
  complex, 383
  dimensioning, 262
  double-precision, 371
  formatting, 683
  integer, 15
  local, 677
  logical, 84
  name, 15
  real, 15
Variance, 646
Vector, 483
Vertical spacing, 34

W

WHILE loop, 76, 91
Width of format specification, 40
Workspace, 7
Workstation, 7
WRITE statement
  formatted, 145, 423
  list-directed, 144

X

X format specification, 37